AF477395

THE BIG PICTURE

New Concepts for a New World

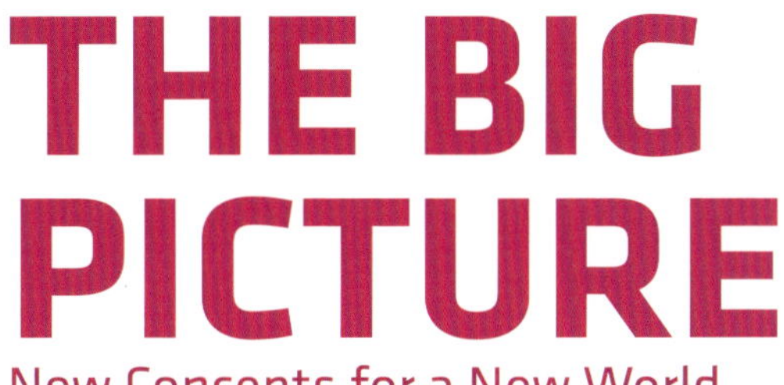

Edited by / *Herausgegeben von*

Hannes Leopoldseder / Gerfried Stocker / Christine Schöpf

Ars Electronica 2012
Festival für Kunst, Technologie und Gesellschaft
Festival for Art, Technology, and Society

30. August – 3. September 2012
August 30 – September 3, 2012
Ars Electronica, Linz

Herausgeber / *Editors:* Hannes Leopoldseder,
Christine Schöpf, Gerfried Stocker

Redaktion / *Editing:* Jutta Schmiederer

Übersetzungen / *Translations:*
(Englisch–Deutsch / English–German): Martina Bauer,
Michael Kaufmann, Sonja Pöllabauer, Wilfried Prantner
(Deutsch–Englisch / German–English): Mel Greenwald
(all texts unless otherwise indicatad)

Lektorat / *Copyediting:* Ingrid Fischer-Schreiber,
Cathy Lewis, Jutta Schmiederer

Grafische Gestaltung und Produktion /
Graphic design and production: Gerhard Kirchschläger,
www.kirchschlaeger.at

Schrift / *Typeface:* Klavika

Druck / *Printed by:* Gutenberg Werbering GmbH, Linz

Papier / *Paper:* BVS matt, 135 g/m²
Galerie Vision, 285 g/m²

© 2012 Ars Electronica
© 2012 für die abgebildeten Werke bei den Künstlern
oder ihren Rechtsnachfolgern / for the reproduced
works: the artists, or their legal successors

Erschienen im / *Published by*
Hatje Cantz Verlag
Zeppelinstrasse 32
73760 Ostfildern
Deutschland / Germany
Tel. +49 711 4405-200
Fax +49 711 4405-220
www.hatjecantz.com

Informationen zu dieser oder zu anderen
Ausstellungen finden Sie unter www.kq-daily.de
*You can find information on this exhibition and
many others at www.kq-daily.de*

Hatje Cantz books are available internationally at
selected bookstores. For more information about our
distribution partners please visit our homepage at
www.hatjecantz.com

ISBN 978-3-7757-3434-9

Printed in Austria

Umschlagabbildung / *Cover illustration:*
Andreas Jalsovec, Ars Electronica Futurelab

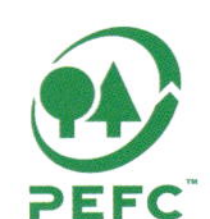

PEFC/06-39-27   **klimaneutral gedruckt** O   CP IKS-Nr.: 53401-1208-1005

ARS ELECTRONICA

HATJE
CANTZ

Ars Electronica 2012

Festival für Kunst, Technologie und Gesellschaft /
Festival for Art, Technology and Society

Organization
Ars Electronica Linz GmbH

Managing Directors
Gerfried Stocker, Diethard Schwarzmair
Ars-Electronica-Straße 1, 4040 Linz, Austria
Tel: +4373272720
Fax: +4373272722
info@aec.at

Co-organizers

ORF Oberösterreich
General Director: Kurt Rammerstorfer

LIVA – Veranstaltungsgesellschaft m.b.H.
CEO: Wolfgang Winkler, Wolfgang Lehner

OK Offenes Kulturhaus im OÖ Kulturquartier
Artistic Director: Martin Sturm
Commercial Director: Gabriele Daghofer

Partners
Universität der Künste Berlin
afo – architekturforum oberösterreich
Lentos Kunstmuseum Linz
Mariendom Linz
Kunstuniversität Linz – Universität für künstlerische
und industrielle Gestaltung
Landesgalerie Linz
Otelo – Offenes Technologielabor
BFI OÖ
Pädagogische Hochschule OÖ
Rotes Kreuz Oberösterreich
Youth Future Project e.V.
jugend innovativ – Austria Wirtschaftsservice GmbH
bm:ukk – Bundesministerium für Unterricht, Kunst und Kultur

Directors Ars Electronica: Gerfried Stocker, Christine Schöpf
Head of Festival: Martin Honzik
Technical Head: Karl Julian Schmidinger
Internal Organization: Veronika Christina Liebl

Production Team: Susanne Aichinger, Florian Bauböck,
Katharina Edlmair, Ingrid Fischer-Schreiber, Rosi Grillmair,
Oliver Haindl, Sarah Hellwagner, Barbara Hinterleitner,
Simon Kopfberger, Christian Korherr, Tobias Michael Kösters,
Romana Leopoldseder, Michael Lettner, Veronika Christina
Liebl, Manuela Naveau, Kathrin Obernhumer, Emiko Ogawa,
Maria Pfeifer, Roland Ploner, Gerald Priewasser, Georg
Pühringer, Julia Rabeder, Miriam Schmeikal, Jutta Schmiederer,
Florian Sedmak, Pia Stöffelbauer, Alice Strunkmann-Müller,
Laura Welzenbach, Susi Windischbauer

Co-curators
u19 - CREATE YOUR WORLD: Susi Windischbauer
Theme Symposium: Ingrid Fischer-Schreiber, Adam Bly
Campus Exhibition: Sam Auinger, Georg Spehr
Pixelspaces: Horst Hörtner, Matthew Gardiner, Christopher
Lindinger, Roland Haring, Roland Reiter
Interface Cultures Exhibition: Faculty: Christa Sommerer,
Laurent Mignonneau, Martin Kaltenbrunner, Marlene
Hochrieser, Michaela Ortner, Georg Russegger; Production:
Ivan Petkov, Maša Jazbec; technical support: Alberto Boem;
graphic design: Veronika Krenn, Vesela Mihaylova
Big Concert Night: Dennis Russell Davies, Wolfgang Winkler,
Heribert Schröder
Deep Space Live: Dietmar Hager

Prix Ars Electronica 2012

Co-organizers

ORF Oberösterreich
General Director: Kurt Rammerstorfer

LIVA – Veranstaltungsgesellschaft m.b.H.
CEO: Wolfgang Winkler, Wolfgang Lehner

OK Offenes Kulturhaus im OÖ Kulturquartier
Artistic Director: Martin Sturm
Commercial Director: Gabriele Daghofer

Idea: Hannes Leopoldseder
Conception: Christine Schöpf, Gerfried Stocker
Coordination: Martin Honzik, Romana Leopoldseder, Barbara Hinterleitner
Technical Management: Karl Julian Schmidinger

Production Team: Susanne Aichinger, Bernhard Böhm, Viktor Delev, Christoph Einfalt, Ingrid Fischer-Schreiber, Sandra Gassner, Gregor Göttfert, Manuel Hartmann, Sarah Hellwagner, Barbara Hinterleitner, Romana Leopoldseder, Michael Lettner, Veronika Christina Liebl, Emiko Ogawa, Johannes Ramsl, Remo Rauscher, Theresa Schubert-Minski, Markus Wipplinger

Press: Christopher Sonnleitner, Robert Bauernhansl, Michael Kaczorowski

Marketing: Sina Balke-Juhn, Cornelia Erber, Isabella Grünauer, Martina Huber

Ars Electronica Archive: Martina Hechenberger, Nicole Höbart, Elvis Pavic, Heinz Sambs, Jutta Schmiederer, Theresa Schubert-Minski

Ars Electronica Linz GmbH

Ars Electronica Center: Andreas Bauer, Christoph Kremer, Renata Aigner, Viktoria Aistleitner, Lisa-Maria Arnreiter, Reinhard Bengesser, Tamara Böhm, Sarah Breinbauer, Blanka Denkmaier, Wolfgang Deutsch, Hans Peter Ecker, Johannes Egler, Karl Federspiel, Julia Felberbauer, Melinda File, Evelyn Fränzl, Andrea Fröhlich, Mitra Gazvini-Zateh, Christian Gerber, Elisabeth Gerhard-Mayrhofer, Fabian Geyerhofer, Tamara Geyerhofer, Nicole Grüneis, Ulrike Gschwandtner, Harald Haas, Gerid Maria Hager, Kathrin Haider, Birgit Hartinger, Florian Heiml, Martin Hieslmair, Thomas Hillinger, Denise Hinger, Gerold Hofstadler, Sri Rahayu Hofstadler, Philip Huemer, Elisabeth Innerwinkler, Thomas Jannke, Erika Jungreithmayr, Katharina Karrer, Elisabeth Kattner, David-Mathias Kemethofer, Daniel Kern, Herwig Kerschner, Viktoria Klepp, Thomas Kollmann, Michael Koller, Wolfgang König, Kristýna Krabatschová, Andreas Leeb, Sabine Leidlmair, Juliane Leitner, Dominic Lengauer, Anna Katharina Link, Kathrin Meyer, Clemens Mock, Horst Morocutti, Marc Mühlberger, Heinrich Niederhuber, Michaela Obermayer, Marlene Penn, Marius Petermandl, Svetlana Petrovic, Katharina Pilar, Armin Pils, Andreas Plakolm, Mathias Pöschko, Karl Hans Rois, Andreas Roth, Benjamin Perndl, Ulrike Rieseneder, Petra Saubolle-Hofmann, Alina Sauter, Birgitt Schäffer, Johann Schauer, Barbara Schmidt, Stefan Schwarzmair, Elio Seidl, Maria Seidl, Manfred Seifriedsberger, Lukas Steindl, Margarethe Stöttner-Breuer, Lioubov Studener, Johannes Stürzlinger, Istvan Szabo, Bhoomesh Tak, Kerstin Tak-Wakolbinger, Michael Thaler, Michael Trebo, Linda Vaňková, Thomas Viehböck, Florian Voggeneder, Karin Wabro, Florian Wanninger, Burak Yolcu, Sebastian Zach, Silvia Zainzinger

Ars Electronica Futurelab: Horst Hörtner, Christopher Lindinger, Roland Aigner, Tamer Aslan, Florian Berger, Sigrid Blauensteiner, Bernhard Böhm, Chris Bruckmayr, Cecile Bucher, Maria Eschlböck, Peter Freudling, Stefan Fuchs, Matthew Gardiner, My Trinh Gardiner, Imanol Gomez, Roland Haring, Yvonne Hauser, Christoph Hofbauer, Peter Holzkorn, Andreas Jalsovec, Martina Karrer, Petros Kataras, Fadil Kujundžić, Anna Lucia Kuthan, Martina Mara, Pascal Maresch, Johanna Maria Mathauer, Benjamin Mayr, Michael Mayr, Kathrin Agnes Meyer, Kristefan Minski, Stefan Mittlböck-Jungwirth-Fohringer, Harald Moser, Patrick Müller, Otto Naderer, Nicolas Naveau, Ali Nikrang, Hideaki Ogawa, Benjamin Olsen, Veronika Pauser, Dietmar Peter, Michael Platz, Andreas Pramböck, Gerald Priewasser, Erwin Reitböck, Roland Reiter, Vanessa Schauer, Roland Schmidt, Alexa Steinbrück, Markus Wipplinger, Claus Zweythurm

Ars Electronica Festival: Martin Honzik, Karl Julian Schmidinger, Susanne Aichinger, Florian Bauböck, Sarah Hellwagner, Barbara Hinterleitner, Romana Leopoldseder, Michael Lettner, Veronika Christina Liebl, Manuela Naveau, Emiko Ogawa, Jutta Schmiederer, Susi Windischbauer

Ars Electronica Management Services: Elisabeth Kapeller, Sina Balke-Juhn, Sebastian Bauböck, Robert Bauernhansl, Bettina Danninger, Florian Deutsch, Cornelia Erber, Michaela Frech, Bettina Gahleitner, Gerhard Grafinger, Michael Grausgruber, Isabella Grünauer, Andrea Hartl, Martina Hechenberger, Nicole Höbart, Gerald Hochhauser, Gerold Hofstadler, Martina Huber, Markus Jandl, Michael Kaczorowski, Heinz Klambauer, Martin Kneidinger, Stephan Kobler, Zulfija Magomedova, Peter J. Nitzschmann, Elvis Pavic, Heinz Sambs, Theresa Schubert-Minski, Christopher Sonnleitner, David Starzengruber, Julia Starzer, Daniel Weihrauch, Michaela Wimplinger

Ars Electronica Solutions: Bernd Albl, Michael Badics, Lukas Bischof, Youri Marko, Stephan Pointner, Gabriele Purdue

OK Offenes Kulturhaus im OÖ Kulturquartier

OK CyberArts Team
Artistic Director: Martin Sturm
Commercial Director: Gabriele Daghofer
Curator: Genoveva Rückert
Public Relations: Maria Falkinger
Technical Manager: Rainer Jessl
Production: Martina Rauschmayer, Aron Rynda
Technical Head: Markus Wallner

Production Team: Jarno Bachheimer, Attila Ferenczi,
Alfred Fürholzer, Martin Haselsteiner, Bernhard Kitzmüller,
Andreas Kurz, Daniel Mandel, Gerald Schreilechner, Andreas
Steindl, André Tschinder, Tom Vens, Hans-Jörg Weidinger,
Gerhard Wörnhörer, Simon Wilhelm

OK Team: Verena Atteneder, Johann Aufreiter, Erika
Baldinger, Julia Brunner, Michael Dalpiaz, Walter
Eckerstorfer, Max Fabian, Maria Falkinger, Michaela
Fröhlich, Andrea Gintner, Manuela Gruber, Sabine
Haunschmid, Evi Heininger, Robert Herbst, Maximilian
Höglinger, Christa Höllhumer, Fritz Holzinger, Simon
Lachner, Katharina Lackner, Elisabeth Lehner, Franz
Minichberger, Walter Mühlböck, Wolfgang Nagl, Josef
Pfarrhofer, Franz Pfifferling, Wilhelm Pichler, Angelika
Pöschl, Franz Quirchtmayr, Brigitte Rosenthaler, Gerda
Sailer, Markus Schiller, Ulrike Schimpl, Alexandra Schlager,
Ulrike Seelmann, Renate Stummer

Brucknerhaus

Romana Gillesberger, Wolfgang Scheibner, Wolfgang
Schützeneder, Ursula Kislinger

afo – architekturforum oberösterreich

Host: Gabriele Kaiser
Symposia Curators: Dietmar Offenhuber, Katja Schechtner

voestalpine Klangwolke 2012

Die voestalpine Klangwolke 2012 wird von tausenden
Menschen gemeinsam gestaltet. Die Realisierung wird
von Ars Electronica und Brucknerhaus geleitet.

Ars Electronica Linz GmbH

Managing Directors: Gerfried Stocker, Diethard
Schwarzmair
Production Management: Martin Honzik, Horst Hörtner
Technical Management: Karl Julian Schmidinger
Production Team: Susanne Aichinger, Lisa Marie Arnreiter,
Sina Balke-Juhn, Florian Bauböck, Andreas Bauer, Sigrid
Blauensteiner, Florian Berger, Tamara Böhm, Christoph
Bruckmayr, Hans Peter Ecker, Horst Eckl, Katharina
Edlmair, Cornelia Erber, Stefan Fuchs, Matthew Gardiner,
My Trin Gardiner, Ray Gardiner, Mitra Gazvini-Zadeh,
Andreas Gruber, Isabella Grünauer, Gerid Maria Hager,
Roland Haring, Yvonne Hauser, Hubert Havel, Barbara
Heinzl, Sarah Hellwagner, Barbara Hinterleitner, Christoph
Hofbauer, Martina Huber, Philip Huemer, Andreas Jalsovec,
Michael Kaczorowski, Katharina Karrer, Harpreet Kaur,
Robert Kolmhofer, Simon Kopfberger, Christian Korherr,
Tobias Michael Kösters, Christoph Kremer, Fadil Kujundžić,
Juliane Leitner, Michael Lettner, Romana Leopoldseder,
Veronika Christina Liebl, Martina Mara, Pascal Maresch,
Michael Mayr, Kristefan Minski, Stefan Mittlböck-
Jungwirth-Fohringer, Harald Moser, Patrick Müller,
Otto Naderer, Manuela Naveau, Sarah Nokes, Kathrin
Obernhumer, Ben Olsen, Emiko Ogawa, Hideaki Ogawa,
Marco Palewitz, David Panhofer, Maria Pfeifer, Michael
Platz, Mathias Pöschko, Andreas Pramböck, Gerald
Priewasser, Georg Pühringer, Julia Rabeder, Erwin
Reitböck, Roland Reiter, Vanessa Schauer, Miriam
Schmeikal, Roland Schmidt, Maria Seidl, Martina
Sochor, Christopher Sonnleitner, Alexa Steinböck,
Pia Stöffelbauer, Alice Strunkmann-Müller, Thomas
Viehböck, Joschi Viteka, Stefan Waschak, Laura
Welzenbach, Susi Windischbauer, Markus Wipplinger,
Burak Yolcu, Claus Zweythurm

LIVA – Veranstaltungsgesellschaft m.b.H.

CEO: Wolfgang Winkler, Wolfgang Lehner
Production Team: Romana Gillesberger, Daniela Haslecker,
Günther Herzog, Ursula Kislinger, Bernhard Lang, Sabine
Rößl, Wolfgang Scheibner, Wolfgang Schützeneder,
Sandra Seitz, Claudia Werner, Hannelore Wojik

ORGANIZATION / VERANSTALTER

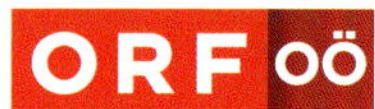 **ARS ELECTRONICA**

Ars Electronica Linz GmbH is a company of the city of Linz.
Ars Electronica Linz GmbH ist ein Unternehmen der Stadt Linz.

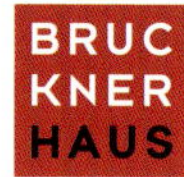 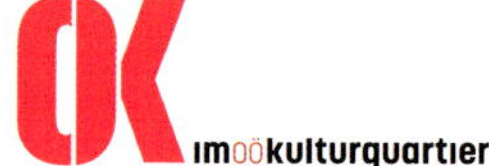

COOPERATION PARTNERS / KOOPERATIONSPARTNER

Universität der Künste Berlin

afo – architekturforum oberösterreich

Lentos Kunstmuseum Linz

Mariendom Linz

Kunstuniversität Linz – Universität für künstlerische und industrielle Gestaltung

Landesgalerie Linz

Otelo – Offenes Technologielabor

BFI OÖ

Pädagogische Hochschule OÖ

Rotes Kreuz Oberösterreich

Youth Future Project e.V.

jugend innovativ – Austria Wirtschaftsservice GmbH

bm:ukk – Bundesministerium für Unterricht, Kunst und Kultur

Seed Media Group

ARS ELECTRONICA RECEIVES SUPPORT FROM / ARS ELECTRONICA WIRD UNTERSTÜTZT VON:

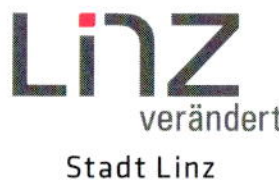
Stadt Linz

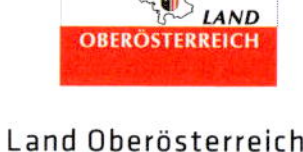
Land Oberösterreich

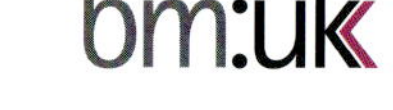
Bundesministerium für
Unterricht, Kunst und Kultur

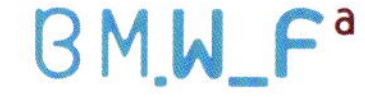
Bundesministerium für
Wissenschaft und Forschung

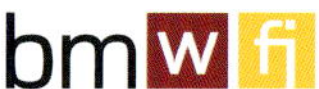
Bundesministerium für
Wirtschaft, Familie und Jugend

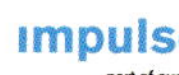 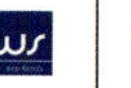
impulse | evolve

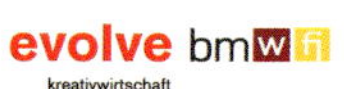 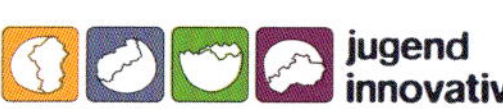
Jugend Innovativ

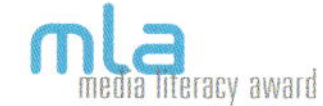
Media Lt. Award

voestalpine KLANGWOLKE 2012

ORGANIZATION / VERANSTALTER

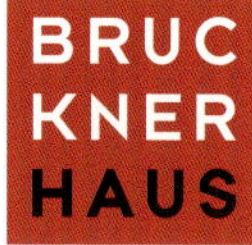 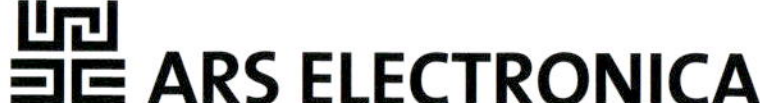 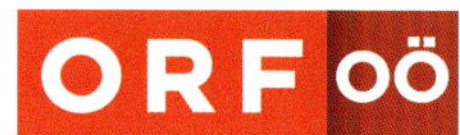

COOPERATION PARTNERS / KOOPERATIONSPARTNER

Heinz Biebl, Wartberg ob der Aist
Grießkogelschnalzer, Abtenau
Linzer Ruderverein Ister
EKRV Linz
Wassersportverein Ottensheim
Wasserskischule Kral
Sportvereinigung Urfahr 1912
ASKÖ Modellflugclub Linz
ASKÖ-Wassersportclub Linz
Freiwillige Feuerwehren aus den Bezirken Linz Stadt, Urfahr Umgebung,
Linz Land, Freistadt, Perg, Steyr Land, Eferding, Wels Land, Rohrbach
Motor Yacht Club Nibelungen Linz
Papp Lab
Musikschule der Stadt Linz
Landesmusikschulen OÖ
Otelo – Offenes Technologielabor
RedSapata Tanzfabrik

Gerfried Stocker

THE BIG PICTURE
New Concepts for a New World

If every crisis is also an opportunity, then what opportunities are we failing to take advantage of on account of our perplexity and our unwillingness to come to terms with the changes happening now?

What we need is a more open-minded attitude that enables us to peer beyond the boundaries of our habitual ways of doing things, our specialized disciplines and our conventional ideologies, and that can also deal with the pluralism and the inherent contradictions of our modern, globally networked world. What we need is a new Big Picture of the world, one that is no longer from a central point of view and isn't projected out of the center of global power, but is instead a patchwork of diverse positions. Interdisciplinary thinking and working, which have been practiced so successfully in science and art, could serve as an effective role model. After all, the whole is more than the sum of its parts only when the individual parts are ready, willing and able to open up to one another and take what the others have to offer. What's called for is a paradigm shift that necessarily pervades all strata, sectors and walks of life.

On the Threshold of a New Epoch?

Amidst the turbulence of humankind's present crises, it's clear that the world of our future will be different. Politically, since the West will no longer be able to afford its leadership role and new powers such as China and India are just getting started playing their parts on the global political stage. Economically, because the financial sector as the engine of growth has run out of gas, and petroleum-based industry as a whole is motoring towards history's junk heap. And not least of all ecologically, since global warming is accelerating and its effects on our planet's ecosystem are becoming more massive by the day. Even if we already know all of this and we're aware that we have to make the necessary changes, we persist in our indecisive hesitation, indulging in the fantasy that everything is going to be OK—whereby OK means: the way it used to be. The fact that this is precisely what is not going to happen is something only a few of us are willing to admit. But by persisting on our well-trodden paths, we ignore precisely those great opportunities that naturally arise in times rocked by crises.

Where Might These Big Pictures of the Future Emerge?
Envisioned by Whom?

Accordingly, the aim of serious approaches to solutions cannot be to restore the status quo; instead, they have to pursue a global vision of our future. But where can this be headed? And who can specify the direction and the speed of our journey? It's obvious that there no longer exists a center of power that can tell the rest of the world what it has to do. Rather, the work of our future is going on at multiple locations and being done by diverse protagonists. And each one of them reserves the right to establish his/her own priorities. Nevertheless, the quality of their collaboration with all the others will be decisive for the success or failure of their undertakings because we all need each other in this globalized, networked world of ours and it's no longer possible to proceed in complete isolation. At the same time, the way we think about the world and our place in it will be determined less and less by politics or religions and increasingly by findings in (natural) science. And because we feel, sense or know that everything around us is getting more and more complicated, what we're seeing as a result is a renaissance of the scientific expert—one that's no longer either an overspecialized nerd or a universal genius but more of a team player.

Imaging Procedures Deliver the Icons of our Age …

Key importance in this process is assumed by new image-generating processes, which are in many instance all that we have available to impressively depict scientific insights and to generate, among other things, true icons. Like the first satellite picture of our Blue Planet that displayed such extraordinary power in demonstrating the fact that we're all in the same boat. Or animated images of the human brain and its gigantic network of synapses, and visualizations of our DNA and thus of the building blocks of life itself.

… and Social Networks Disseminate them Globally

Much of the propagation of sensational news items and images no longer proceeds through conventional media but rather above all via social networks in which they can instantaneously reach hundreds of millions of people, transcending linguistic, cultural and religious barriers to trigger various sorts of delight or horror. This unprecedented circulation of information, in turn, does its part to further undermine traditional power structures and the authority of previously accepted opinion leaders and to nurture the formation of totally new communities and hierarchies.

Best Practice from Art and Science

Nevertheless, all of these sensations propagated via the internet do not coalesce to form a new picture of the world. They're all just parts of a big jigsaw puzzle that attest to the fragmentation, multifaceted nature and complexity of our reality. In order to assemble them into one big whole, the first thing we have to do is get an overview. But a precondition for this is a broader, more open-minded perspective like the one that has been successfully applied only in science and art up to now. Such a point of view would enable us to peer beyond the boundaries of our individual cultures, ideologies, specialized disciplines and habitual ways of doing things, and behold the gigantic patchwork of our globalized world. And this is precisely where the 2012 Ars Electronica Festival comes in—bringing together models that can serve as paragons and best-practice examples from science and art whose interdisciplinary approaches preordain them to provide suitable role models. This, in turn, is meant as the point of departure of a discussion of how a Big Picture of our times ought to be composed and what strategies are conducive to being able to see and take it.

Gerfried Stocker

THE BIG PICTURE
Weltbilder für die Zukunft

Wenn jede Krise auch eine Chance ist, welche Chancen vergeben wir uns dann gerade angesichts unserer Ratlosigkeit und unserem Unwillen, mit den Veränderungen umzugehen? Was uns weiterhelfen könnte, wäre ein breiterer Blickwinkel, eine offenere Haltung, die es uns erlaubt, über die Grenzen unserer Gewohnheiten, unserer Fachdisziplinen und überkommenen gesellschaftlichen und politischen Ideologien hinaus zu blicken. Eine Haltung, die mit der Vielschichtigkeit, Pluralität und Widersprüchlichkeit unserer modernen Welt, der globalen Vernetztheit des Handelns und Denkens auch umgehen kann. Wir brauchen ein neues großes Bild der Welt, eines, das keine Zentralperspektive mehr haben wird. Kein einzelnes Weltbild aus dem Zentrum einer globalen Macht, sei es auch noch so weit gedacht, sondern ein Patchwork aus ganz vielen geopolitischen, kulturellen, religiösen und individuellen Positionen. Das in Wissenschaft und Kunst schon vielfach erfolgreiche, interdisziplinäre Denken und Arbeiten könnte ein wirkungsvolles Rollenbild sein. Denn die Summe ergibt nur dann mehr als ihre Einzelteile, wenn die Einzelteile auch bereit und in der Lage sind, sich aufeinander einzulassen, voneinander anzunehmen. Es ist ein Paradigmenwechsel notwendig, der sich auf alle Bereiche erstrecken muss.

An der Schwelle zu einer neuen Epoche?

Mitten im Strudel der aktuellen Krisen ist klar, dass unsere Welt künftig eine andere sein wird. Politisch, weil sich der Westen seine Führungsrolle nicht länger leisten wird können und neue Mächte wie China und Indien erst damit beginnen, ihre Rollen auf der Bühne der Weltpolitik auszugestalten. Ökonomisch, weil die Finanzwirtschaft als Wachstumsförderer ausgedient hat und die erdölbasierte Industrie insgesamt ein Auslaufmodell ist. Und nicht zuletzt ökologisch, weil die Klimaerwärmung immer schneller voranschreitet und ihre Auswirkungen auf das globale Ökosystem von Tag zu Tag massiver werden. Wenngleich wir das alles wissen und uns bewusst ist, dass wir die notwendigen Veränderungen angehen müssen, verharren wir in unschlüssigem Zögern und hängen der Vorstellung nach, dass alles wieder gut werden wird, wobei wir mit „gut" „so wie früher" meinen. Dass genau das nicht eintreten wird, wollen die Allerwenigsten wahrhaben. Im Beharren darauf, unsere gewohnten Wege weiter zu gehen, ignorieren wir die Chancen, die wir gerade in krisengebeutelten Zeiten eigentlich hätten.

Durch wen und wo könnte ein zukunftsfähiges Big Picture entstehen?

Ernsthafte Lösungsansätze können also kein Wiederherstellen eines Status Quo zum Ziel haben, sondern müssen einer globalen Vision von unserer Zukunft folgen. Wohin aber soll es gehen? Und wer kann die Richtung, wer das Tempo vorgeben? Klar ist, dass es kein Machtzentrum mehr gibt, das dem Rest der Welt sagt, was er zu tun hat, sondern dass an mehreren Orten und von unterschiedlichen Protagonisten an unserer Zukunft gebastelt wird. Protagonisten, die jeweils für sich in Anspruch nehmen, ihre eigenen Prioritäten zu setzen. Über ihren Erfolg oder Misserfolg entscheidet dennoch die Qualität der Zusammenarbeit mit allen anderen, weil in unserer globalisierten vernetzten Welt jeder jeden braucht und rein gar nichts mehr allein geht. Gleichzeitig wird die Art und Weise, wie wir über die Welt und unseren Platz darin denken, immer weniger von Politik oder Religionen und immer mehr von (natur-) wissenschaftlichen Erkenntnissen bestimmt. Und weil wir fühlen, ahnen oder wissen, dass alles um uns herum immer komplizierter wird, stellt sich eine Renaissance des „wissenschaftlichen Experten" ein, der nicht länger Fachidiot oder Universalgenie, sondern ein Teamplayer ist.

Bildgebende Verfahren liefern die Ikonen unserer Zeit ...

Wesentliche Bedeutung kommt in diesem Prozess auch neuen bildgebenden Verfahren zu, die es oft erst möglich machen, wissenschaftliche Erkenntnisse eindrucksvoll darzustellen und mitunter wahre Ikonen hervorzubringen, wie das erste Satellitenbild des blauen Planeten, das so eindringlich wie kein anderes Bild vor Augen führt, dass wir alle im selben Boot sitzen. Oder Animationen unseres Gehirns und seines gigantischen Netzwerks von Synapsen oder Visualisierungen unserer DNA und damit der Bausteine des Lebens selbst.

.. und soziale Netzwerke verbreiten sie rund um den Globus

Ihre Verbreitung erfahren solch sensationelle News und Bilder indes nicht mehr nur über klassische Medien, sondern vor allem über soziale Netzwerke, in denen sie binnen kürzester Zeit hunderte Millionen Menschen erreichen und über nationale, sprachliche, kulturelle und religiöse Barrieren hinweg Begeisterung oder Entsetzen auslösen. Dieses noch nie dagewesene Zirkulieren von Information trägt wiederum seinen Teil dazu bei, traditionelle Machtstrukturen und Meinungsführerschaften weiter zu untergraben und völlig neue Gemeinschaften und Hierarchien auszubilden.

Best-Practice aus Kunst und Wissenschaft

Dennoch fügen sich all diese via Internet herumgereichten Sensationen noch zu keinem neuen Weltbild. Sie alle sind nur Puzzleteilchen, die von der Fragmentierung, Vielschichtigkeit und Komplexität unserer Wirklichkeit zeugen. Um sie zu einem großen Ganzen zusammenzufügen, müssten wir uns erst mal einen Überblick verschaffen. Voraussetzung dafür allerdings wäre ein breiter, offener Blickwinkel, wie er bislang nur in Wissenschaft und Kunst erfolgreich erprobt ist. Erst ein solcher Blickwinkel würde es uns erlauben, über die Tellerränder unserer Kulturen, Ideologien, Fachdisziplinen und Gewohnheiten hinauszuschauen, auf das gigantische Patchwork unserer globalisierten Welt.
Genau hier setzt die Ars Electronica 2012 an und versammelt Vorbilder und Best-Practice-Beispiele aus Wissenschaft und Kunst, die ihrer interdisziplinären Herangehensweise wegen geeignete Rollenbilder liefern können. Davon ausgehend soll auch diskutiert werden, wie ein „Big Picture" unserer Zeit beschaffen sein müsste und mit welchen Strategien wir es realisieren könnten.

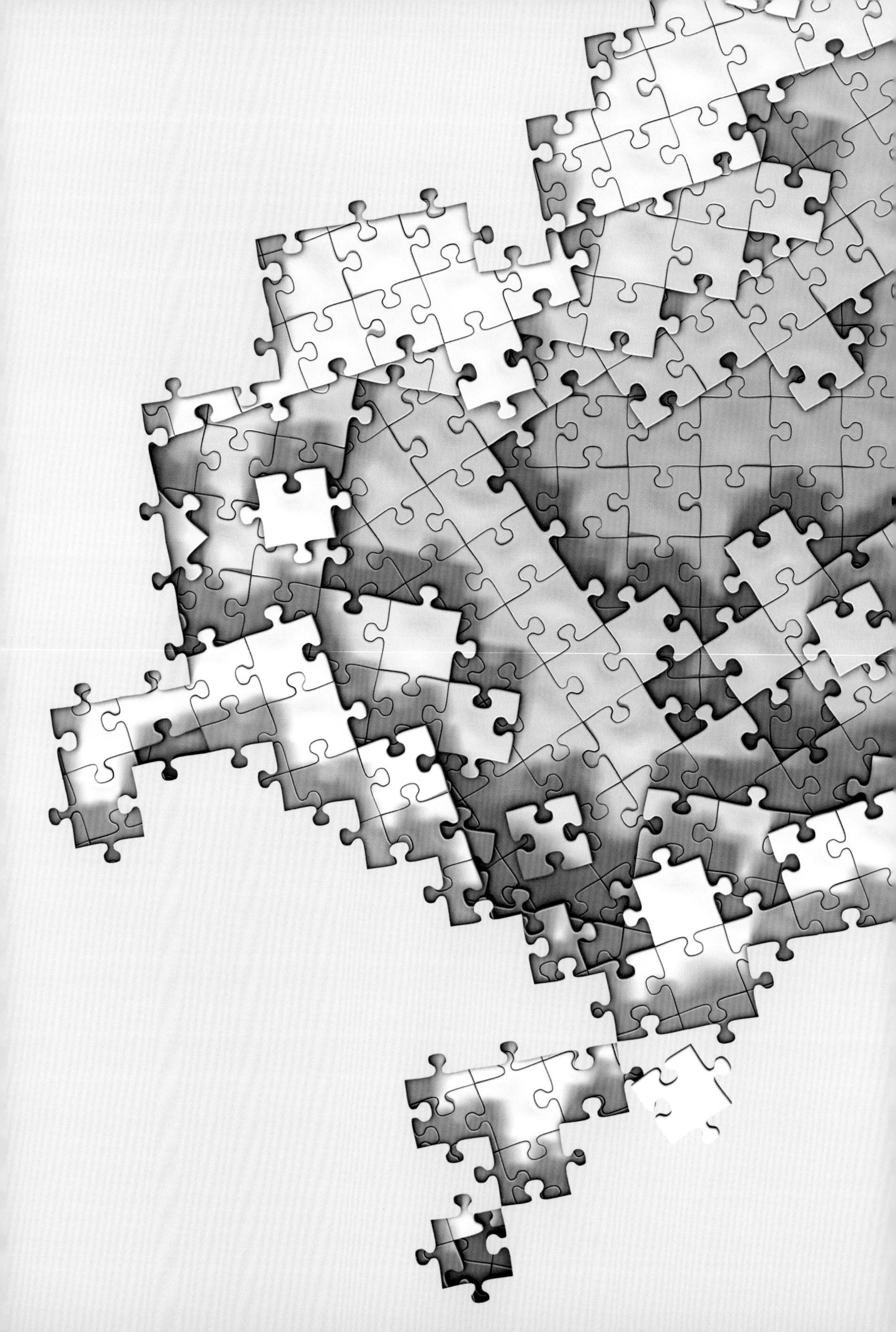

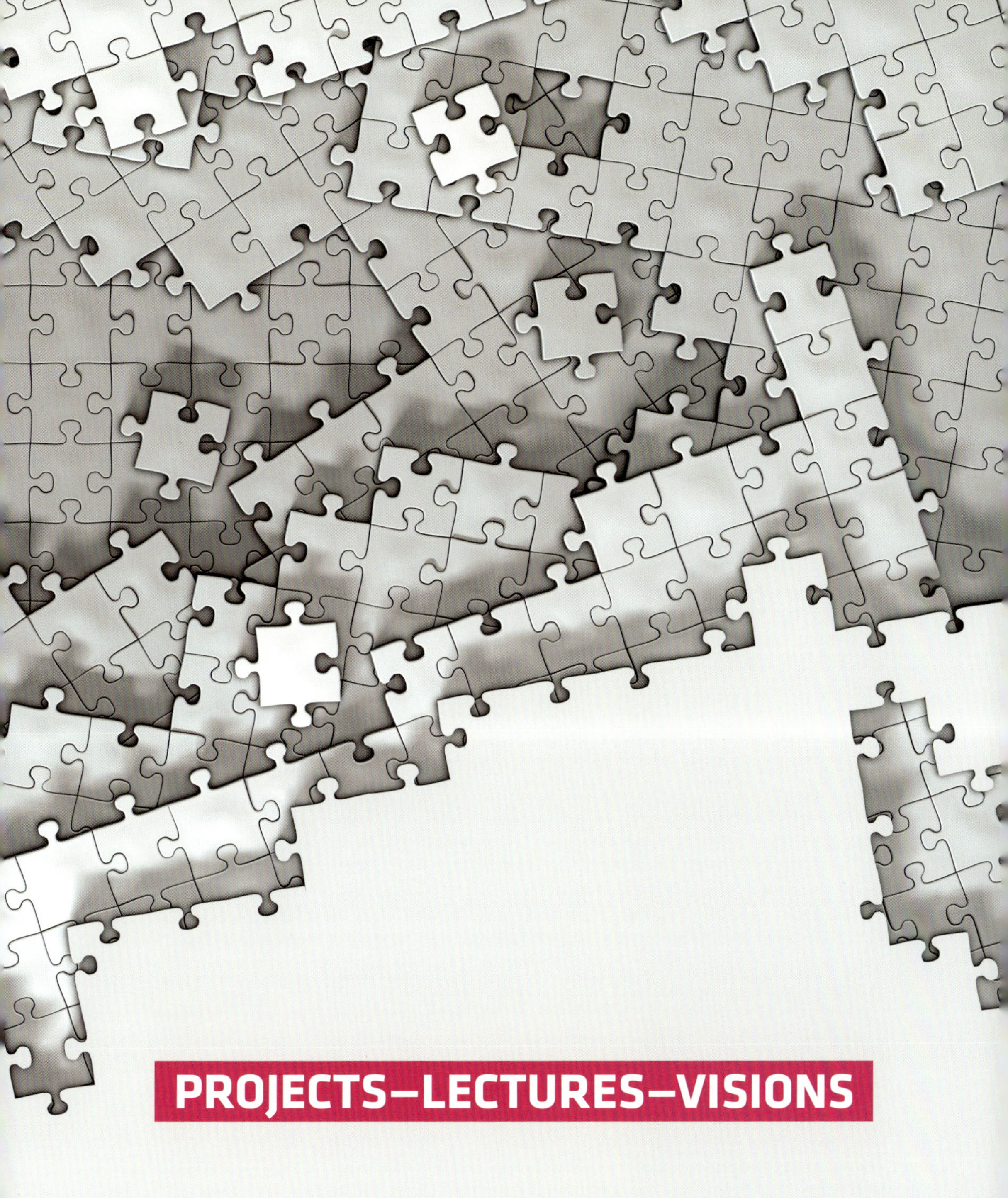
PROJECTS–LECTURES–VISIONS

Thomas Macho

How Do World Pictures Take Shape?

How does a Weltbild, a world picture, emerge? The question sounds simple but possible answers are complex since they pertain to linguistic and visual, narrative and imaginative, epistemic and architectural cultural techniques, to say nothing of the expression itself–Weltbild, a German term that gets a bit blurred when translated into other languages. Is this Weltbild a vision du monde, a world view or big picture, a panorama, or a cosmology as the discussion of the geocentric and Copernican worldviews would seem to suggest? Have all epochs and cultures brought forth their own specific, characteristic pictures of the world? How do we differentiate between a Weltbild and Weltanschauung? "What is it – a 'world picture'? Obviously, a picture of the world. But what is a world? What does 'picture' mean here?"[1] This is how Martin Heidegger framed the issue in a speech entitled "Die Zeit des Weltbildes" he delivered on June 9, 1938 in Freiburg, Germany to an audience of physicians, scientists and art scholars. And he provided an answer: a Weltbild is not simply a depiction of the world or the outcome of scientists' ongoing efforts to obtain a comprehensive view of the world; rather, it is–taken quite literally–the definition of the world as a picture. "Where the world becomes picture, beings as a whole are set in place as that for which man is prepared; that which, therefore, he correspondingly intends to bring before him, have before him, and, thereby, in a decisive sense, place before him. Understood in an essential way, world picture does not mean ›picture of the world‹ but, rather, the world grasped as picture. Beings as a whole are now taken in such a way that a being is first and only in being insofar as it is set in place by representing producing [vorstellend-herstellenden] humanity. Whenever we have a world picture, an essential decision occurs concerning beings as a whole. The being of beings is sought and found in the representedness of beings. Where, however, beings are not interpreted in this way, the world, too, cannot come into the picture – there can be no world picture."[2]

The Weltbild, we may properly conclude, encompasses perception and operation, seeing and establishing, knowledge and power; it serves the purpose of representation, the epistemic strategies of mastery. Herein is the framework (Gestell) that Heidegger describes as a practical entity of imagining, representing, exhibiting and creating. Weltbilder are tantamount to preconceptions (Vorstellungen) that capture the world as a picture (darstellen) in order to be able to technically render and produce (herstellen) it. This is why there are said to be only "modern" Weltbilder, whereby the adjective "modern" serves to tautologically underscore it. In contrast to the editors of a recently published *Atlas der Weltbilder,* whose broad historical arc extends from Ancient Egypt (Henrik Pfeiffer) to the contemporary satellite images of Google Earth (Sybille Krämer),[3] Heidegger expressly emphasized that it makes no sense to speak of Weltbilder in the Middle Ages or Antiquity: "The familiar phrases 'world picture of modernity' and 'modern world picture' say the same thing twice. And they presuppose something that could never before have existed, namely, a medieval and ancient world picture. The world picture does not change from an earlier medieval to a modern one; rather, that the world becomes picture at all is what distinguishes the essence of modernity."[4] These formulations could easily be confused with a critique of culture and media that protests against the dominance of global visualizations manifested in posters, magazines, films, radio & TV shows and, most recently, on websites and cell phones. But actually, Heidegger's assertion that it was not until the early modern period that the world even became a picture has to be considered with reference to his own questions: But what is a world? What does "picture" mean here?

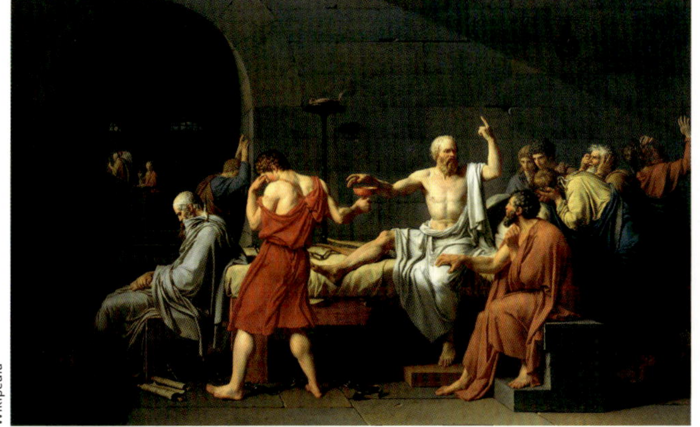

Jacques-Louis David: *The Death of Socrates* (1787)

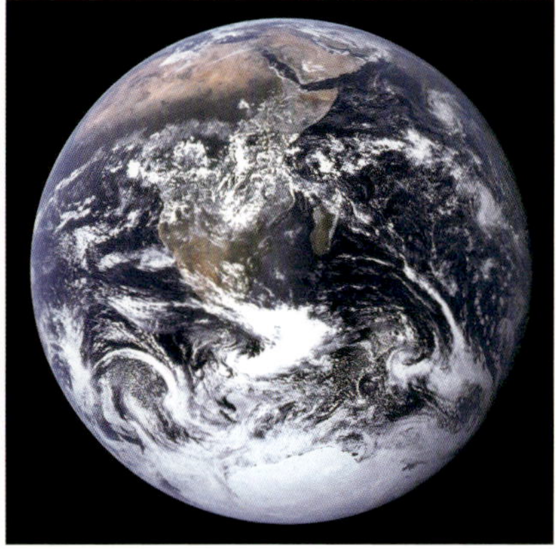

Apollo 17 (December 7, 1972)

When Swiss hotelier Erich von Däniken read the following lines in Plato's *Phaedo* almost 50 years ago, he thought (as he was wont to do) about an outer space expedition: "It is said that the world, if one gaze down on it from above, is to look on like those leathern balls of twelve pieces, variegated in divers colours, of which the colours here—those our painters use—are as it were samples. There, the whole world is formed of such, and far brighter and purer than they; part sea-purple of a wonderful beauty, a part like gold; a part whiter than alabaster or snow; aye, composed thus of other colours also of like quality, of greater loveliness than ours—colours we have never seen. For even those hollows in it, being filled with air and water, present a certain species of colour gleaming amid the diversity of the others; so that it presents one continuous aspect of varied hues."[5] Does this even refer to outer space? Or to the world at all? Socrates did indeed describe Earth as a sphere, as a colorful ball, but not, as the first astronauts did, as the blue planet (whereby the famous photograph taken from Apollo 17 on December 7, 1972 looks less blue than it usually does, and also shows a bit of purple but little gold). Why could the photograph of the blue planet also be characterized as a sort of Weltbild in Martin Heidegger's sense but not the Platonic version? An initial answer is obviously that this has to do with the relation between the image and the narrative. Our own discourse about the blue planet is derived from a photograph taken during a space mission; Socrates' tale is of the cosmic place where immortal souls reside, and as such has just as little to do with a "picture" as it does with the globe as a "world."

Weltbilder from before the early modern period are neither pictures nor do they have anything to do with the world. In most instances, they unfold as myths, the moral punch lines of which are not due to a geometric construction but rather the rhetoric of a narrative. Hence, neither is Socrates a reliable witness for Däniken's speculations about ancient astronauts, nor does the allegory of the cave in Plato's *The Republic* represent a movie theater. "Nothing supports the assumption that those trapped in the cave would become iconoclasts if they would only find out that they would be permitted to derive satisfaction from what is termed actuality."[6] The point is not to see the difference between shadows and ideas, between the sign and the signified; rather, the main thing is the paradoxical effort of all accounts of birth and creation to tell of beginnings. Weltbilder before the Age of the World Picture play up narrative differences such as the one between chaos and cosmos. In the beginning, the Earth was tohu va bohu according to the Book of Genesis, "unformed and void." Only then did a mighty, magical separation transform chaos into cosmos, into ordered systems of meaning. "Draw a distinction," demands the fundamental principle of the *Laws of Form*[7] that British logician George Spencer-Brown published in 1969. And thus "God divided the light from the darkness. And God called the light Day, and the darkness He called Night." (Genesis 1,4). With words and not with images was the chaos converted into distinctions: Sun and Moon, Heaven and Earth, land and sea. In Ancient Greek, *kósmos* meant "world order" as well as "decorum" and "decoration," and is thus the etymological root of the word "cosmetic." Cosmos was an outgrowth of logos, of the harmonious ideals of rightness and beauty, as the Delphic Oracle proclaimed. As an inhabitant of the cosmos—as a *kosmopolites*—is how Diogenes wanted to be identified when he was asked from whence he came, whereby his choice of terminology was emblematic of his contempt for Athenian politics.

culturechange.de

Wikipedia

Wikipedia

museum-frieder-burda.de

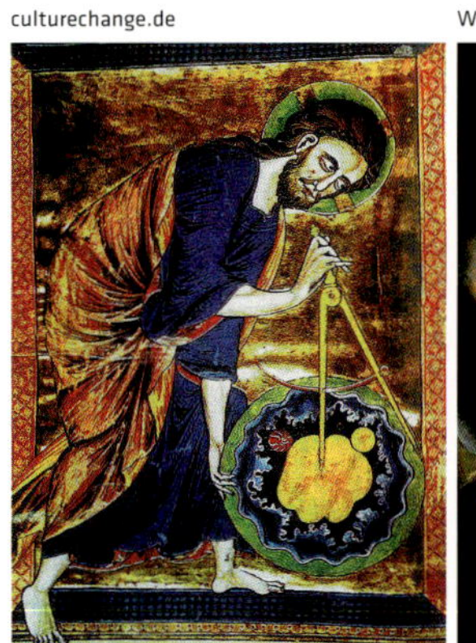

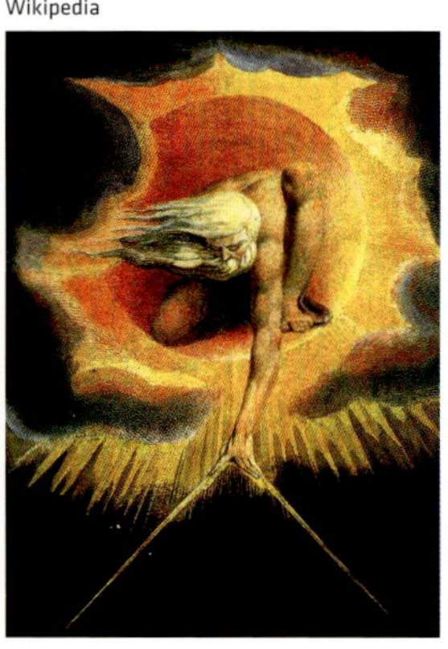

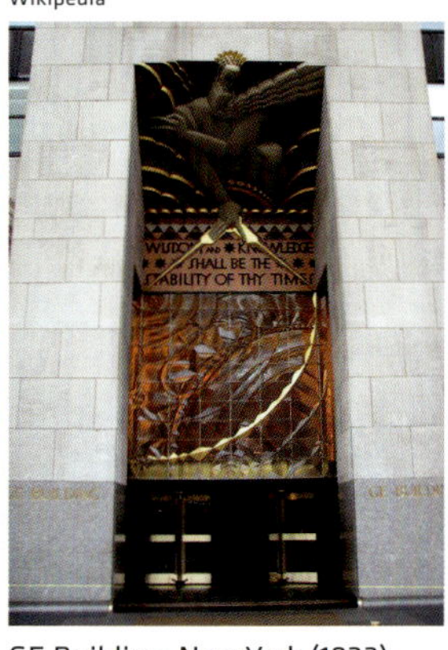

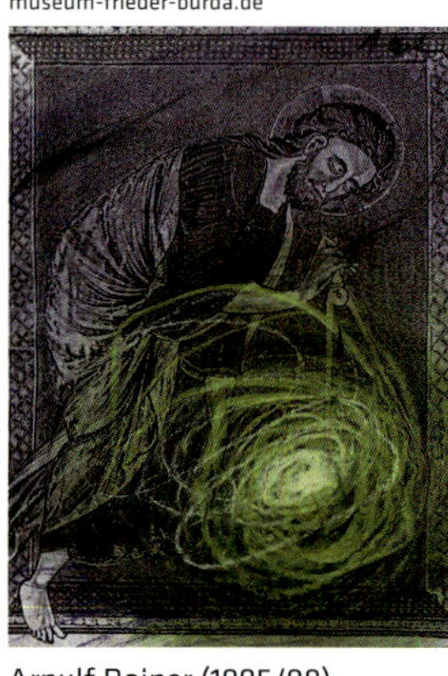

Bible moralisée (1250)   William Blake (1794)   GE Building, New York (1933)   Arnulf Rainer (1995/98)

Creation myths are latently iconoclastic—they are most difficult to depict, just as the Big Bang cannot be simulated in a particle accelerator. Origins remain murky. A famed medieval illustration in the *Bible moralisée* (created around 1250) shows the God of creation—with his right foot stepping outside the miniature's frame—as he goes about taking the measure of the world. A compass set at an angle of about 30° is being used to impart order to a disc that vaguely resembles a discus, a uterus or a placenta. Chaos imagined in more or less feminine terms is to be subordinated to the masculine law of the cosmos, the ordering principles of mathematics and proportions. William Blake, more than 500 years later in "Ancient of Days" (1794), rendered the Creator much differently. Here, God himself—his long hair and beard wafting in the solar wind—comes across like the personification of the chaos that is being thrust out of a blazing star by the right angle of his Freemason's compass. In the extension of the spread fingers of his left hand, the compass points to the empty, black night and towards the corners of the painting. Would-be creation lies beyond the visible depiction, beneath the compass-aimed blitz of the left-handed demiurge who only later reverted to right-handedness above the grand entry portal of the GE (former RCA) Building fronting Rockefeller Center in midtown Manhattan. As we know, creations have to be repeated, whereby the rebellious lefty can be replaced by the authoritarian rightist,[8] or the placental disc by an iridescent green cyclone that threatens to devour the divine compass from the Bible moralisée in Arnulf Rainer's black-and-white play on the rules of creativity and copying. When a portrait of the so-called God particle—the Higgs boson that CERN's Large Hadron Collider had purportedly discovered—was adorning the front page of many newspapers a few weeks ago, I found myself emphatically reminded of Rainer's greenish whirlwind of creation.

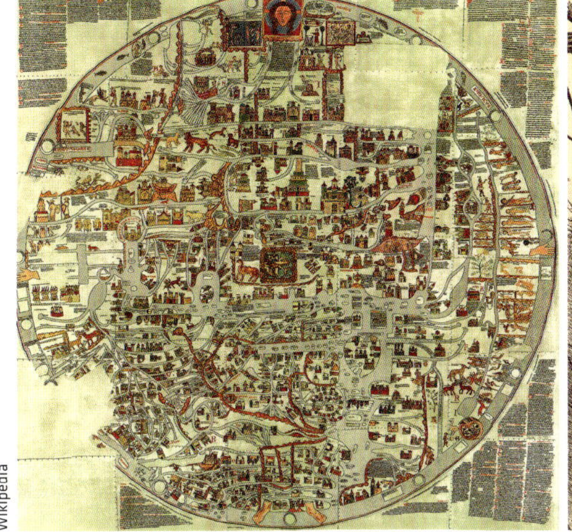

The Ebstorf Map (approximately 1300)

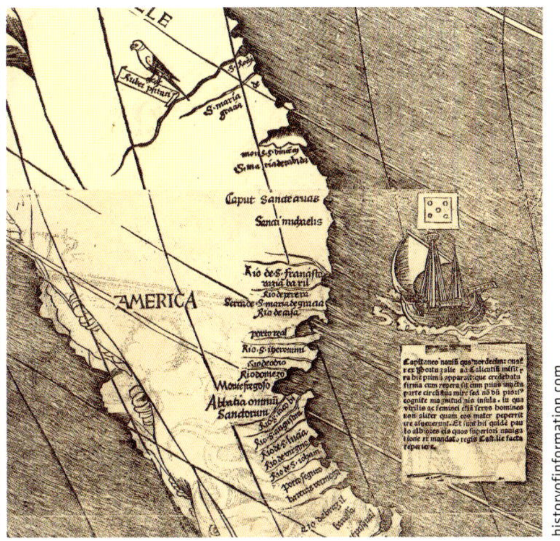

Martin Waldseemüller: World Map (1507)

So, how actually do Weltbilder materialize? They are generated, as it were, by a procedure that projects myths and narratives onto flat surfaces. The traces of this process can still be discovered on old maps of the world, on which they seem to seek connection to a message, to a type of movement that can be associated with narratives. The medieval maps that shaped the picture of the ancient world are often termed T and O maps: into a circle (that is, the O formed by the oceans) is inscribed a T that divides the circle into three parts—the upper semicircle of Asia, the left lower quadrant of Europe and the right lower quadrant of Africa. The T and O maps were "Easternized," so to speak. The East was on top, not the North; orientation was bestowed by the Orient. The T was formed by the rivers Don and Nile (as crossbeams) and the Mediterranean; at the center of all creation was Jerusalem. Some editions of the T and O maps also indicated places that were said to be inhabited by those monstrous-miraculous peoples Pliny had described. Or the apocalyptic nations of Gog and Magog, the upshot of whose labeling were cultural misunderstandings of the Mongol invasions in the 13th century. The famous Ebstorf Map that has been dated to approximately 1300[9] consisted of 30 parchment sheets sewn together into a cartographical work measuring no less than 3.57 meters across. It was discovered in 1830 in the Benedictine convent in Ebstorf in Germany's Lüneburger Heide, and was destroyed in 1943 by the fire a World War II air raid ignited. Endowing this map with its symbolic order are not only the directions of the (magnetic) compass but also the figure of Christ—his head (next to paradise), his right and left hands and both feet, and the city, Jerusalem, as navel. A world map as symbolic circle with cross, as a human gestalt? Rather more abstract, on the other hand, is Martin Waldseemüller's famous 1507 world map that is currently on display as "America's Birth Certificate" in the Treasures Gallery of the Library of Congress in Washington. But even on this map there is yet another ship sailing to the New World, which here, for the first time, is referred to as America.

In his treatise entitled "The Age of the World Picture," perhaps Heidegger actually did have in mind the maps that enabled and accompanied men as they set forth for new worlds and into new times. What is in any case evident is that the maps also became increasingly precise and more exactly organized to the same extent that they became more abstract and further removed from the realm of imagery and myth, in order to better serve the interests and operations of field marshals and conquistadores. But maybe the philosopher was thinking about a completely different kind of Weltbild that was being designed at the same time he was writing *Being and Time* (1927). In those days, economist/philosopher Otto Neurath, briefly head of the Bavarian Soviet

Republic's Office of Central Economic Planning in Munich and, since 1924, director of the Museum of Society and Economy he himself had established in Vienna, was collaborating with graphic artist Gerd Arntz to promulgate Viennese pictorial statistics, a system of pictographic symbols that could be used to portray statistically complex facts and interrelationships in ways that are easily understandable by all kinds of people worldwide. The International System of Typographic Picture Education (ISOTYPE) was closer to Friedrich Kittler's sober insight that, in the wake of World War I, death had ceased to be a category of philosophy and was merely a set of statistics,[10] than Heidegger's "being-toward-death"[11] was. Some of the illustrations Gerd Arntz designed for *Society and Economy* (1930)[12], the fundamental work of pictorial statistics, were visualizations of mortality rates with straightforward symbols like black crosses and red soldiers providing a comparison with war casualties (Table 27), whereby each cross was meant to represent 50,000 (in World War I: 500,000) dead, each anthropomorphic figure 50,000 (after World War I: 500,000) surviving men. Table 92 employs pink dolls, black coffins and coin-like discs to visualize the relationship between infant mortality and income level in various countries of the world. Here, each coffin represents one death in the first year of life per 10 births, and each disc stands for per capita annual income of 100 marks. In the illustrations created by Neurath and Arntz, what Heidegger referred to as the "indeterminacy" of one's own death is liquidated into a calculable mean value. The "being-toward-death" is translated into life expectancy statistics and liberated from the "mysterious power of the individual personality."[13] And even if the intended internationality of the ISOTYPE pictorial language might have been stymied by the use of culturally specific symbols like crosses and caskets, the perspective of actuarial mathematics and demographics, the planning policies of the welfare state (as this term was used by François Ewald[14]) nevertheless became so pervasive as a political attitude and established themselves to such an extent that it is truly difficult to suggest alternatives. In the Age of the Internet too—and especially now—number- and data-based Weltbilder—the very epitomes of big pictures—serve the interests of power and of Heidegger's "framework." Weltbilder are instruments of domination.

1   Martin Heidegger: "The Age of the World Picture". In: *Off the Beaten Track*. Translated and edited by Julian Young and Kenneth Haynes. Cambridge (UK)/New York: Cambridge University Press 2002, p.67.
2   Ibid. p. 67 f.
3   See *Atlas der Weltbilder*. Edited by Christoph Markschies, Ingeborg Reichle, Jochen Brüning and Peter Deuflhard. Berlin: Akademie Verlag 2011.
4   Martin Heidegger: "The Age of the World Picture", p. 83.
5   Plato: *Phaedo*, English translation by Walter Pater in: *Plato and Platonism*, The Echo Library, Middlesex, 2006.
6   Hans Blumenberg: *Höhlenausgänge*. Frankfurt am Main: Suhrkamp 1989. p. 117.
7   George Spencer-Brown: *Laws of Form*. New York: The Julian Press 1972. p. 3.
8   See Robert Hertz: *Die Vorherrschaft der rechten Hand. Eine Studie über religiöse Polarität*. Übersetzt von Hubert Knoblauch. In: *Das Sakrale, die Sünde und der Tod*. Religions-, kultur- und wissenssoziologische Untersuchungen. Edited by Stephan Moebius and Christian Papilloud. Konstanz: UVK 2007. pp. 181-217.
9   See *Die Ebstorfer Weltkarte*. Kommentierte Neuausgabe in zwei Bänden. Edited by Hartmut Kugler with assistance from Sonja Glauch and Antje Willing. Berlin: Akademie Verlag 2007.
10 See Friedrich Kittler: *Il fiore delle truppe scelte*. In: *Der Dichter als Kommandant. D'Annunzio erobert Fiume*. Edited by Hans Ulrich Gumbrecht, Friedrich Kittler and Bernhard Siegert. Munich: Wilhelm Fink 1996. pp. 205-225.
11 See Martin Heidegger: Sein und Zeit. Tübingen: Max Niemeyer[19] 2006. pp. 260-267.
12 See Otto Neurath / Gerd Arntz: *Gesellschaft und Wirtschaft. Bildstatistisches Elementarwerk*. Das Gesellschafts- und Wirt-schaftsmuseum in Wien zeigt in hundert farbigen Bildtafeln Produktionsformen, Gesellschaftsordnungen, Kulturstufen, Lebenshaltungen. Leipzig: Bibliographisches Institut 1930.
13 Otto Neurath: "Statistik und Proletariat". Zitiert nach: Frank Hartmann / Erwin K. Bauer (Eds.): *Bildersprache. Otto Neurath Visualisierungen*. Vienna: Facultas Verlag WUV [2]2006. p. 75.
14 See François Ewald: *Der Vorsorgestaat*. Translated by Wolfram Bayer and Hermann Kocyba. Frankfurt am Main: Suhrkamp 1993.

Thomas Macho

Wie entstehen Weltbilder?

Wie entstehen Weltbilder? Die Frage klingt einfach; mögliche Antworten sind komplex. Denn sie betreffen sprachliche und visuelle, narrative und imaginative, epistemische und architektonische Kulturtechniken, ganz abgesehen vom Begriff des „Weltbilds" selbst, der nur schwer in andere Sprachen übersetzt werden kann. Ist das Weltbild eine *vision du monde,* ein *world view* oder *big picture,* ein Panorama oder eine Kosmologie, wie die Rede vom geozentrischen und kopernikanischen Weltbild nahezulegen scheint? Haben alle Epochen und Kulturen ihre besonderen, charakteristischen Weltbilder ausgebildet? Worin unterscheiden sich Weltbilder und Weltanschauungen? „Was ist das – ein Weltbild? Offenbar ein Bild von der Welt. Aber was heißt hier Welt? Was meint da Bild?"[1] So fragte Martin Heidegger in einem Vortrag über *Die Zeit des Weltbildes,* den er am 9. Juni 1938 vor Ärzten, Natur- und Kunstwissenschaftlern in Freiburg hielt; und er gab zur Antwort: Ein Weltbild sei nicht einfach ein Abbild der Welt oder der Ausdruck rastloser Versuche der Wissenschaften, sich über die Welt ins Bild zu setzen, sondern – ganz wörtlich genommen – die Definition der Welt als Bild. „Wo die Welt zum Bilde wird, ist das Seiende im Ganzen angesetzt als jenes, worauf der Mensch sich einrichtet, was er deshalb entsprechend vor sich bringen und vor sich haben und somit in einem entschiedenen Sinne vor sich stellen will. Weltbild, wesentlich verstanden, meint daher nicht ein Bild von der Welt, sondern die Welt als Bild begriffen. Das Seiende im Ganzen wird jetzt so genommen, daß es erst und nur seiend ist, sofern es durch den vorstellend-herstellenden Menschen gestellt ist. Wo es zum Weltbild kommt, vollzieht sich eine wesentliche Entscheidung über das Seiende im Ganzen. Das Sein des Seienden wird in der Vorgestelltheit des Seienden gesucht und gefunden."[2]
Das Weltbild, so lässt sich folgern, verklammert Wahrnehmung und Operation, Sehen und Stellen, Wissen und Macht; es dient der Repräsentation, den epistemischen Strategien der Beherrschung. Darin besteht das „Gestell", das Heidegger beschreibt: als praktische Einheit von Vorstellen, Darstellen, Ausstellen und Herstellen. Weltbilder sind gleichsam Vor-Bilder *(Vorstellungen),* welche die Welt als Bild erfassen *(darstellen),* um sie technisch entwerfen und erzeugen *(herstellen)* zu können. Darum gebe es nur „neuzeitliche" Weltbilder, wobei das Adjektiv „neuzeitlich" als tautologische Unterstreichung fungiert. Im Gegensatz zu den Herausgebern eines unlängst edierten *Atlas der Weltbilder,* die einen weiten Bogen spannen vom altägyptischen Reich (Henrik Pfeiffer) bis zu den Google-Earth-Satellitenbildern der Gegenwart (Sybille Krämer), betonte Heidegger ausdrücklich, es mache keinen Sinn, von mittelalterlichen oder antiken Weltbildern zu sprechen: „Die Redewendungen ‚Weltbild der Neuzeit' und ‚neuzeitliches Weltbild' sagen zweimal dasselbe und unterstellen etwas, was es nie zuvor geben konnte, nämlich ein mittelalterliches und ein antikes Weltbild. Das Weltbild wird nicht von einem vormals mittelalterlichen zu einem neuzeitlichen, sondern dies, daß überhaupt die Welt zum Bild wird, zeichnet das Wesen der Neuzeit aus."[4] Leicht könnten diese Formulierungen mit einer Kultur- und Medienkritik verwechselt werden, die gegen die Dominanz globaler Visualisierungen protestiert, die sich in Plakaten, Illustrierten, Filmen, Radio- und Fernsehsendungen – und heute auf Websites und Handys – verkörpert. Tatsächlich muss aber Heideggers Behauptung, dass in der Neuzeit die Welt überhaupt zum Bild wird, auf seine eigenen Fragen bezogen werden: Was heißt hier Welt? Was meint da Bild?

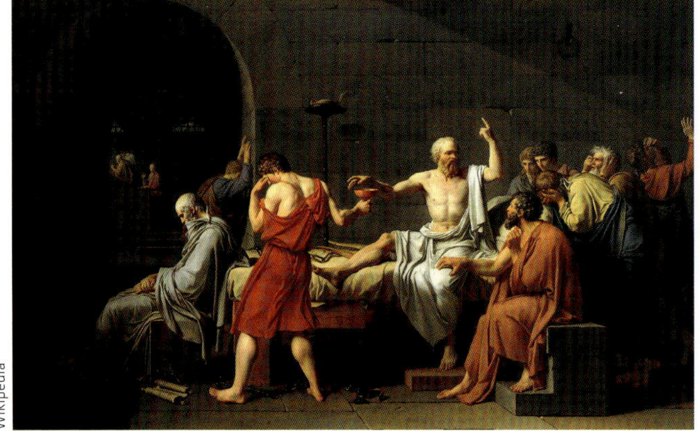
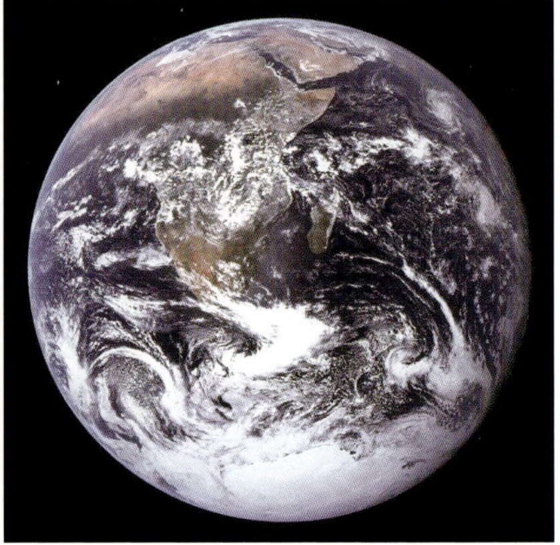

Jacques-Louis David: *La Mort de Socrate* (1787)

Apollo 17 (7. Dezember 1972)

Als der Schweizer Hotelier Erich von Däniken – vor fast einem halben Jahrhundert – folgende Zeilen in Platons *Phaidon* las, dachte er (wieder einmal) an eine Weltraumexpedition: „Man sagt also zuerst, o Freund, diese Erde sei so anzusehen, wenn sie jemand von oben herab betrachtete, wie die zwölfteiligen ledernen Bälle, in so bunte Farben geteilt, von denen unsere Farben hier gleichsam Proben sind, alle die, deren sich die Maler bedienen. Dort aber bestehe die ganze Erde aus solchen und noch weit glänzenderen und reineren als diese. Denn ein Teil sei purpurrot und wunderbar schön, ein anderer goldfarbig, ein anderer weiß, aber viel weißer als Alabaster oder Schnee, und ebenso aus jeder anderen Farbe bestehe einer und aus noch mehreren und schöneren, als wir je gesehen haben. Denn selbst diese Höhlungen der Erde, welche mit Wasser und Luft angefüllt sind, bilden eine eigene Art von Farbe, welche in der Vermischung aller anderen Farben glänzt, so daß sie ganz und gar als ein ununterbrochenes Bunt erscheint."[5] Ist hier vom Weltraum die Rede? Oder überhaupt von der Welt? Zwar beschreibt Sokrates die Erde als Kugel, als bunten Ball, jedoch nicht – wie die ersten Astronauten – als *blue planet* (wobei die berühmte Fotografie von Apollo 17, aufgenommen am 7. Dezember 1972, weniger blau als gewöhnlich aussieht, auch ein paar Purpurtöne und wenige Goldfarben zeigt). Warum könnte die Fotografie des blauen Planeten als eine Art von „Weltbild", auch im Sinne Martin Heideggers, charakterisiert werden, nicht aber die platonische Vision? Eine erste Antwort liegt nahe: Sie betrifft das Verhältnis von Bild und Erzählung. Unser eigener Diskurs über den blauen Planeten folgt einer Fotografie, die während einer Weltraumexpedition aufgenommen wurde; die Erzählung des Sokrates bezieht sich auf die kosmischen Wohnorte unsterblicher Seelen: Sie zielt ihrerseits ebenso wenig auf ein „Bild" wie auf die Erdkugel als „Welt".

Vorneuzeitliche „Weltbilder" sind weder Bilder noch handeln sie von der Welt. Zumeist entfalten sie sich als Mythen, die ihre Pointen keiner geometrischen Konstruktion verdanken, sondern der Rhetorik einer Narration. Sokrates ist darum kein verlässlicher Zeuge für die Spekulationen der Prä-Astronautik Dänikens, und das Höhlengleichnis (aus Platons *Politeia)* schildert keinen Kinosaal: „Nichts läßt die Vermutung zu, daß die Eingeschlossenen der Höhle zu Bilderstürmern würden, wenn sie nur erführen, man lasse sie an Abbildern von dem Genüge finden, was das Wirkliche genannt wird."[6] Nicht auf die Differenz zwischen Schatten und Ideen, zwischen Zeichen und Bezeichnetem, kommt es an, sondern auf den paradoxen Versuch aller Geburts- und Schöpfungsberichte, von Anfängen zu erzählen. Die „Weltbilder" vor der *Zeit des Weltbildes* exponierten narrative Differenzen, etwa zwischen Chaos und Kosmos. Ursprünglich war die Erde *tohu va bohu,* behauptete das Buch *Genesis,* wüst und wirr. Erst ein mächtiger Trennungszauber verwandelte Chaos in Kosmos, in Systeme geordneter Bedeutungen. *Draw a distinction,* fordert daher das Grundgesetz der *Laws of Form,*[7] die der britische Logiker George Spencer-Brown im Jahr 1969 veröffentlichte; und also „schied Gott das Licht von der Finsternis und nannte das Licht Tag und die Finsternis Nacht" *(Gen* 1,4). Mit Worten, nicht mit Bildern wurde das Chaos in Distinktionen übersetzt: Sonne und Mond, Himmel und Erde, Land und Meer. In der altgriechischen Sprache bedeutete *kósmos* die „Weltordnung", aber auch „Anstand" und „Schmuck", etymologische Wurzel des Ausdrucks „Kosmetik". Kosmos entsprang dem Logos, den harmonischen Idealen der Richtigkeit und Schönheit, wie sie das delphische Orakel verkündete. Als Bewohner des Kosmos – als *kosmopolites* – wollte Diogenes anerkannt werden, als er gefragt wurde, woher er denn komme; in diesen Begriff kondensierte er seine Verachtung athenischer Politik.

culturechange.de

Wikipedia

Wikipedia

museum-frieder-burda.de

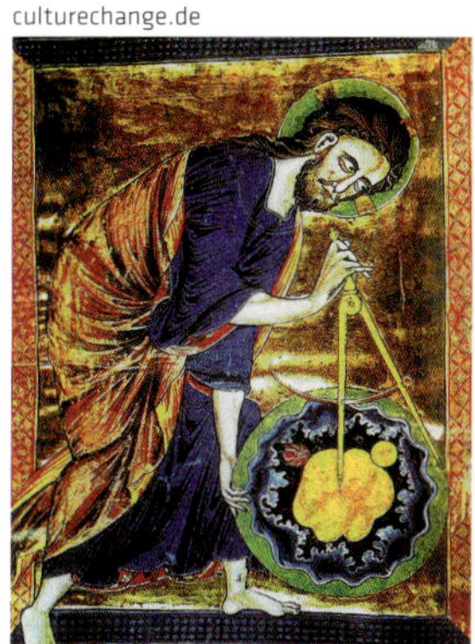

Bible moralisée (1250)

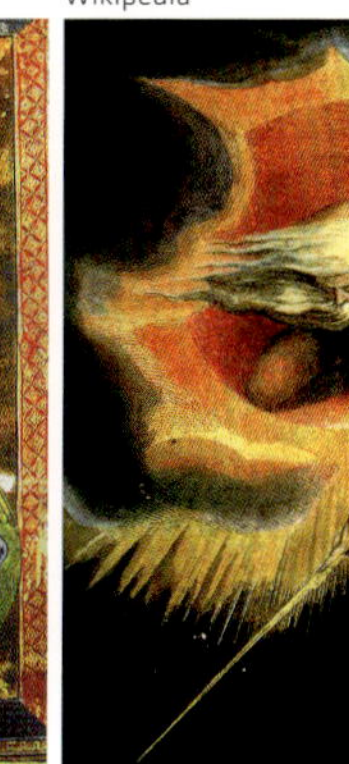

William Blake,
Ancient of Days (1794)

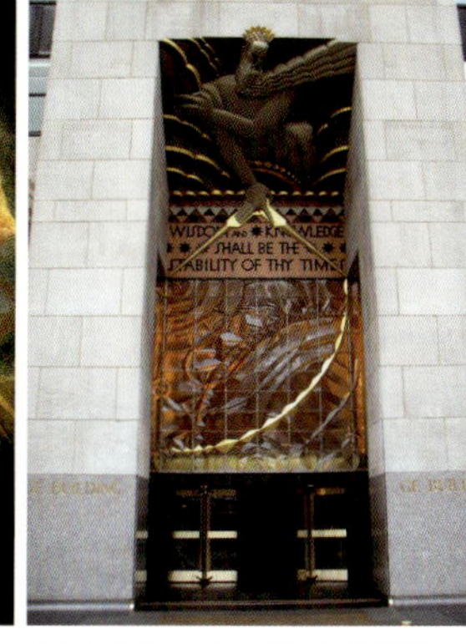

GE Building, New York (1933)

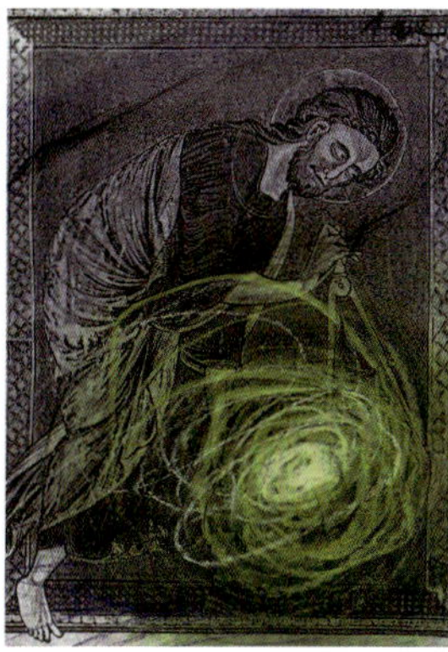

Arnulf Rainer (1995/98)

Schöpfungsmythen sind latent ikonoklastisch; sie lassen sich nur schwer abbilden, ebenso wie der *Big Bang,* der in keinem Teilchenbeschleuniger simuliert werden kann. Ursprünge bleiben dunkel. Eine bekannte mittelalterliche Illustration der *Bible moralisée* (entstanden um 1250) zeigt den Schöpfergott – mit dem rechten Fuß tritt er aus dem Rahmen der Miniatur –, wie er die Welt vermisst. Ein Zirkel, angesetzt im Winkel von etwa dreißig Grad, soll eine Scheibe bändigen, die entfernt an einen Diskus, einen Uterus oder eine Plazenta erinnert. Ein mehr oder weniger weiblich imaginiertes Chaos soll dem männlichen Gesetz des Kosmos, den Ordnungen der Mathematik und der Proportionen, unterworfen werden. Ganz anders zeigt William Blake, mehr als fünfhundert Jahre später – in *Ancient of Days* (von 1794) – den Schöpfer: Gott selbst wirkt hier wie das personifizierte Chaos, das vom rechten Winkel seines freimaurerischen Zirkels, mit wehendem Haarschopf und Bart, aus einem lodernden Gestirn herausgerissen wird. In Verlängerung der gespreizten Finger der linken Hand zielt der Zirkel auf die leere, schwarze Nacht – und auf die Ecken des Bildes. Die mögliche Schöpfung liegt jenseits der sichtbaren Darstellung, unter dem Zirkelblitz des linkshändigen Demiurgen, der erst über dem Eingangsportal zum GE (vormals RCA) Building im Rockefeller Center von Midtown Manhattan wieder zur Rechtshändigkeit bekehrt wurde. Gewiss, Schöpfungen müssen wiederholt werden; dabei kann die rebellische Linke durch die herrische Rechte ersetzt werden,[8] oder die plazentale Scheibe durch einen grün irrlichternden Wirbel, der den göttlichen Zirkel aus der *Bible moralisée* zu verschlingen droht: in Arnulf Rainers Spiel mit den Regeln der Kreativität und des Kopierens (in Schwarzweiß). Als vor wenigen Wochen ein Porträt des sogenannten „Gottesteilchens" – des im Large Hadron Collider von CERN vermutlich entdeckten Higgs-Boson – die Titelseiten zahlreicher Zeitungen schmückte, fand ich mich nachdrücklich erinnert an den grünlichen Schöpfungswirbel Rainers.

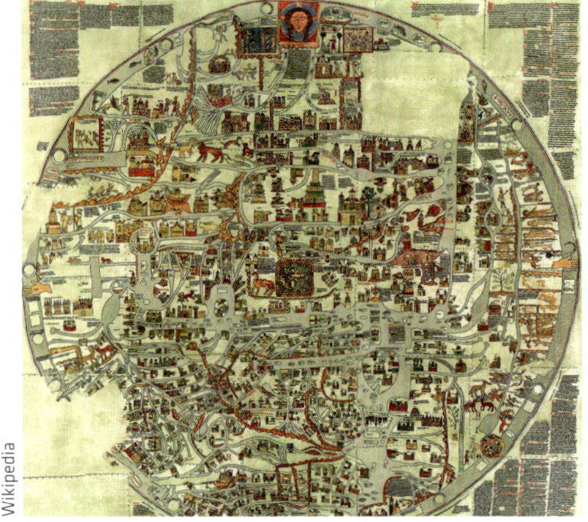
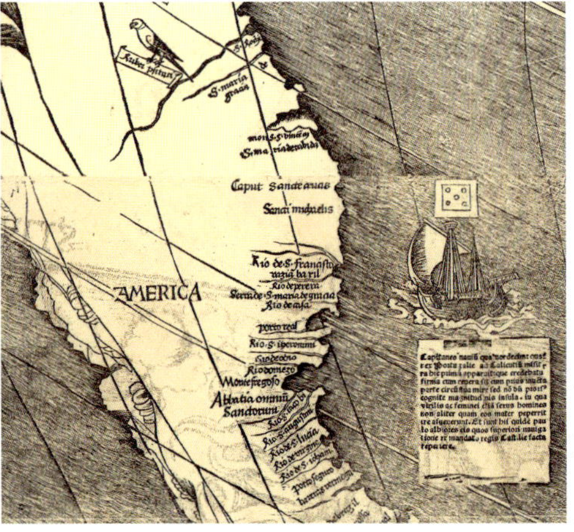

Ebstorfer Weltkarte (um 1300)   Martin Waldseemüller: Weltkarte (1507)

Wie also entstehen Weltbilder? Sie werden gleichsam durch ein Verfahren generiert, das Mythen und Erzählungen auf Flächen projiziert. Die Spuren dieses Verfahrens lassen sich noch auf alten Weltkarten entdecken: Sie scheinen den Anschluss zu suchen an eine Botschaft, an eine Art von Bewegung, die mit Narrationen assoziiert werden kann. Die mittelalterlichen Karten, die das Bild der alten Welt geprägt haben, werden häufig als „TO-Karten" bezeichnet: Einem Kreis (dem O des Ozeans) wurde ein T eingeschrieben, das diesen Kreis in drei Teile schnitt – den oberen Halbkreis Asiens, den linken unteren Viertelkreis Europas und den rechten unteren Viertelkreis Afrikas. Die TO-Karten waren gleichsam „geostet": Der Osten stand oben, nicht der Norden; Orientierung stiftete der Orient. Das T wurde von den Flüssen Don und Nil (als Querbalken) und dem Mittelmeer gebildet; im Zentrum lag Jerusalem. Manche Ausgaben der TO-Karten zeigten auch die Orte, an denen jene monströsen Wundervölker leben sollten, die bereits Plinius beschrieben hatte, oder die apokalyptischen Völker Gog und Magog; so kam es zu kulturellen Missverständnissen der Mongolenstürme des 13. Jahrhunderts. Aus dreißig zusammengenähten Pergamentblättern bestand die berühmte Ebstorfer Weltkarte, die um 1300 entstanden sein soll;[9] sie erreichte einen Durchmesser von 3,57 Metern. Gefunden wurde sie 1830 im Benediktinerinnenkloster von Ebstorf in der Lüneburger Heide; sie verbrannte 1943 bei einem Luftangriff im Zweiten Weltkrieg. Ihre symbolische Ordnung erhielt die Karte nicht nur durch Windrichtungen, sondern auch durch die Gestalt Christi: den Kopf (neben dem Paradies), seine rechte und linke Hand, sowie die beiden Füße und die Stadt Jerusalem als Bauchnabel. Eine Weltkarte als symbolischer Kreis mit Kreuz, als menschliche Gestalt? Abstrakter wirkt dagegen die berühmte Weltkarte Martin Waldseemüllers (1507), die heute – unter dem Titel *America's Birth Certificate* – in der Treasures Gallery der Library of Congress in Washington gezeigt wird. Doch selbst auf dieser Karte segelte noch ein Schiff zur Neuen Welt, die an dieser Stelle erstmals „America" genannt wurde.

Vielleicht dachte Heidegger – in seiner Abhandlung über *Die Zeit des Weltbildes* – tatsächlich an die Karten, die den Aufbruch in neue Welten und neue Zeiten ermöglichten und begleiteten; evident ist jedenfalls, dass die Karten im selben Maße, in dem sie abstrakter, bild- und mythenferner, doch zunehmend präziser und exakter ausgestaltet wurden, den Interessen und Operationen der Feldherren und Eroberer immer besser dienten. Vielleicht dachte der Philosoph aber auch an eine ganz andere Art von Weltbildern, die just zur selben Zeit, in der er *Sein und Zeit* (1927) verfasste, entworfen wurden. Damals initiierte der Ökonom und Philosoph Otto Neurath, kurzfristig Leiter des Zentralwirtschaftsamts der Münchner Räterepublik und seit 1924 Direktor des von ihm gegründeten Gesellschafts- und Wirtschaftsmuseums in Wien, gemeinsam mit dem Graphiker Gerd Arntz das Projekt der Wiener Bildstatistik, eines international leicht verständlichen Zeichen- und Sprachsystems auf Grundlage piktographischer Symbole, mit denen auch statistisch komplexe Sachverhalte übersichtlich dargestellt werden konnten. Das *International System of Typographic Picture Education,* kurz: ISOTYPE, stand der nüchternen Einsicht Friedrich Kittlers, der Tod sei nach dem Ersten Weltkrieg keine Kategorie der Philosophie mehr, sondern schlicht der Statistik,[10] näher als Heideggers „Sein zum Tode".[11] Auf manchen der von Gerd Arntz gestalteten Bildtafeln des „bildstatistischen Elementarwerks" *Gesellschaft und Wirtschaft* (von 1930)[12] wurden auch Mortalitätsraten visualisiert, mit Hilfe von einfachen Symbolen wie schwarzen Kreuzen und roten Soldaten für Kriegsverluste im Vergleich (Tafel 27), wobei jedes Kreuz 50.000 (im Ersten Weltkrieg: 500.000) Tote, jede Figur 50.000 (bzw. 500.000) überlebende Männer anzeigen sollte; mit Hilfe von rosa Puppen, schwarzen Särgen und münzartigen Kreisen wurden die Relationen zwischen Säuglingssterblichkeit und Einkommenshöhe in verschiedenen Ländern der Welt visualisiert (Tafel 92), wobei hier jeder Sarg einen Todesfall im ersten Lebensjahr, gerechnet auf zehn Geburten, jeder Kreis ein Jahreseinkommen von hundert Mark pro Einwohner repräsentieren sollte. Auf den Bildtafeln von Neurath und Arntz wird die „Unbestimmtheit" des eigenen Todes (im Sinne Heideggers) aufgelöst in einen berechenbaren Durchschnittswert; das „Sein zum Tode" wird in die Statistik von Lebenserwartungen übersetzt, befreit von der „geheimnisvollen Macht der Einzelpersönlichkeit".[13] Und obwohl die beabsichtigte Internationalität der ISOTYPE-Bildersprache schon an der Verwendung kulturspezifischer Symbole – Kreuze oder Särge – zu scheitern drohte, hat sich doch die Perspektive der Versicherungsmathematik und Demographie, die Planungspolitik des „Vorsorgestaats" (nach François Ewald[14]), als politische Haltung so weit verbreitet und durchgesetzt, dass es schwerfällt, Alternativen vorzuschlagen. Auch und gerade im Zeitalter des Internet dienen die zahlen- und datenbasierten Weltbilder – *big pictures* schlechthin – den Interessen der Macht und des „Gestells" (nach Heidegger). Weltbilder sind Herrschaftsinstrumente.

1   Martin Heidegger: Die Zeit des Weltbildes. In: *Holzwege.* Frankfurt am Main: Klostermann 1950.
    S. 69–104; hier: S. 81 f.
2   Ebd. S. 82 f.
3   Vgl. *Atlas der Weltbilder.* Herausgegeben von Christoph Markschies, Ingeborg Reichle, Jochen Brüning
    und Peter Deuflhard. Berlin: Akademie Verlag 2011.
4   Martin Heidegger: *Die Zeit des Weltbildes.* A.a.O. S. 83.
5   Platon: Phaidon [110 b–d]. Übersetzt von Friedrich Schleiermacher. In: *Sämtliche Werke.* Herausgegeben
    von Walter F. Otto, Ernesto Grassi und Gert Plamböck. Band III. Hamburg: Rowohlts Klassiker 1958. S. 7–66;
    hier: S. 59.
6   Hans Blumenberg: *Höhlenausgänge.* Frankfurt am Main: Suhrkamp 1989. S. 117.
7   George Spencer-Brown: *Laws of Form.* New York: The Julian Press 1972. S. 3.
8   Vgl. Robert Hertz: Die Vorherrschaft der rechten Hand. Eine Studie über religiöse Polarität. Übersetzt von
    Hubert Knoblauch. In: *Das Sakrale, die Sünde und der Tod. Religions-, kultur- und wissenssoziologische
    Untersuchungen.* Herausgegeben von Stephan Moebius und Christian Papilloud. Konstanz: UVK 2007.
    S. 181–217.
9   Vgl. *Die Ebstorfer Weltkarte.* Kommentierte Neuausgabe in zwei Bänden. Herausgegeben von Hartmut Kugler
    unter Mitarbeit von Sonja Glauch und Antje Willing. Berlin: Akademie Verlag 2007.
10 Vgl. Friedrich Kittler: Il fiore delle truppe scelte. In: *Der Dichter als Kommandant. D'Annunzio erobert Fiume.*
    Herausgegeben von Hans Ulrich Gumbrecht, Friedrich Kittler und Bernhard Siegert. München: Wilhelm Fink
    1996. S. 205–225.
11 Vgl. Martin Heidegger: *Sein und Zeit.* Tübingen: Max Niemeyer 192006. S. 260–267.
12 Vgl. Otto Neurath / Gerd Arntz: *Gesellschaft und Wirtschaft. Bildstatistisches Elementarwerk. Das
    Gesellschafts- und Wirtschaftsmuseum in Wien zeigt in hundert farbigen Bildtafeln Produktionsformen,
    Gesellschaftsordnungen, Kulturstufen, Lebenshaltungen.* Leipzig: Bibliographisches Institut 1930.
13 Otto Neurath: *Statistik und Proletariat.* Zitiert nach: Frank Hartmann / Erwin K. Bauer (Hrsg.):
    Bildersprache. Otto Neurath Visualisierungen. Wien: Facultas Verlag WUV 2006. S. 75.
14 Vgl. François Ewald: *Der Vorsorgestaat.* Übersetzt von Wolfram Bayer und Hermann Kocyba.
    Frankfurt am Main: Suhrkamp 1993.

Friedrich Kittler

The History of Communication Media

What follows is an attempt to discuss the history of communication technologies—as far as this is humanly possible—in general terms. The objective is ultimately the outline of a scientific history of the media—an outline for the simple reason that media sciences is a new field of research which would not exist had it not been for the triumphal advance of modern information technologies. This is why such a history comes up against methodological and practical problems.

One practical problem is that communications technologies themselves are documented to a far lesser extent, or are far less accessible, than their contents, vide the manner in which the intelligence services have remained, despite their frequently decisive role in wars, (to quote the last head of the Wehrmacht intelligence service) "the Cinderella of military-historical research"[1]. Then there is the methodological problem posed by the conundrum of whether the now so self-evident term "communication" can properly be used in connection with times and locations which manifestly were characterised by other terminology (drawn from mythology or religion). At any rate its enthronement in philosophy was based, in John Locke's "Essay on Human Understanding", on the scarcely generalisable assumption that communication means the rendering into speech of perceived ideas, and consequently the linking of isolated individuals through "bonds of language"[2]. The only trouble is that philosophy omits to enquire how, without language, people are supposed to have arrived at their ideas and conceptions in the first place. Liberation from this unfathomable confusion came only with a technical concept of information which, since Shannon's "Mathematical Theory of Communication" avoids any reference to ideas or meanings, and thus to people.

Information systems in the narrowest sense of the word are, it is true, optimised in terms of the storage, processing and transmission of messages. Communication systems on the other hand, because in addition to messages they also control the traffic of persons and goods[3], comprise all kinds of media (in McLuhan's analysis) from road systems to language[4]. There is nonetheless good reason to analyse communication systems in the same way as information systems. Ultimately, communication too depends on control signals, the more so the more complex it's working; even the triad of "things communicated"—information, persons, goods—can be reformulated in terms of information theory:

- Firstly, messages are essentially commands to which persons are expected to react (this definition in the original German is based on the etymology of the German word "Nachrichten"—Tr.).
- Secondly, as systems theory teaches, persons are not objects, but addresses which "make possible the assessment of further communications"[5].
- Thirdly, as ethnology since Mauss and Lévi-Strauss has taught, goods represent data in an order of exchange between said persons.

However if data make possible the operation of storage, addresses that of transmission and commands that of data processing, then every communication system, as the alliance of these three operations, is an information system. It depends solely on whether the three operations are implemented in physical reality to what extent such a system becomes an independent communication technology. In other words the history of these technologies comes to an end when machines not only handle the transmission of addresses and data storage, but are also able, via mathematical algorithms, to control the processing of commands. It is thus no coincidence that not until the start of the computer age, that is, when all operations of communication systems had been mechanised, was Shannon able to describe a formal model of information. This model comprises, as we know, five connected stages[6]:

This elegant model, however, not least because it lays no claim whatever to historicity, cannot simply be applied to the factual history of communication technology. Instead of simply accepting Shannon's five black boxes, as has become customary in linguistics and the humanities too, it seems more important and more rewarding to trace back through history how their evolution must have proceeded in the first place. Taking Luhmann's premise that communication technologies provide a "first-rate demarcation of epochs, magnetising all else"[8], it is reasonable to conclude that the historical transition from orality to the written word equated to a decoupling of interaction and communication, and the transition from writing to the technical media indeed to a decoupling of communication and information. What we have here, therefore, is a process of evolution which has come to a conclusion only in the theory and practice of an information which corresponds to the exact opposite of the energetic concept of entropy[9].

This evolutionary process gives us the possibility of dividing the history of communication media into two main blocks. The first block deals with the history of writing, and itself falls into a section on scripts and one on printing. The second block, on technical media, will take us from the basic invention of telegraphy via the analog media to, finally, the digital medium of the computer.

A Writing

1. Script

The history of the literate cultures, whose "medium" customarily also divides history from prehistory[10], is determined by two series of variables. The first series stands in relation to what philosophy since the Stoics has recognised or failed to recognise as a reference: To the extent that the content of a medium is always another medium[11], and that of writing (even for Aristotle[12]) is speech, scripts can be classified according to whether they process everyday languages into pictographs, or syllabic or phonemic signs[13]. However to the extent that the medium of writing, probably for the first time, also couples storage and transmission, inscription and post, then physical variables relating to writing implements and writing surface decide as to the space and time-frame of the communication. These variables dictate the time needed for transmitting and receiving, the permanence or erasability of what is written, and not least whether the information is transportable or not.

The first series of variables controls developments between speech and writing: degrees of memory performance, degrees of grammatical analysability, the possibilities of coupling speech with other media. As an independent field of anthropological media research it can for our purposes be left to one side. The second series of variables has received considerably less attention, possibly because it is so material in nature. And yet it is such simple things as writing implements and writing surface that determine the gain in power which the introduction of scripts always results in. If priests were interested in the storage of addresses, that is, of gods or the dead, for a maximum length of time; if merchants were interested in the storage of goods over a maximum length of time and in goods transportation over maximum distances, and finally warriors in the transmission of commands over maximum distances in the shortest possible time, then the oldest scripts which were produced some 3,000 years BC in Sumeria and Egypt had economic and religious functions. In warrior circles, however, that which military historians call the oral "stone age of the command flow" ended only with Napoleon[14]. Apart from commands passed from mouth to ear there were only the semiotic use of fire for signalling purposes and fast but equally oral messengers, whose record was probably held by Genghis Khan[15].

The first manifestations of script are of course inscriptions without a writing surface in the accepted sense. Two-dimensional rolls of seals or stamps in the medium of clay enabled goods to be given addresses indicating their owner or their contents. Stone inscriptions named the deceased occupants of tombs[16]. As signals in the absence of the source of information, in other words through the decoupling of communication and interaction, inscriptions opened up, according to Jan Assmann, the possibility in principle of literature[17].

By contrast an administration of those great river irrigation systems, in which cities and high cultures blossomed, presupposed the transition from inscribed tablets to skilfully crafted and optimised, transportable writing surfaces: bamboo and mulberry in China, unfired clay or clay fired for storage purposes in Mesopotamia, papyrus as the monopoly of the Nile delta. Thus the same rivers on which the traffic of slave labour and goods flowed simultaneously carried (on the basis of a calendar or goniometric mathematics) the commands of water allocation and the harvesting of products[18]. The same cities that translated the anthropological schema of head, hand and torso into the architectonic schema of palaces, streets and storehouses[19] needed scripts for the processing, transmission and storage of their data. This establishment of a unified area is reflected in the texts themselves as a spatialisation of speech: since its very beginnings writing has yielded lists without context which bear no traces of oral or written communication networks, but for this precise reason no longer have any equivalent in everyday situations[20].

By contrast, outreachings beyond the unified area—the founding of empires in other words—only became possible when states of both the ancient world and the modern took over control of the warrior messengers and additionally, in the ancient world since 1200 BC, after the crossing of two breeds of horse, made messengers and warriors mobile[21]. In classical times, "There was", in the immortal words of Herodotus, "nothing swifter on earth" than the alliance of media which under the Achaemenides combined Persia's Royal Way with a mounted staging messenger service to carry "urgent messages at a fast trot", in the face of all natural adversities, from rider to rider, from stage to stage[22]. Angareion, the Persian name of this military mail, is the root of the Greek word for messenger and consequently of all Christian angels.

The Greek polis had but one script to set against a communications empire such as the Persian, but in contrast to oriental bureaucracies it was entirely susceptible of orality. Firstly the Greek alphabet (from Indo-European necessities and because it developed in the course of commercial and translation intercourse with Semitic consonant scripts) turned redundant consonants into vowels, thus performing the first total analysis of a spoken language—and in principle of all such[23]. The fact that vowel signs for the first time encoded prosodic-musical elements of speech permitted a musical notation, and in the Pythagorean school, for the simple reason that Greek letters also possessed numerical values[24], a mathematisation of music, to the extent that this remained a matter of abstract intervals.

Secondly, the triumphal progress of the vocalic alphabet seems less to be the result of an overestimated degree of innovation rather than of the unambiguity of its phoneme allocation. This minimised the effort required for literacy and thus transferred palace and temple secrets to the public domain[25]. It became possible for literature firstly to incorporate oral mnemonics (such as airs or rhapsodies) and later also prose[26]. Athenian tyrants founded the first public library; the bookworm Euripides became the "first great reader" among writers[27].

These ancient scrolls got their Biblical name from a papyrus-exporting city in Phoenicia, whose place was taken as of 560 BC by the Nile delta. The Imperium Romanum too, after the conquest of Egypt, based its command network—which is what the empire was—on a combination of mounted staging messengers, made-up military roads and easily transportable papyrus. The empire, in other words, combined despotic transmission mechanisms with a democratic alphabet. The cursus publicus which Augustus set up, with overnight stations at distances of 40 kilometres and staging posts at around 12 kilometres, exclusively for officials and legions[28], became despite this, or perhaps precisely because of it, the crystallisation point for European towns. In combination with beacon telegraphy at sensitive frontiers, a state postal service, which was faster than the fastest ships and was not excelled until Napoleon, transmitted imperial power as such: "Caesarum est per orbem terrae litteras missitare"[29], as a late Roman writer has it—"It is the office of emperors to send written commands across the world." In comparison with this perfect transmission medium for said world and Caesar's news-sheet distribution in the city of Rome, data storage—even if there was an imperial officium sacrae memoriae since Hadrian—remained technically retarded.

Papyrus may be light, but it is fragile and impermanent. It could only be stored in rolls, and read with two hands. In the opinion of Alan Turing, the first computer theorist, "it must have taken some time to look up references in such volumes"[30]. It was not until the arrival of the codex in parchment, used first by the library of Pergamon for circumventing the Egyptian papyrus monopoly, and by Christians since 140 AD, that indexing by location, sheets and finally sides became possible. Books, which were durable, erasable (as in the palimpsest) and addressable with special pages (indices) were worth their extra weight and extra cost. They decoupled increasingly cursory reading from the laboriousness and slowness of orality. When Bishop Ambrose of Milan (according to the testimony of his best-known disciple) read a codex, "his eyes swept over the pages, extracting the essence of the meaning, while he himself remained silent"[31]. In the codex, the transportable, addressable and interpretable scripts of former nomads, the Jews and Arabs, vanquished the immobility of statues and temples of the gods.

The decline of the cursus publicus and the Islamic incorporation of Egypt, which also led to the destruction of the great ancient library, cut off Western Europe from papyrus imports. What was left was the agricultural product, parchment, on which monks were constrained to copy the censored Christian version of what was contained on papyrus, while in the Byzantine Empire the flow of written commands from all past emperors coagulated into the legislation of the Codex Justinianus. Through such bridgings or compressions of time a translatio studii was enabled to take place; but the translatio imperii presupposed new orders of distance and thus more accessible writing surfaces.

In the 13th century, paper, imported from China via Baghdad, arrived in Europe, where it was further developed by cities of the linen trade and the new windmills and watermills into rag-paper. This writing surface was central to the rise of the universities, which with their incorporated bookcopying departments and postal networks broke the storage monopoly of the monasteries. And at the same time it was central, in combination with the Indian numerical system imported via Arabia, to the rise of trading cities[32]. The important thing in this context was not simply the well known invention of double-entry bookkeeping, but above all a mathematical notation which for the first time brought independence from the numerous workaday languages. Greeks, when adding two numbers together, had said kai, and Romans et; since the 15th century however we have had plus and minus, as mute as they are international, as signs for mathematical operators.

2. Printing

Gutenberg's invention of printing using movable letters developed from book-spine stamps which, in contrast to their predecessors in China and Korea, functioned both alphabetically and (after the disappearance of ligatures) discretely, may not have been a revolution of the magnitude of the codex—but it met the demand awakened by paper. As "the first assembly line in the history of technology"[33], printing potentiated the data processing capacity of books. Because all copies of an edition, in contrast to manual copies, had the same texts, woodcuts and engravings in the same places, they could be accessed via unified and for the first time alphabetical indexes. This addressing using page numbers, titles and, since Leibniz, alphabetical library catalogues[34], put the communication system which is science on its reference basis, while book illustrations free of copying errors formed the basis of engineering[35]. Not without reason could Vasari boast that Italy had discovered perspective, as enabling the production of technically accurate drawings, in the same year as Gutenberg invented typography.

New media do not make old media obsolete; they assign them other places in the system. Thus because printing now reproduced the rhetorical-musical performances at tournaments as literature and fictions of the authors, the physical techniques of these tournaments appear (according to Gumbrecht's thesis) to have been transmuted into silent, measurable disciplines[36]. Equally it was only as a development within typography that the intrinsic value of handwriting emerged, the individuality of the hand taking the place of seals on letters and documents, and which became the domain of a state system of post and police. The first state postal systems of early modernity were, after the fashion of the Roman imperial system, still reserved for military and diplomatic networks and protected from interception by a cryptography whose rise began with Vieta's algebraic encoding of alphabetical and numerical signs[37]. The territorial states controlled extensively by post and firearms, on the other hand, opened up their networks to a private traffic which they also monopolised through their sovereign right of posts. When commercial correspondents were included in the public postal network, after 1600 newspapers and journals came into being; when the transport of persons was also included, after 1650 the post-coach networks were established as a scheduled service[38]. However the oft-quoted structural transformation from the aristocratic to the middle-class publicness, whose travels and letters, printed pamphlets and newspaper critiques are supposed to have undermined the old power system of Europe, never took place[39]. Even without its consistent control through secret cabinets and print censorship the middle-class publicness remained an artefact of mercantile states, whose new post office provided half the budget and half the war chest[40]. Only in the intimacy of family circles did the "addiction to reading" of the so-called public[41] promote a record rise in national-language belles-lettres which compensated for the "loss of sensuality"[42] with virtual effects on readers' senses, thus presaging future media technologies[43].

This mediatisation of the printed word presumably had its basis in a routine light reading which was no longer a privilege of the elite, as in Saint Ambrose's time, but which paved the way for democracy through compulsory schooling and general literacy. But precisely this effortless reading triggered a new systemic problem. Because, unlike parchment codices, printed books are storage devices having no possibility of erasure, there was, around 1800, (to quote Fichte) "no branch of knowledge on which a surfeit of books is not available"[44]. As a result literature and science had to revamp their transmission and receiving techniques: away from the literalness of quotes from the scholarly elite, and rhetorical mnemonics, towards an interpretative approach which reduced the quantity of printed data to its essence, in other words to a smaller quantity of data. The consequence for the communication system that is science, since Humboldt's reform, was lectures without textbooks, seminars as exercises in interpretation and the rise at universities of a philosophy whose absolute "spirit" preserved only the "remembrance"of all previous forms of knowledge and of its own textbook, thus becoming the hermeneutic "silhouette" of the totality of books[45].

In the real world this mediatisation of writing amounted to its industrial revolution. In place of Gutenberg's enumerable combinations came, in practical terms too, a calculus of infinites: endless paper machines replaced, as of 1800, the discrete formats and moulded sheets; pulp papers from America's seemingly inexhaustible forests, this material basis of all mass print material since 1850, took the place of rag. And finally the typewriter and linotype have, since 1880, levelled out the difference between writing and printing[46], thus opening up the floodgates of modern literature[47]. It was Mallarmé who first offered the solution of reducing literature to its lexical meaning, the twenty-six letters, and thus not competing with other media at all.

B Technical media

Unlike writing, technical media do not utilise the code of a language. They make use of physical processes which are faster than human perception and are only at all susceptible of formulation in the code of modern mathematics.

1. Telegraphy and Analog Technology

Self-evidently there must always have been technical media, because any sending of signals using acoustic or visual means is in itself technical. However in pre-industrial times channels such as smoke signals or fire telegraphy which exploited the speed of light, or bush telegraphs and calling chains making use of the speed of sound, were only subsystems of an everyday language. The beacon signal from Troy to Mycenae, with which Aeschylus introduces the literary genre of tragedy, announced in one single bit the fall of the besieged fortress, although that depended on prior arrangement[48]. On the other hand it remains questionable whether a form of telegraphy which, according to Polybios, was capable of encoding the Greek alphabet into five times five light signals and thus transmitting random sets, ever saw service[49]. Information rates which exceeded all performance limits of writing were first achieved as a result of the necessity for command flow in conscripted mass armies and wars waged with standardised weaponry. It was one and the same to Lakanai, the politician who presented the revolutionary France of 1793 with an elementary school system and a literary copyright law, who one year later persuaded the national assembly to build optical telegraphy lines. As the official reason for this revolution the argument was pressed into service that, in large nation-states, only Chappe's optical telegraph could make possible that democratic election process which Rousseau had, as we know, picked up from the city-state of Geneva. With Napoleon however a less public, but exclusive use of the optical telegraph network gave rise to a strategy which finally released wars from the stone age of command flow. Independently-operating divisions were able to fight on several fronts at the same time because newly-created general staffs imposed their cartographic knowledge by telegraph on the actual ground[50].

Telegraphy thus separated literary publicness and military secrecy at the same historic moment, since publicness was transferred from elites to entire populations. A new elite of engineering schools and general staffs finally discovered in the 1809 war their new, to all intents and purposes secret medium of electricity. With the move of telegraphy from optics to direct current, not only did the human, and therefore unreliable, relay stations disappear, but also Claude Chappe's grand total of 98 signs. The Morse code with its dots and dashes and pauses put an economy of signs into practice which Leibniz had previously come up with in expressly typographical theory in the form of his binary code[51]. The electric telegraph, optimised on the basis of letter frequency and charged by the number of words, was the first step on the road to infomation technology.

In terms of organisation and technology too, telegraphy had world-wide repercussions. For absolutely the first time, information was decoupled, in the form of a massless flow of electromagnetic waves, from communication. Remote telegraphic control via landline made possible a systematic railroad network[52], railways made possible an accelerated traffic in goods and persons[53] which, from the time of the American Civil War on, was also subject for military purposes to telegraphic command[54]. However, in the form of goods and people traffic the post lost two of its traditional functions. It was forced to become a pure information technology based on the principles of house numbers and letterboxes, prepayment with stamps and the world postal union[55]. This detachment from the ground, whose distances (as in synchronous mathematical topography) are, in contrast to all pre-modern postal systems, no longer calculated because only absolute speed counts, brought internationality: from the stock exchange reports of world trade and the telegraph agencies of the world press, to colonial empires which, like the British Empire, were founded on a "fleet in being" and consequently on a global undersea cable monopoly[56].

Technical repercussions of telegraphy as information time made discrete were consequential inventions which, paradoxically, also processed precisely the continuous signal sources. Of these I shall pass over the analog medium of photography, which requires a treatment of its own, and mention only the telephone, gramophone record, and film.

Bell's telephone, the most lucrative single patent of all time, came about in 1876 not by any means in its familiar function, but in the course of an attempt to transmit several messages over a single telegraph cable at the same time. In exactly the same way, only a year later Edison's phonograph emerged as a spin-off from an attempt to increase the throughput rate of telegraph cables. And finally Muybridge's scientific serial photographs, which in 1895, after the invention of Maltese cross and celluloid, paved the way for cinema, were triggered by electric telegraph relays.

Film and gramophone, these mass-reproduceable competitors to Edison's phonographs, made it possible to store optical and acoustical data as such. Because analog media underbid, first mechanically and subsequently electrically, the perceptual thresholds determined by Fechner, they can recognise in speech phonemes and musical intervals–which is where the Greek analysis as their being the final alphabetical elements stopped–complex frequency mixtures which are open to a further, and since Fourier mathematical, analysis. The modern fundamental concept of frequency[57], which since Euler governs probability calculation, music and optics alike, has replaced the arts with technical media. This physics in the simulation process of the real is no longer partnered in the reception process by a language-based mnemonics or pedagogy, but by a sensory physiology which has guaranteed the media their world-wide and, thanks to Shannon's measure of information, calculable success[58]. At the same time a knowledge gap between unconscious media effects on the one hand and the innovatory thrusts on the other (which since Edison's first laboratory are also plannable) has emerged which, despite the participation of women in telegraph, telephone and typewriter operations[59] is inimical to the general development of literacy and absolutely rules out communication on communication.

A prominent role in this turning-point, whose significance is probably equalled only by the invention of writing[60], was taken by Maxwell's electromagnetic field equations and their experimental substantiation by Heinrich Hertz. Since Christmas 1906, when Fessenden's radio transmitter broadcast low-frequency random events as they occur as amplitude or frequency modulation of a high frequency, there exist non-material channels. Since 1906, when de Forest developed from Edison's light bulb the controllable valve, information is open to any kind of amplification and manipulation. The valve radio, developed as wireless telephony for breaking the imperial cable monopoly, first of all made the new weapons systems of the first World War, the aeroplane and the tank, both mobile and dirigible by remote control[61], and after the end of the war was applied to the civilian populations[62].

In the guise of a "secondary orality"[63], bypassing the written word, radio had the effect of standardising unwritten languages primarily through world-wide short-wave broadcasting[64], thus transforming colonised tribal associations into independent nations[65]. In the same way the telephone, in its progress from the direct dialling system via frequency multiplex to satellite links, has made possible the non-hierarchical networking firstly of cities and ultimately of the "global village"[66]. Yet the publicly accessible wavebands remain, despite their critical overcrowding[67], only fractions of a frequency spectrum which, from long-wave broadcasting to the decimetre radar, exercises governmental or military control functions and taps all public wavebands for the secret services[68].

The electrification of sensory input data through transducers and sensors enabled the entertainments industry to couple analog storage media firstly with one another and secondly with transmission media. The sound film combined optical and acoustic memories; radio, before the introduction of the tape-recorder, largely transmitted gramophone records; the first television systems, prior to the development of electronic cameras, scanned feature films. Thus the content of entertainment media always remains another medium, which in this way they serve to promote.

But all these couplings of technologies which are already individually standardised, even though they gave birth to aesthetic forms from the radio play and electronic music to the videoclip, have one decisive deficiency: there is no general standard which regulates their control and reciprocal translation. This is precisely the point at which the heroes and heroines of Benjamin's theory of media came to the rescue, in the shape of cutters in film studios, and sound engineers for tape, with their celebrated but strictly manual montage techniques[69]. The rendering obsolete of this human intervention, and the automation of a general standard, was reserved for digital technology.

2. Digital technology

Digital technology functions like an alphabet, only on a numerical basis. It replaces the continuous functions into which the analog media transform input data, which are generally also continuous, with discrete scannings at points in time as equidistant as possible, in the same way that the 24 film exposures per second or, at a much higher frequency since the Nipkow screen television did before. This measurement followed by evaluation in the binary number system is the precondition for a general media standard.

According to the scanning theorem of Nyquist and Shannon, any and every form of signal, provided it is frequency-range-limited intrinsically or through filtering, can be biunivocally reconstructed from scanned values of at least twice the frequency[70]. The quantisation noise which necessarily arises in the process can also, in contrast to the physically-determined noise of analog systems, be minimised to any degree simply because it obeys the laws of a digital system[71]. It was in 1936 that Turing's universal discrete machine stated the principle of all digital technology. Extrapolating or reducing the equally discrete typewriter[72], it consisted simply of an endless paper tape, the idea of which goes back to 1800. On this "paper machine" for data storage a write/read/erase head for data processing could write the binary signs 0 and 1, while a transport device for data addressing made it possible to access the neighbouring signs right and left. Turing proved however that this elementary machine, because by contrast to the noisy Laplace universe it knows a finite number of states, is equal not only to any mathematician, but solves all (in Hilbert's sense) decidable problems of mathematics, through simulation of any other correctly-programmed machine[73].

Thus the Turing machine concluded in its universality all developments for the storing, indexing and processing of both alphabetical and numerical data. In the alphabetical field these developments had led from lists and catalogues, via the card indexes from which around 1800 Jean Paul's literature and Hegel's philosophy had sprung[74], to the Hollerith machine of the American census of 1890[75]. In the numeric field a parallel development had led from Schickart's calculator for the four basic types of calculation, via Jacquard's programmable looms[76], to the pioneer of computers, Babbage, whose differential engine of 1822 reduced the time-consuming developments of series in trigonometry and ballistics to recurrent difference equations, while his later planned analytical engine was intended to make the whole of analysis calculable with conditional jump commands[77]. To achieve the alphanumeric universality of Turing machines, alias computers, however, the two development strands had to be brought together by Boole's logical algebra and Goedel's theorem of incompleteness, making statements and axioms as manipulable as figures.

The Turing machine of 1936 was infinitely slow, its paper tape infinitely long, and therefore inexistent. By contrast the computer, its technical successor, is a miracle of economy of time and space called forth by the exigencies of the second World War. At the same time that Shannon was demonstrating that simple relays connected in series or in parallel can automate all operations of Boole's algebra[78], Zuse was building the first computers for Luftwaffe research from telegraph relays, while the cryptography department of the Army rejected his offers of automation[79]. At the end of 1943, by contrast, the British secret service came up with computers based on overmodulated tubes for Turing's war-deciding cryptoanalysis of precisely that secret VHF radio traffic which had made the German blitzkrieg possible[80]. Finally in 1945 John von Neumann designed the now customary architecture of sequential but microsecond-fast computers for the planned American uranium bomb, whose rate of explosion set new standards in the measurement of time[81].

Von Neumann's design postulated the following three system elements:
- Firstly a central processing unit for command-controlled processing of alphanumeric data by either mathematical or logical rules;
- secondly a write-read memory for variable data and a read-only memory for programmed commands;
- and thirdly a bus system for sequential transmission of all these data and commands as biunivocally indicated through binary addresses by pages and columns.

With these three parts, von Neumann machines articulated the fundamental structure of information technology as a functional interrelationship of hardware elements. No matter whether their environment supplies alphabetic or numerical data, that is, writing or media-generated values, the commands, data and addresses are all represented internally by binary numbers. The classic distinction between functions and arguments, operators and numerical values has become permeable. However it is precisely this breakdown of the alphabet which also permits operations to be applied to operations, and ramifications to be automated. Which is why computers in principle comprehend all other media and can subject their data to the mathematical procedures of signal processing[82].

Data throughput and access time depend solely on physical parameters. Since 1948, when the transistor replaced the tubes/printed circuits of the second World War, and 1968 when integrated circuits replaced the single transistor, in each case reducing the space and time requirement by a factor of ten, real time analyses and real time syntheses of one-dimensional data flows (of speech or music for example) are no longer any problem[83]. So the sound engineer can go home. However, for multi-dimensional signal processing in real time, such as is required for television pictures or computer animations, the von Neumann architecture becomes a bottleneck. For this reason large numbers of parallel computers are already in use, and biological and optical circuitry such as is required above all for the simulation of brain functions, is already under development. The day is not far off when signal processing will reach the physical limits of feasibility[84].

This absolute limit is where the history of communication technologies will literally come to an end. Theoretically there remains only the question as to what logic this completion will have obeyed. From Freud[85] to McLuhan the classic answer to this was a generic subject—humanity—which before of an indifferent or interferent natural world would have externalised first its motor and sensory interface, and finally its intelligence, in technical prosthetics. However if Shannon's mathematisation of information rested on his "fundamental idea" of inferring, through a conceptual transfer, the "information efficiency of a jammed transmission" from its cryptoanalytical efficiency[86], interference will only be understandable as the interventions of a hostile intelligence, and the history of communication technologies as a series of strategic escalations. Without reference to the individual or to mankind, communication technologies will have overhauled each other until finally an artificial intelligence proceeds to the interception of possible intelligences in space[87].

First published in:
ON LINE – KUNST IM NETZ, Edt. Dr. Helga Konrad,
Steirische Kulturinitiative, Graz, 1993

In memoriam Friedrich Kittler 1943–2011

Translated from German by Don Briant (1993)

Literature see p. 51

1 Praun 1970, 137
2 Peters 1989
3 Knies 1857, 6
4 McLuhan 1968
5 Luhmann 1988, 901
6 vgl. Hagemeyer 1979, 422-39
7 Shannon 1949a, 10f
8 Luhmann 1985, 21
9 Bell 1955, 35
10 Schiller 1904, XIII 17
11 McLuhan 1968
12 Aristoteles, Herrn. 16a 3-7
13 Derrida 1974
14 Van Creveld 1985
15 Voigt 1965-73, 11/2 830f
16 Schenkel 1983, 53-59
17 Assmann 1983, 80-88
18 Wittfogel 1962
19 Leroi-Gourhan 1980, 228
20 Goody 1977, 86f
21 Innis 1950, 71
22 Herodot, Hist. VII 98
23 Lohmann 1980, 168-74
24 Dornseiff 1922 ,13
25 Vernant 1962, 13
26 Havelock 1962, 32
27 Nietzsche 1922-28, V 218
28 Sueton, Augustus, 49
29 Fronto, zit. Riepl 1913, 241
30 Turing 1987, 187
31 Augustin, Conf. VI 3
32 Innis 1950, 126-140
33 Ong 1987, 119
34 Vorstius/Joost 1977, 30-46
35 Eisenstein 1979, 153
36 Gumbrecht 1988, 42 f
37 Kahn 1967
38 Beyrer 1985, 5 4
39 Habermas 1971, 28-61
40 Voigt 1965-73, 11/ 848
41 Schenda 1970
42 Schön 1987
43 Kittler 1987
44 Fichte 1845, VIII 98

45 Hegel 1952, 564 und 27
46 McLuhan 1968, 283
47 Kenner 1987
48 Aischylos, Agamemnon, V. 281-316
49 Riel 1913, 91-106
50 Oberliesen 1982, 44-62
51 Cajori 1928-29, II 182-85
52 Schivelbusch 1977, 32-34
53 Knies 1857, 16-19
54 Blum 1939, 73
55 vgl. Derrida 1982
56 Kennedy 1979, 75-97
57 Hacking 1975
58 Beck 1974, 37f
59 Faulstich-Wieland/ Horstkemper 1987
60 Leroi-Gourhan 1980, 265-70
61 Virilio 1986
62 Lerg 1970
63 Ong 1987, 136
64 Schwipps 1971, 29
65 Innis 1950, 169
66 Mc Luhan 1968
67 Beck 1974, 38-42
68 Bamford 1986
69 Benjamin 1972-85, 1/2 495 f
70 Shannon 1949 a, 11 f
71 von Neumann 1967, 146f
72 Hodges 1983, 96
73 Turing 1987, 17-60 und 157f
74 Rosenkranz 1844, 15
75 Oberliesen 182, 212-48
76 Coy 1985, 43-48
77 Hyman 1986, 191-279
78 Shannon 1938, 713-23
79 Zuse 1984, 51 f
80 Hodges 1983, 267-88
81 Hagen 1989
82 Rabiner/Gold 1975
83 Sickert 1983, 117-220
84 Cambers 1985
85 Freud 1940-68, XIV 449 f
86 Hagemeyer 1979, 434
87 Posner 1984, 198-202

Friedrich Kittler

Geschichte der
Telekommunikationsmedien

Was folgt, bildet einen ersten Versuch, über die Geschichte der Kommunikationstechniken, soweit das menschenmöglich ist, im ganzen und allgemeinen zu sprechen. Das sollte im
Ergebnis auf den Entwurf einer historischen Medienwissenschaft führen. Einen Entwurf einfach
deshalb, weil die Medienwissenschaft ein junges Forschungsfeld ist, das es ohne den Siegeszug
moderner Informationstechnologien gar nicht geben würde. Deshalb stößt eine solche Geschichte auf methodische und sachliche Probleme.
Ein sachliches Problem liegt schon darin, daß Kommunikationstechniken selber weit weniger
archiviert oder weit weniger zugänglich als ihre Inhalte sind, wie denn das Nachrichtenwesen
trotz seiner oft kriegsentscheidenden Rolle (um den letzten Chef des Wehrmachtnachrichten-
wesens zu zitieren) „ein Stiefkind der militärhistorischen Forschung"[1] geblieben ist. Dazu
kommt als methodisches Problem die Rätselfrage, ob der mittlerweile so selbstverständliche
Begriff Kommunikation zur Beschreibung von Zeiten und Räumen taugt, die ersichtlich anderen
Leitbegriffen (aus Mythos oder Religion) unterstanden. Jedenfalls beruhte seine philosophische
Inthronisierung, in John Lockes „Essay on Human Understanding", auf der schwerlich verallge-
meinerbaren Annahme, Kommunikation besage Versprachlichung wahrgenommener Vorstellungen und infolgedessen Vernetzung von isolierten Individuen durch „das Band der Sprache"[2].
Nur wie Menschen ohne Sprache zu ihren Vorstellungen oder Ideen überhaupt gekommen sein
sollen, vergißt die Philosophie zu fragen. Aus dieser abgründigen Verwirrung hat erst ein technischer Begriff von Information befreit, der seit Shannons „Mathematischer Theorie der Kommunikation" jede Bezugnahme auf Ideen oder Bedeutungen, damit aber auch auf Menschen
unterläuft.
Informationssysteme im engen Wortsinn sind allerdings auf Speicherung, Verarbeitung und
Übertragung von Nachrichten optimiert. Kommunikationssysteme dagegen, weil sie, über
Nachrichten hinaus, den Verkehr auch von Personen und Gütern regeln,[3] umfassen (nach
McLuhans Analyse) unterschiedlichste Medien vom Straßensystem bis zur Sprache.[4] Dennoch
besteht Anlaß, Kommunikationsysteme wie Informationssysteme zu analysieren. Auch Kom-
munikation hängt schließlich von Steuersignalen ab, und zwar um so mehr, je komplexer sie
arbeitet; auch die Dreiheit der Kommunikate – Nachrichten, Personen, Güter – läßt sich informa-
tionstheoretisch reformulieren:
- Erstens sind Nachrichten, das besagt schon ihre deutsche Etymologie, Befehle, „nach" denen
  Personen sich zu „richten" haben.
- Zweitens sind Personen, wie die Systemtheorie lehrt, keine Gegenstandseinheiten, sondern
  Adressen, die „die Berechnung weiterer Kommunikationen ermöglichen".[5]
- Drittens schließlich bilden Güter, wie die Ethnologie seit Mauss und Lévi-Strauss gelehrt hat,
  Daten in einer stellenwertigen Tauschordnung zwischen besagten Personen.
Wenn nun aber Daten die Operation der Speicherung auftun, Adressen die der Übertragung und
Befehle die der Datenverarbeitung, ist jedes Kommunikationssystem als Verbund dieser drei
Operationen ein Informationssystem. Es hängt schlechterdings nur davon ab, ob die drei Opera-
tionen im physikalisch Realen implementiert sind, inwieweit ein solches System zur selbständi-
gen Kommunikationstechnologie wird. Die Geschichte dieser Techniken kommt, mit anderen
Worten, zum Ende, wenn Maschinen nicht nur die Adressen Übertragung und die Datenspeiche-

rung übernehmen, sondern mittels mathematischer Algorithmen auch die Befehlsverarbeitung steuern können. Es ist deshalb kein Zufall, daß Shannon erst zu Beginn des Computerzeitalters, also nachdem alle Operationen von Kommunikationsystemen maschinell realisiert waren, ein formales Modell von Information anschreiben konnte. Dieses Modell umfaßt bekanntlich fünf verschaltete Instanzen:[6]

- Erstens gibt es eine Informationsquelle, die je eine Nachricht pro Zeiteinheit aus der entweder abzählbar-diskreten oder unabzählbar-stetigen Menge möglicher Nachrichten selektiert.
- Zweitens versorgt diese Quelle ein oder mehrere Sender, die durch geeignete Codierung die Nachricht zum technischen Signal verarbeiten (was im diskreten Fall ohne Zwischenspeicherung von Daten gar nicht möglich ist).
- Drittens beschicken diese Sender einen Kanal, der die Signalübertragung in Raum und/oder Zeit gegen physikalisches Rauschen und/oder feindliche Störungen sichert.
- Viertens führen diese Kanäle zu einem oder mehreren Empfängern, die die Nachricht aus dem Signal rekonstruieren, das heißt einem zum Sender inversen Algorithmus der Decodierung unterziehen, so daß schließlich
- Fünftens die rückübersetzte Nachricht an die Adresse einer Informationssenke gelangt.[7]

Dieses elegante Modell kann allerdings, schon weil es keinerlei historischen Ehrgeiz hat, auf die faktische Geschichte der Kommunikationstechniken nicht einfach angewandt werden. Statt allenthalben, wie es auch in Sprach- und Kulturwissenschaften üblich geworden ist, Shannons fünf *black boxes* anzuzeichnen, scheint es dringender und lohnender, durch die Geschichte zu verfolgen, wie ihre Ausdifferenzierung selber erst einmal hat zustandekommen müssen. Unter der Luhmannschen Prämisse, daß Kommunikationstechniken eine „vorrangige, alles andere magnetisierende Epocheneinteilung"[8] leisten, läßt sich plausibel machen, daß der historische Übergang von Mündlichkeit zu Schriftlichkeit einer Entkopplung von Interaktion und Kommunikation gleichkam, der Übergang von Schrift zu technischen Medien dagegen einer Entkopplung auch von Kommunikation und Information. Es geht also um einen Prozeß der Ausdifferenzierung, der erst in Theorie und Praxis einer Information, die dem energetischen Begriff Entropie mit umgekehrtem Vorzeichen entspricht[9], zum Abschluß gekommen ist.

Dieser Ausdifferenzierungsprozeß vergibt die Möglichkeit, die Geschichte der Kommunikationsmedien in zwei größere Blöcke zu zerlegen. Der erste Block behandelt die Schriftgeschichte und zerfällt seinerseits in einen Block über Handschriften und einen über Druckschrift. Der zweite Block über technische Medien wird von der Basiserfindung Telegraphie über die analogen Medien schließlich zum digitalen Medium Computer führen.

A Schrift

1. Handschrift

Über die Geschichte der Schriftkulturen, deren „Medium" üblicherweise auch Geschichte und Vorgeschichte trennt,[10] bestimmen zwei Reihen von Variablen. Die erste Reihe steht in Bezug zu dem, was die Philosophie seit den Stoikern als Referenz er- oder verkannt hat: Sofern der Inhalt eines Mediums immer ein anderes Medium ist[11] und der von Schrift (schon bei Aristoteles[12]) die Rede, lassen sich Schriften danach klassifizieren, ob sie Alltagssprachen zu Bild-, Silben- oder Phonemzeichen verarbeiten.[13] Sofern das Medium Schrift aber auch, wahrscheinlich zum erstenmal, Speicherung und Übertragung, Inschrift und Post koppelt, entscheiden physikalische Variablen von Schreibzeug und Schreibfläche über Raum und Zeit der Kommunikation. Von diesen Variablen rührt der Zeitverbrauch beim Senden und Empfangen, die Permanenz oder Löschbarkeit des Geschriebenen und nicht zuletzt die Ortsfestigkeit oder Mobilität der Nachrichten. Die erste Variablenreihe regelt Ausdifferenzierungen zwischen Rede und Schrift: Grade der Gedächtnisleistung, Grade der grammatischen Analysierbarkeit, Kopplungsmöglichkeiten von Sprache mit anderen Medien. Als Hauptforschungsfeld der kulturwissenschaftlichen Medienforschung kann sie hier am Rand bleiben.

Der zweiten Variablenreihe hat, womöglich weil sie so materiell ist, wesentlich weniger Aufmerksamkeit gegolten. Und doch bestimmen so schlichte Dinge wie Schreibzeug und Schreibfläche über den Machtgewinn, den der Einsatz von Schriften jeweils abwirft. Wenn Priestern an der Speicherung von Adressen, also von Göttern oder Toten, über eine maximale Zeit liegt, Händlern an Güterspeicherung über maximale Zeit und Gütertransport über maximale Räume, Kriegern schließlich an Befehlsübertragung über maximale Räume in minimaler Zeit, dann hatten die ältesten Schriften, um 3000 vor Christus in Sumer und Ägypten entstanden, ökonomische und religiöse Funktionen. In Kriegerverbänden dagegen endete, was Militärhistoriker die orale „Steinzeit des Befehlsflusses" nennen, wohl erst mit Napoleon.[14] Außer Befehlen vom Mund zum Ohr gab es nur semiotische Einsätze des Feuers zu Signalzwecken und schnelle, aber gleichfalls mündliche Botenposten, deren Rekord wahrscheinlich Dschingis Khan hielt.[15]

Die ersten Schriftzeugnisse sind bekanntlich Inschriften ohne genuine Schreibfläche. Zweidimensionale Abrollungen von Siegeln oder Stempeln im Medium Ton versahen Güter mit Adressen ihres Besitzers oder ihres Inhalts, Lapidarinschriften versahen Gräber mit dem Namen ihres Toten.[16] Als Signale in Abwesenheit der Nachrichtenquelle, also durch Entkopplung von Kommunikation und Interaktion, eröffneten Inschriften – nach dem Argument Jan Assmanns – die prinzipielle Möglichkeit von Literatur[17].

Hingegen setzte eine Verwaltung jener großen Flußbewässerungssysteme, in denen Städte und Hochkulturen entstanden, die Ablösung der Inschrift durch handwerklich optimierte und transportable Schreibflächen voraus: Bambus und Maulbeerbaum in China, ungebrannter oder zur Speicherung gebrannter Ton im Zweistromland, Papyrus als Monopol des Nildeltas. Dieselben Flüsse, über die der Verkehr von Fronarbeitern und Gütern lief, übertrugen also gleichzeitig (nach Maßgabe einer kalendarischen oder goniometrischen Mathematik) die Befehle der Wasserzuteilung und Güterabschöpfung.[18] Dieselben Städte, die das anthropologische Schema von Kopf, Hand und Rumpf ins architektonische Schema von Palästen, Straßen und Speichern überführten,[19] brauchten Schriften zur Verarbeitung, Übertragung und Speicherung ihrer Daten. Diese Erschließung eines ökumenischen Raums kehrt in den Texten selber als Verräumlichung der Rede wieder: Die Schrift kennt seit Anbeginn kontextlose Listen, die alle Spuren mündlicher oder graphischer Kommunikationsnetze ausfüllen, eben darum aber auch kein alltäglich-situatives Äquivalent mehr haben[20].

Ausgriffe über die Ökumene hinaus, also Reichsgründungen, wurden dagegen erst möglich, nachdem Staaten der Alten wie der Neuen Welt die kriegerischen Botenposten übernahmen und in der Alten Welt seit 1200 vor Christus, nach Kreuzung zweier Pferderassen, Boten und Krieger darüber hinaus mobil machten.[21] In klassischer Zeit „gab es", nach Herodots unvergeßlicher Formulierung, „auf Erden nichts Schnelleres" als den Medienverbund, der unter den Achämeniden Persiens Königsstraße mit einer berittenen Relaispost kombinierte, um „Eilbriefe im schlanken Trab", also allen Naturstörungen zum Trotz, von Reiter zu Reiter, von Tagereise zu Tagereise zu übertragen.[22] Angareion, der persische Name dieser Militärpost, liegt dem griechischen Namen für Boten und mithin auch allen christlichen Engeln zugrunde.

Einem Kommunikationsimperium wie dem persischen hatte die griechische Polis nur eine Schrift entgegenzusetzen, die im Unterschied zu orientalischen Bürokratien für Mündlichkeit mehrfach transparent blieb. Erstens funktionierte das griechische Alphabet (aus indoeuropäischen Notwendigkeiten und weil es im Handels- und Übersetzungsverkehr mit semitischen Konsonantenschriften entstand) redundant gewordene Konsonanten in Vokale um, leistete also die erste Totalanalyse einer gesprochenen Sprache – und im Prinzip jeder beliebigen.[23] Daß die Vokalzeichen erstmals prosodisch-musikalische Elemente der Rede encodierten, erlaubte eine Notenschrift und in der pythagoräischen Schule, einfach weil griechische Lettern zugleich Ziffernwerte hatten,[24] eine Mathematisierung der Musik, sofern sie nur abstraktes Intervall blieb.

Zweitens scheint für den Siegeszug des Vokalalphabets nicht so sehr sein überschätzter Innovationsgrad als vielmehr die Eindeutigkeit der Phonemzuordnung verantwortlich. Sie minimierte den Aufwand des Schrifterwerbs und überführte damit Palast- oder Tempelgeheimnisse in Öffentlichkeit.[25] Der Literatur wurde es möglich, zunächst mündliche Mnemotechniken (etwa von Weisen oder Rhapsoden) und später auch die Prosa einzubinden.[26] Athenische Tyrannen gründeten die erste öffentliche Bibliothek; Euripides als Büchernarr wurde zum „ersten großen Leser" unter den Dichtern.[27]

Ihren biblischen Namen hatten solche antiken Buchrollen von einer Papyrusexportstadt in Phönizien, deren Stelle ab 560 vor Christus das Nildelta einnahm. Auch das Imperium Romanum stützte nach Eroberung Ägyptens sein Befehlsnetz, das mit dem Imperium ja synonym war, auf einen Verbund aus berittener Relaispost, befestigten Heerstraßen und leicht transportablem Papyrus. Das Imperium, mit anderen Worten, kombinierte despotische Übertragungstechnik mit demokratischem Alphabet. Der *Cursus publicus,* von Augustus mit Übernachtungsstationen in Abständen von 40 Kilometern und Pferdewechselplätzen in Abständen von rund 12 Kilometern ausschließlich für Beamte und Legionen eingerichtet,[28] wurde trotzdem oder gerade deshalb zum Kristallisationspunkt der europäischen Städte. Im Verbund mit Feuertelegraphen an sensitiven Limesstrecken trug eine Staatspost, die die schnellste Schiffahrt übertraf und ihrerseits erst von Napoleon übertroffen werden sollte, die imperiale Gewalt als solche: „Caesarum est per orbem terrae litteras missitare",[29] heißt es bei einem spätrömischen Schriftsteller. „Amt der Kaiser ist es, schriftliche Befehle über den Erdkreis zu schicken." Gegenüber diesem perfekten Übertragungsmedium für besagten Erdkreis und Cäsars Zeitungsdistribution für die Stadt Rom blieb die Datenspeicherung, auch wenn es seit Hadrian ein kaiserliches *officium sacrae memoriae* gab, technisch zurück.

Papyrus ist zwar leicht, aber empfindlich und wenig haltbar. Lagern ließ es sich nur in Buchrollen, lesen nur beidhändig. Nach der Einsicht Alan Turings, des ersten Computertheoretikers, „muß es seine Zeit gebraucht haben, in solchen Volumina Verweise nachzuschlagen"[30]. Erst der Codex aus Pergament, den zunächst die Bibliothek von Pergamon zur Umgehung des ägyptischen Papyrusmonopols und seit 140 nach Christus vorab Christen benutzten, erlaubte eine Indizierung nach Lagen, Blättern und schließlich nach Seiten. Bücher, die haltbar, löschbar (wie im Palimpsest) und durch Blättern adressierbar waren (wie in Konkordanzen) wogen Mehrgewicht und Mehrpreis auf: Sie entkoppelten eine kursorisch werdende Lektüre von der Arbeit und Langsamkeit der Münder. Wenn Bischof Ambrosius von Mailand (nach dem Zeugnis seines berühmtesten Schülers) einen Codex „las, schweiften seine Augen über die Seiten, erforschte das Herz den Sinn, er selbst aber schwieg"[31]. Im Codex siegten die transportierbaren, adressierbaren und interpretierbaren Schriften ehemaliger Nomaden, der Juden und Araber, über die Ortsfestigkeit von Götterstandbildern und Tempeln.

Der Zerfall des *Cursus publicus* und die islamische Einnahme Ägyptens, die ja auch die größte antike Bibliothek zerstörte, schnitten Westeuropa vom Papyrusimport ab. Übrig blieb das

Agrarprodukt Pergament, auf dem Mönche die christlich zensurierte Papyrusüberlieferung abschreiben mußten, während in Ostrom der briefliche Befehlsfluß aller gewesenen Kaiser zur festen Gesetzgebung des *Codex Iustinianus* gerann. Mit solchen Überbrückungen oder Verdichtungen der Zeit gelang zwar eine *translatio studii;* die *translatio imperii* dagegen setzte neue Raumordnungen und damit auch zugänglichere Schreibflächen voraus.

Im 13. Jahrhundert gelangte das Papier, aus China über Bagdad importiert, nach Europa, wo es von Leinwandhandelsstädten und neuen Wind- oder Wassermühlen zum Lumpenpapier weiterentwickelt wurde. Diese Schreibfläche als solche trug den Aufschwung der Universitäten, die mit angeschlossenen Bücherkopierbüros und Postnetzen das Speichermonopol der Klöster sprengten. Sie trug aber auch, im Verbund mit dem aus Indien über Arabien importierten Stellenwertsystem der Zahlen, den Aufschwung von Handelsstädten.[32] Dabei ging es nicht nur um die bekannte Erfindung der doppelten Buchführung, sondern vor allem um eine mathematische Notation, die zum erstenmal von den vielen Alltagssprachen unabhängig machte: Wenn sie zwei Zahlen addierten, hatten Griechen *kai* gesagt und Römer *et;* seit dem 15. Jahrhundert dagegen gibt es, ebenso stumm wie international, das Plus und das Minus, Zeichen also für mathematische Operatoren.

2. Druckschrift

Gutenbergs Erfindung, mit beweglichen, aus Buchrückenstempeln entwickelten Lettern zu drucken, die anders als ihre Vorläufer in China und Korea zugleich alphabetisch und (nach Wegfall der Ligaturen) diskret fungierten, war wohl keine Revolution wie der Codex, deckte aber den durch Papier geweckten Bedarf. Als „erstes Fließband der Technikgeschichte"[33] potenzierte der Druck die Datenverarbeitungskapazität von Büchern. Weil alle Exemplare einer Auflage, im Gegensatz zu manuellen Abschriften, dieselben Texte, Holzstiche und Kupferstiche an derselben Stelle hatten, konnten einheitliche und erstmals alphabetische Register auf sie zugreifen. Diese Adressierung nach Belegen, Buchtiteln und seit Leibniz auch alphabetischen Bibliothekskatalogen[34] stellte das Kommunikationssystem Wissenschaft auf seine Zitierbasis, während Buchillustrationen ohne Überlieferungskorruptelen das Ingenieurswesen begründeten.[35] Nicht umsonst rühmte Vasari, daß Italien die Perspektive als Ermöglichung technisch exakter Zeichnungen im selben Jahr wie Gutenberg seinen Buchdruck erfunden habe.

Neue Medien machen alte nicht obsolet, sie weisen ihnen andere Systemplätze zu. Eben weil der Buchdruck die rhetorisch-musikalischen Performanzen auf Turnieren nurmehr als Literatur der Autoren und Fiktionen abbildete, scheinen die Körpertechniken dieser Turniere (nach Gumbrechts These) in stumme und meßbare Sportarten abgewandert zu sein.[36] Ebenfalls erst als Ausdifferenzierung innerhalb der Typographie entstand ein Eigenwert der Handschrift, deren Signatur auf Briefen und Akten das antike Siegel ablöste und deren Individualität an ein Staatssystem aus Post und Polizei fiel. Die ersten Staatsposten der Frühneuzeit waren nach dem Modell des römischen Imperiums zwar noch für militärischdiplomatische Netze reserviert und durch eine Kryptographie, deren Aufschwung auf Vietas Algebra als Übercodierung von alphabetischen und numerischen Zeichen zurückging,[37] vor Interzeption geschützt. Die durch Post und Feuerwaffen weiträumig kontrollierten Territorialstaaten dagegen öffneten ihre Netze einem Privatverkehr, den sie über ihr Postregal zugleich monopolisierten. Nach Anschluß von Handelskorrespondenten ans öffentliche Postnetz entstanden ab 1600 Zeitungen und Zeitschriften, nach Anschluß auch des Personentransports ab 1650 die Ordinari-Posten als Verkehrsnetze nach Fahrplan.[38] Nur den vielberufenen Strukturwandel von der aristokratischen zur

bürgerlichen Öffentlichkeit, deren Reisen und Briefe, Drucksachen und Zeitschriftenkritiken Europas altes Machtsystem unterhöhlt haben sollen,[39] hat es nie gegeben. Auch ohne ihre durchgängige Kontrolle durch Briefgeheimkabinette und Druckzensur blieb die bürgerliche Öffentlichkeit ein Artefakt merkantilistischer Staaten, deren neues Postregal den halben Staatshaushalt und die halbe Kriegskasse füllte.[40] Nur in der Intimität von Familienzirkeln förderte die „Lesesucht" der sogenannten Öffentlichkeit[41] einen Rekordanstieg nationalsprachlicher Belletristik, die den „Verlust der Sinnlichkeit"[42] durch virtuelle Effekte auf Lesersinne kompensierte, also kommenden Medientechniken vorarbeitete.[43] Ihre technische Basis hatte diese Mediatisierung der Druckbuchstaben vermutlich in einer routinierten leisen Lektüre, die kein elitäres Privileg wie beim heiligen Ambrosius mehr war, sondern durch allgemeine Schulpflicht und allgemeine Alphabetisierung die Demokratie installierte. Eben damit aber löste die mühelose Lektüre ein neues Systemproblem. Weil gedruckte Bücher, anders als Pergamentcodices, Festwertspeicher ohne jede Löschmöglichkeit sind, gab es um 1800 (nach Fichtes Wort) „keinen Zweig der Wissenschaft mehr, über welchen nicht sogar ein Ueberfluss von Büchern vorhanden" gewesen wäre.[44] Literatur und Wissenschaft mußten ihre Sende- und Empfangstechniken folglich umstellen: weg von der Buchstäblichkeit gelehrtenrepublikanischer Zitate oder rhetorischer Mnemotechniken und hin zu einer Interpretation, die gedruckte Datenmengen auf ihren Sinn, eine kleinere Datenmenge also reduzierte. Die Folge im Kommunikationssystem Wissenschaft, seit Humboldts Reform, waren Vorlesungen ohne Lehrbuch, Seminare als Interpretationsübungen und der universitäre Aufstieg einer Philosophie, deren absoluter „Geist" von allen Wissensformen der Geschichte und seinem eigenen Lehrbuch lediglich die „Er-Innerung" aufbewahrte, also zum hermeneutischen „Schattenrisse" des gesamten Buchwesens wurde.[45]
Im Realen entsprach dieser Mediatisierung der Schrift ihre industrielle Revolution. An die Stelle von Gutenbergs abzählbarer Kombinatorik trat auch praktisch eine Analysis von Unendlichkeiten: Endlospapiermaschinen ersetzten seit 1800 die diskreten Formate und geschöpften Bögen, Holzpapiere aus Amerikas scheinbar unerschöpflichen Wäldern, diese materielle Basis aller Massenpresse seit 1850, ersetzten Hadern oder Lumpen. Und schließlich haben Schreibmaschine und Linotype seit 1880 auch noch den Unterschied zwischen Schreiben und Drucken eingeebnet,[46] eben damit aber den Raum moderner Literatur eröffnet.[47] Erst Mallarmé gab ja die Losung aus, Literatur auf ihren Wortsinn, die sechsundzwanzig Lettern, zu reduzieren, mit anderen Medien also gar nicht mehr in Konkurrenz zu treten.

B Technische Medien

Technische Medien, anders als Schrift, arbeiten nicht auf dem Code einer Alltagssprache. Sie nutzen physikalische Prozesse, die die Zeit menschlicher Wahrnehmung unterlaufen und nur im Code neuzeitlicher Mathematik überhaupt formulierbar sind.

1. Telegraphie und Analogtechnik

Selbstredend muß es technische Medien seit jeher gegeben haben, weil alles Zeichengeben mit akustischen oder optischen Mitteln an ihm selbst technisch ist. In vorindustriellen Zeiten jedoch bildeten Kanäle, die wie Rauch- oder Feuertelegraphie die Lichtgeschwindigkeit ausnutzten oder wie Trommelsprachen und Rufketten die Schallgeschwindigkeit, nur Subsysteme einer Alltagssprache. Das Feuersignal von Troja nach Mykene, mit dem bei Aischylos die Literaturgattung Tragödie beginnt, meldete als einziges Bit den Fall der belagerten Festung und auch das nur nach vorheriger Verabredung.[48] Dagegen bleibt es fraglich, ob eine von Polybios angegebene Telegraphie, die das griechische Alphabet in fünf mal fünf Lichtzeichen encodieren, also auch zufällige Sätze übertragen können sollte, je Einsatz gefunden hat.[49]

Informationsraten, die alle Leistungsgrenzen von Schrift überboten, erzwang erst der Befehlsfluß in wehrpflichtigen Massenheeren und waffentechnisch standardisierten Nationalkriegen. Derselbe Abgeordnete Lakanal, der dem revolutionären Frankreich 1793 ein allgemeines Volksschulsystem und ein literarisches Urheberrecht bescherte, brachte den Nationalkonvent ein Jahr später auch zum Bau von optischen Telegraphenlinien. Als offizielle Begründung dieser Revolution fungierte das Argument, in flächendeckenden Nationalstaaten könne nur Chappes optischer Telegraph jenes demokratische Wahlverhalten ermöglichen, das Rousseau bekanntlich dem Stadtstaat Genf abgelernt hatte. Als minder öffentliche, aber ausschließliche Verwendung des optischen Telegraphennetzes trat dagegen mit Napoleon eine Strategie auf den Plan, die Kriege aus der Steinzeit des Befehlsflusses erlöste. Selbständig operierende Divisionen konnten gleichzeitig an mehreren Fronten kämpfen, weil neu geschaffene Generalstäbe ihre kartographische Wissensbasis per Telegraph dem realen Erdboden auferlegten.[50]

Die Telegraphie hat also literarische Öffentlichkeit und militärisches Geheimnis im selben historischen Augenblick wieder getrennt, da Öffentlichkeit von Eliten auf ganze Bevölkerungen überging. Eine neue Elite aus Ingenieursschulen und Generalstäben entdeckte im Krieg von 1809 schließlich ihr neues, schlechthin geheimes Medium Elektrizität. Mit der Umstellung der Telegraphie von Optik auf Gleichstrom verschwanden nicht nur die menschlichen, also unzuverlässigen Relaisstationen, sondern auch Claude Chappes (sage und schreibe) 98 Zeichen. Das Morsesystem mit seinen Punkten, Strichen und Pausen machte eine Zeichenökonomie zur Praxis, die einst Leibniz in ausdrücklich typographischer Theorie mit seinem Binärcode erfunden hatte.[51]

Die Depesche, nach Buchstabenfrequenzen optimiert und nach Wörterzahl verrechnet, war der erste Schritt zur Informatik. Auch organisatorisch und technisch hatte die Telegraphie weltweite Rückwirkungen. Zum absolut ersten Mal war Information als masseloser Fluß elektromagnetischer Wellen abgekoppelt von Kommunikation. Durch telegraphische Fernsteuerung über Landkabel wurde ein systematisches Eisenbahnnetz möglich,[52] durch Eisenbahnnetze ein beschleunigter Verkehr von Gütern und Personen,[53] der seit dem amerikanischen Bürgerkrieg auch militärisch unter Telegraphenbefehl geriet.[54] Mit dem Güter- und Personenverkehr aber büßte die Post zwei ihrer drei altehrwürdigen Funktionen ein. Sie wurde gezwungen, reine Informationstechnik nach Standards des Hausnummerbriefkastens, der Briefmarkenvorfrankierung und des Weltpostvereins zu werden.[55]

Diese Lösung vom Erdboden, dessen Distanzen (wie in der zeitgleichen mathematischen Topologie) im Gegensatz zu allen vormodernen Postsystemen gar nicht mehr berechnet werden, weil nur die absolute Geschwindigkeit zählt, organisierte Internationalität: von den Börsenberichten des Welthandels über die Telegraphenagenturen der Weltpresse bis zu Kolonialreichen, die wie das britische Empire auf einer *Fleet in being* und damit auf einem weltweiten Seekabelmonopol beruhten.[56]

Technische Rückwirkungen der Telegraphie als diskret gemachter Informationszeit waren Folgeerfindungen, die paradoxerweise auch und gerade die stetigen Signalquellen verarbeiteten. Ich übergehe hier das Analogmedium der Photographie, die einen eigenen Vortrag verdient hätte, und erwähne nur Telephon, Schallplatte und Film.

Bells Telephon, dieses lukrativste Einzelpatent der Geschichte, entstand 1876 gar nicht in seiner wohlbekannten Funktion, sondern beim Versuch, mehrere Nachrichten gleichzeitig über ein einziges Telegraphenkabel zu schicken. Ganz entsprechend entstand, nur ein Jahr später, der

Phonograph Edisons beim Versuch, die Durchsatzrate von Telegraphenkabeln zu steigern. Und schließlich wurden Muybridges wissenschaftliche Serienphotographien, die 1895 nach Erfindung von Malteserkreuz und Zelluloid im Kino mündeten, durch elektrische Telegraphenrelais ausgelöst.

Film und Grammophon, diese massenreproduzierbare Konkurrenz zu Edisons Phonographen, haben es möglich gemacht, optische und akustische Daten als solche zu speichern. Weil Analogmedien die von Fechner ermittelten Wahrnehmungsschwellen zunächst mechanisch und später elektrisch unterlaufen, können sie in Sprachphonemen und Musikintervallen, bei denen die griechische Analyse als letzten alphabetischen Elementen ja stehengeblieben war, gerade umgekehrt noch Frequenzgemische erkennen, die dann einer weiteren und seit Fourier mathematischen Analyse offenstehen. Der moderne Grundbegriff Frequenz[57], dem seit Euler Wahrscheinlichkeitsrechnung, Musik und Optik gleichermaßen unterstehen, hat Künste durch technische Medien abgelöst. Dieser Physik im Simulationsverfahren des Realen entspricht im Rezeptionsvorgang denn auch keine Mnemotechnik oder Pädagogik auf Sprachbasis mehr, sondern eine Sinnesphysiologie, die den Medien ihren weltweiten und dank Shannons Informationsmaß auch berechenbaren Erfolg garantiert hat.[58] Zugleich ist zwischen unbewußten Medieneffekten einerseits und den (seit Edisons erstem Labor auch planbaren) Innovationsschüben andererseits ein Wissensgefälle entstanden, das bei aller Frauenemanzipation an Telegraphen, Telephonen und Schreibmaschinen[59] die allgemeine Alphabetisierung konterkariert und Kommunikation über Kommunikation nachgerade ausschließt.

Maßgeblich für diese Zäsur, die wohl nur an der Schrifterfindung ihresgleichen hatte,[60] waren Maxwells elektromagnetische Feldgleichungen und deren experimenteller Nachweis durch Heinrich Hertz. Seit Weihnachten 1906, als Fessendens Radiosender niederfrequente Zufallsereignisse, wie sie in die Sinne fallen, als Amplituden- oder Frequenzmodulation einer Hochfrequenz gefunkt hat, gibt es immaterielle Kanäle. Seit 1906, als de Forest aus Edisons Glühbirne die energielos steuerbare Röhre entwickelte, steht Information beliebigen Verstärkungen und Manipulationen offen. Das Röhrenradio, als drahtlose Telephonie zur Brechung imperialer Kabelmonopole herbeigeforscht, machte im Ersten Weltkrieg zunächst die neuen Waffensysteme Flugzeug und Panzer ebenso mobil wie fernsteuerbar,[61] nach Kriegsende dann auch Zivilbevölkerungen.[62]

Als „sekundäre Oralität"[63] unter Umgehung von Schrift standardisierte das Radio, vor allem im weltweiten Kurzwellenfunk[64], nichtalphabetisierte Sprachen, verwandelte also kolonisierte Stammesverbände in selbständige Nationen.[65] Entsprechend hat das Telephon auf seinem Weg vom Selbstwahlsystem über das Frequenzmultiplex bis zum Satellitenfunk hierarchiefreie Vernetzungen zunächst der Städte und schließlich eines „globalen Dorfs"[66] ermöglicht. Aber die öffentlich zugänglichen Wellenbereiche bleiben trotz ihrer kritischen Überfüllung[67] nur Bruchteile eines Frequenzspektrums, das vom Langwellenfunk bis zum Dezimeterradar staatliche oder militärische Steuerungsaufgaben übernimmt und alle öffentlichen Wellenbereiche geheimdienstlich anzapft.[68]

Die Elektrifizierung sinnlicher Eingangsdaten durch Wandler und Sensoren erlaubte es der Unterhaltungsindustrie, analoge Speichermedien erstens aneinander und zweitens mit Übertragungsmedien zu koppeln. Der Tonfilm kombinierte optische und akustische Speicher, das Radio vor Einführung des Magnetophons übertrug im wesentlichen Schallplatten, die ersten Fernsehsysteme vor Entwicklung elektronischer Aufnahmeröhren tasteten Spielfilme ab. So bleibt der Inhalt von Unterhaltungsmedien stets ein anderes Medium, für das sie Werbung machen. Aber all diese Kopplungen bereits einzeln standardisierter Techniken, auch wenn sie ästhetische Formen vom Hörspiel über die elektronische Musik bis zum Videoclip ins Leben riefen, haben ein entscheidendes Manko: Kein allgemeiner Standard regelt ihre Steuerung und wechselseitige Übersetzung. An genau dieser Leerstelle sprangen vielmehr die Helden und Heldinnen von Benjamins Medientheorie ein: Cutter beim Film, Tonmeister beim Tonband mit ihrer gefeierten, aber bloß handwerklichen Montage.[69] Dieses Menschenwerk abzuschaffen und einen allgemeinen Standard zu automatisieren, blieb der Digitaltechnik vorbehalten.

2. Digitaltechnik

Die Digitaltechnik fungiert, nur eben auf numerischer Basis, wie ein Alphabet: Sie ersetzt die stetigen Funktionen, die die Analogmedien, die im allgemeinen ebenfalls stetigen Eingangsdaten umwandelt, durch diskrete Abtastungen zu möglichst gleichabständigen Zeitpunkten, wie das die 24 Filmaufnahmen pro Sekunde oder das Fernsehen seit der Nipkow-Scheibe viel hochfrequenter vorgemacht haben. Diese Messung mit anschließender Auswertung im Binärzahlensystem ist die Voraussetzung eines schlechthin allgemeinen Medienstandards. Nach dem Abtasttheorem von Nyquist und Shannon können nämlich beliebige Signalformen, wenn sie nur von Haus aus oder durch Filterung frequenzbandbegrenzt sind, aus Abtastwerten der mindestens doppelten Frequenz wieder eindeutig konstruiert werden.[70] Das Quantisierungsrauschen, das dabei notwendig entsteht, erlaubt im Gegensatz zum physikalisch festgelegten Rauschen von Analogsystemen beliebige Minimierungen, einfach weil es Regeln eines Stellenwertzahlensystems gehorcht.[71]

Die Prinzipschaltung aller Digitaltechnik erstellte 1936 Turings Universale Diskrete Maschine. Sie bestand in Fortschreibung oder Reduktion der ja ebenfalls diskreten Schreibmaschine[72] schlicht und einfach aus einem Endlospapierband, dessen Idee ja seit 1800 umging. Auf diese „Papiermaschine" zur Datenspeicherung konnte ein Schreib/Lese/Löschkopf zur Datenverarbeitung die Binärzeichen 0 und 1 schreiben, während eine Transportvorrichtung zur Datenadressierung Zugriffe auf die Nachbarzeichen rechts und links ermöglichte. Turing aber bewies, daß diese schlechthin elementare Maschine, weil sie im Unterschied zum verrauschten Laplace-Universum endlich viele Schaltzustände einnimmt, nicht nur jedem Mathematiker ebenbürtig ist, sondern alle (in Hilberts Wortsinn) entscheidbaren Probleme der Mathematik löst – und zwar durch Simulation jeder anderen korrekt programmierten Maschine.[73]

Die Turingmaschine in ihrer Universalität schloß also alle Entwicklungen zur Speicherung, Indizierung und Bearbeitung sowohl alphabetischer wie numerischer Daten ab. Im Raum des Alphabets hatten diese Entwicklungen von Listen und Katalogen über die Zettelkästen, denen um 1800 Jean Pauls Literatur und Hegels Philosophie entsprungen waren,[74] bis zur Hollerith-Maschine der amerikanischen Volkszählung von 1890 geführt.[75] Im Raum der Ziffern hatte eine parallele Entwicklung von Schickarts Rechenuhr für die vier Grundrechenarten über Jacquards programmierbare Webstühle[76] bis zum Computervorläufer Babbage geführt, dessen *Differential Engine* von 1822 die mannzeitaufwendigen Reihenentwicklungen in Trigonometrie und Ballistik auf rekursive Differenzengleichungen reduzierte, während seine später geplante *Analytical Engine* mit bedingten Sprungbefehlen die gesamte Analysis berechenbar machen sollte.[77] Um die alphanumerische Universalität von Turingmaschinen alias Computern zu erreichen, mußten Booles logische Algebra und Gödels Unvollständigkeitsbeweis allerdings beide Entwicklungsstränge noch zusammenführen, also Aussagen und Axiome gleichermaßen manipulierbar wie Zahlen machen.

Die Turingmaschine von 1936 war unendlich langsam, ihr Papierband unendlich lang, also inexistent. Der Computer als ihre technische Realisierung glänzt dagegen durch eine Ökonomie von Zeit und Raum, wie erst der Zweite Weltkrieg sie nötig machte. Gleichzeitig mit Shannons Beweis, daß schlichte Relais in Reihen- oder Parallelschaltung alle Operationen der Booleschen Algebra automatisieren können,[78] baute Zuse aus Telegraphenrelais erste Computer für die Luftwaffenforschung, während das Chiffrierwesen der Wehrmacht seine Automatisierungsangebote zurückwies.[79] Ende 1943 dagegen entstanden für Turings kriegsentscheidende Kryptoanalyse genau dieses UKW-Geheimfunks, der die deutschen Blitzkriege möglich gemacht hatte, im britischen Geheimdienst Computer auf der Basis übersteuerter Radioröhren.[80] 1945 schließlich konnte John von Neumann für die geplante amerikanische Uranbombe, deren Explosionsgeschwindigkeit neue Zeitmaßstäbe setzte,[81] die seitdem übliche Architektur sequentieller, dafür aber in Mikrosekunden getakteter Computer entwerfen.
Von Neumanns Entwurf sah folgende drei Systemelemente vor:
- Erstens eine Zentraleinheit zur befehlsgesteuerten Abarbeitung alphanumerischer Daten nach entweder arithmetischen oder logischen Regeln;
- zweitens einen Schreiblesespeicher für variable Daten und einen Festwertspeicher für vorprogrammierte Befehle;
- drittens schließlich ein Bussystem zur sequentiellen Übertragung aller dieser Daten und Befehle, wie sie durch binäre Adressen nach Seiten und Spalten eineindeutig indiziert sind.

Mit diesen drei Teilen haben Von-Neumann-Maschinen die Struktur von Informationstechnik überhaupt als einen Funktionszusammenhang von Hardware-Elementen artikuliert. Gleichgültig ob ihre Umwelt alphabetische oder numerische Daten, also Schriften oder Medien-Meßwerte anliefert, sind die Befehle, Daten und Adressen intern sämtlich durch Binärzahlen repräsentiert. Die klassische Unterscheidung zwischen Funktionen und Argumenten, Operatoren und Zahlenwerten ist durchlässig geworden. Gerade dieses Ende des Alphabets erlaubt es jedoch, Operationen auch auf Operationen anzuwenden und Verzweigungen zu automatisieren. Weshalb Computer prinzipiell alle anderen Medien einbinden und ihre Daten den mathematischen Verfahren der Signalverarbeitung unterziehen können.[82]
Datendurchsatz und Zugriffszeit hängen dabei nur von physikalischen Rahmenwerten ab. Nachdem der Transistor ab 1948 die Röhren-Leiterplatten des Zweiten Weltkriegs und der Integrierte Schaltkreis ab 1968 die Einzeltransistoren abgelöst hat, was Raum- und Zeitbedarf jeweils um eine Zehnerpotenz senkte, sind Echtzeitanalysen und Echtzeitsynthesen eindimensionaler Datenströme (etwa von Sprache und Musik) kein Problem mehr.[83] Die Tonmeister können also gehen. Für mehrdimensionale Signalverarbeitung in Echtzeit dagegen, wie Fernsehbilder oder Computer-Animationen sie brauchen, wird die Von-Neumann-Architektur zum Flaschenhals. Deshalb sind massiv parallele Rechner schon im Einsatz, biologische und optische Schaltkreise, wie vor allem die Simulation von Gehirnfunktionen sie voraussetzt, schon in der Entwicklung. Der Tag ist nicht mehr fern, an dem die Signalverarbeitung an die Grenzen physikalischer Machbarkeit stößt.[84]
An dieser absoluten Grenze wird die Geschichte der Kommunikationstechniken buchstäblich abgeschlossen. Theoretisch bleibt damit nur die Frage, welcher Logik die Vollendung gehorcht haben wird. Von Freud[85] bis McLuhan war die klassische Antwort darauf ein Gattungssubjekt, das gegenüber einer gleichgültigen oder störenden Natur nacheinander seine Motorik, seine Sensorik und schließlich auch seine Intelligenz an technische Prothesen veräußert haben soll.

Wenn jedoch Shannons Mathematisierung der Information auf seiner „fundamentalen Idee" beruhte, den „nachrichtentechnischen Effizienzbereich einer gestörten Übertragung" durch Konzept-Transfer aus ihrem kryptoanalytischen Effizienzbereich herzuleiten,[86] werden Störungen erst als Eingriffe einer feindlichen Intelligenz intelligibel und die Geschichte der Kommunikationstechniken als eine Serie strategischer Eskalationen. Ohne Referenz auf den oder die Menschen haben Kommunikationstechniken einander überholt, bis schließlich eine künstliche Intelligenz zur Interzeption möglicher Intelligenzen im Weltraum schreitet.[87]

Ersterschienen in:
ON LINE – KUNST IM NETZ, Hrsg. Dr. Helga Konrad,
Steirische Kulturinitiative, Graz, 1993

In memoriam Friedrich Kittler 1943–2011

Fußnoten siehe Seite 42

Assmann, Jan, Schrift, Tod und Identität. Das Grab als Vorschule der Literatur im alten Ägypten. In: Assmann, Aleida und Jan/Hardmeier, Christof (Hrsg.), *Schrift und Gedächtnis. Beiträge zur Archäologie der literarischen Kommunikation I.* München 1983, 64-93.

Bamford, James, *NSA. Amerikas geheimster Nachrichtendienst.* Zürich/Wiesbaden 1986.

Beck, Arnold H., *Worte und Wellen. Geschichte und Technik der Nachrichtenübermittlung,* Frankfurt/M. 1974.

Bell, D.A., *Information theory and its engineering applications,* 3. Aufl. New York/Toronto/London 1955.

Benjamin, Walter, Das Kunstwerk im Zeitalter seiner technischen Reproduzierbarkeit. Zweite Fassung. In: *Gesammelte Schriften,* hrsg. v. Tiedemann, Rolf/Schwepphäuser, Hermann. Frankfurt/M. 1972-85, Bd.I 2, 471–508.

Beyrer, Klaus, *Die Postkutschenreise.* Tübingen 1985. (Untersuchungen des Ludwig-Uhland-Instituts der Universität Tübingen im Auftrag der Tübinger Vereinigung für Volkskunde, hrsg. v. Hermann Bausinber, Bd.66).

Blake, George G., *History of radio trelegraphy and telephony.* London 1928.

Blum, Prof. Dr. Ing. e.h., Das neuzeitliche Verkehrswesen im Dienste der Kriegsführung. In: *Jahrbuch für Wehrpolitik und Wehrwissenschaften,* 1939, 73–92.

Cajori, Florian, *A History of mathematical notations.* I. Chicago 1928. II. Chicago 1929.

Chambers, William G., *Basics of communication and coding.* Oxford 1985.

Coy, Wolfgang, *Industrieroboter. Zur Archäologie der zweiten Schöpfung.* Berlin 1985.

Derrida, Jacques, *Die Postkarte von Sokrates bis an Freud und jenseits.* I. Berlin 1982.

Dornseiff, Franz, *Das Alphabet in Mystik und Magie.* 1. Aufl. Leipzig 1922.

Eisenstein, Elizabeth, *The printing press as an agent of change. Communications and cultural transformations in early-modern Europe,* 2 Bde., New York 1979.

Faulstich-Wieland, Hannelore/Horstkemper, Marianne, *Der Weg zur modernen Bürokommunikation. Historische Aspekte des Verhältnisses von Frauen und neuen Technologien.* Bielefeld 1987. (Materialien zur Frauenforschung, Bd.4).

Fichte, Johann Gottlieb, Deducierter Plan einer zu Berlin zu errichtenden höheren Lehranstalt. (1817). In: *Sämtliche Werke,* hrsg. v. Immanuel Hermann Fichte. Berlin 1845, Bd. VIII, 97-203.

Freud, Siegmund, Das Unbehagen in der Kultur. In: *Gesammelte Werke, chronologisch geordnet.* London/Frankfurt/M. 1940-68, Bd. XIV, 419–506.

Goody, Jack, *The domestication of the savage mind.* Cambridge 1977.

Gumbrecht, Hans Ulrich, Beginn von „Literatur"/Abschied vom Körper? In: Smolka-Koerdt, Giesela/Spangenberg, Peter M./Tillmann- Barlylla, Dagmar (Hrsg.), *Der Ursprung von Literatur. Medien, Rollen und Kommunikationssituationen zwischen 1450 und 1650.* München 1988, 15–50.

Habermas Jürgen, *Strukturwandel der Öffentlichkeit. Untersuchungen zu einer Kategorie der bürgerlichen Gesellschaft.* 5. Aufl. Neuwied/Berlin 1971.

Hacking, Ian, *The emergence of probability. A philosophical study of early ideas about probability, induction and statistical inference.* Cambridge/London/New York/New Rochelle/Melbourne/Sidney 1975.

Hagemeyer, Friedrich-Wilhelm, *Die Entstehung von Informationskonzepten in der Nachrichtentechnik. Eine Fallstudie zur Theoriebildung in der Technik in Industrie- und Kriegsforschung.* Diss. (masch.) FU Berlin 1979.

Hagen, Wolfgang, Die verlorene Schrift. Über digitales Schreiben an Computern. Erscheint in: Kittler, Friedrich A./Tholen, Georg Christoph (Hrsg.), *Arsenale der Seele. Literatur- und Medienanalyse seit 1870.* München 1989.

Havelock, Eric A., *The literate revolution in Greece and its cultural consequences.* Princeton 1982.

Hegel, Georg Wilhelm Friedrich, *Phänomenologie des Geistes* (1807), hrsg. v. Johannes Hofmeister. 6. Aufl. Hamburg 1952.

Hodges, Andrew, Allan Turing. *The enigma.* New York 1983.

Holmberg, ErikJ., *Zur Geschichte des cursus publicus.* Diss. Uppsala 1933.

Hyman, Anthony, *Charles Babbage, 1791-1871. Philosoph, Mathematiker, Computerpionier.* Stuttgart 1987.

Innis, Harold Adams, *Empire and communications.* Oxford 1950.

Kahn, David, *The codebrakers. The story of secret writing.* London 1967.

Kennedy, Paul M., Imperial cable communications and strategy, 1870-1914. In: Kennedy, Paul M. (Hrsg.), *The war plans of the great powers 1880–1914.* London 1979, 75–79.

Kenner, Hugh, *The mechanic muse.* New York/Oxford 1987.

Kittler, Friedrich A., *Grammophon Film Typewriter.* Berlin 1986.

Kittler, Friedrich A., *Aufschreibesysteme 1800/1900.* 2. Aufl. München 1987.

Knies, Karl, *Der Telegraph als Verkehrsmittel.* Tübingen 1 857.

Lerg, Winfried B., *Die Entstehung des Rundfunks in Deutschland. Herkunft und Entwicklung eines publizistischen Mittels.* 2. Aufl. Frankfurt/M. 1970. (Beiträge zur Geschichte des deutschen Rundfunks, Bd. 1).

Leroi-Gourhan, André, Hand und Wort. *Die Evolution von Technik, Sprache und Kunst.* Frankfurt/M. 1980.

Lohmann, Johannes, Die Geburt der Tragödie aus dem Geiste der Musik. In: *Archiv für Musikwissenschaft 37,* 1980, 167-186.

Luhmann, Niklas, Das Problem der Epochenbildung und die Evolutionstheorie. In: Gumbrecht, Hans Ulrich/Link-Heer, Ursula (Hrsg.), *Epochenschwellen und Epochenstrukturen im Diskurs der Literatur- und Sprachhistorie.* Frankfurt/M. 1985, 1 1-33.

Luhmann, Niklas, Wie ist Bewußtsein an Kommunikation beteiligt? In: Gumbrecht, Hans Ulrich/Pfeiffer, K. Ludwig (Hrsg.), *Materialität der Kommunikation.* Frankfurt/M. 1988, 884-905.

McLuhan, Marshall, *Die magischen Kanäle. Understandig Media.* Düsseldorf/Wien 1968.

Metropolis, Nicholas Constantine/Howlett, Jack/Rota, Gian Carlo (Hrsg.), *A history of computing in the twentieth century. A collection of essays.* New York/London/Toronto/Sydney/San Francisco 1980.

Neumann John von, Allgemeine und logische Theorie der Automaten. In: *Kursbuch 8,* 1967, 1 39-175.

Nietzsche, Friedrich, Geschichte der griechischen Literatur. (Vorlesung Basel 1 874-76). In: *Sämtliche Werke.* München 1922-29, Bd. V, 67-284.

Oberliesen, Rolf, Information, *Daten und Signale. Geschichte technischer Informationsverarbeitung.* Reinbeck 1982.

Ong, Walter J., *Oralität und Literalität. Die Technologisierung des Wortes.* Opladen 1987.

Peters, John Durham, John Locke, the individual, and the origin of communication. Erscheint in: *Quarterly journal of speech,* August 1989.

Posner, Roland, Mitteilungen an die ferne Zukunft. Hintergrund, Anlaß, Problemstellung und Resultate einer Umfrage. In: *Zeitschrift für Semiotik 6*, 1984, 195-227.

Praun, Albert, Vernachlässigte Faktoren in der Kriegsgeschichtsschreibung. Das Nachrichtenverbindungswesen im 2. Weltkrieg, ein Stiefkind der militärischen Forschung. In: *Wehrwissenschaftliche Rundschau*, H.3, 1970, 137-145.

Rabiner, Lawrence R./Gold, Bernhard, *Theory and application of digital signal processing*. Englewood Cliffs 1975.

Riepl, Wolfgang, *Das Nachrichtenwesen des Altertums. M it besonderer Rücksicht auf die Römer. Leipzig/Berlin 1913*.

Rosenkranz, Karl, *Georg Wilhelm Friedrich Hegels Leben*. Berlin 1844.

Schenda, Rudolf, *Volk ohne Buch. Studien zur Sozialgeschichte der populären Lesestoffe 1770-1910*. Frankfurt/M. 1970.

Schenkel, Wolfgang, Wozu die Ägypter eine Schrift brauchten. In: Assmann, Aleida und Jan/Hardmeier, Christof (Hrsg.), *Schrift und Gedächtnis. Zur Archäologie der literarischen Kommunikation I*. München 1983, 45-63.

Schiller, Friedrich, Was heißt und zu welchem Ende studiert man Universalgeschichte? Eine akademische Antrittsrede (Jena 1789). In: *Sämtliche Werke*, hrsg. v. Eduard von der Hellen. Stuttgart-Berlin 1904, Bd. XIII, 3-24.

Schivelbusch, Wolfgang, *Geschichte der Eisenbahnreise. Zur Industrialisierung von Raum und Zeit im 19. Jahrhundert*. München 1977.

Schön, Erich, *Der Verlust der Sinnlichkeit oder die Verwandlung des Lesers*. Stuttgart 1987.

Schwipps, Werner, Wortschlacht im Äther. In: Deutsche Welle (Hrsg.), *Wortschlacht im Äther. Der deutsche Auslandsrundfunk im Zweiten Weltkrieg*. Berlin 1971, 1 1-97.

Shannon, Claude Elwood, A symbolic analysis of relay and switching circuits. In: *Transactions of the American institute of electrical engineers*, 57, 1938, 713-723.

Shannon, Claude Elwood, Communication in the presence of noise. In: *Proceeding of the institute of radio engineers*, 37, 1949a, 1021.

Shannon, Claude Elwood, Communication theory of secrecy systems. In: *Bell system technical journal*, 1949b, 656-715.

Sickert, Klaus (Hrsg.), *Automatische Spracheingabe und Sprachausgabe. Analyse, Synthese und Erkennung menschlicher Sprache mit digitalen Systemen*. Haar 1983.

Stephan, Heinrich von/Satter, Karl, *Geschichte der deutschen Post*. I. Berlin 1928. II. Berlin 1935. III. Frankfurt/M. 1951.

Turing, Allan M., *Intelligence Sevice. Ausgewählte Schriften,* hrsg. v. Dotzler, Bernhard/Kittler, Friedrich. Berlin 1987.

Van Creveld, Martin L., *Command in War*. Cambridge (Mass.)/London 1985.

Vernant, Jean-Pierre, Les origines de la pensée grecque. Paris 1962.

Virilio, Paul, *Krieg und Kino. Logistik der Wahrnehmung*. München 1986.

Voigt, Fritz, *Verkehr*. I. Berlin 1973. II. Berlin 1965.

Vorstius, Joris/Joost, Siegfried, *Grundzüge der Bibliotheksgeschichte*. 7. Aufl. Wiesbaden 1977.

Wittfogel, Karl, *Die Orientalische Despotie. Eine vergleichende Untersuchung totaler Macht*. Köln/Berlin 1962.

Yates, Frances A., *The art of memory*. London 1966.

Zglinicki, Friedrich von, *Der Weg des Films. Die Geschichte der Kinematographie und ihrer Vorläufer*. Berlin 1956.

Zuse, Konrad, *Der Computer. Mein Lebenswerk*. 2. Aufl. Berlin/Heidelberg/N ew York/Tokyo 1984.

Seiko Mikami
Featured Artist Ars Electronica 2012

The Japanese artist Seiko Mikami is "Featured Artist" of this year's Ars Electronica Festival. Since the 1980s, she has created very large-scale installations that deal with the interrelationship between the human body and Information Society. In the 1990s, she turned her attention increasingly to interactive works into which she integrates human perception. Outside of Japan, where the artist holds a chair at Tama Art University, she exhibits her work primarily in Europe and the USA.

Machining Perception
Andreas Broeckmann on the work of Seiko Mikami

Seiko Mikami's works offer a deconstruction of human and machine perception. In *Molecular Informatics,* for Instance, the visitor dons a head-mounted display and can then see the traces of his or her act of looking, visualised as animated lines and shapes, in a virtual space. A projection displays the animation for the gallery audience, offering to them the opportunity of observing perception as an immersive experience. In her various, often ongoing projects of the past two decades, Mikami explores the conditions of perception, whether in the solitary audio-space of *World, Membrane and Dismembered Body* which plunges the participant into the gap between self and perception, or in the complex disposition of *Gravicells* that correlates the physical presence of the visitors with the gravitational forces of the Earth and of communication satellites. All of Mikami's works are strictly interactive in that they primarily use and factor current perceptual and sensor data, creating loops of seeing, of hearing and of sensing, folding what is being perceived back onto the act of perception.

With the new work, *Desire of Codes,* Mikami has conceptually moved from the machining of human perception, towards the deconstruction of machine perception and cognition. A small step, since the differences between human and machine conditions of perception and cognition, of vision and visual data processing, seem to have become negligible. We perceive like machines, and machines perceive like us. At least, that is the openly *fictitious* claim that *Desire of Codes* appears to make, or test. As we enter its space, we are immersed in the robotic sense organs of a machine mind that curiously follows our every move, and into whose workings we gain the most eerie insight when we stand or sit still and wait for it to forget about our presence. That's when the machine, Mikami's contraption, begins to "dream", to reprocess images from its data storage, mixing them to a rumbling sound with current images from the live streams of networked camera eyes.

By presenting an image both of the voyeuristic juissance of the machine, and of its melancholy processing of the past and of the distant, Mikami invites us to reflect on the way in which we ourselves deal with perception, desire and memory, with the emotional surplus that we project onto the data worlds. What is it that distinguishes us from the machines that—selfishly?—aid our perception, and construct our access to the world, to ourselves?

Seiko Mikami

Desire of Codes

Desire of Code expresses the ambiguous boundaries between the *data body in the virtual world* and the *physical body in the real world* in the information-oriented society.

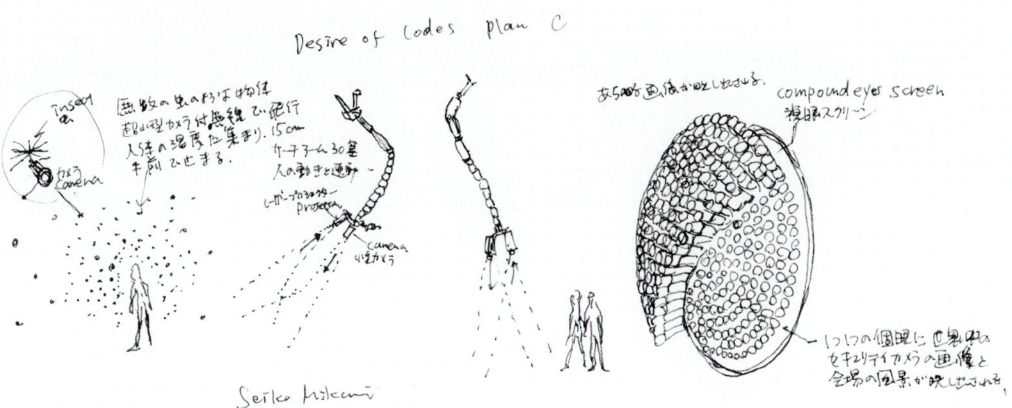

The interactive installation comprises three parts. First, a white wall composed of 90 mechanized rods resembling tentacles with built-in small surveillance cameras (Ninety Wriggling Wall Units). Second, a set of six large robotic arms, equipped with video cameras and laser projectors, which are suspended from the ceiling (Six Multi-perspective Search Arms). And third, a large, round, 4.7 m projection screen that looks like an insect's compound eye, wall-mounted at the back of the exhibition space (Compound Eye Detector Screen).

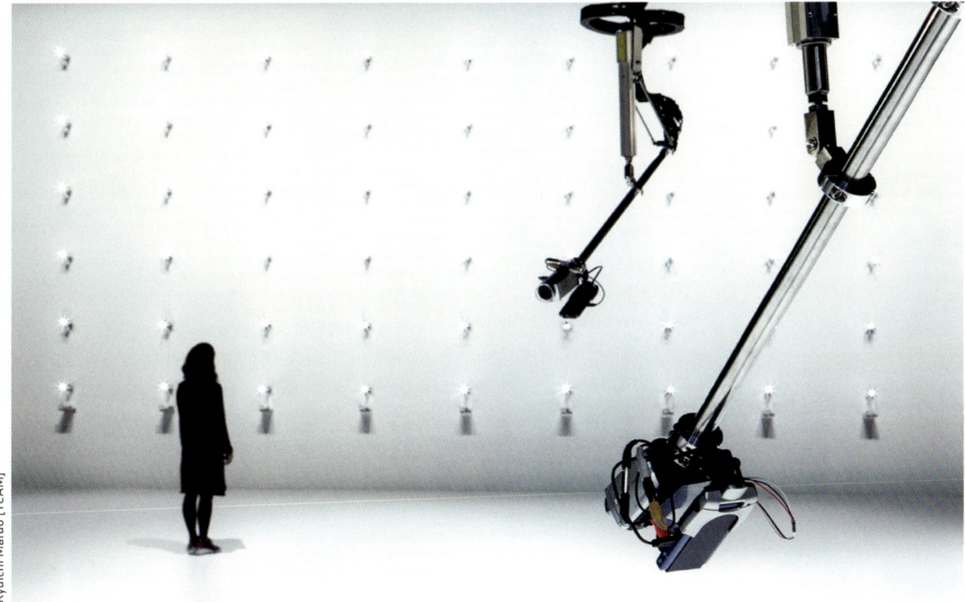

Ryuichi Maruo [YCAM]

57

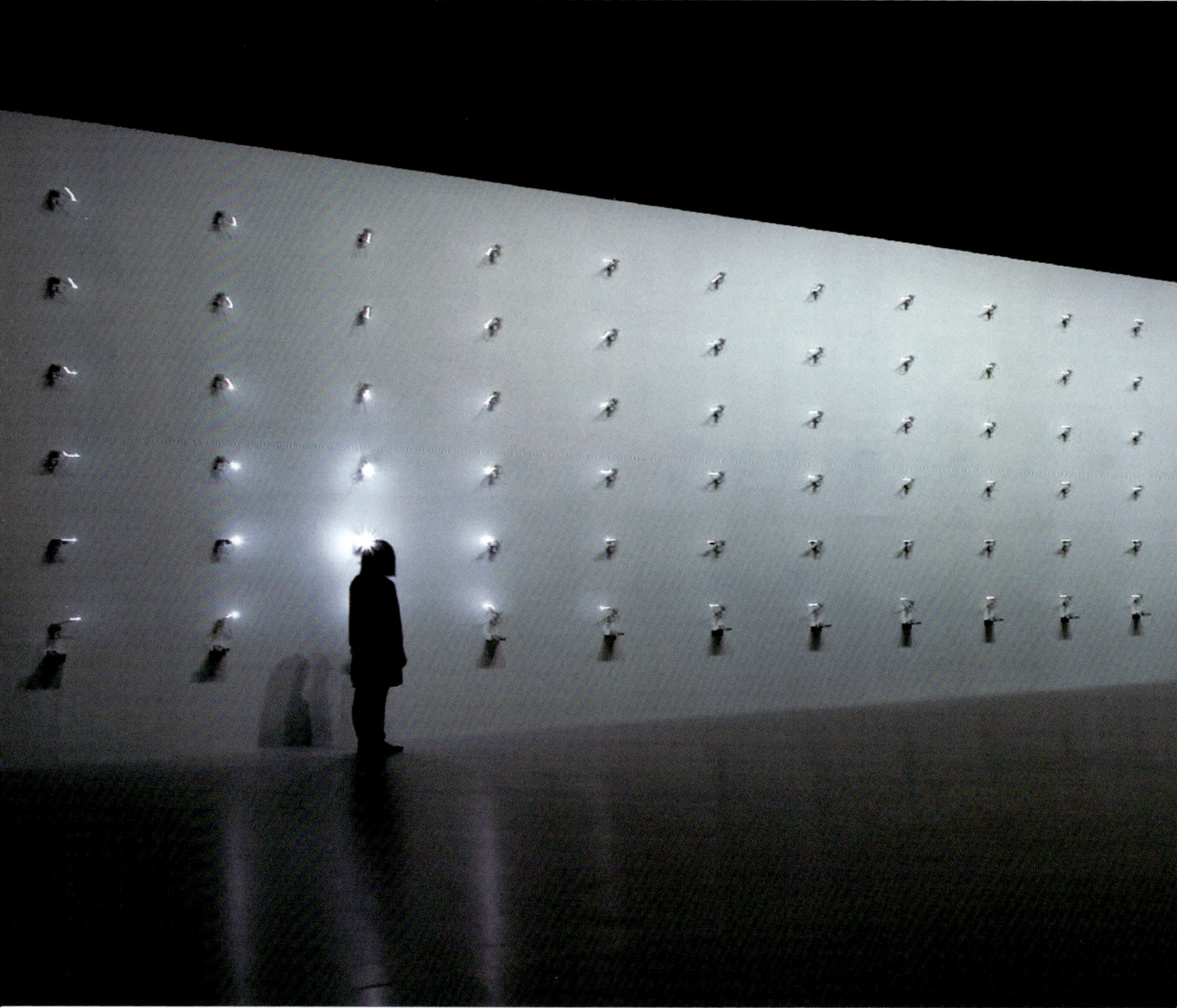

Ryuichi Maruo [YCAM]

Ninety Wriggling Wall Units

Ninety devices are distributed across a 14m × 4.5m wall. As soon as a visitor enters the area in front of the wall, the devices' heads start blinking, and all together they move in the visitor's direction like an insect's tentacles. Highly sensitive cameras (0.00003 lux) and microphones able to detect motion and sound beyond human perception record the visitor's action and send the recorded images and sounds together with the data collected in this work's integrated database, from where they are eventually transmitted to the Compound Eye Detector Screen.

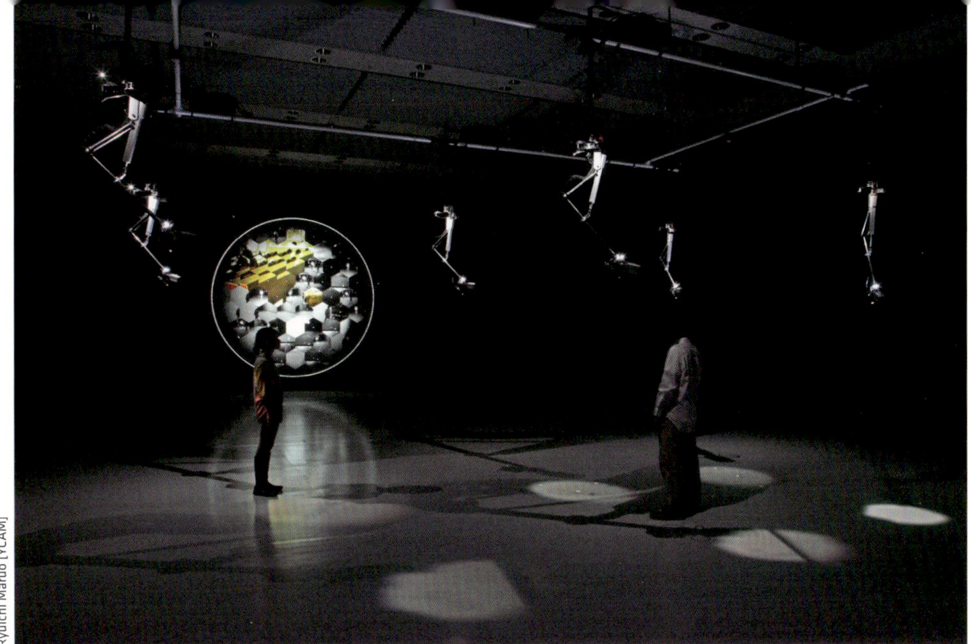

Six Multi Perspective Search Arms

Six robotic search arms resembling an insect's tentacles are suspended from the ceiling. Video cameras and small laser projectors mounted onto the ends of these arms follow and record the movements of approaching visitors, and simultaneously project the recorded images. Through the looped feedback resulting from the search arms' endlessly repeated input (recording) and output (projecting), the visitor perceives reality as a repetition of *voids*.
Data from the search arms' movements are stored in the *Desire of Codes* database, which controls the operation of the work as a whole and is ultimately reflected in the installation's light and sound.

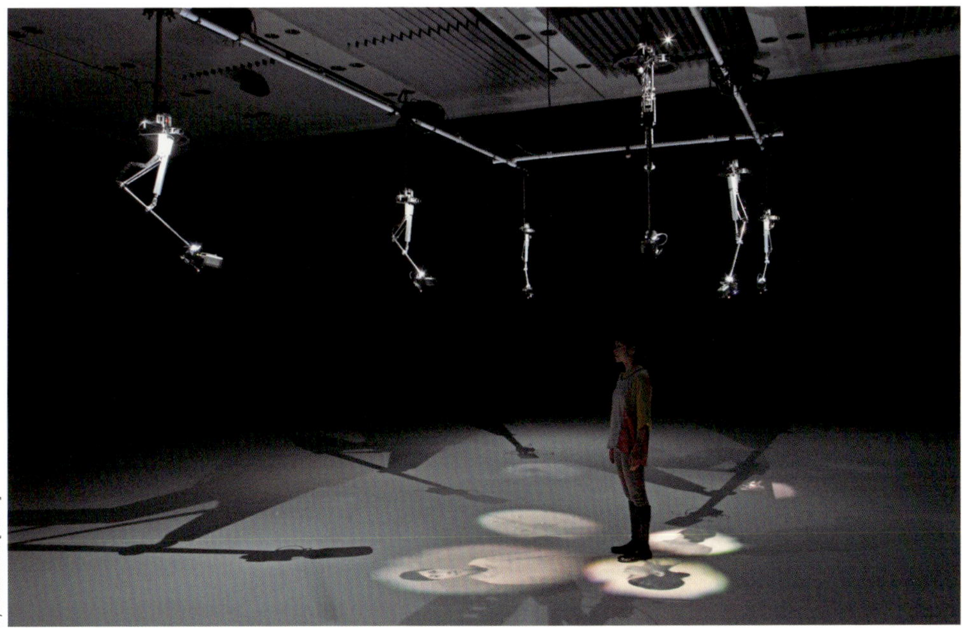

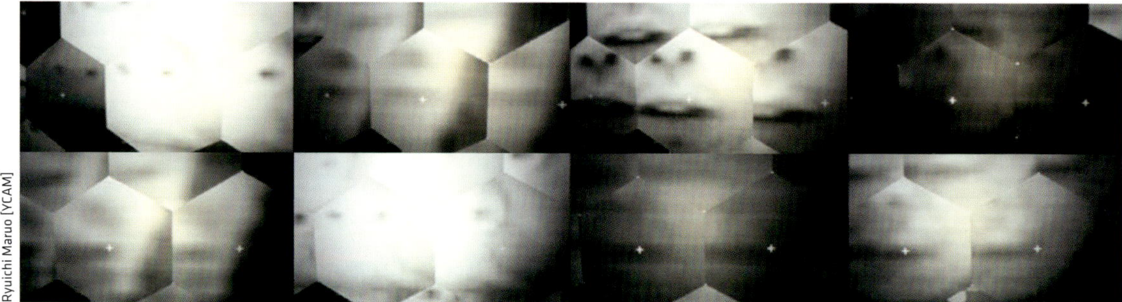

Ryuichi Maruo [YCAM]

Compound Eye Detector Screen

The *Desire of Codes* database contains images from the exhibition venue, such as the visitors' skin, eyes, hair, bags, which are recorded in real-time by the devices on the wall. The footage also includes images recorded seconds, hours and months ago, so that elements from the past and the present are mixed and projected onto the screen.

Additionally surveillance images recorded in public places—airports, parks, hallways or crowded streets around the world—and images in this database are transferred to a 4.7 m round screen that looks like an insect's compound eye and is divided into 61 hexagonal video screens.

Looking at the constantly changing projected scenery with its shifting time axes, the visitors feel as if they are watching a segmentalized dream or memories stored in the brain, and discover the desires that are automatically generated through the act of monitoring. This Compound Eye Detector Screen visualizes a new reality in which fragmentary aspects of space and time are recombined, while the visitor's position as a subject of expression and surveillance at once indicates the new appearances of human corporeality and desire.

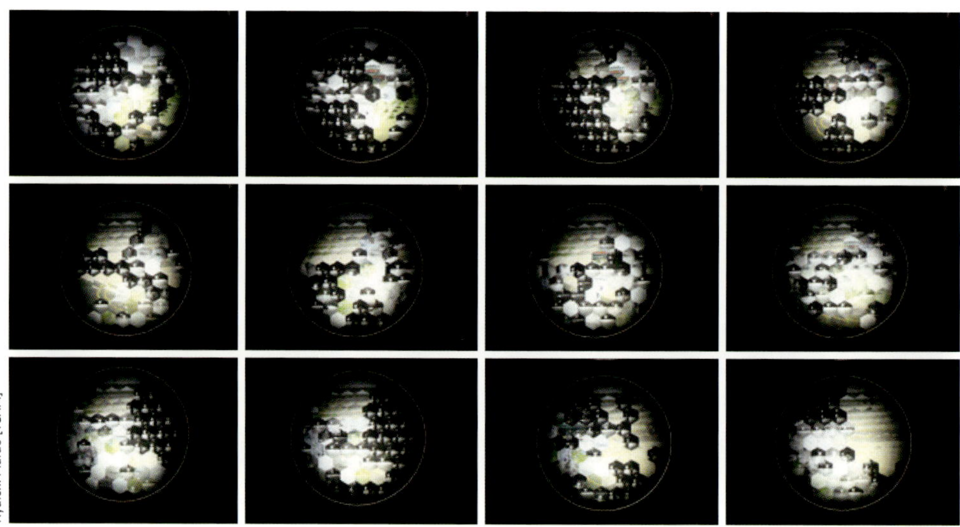

Ryuichi Maruo [YCAM]

Sound

Sound from the audience in the installation space, the sound generated by the machinery and other noise is collected by highly directional microphone. The changes of sound pressure and sound frequency over time are also collected and sent to the database for analysis purposes. New sound space is created when the present sound triggers the recollection of sound recorded in the past that is stored in the database.

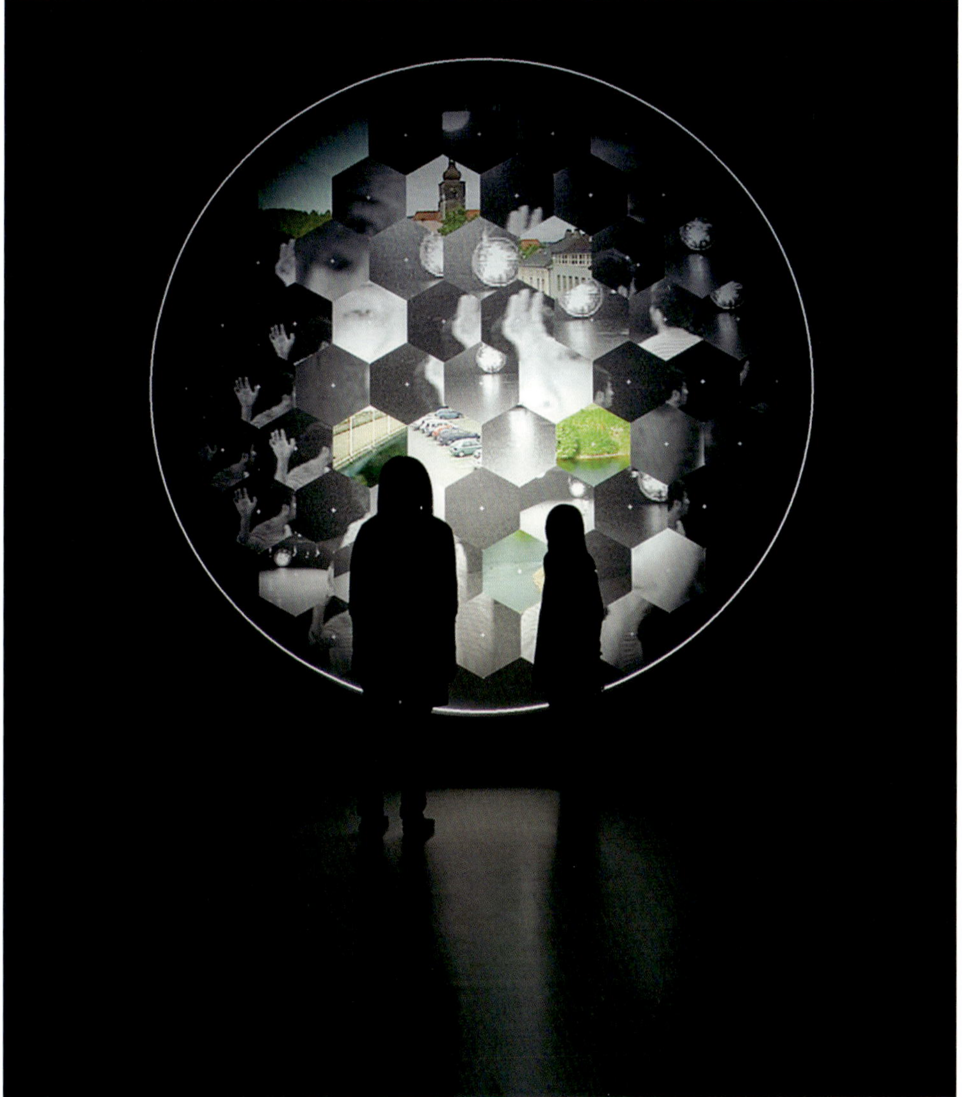

Ryuichi Maruo [YCAM]

Desire of Codes database program

In this installation the monitor displays different aspects of the *Desire of Codes* database program.

- The indicators on the left: 15 horizontal lines are directly related to the cameras mounted on the "wriggle wall" and display a visitor's position and react to his movements
- The indicators on the right hand side show the current video camera source for the images being displayed on the Compound Eye Detector Screen
- Grey: Images from the past
- Light grey: WEB surveillance camera images from across the world in real time
- Dark grey: facial image recognition
- Black: Real-time images from this installation
- Blue: Movement of the line that displays images that the camera is currently recording of visitors in front of the Ninety Wriggling Wall Units
- White vertical lines running from one side to the other indicate when the database is being searched. This software is the program manager of the *Desire of Codes*, combining the past and the present by displaying these composite images on the Compound Eye Detector Screen.

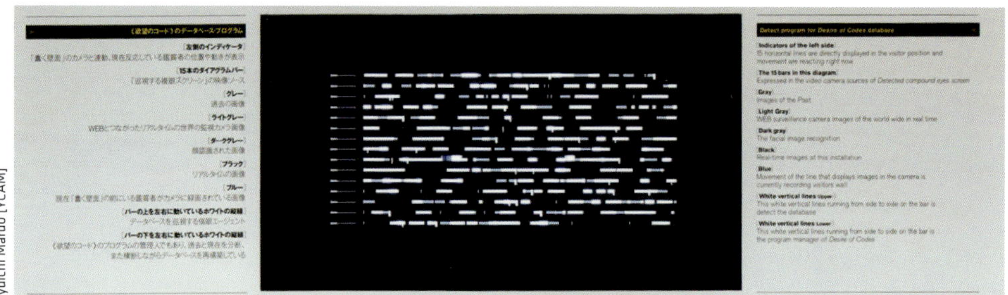

Ryuichi Maruo [YCAM]

Desire of codes is a work commissioned by [YCAM], Yamaguchi, and has been exhibited at ICC, Tokyo, Hartware Media Art Association, Dortmund, and at Kuenstlerhaus Vienna.

[YCAM] Yamaguchi Center for Arts and Media, Kazunao Abe (Curator)
[YCAM] InterLab (Soichiro Mihara, Richi Owaki, Satoshi Hama), Norimichi Hirakawa, Ryota Kuwakubo
TAKEGAHARASEKKEI, Sota Ichikawa, Tama Art University, Course of Media Art

Seiko Mikami
Featured Artist Ars Electronica 2012

Die japanische Künstlerin Seiko Mikami ist „Featured Artist" der Ars Electronica 2012. Seit den 1980ern beschäftigt sie sich in ihren großen, Raum füllenden Installationen mit der Beziehung zwischen dem menschlichen Körper und der Informationsgesellschaft. Seit den 1990ern entwickelt sie vor allem interaktive Arbeiten, in die sie die menschliche Wahrnehmung einbezieht. Außerhalb Japans, wo die Künstlerin einen Lehrstuhl an der Tama Art University innehat, sind ihre Arbeiten vorwiegend in Europa und in den USA gezeigt worden.

Wahrnehmungsmaschinen
Andreas Broeckmann über das Werk von Seiko Mikami

Die Werke von Seiko Mikami liefern eine Dekonstruktion menschlicher und maschinengebundener Wahrnehmung. In *Molecular Informatics* zum Beispiel setzt der Besucher ein *Head-mounted Display* auf und kann dann Spuren des eigenen Schauens sehen, die als animierte Linien und Formen im virtuellen Raum visualisiert werden. Eine Projektion zeigt dieselbe Animation für das übrige Galeriepublikum und bietet diesem so die Gelegenheit einer Beobachtung von Wahrnehmung als immersiver Erfahrung. In den verschiedenen Projekten, die Mikami in den letzten zwanzig Jahren verfolgt und stets weiter entwickelt hat, untersucht sie die Bedingungen der Wahrnehmung, ob in dem einsamen Klangraum von *World, Membrane and Dismembered Body*, der den Teilnehmer auf die Lücke zwischen Selbst und Wahrnehmung aufmerksam werden lässt, oder in der komplexen Anlage von *Gravicells*, die die physische Präsenz der Besucher in Beziehung setzt zu den Gravitationskräften der Erde und von Kommunikationssatelliten. Alle Werke von Mikami sind im engeren Sinne interaktiv, denn sie verwenden vornehmlich aktuelle Wahrnehmungs- und Sensordaten. Sie schaffen Feedbackschlaufen des Sehens, des Hörens und Fühlens und falten das Wahrgenommene zurück auf den Akt des Wahrnehmens.

Mit der neuen Arbeit *Desire of Codes* geht Mikami über von einer Maschinisierung menschlicher Wahrnehmung zur Dekonstruktion von Maschinenwahrnehmung und Maschinenkognition. Ein kleiner Schritt, denn die Unterschiede zwischen den menschlichen und den maschinengebundenen Bedingungen von Wahrnehmung und Verstehen, von Sehen und dem Prozessieren visueller Daten scheinen vernachlässigbar. Wir sehen wie Maschinen, und Maschinen sehen wie wir. Zumindest ist dies die explizit *fiktive* Behauptung, die *Desire of Codes* zu machen oder zu überprüfen scheint. Indem wir ihren Raum betreten, sind wir umgeben von den robotischen Sinnesorganen einer Maschinenintelligenz, die neugierig jede unserer Bewegungen verfolgt und in deren Funktionsweise wir einen geradezu unheimlichen Einblick bekommen, wenn wir still stehen oder sitzen und warten, bis sie unsere Anwesenheit vergessen hat. Dann nämlich beginnt Mikamis Erfindung zu „träumen", die Bilder aus ihrem Datenspeicher erneut zu prozessieren und, begleitet von einem rumpelnden Soundtrack, mit aktuellen Bildern aus den Live-Streams vernetzter Kameraaugen zu mischen.

Indem sie uns ein Bild bietet von der Schaulust der Maschine und ihrem melancholischen Prozessieren von Vergangenheit und Ferne, lädt uns Mikami ein, darüber nachzudenken, wie wir selbst mit Wahrnehmung, Verlangen und Erinnerung umgehen, und mit dem emotionalen Überschuss, den wir auf die Datenwelten projizieren. Was unterscheidet uns von den Maschinen die – eigensinnig? – unsere Wahrnehmung unterstützen und unseren Zugang zur Welt ermöglichen, und zu uns selber?

Seiko Mikami

Desire of Codes

Desire of Codes zeigt die verschwommenen Grenzen zwischen dem *Datenkörper in der virtuellen Welt* und dem *physischen Körper in der realen Welt* in unserer Informationsgesellschaft auf.

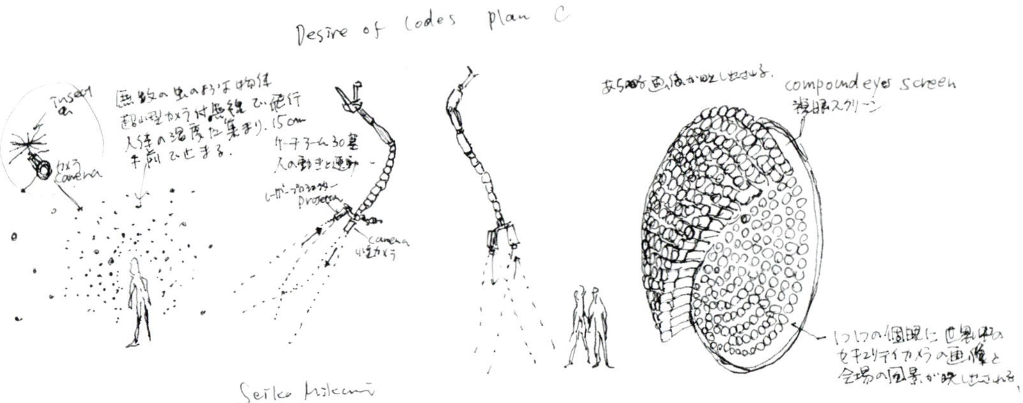

Die interaktive Installation besteht aus drei Teilen: (1) einer weißen Wand, an der 90 an Insektenfühler erinnernde Objekte mit kleinen, eingebauten Überwachungskameras angebracht sind (*Ninety Wriggling Wall Units*), (2) sechs riesenhaften Roboterarmen, die mit Videokameras und Laserprojektoren ausgestattet von der Decke hängen (*Six Multi-perspective Search Arms*) und (3) einer im Durchmesser 4,7 Meter großen, runden Projektionsfläche, die dem Facettenauge eines Insekts gleicht (*Compound Eye Detector Screen*).

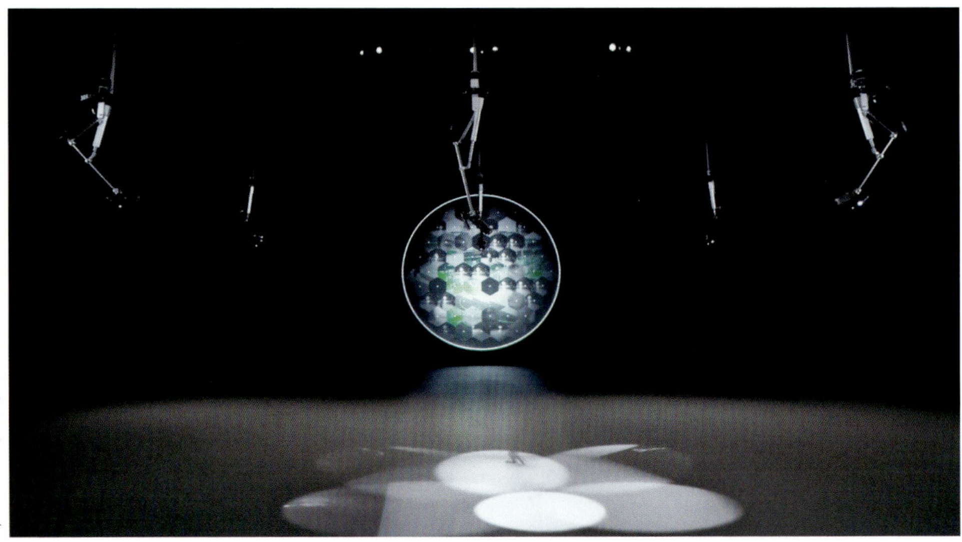

Ryuichi Maruo [YCAM]

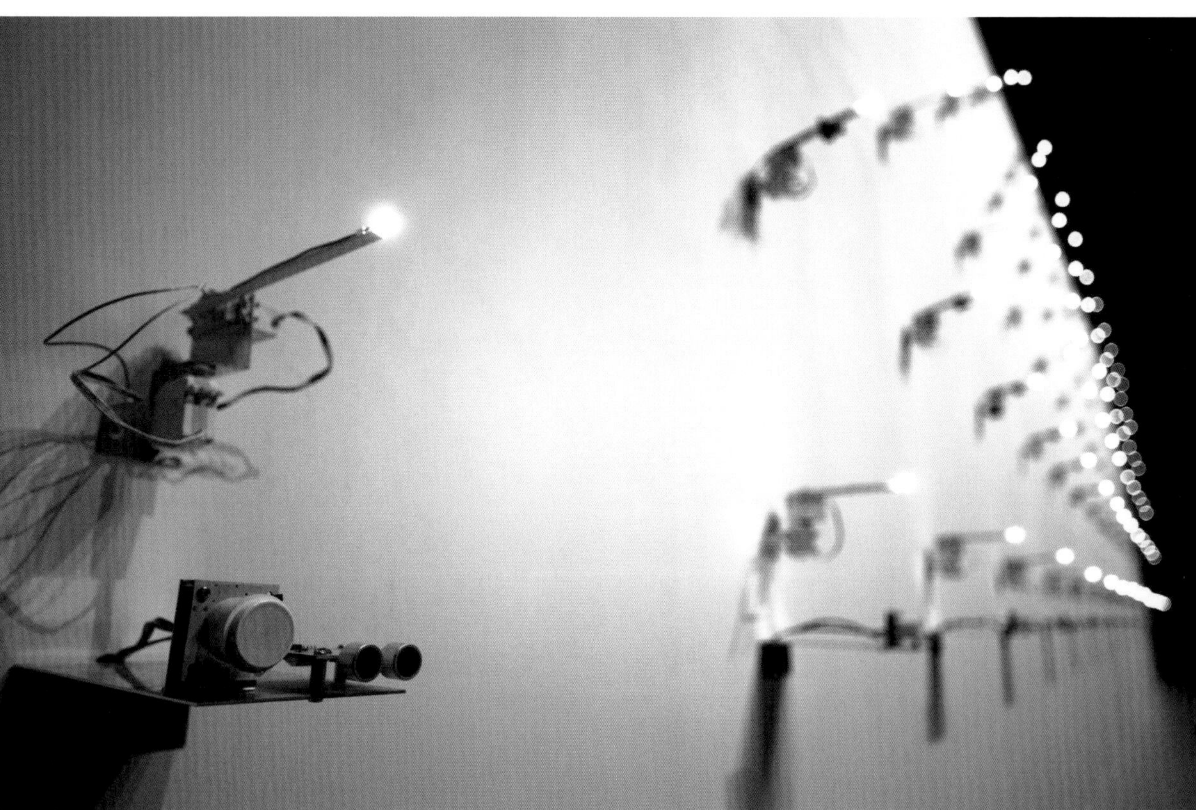

Ryuichi Maruo [YCAM]

Ninety Wriggling Wall Units – Neunzig neugierige Wandelemente

An einer 14 x 4,5 Meter großen Wand sind neunzig Objekte angebracht. Sobald ein Besucher den Bereich vor der Wand betritt, beginnen die Köpfchen der Bauteile zu blinken, die sich dem Besucher wie die Fühler eines Insekts zuneigen. Hochempfindliche Kameras (0.00003 Lux) und Mikrofone, die Bewegungen und Geräusche jenseits der menschlichen Wahrnehmungschwelle erfassen können, zeichnen das Handeln des Besuchers auf und übermitteln die Bilder und Klänge gemeinsam mit den Daten, die in einer integrierten Datenbank gesammelt werden, an den *Compound Eye Detector Screen*.

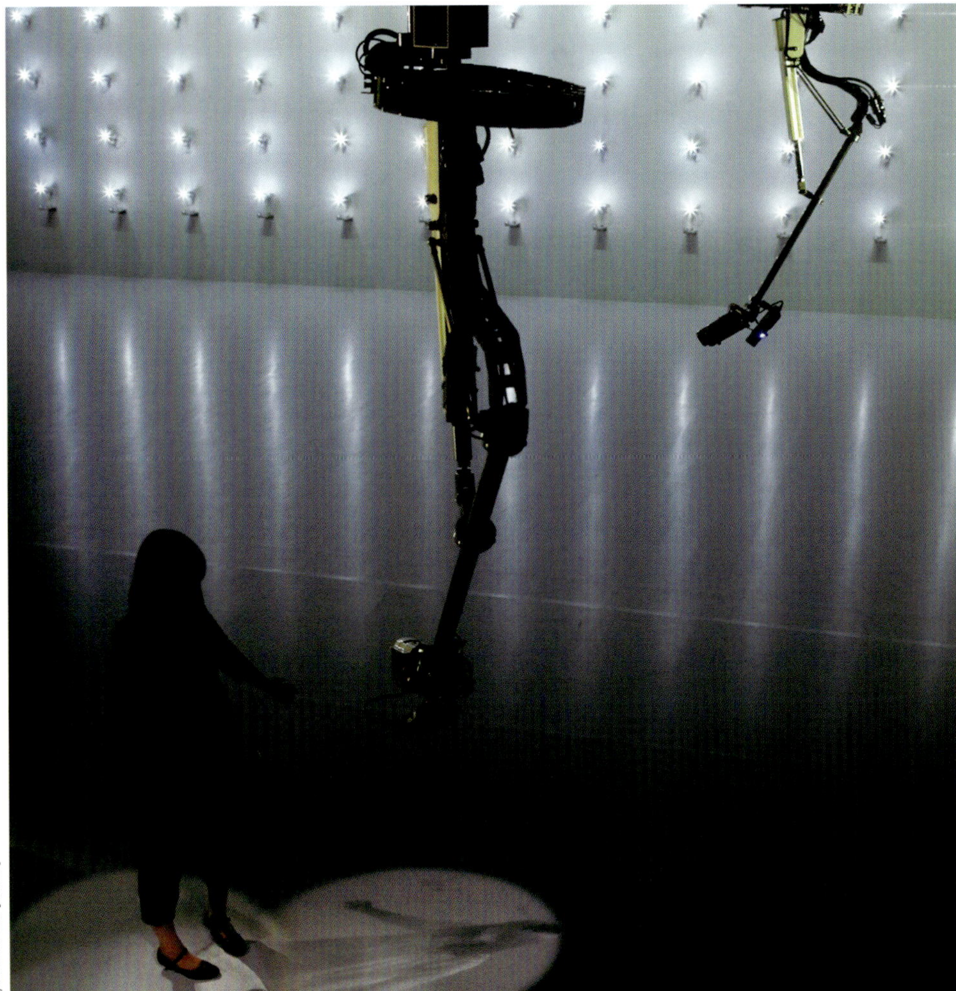

Ryuichi Maruo [YCAM]

Six Multi Perspective Search Arms
Sechs frei bewegliche Überwachungsfühler

Sechs an Tentakel erinnernde robotische Schwenkarme hängen von der Decke. Die an den Enden angebrachten Videokameras und Miniaturlaserprojektoren folgen den Bewegungen sich nähernder Besucher und zeichnen sie auf, während sie die aufgenommenen Bilder gleichzeitig projizieren. Aufgrund der Endlosschleife, die aus dem pausenlos sich wiederholenden Input (Aufzeichnung) und Output (Projektion) der Schwenkarme resultiert, nimmt der Besucher die Realität als eine Wiedergabe von Leere wahr.

Die aus den Bewegungen der Schwenkarme resultierenden Daten werden In der *Desire of Codes*-Datenbank gespeichert, die die gesamte Installation steuert; ferner kommen sie auch im Licht und Klang der Installation zum Ausdruck.

Compound Eye Detector Screen – Projektionsfläche Facettenauge

Die Datenbank *Desire of Codes* enthält Bilder des Ausstellungsorts, die beispielsweise Haut, Haare, Augen oder Taschen der Besucher zeigen und in Echtzeit von den Geräten an der Wand aufgenommen werden. Weiters sind auch Bilder gespeichert, die vor Sekunden, Stunden oder auch Monaten aufgenommen wurden, sodass abwechselnd Ausschnitte aus der Vergangenheit und der Gegenwart projiziert werden.

Zusätzlich werden Überwachungsbilder, die an öffentlichen Plätzen der ganzen Welt, etwa an Flughäfen, in Parks, Gängen oder überfüllten Straßen etc. aufgenommen wurden, und Bilder aus der Datenbank auf eine im Durchmesser 4,7 Meter große Projektionsfläche übertragen, die aus 61 hexagonalen Videomonitoren besteht und an das Facettenauge eines Insekts erinnert.

Beim Anblick der sich unablässig verändernden szenischen Projektionen mit sich verlagernden Zeitachsen haben die Besucher das Gefühl, Bruchstücke eines Traums oder von im Gedächtnis gespeicherten Bildern zu betrachten und entdecken Sehnsüchte, die durch den Prozess des Überwachens automatisch entstehen. Dieser *Compound Eye Detector Screen* visualisiert eine neue Realität, in der fragmentarische Aspekte von Raum und Zeit neu kombiniert werden, während die Stellung des Besuchers im Spannungsfeld zwischen Mitwirkung und Objekt der Überwachung zugleich auf neue Erscheinungsbilder menschlicher Körperlichkeit und Sehnsucht verweist.

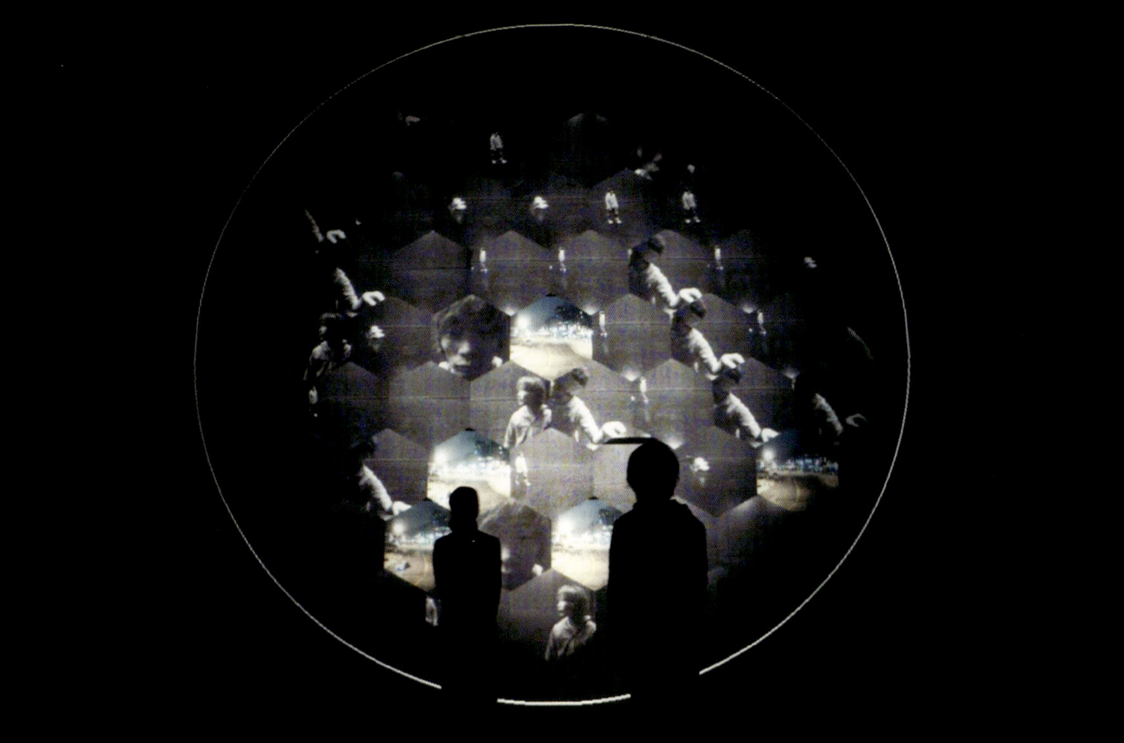

Ryuichi Maruo [YCAM]

Sound

Die vom Publikum im Ausstellungsraum erzeugten Geräusche werden ebenso wie die von den Geräten generierten Sounds von extremen Richtmikrofonen aufgenommen. Zusätzlich werden die über die Zeit erfolgenden Schalldruck- und -frequenzänderungen gesammelt und zur Analyse an die Datenbank übermittelt. Wenn der aktuelle Sound Erinnerungen an Klänge auslöst, die in der Vergangenheit aufgenommen und in der Datenbank gespeichert wurden, entsteht ein neuer Klangraum.

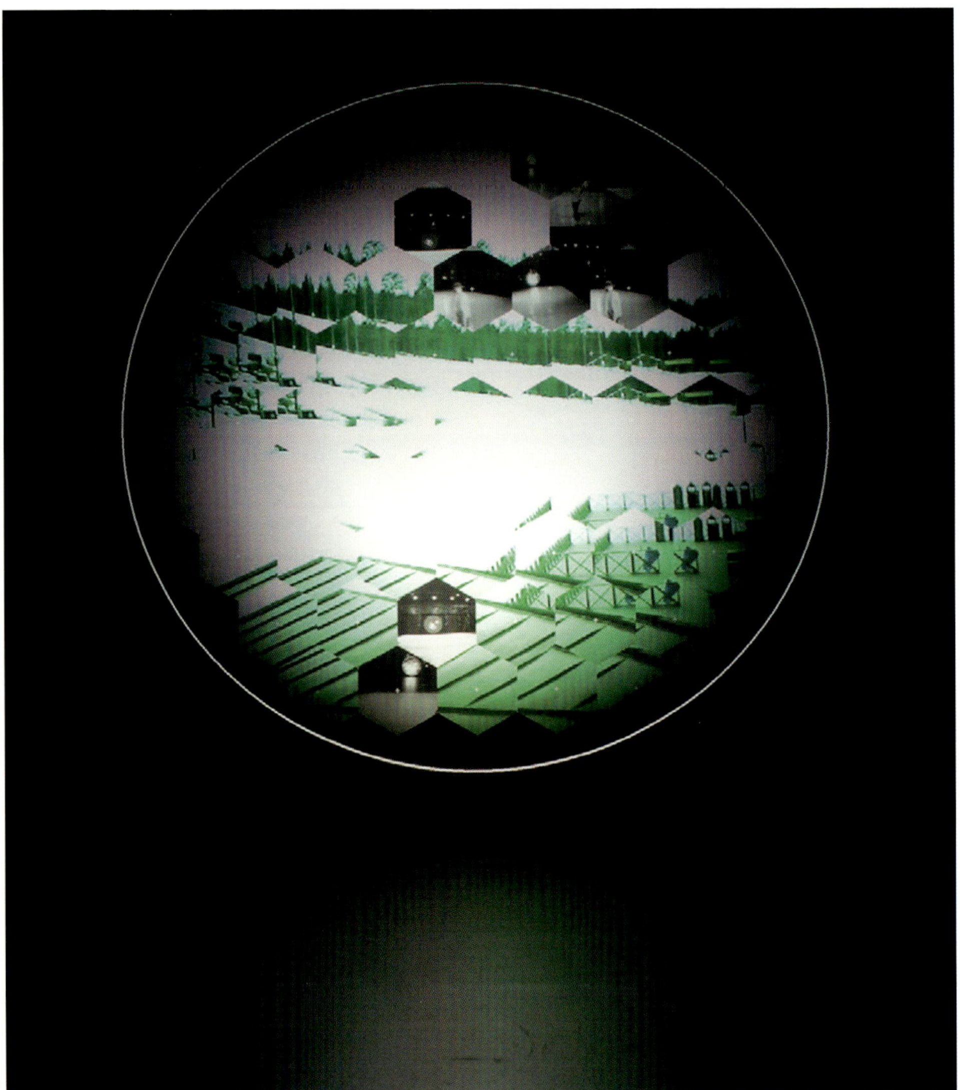

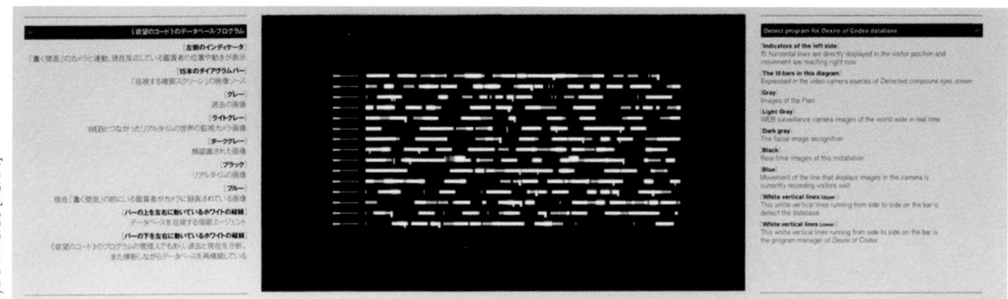

Ryuichi Maruo [YCAM]

Datenbank-Programm *Desire of Codes*

Der Monitor zeigt unterschiedliche Aspekte des Datenbank-Programms *Desire of Codes.*
* Indikatoren auf der linken Seite: 15 horizontale Linien korrelieren mit den auf der „Wriggle Wall" montierten Kameras, zeigen die Position des Besuchers an und reagieren auf seine Bewegungen.
* Die Indikatoren auf der rechten Seite zeigen die aktuelle Quelle der Videokamera für die auf dem *Compound Eye Detector Screen* gezeigten Bilder.
* Grau: Bilder aus der Vergangenheit
* Hellgrau: Web-Bilder von Überwachungskameras in Echtzeit
* Dunkelgrau: Gesichtserkennung
* Schwarz: Echtzeitbilder der Installation
* Blau: Bewegung der Linie, die Bilder zeigt, welche die Kamera gerade von Besuchern aufnimmt, die sich vor den *Ninety Wriggling Wall Units* befinden.
* Weiße vertikale Linien, die von einer Seite zur anderen verlaufen, zeigen an, dass die Datenbank durchsucht wird. Diese Software ist der Programmmanager des *Desire of Codes*-Datenbanksuchprogramms, das Vergangenheit und Gegenwart verknüpft, indem es auf dem *Compound Eye Detector Screen* zusammengesetzte Bilder unterschiedlicher zeitlicher und räumlicher Provenienz zeigt.

Aus dem Englischen von Martina Bauer

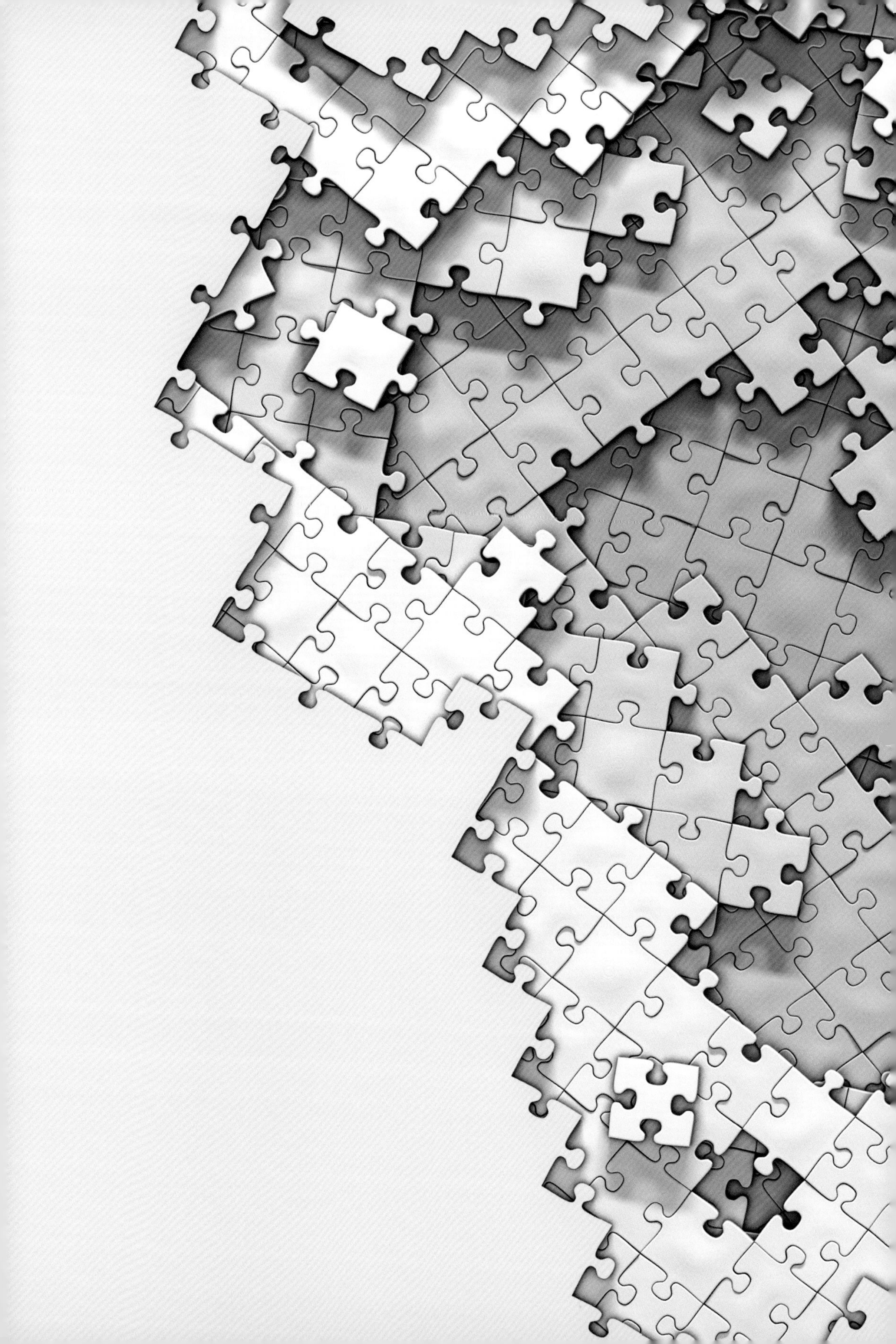

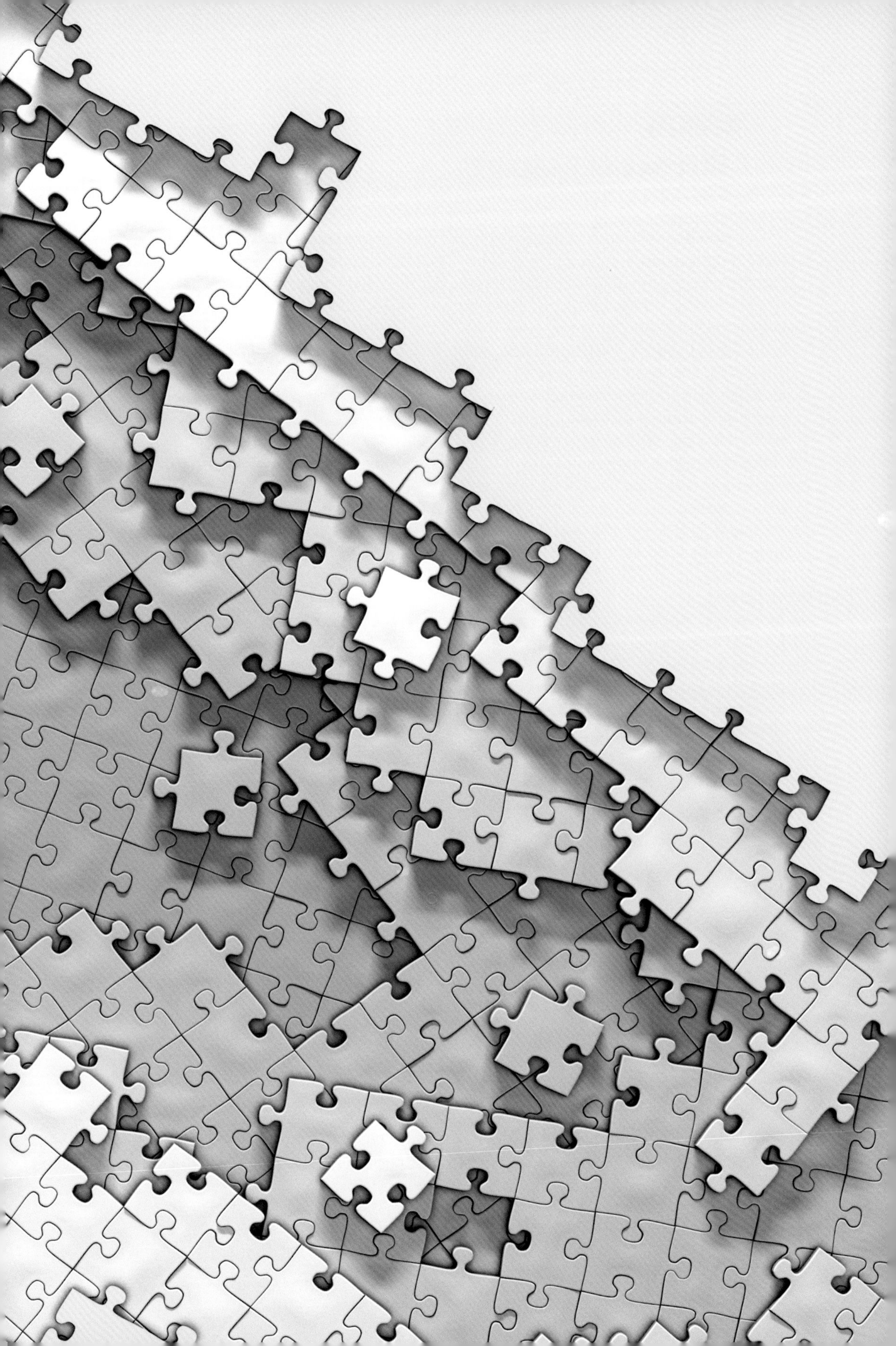

Adam Bly

Science is Culture

When I first jotted "science is culture" down on a mock-up of the cover of *Seed,* it was more of an aspiration than an observation. I started a science magazine during an American administration that not only opposed science but devalued empiricism. This emboldened activists around the world who rejected evolution and sought to reform science education with their own version of truth. But at the same time, in the vitality of this antiscientific movement, you could sense the imminent rise of a cultural shift they sought to prevent. I had the idea that science was becoming the fundamental driver of our times and held unique promise to improve the state of the world. I believed that we were on the cusp of a twenty-first-century scientific renaissance, and I wanted to create a magazine to capture this cultural shift. I called it *Seed* because that's how I saw science: where things start, beneath the surface of all that surrounds us.

Today that tagline seems self-evident: science *is* culture. In the last decade, science has transformed the social, political, economic, aesthetic, and intellectual landscape. It is reshaping our understanding of who we are and where we come from and modernizing our system of values—how we regard our planet and one another. Other forces undeniably affect the state of the world—faith, democracy, and free markets among them. But science is the overwhelming and universal agent of change. Today, science affects every single person on the planet.

These are times for great optimism—about what we can know and accomplish. In the last decade, we mapped the human genome and the cosmic microwave background. We confirmed the existence of dark energy and the age of the universe, and know that it is expanding. We sequenced the rice genome. We found evidence of oceans on Mars and landed for the first time on another planet's (Saturn) moon. We know that we have more in common with Earth's other biota than we once thought. We built a machine capable of approximating the big bang, used the Internet to study human behavior, and produced more data than in all prior human history. We awarded scientists the Nobel Peace Prize.

These are also times of great uncertainty. We now notice that the systems that support life and commerce on this planet are riddled with complexity and interdependence of an unimaginable scale. We see that we cannot solve epidemics, for example, without solving climate change; we cannot solve climate change without rethinking economic growth; we cannot reconsider growth without an understanding of population and demographics; and we cannot anticipate population shifts without considering epidemics. The toolbox that served us well in the twentieth century is inadequate to wrestle with the systemic challenges apparent at the dawn of the twenty-first.

We need a new way of looking at the world. We need to rekindle the conviction that knowledge is good, and more knowledge is better. We need to be reminded that disciplines are man-made creations, useful only to a degree. Like the Renaissance of the fifteenth and sixteenth centuries, the renaissance before us will be characterized by a revolution in how knowledge is gathered, synthesized, and applied to society. And once again, science will mean more to us than its output, than drugs and technologies; more than something to be governed, science will become a way of governing and thinking.

Today, we think scientifically about issues like health and the environment, but soon we will also think scientifically about the size of cities, the reason for poverty, the basis of morality, the resilience of markets, and much more.

Science is a methodology and philosophy rooted in evidence, kept in check by persistent inquiry, and bounded by the constraints of a self-critical and rigorous method. Science is a lens through which we can visualize and solve complex problems, establish international relations, and embolden (even reignite) democracy. More than anything, what this lens offers us is a limitless capacity to handle all that comes our way, no matter how complex or unanticipated.

We are on the cusp of this renaissance, not in the midst of it. For all that science has contributed to our lives in the past half century, it hasn't yet universally changed the way we think. And it won't unless we understand and address why.

In times of uncertainty, fear becomes the overwhelming faculty. People seek out quick and easy answers and comfort, and religion offers both. It is soothing to think that when the ground shakes—killing two hundred thousand people in an already destitute nation—there is a grander purpose to it all, an underlying beneficent plan. Much less comforting is the objective explanation: that the Earth's tectonic plates constantly move and grind against one another, so there is compression and subduction, and the occasional violent rupture—a terrifying, but ultimately random and meaningless event. But it is only by studying those geological forces—and today we can—and embracing the findings, that we will be able to better predict earthquakes and save lives. We're not there yet...

Because science and religion are at war, embroiled in a battle that has not strengthened either side; it has served only to strengthen the bases, not convert the masses. (And the base for religion is a lot bigger than the base for science!) That's not to say the "culture war" has not been an intellectually useful exercise; it has. But religion will not overturn science and science will not overturn religion; both are too fundamentally rooted in society—the global economy is built on science; more than two-thirds of the world's population believes in a God. Pursuing each other's demise is ultimately deleterious to both and compromises the much more important goal of actually improving the state of the world. For the benefit of humanity, we need most of the seven billion people on this planet to embrace science as the way forward—we need them to use vaccines, fund stem cell labs, and support carbon taxes, not march against them.

The trouble with (commonly practiced organized) religion is not God. It is that it offers truth without a way of questioning it. Worse, it punishes you for questioning it. We simply cannot move forward in these times with this dogma.

Every child around the world should be taught to embrace the scientific method (this is what scientific literacy must mean in this century)—before they hear about God. And we should be reminded always that we have the right to question everything—that changing our minds with new evidence is a virtue—not a cause for condemnation. If one then chooses faith and subjects it to permanent scrutiny, then religion is no longer the enemy. In the interest of global stability, science must precede faith, but not seek to overturn it.

I should note that one of the practical problems here is that, unlike religion, science has no ordained leaders with the pulpit to make this plea. Science does not issue talking points. Ironically, this weakness, this absence of idols and enforced consensus, confers unique strength and stability to science. So perhaps instead, the world's priests and sheikhs and rabbis might take up the position.

Richard Feynman, the Nobel Prize-winning physicist, once told this story on television:

> "I have a friend who's an artist and he's sometimes taken a view which I don't agree with very well. He'll hold up a flower and say, "look how beautiful it is," and I'll agree. And he says, "You see, I, as an artist, can see how beautiful this is, but you as a scientist, oh, take this all apart and it becomes a dull thing." And I think he's kind of nutty. First of all, the beauty that he sees is available to other people and to me too, although I might not be quite as refined aesthetically as he is. But I can appreciate the beauty of a flower. At the same time, I see much more about the flower than he sees. I could imagine the cells in there, the complicated actions inside which also have a beauty... The fact that the colors in the flower are evolved in order to attract insects to pollinate it is interesting—it means that insects can see the color. It adds a question—does this aesthetic sense also exist in the lower forms? Why is it aesthetic? A science knowledge only adds to the excitement and mystery and the awe of a flower. It only adds. I don't understand how it subtracts."

It is one thing to accept science; it is another to embrace it. For some, the path to scientific thinking will be perfunctory. For most, though, it will need to be beautiful, inspiring, and fulfilling at the same time.
Millions of Soviet children cheered when Laika became the first living creature to orbit the Earth in 1957. Millions of American kids listened in rapt silence when Neil Armstrong, touching down on the lunar surface, delivered his indelible "One step" communique. An estimated six hundred million people worldwide—many of them children—watched the scene unfold on television: two grainy white shapes bobbing across the rocky moonscape, the first human beings to touch extra-terrestrial soil. Two years earlier, when Robert Wilson, the director of Fermilab, was called to justify the multimillion-dollar particle accelerator to Congress, Wilson argued:

> "It has only to do with the respect with which we regard one another, the dignity of men, our love of culture. It has to do with: Are we good painters, good sculptors, great poets? I mean all the things we really venerate in our country and are patriotic about. It has nothing to do directly with defending our country except to make it worth defending."

We should all see science the way scientists do.
To do advanced physics at Fermilab or CERN takes advanced degrees. And we cannot all study dark matter. But that should not imply that we must remain on the receiving end of science rather than engaging with it as participants. We can all use the methodology, we can all contribute knowledge, and today, we can even all participate in some of the process.
Consider this: You can cook without mastering Escoffier. You can close your eyes and pray without reading Arabic. You can be an artist with just a paintbrush. The perception that the barrier to entry for science is somehow higher is wrong. It is probably even easier and more intuitive to think scientifically than it is to draw well or serve an ace ... because we were once all scientists. It's how we thought as children, when we looked out at the ocean and wondered, "Why is it blue?" When we followed that question with further questions, and then with our own experiments: a jarful of salty water carried home from the beach answered: "Is it blue everywhere?" Creeping down to the waterfront well after dusk clinched the response to: "Does it stay blue at

night?" If you wanted to understand how a butterfly flies, you examined it. You notice it has wings—two forewings and two hindwings, each pair attached to a different part of its body. An ant doesn't have wings, and a beetle doesn't appear to have any either... but there they are, hidden under a hard-shelled coat. Then, if you want to learn more, you crack open a biology book. You start adding information, observing more carefully, making richer hypotheses, and conducting experiments—and you do it because you want to, because it starts to become extremely gratifying. And then you start to understand something, and you begin making connections, seeing relationships and dependencies, and applying that knowledge... and a traffic circle suddenly resembles a horde of food-gathering ants.

The burgeoning "citizen science" movement coupled with the rise of mobile devices and social media allows anyone to participate in the process of science—counting migrating birds, collecting water samples, processing the search for extraterrestrial intelligence.... And the deepening relationship between science and design is opening up new means of physical and emotional interaction with the revolutions that science spurs.

Science is necessarily flat and open. Any idea can be overturned at anytime by anyone. This is fundamental to the culture and stability of science. Although they must ultimately hold up to the other tenets of science—reproducibility and falsifiability among them—the best ideas can come from anywhere. And they do. They come from architects conceiving higher dimensional spaces, from game designers toying with astrobiology, and from novelists thinking about memory.

This is the foundation for a 21st century scientific renaissance.

Reprinted with permission of the author from *Science is Culture: Conversation at the New Intersection of Science + Society,* published by HarperCollins.

Adam Bly

Wissenschaft ist Kultur

Als ich zum ersten Mal die Worte „Science is Culture" auf ein Probe-Cover der Zeitschrift *Seed* kritzelte, entsprang das mehr einem Wunschdenken denn einer Beobachtung. Ich wollte ein Wissenschaftsmagazin zu einer Zeit verlegen, als die amerikanische Regierung der Wissenschaft skeptisch gegenüberstand und die Empirie desavouierte. Das bestärkte weltweit Kräfte, die die Evolution ablehnten und die wissenschaftliche Bildung mit ihrer eigenen Version der Wahrheit zu reformieren suchten. Doch mitten in der Blütezeit dieser antiwissenschaftlichen Bewegung war auch schon die bevorstehende kulturelle Veränderung zu spüren, die sie zu verhindern trachtete. Nach meiner Vorstellung war die Wissenschaft im Begriff, zur maßgeblichen Triebkraft unserer Zeit zu werden, und barg ein einzigartiges Potenzial, den Zustand der Welt zu verbessern. Ich war überzeugt, wir befänden uns an der Schwelle zu einer Wissenschaftsrenaissance des 21. Jahrhunderts – und ich wollte diesen kulturellen Umbruch mit meinem Magazin festhalten. Ich nannte es *Seed* (Samen), denn so sah ich die Wissenschaft: als das, wo alles beginnt, unter der Oberfläche dessen, was uns umgibt.

Heutzutage erklärt sich so ein Motto von selbst: Wissenschaft *ist* Kultur. Die Wissenschaft hat im vergangenen Jahrzehnt die soziale, politische, ökonomische, ästhetische und intellektuelle Landschaft verändert. Sie prägt unser Verständnis davon, wer wir sind und woher wir kommen, und erneuert unser Wertesystem – unsere Sicht des Planeten und unserer selbst. Natürlich üben auch andere Kräfte einen Einfluss auf die Welt aus – Glaube, Demokratie oder freie Märkte – aber die Wissenschaft ist der vorrangige und universelle Motor des Wandels. Sie hat Auswirkungen auf jeden einzelnen Menschen auf dem Planeten.

Wir leben in Zeiten, die Anlass zu Optimismus geben – in Bezug auf das, was wir wissen und erreichen können. In den letzten zehn Jahren haben wir das Humangenom und die kosmische Hintergrundstrahlung entschlüsselt. Wir haben die Existenz dunkler Energie nachgewiesen und das Alter des Universums bestimmt, und wir wissen, dass es expandiert. Wir haben das Reisgenom sequenziert. Wir haben Belege für Ozeane auf dem Mars gefunden und sind zum ersten Mal auf dem Mond eines anderen Planeten (Saturn) gelandet. Wir wissen, dass wir mehr Gemeinsamkeiten mit anderen irdischen Lebensformen haben als ursprünglich angenommen. Wir haben eine Maschine gebaut, die den Urknall simulieren kann, das Internet zur Untersuchung menschlichen Verhaltens eingesetzt und mehr Daten produziert als in der gesamten bisherigen Menschheitsgeschichte. Und wir haben Wissenschaftlern den Friedensnobelpreis verliehen.

Es sind aber auch Zeiten großer Unsicherheit. Wir erkennen, dass die unser Leben und unsere Wirtschaft erhaltenden Systeme unvorstellbar komplex und miteinander verflochten sind. Uns ist klar, dass wir z. B. Epidemien nicht bekämpfen können, ohne den Klimawandel zu lösen. Den Klimawandel aber können wir nur lösen, wenn wir beim Wirtschaftswachstum umdenken. Ein Umdenken beim Wirtschaftswachstum setzt ein Verständnis für Bevölkerungswachstum und Demografie voraus. Und das Bevölkerungswachstum wiederum kann nicht ohne Berücksichtigung von Epidemien prognostiziert werden. Die Werkzeuge, die ihre Aufgaben im 20. Jahrhundert gut erfüllt haben, erweisen sich für die systemischen Herausforderungen zu Beginn des 21. als unzulänglich.

Wir müssen die Welt mit anderen Augen betrachten. Wir müssen die Überzeugung neu beleben, dass Wissen gut und mehr Wissen noch besser ist. Gleichzeitig dürfen wir nicht vergessen, dass Disziplinen künstlich geschaffene Konstrukte und nur zu einem gewissen Grad nützlich sind.

Wie die Renaissance des 15. und 16. Jahrhunderts wird auch die vor uns liegende Renaissance durch eine Revolution in der Sammlung und Synthetisierung von Wissen und seiner Anwendung auf die Gesellschaft bestimmt. Und wieder wird die Wissenschaft mehr sein als ihr Output – Pillen und Technologien; sie wird nicht nur etwas sein, das es zu beherrschen gilt, sondern selbst eine Art zu herrschen und denken sein.

Heute gehen wir an Fragen der Gesundheit oder der Umwelt wissenschaftlich heran. Bald werden wir auch die Größe von Städten, die Gründe für Armut, die Grundlage von Moral, die Mechanismen von Märkten und vieles mehr wissenschaftlich ergründen.

Die Wissenschaft als Methode und Philosophie wurzelt auf Beweisen, in Schach gehalten und begrenzt durch unablässiges Weiterfragen und durch kritische und rigorose Verfahrensweisen.

Die Wissenschaft ist eine Linse, durch die komplexe Probleme visualisiert und gelöst, internationale Beziehungen geknüpft und Demokratien gestärkt (oder sogar neu belebt) werden können. Vor allem aber ermöglicht uns diese Linse, alles in Angriff zu nehmen, was sich uns entgegenstellt, ganz gleich, wie komplex oder unerwartet es ist.

Wir befinden uns an der Schwelle zu dieser Renaissance, nicht mitten drin. Trotz allem, was die Wissenschaft im letzten halben Jahrhundert zu unserem Leben beigetragen hat, hat sie unser Denken noch nicht grundlegend verändert. Was auch nicht geschehen wird, solange wir die Frage nach dem Warum nicht klären.

In Zeiten der Unsicherheit wird die Furcht zum alles bestimmenden Faktor. Die Menschen suchen nach raschen und einfachen Antworten und nach Trost – und die Religion bietet beides. Wenn die Erde bebt – und 200.000 Menschen eines ohnehin verarmten Landes den Tod finden – beruhigt es natürlich zu glauben, dass das einem höheren Zweck dient, Teil eines größeren Heilsplans ist, Die objektive Begründung ist weit weniger tröstlich: Die tektonischen Platten der Erde sind permanent in Bewegung, stoßen aneinander, sodass es ständig zu Kompressionen kommt und eine unter die andere rutscht, was gelegentlich zu heftigen Ausbrüchen führt – ein furchteinflößendes, aber absolut zufälliges Ereignis ohne weiteren Sinn. Aber nur durch das Studium dieser geologischen Kräfte – und dazu sind wir heute in der Lage – und die Anerkennung der Ergebnisse werden wir einmal fähig sein, Erdbeben genauer vorherzusagen und Leben zu retten. Soweit sind wir aber noch nicht...

Denn Wissenschaft und Religion sind miteinander verfeindet und in einen Kampf verwickelt, der keine der beiden Seiten stärkt. Lediglich die jeweilige Basis wurde gefestigt, doch die Massen noch nicht bekehrt. (Und die religiöse Basis ist um vieles größer als die wissenschaftliche!) Ich will damit nicht sagen, dieser „Kulturkampf" sei keine intellektuell nützliche Übung gewesen; er war es. Aber die Religion wird die Wissenschaft nicht stürzen, und die Wissenschaft nicht die Religion. Beide sind zu sehr in der Gesellschaft verwurzelt – die Weltwirtschaft fußt auf der Wissenschaft, und mehr als zwei Drittel der Weltbevölkerung glaubt an einen Gott. Allein der Versuch, den anderen auszulöschen, ist letztendlich für beide verheerend und schadet dem weit wichtigeren Ziel, die Welt besser zu machen. Zum Wohl der Menschheit muss die Mehrheit der sieben Milliarden Erdbewohner die Wissenschaft als den Weg der Zukunft anerkennen. Sie müssen sich impfen lassen, Stammzellenlabors finanzieren und Steuern auf Kohlendioxid unterstützen und nicht dagegen demonstrieren.

Das Problem mit (der meist organisiert praktizierten) Religion ist nicht Gott, sondern dass sie eine Wahrheit anbietet, ohne die Möglichkeit sie infrage zu stellen. Schlimmer noch, sie stellt das Infragestellen sogar unter Strafe. Derlei Dogmatismus aber bringt uns in Zeiten wie diesen nicht weiter.

Jedes Kind sollte mit wissenschaftlichen Methoden (nichts anderes kann wissenschaftliche Bildung in diesem Jahrhundert bedeuten) vertraut gemacht werden, bevor es von Gott hört. Wir sollten stets daran denken, dass wir alles in Frage stellen dürfen – dass es kein Grund zur Verdammnis, sondern eine Tugend ist, seine Meinung mit neuen Erkenntnissen zu ändern. Entscheidet sich dann jemand für den Glauben und hinterfragt ihn ständig, dann ist die Religion nicht mehr länger der Feind. Im Interesse der globalen Stabilität sollte die Wissenschaft dem Glauben vorausgehen, ihn aber nicht zu vernichten suchen.

Ich sollte anmerken, dass ein nicht unwesentliches praktisches Problem darin besteht, dass die Wissenschaft im Gegensatz zur Religion keine ordinierten Führer hat, die das von der Kanzel herunter dekretieren könnten. Die Wissenschaft verfasst keine Leitsätze. Ironischerweise trägt dieses Manko, dieses Fehlen von Götzen und erzwungenem Konsens zu einigender Stärke und Stabilität in der Wissenschaft bei. Vielleicht sollten die Priester, Mullahs und Rabbis der Welt diesen Ansatz übernehmen.

Der Physik-Nobelpreisträger Richard Feynman erzählte im Fernsehen einmal folgende Geschichte:

> „Einer meiner Freunde ist Künstler und manchmal bezieht er eine Position, die ich nicht teilen kann. Er nimmt eine Blume und sagt: „Schau, wie schön sie ist", und ich stimme zu. Dann sagt er aber: „Ich als Künstler kann diese Schönheit erfassen, aber du als Wissenschaftler, ha, du nimmst sie auseinander, und übrig bleibt ein Haufen Dreck." Ich denke mir dann, dass er verrückt ist. Selbstverständlich ist die Schönheit, die er sieht, auch anderen zugänglich, sogar mir. Selbst wenn ich ästhetisch nicht so fein unterscheiden kann wie er. Aber ich kann die Schönheit einer Blume sehr wohl schätzen. Zusätzlich sehe ich noch viel mehr als er. Ich kann mir die Zellen vorstellen, die komplexen Abläufe im Inneren, die ebenso ihre Schönheit haben ... Es ist interessant, dass die Pflanze Farben entwickelt hat, um Insekten zum Bestäuben anzulocken – und das bedeutet, dass Insekten Farben sehen können. Das wirft die Frage auf, ob es diesen Sinn für Ästhetik auch in niedrigeren Lebensformen gibt? Warum ist es ästhetisch?... Wissenschaftliches Wissen steigert die Begeisterung und das Mysterium nur noch, trägt zur Bewunderung für die Blume bei. Es kommt etwas dazu. Ich verstehe nicht, inwiefern es etwas wegnehmen sollte. "

Es ist eine Sache, die Wissenschaft zu akzeptieren; es ist eine andere, sie sich zueigen zu machen. Für einige ist der Weg zu wissenschaftlichem Denken nur ein Mittel zum Zweck. Für die meisten jedoch muss er zugleich auch schön, inspirierend und erfüllend sein.

Als Laika 1957 das erste Lebewesen in einer Umlaufbahn um die Erde war, jubelten Millionen sowjetischer Kinder, Millionen amerikanischer Kinder lauschten ehrfürchtig Neil Armstrongs „Schritt"-Botschaft beim Betreten des Mondes. Geschätzte 600 Millionen Fernsehzuseher weltweit – viele davon Kinder – beobachteten, wie zwei grobkörnige weiße Gestalten, die ersten Menschen, die außerirdischen Boden betraten, durch eine felsige Mondlandschaft hüpften. Zwei Jahre zuvor hat Robert Wilson, der Direktor von Fermilab, zur Rechtfertigung des mehrere Millionen teuren Teilchenbeschleunigers vor dem Kongress argumentiert: „Das hat nur mit dem Respekt zu tun, den wir einander entgegenbringen, mit der Würde des Menschen und unserer Liebe zur Kultur. Wir fragen: Sind wir gute Maler, gute Bildhauer, geniale Poeten? Ich meine all die Dinge, die wir in unserem Land verehren, weswegen wir darauf stolz sind. Das alles hat nicht direkt etwas mit der Verteidigung des Landes zu tun, sondern damit, dass das Land überhaupt verteidigenswert wird."

Wir alle sollten die Wissenschaft so wie die Wissenschaftler sehen.

Für komplexe physikalische Experimente im Fermilab oder CERN bedarf es einer höheren Ausbildung. Und wir können nicht alle die dunkle Energie untersuchen. Das sollte aber nicht heißen, dass wir auf der Empfängerseite der Wissenschaft bleiben müssen und uns nicht aktiv einbringen können. Wir alle können die Methode einsetzen, wir können Wissen beisteuern, und heutzutage können wir aktiv an dem einen oder anderen Prozess teilhaben.

Überlegen Sie nur: Sie können kochen, ohne ein Auguste Escoffier zu sein. Sie können ihre Augen schließen und beten, ohne Arabisch zu können. Und ein Pinsel genügt, um sie zum Künstler zu machen. Die Vorstellung, dass die Zutrittsschranke zur Wissenschaft höher sei, ist falsch. Es ist vielleicht sogar einfacher und intuitiver, wissenschaftlich zu denken, als gut zeichnen oder ein Ass servieren zu können ... denn einst waren wir alle Wissenschaftler. So dachten wir als Kinder, wenn wir das Meer betrachteten und uns fragten: „Warum ist es blau?" Darauf folgten weitere Fragen und dann oft unsere eigenen Experimente: Ein vom Strand mitgebrachtes Glas Salzwasser beantwortete die Frage: „Ist es überall blau?" Wenn wir uns weit nach Einbruch der Nacht zum Strand schlichen, erhielten wir die Antwort auf: „Bleibt es auch in der Nacht blau?". Wenn man verstehen wollte, wie ein Schmetterling fliegt, untersuchte man ihn. Man bemerkte, dass er Flügel hat – zwei Vorder- und zwei Hinterflügel, von denen jedes Paar an einem anderen Teil des Körpers angewachsen ist. Eine Ameise hat keine Flügel, und ein Käfer scheint auch keine zu haben ... dabei sind sie nur unter einer harten Schale verborgen. Möchte man mehr erfahren, schlägt man ein Biologiebuch auf. Man sammelt Informationen, beobachtet aufmerksamer, stellt gewagtere Hypothesen auf und führt Experimente durch – und das alles, weil man es machen möchte, weil es sich als äußerst lohnend entpuppt. Und plötzlich versteht man etwas, stellt Verbindungen her, sieht Beziehungen und Abhängigkeiten ... und auf einmal ähnelt ein Kreisverkehr einem Nahrung sammelndem Ameisenvolk.

Die wachsende Bewegung der „Bürgerwissenschaft" zusammen mit dem Aufschwung mobiler Geräte und sozialer Medien erlaubt jedem, am Wissenschaftsprozess teilzunehmen – indem man Zugvögel zählt, Wasserproben nimmt, die Suche nach außerirdischer Intelligenz weiterführt ... Die sich vertiefende Beziehung zwischen Wissenschaft und Design eröffnet neue Wege physischer und emotionaler Interaktion mit den von der Wissenschaft initiierten Revolutionen. Die Wissenschaft ist notwendigerweise flach und offen. Jeder kann jederzeit eine These umwerfen. Das ist für die Kultur und Stabilität der Wissenschaft grundlegend. Auch wenn sie letztlich den übrigen Prinzipien der Wissenschaft – wie Reproduzier- und Falsifizierbarkeit – genügen müssen, so können die besten Thesen doch von überall her kommen. Was auch geschieht: Sie kommen von Architekten, die höhere räumliche Dimensionen postulieren, von Spieleentwicklern, die sich in Astrobiologie versuchen und von Romanschriftstellern, die sich mit dem Gedächtnis auseinandersetzen.

Das ist die Grundlage für eine wissenschaftliche Renaissance des 21. Jahrhunderts.

Aus dem Englischen von Michael Kaufmann

Nachdruck mit freundlicher Genehmigung des Autors aus *Science is Culture: Conversation at the New Intersection of Science + Society,* herausgegeben von HarperCollins.

George M. Church

The Future of Practical Arts

" It is not the function of the poet to relate what has happened, but what may happen—
what is possible according to the law of probability or necessity. "
from Aristotle's Poetics, 350 BCE; translated by S.H. Butcher

Epic poems, fire songs and dances, athletic games and cave paintings. These enabled our
ancestors to remember past hunts, floods and seasons, to predict the future and to practice for
it. For each instance of adaptive evolution we find parasitic forms. Our ancestors had just enough
art to survive, but our technology + art evolved fruit into candy, history into soap opera, herbal
salves into addictions, procreation into porn, spear practice into billion dollar stadiums.
Our brand of synthetic biology aims at reassessing such unintended consequences and new
approaches to safety. Our future: In the practical arts we paint on an earth-sized canvas with
atom-sized brushes. We use computer-aided design *(caDNAno.org)* to deal with the intermediate levels. We build nanorobots that combine sensors, actuators and logic *(www.sciencemag.
org/content/335/6070/831)* to handle some of the detail-work. Cells still provide only nanotech-
nology capable of self-replication and extensive synthetic change. We now have not merely in
labs, but in production *(LS9.com, JouleUnlimited.com)*, bacteria that turn carbon dioxide and
sunlight into hydrocarbon fuels—totally compatible with current engines. We do not accept our
genetic destiny. Some of us have made their bodies resistant to HIV-AIDS by atomically manipulating both copies of each CCR5 gene in their blood cells. This is successful enough to already be
in Phase II clinical trials. We are reading the genomes of many youthful centenarians now—and
many others willing to share their genomic fortunes and issues *(www.personalgenomes.org)*. We
have added a year to our lives every 4 years, like clockwork for 170 years, but what happens if this
changes to one year per year? In addition to steady linear progress, technologies improve expo-
nentially or in leaps—computer reading and writing by 1.5 fold per year, DNA reading and writing
by 9-fold per year. The DIYbio movement is growing. As Joe Davis pioneered in 1986 *(http://goo.
gl/IUz0x)*, analo-digital datart can be encoded in DNA. Today this whimsy begins to look practical, competitive with other recording media—a billion times denser than Blu-ray and 400,000
year track record for long-term storage. We can design 3D computer circuits with 3 nanometer
features so that these can fit inside 10-micron cells to exchange messages with every neuron in
our brains. To gaze on the dark matter that comprises 84% of our universe, we design stalactites
of DNA to detect WIMPs. Will we cure disease and poverty to free the resources needed to backup our species outside of our earthly meteor target? What limits us? Our practical arts. What
limits that? Our imagination.

Die Zukunft der praktischen Künste

" ... dass es nicht Aufgabe des Dichters ist mitzuteilen, was wirklich geschehen ist, sondern vielmehr, was geschehen könnte, d.h. das nach den Regeln der Wahrscheinlichkeit
oder Notwendigkeit Mögliche. "
Aristoteles Poetik, 350 v. Chr., übersetzt von M. Fuhrmann

Epen, Feuergesänge und -tänze, sportliche Wettkämpfe und Höhlenmalereien – das waren die Mittel, über die unsere Vorfahren verfügten, um vergangener Jagden, Überflutungen und jahreszeitlicher Rituale zu gedenken, die Zukunft vorauszusagen und sich dafür zu rüsten. Für jedes Beispiel adaptiver Evolution finden sich immer auch parasitäre Formen. Unsere Vorfahren beherrschten gerade einmal die Kunst des Überlebens, während wir mit unserer Kombination von Kunst und Technologie Früchte in Bonbons, Geschichte in Seifenopern, Heilkräutersalben in Abhängigkeiten oder Fortpflanzung in Porno verwandeln und für den Speerwurf aberwitzig teure Stadien bauen.

Unser Unternehmen für synthetische Biologie hat sich zum Ziel gesetzt, derlei ungewollte Folgen zu verhindern und neue Sicherheitskonzepte zu prüfen. Unsere Zukunft: In den praktischen Künsten bemalen wir eine Leinwand in Größe der Erde mit Pinseln in der Größe von Atomen. Für die Zwischenebenen verwenden wir CAD *(http://caDNAno.org)*. Wir entwickeln Nanoroboter, die mithilfe einer Kombination von Sensoren, Aktoren und Logikgattern *(http://sciencemag.org/content/335/6070/831)* die Detailarbeit übernehmen. Zellen liefern nach wie vor die einzige Nanotechnologie, die zur Selbstreplikation und umfassenden synthetischen Veränderung fähig ist. Wir verfügen heute nicht nur in den Laboratorien über Bakterien, die Kohlendioxid und Sonnenlicht in Kohlenwasserstoff-Treibstoffe verwandeln, sie werden bereits produktiv eingesetzt *(http://LS9.com, http://JouleUnlimited.com)* – und sind mit heutigen Motoren absolut kompatibel. Wir ergeben uns nicht in unser genetisches Schicksal. So gelang es bereits, den menschlichen Körper durch eine Manipulation beider Kopien des CCR5-Gens in den Blutzellen resistent gegen den HIV-Virus zu machen. Dieser Erfolg rechtfertigt eine klinische Studie der Phase II. Wir entschlüsseln heute die Genome rüstiger Hundertjähriger – und vieler anderer, die bereit sind, ihr genetisches Schicksal und Erbgut öffentlich zugänglich zu machen *(http://www.personalgenomes.org)*. Seit 170 Jahren steigt die durchschnittliche Lebenserwartung – präzise wie ein Uhrwerk – alle vier Jahre um ein Jahr, doch was geschieht, wenn sich dies auf ein Jahr pro Jahr beschleunigt? Zusätzlich zu einem kontinuierlichen linearen Fortschritt verbessern sich die Technologien auch exponenziell oder sprunghaft – die Leistung von Computern wird sich pro Jahr um den Faktor 1,5 steigern, das Lesen und Schreiben der genetischen Information um den Faktor 9 seit dem Durchbruch im Jahr 2005. Die DIYBio-Bewegung wächst unaufhörlich. Wie Joe Davis 1986 *(http://goo.gl/IUz0x)* in seiner Pionierarbeit demonstrierte, lässt sich die DNA als Träger nicht-biologischer Information einsetzen. Heute hält diese kapriziöse Idee Einzug in die Praxis und läuft anderen Aufzeichnungsmedien den Rang ab – mit einer eine Milliarde Mal höheren Datendichte als Blue-ray und dem Vorzug einer langfristigen Sicherung von 400.000 Jahren. Wir können 3D-Schaltkreise auf 3-Nanometer-Bauelementen entwickeln, die in 10 Mikrometer große Zellen eingeschleust werden können, um Informationen mit jedem Neuron des Gehirns auszutauschen. Wir designen hängende DNA-Stränge, um WIMPs zu entdecken und einen Blick auf die Dunkle Materie, die 84 Prozent unseres Universums ausmacht, zu erhaschen. Werden wir Krankheit und Armut heilen können, um die Ressourcen freizusetzen, die benötigt werden, um ein Backup unserer Spezies außerhalb der Erde zu machen, die Zielscheibe von Meteoriten ist? Was setzt uns Grenzen? Unsere praktischen Fertigkeiten. Was setzt ihnen Grenzen? Unsere Vorstellungskraft.

Aus dem Englischen von Martina Bauer

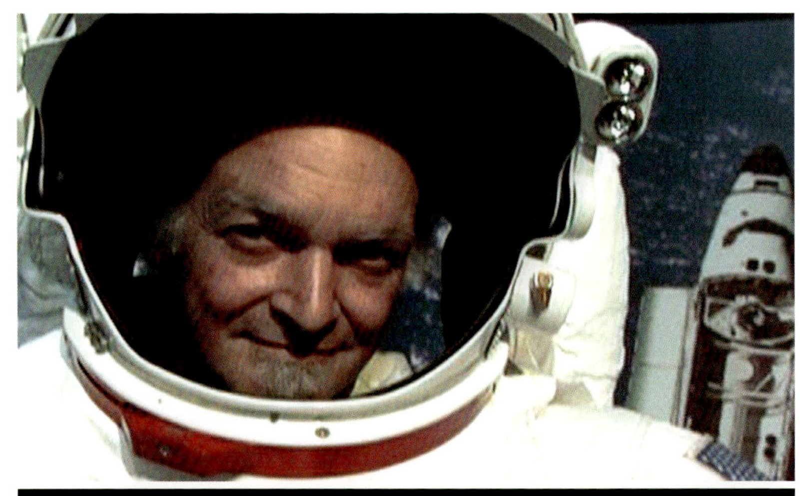

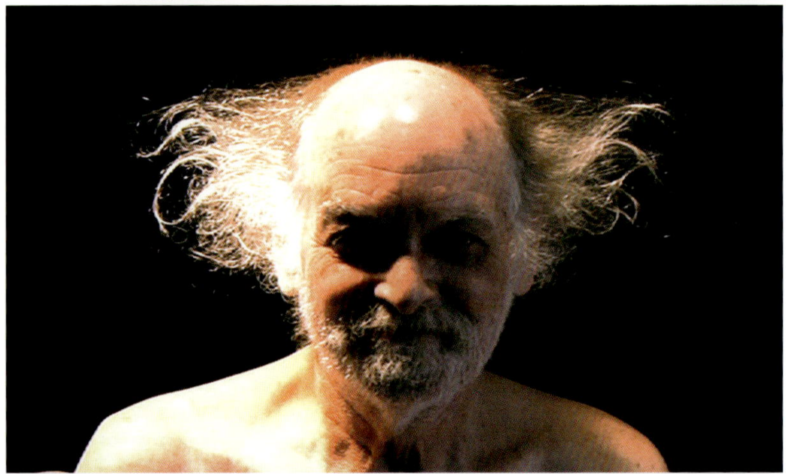

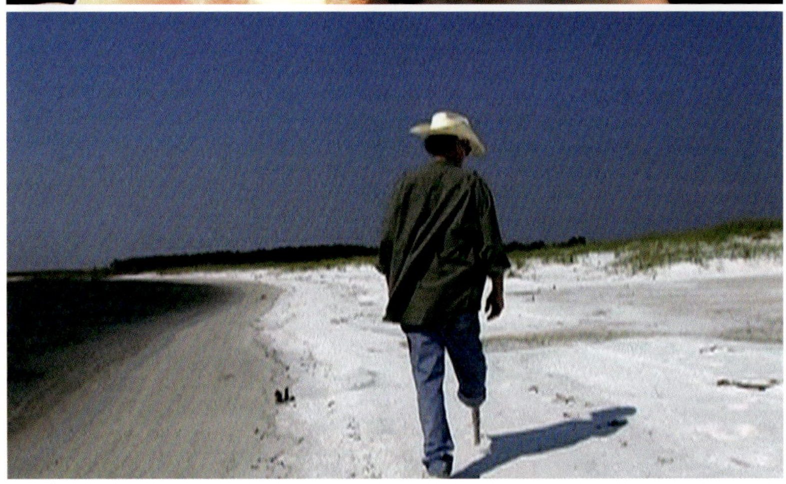

Peter Sasowsky

HEAVEN+EARTH+JOE DAVIS

Thirty years ago a peg-legged motorcycle mechanic from Mississippi walked into the Center for Advanced Visual Studies at MIT. They had not returned his calls. The police were summoned. Forty-five minutes later he walked out with an academic appointment. Since that time, Joe Davis has sent vaginal contractions into deep space to communicate with aliens, encoded poetry into DNA, and designed a sculpture to save the world. It's a great life for a man driven by imagination—except when it's not. There is no funding for this work. He is evicted from apartments and labs. His uncompromising approach to art and life collides with the world's banal requirements. This is a story of self-discovery, sacrifice and the complexity of human endeavor; of the price of art and the ecstatic joy of discovery.

Vor dreißig Jahren spazierte ein in Mississippi beheimateter Motorradmechaniker mit einem Holzbein in das Center for Advanced Visual Studies am Bostoner Massachusetts Institute of Technology (MIT), weil seine Anrufe unbeantwortet geblieben waren. Man rief die Polizei. Fünfundvierzig Minuten später verließ er das Gebäude mit einem Auftrag als wissenschaftlicher Mitarbeiter. Seither hat Joe Davis vaginale Kontraktionen in den Weltraum geschickt, um mit Außerirdischen zu kommunizieren, poetische Textfragmente in der DNA kodiert und eine Skulptur geschaffen, um die Welt zu retten. Das Leben ist großartig für einen Mann, dessen Vorstellungskraft keine Grenzen kennt – außer man erschwert ihm sein Dasein. Er erhält für seine Arbeit keine finanziellen Mittel, wurde wiederholt delogiert und aus Labors hinausgeworfen. Seine kompromisslose Herangehensweise an Kunst und Leben kollidiert mit der Banalität der Welt. Diese Geschichte erzählt von Selbstfindung, Opfern und der Komplexität menschlichen Strebens, vom Preis der Kunst und der ekstatischen Freude an der Entdeckung.

Aus dem Englischen von Martina Bauer

Serious Motion Pictures presents *HEAVEN+EARTH+JOE DAVIS*
Directed and edited by: Peter Sasowsky
Produced by: Peter Sasowsky, Amy Grumbling
Director of photography: Peter Sasowsky
Additional photography: Andrew Neumann, Cécile Bouchier
Additional editing: Brett Nicoletti, Jay Miracle, Charlene Rule
Music by: DO.MAKE.SAY.THINK
Sound mix: Pete Romano
Colorist and on-line editor: Patrick Inhofer, FINI.TV
Additional music: Tom Martin, Tom Phillips
Music rights: Brooke Wentz, The Rights Workshop
Legal services: Karen Schatzkin, Schatzkin and Mayer
Poster design: Bill Bramble
Poster photo:Cha-Ling O'Connell
Website design: Lorena Turner
Made possible in part by a grant from the New York State Council for the Arts

Jon McCormack

Fifty Sisters

Fifty Sisters is a commissioned work for the Ars Electronica Center foyer. It consists of fifty 1m x 1m images of computer-synthesized plant-forms, created using artificial evolution. Each form is derived from the elements of oil company logos. The title of the work refers to the original "Seven Sisters"—a cartel of seven oil companies that dominated the global petrochemical industry and Middle East oil production from the mid-1940s until the oil crisis of the 1970s. Oil has shaped our civilization and driven its unprecedented growth over the last century. We have been seduced by oil and its bi-products as they are used across almost every aspect of human endeavor, providing fuels, fertilizers, feedstocks, plastics, medicines and more. But oil has also changed the environment, evident from the petrochemical haze that hangs over many a modern metropolis, the environmental damage due to oil spills, and the looming specter of global climate change. With worldwide demand for oil now around 88 million barrels per day, humanity's appetite for oil is unrelenting. Oil companies regularly report many of the all-time highest annual earnings in corporate history.

Fossil fuels began as plants that were transformed over millions of years by geological processes into the coal and oil that powers our civilization today. To create this artwork, a variety of digital genes (a computer equivalent of DNA) were generated to replicate the structure and form of Mesozoic plants. These digital genes were used to "grow" imaginary plant species in the computer, being then subject to evolutionary processes of mutation and crossover. Through a process of selective breeding, new and exotic species were evolved. The geometric elements of these digital organisms were derived from the geometric abstractions of oil company logos, which often subtly reference plants and the environment. In the final images, some of the original elements remain quite obvious, others are so strangely distorted or changed by evolution, that they are only subliminally recognizable.

The 21st century is likely to be one of the most challenging that humanity has faced. Our dependence on oil's cheap energy has led to massive and rapid growth, but this dependence cannot continue indefinitely. Ironically, the plants that existed in the Jurassic period when the Earth was at its warmest are now a major cause of our world warming and returning to climate conditions that favored the organisms from which oil originated. *Fifty Sisters* reminds us that the current dominance of oil commerce originated from plants. What once took evolutionary time scales of millions of years can now be superficially replicated by technology in an instant. But while we can evolve species that satisfy our desires, technology has done nothing to change them.

This project was developed in collaboration with the Ars Electronica Futurelab and with support from Monash University and the Australian Research Council (Discovery Project DP1094064) and is part of Studiolab funded by the EC Seventh Framework Programme. The Australian Artist-in-Residence program at the Futurelab was initiated and produced by Novamedia in partnership with the Australia Council for the Arts and Ars Electronica.

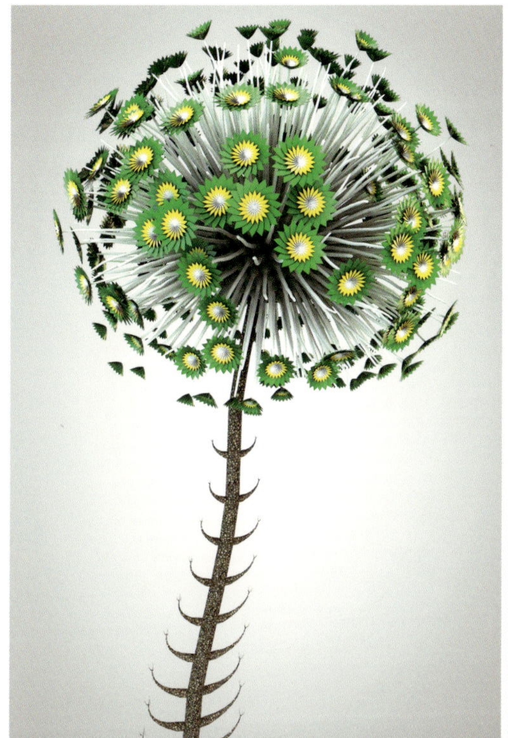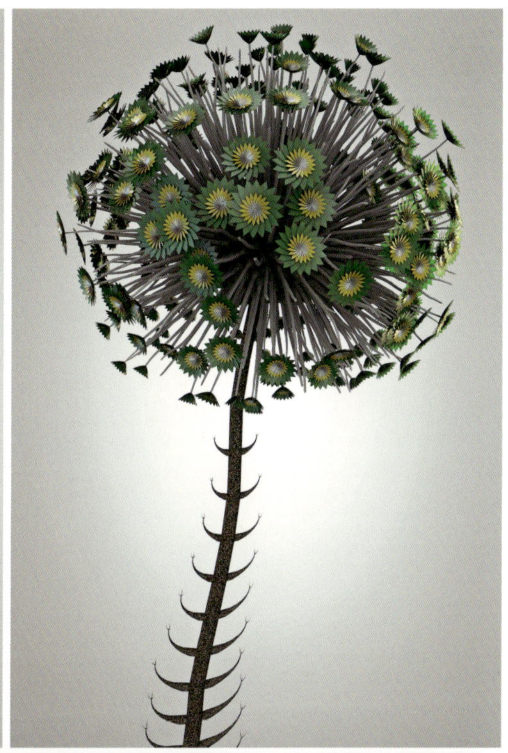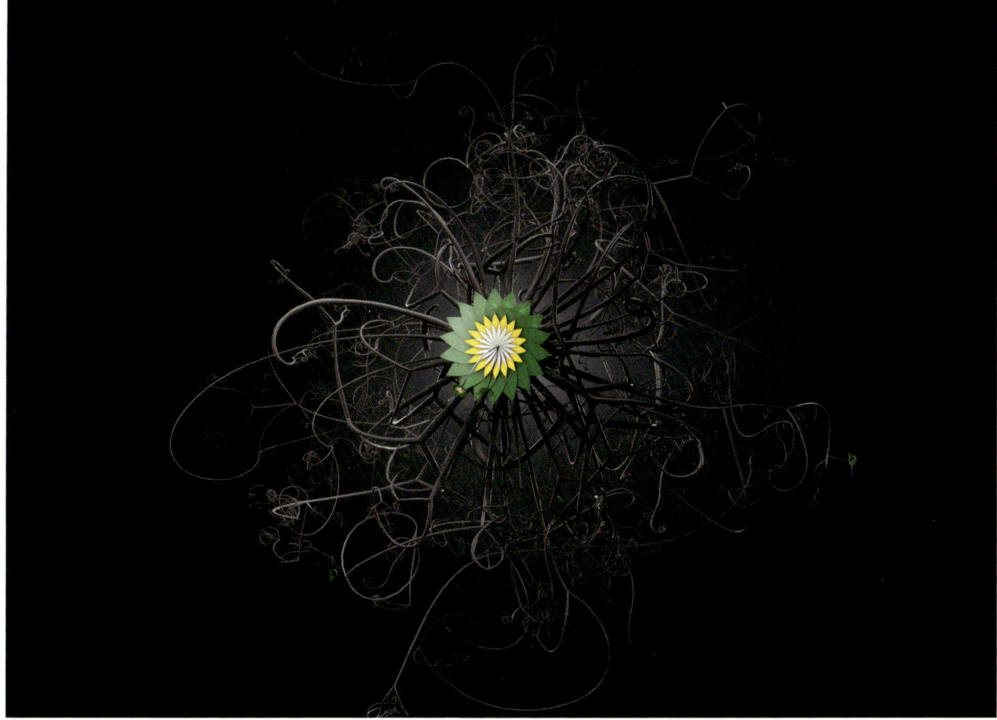

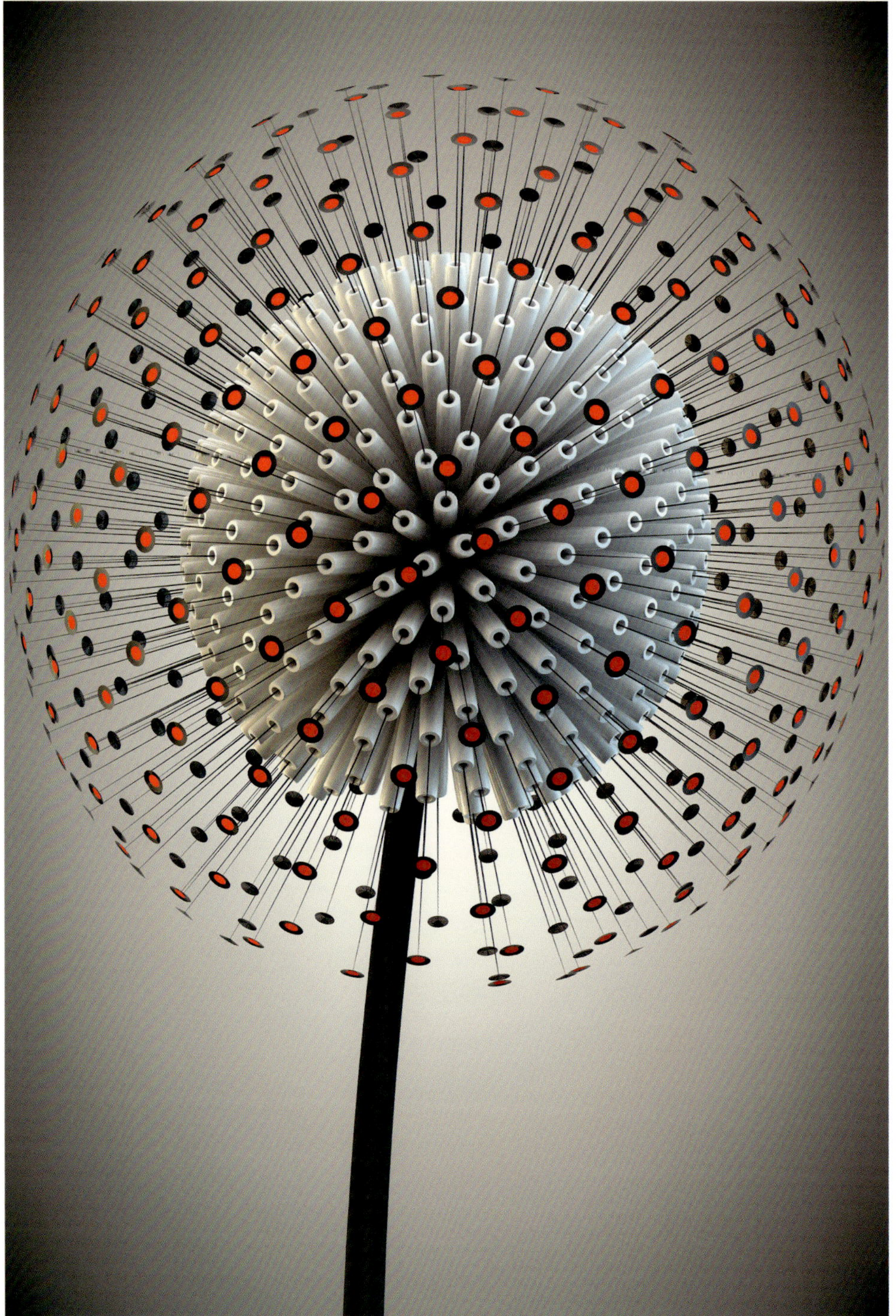

Jon McCormack

Fifty Sisters

Fifty Sisters ist eine Auftragsarbeit für das Foyer des Ars Electronica Center. Sie besteht aus fünfzig 1 x 1 Meter großen Bildern computersynthetisierter Pflanzenformen, die mittels künstlicher Evolution jeweils aus Teilen von Ölfirmenlogos entwickelt wurden. Der Titel der Arbeit spielt auf die „Sieben Schwestern", ein Kartell von sieben Ölgesellschaften an, die von Mitte der 1940er bis zur Ölkrise der 1970er Jahre die globale Petrochemie und die Ölproduktion im Nahen Osten beherrschten. Öl war der prägende Faktor unserer Zivilisation im letzten Jahrhundert und der Motor ihres beispiellosen Wachstums. Wir haben uns von ihm verführen lassen: Als Lieferant von Brennstoffen, Düngemitteln, Rohmaterialien, Plastik, Arzneien und allerlei anderen Dingen ist es in alle Lebensbereiche eingedrungen. Es hat aber auch unsere Umwelt verändert, wie sich an den über unseren Metropolen hängenden petrochemischen Dunstglocken, den Folgeschäden von Ölkatastrophen und dem drohenden Gespenst des globalen Klimawandels zeigt. Bei einem weltweiten Verbrauch von aktuell 88 Millionen Barrel pro Tag, ist der Öldurst der Menschheit immer noch ungestillt. Die Ölgesellschaften melden Jahr für Jahr neue Rekordumsätze.

Die fossilen Brennstoffe, die unsere Zivilisation antreiben, sind durch geologische, Jahrmillionen dauernde Prozesse aus Pflanzen entstanden. Für dieses Kunstwerk wurden mittels einer Reihe digitaler Gene (ein Computeräquivalent der DNA) Struktur und Form mesozoischer Pflanzen nachgebildet. Ausgehend von diesen digitalen Genen wurden im Computer imaginäre Pflanzenarten „gezüchtet" und diese dann evolutionären Prozessen wie Mutation und Kreuzung unterworfen. Durch Zuchtwahl entstanden daraus neue, exotische Arten. Die geometrischen Grundelemente dieser digitalen Organismen wurden durch geometrische Abstraktion von Ölfirmenlogos abgeleitet, die sich ihrerseits häufig auf Pflanzen und Umweltaspekte beziehen. In den fertigen Bildern bleiben einige dieser Elemente ganz deutlich erhalten, während andere durch die Evolution dermaßen verzerrt und verändert wurden, so dass sie kaum noch zu erahnen sind.

Das 21. Jahrhundert dürfte eines der herausforderndsten in der Geschichte der Menschheit werden. Die billige Energie fossiler Brennstoffe hat ein massives und rasantes Wachstum hervorgerufen, aber diese billige Energie wird nicht ewig zur Verfügung stehen. Ironischerweise sind die Pflanzen der Jurazeit, des wärmsten aller Erdzeitalter, nun auch die Hauptursache für die Erderwärmung und die Rückkehr zu Klimabedingungen, die das Wachstum genau jener Organismen begünstigen, aus denen das Öl entstanden ist. *Fifty Sisters* erinnert daran, dass die aktuelle Vorherrschaft der Ölindustrie eine pflanzliche Grundlage hat. Was zu seiner Entwicklung Zeitspannen von Jahrmillionen benötigte, kann heute – zumindest äußerlich – im Handumdrehen repliziert werden. Doch auch wenn uns die Technologie heute die Entwicklung von Spezies nach unseren Wunschvorstellungen erlaubt, so hat sie doch nichts dazu beigetragen, diese selbst zu verändern.

Aus dem Englischen von Wilfried Prantner

Jon McCormack

Codeform

Codeform is a real-time 3D stereoscopic work developed specifically for Deep Space in the Ars Electronica Center. Visitors to Deep Space can use their museum entry tickets to generate the "DNA" of a virtual creature that grows and develops in an electronic ecosystem. The QR code on each ticket is used to generate an artificial life form that is unique to each visitor. Each new life form develops from an egg that floats in a pool on the floor. After a short time the embryo develops and hatches, beginning to move around within Deep Space. Here the creature may join other creatures that have been created by previous visitors in a digital ecosystem. Creatures mate and create offspring. Some creatures may die and others survive, creating a dynamic environment unique to each group of visitors. The most adapted creatures live on until the next show, moving about the floor. A visitor who returns to a later show, can track the progress of their creature over evolutionary time and see how it has fared in the ecosystem and what it has evolved to become. While visually strange and electronic, the ecosystem of *Codeform* suggests a biophilia from the process and behaviors of the system.

Codeform is a reflection of popular concepts of genetics, it questions the influence of an individual in a collective society and the "codification" of the individual by technology. Inspired by the diminishing and changing relationship between natural and human-made environments, *Codeform* provides a glimpse into a new form of electronic nature.

Codeform wurde eigens für den Deep Space im Ars Electronica Center entwickelt und zeigt stereoskopische Echtzeit-3D-Darstellungen. Die Besucher generieren mit ihrer Eintrittskarte die DNA eines virtuellen Wesens, das in einem elektronischen Ökosystem heranwächst. Der QR-Code jeder Eintrittskarte schafft jeweils eine künstliche Lebensform. Jedes dieser Wesen entwickelt sich aus einem Ei in einem Wasserbecken am Boden des Deep Space. Nach kurzer Zeit wächst ein Embryo heran. Er schlüpft und beginnt den Deep Space zu erkunden. Dabei stößt er in diesem digitalen Ökosystem auf andere, von früheren Besuchern geschaffene Wesen. Die künstlichen Lebensformen paaren und vermehren sich. Manche sterben, andere überleben und schaffen eine dynamische Umgebung, die jeweils für eine Besuchergruppe typisch ist. Die den Umweltbedingungen am besten angepassten Kreaturen überleben sich am Boden bewegend bis zur nächsten Vorführung. Kehrt ein Besucher in den Deep Space zurück, kann er die Evolution „seines" Wesens verfolgen und dessen Entwicklung innerhalb dieses Ökosystems betrachten. Auch wenn das von *Codeform* geschaffene Ökosystem visuell fremd und elektronisch anmutet, lassen die in diesem System ablaufenden Prozesse und das Verhalten der Lebewesen das Prinzip der Biophilie vermuten.

Codeform greift gängige Konzepte der Genetik auf und hinterfragt den Einfluss des Individuums in einer kollektivistischen Gesellschaft ebenso wie die „Kodifizierung" des Individuums durch die Technik. Vor dem Hintergrund der abnehmenden und sich verändernden Beziehungen zwischen natürlichen und vom Menschen geschaffenen Lebenswelten lässt *Codeform* einen Blick in eine neue Form elektronischer Natur zu.

Aus dem Englischen von Sonja Pöllabauer

This project was developed in collaboration with the Ars Electronica Futurelab and with support from Monash University and the Australian Research Council (Discovery Project DP1094064) and is part of Studiolab funded by the EC Seventh Framework Programme. The Australian Artist-in-Residence program at the Futurelab was initiated and produced by Novamedia in partnership with the Australia Council for the Arts and Ars Electronica.

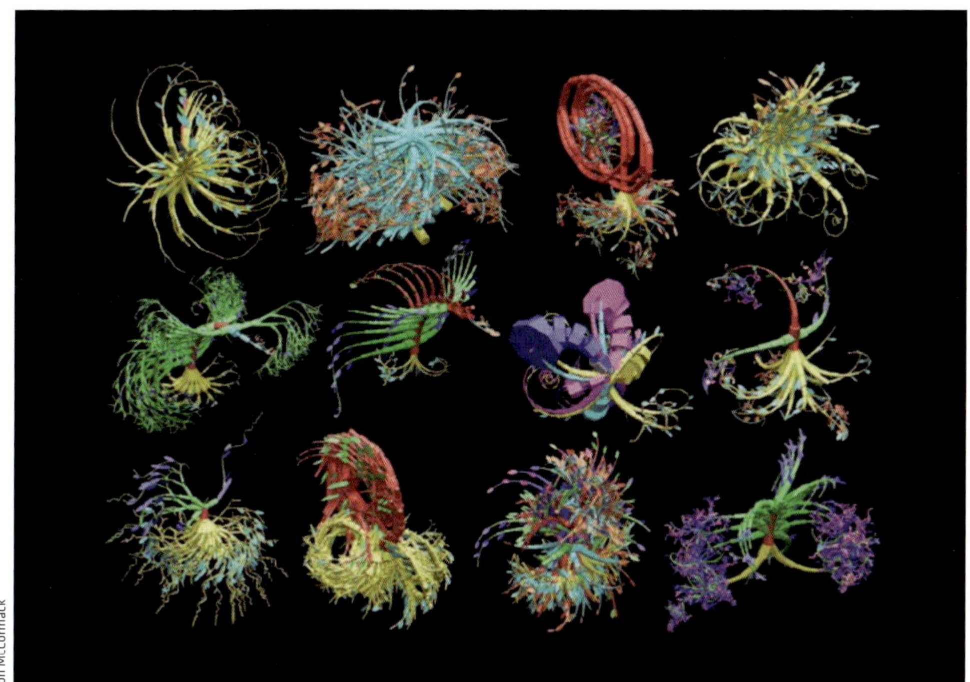

Jon McCormack

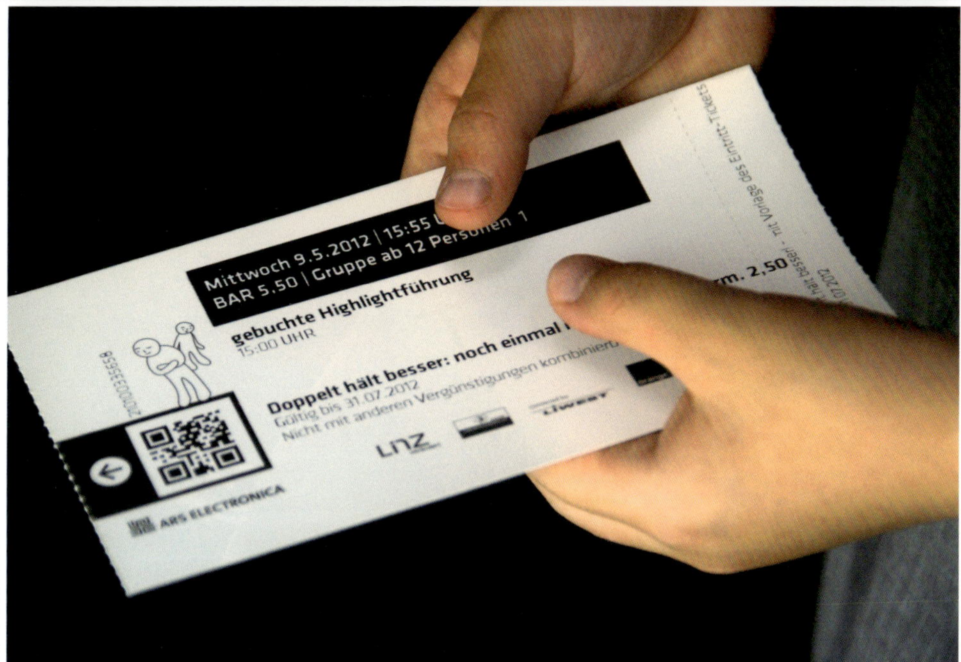

AEC, Matthew Gardiner

Hugvie

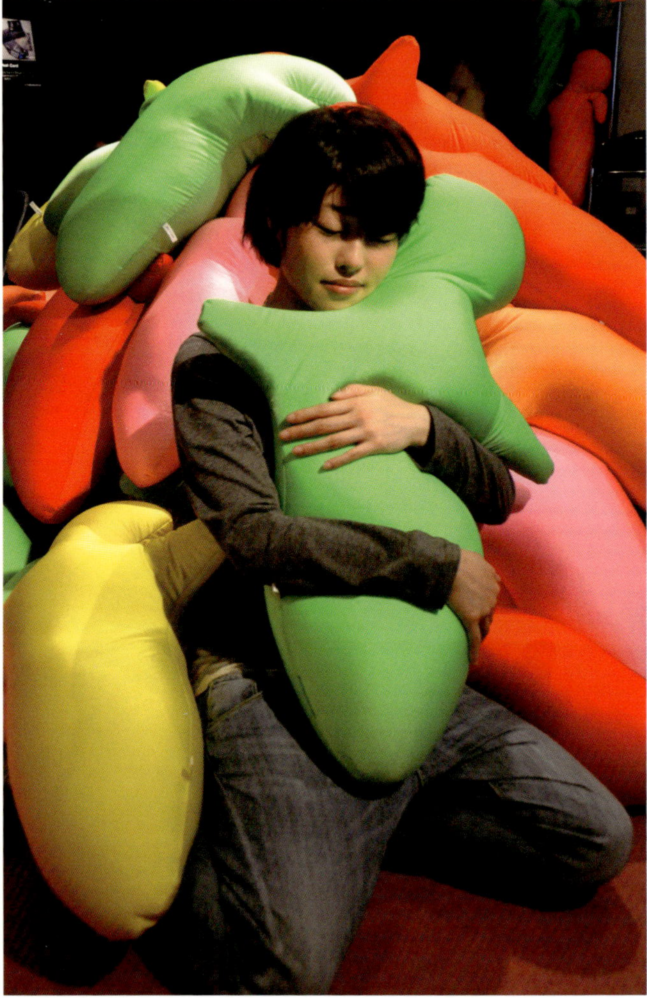

Our tele-operated androids *Telenoid* and *Elfoid,* which are designed with just the most basic human features and movements, implement new telecommunication media to convey the sense of a human presence. Our development and research showed us that physical interaction, such as holding or hugging the androids, conveys not only auditory information, but also touch information from the other person and it can become an effective way to strongly feel the partner's presence.

Hugvie is a newly developed "hug pillow" type of communication media for talking while enjoying hugging. Its body is basically a cushion, similar in form to *Telenoid* and *Elfoid,* that effectively conveys the sense of a human presence. While holding *Hugvie* close to the body, users speak through their cellphones—inserted into a pocket in its head—to people far away.
Hugvie is equipped with a vibrator that simulates heartbeat vibrations and effectively evokes a human presence and human emotions. The heartbeat vibrations vary in accordance with the changes in the partner's tone and reinforce the sense of presence originally conveyed by the voice. The comfortable feel of the cushion, the sensation of hugging one's partner, the sound of the partner's voice close to ear, and the heartbeat vibrations in harmony with that voice, all help to create and enhance the sensation of the partner's actual presence and to intensify the affinity towards him/her. It is an innovative communication medium that embodies the minimum elements required to convey a humanlike presence.
Hugvie, which is a combination of the English word "hug" + the French word "vie", means "embracing life", which is very appropriate for a medium that makes you feel as if you are embracing your partner.

Die von uns entwickelten ferngesteuerten Androiden *Telenoid* und *Elfoid* setzen auf neue Telekommunikationsmedien, die Empfindungen wie menschliche Nähe auf Roboter übertragen sollen. Ihr grundlegendes Design erinnert in Aussehen und Bewegungen entfernt an Menschen. Unsere Android-Forschung hat gezeigt, dass bei der Umarmung eines Androiden nicht nur auditive, sondern auch haptische Signale übermittelt werden, die ein besonders intensives Gefühl des Gegenübers entstehen lassen.
Unser neuester Prototyp *Hugvie* ist ein „Kuschelkissen", das gleichzeitig auch ein Kommunikationsgerät ist: Während der Nutzer *Hugvie* umarmt, unterhält er sich mit einem Gesprächspartner. Wie schon bei *Telenoid* und *Elfoid* ist der Körper von *Hugvie* wie ein Kissen geformt, das dem menschlichen Körper nachempfunden ist und eindrucksvoll das Gefühl menschlicher Präsenz vermittelt. Die Nutzer kuscheln mit *Hugvie* und sprechen über ihr Mobiltelefon, das in eine Tasche im Kopf von *Hugvie* gesteckt wird, mit einem Gesprächspartner, der sich nicht vor Ort befindet. Der Android verfügt zusätzlich über eine Vibrationsfunktion, die das Pochen des menschlichen Herzschlags simuliert und dadurch mehr Ähnlichkeit mit dem Menschen und menschlichen Emotionen vermitteln soll. Der Herzschlag des Androiden ändert sich entsprechend dem Tonfall und der Lautstärke des Gesprächspartners und verstärkt das durch die Stimme vermittelte Gefühl besonderer Nähe. Die angenehm kuschelige Beschaffenheit des Kissens, das Gefühl, den Gesprächspartner zu umarmen und dessen Stimme nahe dem eigenen Ohr zu vernehmen, sowie der an die Stimme angepasste Herzschlag – all das schafft und verstärkt das Gefühl, der Partner sei tatsächlich anwesend. *Hugvie* ist ein innovatives Kommunikationsgerät, das all jene Elemente in sich vereint, die notwendig sind, um eine menschenähnliche Präsenz zu vermitteln.
Der Name *Hugvie* ist ein Kompositum aus dem englischen Verb „hug" (dt. *umarmen*) und dem französischen Nomen „vie" (dt. *Leben*) und kann wörtlich mit „das Leben umarmen" übersetzt werden. Der Name ist treffend, da *Hugvie* das Gefühl vermittelt, man umarme sein Gegenüber.

Aus dem Englischen von Sonja Pöllabauer

New Images and New Concepts of our Brain

To study the brain is to study a physical object—and with that comes the challenge of rendering our findings visually intelligible. Alongside the developments in analytic methods, the elaboration of conceptual models, and the methodologies of data acquisition, how we visualize our findings about the brain is tantamount to our understanding.

Das Gehirn zu erforschen heißt, ein physisches Objekt erforschen, und stellt uns damit vor die Herausforderung, unsere Erkenntnisse visuell nachvollziehbar darzustellen. Die Visualisierung unserer Forschungsergebnisse über das Gehirn ist ebenso wichtig für unser Verständnis wie die Entwicklungen analytischer Methoden, die Erarbeitung konzeptueller Modelle und Datenerfassungsmethoden.

Brain Art Competition

The Brain-Art Competition was launched in 2011 by the Neuro Bureau, with the support of the Child Mind Institute, as a way to offer a platform for the neuroimaging community to encourage novel developments in data presentation. It was our hope that the competition would further ideas and techniques for communicating scientific ideas and findings. The entries in the 2012 competition consisted of 55 submissions across five categories: abstract, connectome, humorous, educational, and video illustration, and the winners in each category were announced at the annual conference of the Organization for Human Brain Mapping, held in June in Beijing.

Die *Brain-Art Competition* wurde 2011 mit der Unterstützung des Child Mind Institute vom Neuro Bureau ins Leben gerufen, um der Neurobildgebungs-Community eine Plattform zur Förderung neuer Entwicklungen in der Datenaufbereitung zu bieten. Wir hofften, dass der Wettbewerb Ideen und Techniken für die Kommunikation wissenschaftlicher Ideen und Erkenntnisse unterstützen würde. Bei dem Wettbewerb 2012 wurden 55 Beiträge in den folgenden fünf Kategorien eingereicht: abstrakt, Konnektom, humorvoll, didaktisch und Videoillustration; die Gewinner der jeweiligen Kategorie wurden bei der Jahreskonferenz der Organization for Human Brain Mapping im Juni in Beijing verkündet.

Texts compiled by Daniel Margulies

Space Ship
Alexander Schäfer

The aim of the project is to establish a novel clustering technique in the field of neuroscience, which promises a better understanding of brain organization. The neuronal activation of the brain is measured indirectly via blood oxygenation using magnet resonance imaging. The cortex of the brain was divided into 463 anatomical regions. Pairs of regions that oscillate synchronously are denoted as being functionally connected and form a network for each individual. The visualized data is showing the average connectivity from 102 individuals with an age range from 18 to 60 years.

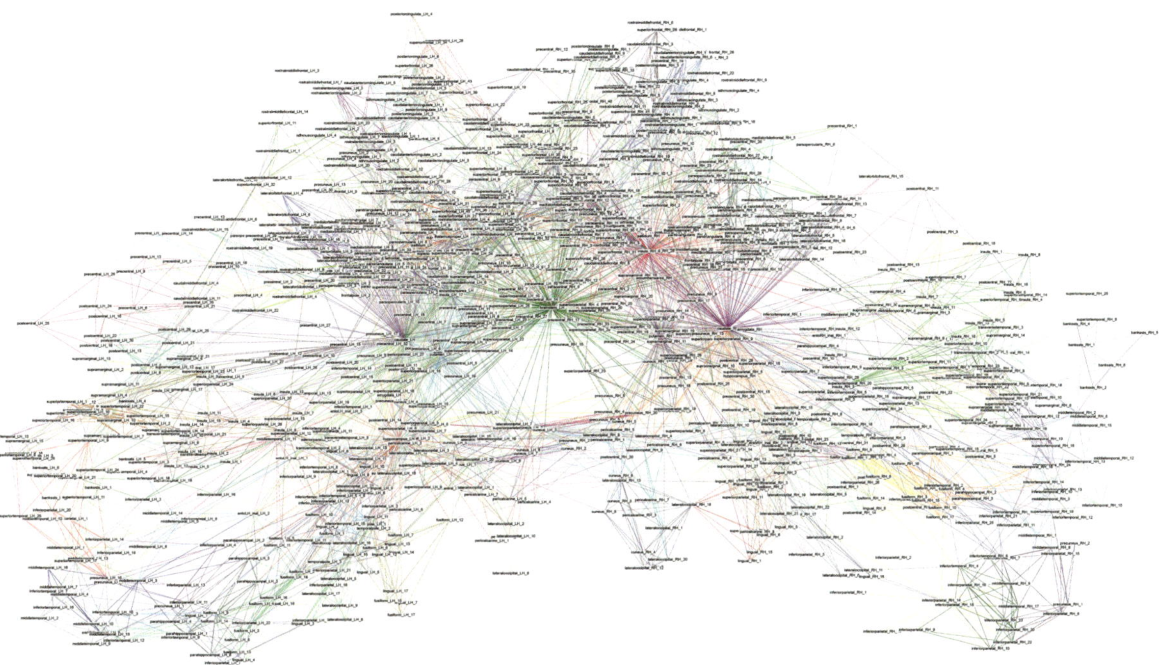

Here, this network is represented as a graph. The colors are derived from the novel clustering algorithm. The position of the regions is derived from the Yifan Hu proportional layout algorithm, which treats the network as a physical system where the regions are bodies in a physical system and the connections as forces between them. The layout algorithm aims to position the regions in a way that minimizes the energy of the physical system. The left and right half of the resulting "spaceship" resembles well the two hemispheres of the brain.

Ziel des Projekts ist es, eine neue Clustering-Technik in den Neurowissenschaften einzuführen, die ein besseres Verständnis der Gehirnorganisation verspricht. Die neuronale Aktivierung des Gehirns wird per Magnetresonanztomographie indirekt über die Blutoxygenierung gemessen. Die Großhirnrinde wurde in 463 anatomische Regionen unterteilt. Paarweise verbundene Regionen, die synchron oszillieren, werden als funktional miteinander verbunden bezeichnet und bilden bei jedem Einzelnen ein Netzwerk. Die dargestellten Daten zeigen die durchschnittliche Konnektivität von 102 Personen im Alter zwischen 18 und 60 Jahren.
Hier wird dieses Netzwerk als Graph dargestellt. Die Farben werden von einem neuen Clustering-Algorithmus und die Position der Regionen vom proportionalen Layout-Algorithmus nach Yifan Hu abgeleitet, der das Netzwerk als physisches System betrachtet, in dem die Regionen Körper in einem physischen System sind und die Verbindungen als zwischen ihnen wirkende Kräfte betrachtet werden. Der Layout-Algorithmus zielt darauf ab, die Regionen so zu positionieren, dass die Energie des physischen Systems minimiert wird. Die linke und die rechte Hälfte des daraus resultierenden „Raumschiffs" gleichen den beiden Hemisphären des Gehirns.

Mapping Morphometry and Connectedness of the Human Brain

John Van Horn

A representation of brain morphometry and connectivity obtained from anatomical and diffusion magnetic resonance imaging (MRI) of N=110 adult human subjects. Colors of the outermost ring map to the regionally-specific colored parcellations. The innermost rings represent average regional volume, surface area, thickness, curvature, and degree of regionally-specific connectedness, respectively. Connections between regions obtained using 30-direction diffusion weighted imaging are weighted by color (reflecting white matter fiber integrity; low=blue; medium=green; high=red) and opacity (reflecting fiber bundle density). Such maps provide a comprehensive picture of the brain's information processing architecture as viewed using in vivo neuroimaging methods.

Eine Darstellung der Morphometrie und der Vernetzung des Gehirns durch anatomische und diffusionsgewichtete Magnetresonanztomographie (DW-MRI) bei einer Versuchsgruppe der Größe von n=110 Erwachsenen. Die Farben des äußersten Rings korrespondieren mit den regional spezifisch eingefärbten Parzellen. Die innersten Ringe stellen die durchschnittlichen Werte für das Volumen, die Überfläche, Dicke, Wölbung und den Grad der Konnektivität der jeweiligen Regionen dar. Die Verbindungen zwischen den Regionen, die man erhält, wenn man diffusionsgewichtete Bildgebung in 30 Richtungen verwendet, werden nach Farbe (spiegelt die Faserintegrität der weißen Substanz wider, niedrig = blau, mittel = grün, hoch = rot) und Opazität (gibt die Faserbündeldichte wieder) gewichtet. Solche Karten vermitteln ein umfassendes Bild der Informationsverarbeitungsarchitektur des Gehirns, wie es In-vivo-Neurobildgebungsmethoden zeigen.

Courtesy of C. Torgerson, M. Chambers, A. Irimia, and J. Van Horn, Laboratory of Neuro Imaging (LONI).

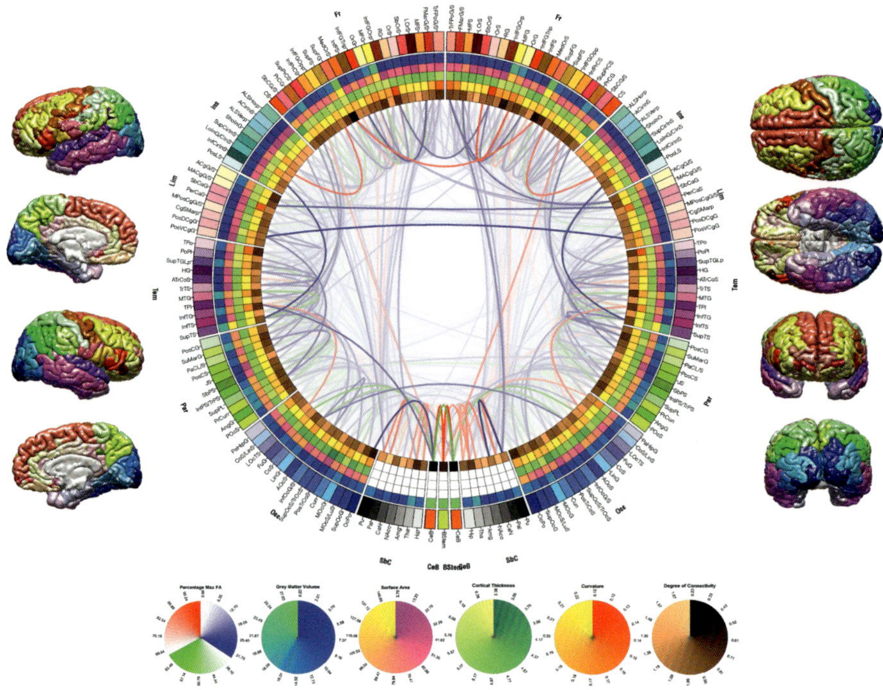

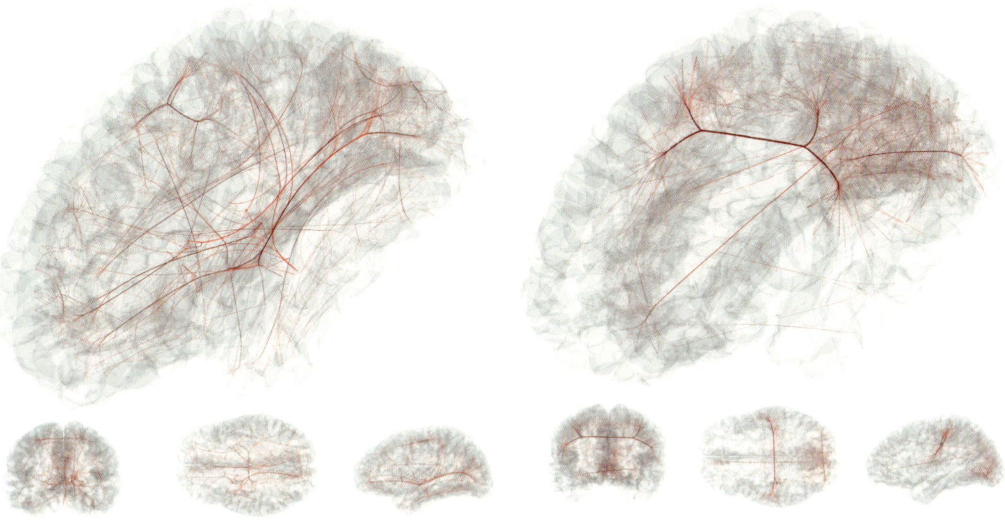

Edge-bundled DSI and Resting-State Connectivity

Joachim Böttger

The images show the result of the application of a method from the field of information visualization, force directed edge-bundling, to two graphs containing different aspects of connectivity in the brain. The left graph is derived from Diffusion Spectrum Imaging (DSI), which allows tracing the anatomical shape of white matter fibers by measuring the diffusion of molecules in the brain. The right graph is based on functional connectivity as derived from resting-state functional MRI, which makes it possible to detect functionally linked gray matter areas by calculating similarities in their intrinsic metabolic activity. Both graphs contain nearly 4000 single connections between 1015 regions of interest, which makes their visualization in anatomical 3D brain space a challenge: Simply drawing all the connections as straight lines leads to a very cluttered image, making it impossible to discern how different parts of the brain are connected. Edge-bundling visually groups together similar connections through the simulation of electrostatic attraction forces, and thus helps to make underlying structure visible.

Die Bilder zeigen das Ergebnis einer Methode aus dem Bereich der Informationsvisualisierung – des Force-Directed Edge-Bundling – an zwei Graphen, in denen verschiedene Aspekte der Konnektivität im Gehirn erfasst sind. Der linke Graph ist von einem Diffusion Spectrum Imaging (DSI) abgeleitet, das es ermöglicht, die anatomische Form von Fasern weißer Substanz zu tracen, indem die Diffusion der Moleküle im Gehirn gemessen wird. Der rechte Graph basiert auf der funktionalen Konnektivität, wie man sie von einer funktionellen MRT im Ruhezustand erhält, die funktional verbundene Bereiche grauer Substanz zu entdecken hilft, indem Ähnlichkeiten in deren intrinsischer metabolischer Aktivität berechnet werden. Beide Graphen enthalten nahezu 4.000 einzelne Verbindungen zwischen 1.015 ausgewählten Regionen, was ihre Visualisierung im anatomischen 3D-Gehirnraum zu einer Herausforderung macht: Zeichnet man einfach alle Verbindungen als gerade Linien, ist das Ergebnis ein sehr unübersichtliches Bild, bei dem unmöglich zu unterscheiden ist, wie unterschiedliche Teile des Gehirns verbunden sind. Beim Edge-Bundling werden ähnliche Verbindungen durch die Simulation elektrostatischer Anziehungskräfte visuell gebündelt, wodurch die zugrunde liegende Struktur sichtbar gemacht werden kann.

HIV in the Elderly Human Connectome

Neda Jahanshad

About one-third of HIV patients are over the age of 50 and with the availability of anti-retroviral therapies, this proportion is sharply increasing. It has been shown that the aged brain itself shows altered and deteriorating network organization, yet the additional effect of this prevalent virus is unknown and of great interest. Testing differences between 55 patients and 30 controls (all aged 60-80), through use of high angular resolution diffusion imaging tractography, we map the alterations in the human connectome with respect to the virus in a floating brain representation. The proportion of traced fibers that connect and intersect regions of the HIV+ brain as compared to controls are found to differ significantly, particularly in fronto-parietal connections. Blue connections represent those where the degree of connectivity between nodes is reduced in HIV patients as compared to age-matched controls. The connection strength (defined as the total fiber density for each region) is significantly lower in the presence of the virus (green spheres). Larger spheres indicate greater effect sizes (lower p-values). The axial slice, on which the brain floats, is segmented into the cortical regions of interest; red-yellow coloring represents the right and the blue-green coloring the left hemisphere. Non-significant tested connections and nodes are displayed in black.

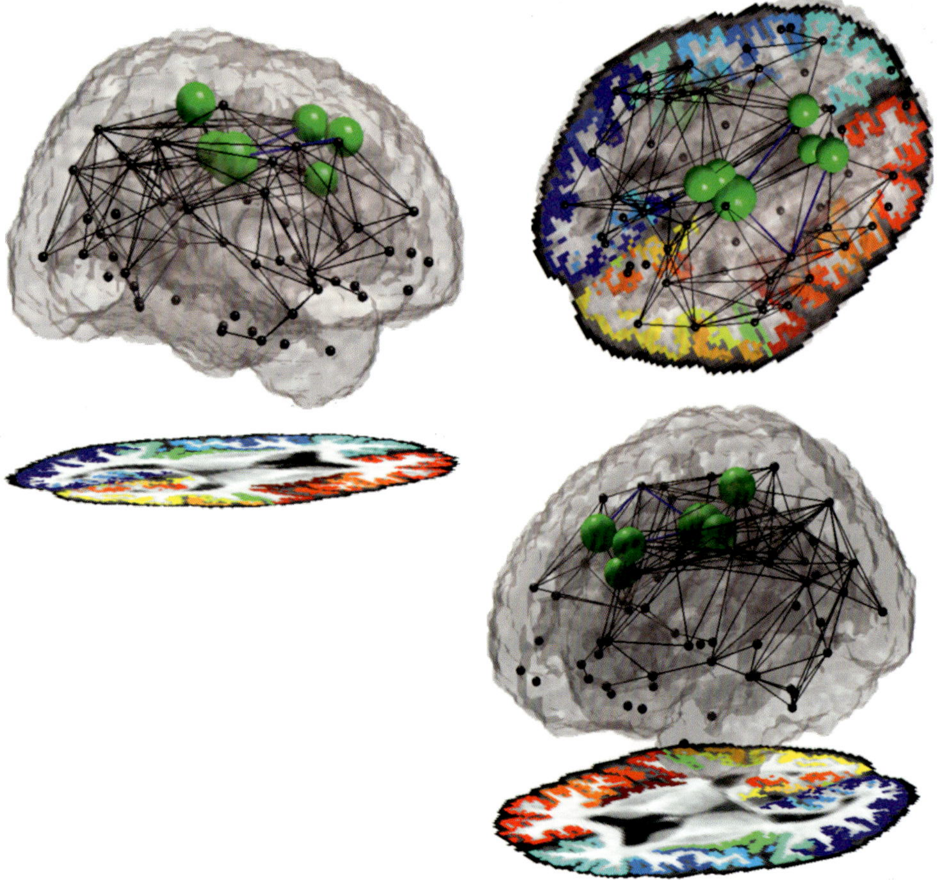

Etwa ein Drittel der HIV-Patienten sind älter als 50 Jahre, wobei der Anteil dieser Altersgruppe durch die Verfügbarkeit antiretroviraler Therapien deutlich steigt. Es wurde nachgewiesen, dass ein gealtertes Gehirn an sich eine veränderte und verschlechterte Netzwerkorganisation aufweist. Welche zusätzliche Auswirkung dieses Virus hat, ist bislang unbekannt und von höchstem Interesse. Dazu werden 55 Patienten und 30 Kontrollpersonen (alle aus der Altersgruppe 60–80 Jahre) mittels Diffusions-Traktografie mit hoher Winkelauflösung untersucht und die Veränderungen im menschlichen Konnektom durch das Virus in einer flexiblen Darstellung des Gehirns abgebildet. Der Anteil der nachverfolgten Fasern, die Regionen in einem HIV-positiven Gehirn verbinden und kreuzen, unterscheidet sich im Vergleich zu den Kontrollpersonen signifikant, insbesondere für frontoparietale Verbindungen. Blaue Verbindungen repräsentieren jene, in denen der Grad der Konnektivität zwischen den Knoten bei HIV-Patienten, verglichen mit gleichaltrigen Kontrollpersonen, reduziert ist. Die Verbindungsstärke (definiert als gesamte Faserdichte für jede Region) ist bei Vorhandensein des Virus signifikant niedriger (grüne Kugeln). Größere Kugeln bedeuten größere Effektstärke (geringere p-Werte). Im Achsialschnitt ist das Gehirn in die kortikalen Regionen unterteilt, die von Interesse sind; eine rotgelbe Färbung repräsentiert die rechte und eine blaugrüne die linke Gehirnhälfte. Nicht signifikante Verbindungen und Knoten werden in Schwarz dargestellt.

CogniToo

CogniToo Team

Everyone's individuality is expressed by unique neural signaling in the brain. Likewise, we observe a growing desire of the society to express the individuality through fancy tattoos. With our new start-up we take the opportunity and satisfy this need with the most unique and individual solution the world of science currently offers. Bringing together state-of-the-art neuroscience and recommended international sculptors, painters, and tattoo artists. The CogniToo (i.e. Cognition Tattoo) is the best way to express one's individuality. This new brand label offers a broad range of high-quality visually brain-art products.
A CogniToo consists of the individual neural activation upon thinking, feeling or experiencing highly personal moments captured in a painting, a sculpture or a tattoo. Depending on the theme one's neural activity is modelled in a unique fashion. To extract the brain's neural signaling functional magnetic resonance techniques are used. It is the most recently developed form of neuroimaging and has dominated the last decade of neurosciences due to its non-invasity and the high spatial resolution.
Our service includes: airfares, hotel, consulting with the neuroscience and CogniToo experts, personal CogniToo selection and development of the appropriate scanning protocol, scanning, cognitooing and refreshing of the CogniToo after a period of two weeks, or alternatively sculpting or painting the CogniToo.
CogniToo.com

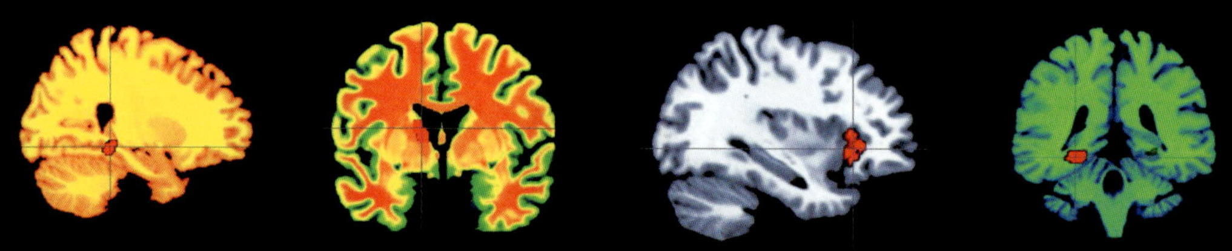

Die Individualität einer Person kommt durch den einzigartigen neuralen Signaltransfer im Gehirn zum Ausdruck. Gesellschaftlich ist ein wachsendes Interesse zu beobachten, Individualität durch extravagante Tatoos auszudrücken. Mit unserem Startup-Unternehmen möchten wir diesen Trend aufgreifen und diesem Bedürfnis nach Individualität mit einer der einzigartigsten Lösungen Rechnung tragen, die die Welt der Wissenschaft derzeit zu bieten hat und für die wir renommierte internationale Bildhauer, Maler und Tattoo-Künstler mit dem neuesten Stand der Neurowissenschaften zusammenbringen. Besser als mit *CogniToo* (d. h. *Cognition Tattoo*, Erkenntnis-Tattoo) lässt sich Individualität nicht ausdrücken. Das neue Label bietet ein breites Spektrum an qualitativ hochwertigen Brain-Art-Produkten.

Ein CogniToo entsteht durch die individuelle neurale Aktivierung beim Denken, Fühlen oder Erleben höchst persönlicher Momente, die in einem Bild, einer Skulptur oder einem Tattoo festgehalten werden. Je nach Thema wird die neurale Aktivität auf einzigartige Weise festgehalten. Mittels Magnetresonanz werden die neuralen Signale des Gehirns extrahiert. Dies ist die neueste Form der Neurobildgebung, die das letzte Jahrzehnt in der Neurowissenschaften aufgrund ihrer Nicht-Invasivität und der hohen räumlichen Auflösung dominiert hat. In unserem Service ist inbegriffen: Flugpreis, Hotel, Beratung durch Neurowissenschaftler und CogniToo-Experten, Auswahl des individuellen CogniToos und Entwicklung des entsprechenden Scanning-Protokolls, Scanning, Cognitooing und Auffrischen des CogniToos nach zwei Wochen oder alternativ Modellage oder Malen des CogniToo.

Aus dem Englischen von Martina Bauer

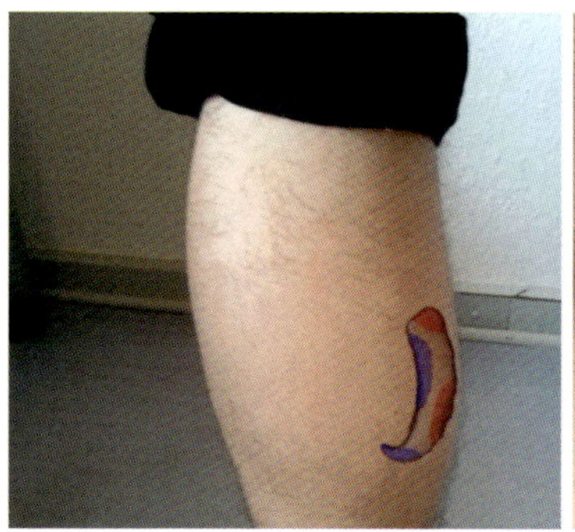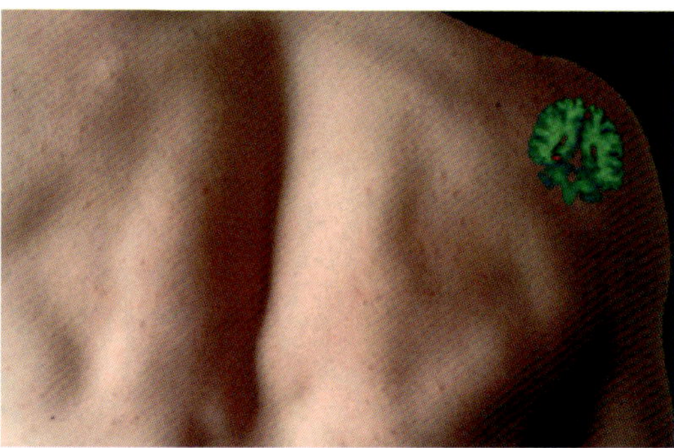

The individuals responsible for organizing the 2012 Brain Art Competition:
Daniel Margulies (Max Planck Institute for Human Cognitive and Brain Sciences)
Michael Milham (Child Mind Institute)
Cameron Craddock (Child Mind Institute)
Institutions: Organized by The Neuro Bureau: *www.neurobureau.org*
Sponsored by Child Mind Institute: *www.childmind.org*
Made possible through the generosity of Stavros Niarchos Foundation: *www.snf.org/*

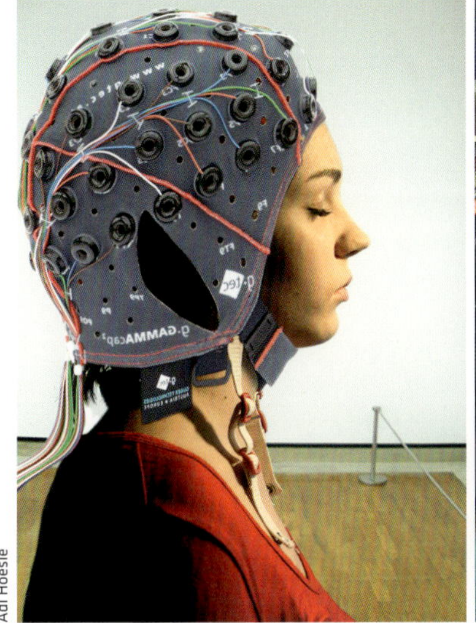
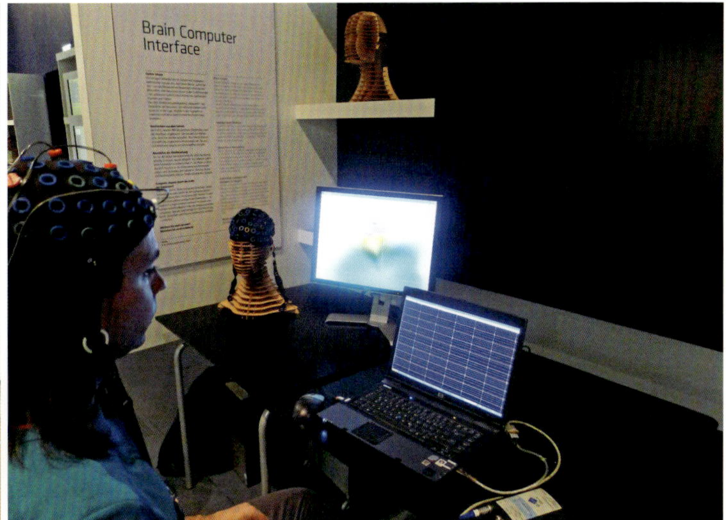

Adi Hoesle

Brain Painting

Paint pictures at a computer without the use of your hands, keyboard or mouse. *Brain Painting* lets you produce images with the conscious activity of your brainwaves, which a brain-computer interface (BCI) and special software translate into actual pictures. There's no need for a brush, pen or chisel to create a work of art; this astounding technology brings forth images directly from the human mind.

Produced in collaboration with artist Adi Hoesle, *Brain Painting* is the spinoff of a scientific research approach developed at the University of Würzburg's Department of Intervention Psychology. It investigates which brain activities or neuronal patterns can be used to foster creativity and thus, in the broadest sense, to create art. Neuronal activity is harnessed with the help of brain-computer interfaces (BCI) and Brain Painting software. From a medical perspective, Brain Painting makes an absolutely unprecedented form of communication and artistic creation available to people such as paraplegics whose physical incapacity cuts them off from the outside world.

Am Computer Bilder malen, ohne dabei Hände, Tastatur und Maus einzusetzen: Beim *Brain Painting* entstehen die Werke durch die bewusste Aktivität der Hirnströme, die mit einem Brain-Computer-Interface (BCI) und einer speziellen Software in Bilder umgesetzt werden. Statt Pinsel, Stift oder Meißel für ein Kunstwerk zu verwenden, wagt der Mensch so die direkte Verbindung seines Geistes mit der Technologie.

Brain Painting ist in Kooperation mit dem Künstler Adi Hoesle aus einem wissenschaftlichen Forschungsansatz der Abteilung für Interventionspsychologie der Universität Würzburg entstanden. Untersucht wird, welche Hirnaktivitäten oder neuronalen Muster genutzt werden können, um Kreativität und damit im weitesten Sinn Kunst zu schaffen. Erschlossen wurde die neuronale Aktivität mithilfe von Gehirn-Computer-Schnittstellen (BrainComputerInterfaces) und dem Malprogramm Brain Painting. Aus medizinischer Sicht bietet *Brain Painting* Menschen, die an dem Locked-in Syndrom leiden, also die in ihrem gelähmten Körper vollständig eingeschlossen sind, eine zuvor undenkbare Art der Kommunikation und künstlerischen Ausdrucksform.

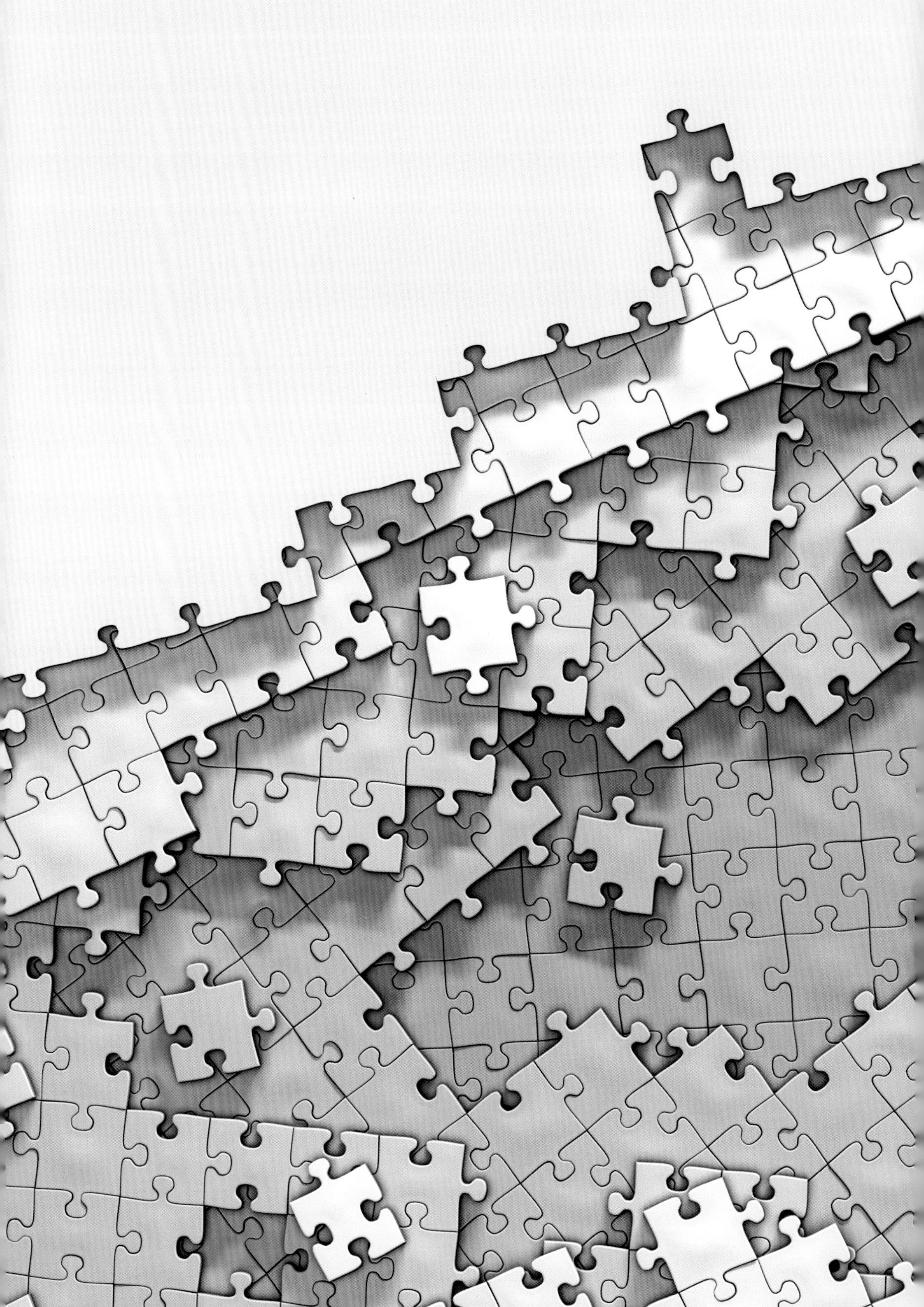

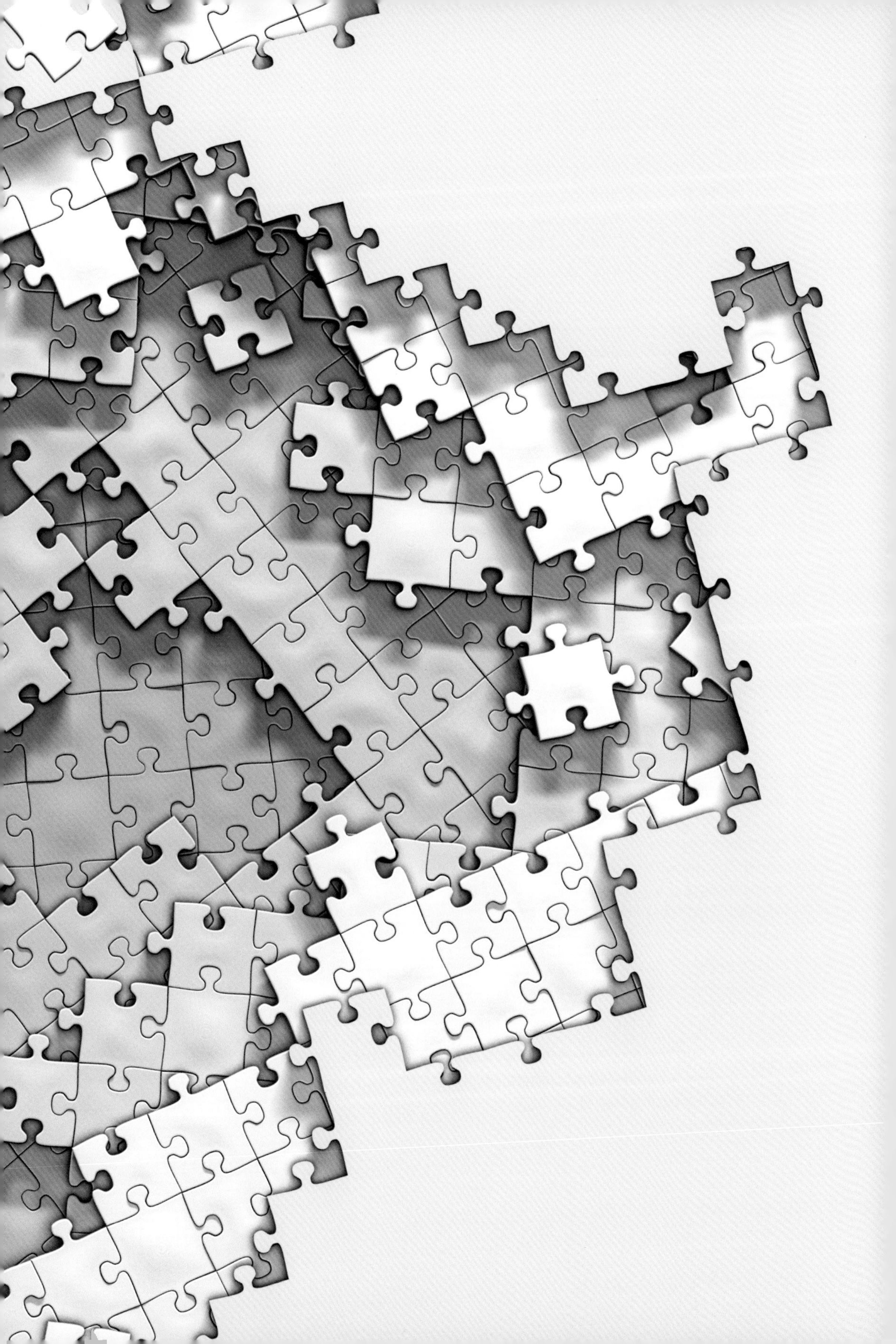

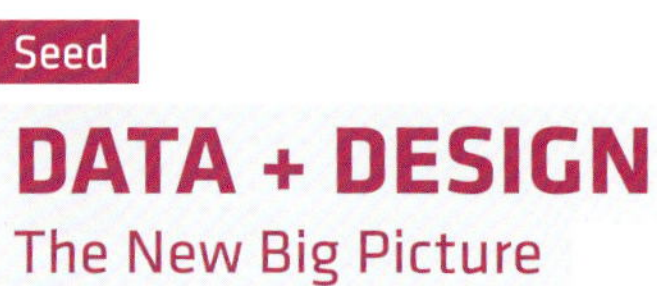

DATA + DESIGN
The New Big Picture

Data. It's the atomic unit of science. The stuff that observations are made of and results are based on. It's the currency of discovery and the foundation of knowledge.

Always paramount to science, data is now grabbing hold of society. We now produce such an unprecedented volume of data each day, both actively (e.g. electronic health records and patent databases) and passively (e.g. mobile and social), that new fields—like data science, computational social science, and data visualization—are emerging to help make sense of it all. Most exciting, this burgeoning intellectual, creative, economic, and social revolution is starting to yield new findings, insights, and pictures about our cities, our planet, and ourselves.

Scientific Thinking™. It's a different way of looking at the world. It's about using data to uncover patterns and design to confront complexity. It's about connecting things to reveal systems. It's about traversing scales and disregarding disciplines, applying neuroscience to economics, math to global health, virology to manufacturing, and genetics to law... It's about experimenting all the way to understanding. It's about changing your mind with new evidence—and getting as close to truth as humanly possible.

Getting 7 billion people to think scientifically has never been a small mission. And it has never been more important. Since 2005, we have offered ideas and stories to help people think scientifically (through *seedmagazine.com, scienceisculture.com, scienceblogs.com, phylotaxis.com, researchblogging.com, visualizing.org*). Now we're taking the next big step in this journey by creating tools and services to help institutions—companies, governments, and international organizations—do the same. We're taking our way of seeing and thinking to parliaments, courtrooms, hospitals, construction sites, boardrooms ... around the world—to catalyze scientific thinking at scale.

For the Ars Electronica Festival 2012 THE BIG PICTURE, Seed and Ars Electronica have partnered to explore how the convergence of data and design is forging a new Big Picture. The two principal questions we will explore are: What is the new "Big Picture" being created through the convergence of data and design? And, as seeing the Earth from the Moon catalyzed environmentalism, can this new "Big Picture" compel some new collective emotion or insight that results in social action?

Seed sees science not only as an object of study or a source of new technology, but as a lens through which to understand and manage the world around us. Seed uses scientific discoveries, tools, and methods to reach new insights, strategies, and solutions.

Seed started as a magazine *(seedmagazine.com)*; today the company is focused on bringing the ideas and methods advanced in its pages to scale through technology and services, helping some of the world's most innovative companies, governments, and organizations become more scientific in their way of thinking.

seedscientific.com

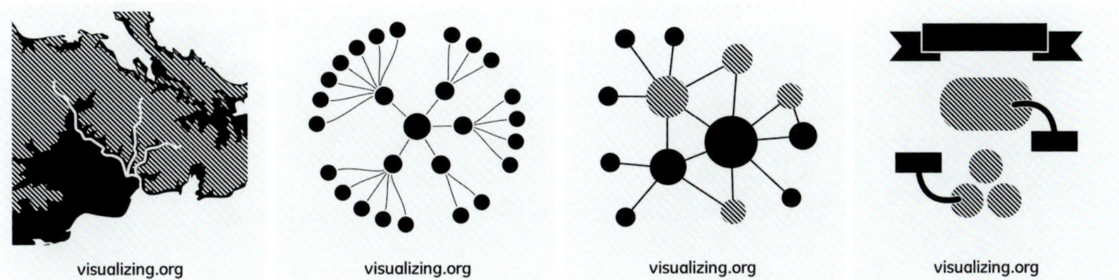

Seed's program at Ars Electronica will include three components:

SEED SYMPOSIUM

What is the new Big Picture we are creating through data and design? How should we interpret these new pictures? What is the emotional consequence of seeing these new pictures? And using data and design, what questions are we now able to ask about ourselves and our environment? Leading thinkers and practitioners in data visualization and data science will explore these questions.

VISUALIZING.ORG GALLERY

As our world becomes increasingly global and interconnected, new perspectives are ever more important. Patterns of movement, communication, and exchange now happen on a scale never previously imagined. Data visualization can offer a "big picture" perspective on the patterns, flows, and forces that underpin modern life, prompting new ideas and insights. Visualizing.org will present a gallery of data visualizations that capture the spirit of The Big Picture. Launched by Seed and GE, Visualizing.org is a global community of creative people making sense of complex issues through data and design. Together with 100 partner universities, international organizations, companies, and NGOs, Visualizing.org is helping to improve understanding and uncover insights about the systems that make up our world.

DATA VISUALIZATION WORKSHOP

Join us for a hands-on workshop on the semantics of graphical representations and the aesthetics of information design, covering both conceptual and practical dimensions of the craft. Theoretical discussions will cover subjects such as how to use the space of the canvas, what the legend means, as well as what colors, shapes and patterns are suitable for representing a variety of data types. In the practical part of the workshop, we will guide participants through the creation of a data visualization sketch using JavaScript libraries. Based on a dataset that is provided, each participant will create a network visualization.

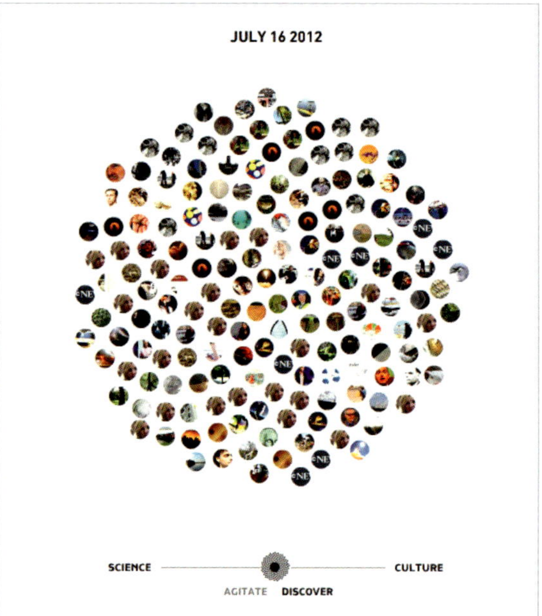

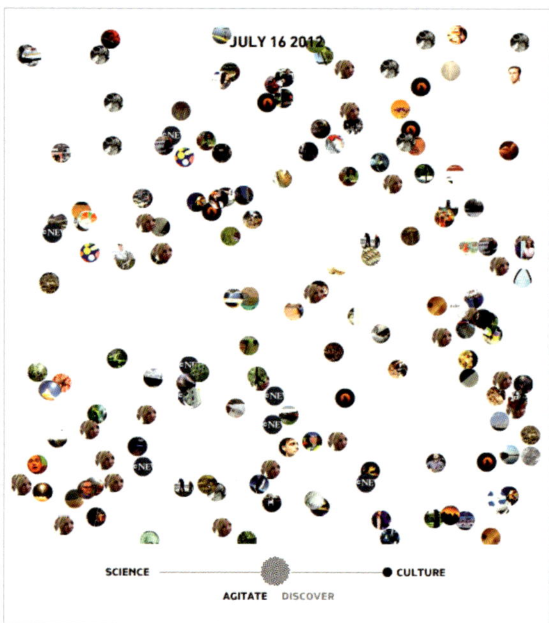

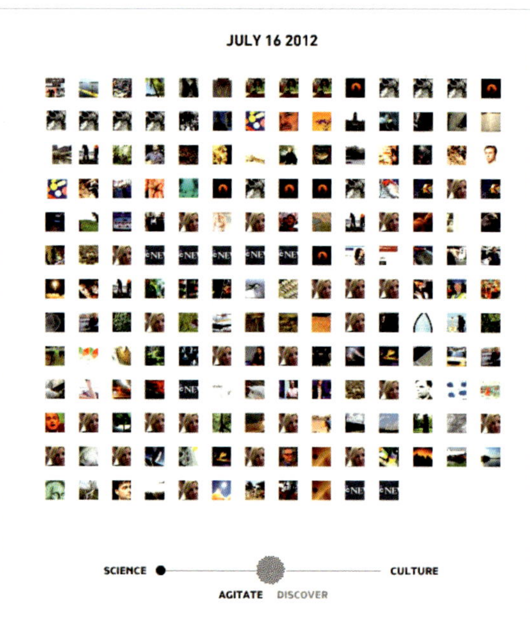

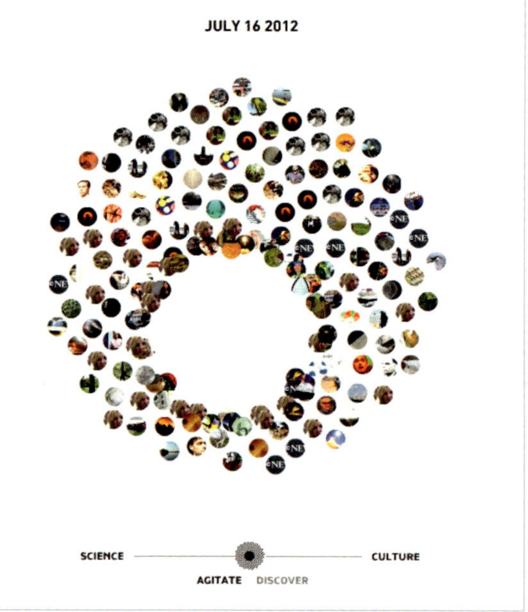

A visualization project commissioned by Seed that explores the space where science meets culture. Designer: Jonathan Harris. / Ein von *Seed* in Auftrag gegebenes Visualisierungsprojekt zum Aufeinandertreffen von Wissenschaft und Kultur. Designer: Jonathan Harris.

Daten. Die kleinste Einheit der Wissenschaft. Das Fundament aller Beobachtungen und Resultate. Die Währung der Wissenschaft und der Grundstock allen Wissens.

Was für die Wissenschaft von jeher von höchster Wichtigkeit war, fasst nun auch in der Gesellschaft Fuß. Wir produzieren täglich – aktiv (z. B. elektronische Patientenakten und Patentdatenbanken) wie auch passiv (z.B. Mobiltelefone, soziale Netzwerke) – eine derart gewaltige Menge an Informationen, dass neue Wissenschaftsfelder zur Bewältigung dieser Datenexplosion entstehen (Data Science, Computational Social Science und Datenvisualisierung). Und was besonders spannend ist: Diese aufkeimende intellektuelle, kreative, wirtschaftliche und soziale Revolution liefert bereits erste neue Erkenntnisse über unsere Städte, unseren Planeten und uns selbst.

Scientific Thinking™ – eine neue Sicht auf die Welt. Was zählt, ist die Verknüpfung von Daten zur Identifikation gleichbleibender Strukturen und Designs zur Reduktion von Komplexität. Was zählt, ist die Vernetzung von Einzelelementen zur Sichtbarmachung der darunter liegenden Systeme. Was zählt, ist das Verlassen festgefahrener Bahnen und das Aufbrechen traditioneller Disziplinen, die Anwendung neurowissenschaftlicher Theorien in der Wirtschaftswissenschaft, von Mathematik im Bereich globaler Gesundheit, von Virologie in der Industrie oder von Genetik in der Rechtswissenschaft ... Was zählt, ist Experimentierfreudigkeit, die neues Wissen schafft. Was zählt, ist dass eine neue Datenlage eine andere Sicht erlaubt – und dass man sich der Wahrheit so weit wie nur irgend möglich nähert.

Sieben Milliarden Menschen für die Wissenschaft zu begeistern, ist eine große Aufgabe. Nie zuvor war es so wichtig, sich dieser Herausforderung zu stellen. Seit 2005 liefern wir Ideen und Geschichten, die unsere Leser motivieren sollen, wissenschaftlich zu denken (in *seedmagazine. com, scienceisculture.com, scienceblogs.com, phylotaxis.com, researchblogging.com, visualizing. org*). Jetzt wagen wir den nächsten großen Schritt und entwickeln Tools und Services, die Institutionen (Unternehmen, Regierungen, internationale Organisationen) dabei unterstützen, auf das gleiche Ziel hinzuarbeiten. Wir tragen unsere Sicht- und Denkweise hinaus in Parlamente, Gerichtssäle, Krankenhäuser, auf Baustellen und in die Vorstandsetagen der Welt, um wissenschaftliches Denken in einer neuen Dimension voranzutreiben.

Im Rahmen der Ars Electroncia 2012 THE BIG PICTURE untersuchen *Seed* und Ars Electronica gemeinsam, wie die Konvergenz von Daten und Design ein neues „Big Picture" hervorbringen. Die zwei Leitfragen sind: Welche neue Sicht entsteht durch die Konvergenz von Daten und Design? Und kann diese veränderte Sicht neue kollektive Emotionen oder Einsichten hervorbringen, die – so wie der Blick vom Mond auf die Erde zu neuem Umweltbewusstsein führte – soziales Handeln bewirken?

Seed betrachtet Wissenschaft nicht nur als Objekt oder Quelle neuer Technologien, sondern als Möglichkeit zur Erweiterung unseres Weltverständnis' und nutzt wissenschaftliche Erkenntnisse, Hilfsmittel und Methoden, um einen neuen Erkenntnisgewinn zu erhalten und neue Strategien und Lösungen zu entwickeln. *Seed* begann als Zeitschrift *(seedmagazine.com)*. Heute strebt das Unternehmen eine umfassende Umsetzung der in seinen Medien vorgestellten Ideen und Methoden an und unterstützt innovativ denkende Unternehmen, Regierungen und Organisationen in deren Bemühen, wissenschaftliches Denken in den eigenen Reihen umzusetzen. *seedscientific.com*

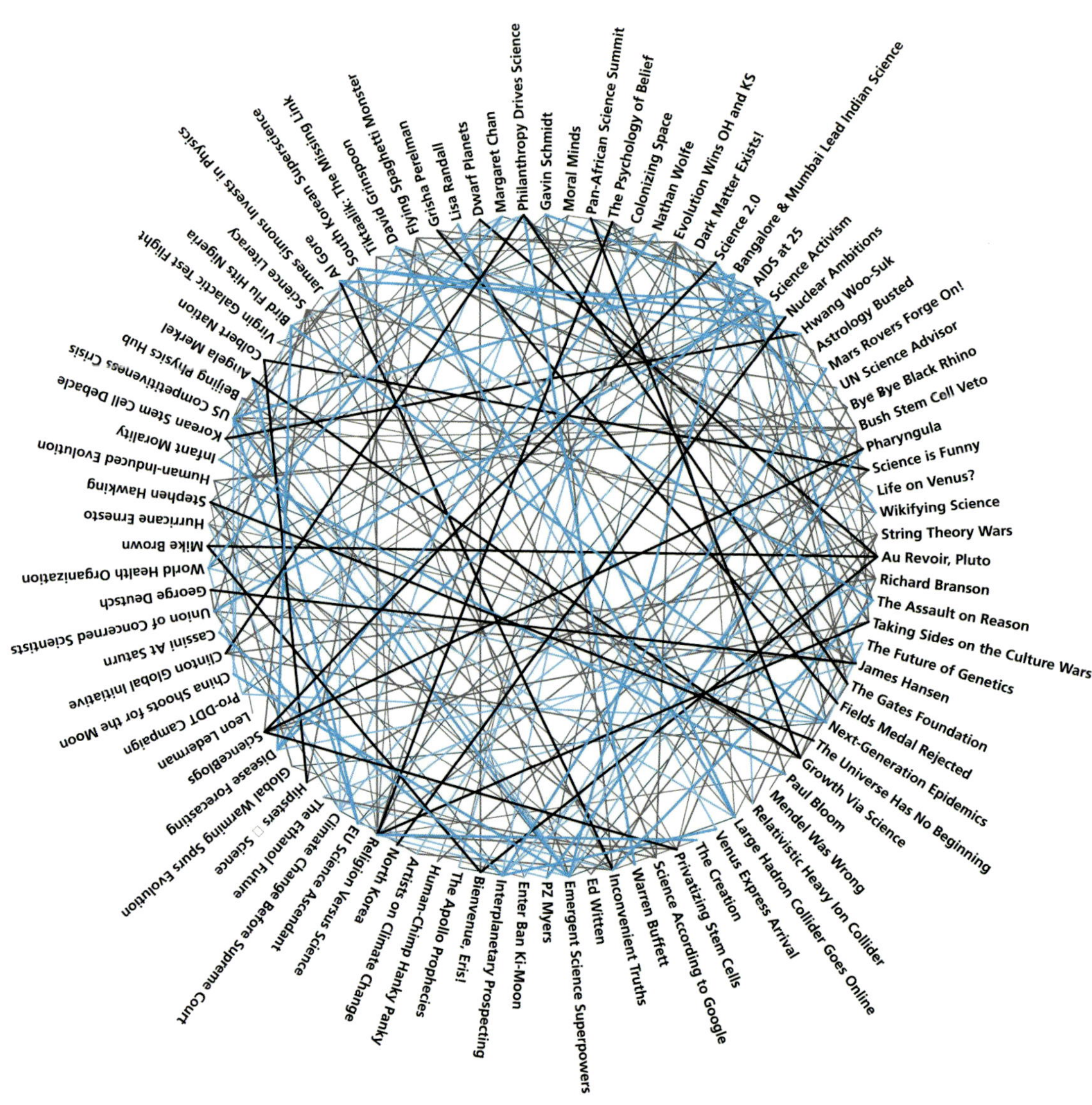

Visualizing the inter-connectedness of current affairs / Visualisierung der Vernetzungen im aktuellen Zeitgeschehen

Seed ist auf der Ars Electronica mit folgenden drei Schwerpunkten vertreten:

SEED SYMPOSIUM

Welches neue „Big Picture" schaffen wir durch die Kombination von Daten und Design? Wie sollen wir diese neuen Erkenntnisse interpretieren? Wie gehen wir emotional mit diesen neuen „Bildern" um? Und zu welchen neuen Fragestellungen über uns selbst und unsere Umwelt führt die Verbindung von Daten und Design? Führende Wissenschaftler und Praktiker im Bereich Datenvisualisierung und Data Science erörtern diese Fragen.

VISUALIZING.ORG GALLERY

Infolge der Globalisierung und der zunehmenden weltweiten Vernetzung sind neue Perspektiven wichtiger denn je. Mobilität, Kommunikation und Austausch haben eine bislang ungeahnte Dimension erreicht. Eine Datenvisualisierung kann ein neues Licht auf die unser modernes Leben prägenden Muster, Ströme und Kräfte werfen und neue Ideen und Erkenntnisse entstehen lassen. *Visualizing.org* präsentiert eine Galerie visualisierter Daten, die den Geist des großen Ganzen, des „Big Picture", einfangen soll.

Visualizing.org wurde von Seed und General Electric gegründet und ist eine globale Gemeinschaft Kreativschaffender, die mittels Daten und Design versucht, komplexen Fragen Sinn zu verleihen. Gemeinsam mit 100 Partneruniversitäten, internationalen Organisationen, Unternehmen und NGOs trägt *Visualizing.org* für ein besseres Verständnis bei und versucht neue Einblicke in die unsere Welt ausmachenden Systeme zu ermöglichen.

WORKSHOP ZUR DATENVISUALISIERUNG

Nehmen Sie teil an einem praxisorientierten Workshop zur Semantik grafischer Repräsentationen und zur Ästhetik des Informationsdesigns, der sowohl auf konzeptionelle als auch praktische Fragen der Datenvisualisierung eingeht.

Themen wie die Nutzung der Arbeitsflächen, die Bedeutung von Legenden oder der Einsatz von Farben, Formen und Mustern für die Darstellung verschiedener Datentypen werden theoretisch behandelt. Im Praxisteil erstellen die Teilnehmer anhand von uns zur Verfügung gestellten Datensätzen eine Netzwerkvisualisierung mittels JavaScript Libraries.

Aus dem Englischen von Sonja Pöllabauer

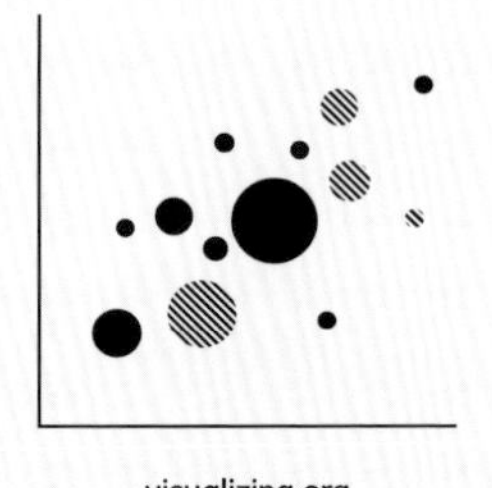

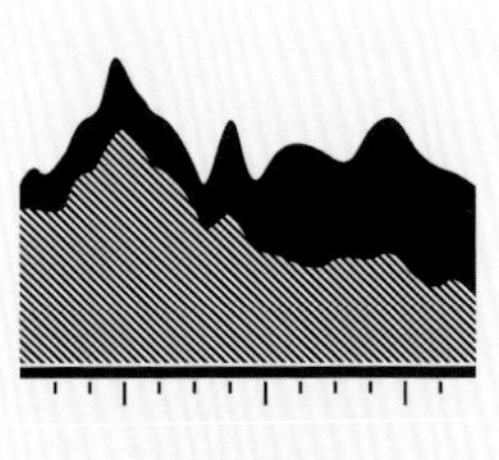

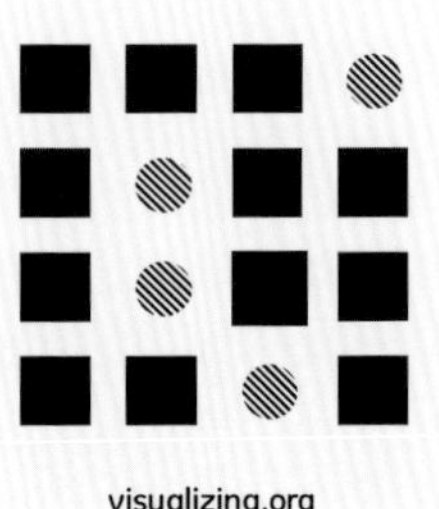

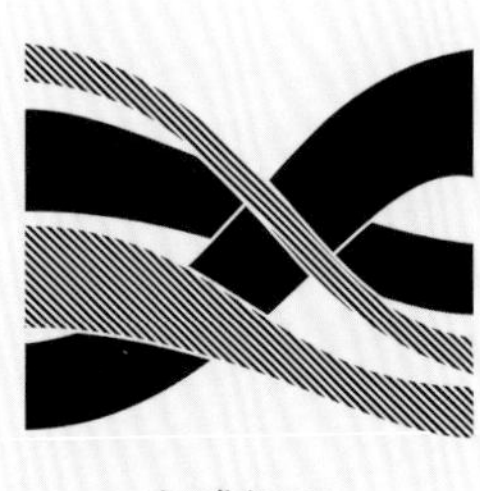

Dietmar Offenhuber, Katja Schechtner

Sensing Place / Placing Sense II
Accountability Technologies

A growing part of the general public is concerned that cities are planned and governed in a responsible way. Accountability technologies stand for new innovative approaches to make sure that urban governments and players who make decisions that affect the public are held accountable for their actions.

In the contemporary information society, the democratic obligation of the citizens to rigorously inform themselves so that they can participate in public affairs has become impossible to fulfill. Rather than submitting to the opinions of self-proclaimed experts, citizens need new ways to make sense of what is going on around them. In this context, Michael Schudson coined the term of the "monitorial citizen", who "scans (rather than reads) the informational environment", ready to mobilize when alerted.[1]

And citizens indeed have questions about where their trash goes, about the air quality in their neighborhood or whether their streets are managed well. The past few years have seen an emerging practice dedicated to this concern—a practice involving DIY sensing, social software and visualization for uncovering facts, coordinating action and influencing decisions in cities and industry. Examples of such practices are abundant—citizen sensing of traffic noise or congestion, pollution; data journalism scrutinizing mobility infrastructures and urban energy consumption; whistleblowers revealing corruption and misuse of power. Ultimately, accountability technologies are both tools allowing citizens to challenge the authority of political elites, as well as tools for public administrations to explain, discuss and adjust their decisions.

We are interested in such projects and technologies that have actually made an impact on the reality of the city. We are interested in the motivations, strategies and tactics of the people who create and use these technologies, both on an individual and a governmental level. We are also interested in the role of representation—does it make a difference how information is presented? Finally, how can information and insights generated by citizens be integrated with the official structures and put into action?

We use the term Accountability Technologies for a collection of different tools and practices that are sometimes used in combination, sometimes separately. These practices include (1) collecting previously unavailable environmental data through a collective of volunteers using DIY sensing technologies. (2) Connecting and harmonizing existing data sources in a common electronic platform for making urban planning and governance more transparent, as practiced for example in open governance initiatives. (3) Platforms for documenting instances of misuse of power or corruption, including dedicated whistleblower websites or the use of online video websites for documenting civic protests. (4) Online visualization tools for analyzing data sets, deeply integrated into journalistic formats, recently termed as data driven journalism. (5) Finally, strategies for maximizing the impact in the public realm, often described as advocacy tools. More broadly, accountability technologies are concerned with three different aspects: the collection and generation of data, the analysis and dissemination of this data, and finally, its strategic use in the public discourse, in the legal system or political processes.

However, the ways in which accountability technologies can have an impact in the public sphere are manifold and often convoluted, matching the ambiguity of the term accountability itself.[2] One meaning of the term is narrative, often circumscribed as answerability: it requires someone who makes decisions to offer a rational explanation of these decisions. The second meaning is related to responsibility and enforcement, meaning the presence of instruments to make sure

License: Public Domain
Ground resolution: 8.31 cm/px
Bounding box: POINT(-88.8701993896 29.798690641)
POINT(-88.8620380748 29.8071316946)
Capture date: May 9, 2010
Publication date: May 16, 2010
Mappers: Shannon Dosemagen Stewart Long Mariko Toyoji
Cartographer: Stewart Long

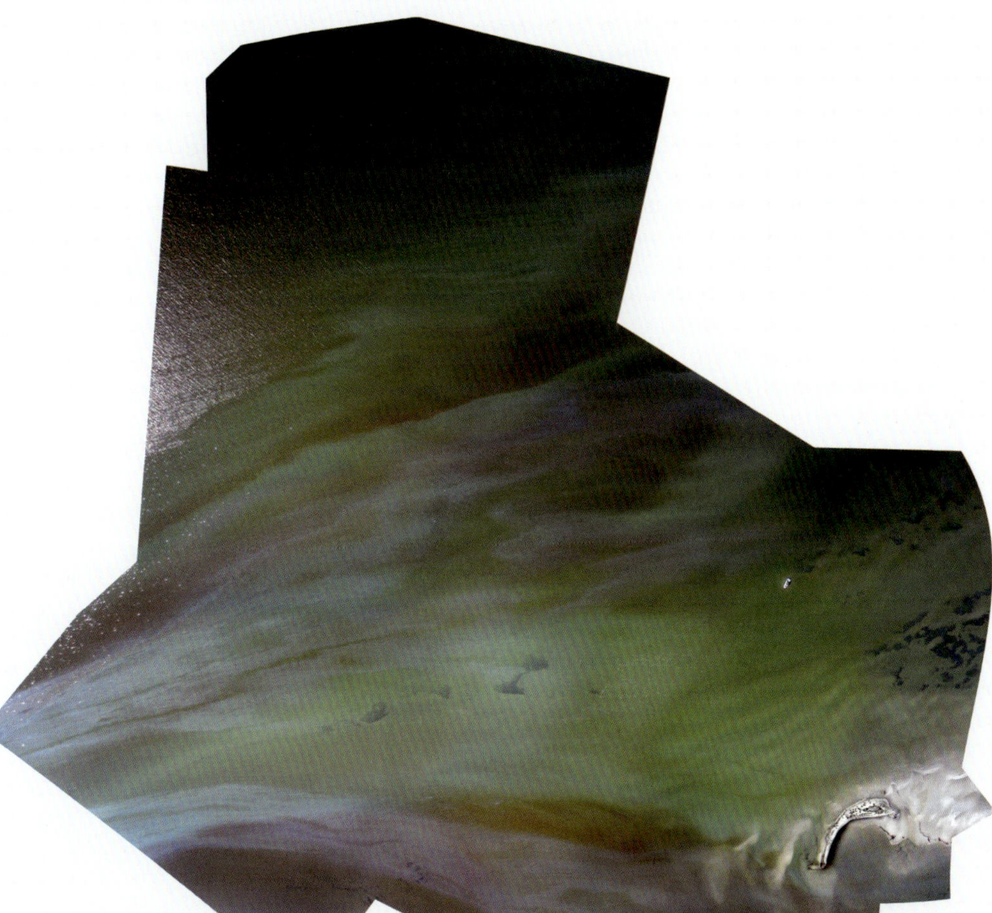

This map was produced by a group of activists in a fishing boat during the 2010 Deepwater Horizon oil spill. It depicts an oil slick entering the Breton Sound during a "media blackout" when no civilian aircraft were allowed to fly under 3,000 feet, and when journalists were being kept off of public beaches. By launching a balloon to roughly 500 meters, they produced an independent record of the damages which was such high resolution (10x that of Google Maps, and 10,000x that of NOAA's daily satellite imagery) that it shows individual pelicans and terns, as well as coral reef. The imagery was captured using open source tools for a total cost of <$200 and we have released it into the public domain as open data.

that the one who makes decisions maintains some responsibility for its consequences. Both meanings of accountability depend on a functioning democratic system that honors both justification and responsibility. Accountability technologies rely on a cooperative relationship between the individual and the government, since these technologies interface with mechanisms that need to be, at least in principle, already built into the system. The notion of accountability acknowledges the fact that full transparency is not possible where humans make decisions, and is probably also not desirable since it would make it very difficult to make any decisions at all. The technologies and practices discussed in this symposium operate at this interface between the citizens, activists and the government, tackling the question of how public responsibility and democratic participation can happen in an information-saturated society.

Symposium in the afo architekturforum oberösterreich–curated by Dietmar Offenhuber and Katja Schechtner. This symposium is a cooperation between the Austrian Institute of Technology, Massachusetts Institute of Technology, afo architekturforum oberösterreich and Ars Electronica.

1   Schudson, Michael (1999). *The Good Citizen: A History of American Civic Life.* New York: Martin Kessler Books.
2   Schedler, Andreas (1999). *Conceptualizing accountability. The self-restraining state: Power and accountability in new democracies*, 13–28.

Dietmar Offenhuber, Katja Schechtner

Sensing Place / Placing Sense II
Accountability Technologies

Immer mehr Menschen machen sich Gedanken über verantwortungsvolle Städteplanung und -verwaltung. Unter *Accountability Technologies* können innovative Praktiken subsummiert werden, die sicherstellen, dass Stadtverwaltungen und öffentliche Entscheidungsträger für ihr Handeln zur Verantwortung gezogen werden.
In der modernen Informationsgesellschaft können Bürger ihrer demokratisch verankerten Pflicht zur Einholung umfassender Informationen, die ihnen Partizipation an öffentlichen Angelegenheiten erlaubt, nicht länger nachkommen. Um nicht der Meinungsmache selbstdeklarierter „Experten" ausgeliefert zu sein, benötigen Bürger neue Wege und Mittel, umd das, was rund um sie geschieht, auch verstehen zu können. Michael Schudson prägte in diesem Zusammenhang den Begriff des *monitorial citizen*, der „sein Informationsumfeld scannt (nicht liest)" und auf gewisse Warnsignale hin mobilisiert werden kann.[1]
So hinterfragen Bürger, was mit ihrem Müll passiert oder wie die Luftqualität und das Straßenmanagement in ihrem Viertel aussehen. Seit einigen Jahren widmet man sich verstärkt derartigen Fragen und nutzt dazu DIY-Datenerfassungssysteme, Social Software und Visualisierungsprogramme. Ziel ist es, Fakten aufzudecken, Maßnahmen zu koordinieren und Einfluss auf Entscheidungsprozesse in Städten und der Industrie zu nehmen. Es finden sich unzählige Beispiele für derartige Initiativen: Engagierte Bürger erfassen Daten zur Verkehrslärm- und Stausituation sowie zur Umweltverschmutzung; es wird Datenjournalismus zur Analyse der Mobilitätsinfrastruktur oder des städtischen Stromverbrauchs betrieben; Korruption und Machtmissbrauch werden durch Whistleblowers aufgedeckt. Derartige Technologien geben Bürgern die Möglichkeit, die Autorität politischer Eliten zu hinterfragen, ebenso wie sie öffentlichen Verwaltun-

gen die Möglichkeit zur Darstellung, Diskussion und Anpassung von Entscheidungen geben. Uns interessieren jene Projekte und Technologien, die tatsächlich die Wirklichkeit der Stadt veränden. Unser Interesse richtet sich einerseits auf die Motivation, Strategien und Taktiken der Entwickler und Nutzer hinter diesen Methoden (auf der Ebene des Individuums ebenso wie auf der Verwaltungsebene). Andererseits sind wir auch an der Darstellung von Informationen interessiert: Macht es einen Unterschied, wie Informationen präsentiert werden? Als drittem Themenstrang widmen wir uns der Frage, wie von Bürgern generierte Daten in die staatlichen Systeme integriert und für konkretes Handeln genutzt werden können.

Unter *Accountability Technologies* verstehen wir Mittel und Praktiken, die kombiniert oder isoliert eingesetzt werden können: (1) die Erfassung bisher nicht vorhandener Umweltdaten durch Freiwillige unter Einsatz von DIY-Messtechniken; (2) die Integration und Harmonisierung verfügbarer Datensätze in einer gemeinsamen Online-Plattform zur Gewährleistung einer transparenteren Städteplanung und –verwaltung, wie etwa bei Open-Governance-Initiativen; (3) Plattformen zur Dokumentation von Machtmissbrauch und Korruption, darunter Whistleblower-Website oder die Verwendung von Online-Video-Websites zur Dokumentation von Bürgerprotesten; (4) Online-Visualisierungsprogramme zur Datenanalyse, die eng mit journalistischen Formaten verzahnt werden, was neuerdings als Datenjournalismus bezeichnet wird; (5) und schließlich Strategien zur Maximierung der Auswirkungen derartiger Praktiken auf die Öffentlichkeit, oft als *Advocacy Tools* (Mittel zur politischen Einflussnahme und Lobbying) bezeichnet. *Accountability Technologies* fokussieren auf drei verschiedene Bereiche: Datenerfassung und -generierung, Datenanalyse und -disseminierung und schließlich strategische Nutzung dieser Daten im öffentlichen Diskurs, in juristischen oder politischen Systemen.

Accountability Technologies nehmen auf sehr unterschiedliche und komplexe Weise Einfluss auf den öffentlichen Bereich und spiegeln so die begriffliche Ambiguität des Konzepts Accountability wider.[2] Zum einen erhält der Begriff eine narrative Bedeutung zugewiesen, etwa wenn es um Rechenschaftspflichtigkeit geht *(answerability):* Ein Entscheidungsträger ist angehalten seine Entscheidungen rational zu begründen. Zum anderen steht die Bedeutung des Begriffs in Zusammenhang mit dem Begriffspaar Verantwortung *(responsibility)* und Durchsetzung *(enforcement):* Hier sind Instrumente gefragt, die sicherstellen, dass Entscheidungsträger zumindest in gewissem Maß Verantwortung für die Folgen ihrer Entscheidungen übernehmen. Beide Bedeutungen von Accountability setzen ein funktionierendes demokratisches System voraus, in dem Rechtfertigung *(justification)* und Verantwortung *(responsibility)* als zentrale Werte verankert sind. *Accountability Technologies* setzen Kooperation zwischen dem Individuum und der Regierung voraus, da Schnittstellen genutzt werden, die zumindest in Ansätzen bereits Teil des Systems sein müssen. Der Begriff Accountability anerkennt die Tatsache, dass bei von Menschen getroffenen Entscheidungen vollständige Transparenz unmöglich und vermutlich auch nicht wünschenswert ist, da in diesem Fall die Entscheidungsfindung sehr schwierig würde. Die im Rahmen dieses Symposiums diskutierten Techniken und Praktiken operieren an der Schnittstelle zwischen Bürgern, Aktivisten und Regierung und gehen der Frage nach, wie öffentliche Verantwortung und demokratische Partizipation in einer informationsübersättigten Gesellschaft gestaltbar sind.

Aus dem Englischen von Sonja Pöllabauer

1   Schudson, Michael:. *The Good Citizen: A History of American Civic Life,* Kessler Books, New York 1999.
2   Schedler, Andreas: „Conceptualizing accountability" in *The self-restraining state: Power and accountability in new democracies,* S. 13–18, 1999.

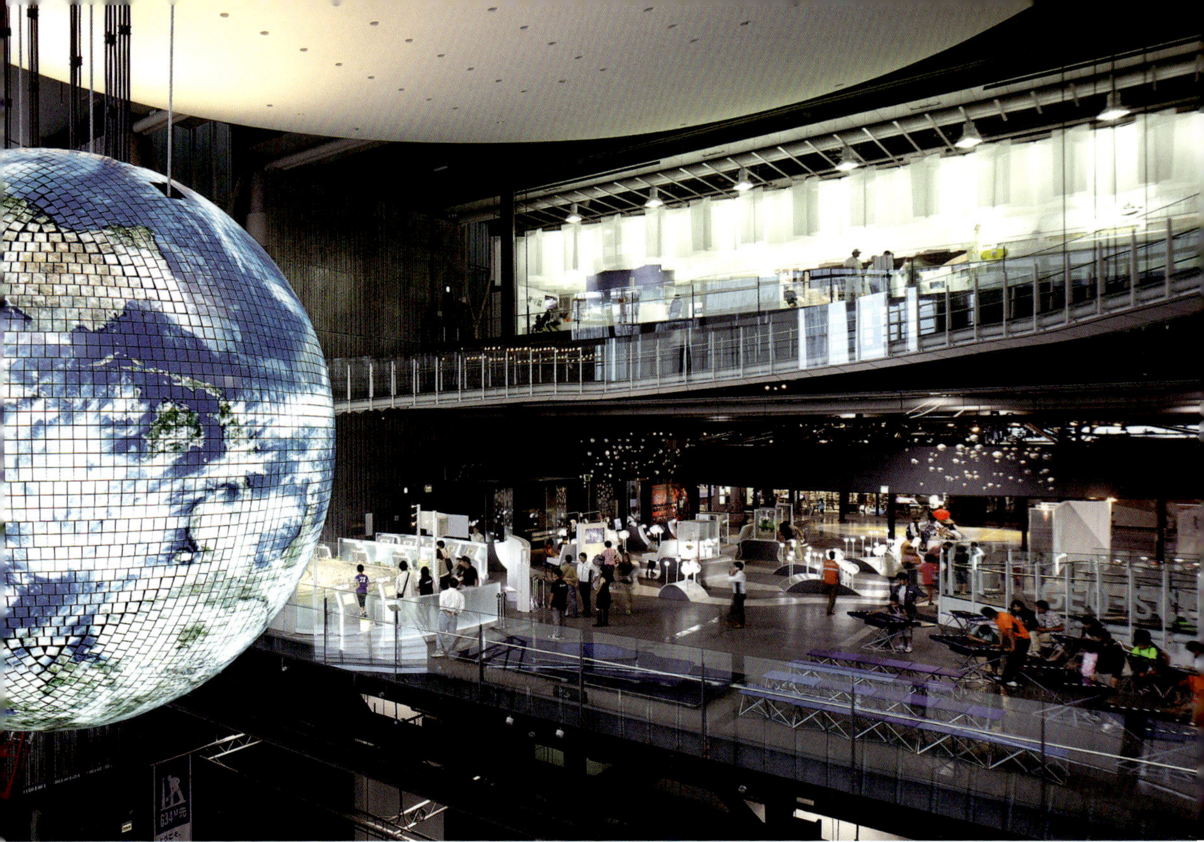

The Miraikan TSUNAGARI Project

How much do we really know about the earth, and ourselves? In the innovative *TSUNAGARI Project* we share scientific information and knowledge about our planet and our species with the world through a new form of visual expression and create a better vision for our future. The *TSUNAGARI Project* helps you to understand the links *(TSUNAGARI)* between life forms in the Earth's ecosystem, and the relations *(TSUNAGARI)* between the Earth and you. The project helps you to identify your own relationship *(TSUNAGARI)* with the Earth and to consider what can be done for the interrelationship between the Earth and future generations.

Three tools, Geo-Cosmos, Geo-Scope, and Geo-Palette serve to develop these links *(TSUNAGARI)*. By utilizing these tools, a new perspective of Earth based on the many forms of *TSUNAGARI* contributed by ideas from people all over the world, by research data related to Earth, and by artists is revealed.

This fusion creates a "new Earth awareness" as we transverse boundaries and integrate knowledge. The *TSUNAGARI Project* will be available throughout the world as a means of sharing information concerning the Earth.

Geo-Cosmos—Feel the Earth

The Geo-Cosmos, Miraikan's symbol exhibit, reveals a super high precision view of the Earth shining brightly in space (>10 million pixels). It is the world's first 'globe-like display' using organic LED panels and created by Miraikan's Chief Executive Director Mamoru Mohri.

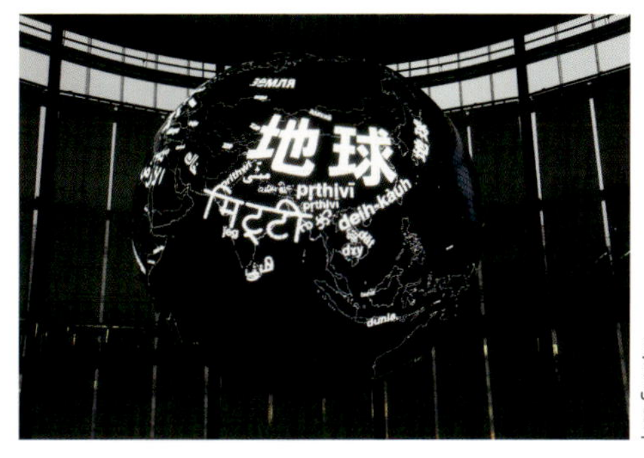
Ingo Guenter

The images of clouds on the globe reflect the everyday image data collected by weather satellites. Geo-Cosmos also provides graphic images such as ocean acidification, temperature change and various scientific observation data related to Earth. With Geo-Cosmos you can see the current image of Earth, which changes every minute, and you can see how the Earth will look in the future.

The Geo-Cosmos' exhibit content is from scientists and research institutes around the world. As you gaze upon its beauty, you perceive the Earth as one celestial body amongst countless others in the immense universe.

Geo-Scope—Search for the Earth

This interactive board allows you to access various Earth observation data collected from national and international scientists and research institutes. Thirteen boards in different sizes are aligned on the exhibition floor and you can search for information on the scale of the Earth via an easily operated touch panel. The regularly updated content covers seasonal changes in ecology, climate change, and the predicted future image of the Earth's environment. You can also view detailed data for an even deeper understanding,

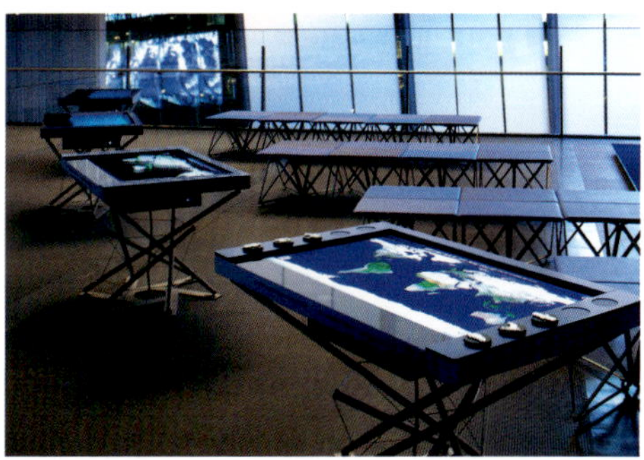

find relationships between data and discover new perspectives of the Earth via your search. Due to the size of the Geo-Scope, it is possible for groups to use it too.

Geo-Palette—Portray the Earth

This online service allows you to draw your own world map based on the available information relating to the countries of the world. Besides the basic data such as population distribution, the website offers several hundred other types of data, including scientific and statistical data such as the Gross Domestic Product figures. By combining various data, the user may make new discoveries that are not possible by viewing just one type of data. The user can select the data freely and can discover many aspects of the earth's environment and human activities by overlapping various data elements on a single map. The user can then post his/her map on the site to share these discoveries with other users.

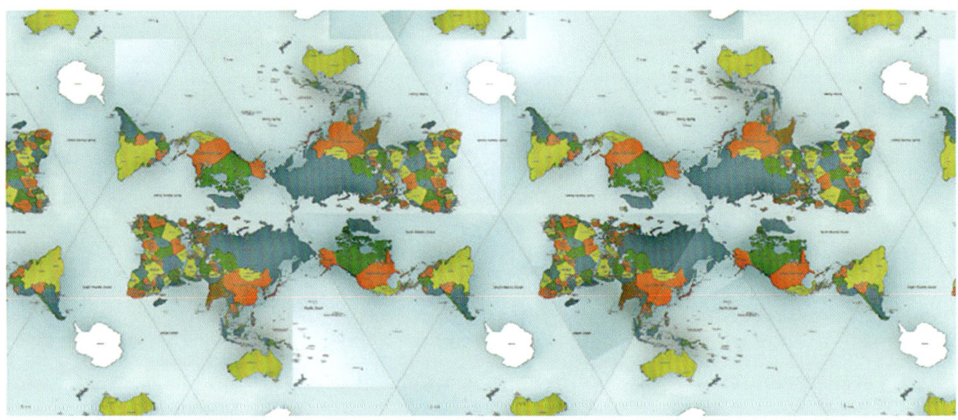

AuthaGraph

This projection method, which was invented by architect Hajime Narukawa and colleagues in 1999, transfers a 3-dimensional sphere into a 2-dimensional rectangle while maintaining area proportions. With this method, an image of the spherical Earth is transferred to a flat surface, evenly distributing distortion on the "AuthaGraph world map".

Mercator projection, invented in the late 16th century, exaggerates scale at higher latitudes. In the Polar Regions the distortion is so great that it is hard to figure out the actual shape. The AuthaGraph world map, on the other hand, is able to frame continents and islands in a rectangle without distorting their area ratios. Miraikan uses the AuthaGraph world map and applies it to Geo-Palette and Geo-Scope for the *TSUNAGARI Project*.

Planning and Production: Miraikan (National Museum of Emerging Science and Innovation), Tokyo
Realization: Geo-Cosmos, DENTSU INC., Mitsubishi Electric Corporation, Go and Pertners, Inc., GK Tech Inc.
Geo-Palette: Internet Initiative Japan Inc.
Geo-Scope: GK Tech Inc.
Schematic Design and Adviser: AuthaGraph Co., Ltd., Ingo Günther

Das Miraikan TSUNAGARI-Projekt

Was wissen wir wirklich über die Erde und uns selbst? Das innovative *TSUNAGARI*-Projekt ermöglicht mit einer neuen Form visueller Darstellung den Austausch wissenschaftlicher Informationen mit der Welt und die Vermittlung von Wissen über unseren Planeten und unsere Spezies. Mithilfe von *TSUNAGARI* können wir gemeinsam an einer besseren Zukunft bauen.

Das *TSUNAGARI*-Projekt fördert das Verständnis für die Verbindungen (so die Bedeutung des japanischen Worts *tsunagari)* zwischen Lebewesen und dem Ökosystem Erde, aber auch zwischen einem selbst und der Erde. Ziel des Projekts ist es, sich innerhalb dieser Verbindungen zu verorten und zu prüfen, was wir für die Verbindung zwischen unserer Erde und künftigen Generationen tun können.

Die drei Werkzeuge des Projekts – *Geo-Cosmos, Geo-Scope* und *Geo-Palette* – sollen eine realistische Wahrnehmung dieser Verbindungen ermöglichen. Mit ihrer Hilfe soll eine neue Sicht und Darstellung der Erde entstehen – eine, die auf den vielen verschiedenen Verbindungen beruht, welche sich aus Ideen von Menschen in aller Welt, erdbezogenen Forschungsdaten und Formen künstlerischen Ausdrucks ergeben.

Mit seinem grenzüberschreitenden Ansatz und seiner Integration aller Wissensbereiche schafft das *TSUNAGARI*-Projekt ein neues „Erdbewusstsein". Es wird weltweit als Modell zur Vermittlung von Informationen über unseren Planteten angeboten.

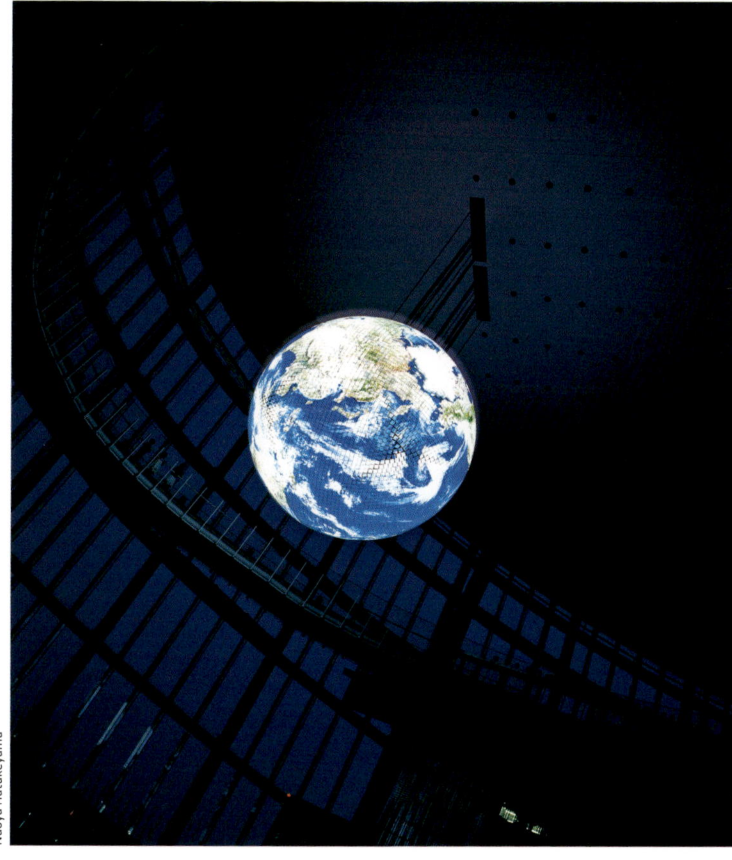

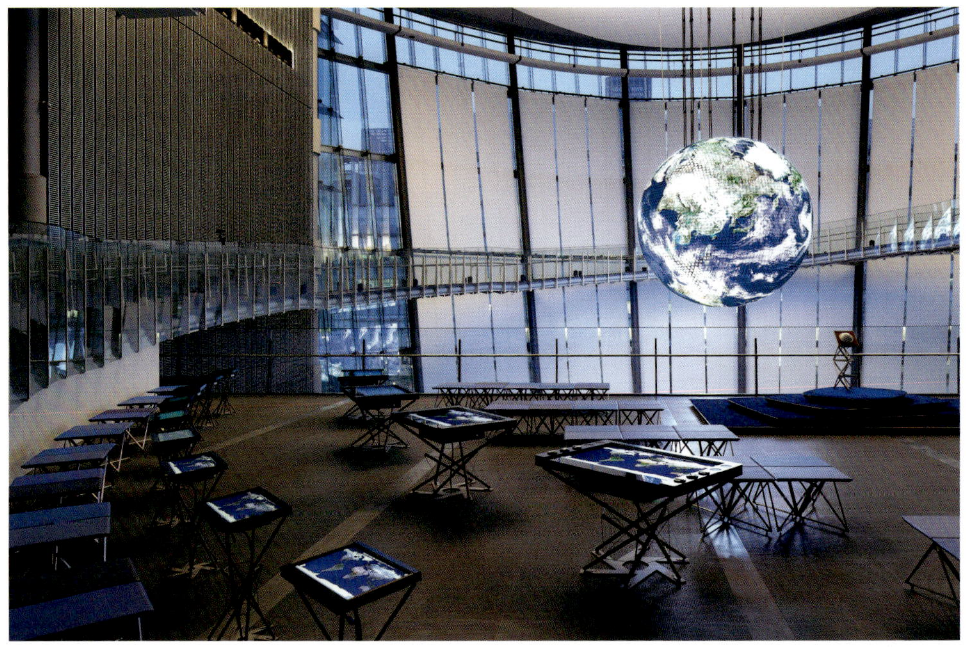

Geo-Cosmos – die Erde erfassen

Geo-Cosmos, das zentrale Symbol der Miraikan-Ausstellung, ist eine mit über 10 Megapixel hochauflösende Wiedergabe unseres prachtvoll im All leuchtenden Planeten. Es ist das weltweit erste kugelförmige Display und basiert auf organischen LED-Panels. Mamoru Mohri, geschäftsführender Direktor von Miraikan, wollte damit einen Eindruck vom „herrlichen Anblick unseres Planeten aus dem All" vermitteln.
Die Wolkenbilder auf diesem Globus spiegeln die aktuellen Bilddaten von Wettersatelliten wider. Dazu bekommt man grafische Darstellungen vom Säuregehalt der Ozeane, Temperaturveränderungen und von anderen wissenschaftlichen Geodaten geliefert. *Geo-Cosmos* bietet aber nicht nur ein aktuelles, sich von Minute zu Minute änderndes Bild der Erde, sondern gestattet auch einen Blick in die Zukunft des Planeten.
Die Inhalte für *Geo-Cosmos* kommen von Wissenschaftlern und Forschungsinstituten aus aller Welt. Dieser Anblick der Erde in ihrer vollen Pracht macht auch klar, dass sie lediglich einer von zahllosen Himmelskörpern in einem unermesslichen Universum ist.

Geo-Scope – die Erde erkunden

Geo-Scope sind interaktive Tafeln zum Abrufen verschiedener Erdbeobachtungsdaten japanischer wie internationaler Wissenschafts- und Forschungsinstitute. In der Ausstellung sind dreizehn unterschiedlich große Tafeln dieser Art aufgestellt, auf denen man mit einem leicht bedienbaren Touchscreen nach Informationen über den Planeten als Ganzes suchen kann. Die regelmäßig aktualisierten Inhalte umfassen etwa Daten zu jahreszeitlich bedingten

Umweltveränderungen, zum Klimawandel oder zur voraussichtlichen ökologischen Entwicklung des Planeten. Zur Vertiefung des Verständnisses kann man Detailinformationen abrufen, Relationen zwischen den Daten herstellen und auf Basis der eigenen Suche neue Bilder der Erde entdecken. Dank ihrer Größe eignen sich die *Geo-Scope*-Tafeln außerdem ideal für die Gruppenarbeit. Beim Diskutieren eigener Entdeckungen mit anderen lernt man, die Erde aus anderen Perspektiven zu sehen. Miraikan wollte mit dieser Ausstellung eine Schnittstelle für Daten zum gegenwärtigen Zustand des Planeten Erde schaffen.

Geo-Palette – die Erde darstellen

Der Online-Dienst *Geo-Palette* ermöglicht es, eine eigene Weltkarte auf der Grundlage unterschiedlicher länderspezifischer Informationen zu erstellen. Die Website bietet etwa grundlegende Daten zur Bevölkerungsverteilung und Hunderte weiterer wissenschaftlicher und statistischer Datenbestände wie z. B. Zahlen zum Bruttoinlandsprodukt. Nutzer können auf diese frei zugreifen und, indem sie diese Informationen auf einer Karte miteinander verknüpfen, viele auf Umwelt und menschliches Handeln bezogene Aspekte unserer Erde entdecken. Durch die Verknüpfung der verschiedenen Daten können Entdeckungen gemacht werden, die durch die Betrachtung nur einer Datenart nicht möglich wären. Der User kann diese selbst erstellten Karten auf unserer Website publizieren und mit anderen teilen.

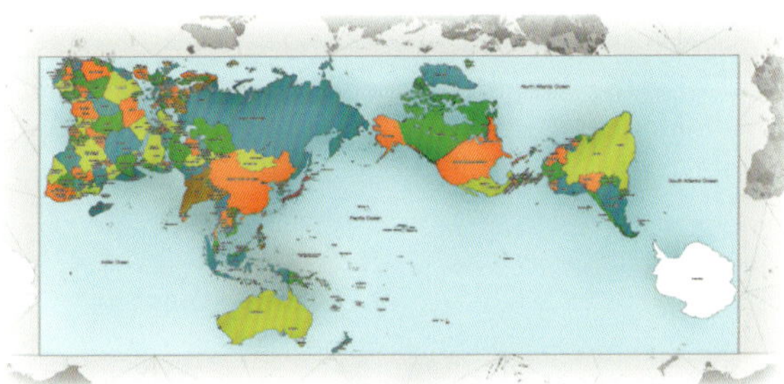

AuthaGraph

AutaGraph ist eine 1999 vom Architekten Hajime Narukawa und seinem Team erfundene Projektionsmethode zur verzerrungsneutralen Übertragung einer Kugel auf eine rechteckige Fläche. Bei der *AutaGraph*-Weltkarte wird mithilfe dieser Methode ein Bild der Erdkugel verzerrungsneutral auf eine Fläche projiziert.

Bei der im späten 16. Jahrhundert erfundenen Mercator-Projektion nimmt die Verzerrung bekanntlich bei den höheren Breitengraden zu. Vor allem in den Polarregionen wird sie dermaßen stark, dass die ursprüngliche Form der Territorien kaum noch zu erkennen ist. Mit der *Auta-Graph*-Weltkarte lassen sich sämtliche Erdteile und Inseln unter Wahrung ihrer richtigen Relationen in ein Rechteck einschreiben.

Miraikan übernimmt die *AuthaGraph*-Projektion als neuen Weltkartenstandard und verwendet sie beim *TSUNAGARI*-Projekt sowohl für *Geo-Palette* wie auch für *Geo-Scope*.

Aus dem Englischen von Wilfried Prantner

Buckminster Fuller Institute Austria

World Game Lab: On the Fly
A game inspired by Richard Buckminster Fuller

Richard Buckminster Fuller was way ahead of his time in many ways. He was an American all-rounder who flashed his wide-ranging genius as a discoverer, inventor, constructor, engineer, scientist, philosopher, writer, cult figure, university professor, humanist and citizen of the world. "Think globally, act locally" was one of the many maxims he made famous. Fuller coined the term "Spaceship Earth" to make us humans cognizant of our responsibility for our planet.
In the 1930s and '40s, Fuller went about developing a world map that depicted our globe without the national borders that were typical up to then. The principles he employed in his cartographic work were utilized again years later by Fuller to come up with the geodesic dome, a lattice shell structure that made him world famous and was designed, among other purposes, to relieve the planet's acute housing shortage.
In World Game, Fuller's aim was to develop a sort of instruction manual for optimal operation of Spaceship Earth. The Dymaxion World Map makes it possible to visualize flows of energy and goods, migrations of peoples, movements of money, and phenomena affecting the climate and raw materials, and is the basis of this game in which players take over as navigators of Spaceship Earth. Dymaxion, a portmanteau Fuller coined in the '20s, puts the object of the game in a nutshell: dynamic maximum. It calls for ongoing adaptation to achieve optimization defined as maintaining a favorable balance of the economy, the environment, and the social status of the world population.

Apply Fuller

When we subject Fuller's ideas to a process of rethinking, redoing and replaying, we're not proceeding in the spirit of a so-called update but rather of an application.
At Ars Electronica 2012, we're demonstrating a game development that the Institute has been investigating in recent years. These are game experiments with systemic interdependencies among natural resources, environmental pollution, agricultural yields, economic growth, technological development, health and world population that we want to shed light on. Data, estimates and opinions of Ars Electronica festivalgoers will be fed into a simplified world model. The resulting simulated course of the world will be repeated hourly, visualized and documented. Nevertheless, the focus isn't on the computer simulation itself (which only makes the game proceed a lot faster), but rather on the expertise gleaned from the audience.

Enrique Guitart, Thomas Thurner, Günther Friesinger, Ronald Strasser
Kiesler Stiftung Wien / Kiesler Foundation Vienna
Az W – Architekturzentrum Wien
Paraflows
Followers of the Buckminster Fuller Institute Austria

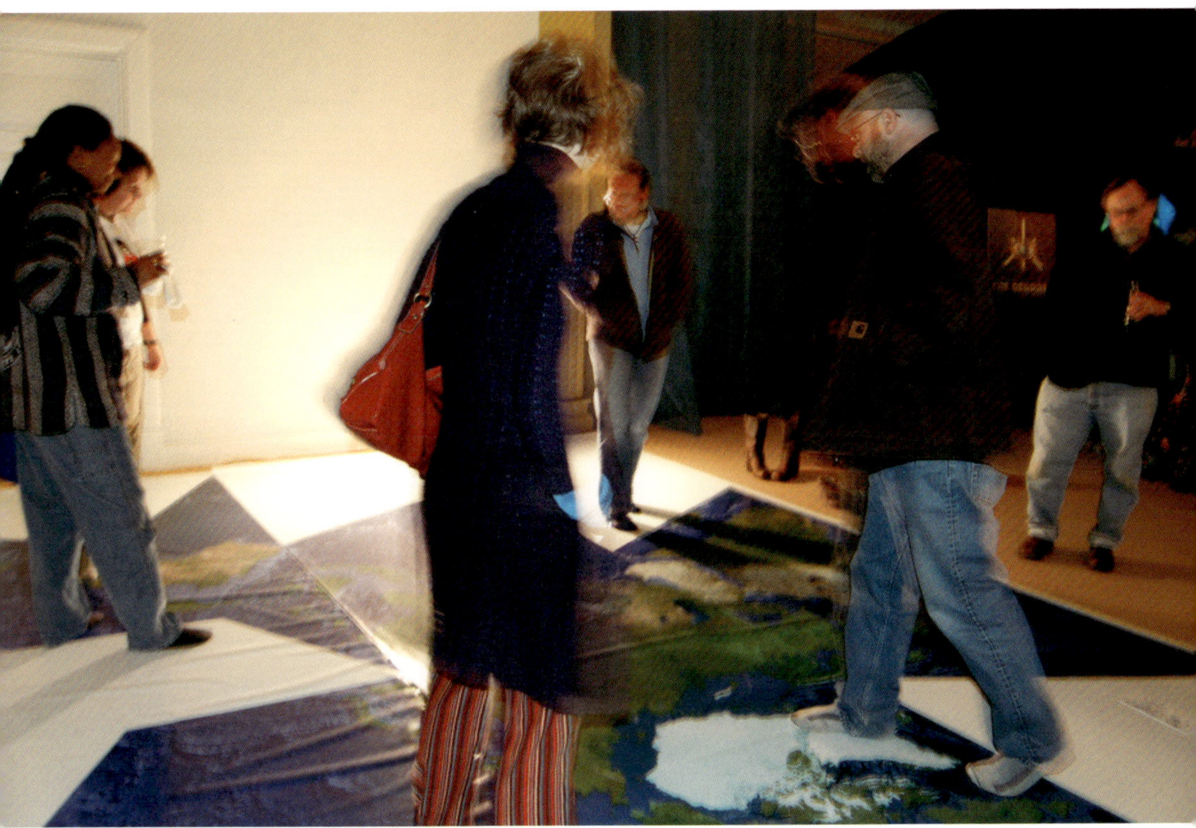

nc jennifer saylor

World Game Lab: On the Fly
A game inspired by Richard Buckminster Fuller

Richard Buckminster Fuller war seiner Zeit in vielem weit voraus. Ein amerikanisches Universaltalent mit genialen Zügen: Entdecker, Erfinder, Konstrukteur, Ingenieur, Naturwissenschaftler, Philosoph, Literat, Kultfigur, Hochschullehrer, Menschenfreund und Weltbürger.
„Denke global, handle lokal" - das war eine seiner vielen berühmt gewordenen Maximen. Fuller erfand den Begriff „Spaceship Earth", „Raumschiff Erde", um unser Verantwortungsbewusstsein für „unseren" Planeten zu schärfen.
In den 1930er und 1940er Jahren ging Fuller daran, jene Weltkarte zu entwickeln, die unseren Globus ohne die bis dahin üblichen Staatsgrenzen anschaulich macht. Die Berechnungsprinzipien für seine *World Map* führten Fuller Jahre später zur Entwicklung seiner „geodätischen", aus Großkreisen zusammen gesetzten Kuppelhauben, die ihn als Konstrukteur weltberühmt machten und nicht zuletzt der Behebung akuter Wohnungsnot dien(t)en.
In *World Game* versuchte Fuller eine Art „Bedienungsanleitung" zur bestmöglichen Steuerung des „Raumschiffs Erde" zu entwickeln. Die *Dymaxion World Map* erlaubt die Visualisierung von Energie- und Handelsströmen, von Migrations- und Geldbewegungen, von Klima- und Rohstoffphänomenen und ist die Basis eines als Weltenspiel angelegten stetigen Navigierens des Spaceship Earth. *Dymaxion* – ein Kunstwort Fullers aus den 1920er Jahren – legt dabei auch das Spielziel fest: Dynamik und Maximum. Stetige Anpassung im Sinne der Verbesserung und Verbesserung im Sinne maximaler Erreichung eines ausgewogenen ökonomischen, ökologischen und sozialen Status für die Welt.

Apply Fuller

Wenn wir Fullers Ideen einem „Rethinking", „Redoing" und „Replaying" zuführen, ist der Gestus nicht der des sogenannten „Updates", sondern vielmehr jener der Anwendung. Bei Ars Electronica 2012 zeigen wir die Spielentwicklung, die das Buckminster Fuller Institute – Austria in den letzten Jahren erforscht hat. Es sind Spielversuche, die die systemischen Abhängigkeiten zwischen Bodenschätzen, Umweltverschmutzung, Agrarertrag, Ökonomie, Technologieentwicklung, Gesundheit und Weltbevölkerung beleuchten wollen. Ein simplifiziertes Weltmodell wird mit Daten, Einschätzungen und Meinungen des Publikums des Festival Ars Electronica gespeist. Der daraus simulierte Weltenverlauf wird stündlich wiederholt, visualisiert und dokumentiert. Nicht die Computersimulation steht dabei im Mittelpunkt (sie kürzt hier nur das Spiel ab), sondern die eingesammelte Expertise des Publikums.

Text: Enrique Guitart

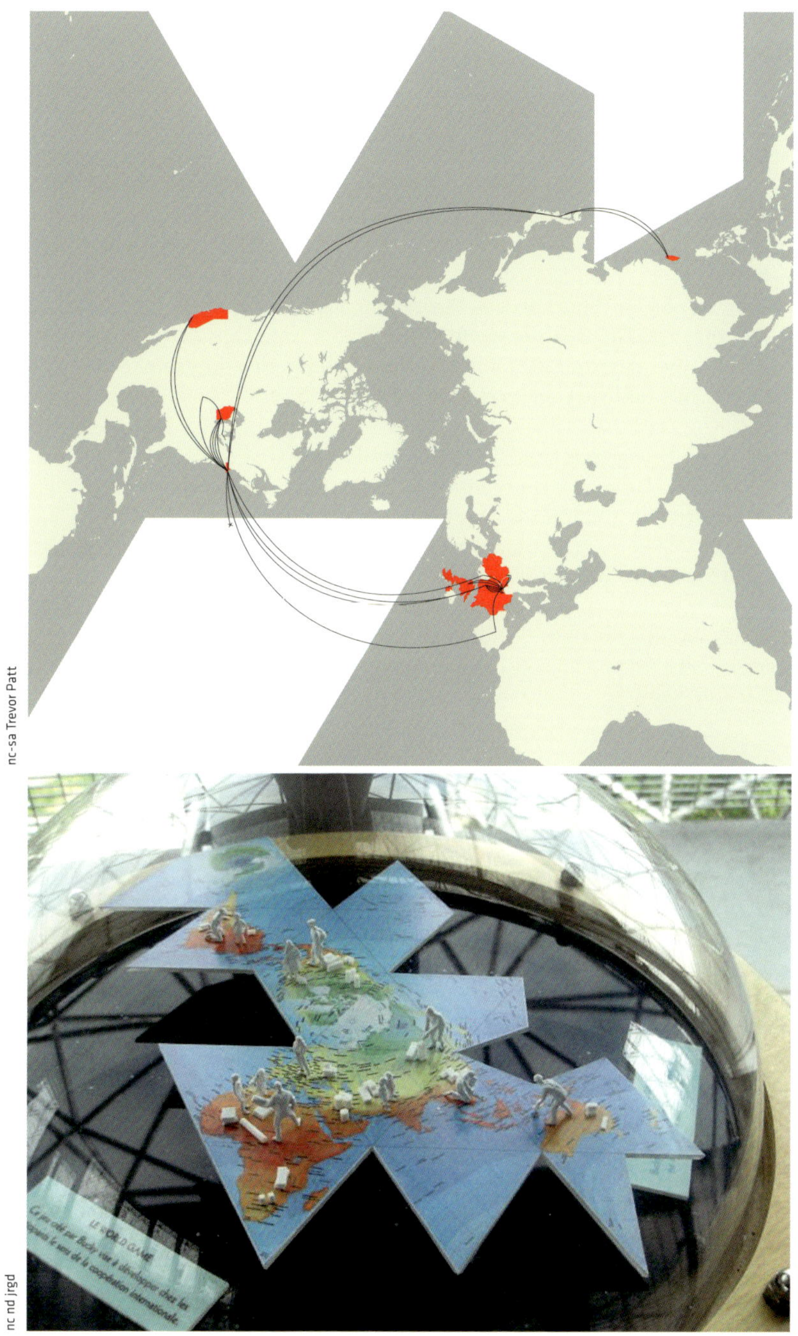

nc-sa Trevor Patt

nc nd jrgd

Brandon Litman, Kyle Ruddick

One Day on Earth

One Day on Earth is the first film made in every country of the world on the same day and the largest collaboration of media creation in the world's history. We see both the challenges and hopes of humanity from a diverse group of volunteer filmmakers assembled by a participatory media experiment. The film shows a world that is greatly interconnected, enormous, perilous, and wonderful.

The hope of *One Day on Earth* has always been to inspire people across the world to create and share whatever they choose. It is the world's new media time capsule. In making this film we were charged with the awesome responsibility to combine many different stories to tell the world's story, an effort that took an incredible amount of listening and discovery in the creative process.

What was the world trying to tell us? We took the full exhaustive review of all 3000 hours of footage very seriously. Through the organization of footage we found certain themes developing. We roughly used the cycle of life to organize these themes. As the process went on, we added statistics to introduce each theme and reinforce the enormity of the current state of life on our planet. After watching this movie, we hope the audience walks away feeling a deeper understanding of interconnectivity of the world we live in and that we all have an amazing opportunity every day we are alive. The world is a challenged place, but we do believe humanity has the opportunity to sustain and we hope this project and film inform us of the shared path we are traveling.

The Back-story

The project links together the world's most established non-profits, filmmakers, students, and other inspired groups. The shared experience of filming throughout the world on the same day galvanized an incredible sense of togetherness and team spirit.

What started as a small group of interested filmmakers, directly approached via platforms such as Vimeo, quickly grew into a worldwide social network, including both large and small Non Profit Organizations and the United Nations. Using a "white label" social networking platform called Ning, *One Day on Earth* invited interested participants to join an online community where they would not only be able to share their plans for the collaboration, but also receive public recognition for their contribution—a key element to the project's success.

From the project's inception to the collaboration event day, organizers focused attention on three main areas of community growth in the hope of fostering broad coverage and a deeper perspective on issues and culture worldwide. Educational groups, cause-based organizations, and professional media creators were all actively pursued.

A big breakthrough in the project came in April 2010, with the first of many meetings with the United Nations. This marked the beginning of what has become an unprecedented production agreement, allowing *One Day on Earth* to ship cameras worldwide and to retrieve footage from areas that do not have access to high speed internet.

Critical for a community-driven movement, the project needed to promote the vision and purpose of the event, and did so with a promotional trailer made from *One Day on Earth* members'

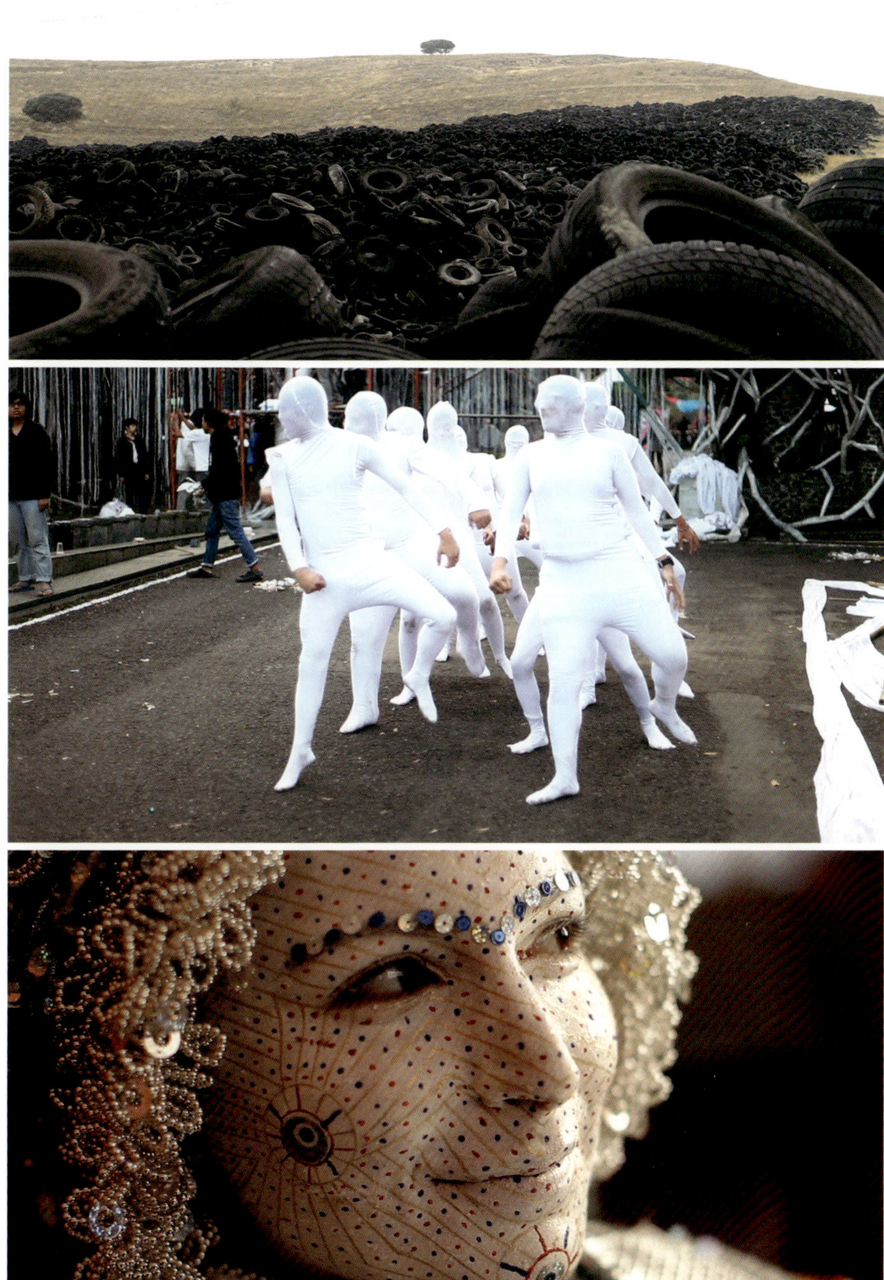

archive footage. Asking members to share footage previously shot revealed not only the incredible talent of the community, but also the participants' profound interest in using *One Day on Earth* to communicate diverse and important subject matter. It also showed incoming members the sincere commitment to the organization's goals.

On 10/10/10 *One Day on Earth* became the first project and film to record life in every country in the world on the same day. The aggregation technology used allowed contributors to tag and add important information to their submissions, which greatly informed the footage review process. Over 3,000 hours of footage were collected and a dedicated staff of reviewers watched every minute. In the end, over 240 hours of dialogues were translated, in more than 75 different languages.

As the film took shape, it was clear that important topics would be shared in a way never before seen, given the same day context. That said, one of the most popular sections of the film is the music section, which weaves together natural sounds and performances of the day into a musical collage that spans the world.

After over 14 months of editing, the film was scheduled for a historic premiere on April 22nd, 2012, Earth Day. With the help of the online community and the United Nations, *One Day on Earth* was shown in 160 countries on the same day, breaking a world record.

During the postproduction process of the first *One Day on Earth* film, the United Nations extended the current production agreement to December 2015, paving the way for expanding the collaboration and ensuring the necessary logistic support to continue *One Day on Earth* as an annual event. With this in mind, the community came together once again on 11/11/11 to film throughout the world and intends to hold its third annual filming event on 12/12/12. Of course, this begs the question, "what will be done in 2013?" To which the project organizers reply, "Keep the momentum going and pick a new day."

The impact

The philosophy of *One Day on Earth* is based on the principle that a collaborative community can share in a process to create insight and perspective. A more informed world is a critical element in making a more sustainable world. And by establishing a shared space of time, a one-day period, we can truly grasp the vastness of the human experience and begin to see the common threads of humanity in greater detail. The shared moment in time creates a fellowship that uncovers great reasons for empathy.

While the 104-minute feature film offers a fair and balanced look at many high priority issues, it is still just a single interpretation of the day's archive. For this reason, all participants have downloadable access to the archive and have been encouraged to share their versions.

The use of technology to connect interested participants and onlookers with ideas and projects, such as *One Day on Earth,* is pivotal in promoting the theory of global citizenship. Participants are given opportunities to not only expand their reach, but also to establish a communication pathway to the issue itself. When exercising this global muscle, it becomes clear that many local issues are actually tied to global issues.

The balance between what is picked for the headlines and what drives change and insight is always in flux. And while the big picture is actually a moving mosaic, *One Day on Earth* is a snapshot of that image of humanity and environment, no matter what angle you view it from.

Brandon Litman, Kyle Ruddick

One Day on Earth

One Day on Earth ist der erste Film, der an einem einzigen Tag in allen Ländern der Erde gedreht wurde. Dieses größte gemeinschaftliche Medienprojekt der Weltgeschichte schildert die Herausforderungen und Hoffnungen der Menschheit aus der Sicht einer Vielzahl von freiwilligen Filmemachern, verbunden durch ein partizipatorisches Experiment. Der Film zeigt eine stark ineinander verflochtene, ausufernde, gefahrvolle und großartige Welt.

One Day on Earth war immer von der Hoffnung getragen, Menschen in aller Welt dazu zu inspirieren, etwas Eigenes zu schaffen und es mit anderen zu teilen. Der Film ist die neue mediale Zeitkapsel der Welt. Bei seiner Herstellung waren wir mit der überwältigenden Aufgabe konfrontiert, eine Vielzahl unterschiedlicher Geschichten zur Geschichte der Welt zu verbinden, ein Unterfangen, dessen kreative Prozesse eine enorme Zuhör- und Entdeckungsbereitschaft erforderten.

Was wollte uns die Welt sagen? Wir nahmen die Sichtung der gesamten 3.000 Stunden Filmmaterial sehr ernst. Bei der Organisation des Materials kristallisierten sich bestimmte Themen heraus. Diese wiederum ordneten wir grob nach dem Zyklus des Lebens. Im Lauf der Arbeit fügten wir Statistiken zur Einleitung der einzelnen Themen als Hinweis auf die ungeheure Fülle gegenwärtigen Lebens auf unserem Planeten hinzu. Wir hoffen, der Film vermag seinem Publikum ein tieferes Verständnis dafür zu vermitteln, wie verflochten die Welt ist, in der wir leben, und welche erstaunlichen Möglichkeiten sich uns täglich bieten. Die Erde steht vor großen Herausforderungen. Wir glauben aber, dass die Menschheit die Chance hat, sich zu behaupten, und hoffen, dass uns dieses Projekt und dieser Film etwas über den Weg sagt, den wir gemeinsam gehen können.

Hintergrund

Das Projekt bringt die renommiertesten Non-Profit-Organisationen der Welt, Filmemacher, Studenten und andere engagierte Gruppen zusammen. Die Erfahrung des gleichzeitigen, gemeinsamen Filmens rund um den Globus ließ ein unglaubliches Zusammengehörigkeitsgefühl entstehen.

Was als kleine, über Plattformen wie Vimeo zusammengetrommelte Gruppe interessierter Filmemacher begann, weitete sich rasch zu einem weltumspannenden sozialen Netzwerk, dem auch verschiedene Non-Profit-Organisationen und die Vereinten Nationen angehören. Mithilfe von Ning, einer White-Label-Plattform zur Erstellung sozialer Netzwerke, lud *One Day on Earth* zur Teilnahme an einer Online-Community ein, die Interessierten nicht nur die Möglichkeit bot, ihre Pläne für eine Zusammenarbeit vorzustellen, sondern auch öffentliche Anerkennung für ihren Beitrag zu finden – ein wichtiger Faktor für den Erfolg des Projekts.

Von der Initiierung des Projekts bis zum Tag des eigentlichen Filmens bauten die Organisatoren bei der Erweiterung der Community und der Sicherstellung einer möglichst breiten und tiefen Berichterstattung über Themen und Kulturen aus aller Welt vor allem auf drei Bereiche: Bildungsinstitutionen, anlassbezogene Organisationen und professionelle Medienschaffende.

Einen großen Schub erhielt das Projekt im April 2010 mit dem ersten einer langen Reihe von

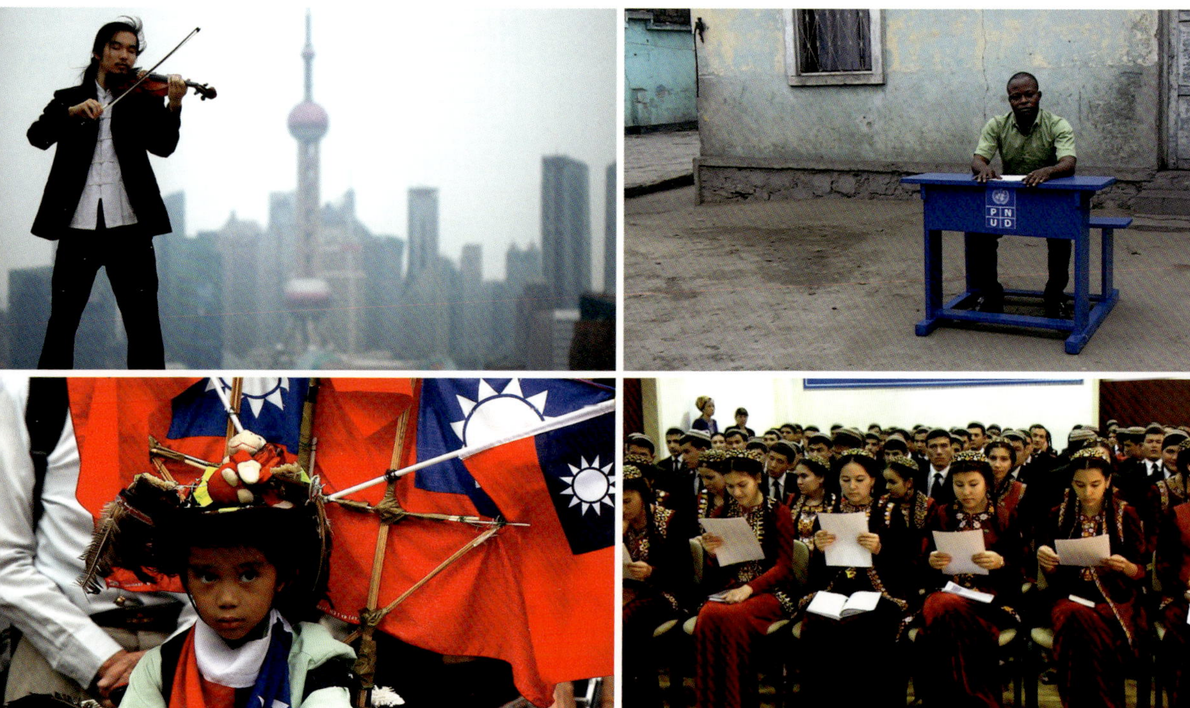

Arbeitsgesprächen mit den Vereinten Nationen. Es markierte den Anfang einer beispiellosen Produktionsvereinbarung, die *One Day on Earth* die Möglichkeit eröffnete, Kameras in alle Welt zu schicken und Bildmaterial aus Gegenden heranzuschaffen, in denen es keinen schnellen Internetzugang gab.

Nicht unerheblich für eine Community-basierte Bewegung war auch die Vermittlung des Projektziels und der Vision des Unterfangens; das geschah mithilfe eines Trailers, der aus Archivmaterial einzelner Projektteilnehmer zusammengestellt wurde. Die Aufforderung zur Bereitstellung von früheren Arbeiten war nicht nur eine Gelegenheit, das in der Community vorhandene ungeheure Talent zu zeigen, sondern auch das ernsthafte Interesse, das die Teilnehmer daran hatten, *One Day on Earth* zur Vermittlung vielfältiger und dringlicher Themen zu nutzen. Zudem zeigte es neu hinzukommenden Mitgliedern, mit welchem Engagement die Organisation ihr Ziel verfolgte.

Am 10.10.10 kam es dann zur Realisierung des ersten Film- und Medienprojekts, das das Leben an ein und demselben Tag in allen Ländern der Erde dokumentiert. Die dabei verwendete Aggregationstechnologie ermöglichte es den Teilnehmern, ihre Einreichungen mit Zusätzen und Anmerkungen zu versehen, was einen starken Einfluss auf die Sichtung des Materials hatte. Über 3.000 Stunden Filmmaterial kamen zustande, das es Minute für Minute zu sichten galt. Mehr als 240 Stunden Dialog in mindestens 75 Sprachen wurden übersetzt.

Als der Film Gestalt annahm, zeigte sich bald, dass er wichtige Themen durch den Kontext ein und desselben Tages auf eine nie zuvor gesehene Art und Weise vermittelte. Einer der populärsten Teile des Films ist die Musiksektion, die natürliche Klänge und musikalische Darbietungen eines Tages zu einer weltumspannenden Musikcollage verwebt.

Nach über 14 Monaten Schnitt hatte *One Day on Earth* schließlich am 22. April 2012, am Tag der Erde, seine historische Premiere. Mithilfe der Online-Community und der Vereinten Nationen wurde *One Day on Earth* an ein- und demselben Tag in 160 Ländern gezeigt – neuer Weltrekord. Während der Postproduktionsphase des Films verlängerten die Vereinten Nationen die bestehende Produktionsvereinbarung bis Dezember 2015. Das ebnete den Weg für eine Intensivierung der Zusammenarbeit und sicherte die notwendige logistische Unterstützung für eine jährliche Fortführung von *One Day on Earth*. Angesichts dieser Entwicklung kam die Community am 11.11.11 erneut zu weltweiten Dreharbeiten zusammen und will das jährliche Filmereignis am 12.12.12 zum dritten Mal stattfinden lassen. Da stellt sich natürlich die Frage, wie das 2013 weitergehen soll. Dazu die Projektorganisatoren: „Behalten wir den Schwung bei und suchen wir uns einen neuen Tag."

Wirkung

One Day on Earth geht vom Grundsatz aus, das es möglich ist, in einem kollaborativen Prozess neue Einsichten und Erkenntnisse zu generieren. Eine besser informierte Welt ist auch ein wesentlicher Faktor für die Schaffung einer nachhaltigeren Welt. Die Festlegung auf einen gemeinsamen Zeitraum – den Zeitraum eines Tages – versetzt uns in die Lage, das menschliche Dasein in seiner ganzen Fülle zu erfassen und einen klareren Begriff von den Gemeinsamkeiten zwischen den Menschen zu gewinnen. Durch den gemeinsamen Zeitraum entsteht ein das Einfühlungsvermögen förderndes Gefühl der Zusammengehörigkeit.

Der abendfüllende 104-Minuten-Film bietet zwar eine gute und ausgewogene Darstellung vieler vordringlicher Probleme, ist aber trotzdem lediglich eine von vielen möglichen Interpretationen des Tagesarchivs. Deshalb können auch alle Mitglieder Material aus dem Archiv downloaden und sie werden zum Erstellen und Weitergeben eigener Versionen ermutigt.

Die technologische Vernetzung interessierter Teilnehmer und Betrachter durch Ideen und Projekte wie *One Day on Earth* spielt eine wichtige Rolle für die Förderung des Weltbürgertums. Sie ermöglicht den Teilnehmern nicht nur eine Reichweitensteigerung, sondern auch die Öffnung eines Kommunikationskanals zum Thema selbst. Wer bei diesem globalen Spiel mitmischt, erkennt schnell, dass viele lokale Probleme eng mit den Problemen der Welt zusammenhängen. Das Verhältnis zwischen den Dingen, die in die Schlagzeilen kommen, und den eigentlichen Triebkräften von Wandel und Erkenntnis befindet sich ständig im Fluss. Wenn das Bild des großen Ganzen ein nie zur Ruhe kommendes Mosaik ist, so ist *One Day on Earth* eine Momentaufnahme dieses Mosaiks, egal aus welchem Blickwinkel man es betrachtet.

Aus dem Englischen von Wilfried Prantner

Arthur Lipsett–The Image Machine

Arthur Lipsett (1936–1986) was a Canadian avant-garde director of short collage films. In the 1960s he was employed as an animator by the National Film Board of Canada (NFB). Lipsett's particular passion was sound. He collected pieces of sound from a variety of sources and fit them together to create an interesting auditory sensation. His first short film *Very Nice, Very Nice* was nominated for the Academy Award for Best Short Subject, Live Action Subjects in 1962. Lipsett's meticulous editing and combination of audio and visual montage was both groundbreaking and influential to famous directors like Stanley Kubrick and George Lucas. In 1965, he completed *A Trip Down Memory Lane,* utilizing newsreel footage from over a fifty-year period, and intended as a kind of cinematic time capsule.

(Source: *http://en.wikipedia.org/wiki/Time_capsule*)

Arthur Lipsett, made visual poetry out of film that others threw away. Working as an editor at the National Film Board, he scavenged scraps of other people's documentaries from trash bins, intercutting shots of trapeze artists and runway models with his own footage of careworn faces passing on the streets of New York and Montreal.

(Source: Steve Silberman in *Wired* 13.05)

Arthur Lipsett (1936–1986) war ein kanadischer Experimentalfilmer, der durch seine collagenartigen Kurzfilme bekannt wurde. In den 1960ern war er als Schnitttechniker am National Film Board of Canada (NFB) beschäftigt. Er sammelte Tonfragmente aus unterschiedlichsten Quellen und montierte sie zu einem beeindruckenden Hörerlebnis. Sein erster Kurzfilm *Very Nice, Very Nice* wurde 1962 für den Oscar in der Kategorie bester Live-Action-Kurzfilm nominiert.
Lipsetts akribische Filmbearbeitung und die Kombination von akustischer und visueller Montage waren bahnbrechend und beeinflussten namhafte Regisseure wie Stanley Kubrick und George Lucas. 1965 stellte er den als eine Art cinematische Zeitkapsel konzipierten Film *A Trip Down Memory Lane* fertig, für den er Material aus Nachrichtensendungen von mehr als fünfzig Jahren verwendete.

(Quelle: *http://en.wikipedia.org/wiki/Time_capsule*)

Arthur Lipsett schuf aus Filmmaterial, das andere wegwarfen, visuelle Poesie. Er arbeitete als Cutter am National Film Board und las weggeworfene Filmschnipsel aus Dokumentarfilmen anderer auf, um sie mit Bildern von Trapezkünstlern und Models auf dem Laufsteg sowie eigenen Aufnahmen von sorgengeplagten Gesichtern in den Straßen New Yorks und Montreals zu kombinieren.

(Quelle: Steve Silberman in *Wired*, 13.05.)

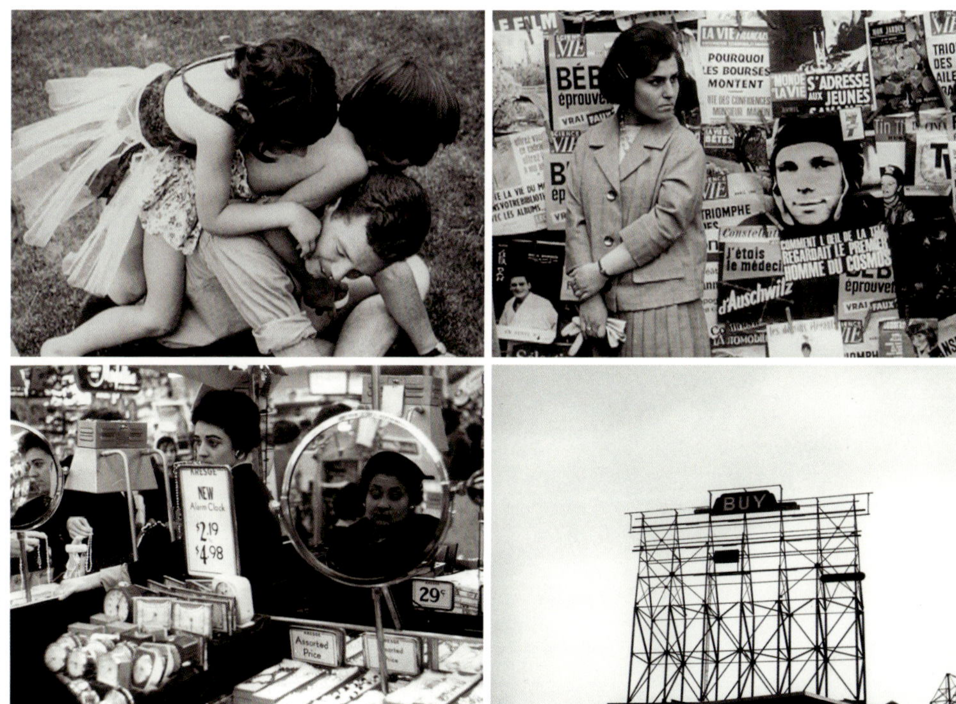

Very Nice, Very Nice

Arthur Lipsett's first film is an avant-garde blend of photography and sound. It looks behind the business-as-usual face we put on life and shows anxieties we want to forget. It is made of dozens of pictures that seem familiar, with fragments of speech heard in passing and, between times, a voice saying, "Very nice, very nice."

(Source: *http://www.nfb.ca/film/very_nice_very_nice/*, National Film Board of Canada)

Arthur Lipsetts erster Film basiert auf einem avantgardistischen Zusammenspiel von Fotografie und Sound. Der Film blickt hinter die Alltagsmaske des modernen Lebens und zeigt Ängste, die wir gerne verdrängen. Er besteht aus Dutzenden von vertrauten Bildern, ergänzt durch fragmentarische Aussagen von Passanten, und dazwischen ist eine Stimme zu hören, die sagt: „Very nice, very nice."

(Quelle: *http://www.nfb.ca/film/very_nice_very_nice/*, National Film Board of Canada)

A Trip Down Memory Lane

In this short film made by Arthur Lipsett in 1965 he looks at human might, majesty and mayhem. Compiled from some peculiar newsreel items of the last 50 years, the film-maker calls this a time capsule yet his arrangement of pictures makes it almost explosive. There are hundreds of items, once front-page stuff, but all wryly grotesque when seen in this reshuffle of the past.

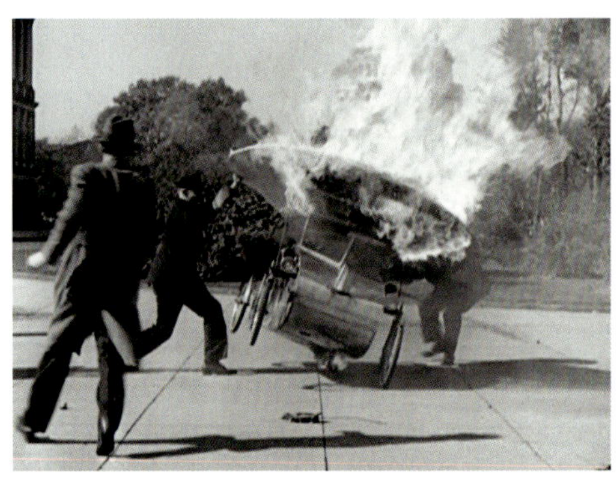

(Source: *http://www.nfb.ca/film/trip_down_memory_lane/*, National Film Board of Canada)

In diesem Kurzfilm aus dem Jahr 1965 thematisiert Arthur Lipsett das Streben des Menschen nach Höhenflügen und sein Scheitern. Der Filmemacher bezeichnete den aus kuriosen Nachrichten der letzten fünfzig Jahre zusammengestellten Film als Zeitkapsel. Durch das Arrangement der Bilder hat diese allerdings einen fast explosiven Charakter. Zu sehen sind Hunderte von Begebenheiten, die einst auf Titelseiten prangten und in diesem Remake der Vergangenheit seltsam grotesk anmuten.

(Quelle: *http://www.nfb.ca/film/trip_down_memory_lane/*, National Film Board of Canada)

21-87

21-87, is Lipsett's masterpiece. In it, he investigates the spiritual nature of humanity. The opening montage sets the scene: an X-ray of a skull cuts to a trapeze artist then to a corpse being cut up. The soundtrack moves from the drill and saw used to dismember corpses to a gospel performance of "Every child of God." Though there are some crowd shots, Lipsett emphasizes individuals throughout the film—street sweepers, department store customers riding an escalator, dancers. A voice states, "They become aware of a force behind this apparent mask in front of us. They call it God." Never allowing one thought to dominate, Lipsett contrasts that pronouncement with the satirical statement, "Then the people say, your number is *21-87* isn't it? Boy does that person really smile." It is often cited as an influence on George Lucas's Star Wars and his conceptualization of "The Force."

(Source: *http://www.nfb.ca/film/21-87/*, National Film Board of Canada)

21-87 ist Lipsetts Meisterwerk und setzt sich mit Spiritualität auseinander. Die Eröffnungssequenz steckt bereits den Rahmen ab: eine Röntgenaufnahme eines Schädels, Schnitt auf einen Trapezkünstler, dann auf einen Leichnam, der seziert wird. Der Soundtrack wechselt vom Bohren und Sägen, das beim Sezieren von Leichnamen zu hören ist, zu einer Gospelaufnahme von „Every child of God." Obwohl es auch Aufnahmen von Menschenmengen gibt, steht der Einzelne im Mittelpunkt des Films – Straßenkehrer, Kaufhauskunden auf der Rolltreppe, Tänzer. Eine Stimme sagt: „Sie werden hinter dieser sichtbaren Maske, die wir vor uns sehen, einer Kraft gewahr und sie nennen diese Gott." Lipsett, der nie zulässt, dass ein Gedanke dominiert, stellt dieser Äußerung ein satirisches Statement gegenüber: „Dann sagen die Leute, deine Nummer ist *21-87*, oder? Mann, beginnt die Person dann zu strahlen." *21-87* soll George Lucas für „Krieg der Sterne" und das Konzept *The Force* inspiriert haben.

(Quelle: *http://www.nfb.ca/film/21-87/*, National Film Board of Canada)

Aus dem Englischen von Wilfried Prantner

Pictures of Our World
Taken by Google Street View and Google Earth

Google Street View and Google Earth let you take a 'round-the-world trip in the privacy of your own home. Magnificent Caribbean beaches, the hustle and bustle of Times Square or your own hometown—pictures of the whole world are just a mouse click away. But note: these images' objective view is as beautiful as it is brutally honest. The arbitrariness of the captured moment and of its endless perspective reveals the synchronicity of both big and small moments of beauty as well as the world's dark side: prostitutes in a seemingly pristine vacation paradise; environmental pollution in a glitzy tourist metropolis; a solitary kiss amidst urban chaos. Here, viewers have a choice—beholding these images from a safe distance, or going on a journey of discovery of their own.

Eine Weltreise von zu Hause aus ermöglichen uns Google Street View und Google Earth. Karibische Traumstrände, der Trubel des Times Square oder der eigene Heimatort – Aufnahmen (aus) der ganzen Welt sind nur einen Mausklick entfernt. Doch der objektive Blick dieser Weltbilder ist genauso wunderschön wie gnadenlos ehrlich. Denn die Willkürlichkeit des aufgenommenen Augenblicks und seiner endlosen Blickwinkel enthüllt die Synchronität sowohl der kleinen und großen Momente der Schönheit als auch der Schattenseiten der Welt: Prostituierte im scheinbar unberührten Urlaubsparadies, Umweltverschmutzung in der glitzernden Touristenmetropole oder ein einsamer Kuss im urbanen Chaos. Der Betrachter hat dabei die Wahl, ob er sich die Bilder aus der sicheren Ferne anschauen will oder sich selbst auf Entdeckungsreise begibt.

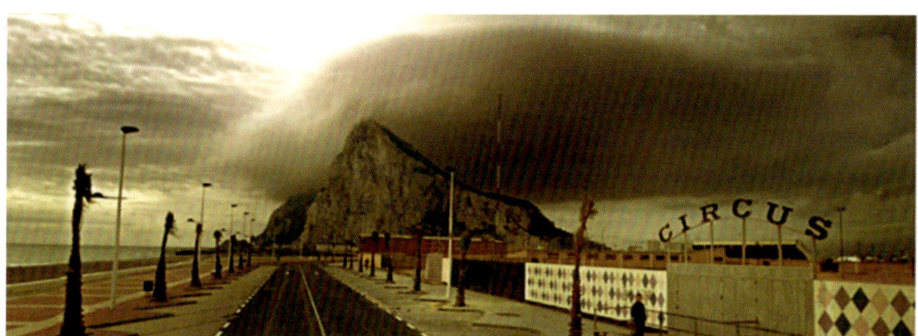

Aaron Hobson (US) combs through Google Street View in search of landscape photographs in which the image's aesthetics can easily stand up to comparison to the work of a pro. In doing so, he also calls into question the role of the photographer as the selective portrayer of our world.

Aaron Hobson (US) durchforstet Google Street View nach Landschaftsfotografien, deren Ästhetik der eines professionellen Fotografen in nichts nachstehen. Er hinterfragt damit zugleich die Rolle des Fotografen als selektiver Bildgeber unserer Welt.

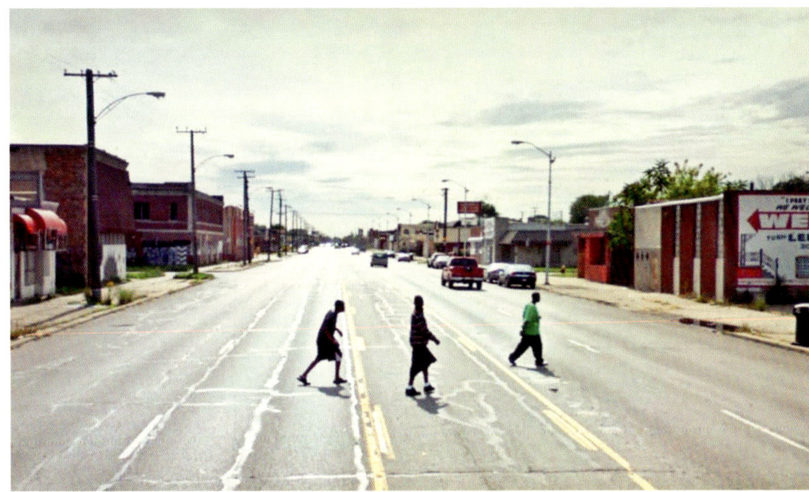

Doug Rickard (US) takes us on a trip through impoverished small-town America in *A New American Picture*. Voyeuristic scrutiny of the ruins of the American dream makes faces that software has rendered anonymous come across like intentionally selected stylistic devices.

Doug Rickard (US) nimmt in uns in *A New American Picture* auf eine Reise in die verarmten amerikanischen Vorstädte. Voyeuristische Blicke auf die Trümmer des amerikanischen Traumes lassen die von der Software anonymisierten Gesichter wie ein bewusstes Stilmittel wirken.

In his *Paris Street View* series, Michael Wolf (DE) captured intimate glimpses of urban life. One shot is of a couple kissing passionately amidst the maelstrom of metropolitan traffic. Another frames a brief moment of personal resistance against surveillance in the public sphere by Google's cameras.

Michael Wolf (DE) fing in der Reihe *Paris Street View* intime Großstadtszenen ein. So zeigen seine Aufnahmen sowohl ein sich im Verkehrstrubel der Metropole innig küssendes Paar, als auch einen kurzen Moment des persönlichen Widerstands gegen die Überwachung des öffentlichen Raumes durch die Google-Kameras.

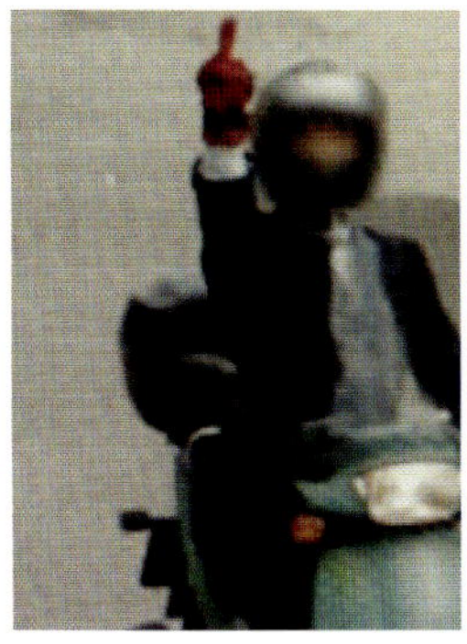

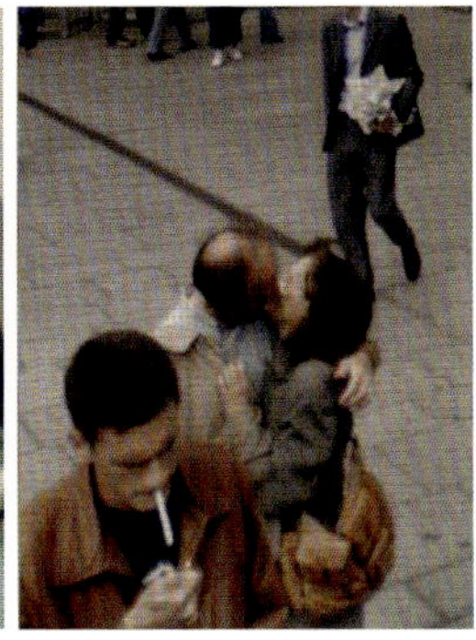

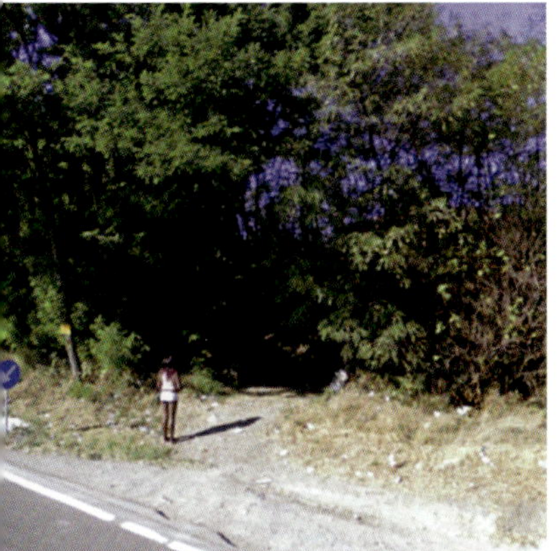

Mishka Henner (UK) decided to publish *No Man's Land*, Google Street View images of street prostitutes in Italy, after learning that members of online communities are using the service to find prostitutes. A sharp contrast is provided by his *Oil Fields* and *Cattle Farms* projects that feature macrovisions made up of individual high-definition images of environmental destruction and exploitation. Their aesthetics are vaguely reminiscent of abstract expressionism.

Mishka Henner (UK) entschied sich dazu, Google-Street-View-Aufnahmen von Straßenprostituierten in Italien unter dem Namen *No Man's Land* zu veröffentlichen, als er herausfand, dass Online-Communities den Service nutzten, um Prostituierte zu finden. Seine Projekte *Oil Fields* und *Cattle Farms* dagegen zeigen aus einer Vielzahl von hochauflösenden Einzelbildern zusammengesetzte Makrovisionen von Umweltzerstörung und -ausbeutung, deren Ästhetik fast an abstrakten Expressionismus erinnert.

Text: Tobias Kösters

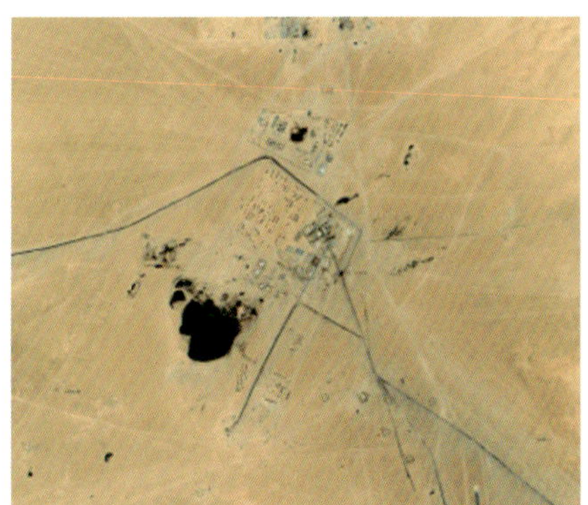

Oil field in Libya during the war
Ölfeld in Lybien während dem Krieg

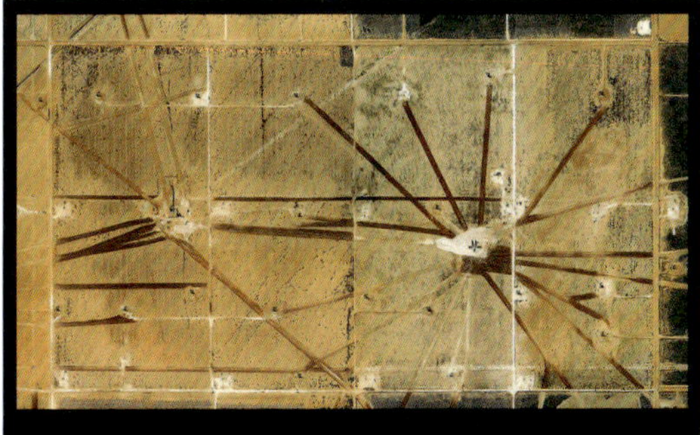

US oil pumping stations
US-Ölpumpstationen

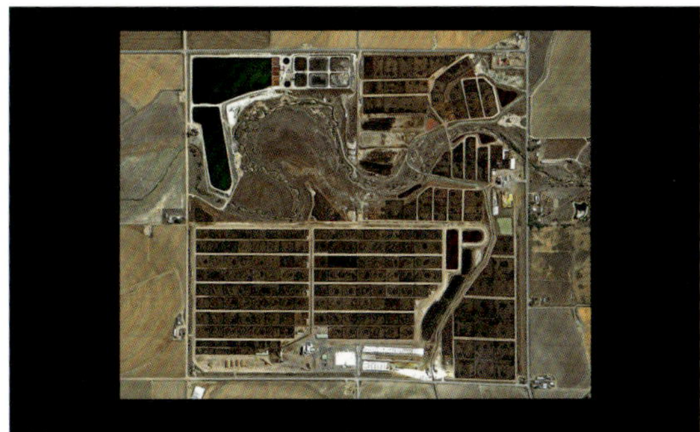

US mega-farm (100,000 head of cattle, liquid manure pit top left)
US Riesenfarm (100,000 Kühe, Jauchegrube oben links)

The Big Picture of 3.11

The Great East Japan Earthquake on 11 March 2011 made it a fateful year for the Japanese people. It is the winners of the Japan Media Arts Festival 2011 who were selected for the Ars Electronica Festival 2012. In the aftermath of the earthquake, each project reveals a unique perspective on the world and the individual and provokes reflection about what "the big picture of 3.11" is.

Das Erdbeben vom 11.3.2011 war ein schicksalsträchtiges Ereignis für Japan. Die Gewinner des Japan Media Arts Festival 2011 wurden ausgewählt, ihre Projekte im Rahmen der Ars Electronica 2012, THE BIG PICTURE – Weltbilder für die Zukunft, zu präsentieren. Vor dem Hintergrund des Erdbebens betrachtet jedes Projekt die Welt und den Menschen aus einer anderen Perspektive und lässt uns darüber nachdenken, wie diese Katastrophe im großen Ganzen, als „The Big Picture 3.11", gesehen werden kann.

micro sievert: Visualization of environmental radiation levels in the Kanto region, Japan

YOSHIHARA Jun / OGAWA Yukihiro / Junko & Richard HOLBROOK / CHONO Kaoru

micro sievert depicts radiation data like rain to visualize the impact of 3.11. It is a web service designed to present visual, easily understood information on radiation levels and potential dangers arising from the nuclear accident at the Fukushima Daiichi Nuclear Power Plant following the Great East Japan Earthquake on March 11, 2011. Based on readings of environmental radioactivity levels, the site presents radiation levels for the Fukushima Prefecture and the Kanto region in an easy-to-understand visual form using Flash and HTML5.

micro sievert stellt zur Visualisierung der Ereignisse des 11.3.2011 Strahlenwerte in Form von Regen dar. Dieser Webservice erlaubt die Darstellung visueller, einfach erfassbarer Informationen zur Strahlenbelastung und zu möglichen Gefahren nach der Unfallserie im Atomkraftwerk Fukushima Daiichi, die mit dem schweren Erdbeben vom 11. März 2011 im Osten Japans ihren Anfang nahm. Strahlenmesswerte des japanischen Ministeriums für Bildung, Kultur, Sport, Wissenschaft und Technik dienen als Grundlage für eine einfach verständliche, mittels Flash und HTML5 visualisierte Darstellung der Strahlenbelastung in der Präfektur Fukushima und der Region Kanto.

Jury Selection / 15th Japan Media Arts Festival 2011 Art Division

microsievert.net

Tunagaru-TENKI

KATAYAMA Yoshiyuki

This website shows weather conditions from August 2010 to July 2011, which have been edited into one video, including photographs. *Tunagaru-TENKI* seamlessly archives the daily weather over a one-year period. Everyone has experienced looking up at the sky and gazing at the vast space above. We know that this sky is constantly changing and we often see photographs, paintings and videos that capture images of these changes. At the same time, however, we are also aware that these images are always presented as fragments and that these images do not really capture the whole sky. This work archives the spectacular changes and vastness of the sky. In the Web's seemingly infinite connectedness, we can see the weather's connectedness, extending in all directions through time and space. Photographs from March 11, 2011 are included, but by selecting only completely mundane, everyday scenes in which everything appears to be normal and joining them together, the creator depicts the steady contours of our lives.

Auf dieser Website wird der Wetterverlauf im Zeitraum eines Jahres (August 2010 bis Juli 2011) durch nahtlos aneinandergereihte und zu einem Video montierte Bilder dargestellt. Wer hat noch nie zum Himmel geblickt und die sich endlos erstreckende Weite bewundert? Wir sind uns der ständigen Veränderungen am Himmel bewusst, die regelmäßig in Fotografien, Bildern und Videos dokumentiert werden. Gleichzeitig wissen wir, dass derartige Darstellungen immer nur Fragmente der Realität sind und nie das ganze Firmament in Bildern einfangen können. *Tunagaru-TENKI* dokumentiert auf spektakuläre Weise die Unbeständigkeit und Weite des Himmels. In der scheinbar unendlichen Vernetztheit des Webs spiegelt sich die Vernetztheit des Wetters wider, das sich durch Raum und Zeit hinweg in alle Richtungen erstreckt. Die Fotostrecke inkludiert auch den 11. März 2011. Gezeigt werden allerdings nur profane Ausschnitte des täglichen Lebens, in denen alles seinen gewohnten Gang zu gehen scheint. Durch die nahtlose Aneinanderreihung dieser Bilder zeichnet der Künstler die festen Konturen unseres Lebens nach.

Excellence Prize / 15th Japan Media Arts Festival 2011 Art Division

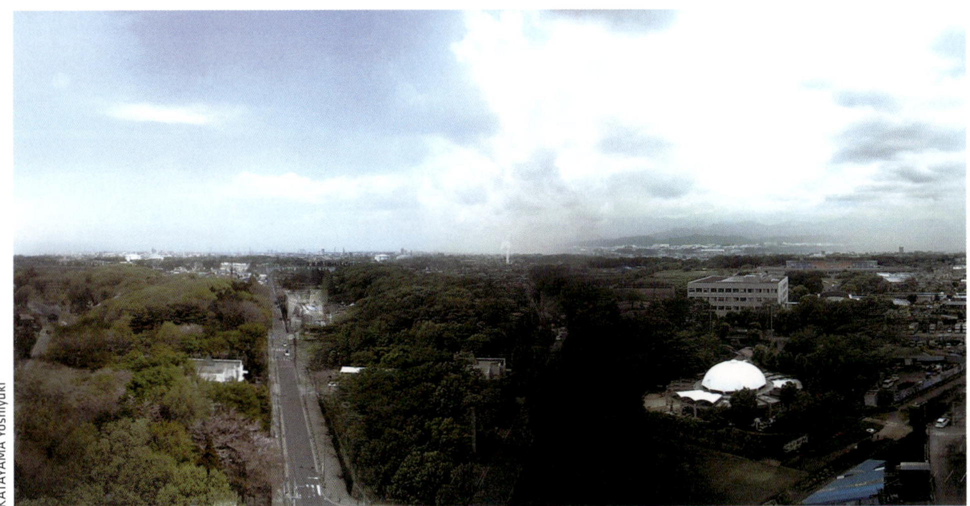

KATAYAMA Yoshiyuki

The Museum of Me

TANAKA Koichiro / TANIGAWA Eiji / SAITO Seiichi / SAKAMOTO Masanori / MURAYAMA Ken

One of the topics for 2011 was how social networking services like Twitter and Facebook have infiltrated our lives and become an indispensable kind of infrastructure. *The Museum of Me* is incorporated into Facebook and the user's previous Facebook activities, photographs of friends and other information and videos, are displayed in various forms–like works of art that are exhibited in a museum just for oneself. By visualizing the changing links between oneself and others, as well as the communication itself, a once-in-a-lifetime visual experience is created. It is stirring to see one's network of friends visually constructed from Facebook wall photographs that express each individual's unique social environment.

Eines der beherrschenden Themen von 2011 war, wie soziale Netzwerke wie Twitter und Facebook sich in unser Leben eingeschlichen haben und für viele unverzichtbar geworden sind. Das *Museum of Me* ist eine Facebook-Applikation, die Informationen, Videos, Facebook-Aktivitäten des Nutzers und Fotos seiner Facebook-Freunde wie Kunstwerke in einem Museum arrangiert, die sich nur um die eigene Person dreht. Durch die Visualisierung der wechselnden Beziehungen zwischen sich selbst und den anderen sowie der sich ändernden Kommunikationsmuster auf Facebook taucht man in eine einzigartige visuelle Welt ein. Verblüfft nimmt man den aus Fotos von der Facebook-Pinnwand visuell rekonstruierten eigenen Freundeskreises wahr und erkennt sich selbst als Teil eines einzigartigen sozialen Netzwerks.

Excellence Prize / 15th Japan Media Arts Festival 2011 Entertainment Division

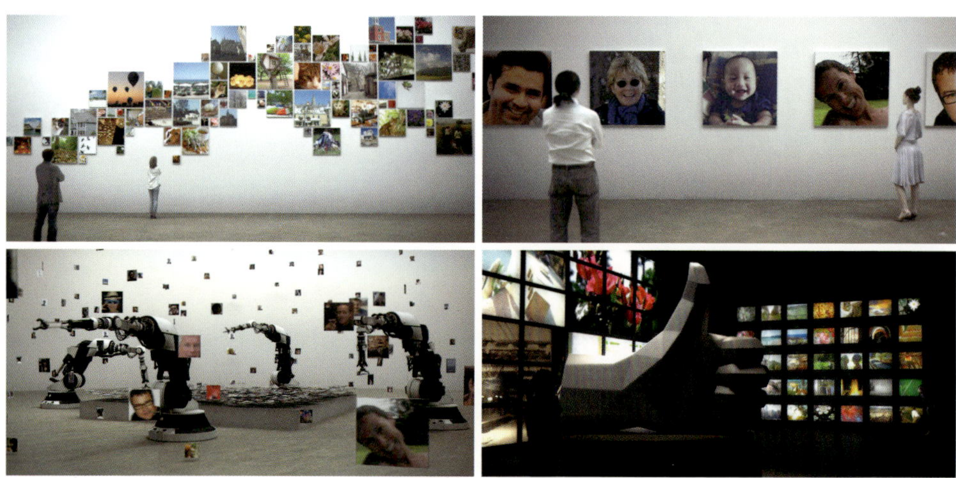

Projector, Intel Corporation

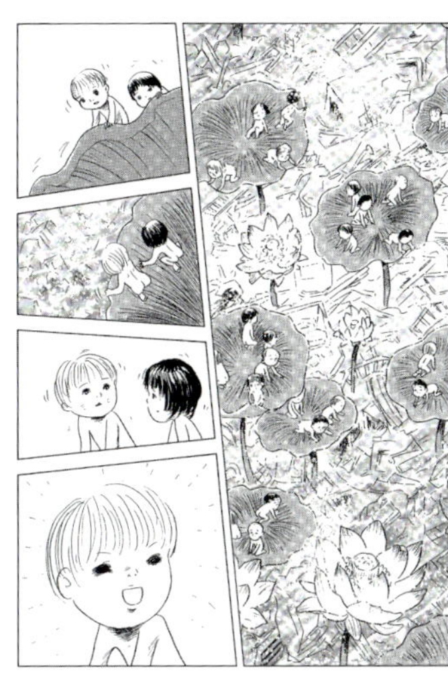 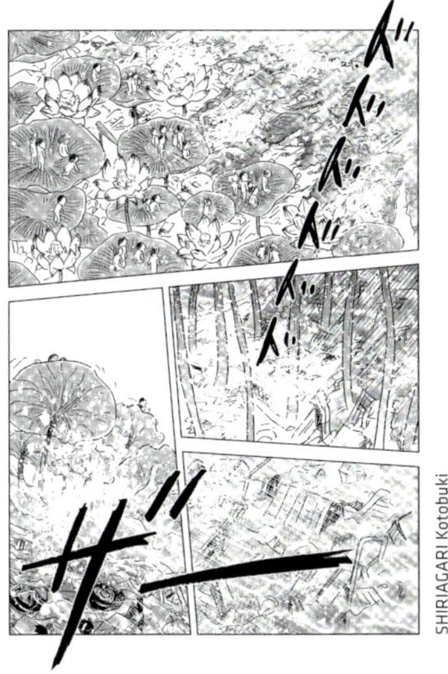

Ano-hi kara no Manga; Manga after 3.11
SHIRIAGARI Kotobuki

Were we just living in a dream world before 3.11? Is the nightmarish present the true reality? From mass media to artwork, that day transformed everything, making it seem like hollow fiction. Manga artist, SHIRIAGARI Kotobuki embraced the new reality and expressed it in post 3.11 Manga, without succumbing to either criticism or despair. Amongst the four-frame manga published each day in the evening edition of the Asahi Shimbun were many that depicted the real state of mind and behavior of people at the time, based on the artist's personal experiences as a volunteer in the disaster-struck area. Moreover, the new awareness, the fear, the sense of hopelessness and the sadness that have afflicted every Japanese since the nuclear power plant disaster have found all sorts of expressive forms. That a manga can turn even the nuclear power plant itself into a character and depict this horrific incident with such extraordinary realism is nothing short of incredible. The work expresses the emotions of that time—which will never be forgotten—but may also provide cathartic release and offer a perspective for reconstruction and the future.

Haben wir vor dem 11.3.2011 in einer Traumwelt gelebt? Ist der Albtraum der Gegenwart die wahre Realität? Dieser Tag veränderte alles, von den Massenmedien bis zur Kunst, ließ alles zur blassen Fiktion werden. Der Manga-Künstler SHIRIAGARI Kotobuki tauchte in diese neue Realität ein und hielt sie in Mangas fest, ohne dabei in Kritik oder Hoffnungslosigkeit zu versinken. Von den 4-Panel-Mangas, die jeden Tag in der Abendausgabe der Tageszeitung *Asahi Shimbun* erschienen, thematisierten viele den Gemütszustand und das Verhalten der Menschen nach dem Erdbeben, wie der Künstler sie als freiwilliger Helfer bei seinen Einsätzen im Krisengebiet erlebt hatte. Das neue Bewusstsein, die Angst, Hoffnungslosigkeit und Traurigkeit, die nach der Unfallserie im Atomkraftwerk Fukushima Daiichi die Japaner begleiten, finden in verschiedenen Formen der künstlerischen Darstellung Ausdruck. Dass ein Manga, in dem sogar das Kernkraftwerk als Manga-Figur dargestellt wird, den katastrophalen Super-GAU im Atomkraftwerk derart realistisch darzustellen vermag, ist eine grandiose Meisterleistung. Es ruft die Emotionen jener Zeit wieder in Erinnerung – die nie in Vergessenheit geraten dürfen –, und bietet gleichzeitig sowohl eine Möglichkeit der Katharsis wie auch eine Zukunftsperspektive für den Wiederaufbau.

Excellence Prize / 15th Japan Media Arts Festival 2011 Manga Division

Aus dem Englischen von Sonja Pöllabauer

Manfred Litzlbauer

Global-Mind-Spirit

Global Spirituality and Global Consciousness – Evidence on the Internet

Spirituality and consciousness are extant themes that are, nevertheless, difficult to grasp. Spirituality in particular is something that is very often experienced in an esoteric context. From a theological point of view, this phenomenon is connected with locations and actions. One of these locations is the internet, which has taken on a real existence. In a globalized world pervaded by a data network, spirituality could be found there as well.

This work conducts research on spirituality and consciousness in a global framework as manifested by evidence found on the internet. To accomplish this, a special context-oriented graphic browser was developed. This made it possible to scrutinize and analyze various domains (entities) within a predefined conceptual framework. The browser functions like a radar screen—for each link found, it renders in graphic form a point within the prescribed context.

The context for spirituality and consciousness was worked out on the basis of relevant literature that deals with this global phenomenon. Four English-language terms as variables were allocated to each of the eight variables for spirituality generated in this way. It was within this framework that an internet search based on five global phenomena was carried out. From a systemic point of view, global phenomena are those that display long-distance effects, side-effects and non-linearity. The fields selected were global problem areas, (Illustration 3), powerful persons, strongest brand names, and worldwide cinematic films. As for the reference to spirituality, there were the traditional major world religions as well as a few newer spiritual movements.

The analysis of the 50 results that were generated display varying densities in the individual domains. The field of global problems displays a very high level of intensity. It would thus be quite justifiable to maintain that humankind is also dealing with them very intensively from a spiritual perspective. At least, the consciousness of global problems is very intensive. Among global brands, more recently founded enterprises and technologically oriented companies are the ones with spiritual substance. This is generally higher among the personalities investigated. The highest density of spirituality is attributable to His Holiness the Dalai Lama (Illustration 2). Contrary to expectations, global films display little creativity. The dimension of creativity is likewise underdeveloped among globally powerful personalities. It can generally be concluded that "the godly and holy" (Illustration 4) is the dominant magnitude in all domains. Power and fear are likewise very pronounced and especially prevalent among the personalities. The overall picture (Illustration 1) of all domains analyzed offers the possibility of working out patterns, irregularities and interrelationships with respect to global spirituality and global consciousness.

This project is an interdisciplinary work of theology, computer science and business. It was carried out in conjunction with the Spiritual Theology in an Intercultural Context master's program. The author received input from the Universities of Salzburg and Linz and Energie AG Oberösterreich Data GmbH. This project was subsidized by the Austrian Federal Ministry for Transport, Innovation and Technology.
Scholarly Fundamentals, Spirituality: University of Salzburg, Center for Intercultural Theology and Study of Religions, Prof. Ulrich Winkler
Master's Thesis Project Work by Manfred Litzlbauer: University of Salzburg, Department of Systematic and Ecumenical Theology, Prof. Hans-Joachim Sander
Computer Science and Software Development: University of Linz's Department of Information Processing and Microprocessor Technology, Prof. Jörg Mühlbacher, Asst. Prof. Florian König
Project assistants: Energie OÖ Data GmbH, Markus Fellhofer, Josef Beham, Andrea Kraft-Pils
Search engine: YAHOO!Search

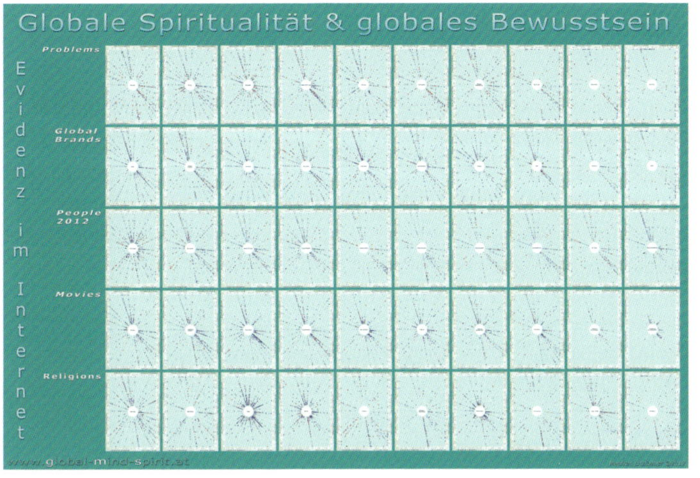

Globale Spiritualität & globales Bewusstsein
Evidenz im Internet
Problems
Global Brands
People 2012
Movies
Religions
www.global-mind-spirit.at

WELTETHOS & VERANTWORTUNG
BEZIEHUNG & EMPATHIE
WISDOM
ETHOS
RESPONSIBLE
OBLIGATE
HUMANITY
RELATIONS
EMPATHY
TRUST
DEVOTION
ERLEUCHTUNG & ERKENNTNIS
ENLIGHTENMENT
CONSCIOUS
COGNITION
GÖTTLICHE & HEILIGE
GOD
BLESSED
SACRED
CREATIVITY
KREATIVITÄT & DESIGN
DESIGN
VISION
INSPIRATION
ACHTSAMKEIT & MITGEFÜHL
MINDFUL
COMPASSION
Dalai Lama
HOLY
POWER
FORCE
ANXIETY
FEAR
ABSOLUTE
ENTIRE
INTEGRAL
WHOLENESS
FEELING
AWARE
ANGST & MACHT
EINS SEIN & NONDUALITÄT

WELTETHOS & VERANTWORTUNG
BEZIEHUNG & EMPATHIE
WISDOM
ETHOS
RESPONSIBLE
OBLIGATE
HUMANITY
RELATIONS
EMPATHY
TRUST
DEVOTION
ERLEUCHTUNG & ERKENNTNIS
ENLIGHTENMENT
CONSCIOUS
COGNITION
GÖTTLICHE & HEILIGE
GOD
BLESSED
SACRED
CREATIVITY
KREATIVITÄT & DESIGN
DESIGN
VISION
INSPIRATION
ACHTSAMKEIT & MITGEFÜHL
MINDFUL
COMPASSION
Poverty
HOLY
POWER
FORCE
ANXIETY
FEAR
ABSOLUTE
ENTIRE
INTEGRAL
WHOLENESS
FEELING
AWARE
ANGST & MACHT
EINS SEIN & NONDUALITÄT

(1)

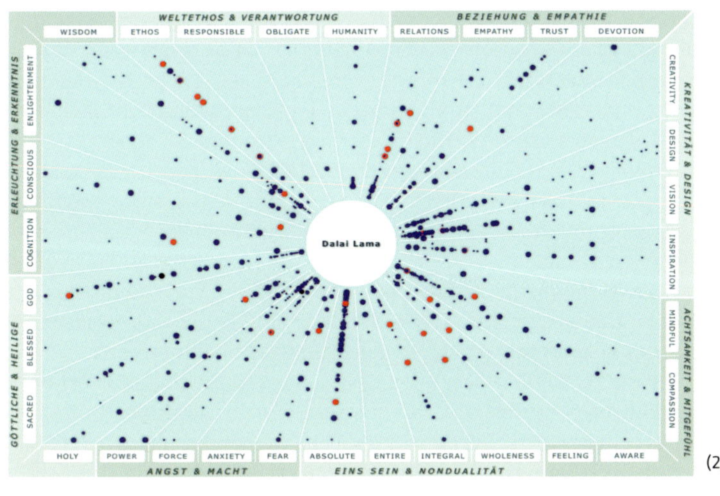

(2)

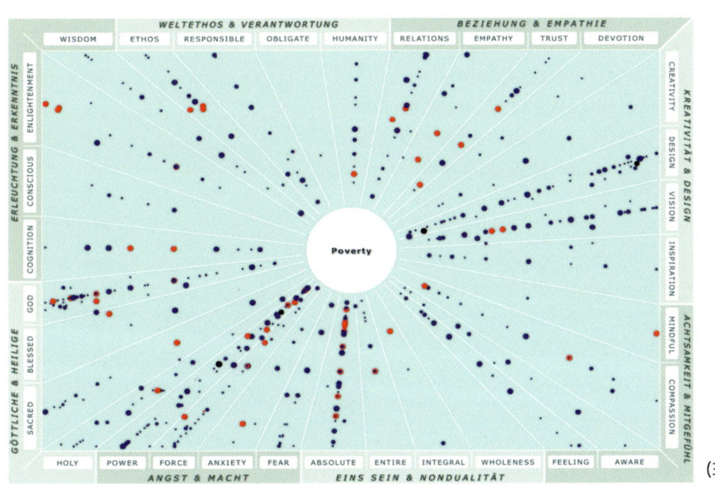

(3)

Globale Spiritualität und globales Bewusstsein – Evidenz im Internet

Spiritualität und Bewusstsein sind existente Themen, die allerdings schwer greifbar sind. Gerade Spiritualität ist ein Thema, welches sehr häufig im esoterischen Kontext erlebt wird. Aus theologischer Sicht ist dieses Phänomen an Orte und Handlungen gebunden. Einer dieser Orte ist das Internet, welches zwischenzeitlich zu einer realen Existenz geworden ist. In einer globalen Welt, die vom Datennetz durchdrungen ist, könnte Spiritualität auch dort gefunden werden.

Die vorliegende Arbeit beschäftigt sich damit, Spiritualität und Bewusstsein im globalen Rahmen als Evidenz im Internet zu erforschen. Für diesen Zweck wurde ein spezieller kontextorientierter grafischer Browser entwickelt. Damit war es möglich, in einem vordefinierten begrifflichen Rahmen verschiedene Domains (Entitäten) durchzusehen und zu analysieren. Der Browser funktioniert ähnlich einem Radarbildschirm und zeichnet in grafischer Form für jeden gefundenen Link einen Punkt innerhalb des vorgegebenen Kontexts.

Der Kontext für Spiritualität und Bewusstsein wurde anhand von einschlägiger Literatur, die sich mit diesem globalen Phänomen auseinandersetzt, herausgearbeitet. Den so gefundenen acht Variablen für Spiritualität wurden jeweils vier englischsprachige Begriffe als Variable zugeordnet. In diesem Rahmen wurde dann die Suche – basierend auf fünf globalen Phänomenen – durchgeführt. Aus systemischer Sicht sind globale Phänomene solche, die über Fernwirkung, Nebenwirkung und Nichtlinearität verfügen. Ausgewählt wurden die Bereiche „globale Problemfelder" (Bild 3), „mächtige Personen", „stärkste Markennamen" und „weltweite Kinofilme". Als Referenz zur Spiritualität kamen noch die großen traditionellen Weltreligionen und einige neuere spirituelle Bewegungen hinzu.

Die Analyse von 50 vorliegenden Ergebnissen zeigen unterschiedliche Dichten in den einzelnen Domains. Eine sehr große Intensität haben die Felder der globalen Probleme. Man könnte also durchaus zur Meinung kommen, dass sich die Menschheit auch aus spiritueller Sicht intensiv damit auseinandersetzt, zumindest ist das Bewusstsein über globale Probleme sehr intensiv. Bei globalen Marken sind es jüngere Unternehmen und eher Technologieunternehmen, die spirituellen Gehalt haben. Dieser ist bei den untersuchten Persönlichkeiten generell höher. Mit der höchsten Dichte an Spiritualität ist seine Heiligkeit der Dalai Lama (Bild 2) anzuführen. Entgegen der Erwartungen haben globale Filme wenig Kreativität. Ebenso ist die Dimension Kreativität bei den global mächtigen Persönlichkeiten unterentwickelt. Generell ist festzustellen, dass „das Göttliche und Heilige" (Bild 4) die dominante Größe in allen Domains ist. Macht und Angst sind ebenfalls sehr stark ausgeprägt und insbesondere bei den Persönlichkeiten vorherrschend. Das Gesamtbild (Bild 1) über alle analysierten Domains bietet die Möglichkeit Muster, Fehlstellen und Zusammenhänge über globale Spiritualität und globales Bewusstsein zu bearbeiten.

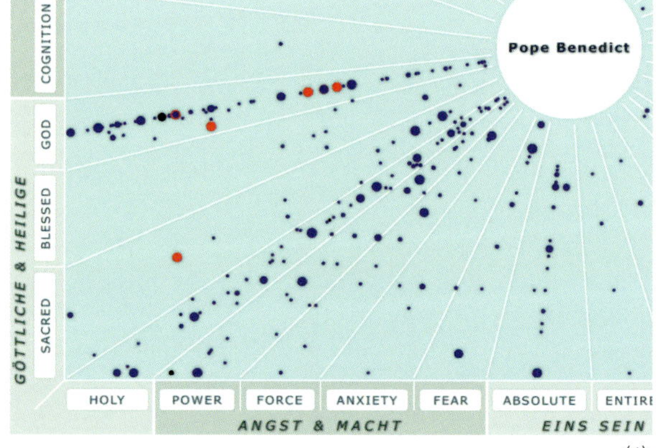

(4)

Wandering Eyes
Video Art from Shanghai

The Landesgalerie is screening *The cold winter* (102 min., 2012), Zheng Kuo's documentary film that Ella Raidel has selected as a special featured presentation at the Festival. The film depicts a group of artists' struggle to preserve their atelier located near Beijing's famous 798 Art Zone. In 2009-10, several such gallery districts were forcibly cleared by the government. The film shows how artists fended off the incursions and orders to vacate the premises. They resisted with public demonstrations and performances. It was a frigid winter in which their electricity and heat were turned off. And as if that weren't enough, over the course of the negotiations, the artists became embroiled in an increasingly intractable dispute among themselves too. The resistance they sought to put up against the power of the state spawned an internecine power struggle.

This film screening is part of a lineup of special events accompanying the *Wandering Eyes: Video Art from Shanghai* exhibition that's running at the Landesgalerie during the Ars Electronica Festival and features works by Liang Yue, Lin Zhele, Ling Yingjie, Miao Ying, Qiu Anxiong, Yang Fudong. This show is the outcome of an agreement the Province of Upper Austria's gallery reached with the Shanghai Art Museum to cooperatively stage exhibitions. Following screenings on site, curators selected six videos.

The works by a young generation of media artists function on various formal, dramaturgical and substantive levels in elaborating on political, social and cultural processes of change in China. As part of an ongoing effort by Landesgalerie Linz to develop a series of exhibitions that are completely site-specific and take creative new approaches to displaying works of art, two project decisions were reached. First, the Landesgalerie awarded a work & travel grant to Norbert Artner, an artist living in Linz and Berlin. This funding enabled him to visit Shanghai, Beijing and Hangzhou to photograph the ateliers and working situations of the Chinese artists showcased in *Wandering Eyes* and thereby develop the *Studios / China / 2012* contribution to that exhibition. The second was to engage Viennese artist Karl-Heinz Klopf to conceive the exhibition architecture. The design concept that he came up with is itself a take on transformation, one in which the transport containers morphed into sculpturally conceived video boxes arranged on the premises of the Landesgalerie. Accordingly, the *Wandering Eyes: Video Art from Shanghai* exhibition encompasses a fascinating array of translational strategies manifested by individual and collective spaces in which to experience Chinese identities.

Shanghai Art Museum, Landesgalerie Linz; films selected by Ella Raidel

Wandering Eyes
Videokunst aus Shanghai

Als speziellen Beitrag zum Festival präsentiert die Landesgalerie den Dokumentarfilm *The cold winter* (102 Min., 2012) von Zheng Kuo. Dieser von Ella Raidel ausgewählte Film zeigt den Kampf einer Gruppe von KünstlerInnen um ihre Ateliers in der Nähe der bekannten Kunstzone Pekings 798. In der Zeit von 2009/2010 wurden mehrere dieser Atelierbezirke von der Regierung geräumt. Der Film zeigt, wie sich die KünsterInnen gegen die Räumung und Einmischung wehren. Mit öffentlichen Demonstrationen und Performances wollen sie Widerstand leisten. Es herrscht ein extrem kalter Winter, und man dreht ihnen auch noch den Strom und die Heizung ab. Im Laufe der Verhandlungen geraten auch die KünstlerInnen unter einander in einen immer vertrackteren Streit. Der Widerstand, den sie gegen die Staatsgewalt richten wollten, mündet in einem persönlichen Machtkampf.

Die Filmpräsentation ist Teil des Begleitprogrammes zur ebenfalls während des Ars Electronica Festivals laufenden Ausstellung *Wandering Eyes – Videokunst aus Shanghai* mit Arbeiten von Liang Yue, Lin Zhele, Ling Yingjie, Miao Ying, Qiu Anxiong und Yang Fudong in der Landesgalerie. Diese Ausstellung ist Ergebnis einer mit dem Shanghai Art Museum getroffenen Vereinbarung über die Realisierung einer Ausstellungskooperation beider Institutionen. Nach einer Sichtung vor Ort wurde eine Auswahl von sechs Videoarbeiten getroffen.

Die Werke einer jungen Generation von MedienkünstlerInnen vermitteln auf unterschiedlichen formalen, dramaturgischen und inhaltlichen Ebenen politische, gesellschaftliche und kulturelle Veränderungsprozesse in China. Im Sinne des permanenten Versuchs der Landesgalerie Linz, ihr gesamtes Ausstellungsprogramm ortsbezogen und mit einem speziellen Displayanliegen zu entwickeln, erfolgten zwei Projektentscheidungen: Erstens vergab die Landesgalerie ein Arbeits- und Reisestipendium an den in Linz und Berlin lebenden Künstler Norbert Artner. Dank dieses Stipendiums konnte er in Shanghai, Peking und Hangzhou die Ateliers bzw. Arbeitssituationen der chinesischen KünstlerInnen des Projektes *Wandering Eyes* fotografieren und somit auch den Ausstellungsbeitrag *Studios / China / 2012* entwickeln. Die zweite Projektentscheidung galt der Einbindung des in Wien lebenden Künstlers Karl-Heinz Klopf für die Konzeption des Ausstellungsdisplays. Seine Gestaltungsidee erwies sich dabei selbst als eine Transformationsüberlegung, die die Form von Transportcontainern in skulptural gedachte und installativ in der Landesgalerie arrangierte Videoboxen übersetzte. In Summe definiert die Ausstellung *Wandering Eyes: Videokunst aus Shanghai* ein spannendes Spektrum von Übersetzungsstrategien an individuellen und kollektiven Erfahrungsräumen chinesischer Identitäten.

Text: Martin Hochleitner

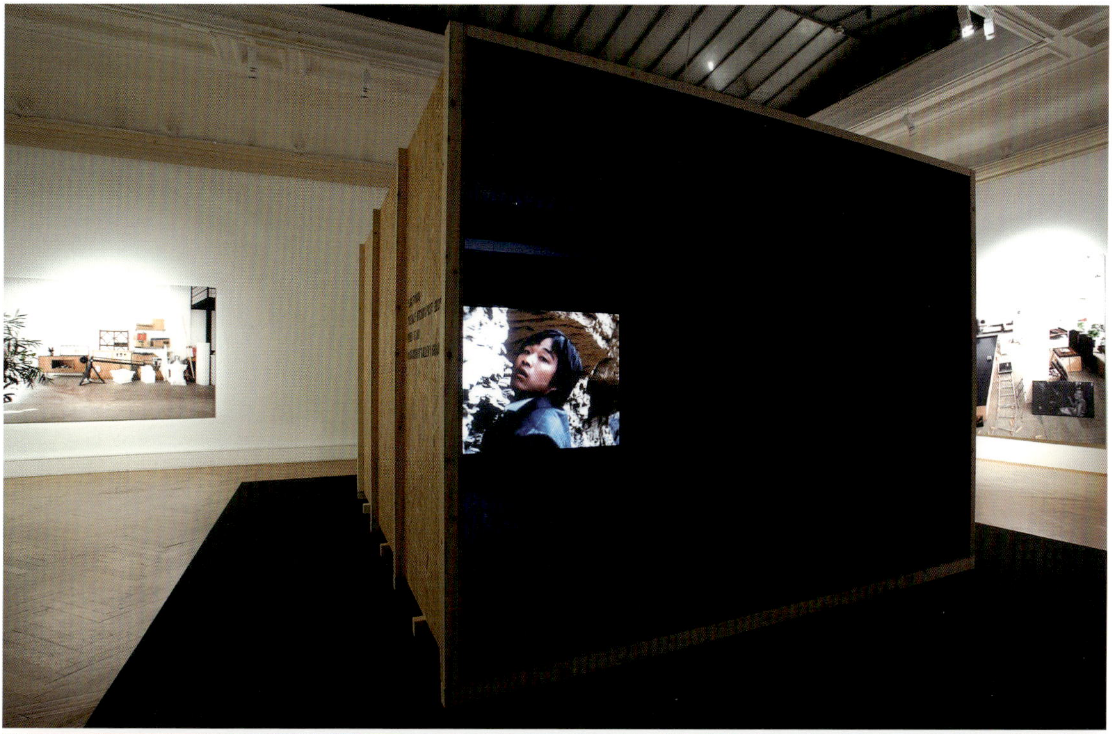

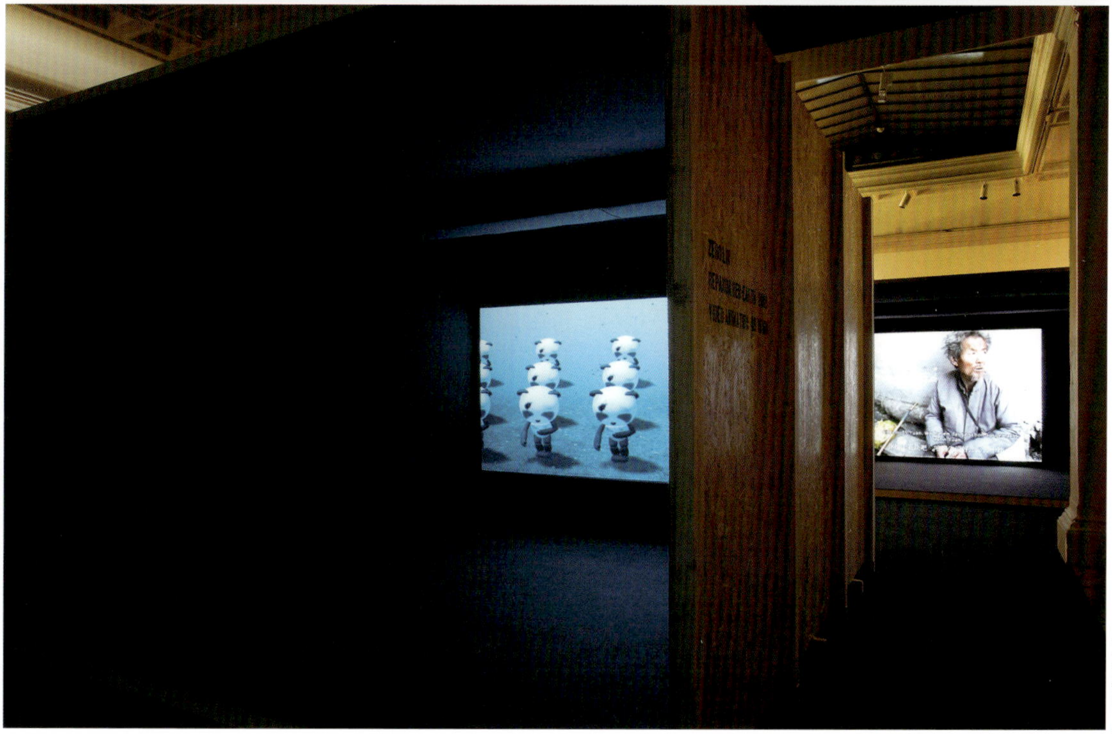

View of the *Wandering Eyes – Video Art from Shanghai* exhibition at Landesgalerie Linz, 2012

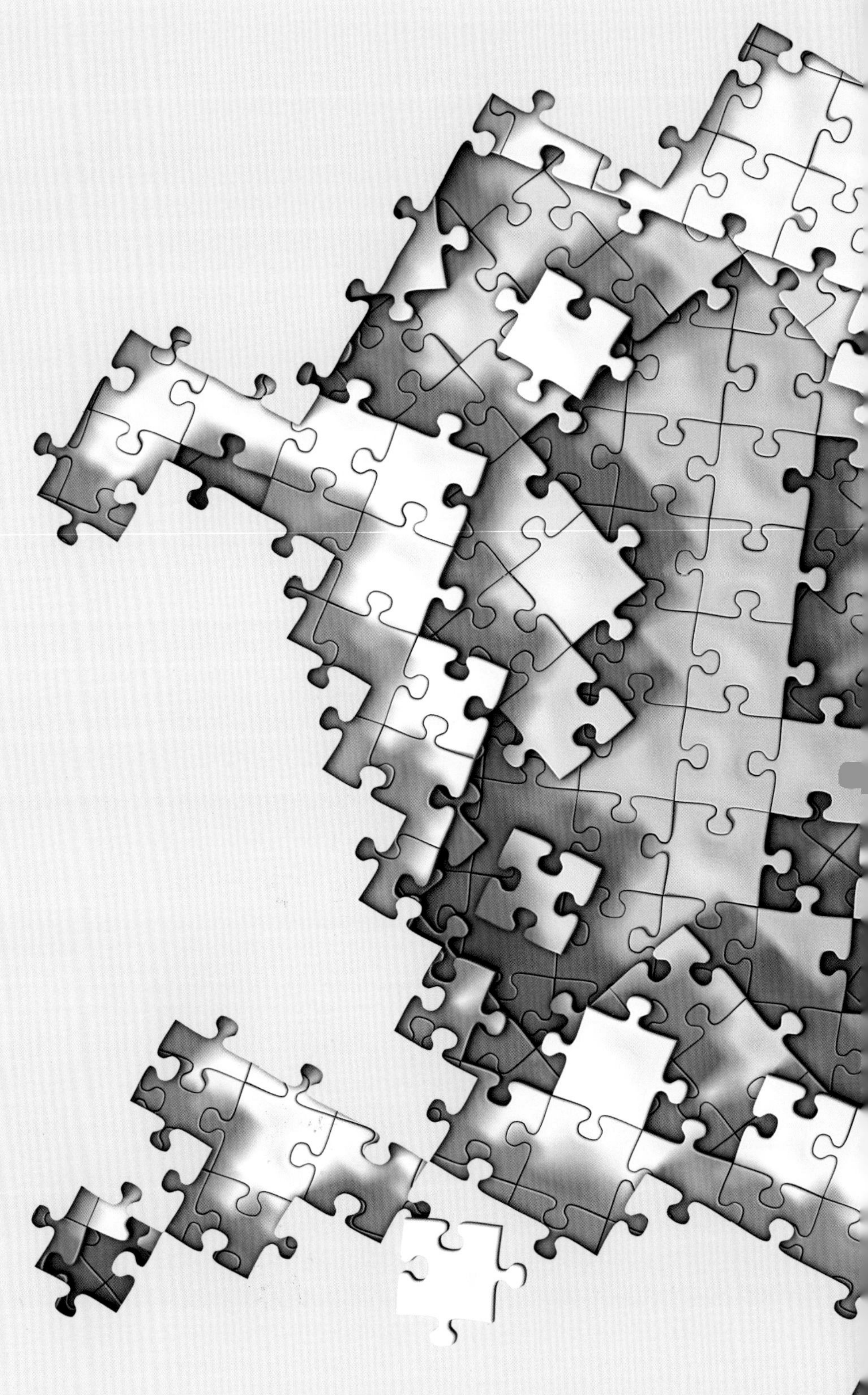

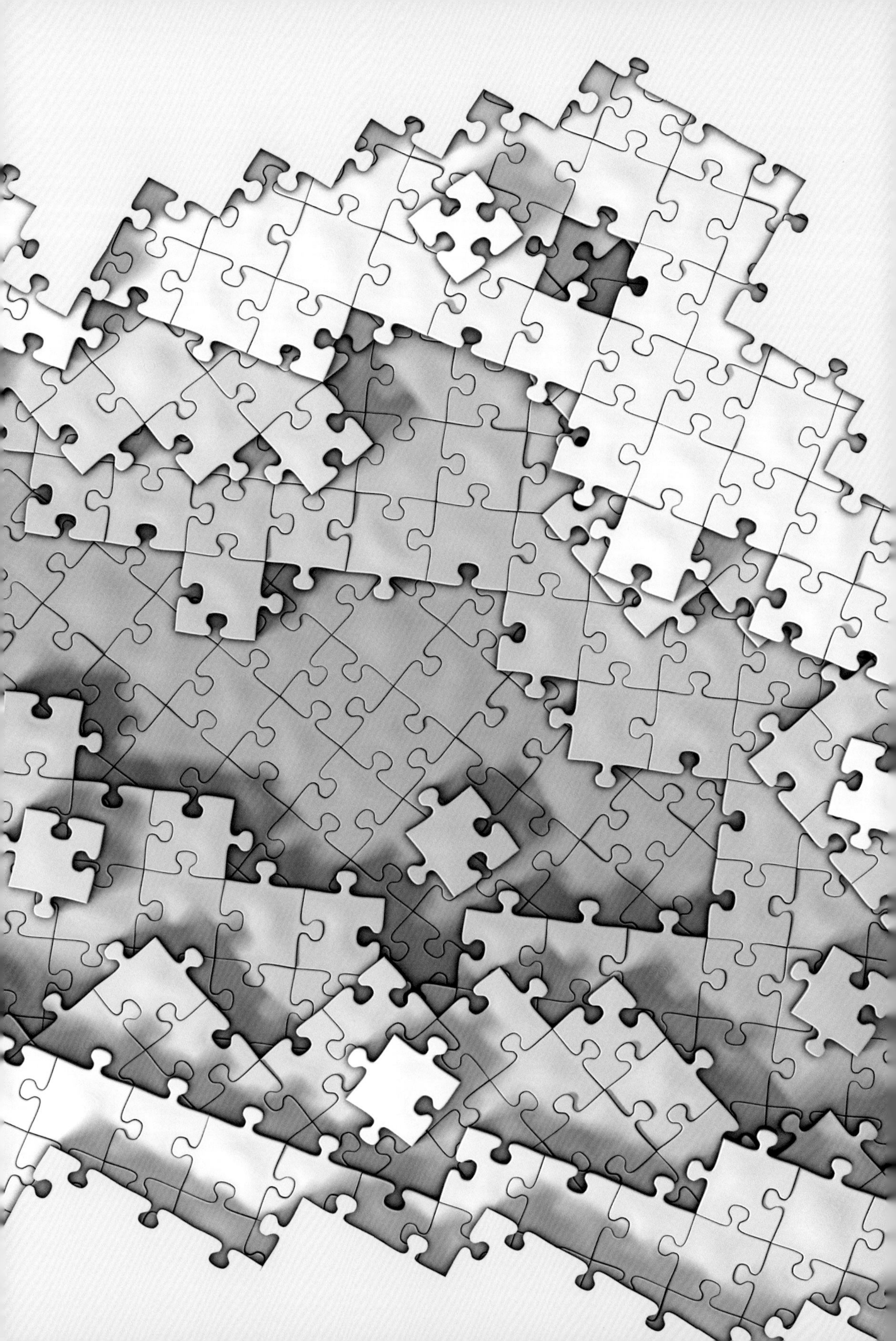

Arash & Arman T. Riahi

Everyday Rebellion

Stop hoping. Make it happen!

Everyday Rebellion pays homage to the creativity of nonviolent resistance. This project is an account of the new and old limits of political and social paradigms that, in numerous respects and in common, everyday ways, are being called into question by people and technologies. Both a documentary film and a cross-media project, *Everyday Rebellion* also breaks down genre boundaries by continuing its narrative and transposing its cinematic texture onto the multifarious characteristics and parameters of modern online media. *Everyday Rebellion* is an ode to the imaginativeness of people rethinking our world, a hymn to the courage and power they display in fighting for their visions.

At the heart of this essayistic documentary film are observations and analyses of the diverse creative methods of nonviolent protest that are currently being practiced worldwide by a rapidly growing number of people. The film features portraits of artists, activists and groups who are no longer prepared to accept the current state of our world as a given, and are fighting for new forms of political, economic and social coexistence.

The point of departure of our observations is the Iranian democracy movement. We proceed on to the Arab Spring, to protests against the Chavez regime in Venezuela, and to democracy movements like Occupy that have been flaring up, seemingly at random, worldwide. Over and over again, we confront essential questions: When is a protest movement successful and when isn't it? How does resistance continue amidst everyday life in dictatorial systems? Where and how does protest intrude into the public sphere? What are the irreversible consequences of this resistance, both for the individual and for society as a whole?

Everyday Rebellion provides a glimpse into the lives of activists who not infrequently risk their lives so that others might have a brighter future. Accompanying them as they go about their work, we learn of their motivations and objectives, their tactics and methods, but also of their doubts, their rage and the luck they've had. This isn't just a matter of up-close-and-personal encounters with individuals; we come face to face with real-life manifestations of the deep fault lines—yawning abysses too wide to cover up—running through today's world and its "structural order" that's in the process of crumbling. What began as localizable and geographically discrete has since become de-territorialized, delimited, and is no longer easy to pinpoint. Resistance has become a global, everyday situation.

The protagonists portrayed as they go about their efforts are activists in the classic sense as well as cyber-activists, bloggers, institutions and, above all, artists. In numerous instances, their works of art are not only interwoven into the film but also put on display in a multimedia exhibition space consisting of the various levels of the cross-media project such as a website and a series of videos broadcast on arte.tv. In addition to the classic, conventional protest methods—strikes, solidarity marches, charitable & educational initiatives—utilized by workers and producers, the fundamental demographic stratum of every economy, *Everyday Rebellion* also scrutinizes trans-medial art projects, individualists, theoreticians and their trailblazing works that often constitute the vanguard of everyday protests.

everydayrebellion.com

The film is a wrap, but the plot continues to thicken. That means "everyday rebels" will continue to spread the word, protest and discuss. The project's cross-media platform is divided into several phases and sectors running parallel: the *everydayrebellion.com* website, online videos and documentary film series in cooperation with ARTE / Creative and arte.tv / lemondearabe, as well as a mobile revolution app and a desktop game with which to practice nonviolent resistance on virtual streets.

The project's homepage is by no means a run-of-the-mill film website; rather, it's a video platform and an important resource for people to get to know and understand the struggle of worldwide nonviolent resistance. It's meant to serve as a discussion forum and a source of information, inspiration, and examples that illustrate, with a wide array of forms and in diverse styles, the necessity of nonviolent resistance. With the accent on video, the website's mission is not only to disseminate information but also to inspire users to get actively involved by enabling them to upload videos and content to the website themselves. This takes place via a secure server and modern encryption technology that protect the prosumer's privacy.

Another key objective is the collection of material and resources on the subject of nonviolence. Access will be provided to basic theoretical elaborations and background information in step-by-step fashion; the most important standard works will be made available to users in cooperation with various institutions and translated into as many languages as possible. Collaboration with organizations such as the Global Nonviolent Action Database is also being planned.

Partners & Associates

In cooperation with creative.arte.tv and in conjunction with the Summer of Rebels that has been running recently on the ARTE channel, we are screening a weekly series of short videos about the methods of nonviolent resistance. "Creative Resistance" features descriptions and demonstrations by some of the iconic figures of the movement, activists, artists and creative users. Yes Men!, Srdja Popovic of CANVAS – Center for Applied Nonviolent Action and Strategies, John Jackson, author of the standard work *Small Acts of Resistance,* and the proprietors of *wagingnonviolence.org* are some of the artists and activists we've been working together with. Since this series is essentially about insiders telling all, these activists talk right into the camera as they speak frankly and directly about their creative resistance methods. And outtakes, excerpts, special features and videos about nonviolence shot especially for this website will regularly be made available on *everydayrebellion.com*. Thanks above all to the enormous amount of material that's been filmed and collected over time, a highly diversified and multi-textual historical document about modern nonviolent resistance will take shape over the coming years.

We will also be working together with ARTE G.E.I.E. and ARTE Deutschland over the course of several months to produce brief portraits of and videos about activists in the Arab world for arte. tv's "The Arab World in Revolution(s)." This platform is composed of several series including "Generation Revolution" and "Shankaboot," the first work of Web fiction from Lebanon. *Every-*

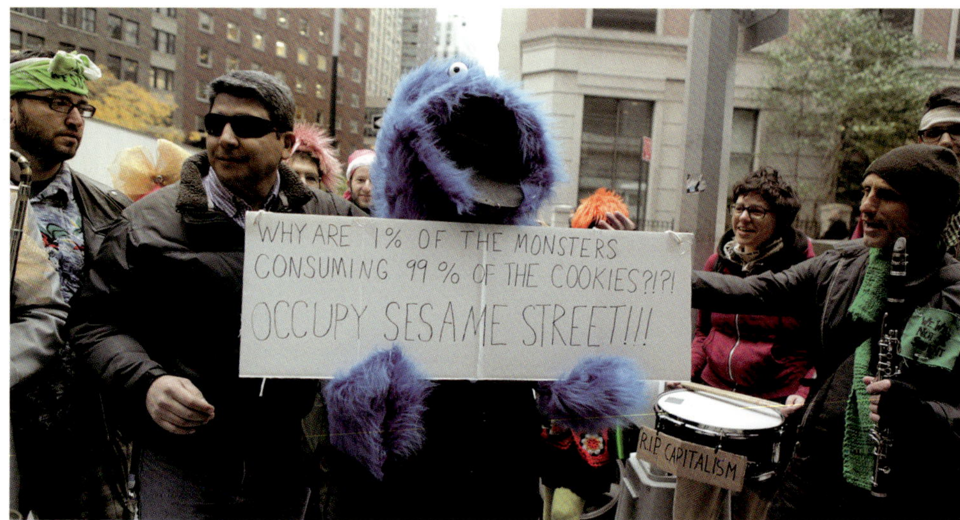
WHY ARE 1% OF THE MONSTERS CONSUMING 99% OF THE COOKIES?!?!
OCCUPY SESAME STREET!!!
R.I.P CAPITALISM

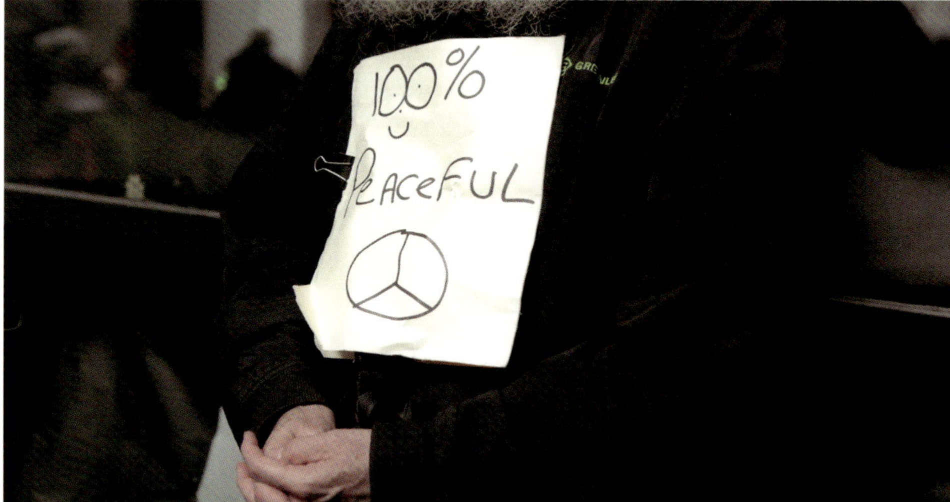
100%
PEACEFUL

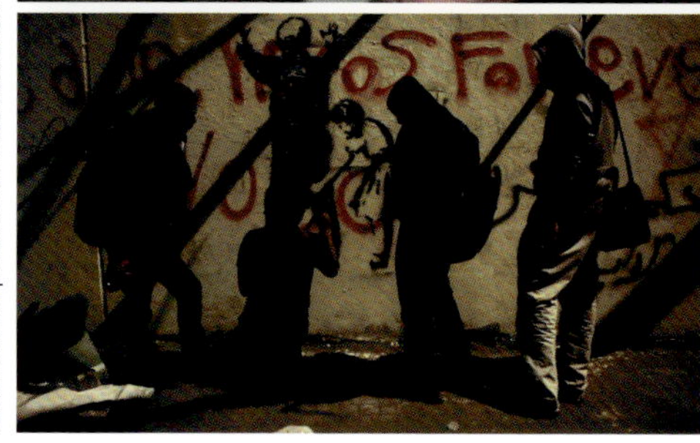

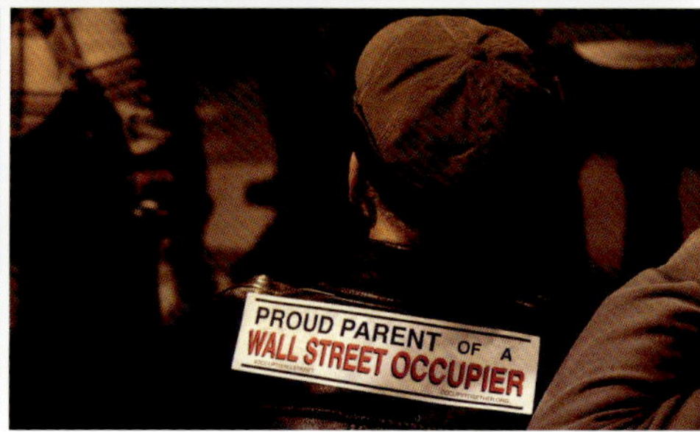
PROUD PARENT OF A
WALL STREET OCCUPIER

148

day Rebellion will also have a series of its own primarily featuring creative activists and their actions, or, alternatively, will have a series of specials identified by the *Everyday Rebellion* brand within the scope of *Generation Revolution.*

The reportage and portraits of the protagonists of creative nonviolent resistance produced in cooperation with arte.tv's "The Arab World in Revolution(s)" is making a name for *Everyday Rebellion* among arte's German-French online audience. Moreover, presenting content on ARTE's website yields the opportunity to productively and creatively work with existing material instead of simply letting it languish on assorted hard drives, as is the case with most documentary films.

The Rebel App

The *Everyday Rebellion Mobile App* will be a free downloadable application available at Apple's App Store and Android Market. It's being partially financed by crowd funding at *kickstarter.org.* In collaboration with CANVAS and the Avaaz organization, we're developing an app designed to assist activists all over the world as they go about their daily nonviolent resistance struggle. In addition to a compendium of the essential principles of nonviolent resistance by Gene Sharp, Mohandas Ghandi and Martin Luther King, it will above all provide practical tips to help activists solve the problems they're faced with on a daily basis—for instance: What do I do when security forces deploy tear gas? How can I circumvent the authorities' efforts to deny internet access? What should I do if I'm arrested? Responses to lots of activists' FAQs will include numerous examples from the history of nonviolent resistance.

Plus, we plan to work together with CANVAS and Avaaz to develop infographics-style animated shorts depicting the most important methods of nonviolence with tips for implementing them successfully, and to integrate this material into the app. This will explain the most essential know-how of the nonviolence movement and provide sketches of it for the activists. We seek to collaborate with organizations like Witness, which already makes instructions available online for amateur photographers and cell phone shutterbugs on how best to film human rights violations. For the app animation, this how-to info will be divided into short, succinct steps and expressed in universally understandable graphics that ideally require no explanatory text. Plus, the file size will be kept to a minimum to make for convenient access by activists. The aim of this app is, on one hand, to put a practical tool into the hands of current and would-be activists, and, on the other hand, to be comprehensible to people throughout the world. To accomplish this, we're having it translated into as many languages as possible by native speakers.

> „Never doubt that a small group of committed people can change the world. Indeed, it is the only thing that ever has."
>
> Margaret Mead

Screenwriter & director Arash & Arman T. Riahi
With: Srdja Popovic, The Yes Men!, John Jackson, Reverend Billy et al.
Subsidized by Media, BMUKK – Innovative Film Austria, ORF Film / Fernseh-Abkommen, Filmfonds Wien,
Bundesamt für Kultur BAK, ZDF / ARTE, SRF Schweizer Radio und Fernsehen
Produced by Golden Girls Filmproduktion & Filmservices GmbH (Vienna)
Coproduced by Mira Film GmbH (Zürich)

Arash & Arman T. Riahi

Everyday Rebellion

Stop hoping. Make it happen!

Everyday Rebellion ist eine Hommage an die Kreativität des gewaltlosen Widerstandes. Das Projekt erzählt von neuen und alten Grenzen politischer und gesellschaftlicher Paradigmen, die vielfach und in alltäglicher Weise von Menschen und Technologien in Frage gestellt werden. Sowohl Kinodokumentarfilm als auch Crossmedia-Projekt, sprengt *Everyday Rebellion* auch die Grenzen der Genres durch die Fortführung der Narration und die Erweiterung der Textur des Kinos auf die vielfältigen Beschaffenheiten und Parameter moderner Online-Medien. *Everyday Rebellion* ist eine Ode an die Fantasie, unsere Welt neu zu denken, und an den Mut und die Kraft, für diese Visionen zu kämpfen.

Im Zentrum des essayistischen Dokumentarfilms stehen die Beobachtung und die Analyse der vielfältigen kreativen Methoden des gewaltlosen Protestes, die derzeit von einer rasant anwachsenden Zahl von Menschen weltweit praktiziert werden. Porträtiert werden KünstlerInnen, AktivistInnen und Bewegungen, die den derzeitigen Zustand unserer Welt nicht mehr als gegeben hinnehmen wollen und für neue Formen des politischen, wirtschaftlichen und gesellschaftlichen Zusammenlebens kämpfen.

So nehmen unsere Beobachtungen ihren Ausgang in der iranischen Demokratiebewegung, führen zum Arabischen Frühling, zu den Protesten in Venezuela gegen das Chavez-Regime bis zu den weltweiten, scheinbar unberechenbar aufflammenden Demokratiebewegungen wie Occupy. Immer wieder stellen sich uns die Fragen: Wann ist eine Protestbewegung erfolgreich, wann nicht? Wie geht der Widerstand im alltäglichen Leben in diktatorischen Systemen weiter? Wo und wie dringt der Protest ins öffentliche Leben? Was sind die unwiderruflichen Folgen dieses Widerstandes, sowohl für das Individuum als auch für die Gesellschaft als Ganzes?

Everyday Rebellion ermöglicht einen Einblick in das Leben von AktivistInnen, die nicht selten ihr Leben riskieren, um eine andere Zukunft zu ermöglichen: Ihre Arbeit begleitend, erfahren wir von ihren Motivationen und Zielen, ihren Taktiken und Methoden, aber auch von ihren Zweifeln, ihrer Wut und ihrem Glück. Dadurch lernen wir nicht nur Individuen kennen, sondern erfahren und erleben exemplarisch die tiefen, nicht mehr zu überdeckenden Verwerfungs- und Bruchlinien, die sich durch die heutige Welt und ihre sich derzeit auflösende „Ordnungsstruktur" ziehen. Was örtlich begrenzt und lokalisierbar begann, hat sich deterrorialisiert, ausgegrenzt, ist nicht mehr leicht zu verorten. Der Widerstand ist zum globalen und alltäglichen Zustand geworden.

Dazu werden AktivistInnen im klassischen Sinne und deren Arbeit genauso begleitet wie Cyber-aktivistInnen, BloggerInnen, Institutionen und vor allem auch KünstlerInnen. Ihre Arbeit wird in vielen Fällen nicht nur in den Film verwoben, sondern zusätzlich durch die verschiedenen Ebenen des Crossmedia-Projektes, wie Webplattform, Videoreihen auf arte.tv usw., in einen multimedialen Rezeptionsraum gestellt. Neben den klassischen und etablierten Protestmethoden – Streiks, Solidarisierungen, karitativen und aufklärerischen Projekten –, die von Arbeitern und Produzenten, den tragenden Bevölkerungsgruppen jeder Volkswirtschaft ausgehen, beobachtet *Everyday Rebellion* auch transmediale Kunstprojekte, IndividualistInnen, TheoretikerInnen und ihre bahnbrechenden Arbeiten, die oftmals die Vorhut des alltäglichen Protestes darstellen.

everydayrebellion.com

Nach dem Film geht die Narration weiter, die *Everyday Rebels* werden weiterhin erzählen, protestieren und diskutieren. Die Cross-Media-Plattform des Projektes ist unterteilt in mehrere, parallel laufende Phasen und Projektbereiche: die Webseite *everydayrebellion.com*, Online-Video-Reihen und serielle dokumentarische Formate in Kooperation mit ARTE / Creative und arte.tv / lemondearabe sowie eine mobile „Revolutions-App" und ein Desktop-Game, mit dem der gewaltlose Widerstand virtuell geübt werden kann.

Die Website des Filmes ist keine klassische Film-Website, sondern vielmehr eine Videoplattform und eine wichtige Ressource, um den Kampf des weltweiten gewaltlosen Widerstandes kennen- und verstehen zu lernen. Sie soll als Informations-, Diskussions- und Inspirationsplattform dienen und mit vielen Beispielen unterschiedlicher Form und Ästhetik die Notwendigkeit des gewaltlosen Widerstandes veranschaulichen. Mit dem Schwerpunkt Video soll die Website nicht nur Information verbreiten, sondern die UserInnen zur aktiven Teilnahme inspirieren, in dem sie selbst Videos und Content auf die Website uploaden können. Das geschieht über sichere Server und eine moderne Verschlüsselungstechnik, die die Privatsphäre der Prosumer gewährleistet.

Ein weiteres wichtiges Ziel ist die Material- und Ressourcensammlung zum Thema „Nonviolence", theoretische Grundlagen und Hintergründe sollen schrittweise für die UserInnen zugänglich gemacht werden; wichtigste Standardwerke sollen in Zusammenarbeit mit verschiedenen Institutionen verfügbar gemacht und in möglichst viele Sprachen übersetzt werden. Dazu ist geplant, mit Organisationen wie der Global Nonviolent Action Database zusammenzuarbeiten.

Kooperationen

In Kooperationen mit creative.arte.tv startet mit Sommer 2012 im Zuge des „Summer of Rebels" von Arte eine wöchentliche Reihe von Kurzvideos über Methoden des gewaltlosen Widerstandes mit dem Titel „Creative Resistance – Die Kreativität gewaltloser Widerstandsbewegungen", die von Ikonen der Bewegungen, AktivistInnen, KünstlerInnen, aber auch von kreativen UserInnen vorgestellt und vorgetragen werden. Hier wird beispielsweise mit KünstlerInnen und AktivistInnen wie den Yes Men!, Srdja Popovic von CANVAS (Center for Applied Nonviolent Action and Strategies), John Jackson, dem Autor des Standardwerkes *Small steps of resistance,* oder den Betreibern der Website *wagingnonviolence.org* zusammengearbeitet. Da die AktivistInnen in dieser Reihe quasi wie aus dem Nähkästchen plaudern, sprechen sie in die Kamera und erzählen sehr direkt und unmittelbar von ihren kreativen Widerstandsmethoden. Auf *everydayrebellion.com* werden weiters regelmäßig Outtakes, Ausschnitte, Special Features und eigens gefilmte Videos zum Thema Nonviolence vorgestellt. Vor allem in Anbetracht des enormen Materials, das über die Zeit gedreht und gesammelt wurde, entsteht in den kommenden Jahren ein vielfältiges und multitextuales Zeitdokument über den modernen gewaltlosen Widerstand. In Zusammenarbeit mit ARTE G.E.I.E. und ARTE Deutschland werden zudem über den Zeitraum von mehreren Monaten für die Plattform arte.tv / arabischewelt Kurzportraits bzw. Videos über

AktivistInnen der arabischen Welt lanciert. Die Plattform ist aus mehreren unterschiedlichen Reihen und Serien zusammengesetzt, unter anderem „Generation Revolution" oder „Shankaboot", der ersten Web-Fiktion aus dem Libanon. *Everyday Rebellion* bekommt eine eigene Rubrik, die in erster Linie von kreativen AktivistInnen und ihren Aktionen handelt bzw. wird in der Rubrik *Generation Revolution* zu einer Sonderreihe, die eigens mit dem Projektnamen gebrandet wird.

Everyday Rebellion etabliert sich in der Kooperation mit arte.tv / arabischewelt durch die Kurzbeiträge und -portraits beim deutsch-französischen (Netz)Publikum als eigenständiges Projekt in Hinblick auf Protagonisten des kreativen gewaltlosen Widerstandes. Zusätzlich ergibt sich durch die Präsentation auf der Plattform von ARTE eine Möglichkeit, bestehendes Material produktiv und effektiv zu verarbeiten statt es auf den Festplatten dahinvegetieren zu lassen, wie es sonst bei den meisten Dokumentarfilmen üblich ist.

Die Rebel-App

Das *Everyday Rebellion Mobile App* wird eine downloadbare Gratis-Applikation auf Apples App-Store oder dem Android-Markt, die teilweise auch durch Crowdfunding auf *kickstarter. org* finanziert wird. Gemeinsam mit CANVAS, dem Center for Applied Non-Violent Action and Strategies, und der Organisation Avaaz wird eine App entwickelt, die den Aktivisten auf aller Welt bei ihrem täglichen, gewaltlosen Widerstandskampf helfen soll. Neben den wichtigsten theoretischen Grundlagen des gewaltlosen Widerstandes von Gene Sharp, Mohandas Ghandi oder Martin Luther King sollen vor allem praktische Tipps dabei helfen, die alltäglichen Probleme, mit denen AktivistInnen kämpfen müssen, zu lösen. Dazu gehören Fragen wie: Was mache ich, wenn die Sicherheitskräfte Tränengas einsetzen? Wie kann ich die Internetsperren der Behörden umgehen? Wie reagiere ich, wenn ich festgenommen werde? Anhand von vielen Beispielen aus der Geschichte des gewaltlosen Widerstandes werden viele für die Aktivisten wichtige Fragen beantwortet.

Zudem sollen gemeinsam mit CANVAS und Avaaz Animationen der wichtigsten Methoden und Nonviolence-Tipps im Stile von Infografiken entwickelt und in die App eingebunden und das Wichtigste Know-How der Nonviolence-Bewegung erklärt und für die AktivistInnen skizziert werden. Beispielsweise wird mit einer Organisation wie Witness, die ihre bereits im Netz weit verbreitete Anleitung zum richtigen Filmen von Menschenrechtsverletzungen für Amateur- und Handyfilmer zur Verfügung gestellt hat, eine Kooperation angestrebt. Diese Anleitung wird in kurzen und prägnanten Schritten für die App animiert und als universell verständliche Anleitung im Idealfall ohne Sprache und in kleiner Datengröße für die AktivistInnen jederzeit abrufbar sein. Ziel der App ist es, einerseits ein praktisches Werkzeug für die AktivistInnen und jene, die welche werden wollen, herzustellen, und gleichzeitig so universell verständlich wie möglich zu bleiben. Dazu wird die App unter Mitarbeit von Native Speakern in so viele Sprachen wie möglich übersetzt.

> „Never doubt that a small group of committed people can change the world. Indeed, it is the only thing that ever has."
>
> Margaret Mead

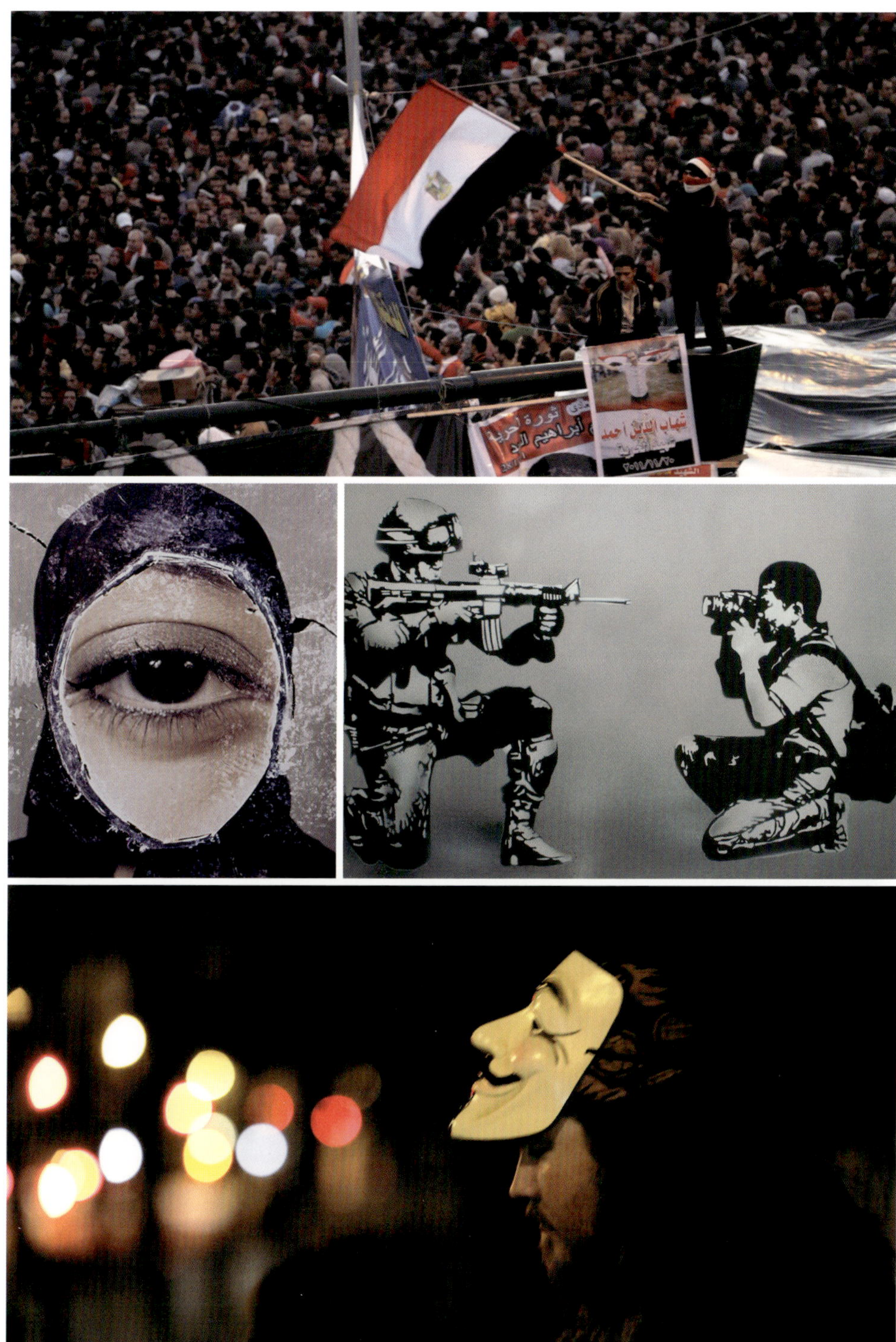

Open Commons 2012
Living with Digital Community Property

Open Commons 2012: Living and Working Together with Digital Community Property is one of two conferences—the other is *WikiSym*—addressing social issues associated with digital communities. How can the open commons—digital community property—be integrated into everyday life in a society? This matter of a smooth transition between digital and real, between theory and practice, and between collaboration and communal use/benefit is simultaneously The Big Picture and The Big Question of the Open Commons movement.

This year's symposium on the subject of the open commons is being organized by Open Commons Region Linz and the University of Linz. The aim is to stage an encounter that is as wide-ranging as possible, spotlighting the general current situation with respect to open digital collaboration, plans to drastically tighten national copyright laws, and specific areas in which people are already living and working within the open commons. At OC12, experts in education, art, business and public administration will discuss the potential, implications and challenges of the open commons in actual practice.

From Digital Village Greens to Digital Village Green

Digitization as a social phenomenon—defined, in the broadest sense, as unlimited access to digital data, the proliferation of digital communication, and using the Web as a social space—has become increasingly important in recent years and attracted the attention of politicians, cultural leaders, educators and businesspeople. At the same time, there have been heated debates—especially among scholars—about digital community property, open collaboration (with which Wikipedia has become synonymous) and how best to organize it, but these debates often occur in isolation and thus far removed from the people who are affected by them. Teachers suddenly find themselves confronted by aspects of copyright law when they download material from the internet and want to use it in classroom instruction. The private and public sectors are making an effort to integrate this open collaboration into their administrative processes, and artists have been creating approaches of their own to the question of the collective as creator on a digital level. Behind these examples—instances of use in actual practice—are fundamental social questions about value, output, property and the role of communities in the increasingly individualized worlds people live in.

Each one of these communities—teachers, artists, administrators, and businesspeople—has come up with its own answers to these questions, and developed ways of proceeding and models for working with the open commons. To express it in the metaphor of the Open Commons movement: each community has set up its own "village green." Teachers refer to *open educational resources;* in business and public administration, *open collaboration* and *open government data* are hot topics; and artists are scrutinizing *crowdsourcing* and the boundaries and edges of this shared space. Now, OC12 extends an invitation to make these discrete village greens into a joint digital one—which means getting connected and interconnected, discussing similarities and differences among various types of shared digital property in the various social domains, and, in accordance with the very nature of the open commons, finding new possibilities for cooperation and participation.

Community Property: Education and Scholarship

One of this year's three tracks has to do with modes of access to the open commons in teaching and research. The school as key social institution for imparting values and sensitization assumes a central role in the open commons debate. *Web literacy*—i.e. actually being able to read and process information received via new media and new channels for conveying information such as Tumblr, Twitter and Feedreader—is an important issue in this track, since this form of literacy enables people, on the one hand, to move about in the digital world, and, on the other hand, to differentiate between commercial goods and community property. Participants will confront the question of *open educational resources*—i.e. free, public documents, reference works and instructional materials—the integration of Web 2.0 in classroom instruction, and pedagogical concepts of *collaborative teaching* in general.

Community Property: Art and Culture

Where are the limits of the collaborative? What relationship exists between authors and those partaking of their work in a society whose open commons consists of things that have been spun off, remixed and modified? How can the community's thoughts and digital community property not only be considered as a frame of reference but also be directly involved in the working process? The "Art & Culture" track at this year's OC12 will look into these and other questions. Since time immemorial, art and culture have been exploring the limits and edges of a particular society's conception of normality, dissecting it and holding a distorting mirror up to it. And the same goes for the open commons and the (compulsory) communities engendered by it.

Community Property: Business and Public Administration

Both the public and private sectors are confronted by structural questions having to do with the open commons. This track focuses on the question of public responsibility towards this digital community property—for example, *open government data*—and its potential for the society and the economy. The potential for working together more intensively, for *open collaboration* among companies, government agencies and members of society is one of the most exciting developments that can be credited to the Open Commons movement.

The Big Picture of Open Collaboration

"Free," "free of charge" and "open" are terms that, in connection with the open commons, are neither empty phraseology nor synonyms; rather, they demarcate the prevailing misunderstandings surrounding this issue. The open commons doesn't just mean making content available at no cost on the internet. It's a philosophy which posits that the Web—and Web 2.0 above all—is based on openness to sharing information, resources, and goods in accordance with the conviction that these things in the hands of the community are more than the sum of their parts. The 2012 Open Commons Conference is dedicated to this idea and its practical implementation.

Open Commons Region Linz: Founded by the City of Linz in 2010 to implement the principle of digital community property on the municipal administrative level, this initiative has become one of the driving forces behind Open Commons in German-speaking Europe.
Johannes Kepler University of Linz: With its outstanding Department of Computer Science and its Open Source, Data und Commons initiatives, JKU has made a name for itself worldwide in this field.

Open Commons 2012
Leben mit digitalen Gemeingütern

Open Commons 2012: Leben und Zusammenarbeiten mit digitalen Gemeingütern setzt sich gemeinsam mit ihrer Schwesterkonferenz – der *WikiSym* – mit den gesellschaftlichen Fragen digitaler Gemeinschaften auseinander: Wie können *Open Commons* – digitale Gemeingüter – in das tägliche Leben einer Gesellschaft integriert werden? Diese Frage nach dem nahtlosen Übergang zwischen digital und real, zwischen Theorie und Praxis und zwischen Zusammenarbeit und gemeinschaftlichem Nutzen ist gleichsam „The Big Picture" und „The Big Question" der Open-Commons-Bewegung.

Das diesjährige Symposium zum Thema Open Commons, organisiert von der Open Commons Region Linz und der Johannes Kepler Universität, hat es sich zum Ziel gesetzt, einen möglichst großen Bogen zu spannen: von der allgemeinen und aktuellen Situation offener, digitaler Gemeinschaftsarbeiten über die geplanten erheblichen Verschärfungen nationaler UrheberInnenrechte zu ganz konkreten Bereichen, in denen mit Open Commons gelebt und gearbeitet wird. Die OC12 diskutiert mit ExpertInnen aus den Bereichen Bildung, Kunst, Wirtschaft und öffentliche Verwaltung über die Potenziale, Implikationen und Herausforderungen von Open Commons in der Praxis.

Von digitalen Allmenden zur digitalen Allmende

Digitalisierung als gesellschaftliches Phänomen – das heißt im weitesten Sinne der unbeschränkte Zugang zu digitalen Daten, die zunehmende Wichtigkeit digitaler Kommunikation und das Web als sozialer Raum – hat in den letzten Jahren rasant an Bedeutung und Aufmerksamkeit seitens Politik, Kultur, Bildung und Wirtschaft gewonnen. Gleichzeitig werden Fragen über digitale Gemeingüter, offene Zusammenarbeit (*Wikipedia* ist mittlerweile ein Synonym dafür) und die Organisation ebendieser vor allem in der Wissenschaft heftig diskutiert. Diese Debatten finden aber oft isoliert und fernab von jenen Personen statt, die sie betreffen. LehrerInnen sehen sich plötzlich mit Aspekten des UrheberInnenrechts konfrontiert, wenn sie Material aus dem Internet im Unterricht verwenden wollen. Wirtschaft und Verwaltung versuchen, diese offene Zusammenarbeit in ihre Prozesse zu integrieren, und KünstlerInnen nähern sich der Frage nach dem Kollektiv als SchöpferInnen auf einer digitalen Ebene. Hinter diesen – in der Praxis verorteten – Beispielen stehen grundlegende gesellschaftliche Fragen über Wert, Leistung, Eigentum und der Rolle von Gemeinschaften in zusehends individualisierten (Lebens-) Welten.

Jede dieser Communities – ob Lehrende, KünstlerInnen, Administratoren und Wirtschaftstreibende – hat für sich Antworten auf diese Fragen gefunden und Handlungsmöglichkeiten und Modelle entwickelt, um mit digitalen Gemeingütern zu arbeiten. Um es mit der Metapher der Open-Commons-Bewegung zu sagen: Jede Community hat ihre eigene Allmende bestellt – für die Lehrenden heißt sie *Open Educational Resources*, für Wirtschaft und Verwaltung sind *Open Collaboration* und *Open Government Data* spannend, und KünstlerInnen beschäftigen sich mit *Crowdsourcing* und den Grenzen und Rändern dieser Allmende. Die OC12 lädt nun dazu ein, diese Allmenden zu einer gemeinsamen digitalen Allmende zu machen, das heißt, sich miteinander und untereinander zu vernetzen, über Parallelen und Unterschiede dieser digitalen Gemeingüter in den jeweiligen gesellschaftlichen Bereichen zu diskutieren und – dem Wesen der Open Commons folgend – neue Möglichkeiten zur Zusammenarbeit und Partizipation zu finden.

Gemeingut: Bildung und Wissenschaft

Einer der drei diesjährigen Tracks beschäftigt sich mit den Zugängen von Bildung und Wissenschaft zu digitalen Gemeingütern. Die Schule als zentrale gesellschaftliche Institution zur Vermittlung von Werten und zur Sensibilisierung nimmt in der Open-Commons-Debatte eine wichtige Rolle ein. *Web Literacy,* das heißt, Informationen, die über neue Medien und neue Arten der Vermittlung von Information (über Tumblr, Twitter, Feedreader) empfangen werden, tatsächlich lesen und verarbeiten zu können, ist ein wichtiges Thema in diesem Track, denn diese Literacy befähigt Menschen, sich einerseits in dieser digitalen Welt zu bewegen und andererseits zwischen kommerziellen und gemeinschaftlichen Gütern zu unterscheiden. Die Frage nach *Open Educational Resources,* also nach freien und öffentlichen Unterlagen, Nachschlagewerken und Unterrichtsmaterialien wird ebenso behandelt wie die Integration des Web 2.0 in den Unterricht und pädagogische Konzepte von *Collaborative Teaching* im Allgemeinen.

Gemeingut: Kunst und Kultur

Wo sind die Grenzen des Kollaborativen? Welches Verhältnis besteht zwischen den AutorInnen und den RezipientInnen in einer Gesellschaft, deren digitale Gemeingüter aus Weiterverarbeitung, Remixing und Veränderung bestehen? Wie kann der Gedanke der Gemeinschaft und der digitalen Gemeingüter nicht nur als Referenzrahmen betrachtet, sondern auch direkt in den Arbeitsprozess eingebunden werden? Diese und andere Fragen geht der Track „Kunst und Kultur" auf der diesjährigen OC12 nach. Kunst und Kultur loten seit jeher die Grenzen und Ränder des jeweiligen Verständnisses einer Gesellschaft von Normalität aus, sezieren sie und setzen sie ihr dann unter einem Zerrspiegel vor. Das verhält sich auch im Bereich der digitalen Gemeingüter und der daraus resultierenden (Zwangs-) Gemeinschaften so.

Gemeingut: Wirtschaft und Verwaltung

Die Sphären der Wirtschaft und der öffentlichen Verwaltung sehen sich mit strukturellen Fragen der digitalen Gemeingüter konfrontiert. Die Fragen nach öffentlicher Verantwortung gegenüber dieser digitalen Allmende – am Beispiel von *Open Government Data* (offenen Regierungs- und Verwaltungsdaten) – und deren Potenzial für Gesellschaft und Wirtschaft stehen in diesem Track im Vordergrund. Alleine das Potenzial zur verstärkten Zusammenarbeit, zur *Open Collaboration* zwischen Wirtschaft und öffentlicher Verwaltung mit der Gesellschaft, ist eine der aufregendsten Entwicklungen, die der Open-Commons-Bewegung zugeschrieben werden kann.

The Big Picture of Open Collaboration

„Frei", „gratis" und „offen" sind im Zusammenhang mit digitalen Gemeingütern weder leere Floskeln noch Synonyme, sondern beschreiben die Missverständnisse, die rund um das Thema herrschen. Digitale Gemeingüter meint nicht das „bloße kostenlose Zurverfügungstellen" von Inhalten im Internet, sondern beschreibt eine Philosophie: Das Web – und vor allem das Web 2.0 – basiert auf einer Offenheit gegenüber dem Teilen von Information, Ressourcen und Gütern, vor dem Hintergrund der Überzeugung, dass diese Dinge in den Händen der Gemeinschaft mehr sind als die Summe ihrer Teile. Diesen Gedanken und vor allem ihrer praktischen Umsetzung widmet sich die Open Commons Conference 2012.

Text: Laura Kepplinger

Wikisym 2012
Wikis and Open Collaboration

The 8th Annual Symposium on Wikis and Open Collaboration (Wikisym) is collocated with Ars Electronica from August 27–29. Wikisym brings together academic researchers, practitioners, and thinkers working to foster open collaboration with technical systems. Open collaboration has helped propel areas like open source software, open government, open science, and of course individual projects like Wikipedia led by keynote speaker Jimmy Wales. Wikisym features cutting edge research in how people use technologies like wikis that foster open collaboration, shows off new systems that promote open collaboration, and discusses topics essential to the success of Openness, including:

Das Internationale Symposium zu Wikis und offener Zusammenarbeit *(Wikisym)* findet dieses Jahr im Vorfeld der Ars Electronica vom 27. bis 29. August in Linz statt. Die *Wikisym* versammelt Akademiker, Praktiker und Denker zur Vertiefung der offenen Zusammenarbeit mit technischen Systemen. Offene Zusammenarbeit brachte Entwicklungen wie Open-Source-Software, offene Regierung, offene Wissenschaft und natürlich auch eigenständige Projekte wie die von Keynote Speaker Jimmy Wales geleitete *Wikipedia* mit sich. Die *Wikisym* stellt neueste Untersuchungen über den Umgang mit Technologien vor, die offene Zusammenarbeit fördern (z. B. Wikis), präsentiert neue Systeme zur Weiterentwicklung offener Zusammenarbeit und erörtert zum Gelingen von Offenheit beitragende Fragen und Themen wie zum Beispiel:

Language, Knowledge, Culture, and Wikipedia

Open collaboration is global, so understanding the relationships between language, knowledge, and culture in these projects is vital. Keynote speaker Brent Hecht will present Omnipedia, which provides users with structured access in their native language to over 8 million concepts from up to 25 language editions of Wikipedia. Other papers explore how translation has shaped Wikipedia's content, how cultures and languages connect through people's biographies, and how to explore the linguistic points of view revealed by articles in different Wikipedias.

Offene Zusammenarbeit findet im globalen Maßstab statt. Das Verständnis der Beziehungen zwischen Sprache, Wissen und Kultur spielt daher eine wesentliche Rolle. Keynote Speaker Brent Hecht präsentiert *Omnipedia,* einen strukturierten Zugang in der Muttersprache des jeweiligen Nutzers zu über acht Millionen Begriffen aus bis zu 25 verschiedenen Wikipedia-Ausgaben. Andere Beiträge spüren der Veränderung der Wikipedia-Inhalte durch Übersetzungen, der Verknüpfung von Kulturen und Sprachen durch Biografien und dem sprachlichen Zugang von Artikeln in verschiedenen Wikipedia-Ausgaben nach.

Measuring and Motivating Participation in Open Collaboration

A key challenge for open collaboration is understanding who contributes and encouraging more people to do better work. We have a robust selection of papers about understanding contributors: how do new members learn the ropes and how can good etiquette help them stay longer, what are they like ("Smart but Fun") and when and why do they leave? We also expect lively discussion around these topics in a featured panel, "Barriers to Participation and Representation in Wikipedia".

Zu verstehen, wer die Beiträger sind, und noch mehr Leute zu besserer Arbeit anzuregen, sind wichtige Aspekte offener Zusammenarbeit. Wir haben ein breites Spektrum an Vorträgen zu diesem Thema zu bieten: Wie arbeiten sich neue Mitglieder ein und wie können sie durch eine entsprechende Etikette länger gehalten werden, welche Eigenschaften haben sie („intelligent, aber nicht langweilig") und wann und warum steigen sie aus? Eines der Hauptpodien – „Teilnahme- und Darstellungsbarrieren bei Wikipedia" – verspricht eine lebhafte Diskussion über diese und ähnliche Fragen.

Studying Collaboration Patterns

Coordinating the work and ensuring its quality is another major challenge. Our other featured panel, "What Aren't We Measuring? Methods for Quantifying Wiki-Work" will open the topic of understanding collaboration, which a number of papers address. From linguistic examination of the psychology of writing about disaster and the emotions associated with conflict, through network analysis of the dynamics of news articles and the quality of articles overall, to models for identifying and resolving controversial and deletable articles, we will take a thorough look at the dynamics of collaboration through the lens of Wikipedia.

Einen weiteren wichtigen Aspekt bilden Arbeitskoordination und Qualitätssicherung. Ein zweites Hauptpodium – „Was wird nicht gemessen? Quantifizierungsmethoden für das Arbeiten mit Wikis" – leitet den Themenblock „Verstehen von Zusammenarbeit" ein, zu dem es ebenfalls eine Reihe von Vorträgen gibt. Von linguistischen Untersuchungen zur Psychologie des Schreibens über Katastrophen und zu mit Konflikten einhergehenden Emotionen über Netzwerkanalysen der Dynamik von Nachrichtenartikeln und der Qualität von Artikeln im Allgemeinen bis zu Identifikations- und Lösungsmodellen für strittige und zu löschende Artikel werfen wir aus der Perspektive von Wikipedia einen gründlichen Blick auf Dynamik der Zusammenarbeit.

Tools and Systems for Open Collaboration

Wikisym also features lively interactive sessions with around thirty demos and posters that use techniques including natural language processing, semantic web technologies, decision support models, user-defined annotation layers, hypervideo, and other technologies to make open collaboration richer, easier, and more efficient. They address a number of domains beyond Wikipedia, including geospatial data, statistics, education, healthcare, and open source. A number of papers present these technologies and explore these domains in more detail.

In einer Reihe interaktiver Sitzungen werden rund dreißig Demos und Poster präsentiert, die mit Techniken wie natürlicher Sprachverarbeitung, semantischen Webtechnologien, Entscheidungsunterstützungssystemen, benutzerdefinierten Annotationsebenen, Hypervideo etc. die offene Zusammenarbeit vertiefen, erleichtern und effizienter machen. Sie erstrecken sich auf verschiedene Bereiche jenseits von Wikipedia wie z. B. Geodaten, Statistik, Bildung, Gesundheitswesen und Open Source. In mehreren Vorträgen werden diese Technologien und Bereiche näher vorgestellt und erläutert.

Open Spaces

There are many other issues and interests in the open collaboration community, and as always, we will have open spaces sessions where you can propose and discuss topics with like-minded attendees and make the conference your own. Wikisym attendees believe that open collaboration can make a better world, and we hope you join us to discuss the future of wikis and open collaboration in Linz!

Darüber hinaus kursieren in der Open-Collaboration-Community natürlich noch viele andere Themen und Interessen, und wie immer wird es offene Räume geben, in denen man mit Gleichgesinnten eigene Themenvorschläge diskutieren und eine Konferenz in der Konferenz abhalten kann. Wer an der Wikisym teilnimmt, glaubt, dass offene Zusammenarbeit zu einer Verbesserung der Welt beiträgt, und wir hoffen, ihr schließt euch uns in Linz an, um mit uns über die Zukunft von Wikis und offener Zusammenarbeit zu diskutieren!

Text: Dan Cosley, Cliff Lampe   Aus dem Englischen von Wilfried Prantner

Verband Freier Radios Österreich (VFRÖ) / Radio FRO

Free Access is Preferable to Controlled Exclusion
A Plea for the Opening of Digital Archives

The *Archivia* conference focuses on an aspect of digitization that is often overlooked in debates about free access to information—namely, the redefinition of the role and function of archives. Archives were long used primarily for professional purposes by journalists and scholars since access to them was usually restricted, often by the very fact of their geographical inaccessibility. This situation has changed radically in the last 15 years. Today, archives can—or rather, could—be a resource accessible worldwide by a global public. But even though the technical preconditions for such use have already been in place for over a decade, the legal situation has been slow to catch up with reality. Accordingly, legal uncertainty prevails. This makes archives less readily available to users and thus impedes access to information. Due to the high transaction costs attributable to clarification of copyright ownership as well as the potential threat of copyright lawsuits arising from the use of so-called orphan works, many archives recoil in horror from digital publication.

Digital technologies have revolutionized the possibilities for the production and exchange of cultural and artistic works. Production and access have been greatly simplified technically. Modes of production have also changed in accordance with technological progress, which, above all from a legal perspective, has been the source of further confusion. For one thing, there's been an increase in the speed at which people have reacted to new phenomena and modified and adapted information; for another, the number of works that are the result of collaborative and/or decentralized forms of production has grown rapidly. Archives in the digital realm as well can be set up and administered collaboratively, which in turn can give rise to dynamics that can develop a life of their own. Hence, there is not necessarily a central administrative hub that can control everything that transpires. Here as well, there's a wide gap between copyright law and real-world practice, since the setup of digital archives is often a collective process that requires framework conditions which allow for disorderly, unplanned growth.

Another problem for digital archives in the context of existing copyright laws is their function as resources for research and stimuli for ideas. Traditionally, knowledge and cultural production build upon prior knowledge and extant works, which is why both archiving existing works and providing open access to them are essential to future productions. Protection by means of copyright determines not only the level of protection for works; it also regulates access to the most important resources for innovation. The stronger copyright protects extant works, the slower creative processes are in producing new ones.

The contribution that open archives make to democracy, cultural diversity and the conservation of humankind's cultural heritage is evident in light of the UNESCO Declaration and the Convention on the Protection and Promotion of the Diversity of Cultural Expressions. Moreover, a direct corollary of these principles is a mandate for states to foster the existence of such open archives, which means creating the legal and financial framework conditions that ensure open access to as many such archives as possible.

The Nature of the Problem

The main problem of archiving at present isn't a technical but rather a legal one. In many cases—free radio, for instance—the production of content is publically subsidized. From this, we can, in turn, impute the social relevance that the subsidy providers attribute to this content. Nevertheless, this content is permitted to be made public only in conjunction with a radio broadcast and not in an archive. Needless to say, this proscription also applies to public broadcasting companies, numerous artistic & cultural projects, as well as libraries and museums. No sooner does open access become technically feasible than an effort is launched to find new possibilities to restrict it again in line with special interests. If government officials and politicians are really serious about free access to information, now's the time to demonstrate that actions—i.e. laws— speak louder than words.

In her speech entitled *A digital world of opportunities*[1] EU Commissioner Neelie Kroes underscored the potential of digitization of cultural works for artists, for the European public, and for cultural diversity. However, she expressly mentioned the fact that differing copyright laws would severely limit these possibilities, and gave several reasons why the existing system doesn't work. By way of example, she cited the *Europeana,* a collection of 12 million books, images, maps, pieces of music and videos that could remain unused due to unresolved copyright issues.

> " Europeana could be condemned to be a niche player rather than a world leader if it cannot be granted licenses and share the full catalogue of written and audio-visual material held in our cultural institutions. (...) Today our fragmented copyright system is ill-adapted to the real essence of art, which has no frontiers. Instead, that system has ended up giving a more prominent role to intermediaries than to artists. It irritates the public who often cannot access what artists want to offer and leaves a vacuum, which is served by illegal content, depriving the artists of their well deserved remuneration. And copyright enforcement is often entangled in sensitive questions about privacy, data protection or even net neutrality. "

Thus, a solution is urgently needed so that those who make available content in the digital domain can do so completely legally and are no longer relegated to a legal grey area. It's necessary to eliminate legal uncertainties and create possibilities for non-commercial publication.

Solutions

There are various potential solutions to the problem of adapting European copyright laws to the requirements of the internet. Above all, two approaches seem to be particularly relevant to the usage of material from archives: legal licensing and transformative (free) use of works. Legal licensing makes it possible to provide access so that—in the case of radio, for instance—programming could be made available without having to obtain individual authorization for each and every copyright-protected work included in it. Nevertheless, there still remains an obligation to compensate the copyright holder. Especially for radio programming, this legal arrangement would probably be among the most sensible since such material could then be archived and aired under the same conditions.

The introduction of the transformative (free) use of works would be another possibility of solving this problem. Essentially, the free use of a work is based on the concept of free use as long as exploitation possibilities are in no way diminished. With respect to the situation of archives, this would at least be a solution for those facilities that archive their own in-house productions, even if they contain other works. Certainly, there is general agreement that nobody wants to repeatedly listen to archived radio shows as a means of avoiding having to purchase music. Thus, if music is audible in the background of an interview, then it can be assumed that this is not going to have a deleterious effect on the music's sales.

In the present situation in which, due to legal uncertainty (orphan works) and immense transaction costs (clarification of copyright), information produced with public funds has to be withheld, there are no winners. Radio producers invest their labor in one-shot-deal broadcasts, taxpayers finance productions that, after being aired, cannot be made accessible appropriately, and neither collecting societies nor copyright holders profit from restrictions obligatory under copyright law.

The ARCHIVIA Conference hosted by the Verband Freier Radios and Radio FRO in cooperation with the Ars Electronica Festival is made possible by financial support from the City of Linz, the Province of Upper Austria and RTR GmbH.
Production associates: Wissensturm Linz (VHS, Medienwerkstatt), Creative Commons Austria hosted by ALLMENDA Gemeinwohl Genossenschaft, dorf tv.

1   Address on November 5, 2010; online at *http://europa.eu/rapid/pressReleasesAction.do?reference= SPEECH/10/619&format=HTML&aged=0&language=EN&guiLanguage=en* (as of January 4, 2011)

Verband Freier Radios Österreich (VFRÖ) / Radio FRO

Freier Zugang vor kontrolliertem Ausschluss
Ein Plädoyer für die Öffnung von digitalen Archiven

Die Konferenz *Archivia* fokussiert auf einen Aspekt der Digitalisierung, der in Debatten um den freien Zugang zu Information oftmals verloren geht, nämlich auf die Neudefinition der Rolle und Funktion von Archiven. Über lange Zeit sind Archive vorwiegend für den professionellen Gebrauch von JournalistInnen und WissenschaftlerInnen genutzt worden, da die Zugänglichkeit oft schon auf Grund von geografischen Distanzen beschränkt war. Diese Situation hat sich in den letzten fünfzehn Jahren radikal verändert: Heute können oder vielmehr könnten Archive eine weltweit zugängliche Ressource für eine globale Öffentlichkeit sein. Doch obwohl die technischen Voraussetzungen für eine solche Nutzung bereits seit mehr als einem Jahrzehnt bestehen, hinkt die rechtliche Situation hinterher, sodass Rechtsunsicherheit herrscht, die die Bereitstellung von Archiven und somit den Zugang zu Information erschwert. Viele Archive schrecken auf Grund von hohen Transaktionskosten, die durch die Rechteabklärung entstehen, sowie vor der Gefahr möglicher Urheberrechtsklagen, die durch verwaiste Werke entstehen können, vor der digitalen Veröffentlichung zurück.

Digitale Technologien haben die Möglichkeiten für die Produktion und den Austausch kultureller und künstlerischer Werke revolutioniert – Produktion und Zugang wurden technisch stark vereinfacht. Auch die Produktionsweisen haben sich entlang der Technologien verändert, was vor allem in rechtlicher Hinsicht für zusätzliche Konfusion sorgte. Zum einen erhöhte sich die Geschwindigkeit, mit der auf neue Phänomene reagiert wurde und Informationen adaptiert und verändert werden konnten, und zum anderen nahm die Zahl von einerseits kollaborativ und andererseits dezentral entstandenen Werke rapide zu. Auch Archive können im digitalen Raum kollaborativ aufgebaut und verwaltet werden, wodurch wiederum eine eigene Dynamik entstehen kann. Folglich gibt es aber auch nicht notwendigerweise eine zentrale Stelle, die alle Vorgänge kontrollieren kann. Auch hier klaffen Praxis und Urheberrecht auseinander, denn der Aufbau digitaler Archive ist oft ein kollektiver Prozess, der Rahmenbedingungen benötigt, die ungeordnetes, ungeplantes Wachstum erlauben.

Ein weiteres Problem für digitale Archive mit dem bestehenden Urheberrecht liegt in ihrer Funktion als Ressource für Recherche und als Stimulus für Ideen. Traditionellerweise bauen Wissen und kulturelle Produktion auf bereits bestehendem Vor-Wissen und bestehenden Werken auf, weshalb sowohl Archivierung wie auch der offene Zugang zu bestehenden Werken essenziell für künftige Produktionen sind. Der Schutz durch das Urheberrecht legt nicht nur das Schutzniveau für Werke fest, sondern bestimmt auch die Zugänglichkeit zur wichtigsten Ressource für Neues: Je stärker das Urheberrecht vorhandene Werke schützt, desto langsamer werden auch kreative Prozesse, die Neues schaffen.

Der Beitrag, den offene Archive für Demokratie, kulturelle Vielfalt und die Erhaltung des kulturellen Erbes leisten, ist im Sinne der UNESCO-Deklaration und des „Übereinkommens zum Schutz und der Förderung der Vielfalt kultureller Ausdrucksformen" evident. Daraus leitet sich auch direkt der Auftrag an Staaten ab, zur Existenz solcher offener Archive beizutragen, das heißt rechtliche und finanzielle Rahmenbedingungen zu schaffen, um einen offenen Zugang zu möglichst vielen Archiven zu gewährleisten.

Problemstellung

Das Hauptproblem bei der Archivierung ist derzeit kein technisches, sondern ein rechtliches. In vielen Fällen – wie auch bei den freien Radios – wird die Produktion der Inhalte öffentlich gefördert, woraus sich wiederum die gesellschaftliche Relevanz ableiten lässt, die die FördergeberInnen diesen Inhalten beimessen. Dennoch dürfen diese Inhalte nur im Rahmen einer Radiosendung veröffentlicht werden, nicht aber in einem Archiv. Dies gilt selbstverständlich auch für den öffentlichen Rundfunk, zahlreiche Kunst- und Kulturprojekte sowie Bibliotheken und Museen. Just in dem Moment, wo ein öffentlicher Zugang technisch möglich geworden ist, wird nach Möglichkeiten gesucht, diesen auf Grund von Partikularinteressen wieder einzuschränken. Wenn es der Politik mit dem freien Zugang zu Information wirklich ernst ist, dann ist es an der Zeit, den Worten Taten oder, besser noch, Gesetze folgen zu lassen.

In ihrer Rede mit dem Titel *Eine digitale Welt der Möglichkeiten*[1] unterstrich EU-Kommissarin Neelie Kroes die Potenziale der Digitalisierung kultureller Werke für KünstlerInnen, für die europäische Öffentlichkeit und für die kulturelle Vielfalt. Sie wies allerdings ausdrücklich darauf hin, dass die unterschiedlichen Urheberrechtsgesetze diese Möglichkeiten stark einschränken würden, und führte mehrere Gründe an, warum das bestehende System nicht funktioniere. Als Beispiel nannte sie die *Europeana,* eine Sammlung von 12 Millionen Büchern, Bildern, Karten, Musikstücken und Videos, die auf Grund ungeklärter Urheberrechtsfragen ungenutzt bleiben könnte:

> Europeana could be condemned to be a niche player rather than a world leader if it cannot be granted licenses and share the full catalogue of written and audio-visual material held in our cultural institutions. (...) Today our fragmented copyright system is ill-adapted to the real essence of art, which has no frontiers. Instead, that system has ended up giving a more prominent role to intermediaries than to artists. It irritates the public who often cannot access what artists want to offer and leaves a vacuum, which is served by illegal content, depriving the artists of their well deserved remuneration. And copyright enforcement is often entangled in sensitive questions about privacy, data protection or even net neutrality.

Es bedarf also dringend einer Lösung, Inhalte im digitalen Raum nicht nur in einer legistischen Grauzone, sondern vollständig legal verfügbar zu machen, die Rechtsunsicherheiten zu beseitigen und Möglichkeiten für nichtkommerzielle Veröffentlichungen zu schaffen.

Lösungen

Es gibt verschiedene Lösungsansätze, um das europäische Urheberrecht an die Anforderungen des Internet anzupassen. Vor allem zwei Ansätze erscheinen für die Nutzung von Archiven besonders relevant: Gesetzliche Lizenzen und transformative (freie) Werknutzung. Gesetzliche Lizenzen ermöglichen den Zugang, sodass – wie auch beim Radio selbst – Sendungen bereitgestellt werden dürfen, ohne für jedes einzelne urheberrechtlich geschützte Werk eine Einzelgenehmigung erwirken zu müssen. Dennoch besteht eine Kompensationspflicht gegenüber den UrheberInnen. Gerade für Radiosendungen wäre diese Regelung wohl eine der nachvollziehbarsten, da sie dann unter den gleichen Bedingungen archiviert wie auch über den Äther verbreitet würden.

Die Einführung einer transformativen (freien) Werknutzung wäre eine weitere Möglichkeit, dieses Problem zu lösen. Im Wesentlichen basieren freie Werknutzungen auf dem Gedanken der freien Nutzung, solange die Verwertungsmöglichkeiten nicht beeinträchtigt werden. Auf die Situation der Archive bezogen wäre dies zumindest eine Lösung für jene Archive, die Eigenproduktionen archivieren, auch wenn andere Werke darin enthalten sind. Es ist einsichtig, dass niemand archivierte Radiosendungen wiederholt hören will, um dem Kauf der Musik zu umgehen. Ist also im Hintergrund eines Interviews Musik zu hören, so kann davon ausgegangen werden, dass dies die Verkaufszahlen der Musik nicht beeinträchtigt.

In der derzeitigen Situation, in der auf Grund von Rechtsunsicherheit (verwaiste Werke) und immensen Transaktionskosten (Rechteabklärung) mit öffentlichen Mitteln produzierte Information zurückgehalten werden muss, gibt es keine GewinnerInnen. Die RadiomacherInnen investieren ihre Arbeit für eine einmalige Sendung, die SteuerzahlerInnen finanzieren Produktionen, die nach der Ausstrahlung nicht entsprechend zugänglich gemacht werden dürfen, und weder Verwertungsgesellschaften noch RechteinhaberInnen profitieren von den urheberrechtlich bedingten Einschränkungen.

Text: Alexander Baratsits, Margarita Köhl, Paul Stepan

1   Rede vom 5.11.2010 online unter *http://europa.eu/rapid/pressReleasesAction.do?reference= SPEECH/10/619&format=HTML&aged=0&language=EN&guiLanguage=en* (Stand 4.1.2011).

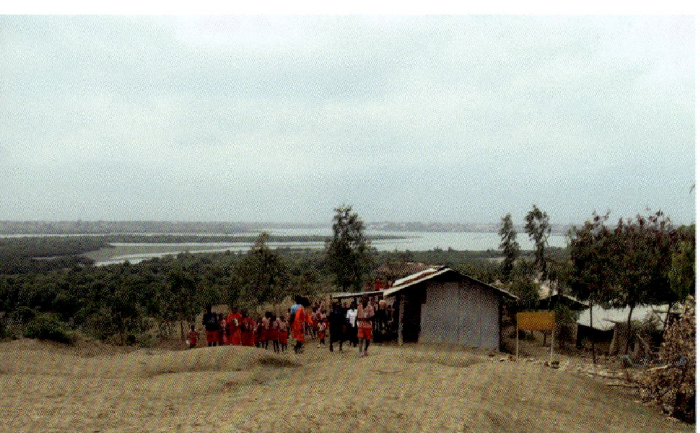 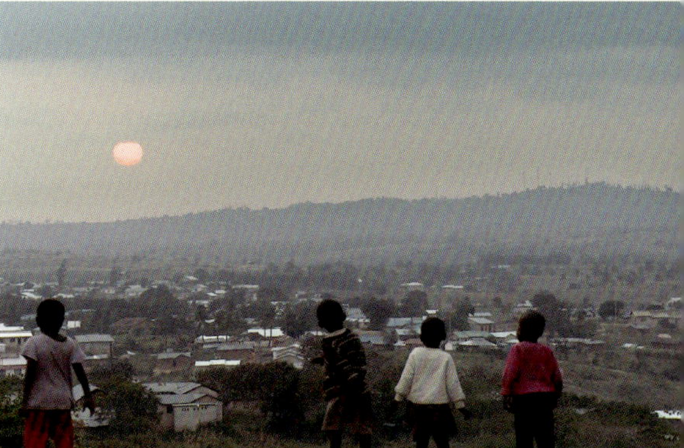

Sebastian Frisch

Whisper down the lane

Whisper down the lane is a multimedia project that aims to reach people in many different cultures to heighten awareness of HIV/AIDS, a complex of issues that has lost none of its explosiveness even after years of media coverage.

To carry out this project, a team of eight undergrads in the Salzburg University of Applied Sciences' MultiMediaArt bachelor's program traveled to Kenya to investigate rumors about HIV and AIDS that are circulating in numerous African states, as well as their impact on society. These rumors are an aspect that has played a subsidiary role at best in previous confrontations with these issues; nevertheless, they make a major contribution to the spread of HIV and to the social discrimination that besets its victims. Women and children in particular suffer from the negative consequences that accompany these rumors and how people deal with them.

Working closely with local organizations, the team produced a 45-minute documentary film as well as a poster campaign designed to motivate local people to reconsider their attitudes about HIV and AIDS and to openly discuss topics that many treat as taboo.

This project's aim is by no means to proselytize people or to indoctrinate them with behavioral norms and putative values from a Eurocentric perspective.

Rather, it's meant to give people food for thought and to foster active encounters with these issues, to prompt reflection on existing taboos and generally accepted modes of behavior, and to enable people to take new approaches.

In conjunction with this project, the team set up the *http://www.whisperdownthelane.com* website that makes available all relevant content, the trailer for the documentary, the poster, and additional info about the project.

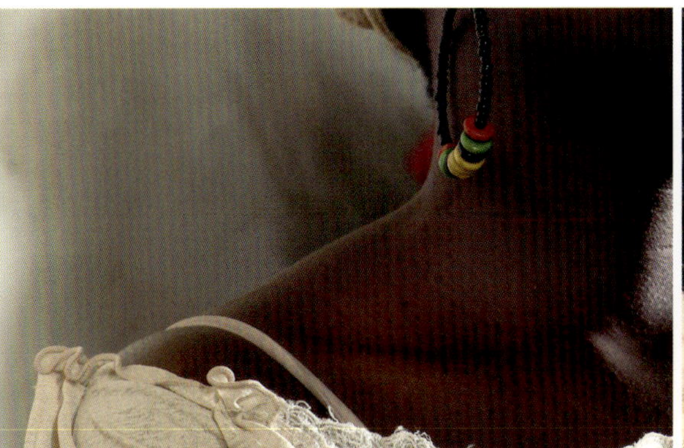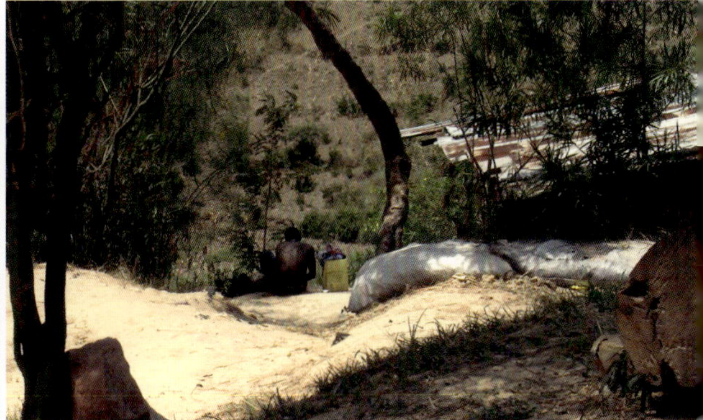

Whisper down the lane ist ein multimediales Projekt mit dem Ziel, Menschen aller Kulturkreise für den Themenkomplex HIV/AIDS zu sensibilisieren, der auch nach Jahren medialer Präsenz nicht an Brisanz verloren hat.

Ein Team aus acht Studenten und Studentinnen des Bachelor-Studiengang MultiMediaArt der Fachhochschule Salzburg reiste dazu nach Kenia, um die Gerüchte, die in vielen afrikanischen Staaten rund um HIV und AIDS kursieren sowie deren Auswirkungen auf die Gesellschaft zu thematisieren. Diese Gerüchte sind ein Aspekt, dem in der bisherigen Auseinandersetzung mit der Thematik allenfalls eine untergeordnete Rolle zukommt, sie tragen jedoch einen wesentlichen Teil zur Verbreitung von HIV und der sozialen Diskriminierung Betroffener bei. Besonders Frauen und Kinder sind von den negativen Folgen, die mit diesen Gerüchten und dem Umgang damit einhergehen, betroffen.

So entstand in enger Zusammenarbeit mit Organisationen vor Ort neben einer filmischen Dokumentation mit 45 Minuten Spielzeit eine Plakatkampagne, die die Menschen vor Ort anregen sollte, ihre Einstellung bezüglich HIV und AIDS zu überdenken und über die Thematik zu sprechen, die oftmals als Tabuthema gehandelt wird.

Ziel des Projekts ist keinesfalls, Menschen zu missionieren oder aus einer eurozentristischen Sichtweise Verhaltensnormen und vermeintliche Werte zu indoktrinieren. Vielmehr sollen Denkanstöße gegeben und die aktive Auseinandersetzung mit der Thematik gefördert werden, um bestehende Tabus und inhärente Verhaltensweisen zu reflektieren und neue Zugänge zu ermöglichen.

Im Zuge des Projekts wurde die Website *http://www.whisperdownthelane.com* eingerichtet, auf der alle relevanten Inhalte, der Trailer zur Dokumentation, die Plakate sowie weitere Informationen zum Projekt zur Verfügung stehen.

Institute: MultiMediaArt, Salzburg University of Applied Sciences; Director: Sebastian Frisch; Executive Producers: Sebastian Frisch, Julia Zisser, Julia-Pia Huemer; Screenplay: Victoria Preuer, Christina Schmölz; Editing: Julia Zisser; Screenplay Editors: Sebastian Frisch, Julia Zisser; Head of Camera Department: Christina Schmölz Camera: Martin Keindl, Andreas Steger; Assistant Director: Julia-Pia Huemer; Color Correction: Christina Schmölz; Music: Sebastian Frisch, Mary, Matabibu, Sticko; Head of Audio Department: Sebastian Frisch; Audio Post Production: Hannah Langhagel Key; Technician: Andreas Steger Graphic Design / Poster Campaign: Victoria Preuer; Translation: Andrew Nyenya Nyambeau, Luke Fredrick, Charles Kiamba, Peter Ngara; Subtitles: Andreas Steger, Martin Keindl; Production Assistants: Betty Kitili, Andrew Nyenya Nyambeau, Angela Kisangau Interview Assistants: Betty Kitili, Angela Kisangau, Akullah Khamisi, Andrew Nyenya Nyambeau; Press: Martin Keindl

ARS ELECTRONICA CENTER

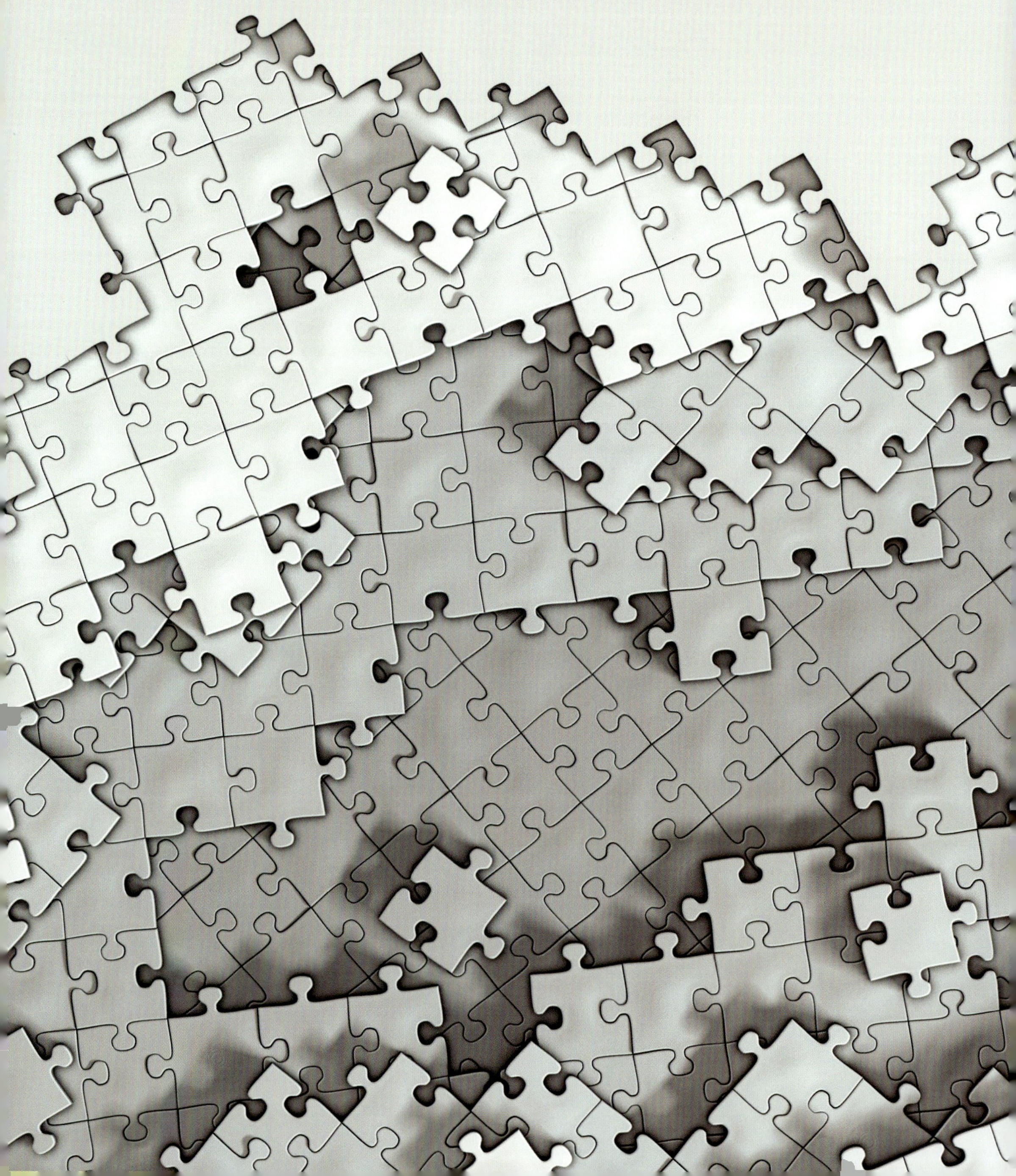

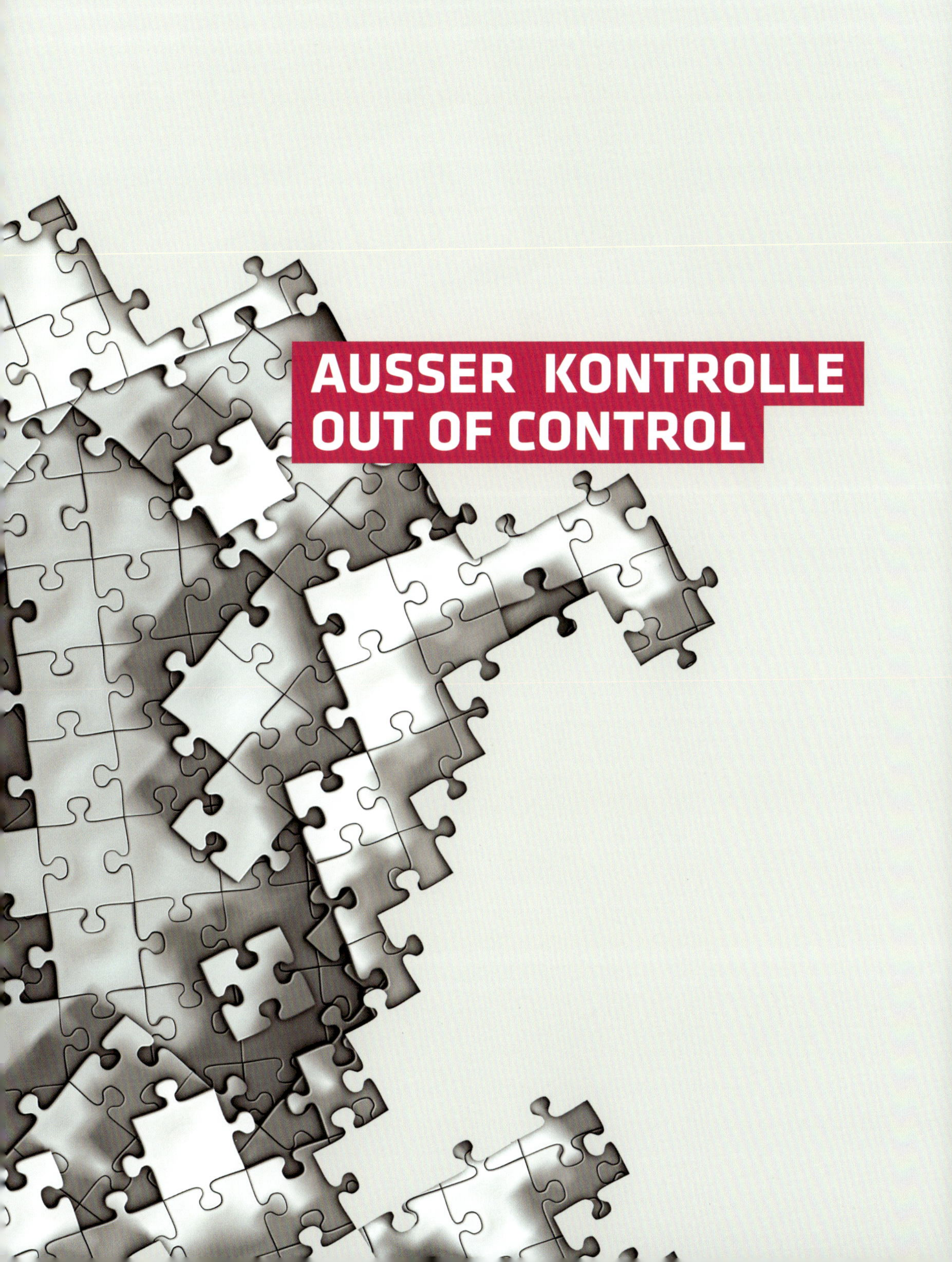
AUSSER KONTROLLE
OUT OF CONTROL

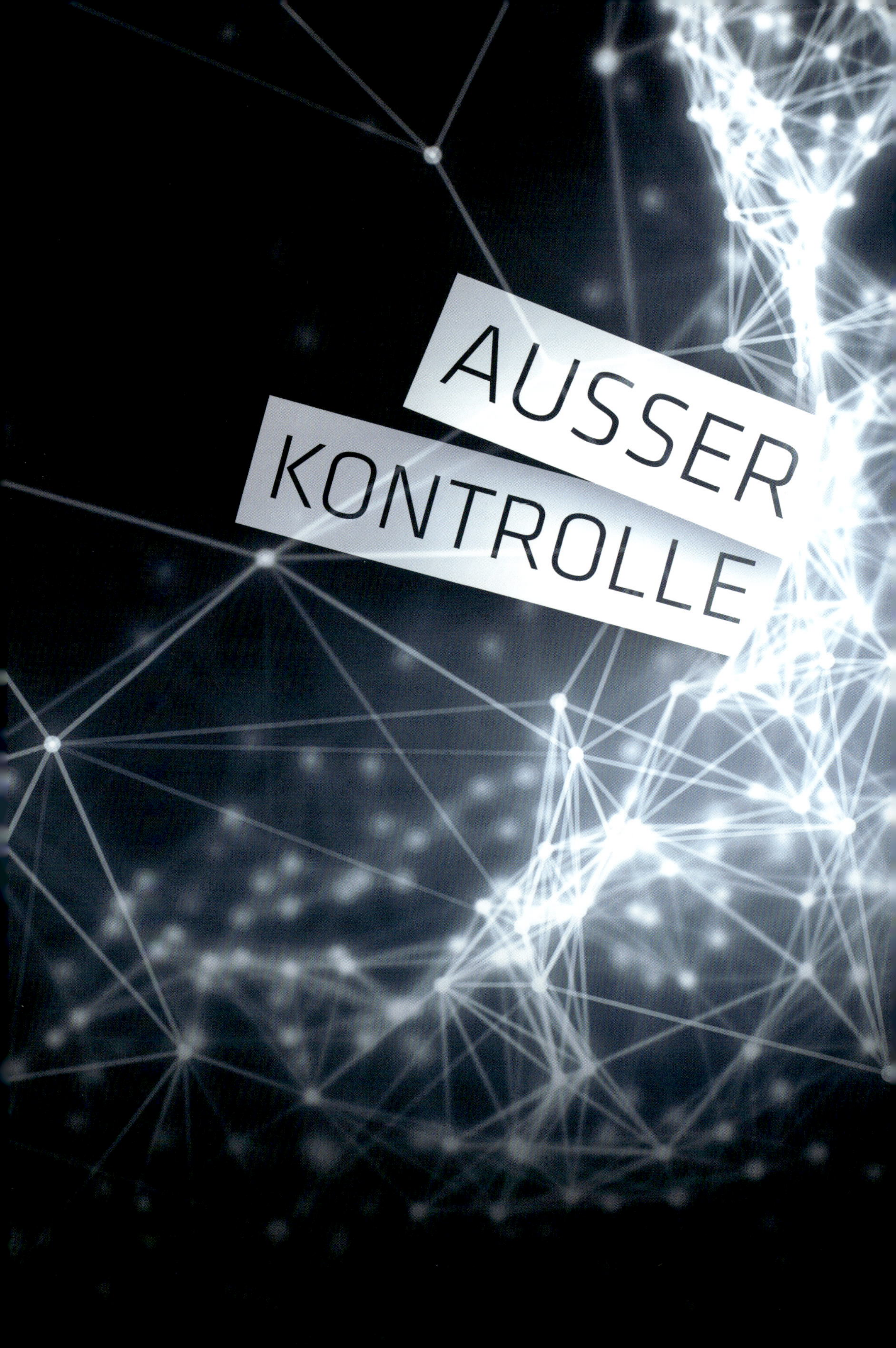

AUSSER
KONTROLLE

OUT OF CONTROL
What the Internet Knows about You

A clash over the possession and dissemination of personal data is now raging worldwide. Politicians and bureaucrats, corporate executives and civil rights activists—it seems they're all squabbling about who may, should or must know what about us and retain it how long! And regardless of who finally prevails in this skirmish, the victory comes with a short expiration date. Why? Because the internet and the services that make it up are changing so rapidly that we users and our elected officials can hardly keep pace. Social networks like Facebook, search engines like Google and all the rest—they know so much about us it's scary! From the moment we get logged into our Google account, our online activities are comprehensively registered— what we buy, the vacations we book, which songs, films and books we like, the videos we view. Thus, because it's completely automatic, it's a simple matter for Google to figure out if we're single or have a family, what income bracket we're in, what we devote most of our energies to and what our sexual preferences are. And Facebook already has its feelers stretched out far beyond its home turf. There are more and more websites we can log on to with our Facebook profile, and, sure, that's really convenient, but it also gives a growing number of services the ability to gain access to the data that we've—voluntarily—revealed on Facebook. Whereby "voluntarily" is true only to a certain extent here, since in many cases all that's necessary is for our Facebook friends to register on a particular website.

Out of Control—What the Internet Knows about You, the Ars Electronica Center's new exhibition produced jointly with the Department of Secure Information Systems at the Upper Austria University of Applied Sciences' Hagenberg Campus, scrutinizes the constantly shifting border between the public and private spheres, and the opportunities and risks this entails for us users.

In cooperation with the Department of Secure Information Systems at Upper Austria University of Applied Sciences' Hagenberg Campus

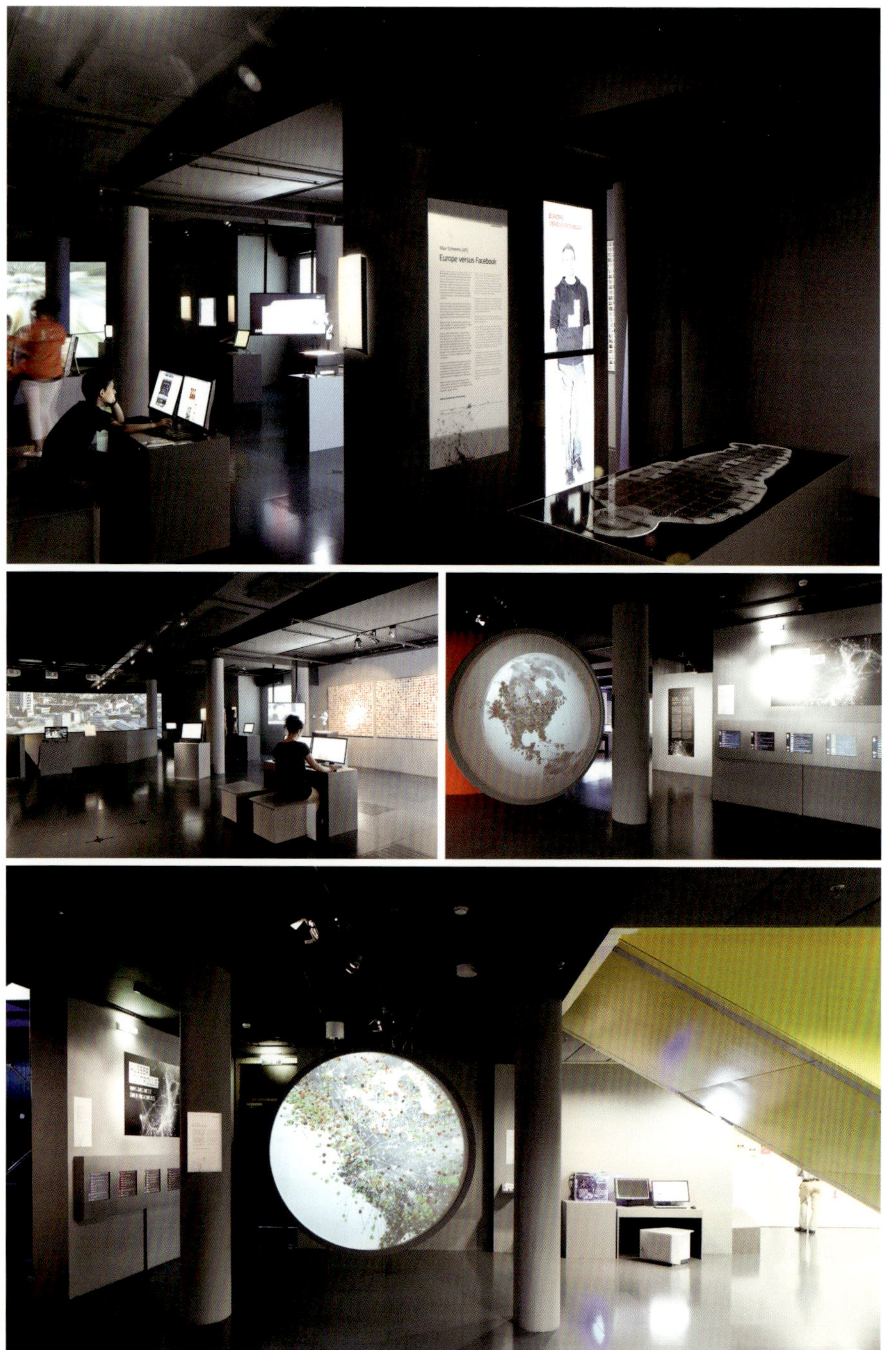

AUSSER KONTROLLE
Was das Netz über dich weiß

Weltweit tobt ein Streit rund um den Besitz und die Weitergabe personenbezogener Daten. PolitikerInnen und Behörden, Unternehmen, AktivistInnen und BürgerrechtlerInnen – sie alle diskutieren darüber, wer was wie lange über uns wissen soll, darf oder muss. Und ganz egal, wer sich dabei durchsetzt, es wird bei einem „Erfolg auf Zeit" bleiben. Warum? Weil das Netz und die darin versammelten Services sich so schnell verändern, dass UserInnen wie Gesetzgeber kaum noch mitkommen. Ob soziale Netzwerke wie Facebook oder Dienste wie Google, sie alle wissen mittlerweile beängstigend viel über uns. Einmal mit unserem Google-Konto eingeloggt, werden alle unsere Online-Aktivitäten lückenlos dokumentiert: was wir kaufen, wo wir unseren Urlaub buchen, welche Musik, Filme und Bücher uns gefallen, welche Videos wir uns ansehen. Und so ist es für Google auch ein Leichtes – weil automatisiert – festzustellen, ob wir Singles sind oder eine Familie haben, welcher Einkommensschicht wir angehören, wo wir unseren Lebensmittelpunkt und welche sexuellen Vorlieben wir haben. Auch Facebook hat seine Fühler schon weit über den eigenen Tellerrand hinaus ausgestreckt. Auf immer mehr Websites können wir uns mit unserem Facebook-Profil anmelden, und so bequem das ist, eröffnet dies gleichzeitig immer mehr Diensten die Möglichkeit, auf unsere Daten zuzugreifen, die wir – freiwillig – auf Facebook geparkt haben. Wobei „freiwillig" nur bedingt richtig ist, weil es häufig schon reicht, dass sich unsere FreundInnen via Facebook auf einer Website anmelden.

Mit der neuen Ausstellung *Außer Kontrolle – Was das Netz über dich weiß* widmet sich das Ars Electronica Center gemeinsam mit dem Department Sichere Informationssysteme der FH OÖ Campus Hagenberg dem sich stetig verschiebenden Verhältnis von Öffentlichkeit und Privatheit und den Chancen wie Risiken, die sich daraus für uns UserInnen ergeben.

In Kooperation mit dem Department Sichere Informationssysteme der FH Oberösterreich, Campus Hagenberg

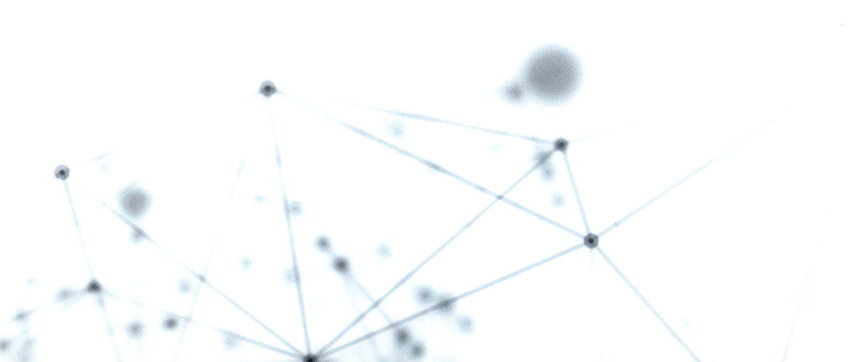

Ingrid Schaumüller-Bichl

Protection of Privacy

Never before has there been so much discussion about the protection of privacy and the threats to it. And it's no wonder. Never before in human history has it been possible to gather so much information about an individual in so short a time. Whether we're using Google, Facebook or location-based services, we all leave behind traces of our activities online. And at the click of a button, all of us have access to more information about other people than we would have even dreamed possible a few years ago. To say nothing of information gathering via video surveillance, telecommunications data retention and data mining.

It is definitely necessary to conduct a comprehensive discourse in which scholars and the general public discuss how we ought to deal with these issues in the future.

In the area of tension and interplay at the nexus of individual liberties, safeguarding privacy, and the protection of the polity and the community, there has to be balanced consideration of the interests of all parties involved.

Essential preconditions for the protection of privacy are the creation of a legal framework as well as fostering people's awareness of these problematic issues. But it also calls for techniques and procedures for implementing these circumstances in actual practice.

The field of information security has come up with a whole series of technical and organizational solutions that can contribute to protecting personal privacy. Classic procedures like encryption and digital signatures are being supplemented with new methods designed to enable people to use the internet securely and anonymously.

Nevertheless, the decisive role is played by people, by each and every one of us. A conscious, cautious mode of dealing with our own data, basic knowledge about correct security settings, and awareness of the dangers and risks that new media entail are essential preconditions for not completely ceding sovereignty over one's private sphere.

At the Department of Secure Information Systems at the University of Applied Sciences Upper Austria in Hagenberg, we're working on technical and organizational solutions to protect individual privacy as well as corporate data. The *Out of Control—What the Internet Knows about You* exhibition is an interesting opportunity to address these technical issues within the context of a broad-based social as well as artistic discourse.

The Upper Austria University of Applied Sciences is the largest such educational institution in Austria. At its Hagenberg Campus, the school offers practice-oriented higher education in the fields of computer science, communications and media. Since 2000, the Department of Secure Information Systems has offered both bachelor's and master's programs in Secure Information Systems (formerly Computer & Media Security) to train security experts in information & communication technology including data security, network security, system security, secure business organization as well as in such cutting-edge areas as cyber-criminality, mobile security, social network security and forensics.

Ingrid Schaumüller-Bichl

Schutz der Privatsphäre

Nie zuvor wurde so viel über den Schutz und die mögliche Gefährdung der Privatsphäre diskutiert wie heute. Das ist nicht verwunderlich: Nie zuvor in der Geschichte der Menschheit war es möglich, so viele Informationen in so kurzer Zeit über ein Individuum zu sammeln. Ob Google, Facebook oder Location Based Services – wir alle hinterlassen Spuren im Netz, und wir alle haben auf Knopfdruck mehr Informationen über andere zur Verfügung, als wir es uns noch vor wenigen Jahren hätten träumen lassen. Von gezielter Datensammlung durch Videoüberwachung, Vorratsdatenspeicherung oder Data Mining ganz zu schweigen.

Mit Sicherheit ist es notwendig, einen umfassenden wissenschaftlichen und gesellschaftlichen Diskurs darüber zu führen, wie wir mit dem Thema in Zukunft umgehen wollen. Im Spannungsfeld zwischen persönlicher Freiheit des Einzelnen, Schutz der Privatsphäre („Privacy") und Schutz des Staates und des Gemeinwesens müssen die Interessen aller Beteiligten abgewogen werden. Es ist ein Konsens zu schaffen, der immer wieder neu zu diskutieren und den sich ändernden gesellschaftlichen Anforderungen anzupassen ist.

Wichtige Voraussetzungen für die Gewährleistung von Privacy sind die Schaffung von rechtlichen Rahmenbedingungen sowie die Förderung eines gesellschaftlichen Bewusstseins für diese Problematik. Doch es braucht auch Techniken und Verfahren, diese Rahmenbedingungen in der Praxis umzusetzen. Die moderne Informationssicherheit kennt eine ganze Reihe technischer und organisatorischer Lösungen, die zum Schutz der Privatsphäre beitragen können. Klassische Verfahren wie Verschlüsselung und digitale Unterschriften werden ergänzt durch neue Lösungen, die es ermöglichen, sich sicher und anonym im Netz zu bewegen.

Doch die ganz entscheidende Rolle kommt dem Menschen, kommt uns allen zu: ein bewusster, sorgfältiger Umgang mit den eigenen Daten, das Grundwissen über korrekte Sicherheitseinstellungen sowie das Bewusstsein über Gefahren und Risiken der neuen Medien sind wesentliche Voraussetzungen dafür, dass wir nicht völlig zum viel zitierten „gläsernen Menschen" werden.

Als Studiengang „Sichere Informationssysteme" der FH OÖ, Campus Hagenberg, arbeiten wir an technischen und organisatorischen Lösungen, um den Schutz der Privatsphäre jedes Einzelnen, aber auch die Sicherheit von Unternehmensdaten zu gewährleisten. Die Ausstellung *Außer Kontrolle – Was das Netz über dich weiß* gibt die spannende Möglichkeit, diese wissenschaftlichen Fragestellungen in einem breiten gesellschaftlichen und auch künstlerischen Diskurs zu thematisieren.

Die FH Oberösterreich ist die größte FH in Österreich. In Hagenberg bietet sie praxisorientierte Hochschulausbildung in den Bereichen Informatik, Kommunikation und Medien an. Das Department für Sichere Informationssysteme mit dem Bachelor- und dem Masterstudium "Sichere Informationssysteme" (ehemals "Computer- und Mediensicherheit") bildet seit dem Jahr 2000 ExpertInnen für IKT-Sicherheit in den Themenbereichen Datenschutz, Netzwerksicherheit, Systemsicherheit, Sichere Unternehmensorganisation und in neuen Gebieten wie Cyberkriminalität, Mobile-Security, Social-Network-Security und Forensik aus.

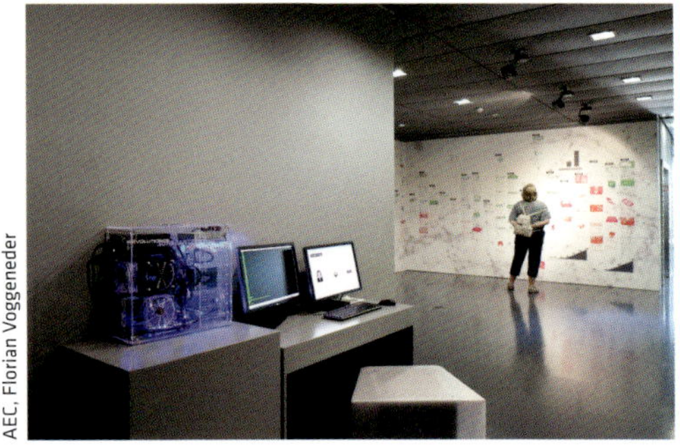
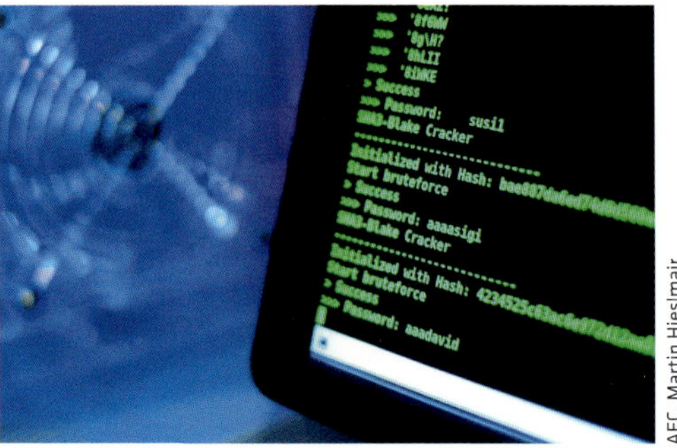

AEC, Florian Vogeneder

AEC, Martin Hieslmair

Password Hacker
Sichere Informationssysteme FH OÖ

A good password is hard to guess. A so-called *password recovery tool* is a readily available computer program that lets users quickly test passwords. Here, visitors can see how hard it is to figure out a particular password and how long that would take. Simple passwords can even be hacked live with a gamer PC. Of course, there are also suggestions for coming up with strong passwords.

Ein gutes Passwort ist schwer zu erraten. Unter dem Namen *Password Recovery Tool* sind Programme zum schnellen Probieren von Passwörtern erhältlich. Hier kann mit selbstge-wählten Passwörtern experimentiert werden, wie schwer sie zu erraten sind und wie lange es dauern würde, sie zu finden. Einfache Passwörter lassen sich mit einem Gamer-PC auch live „knacken". Tipps für gute Passwörter gibt es natürlich ebenso.

Andreas Vogl, Marco Macala, Andrea Mayrhofer

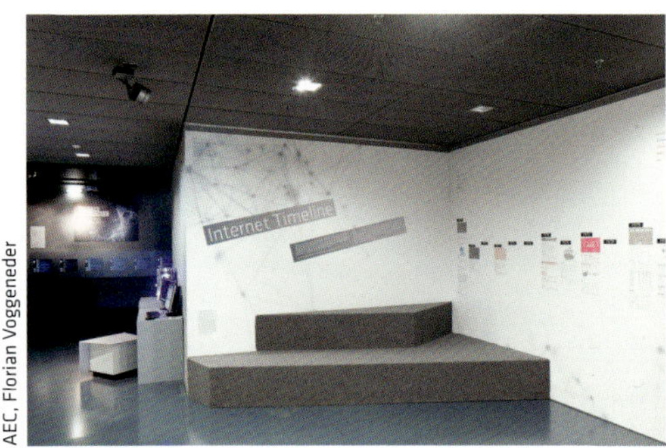

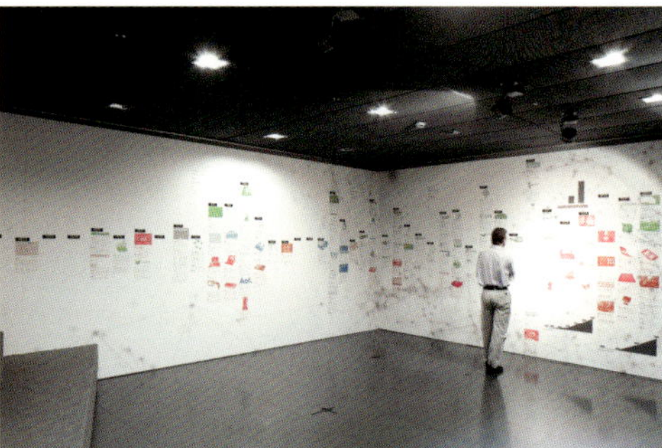

AEC, Florian Vogeneder

Timeline
Ars Electronica, Sichere Informationssysteme FH OÖ

An extensive timeline installed in the Ars Electronica Center elaborates on the history and development of the World Wide Web. The graphics range from a depiction of the Unix multiuser operating system developed at Bell Laboratories in 1963 to the telecommunications data retention law that just went into effect in Austria.

Mit einer meterlangen Timeline zeichnet das Ars Electronica Center Geschichte und Entwicklung des World Wide Web nach. Die Grafik reicht vom 1963 an den Bell Laboratories entwickelten Mehrbenutzerbetriebssystems Unix bis zur gerade eben auch in Österreich eingeführten Vorratsdatenspeicherung.

Recherche: David Starzengruber, Florian Bauböck, Text: Martin Hieslmair, Grafik: Nicolas Naveau

Telecommunications Data Retention
Ars Electronica Futurelab

Since April 1, telecommunications data retention has been in force in Austria too. The Ars Electronica Center's interactive station lets the history of this legislation pass in review. Users can see exactly what information is being gathered and stored about their cell phone and computer usage, and join a discussion—on-site as well as online—about various aspects of telecommunications data retention.

The right to privacy, data protection and copyright are issues that affect us all. Visitors can take advantage of this opportunity to participate in an exchange of views, or get involved in the discussion from their home via the internet. By touching one of the various nodes the posted comments can be read. By turning the net, participants can access other topics. "Link Up" within a comment allows participants to input their own opinion on a topic.

Seit 1. April ist die Vorratsdatenspeicherung (VDS) nun auch in Österreich Realität. Mit einer interaktiven Station rollt das Ars Electronica Center die Geschichte der VDS noch einmal auf. Jede/r kann sich hier ansehen, was genau von der VDS künftig erfasst wird und was nicht. Vor Ort und via Internet kann dann über die verschiedenen Aspekte der VDS diskutiert werden. Themen wie Privatsphäre, Datenschutz und Urheberrecht betreffen uns alle. Hier können Besucher am Meinungsaustausch teilnehmen – oder sich zu Hause über das Internet der Diskussion anschließen. Durch Berühren der vorhandenen Knotenpunkte kann man die Kommentare lesen und durch Drehen des Netzes gelangt man zu anderen Themen. Wählt man „Anknüpfen" innerhalb eines Kommentars, kann man selbst seine Meinung zu einem Thema abgeben.

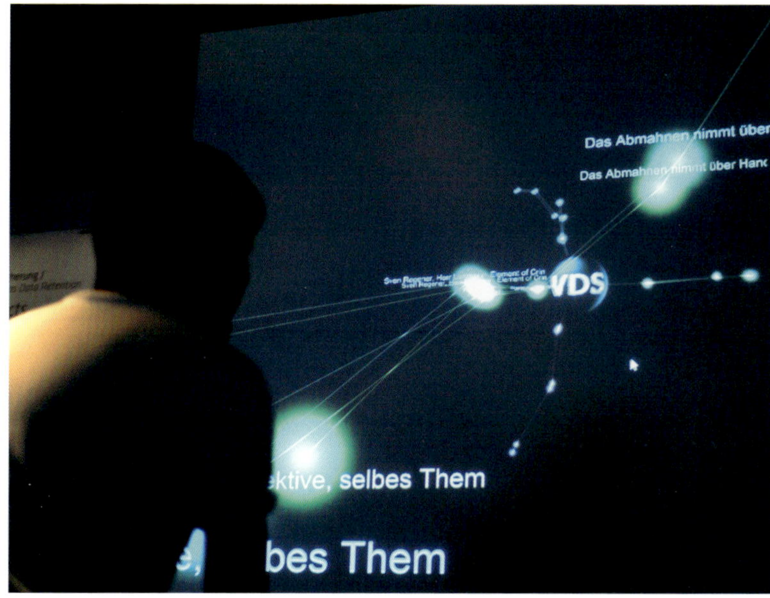

AEC, Martin Hieslmair

Newstweek
Julian Oliver, Danja Vasiliev

Newstweek is a device for manipulating news that can be accessed at WLAN hotspots. Equipment built into a conventional electrical outlet plug makes it possible to alter news being read on laptops, cell phones and tablets without users getting suspicious (initially). The point of *Newstweek* is to point out that our reality is increasingly imparted via media and determined by them. Whereas news is read ever more frequently in digital form, its propagation is still done according to a traditional top-down model that, in turn, makes it susceptible to influence exerted by politicians and businesspeople. *Newstweek* represents an intervention in precisely this model, offering citizens an opportunity to manipulate the media themselves and do a little spin-doctoring of their own.

Newstweek ist ein Gerät zur Manipulation von Nachrichten, die an WLAN-Hotspots abgerufen werden. Das in einen unauffälligen Netzstecker verbaute Gerät ermöglicht es, auf Laptops, Mobiltelefonen und Tablets gelesene Nachrichten zu verändern, ohne dass die UserInnen etwas davon bemerken. „Newstweek" will darauf aufmerksam machen, dass unsere Realität zunehmend über Medien vermittelt und von diesen bestimmt wird. Während Nachrichten immer häufiger digital gelesen werden, folgt ihre Verbreitung hingegen immer noch einem traditionellen Top-down-Modell, was sie wiederum anfällig für die Einflussnahme durch Politik und Wirtschaft macht. In genau dieses Model greift *Newstweek* ein und bietet den BürgerInnen die Möglichkeit, ihrerseits Medien zu manipulieren und ein wenig „an den Fakten zu drehen".
http://newstweek.com/

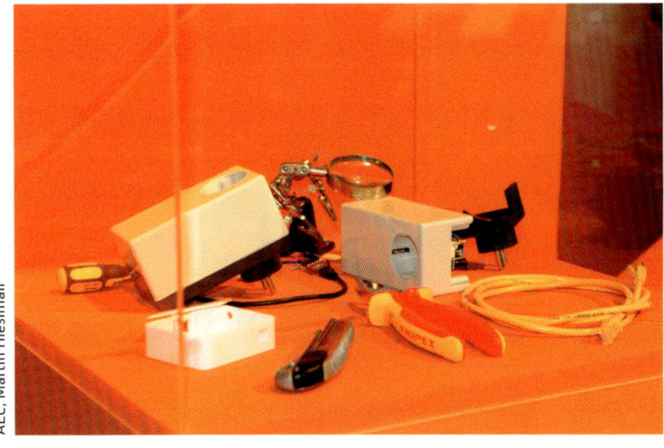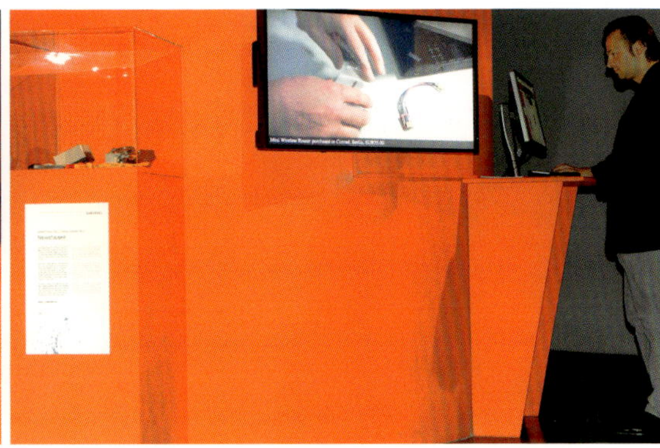

Faceless
Manu Luksch

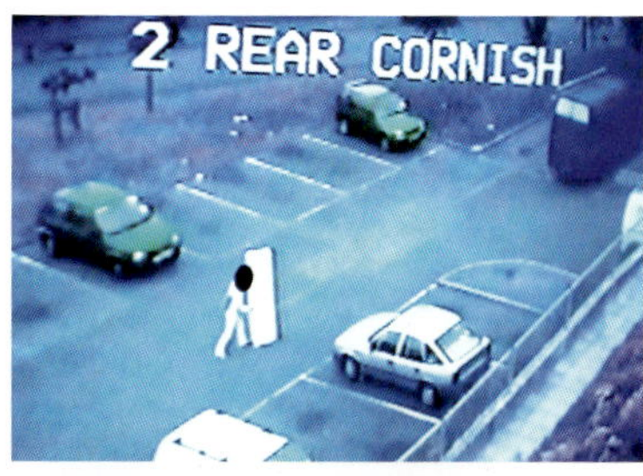

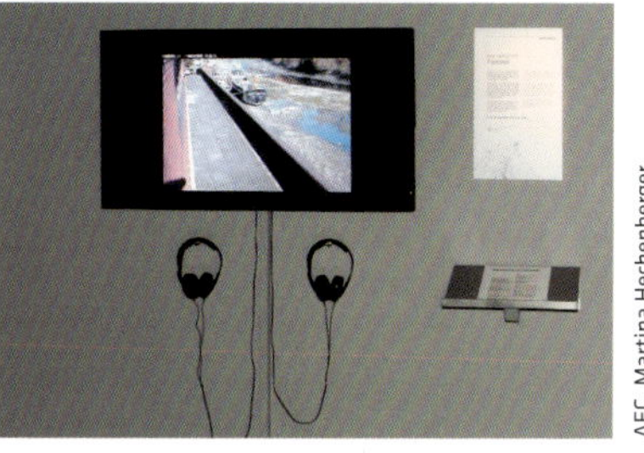

Austrian artist Manu Luksch shot her film *faceless* without the slightest cinematography on her part. The filming was done exclusively by public surveillance video cameras. London was the location of this unusual shoot. Once the filming was completed, the artist sued to obtain all footage in which she appeared. The faces of all other—unintentional—cast members were erased or concealed in consideration of their right to privacy. The end product is a film well worth seeing, one that focuses on increasingly pervasive surveillance in public spaces.

Mit *faceless* drehte die österreichische Künstlerin Manu Luksch einen Film, ohne auch nur eine eigene Kamera einzusetzen. Gefilmt wurde ausschließlich mit Kameras der öffentlichen Videoüberwachung, Schauplatz dieser ungewöhnlichen Dreharbeiten war London. Nachdem die Dreharbeiten abgeschlossen waren, klagte die Künstlerin alles Bildmaterial ein, auf dem sie zu sehen war. Die Gesichter aller anderen – unbeteiligten – Personen dagegen wurden aus datenschutzrechtlichen Gründen gelöscht bzw. durch Farbpunkte abgedeckt. Ergebnis ist ein sehenswerter Film, der auf die immer lückenlosere Überwachung des öffentlichen Raums aufmerksam machen will.
http://www.ambienttv.net/pdf/facelessproject.pdf

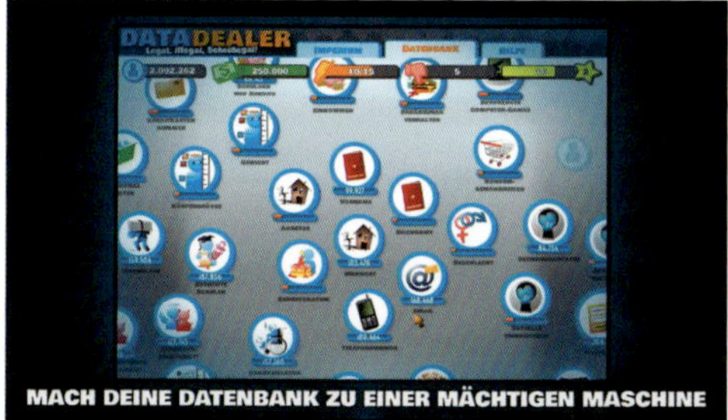

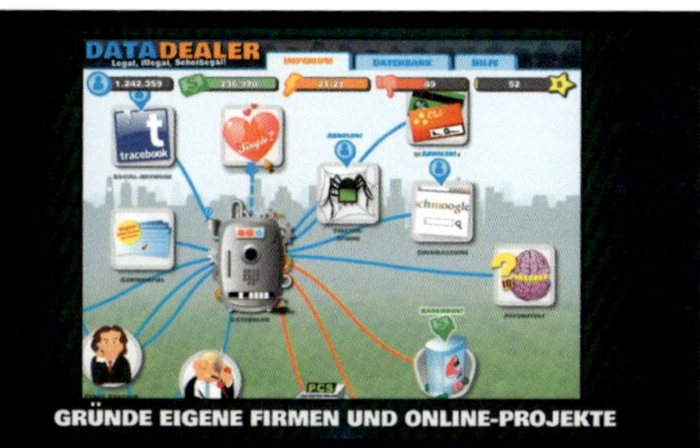

Data Dealer
Ivan Averintsev, Wolfie Christl, Pascale Osterwalder, Ralf Traunsteiner

Collecting, sorting, collating and marketing information has long since become a big business. *Data Dealer* is an online game that aims to make people aware of this. The object is for players to collect as much info as possible about private users and then sell it at a profit to all sorts of enterprises.

Das Sammeln, Sortieren, Verknüpfen und Vertreiben von Information ist längst ein riesiger Industriezweig geworden. Das Online-Game *Data Dealer* will darauf aufmerksam machen und fordert die SpielerInnen auf, möglichst viele Daten von privaten UserInnen zu erfassen und an diverse Unternehmen gewinnbringend zu verkaufen.
http://www.datadealer.net/

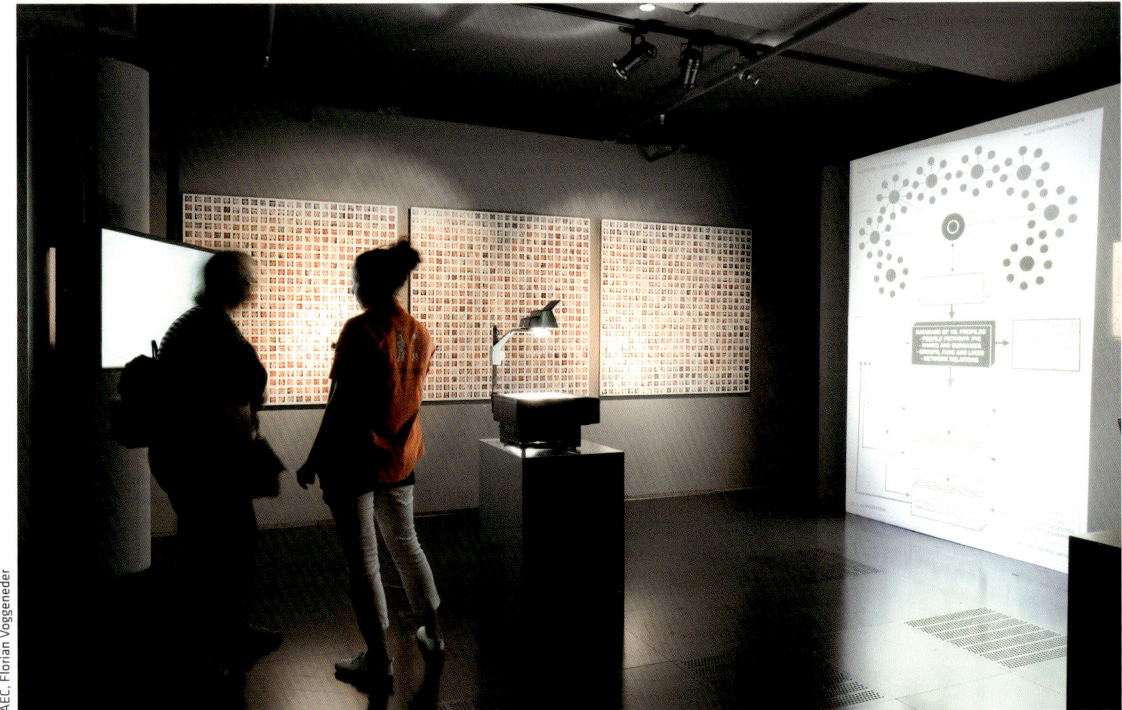

AEC, Florian Voggeneder

face to facebook
Paolo Cirio, Alessandro Ludovico

To conclude their *Hacking Monopolism* trilogy, the two Italian artists took aim at big game online: Facebook. Using a home-brew computer program, they harvested a million Facebook profiles, filtered them with facial recognition software, and then grouped them according to similarities of the data as well as the faces. Finally, the profiles reordered in this way were displayed on a dating site the duo set up, and the profiled individuals were introduced to each other via e-mail. Within the very first week of its existence online, *face to facebook* was already making one hell of a splash, ranging from coverage in media worldwide to death threats and lawsuits. Paolo Cirio and Alessandro Ludovico were ultimately forced to take their project off the internet.

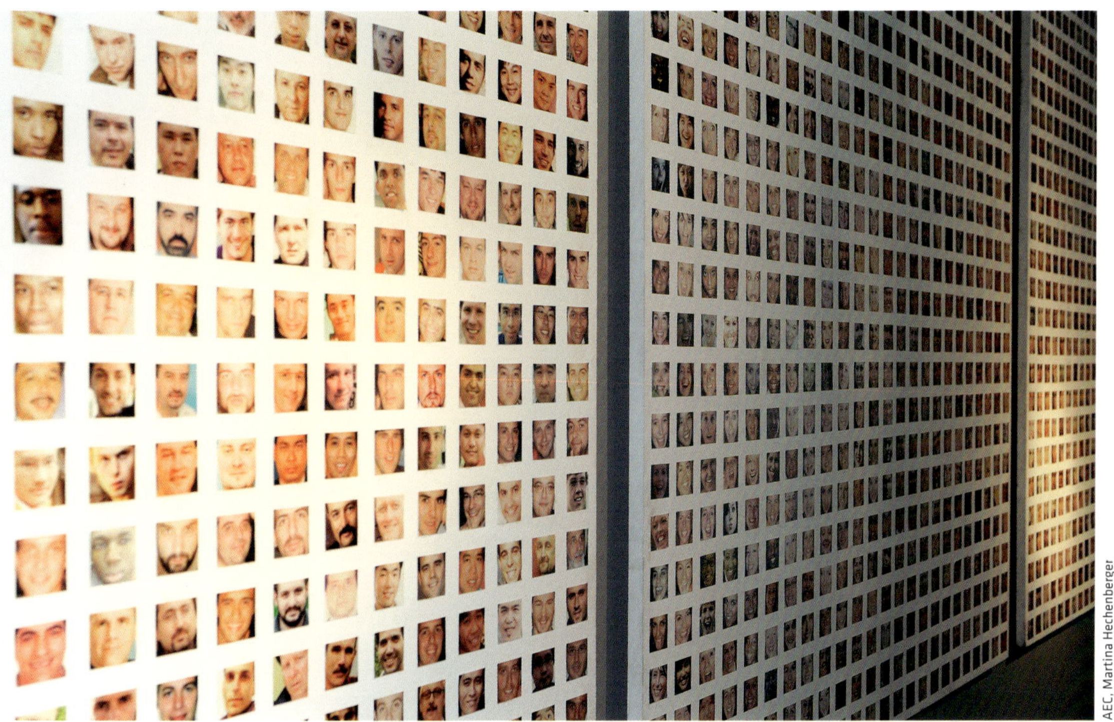

AEC, Martina Hechenberger

Zum Abschluss ihrer Trilogie *Hacking Monopolism* nahmen die beiden italienischen Künstler den Online-Giganten Facebook ins Visier. Mithilfe einer eigens entwickelten Software entwendeten sie eine Million Facebook-Profile, filterten diese mit einem Gesichtserkennungsprogramm und gruppierten sie nach Daten- und Gesichtsähnlichkeiten. Die auf diese Weise neu geordneten Profile wurden schließlich auf eine eigene Partnerbörse gestellt und ihre BesitzerInnen per E-mail miteinander bekannt gemacht. Gerade einmal eine Woche online, rief *face to facebook* ein enormes Echo hervor, das von Medienberichten in aller Welt bis hin zu Morddrohungen und Klagen reichte. Paolo Cirio und Alessandro Ludovico mussten das Projekt letztlich vom Netz nehmen.
http://www.face-to-facebook.net/

Security/Privacy Check
Sichere Informationssysteme FH OÖ

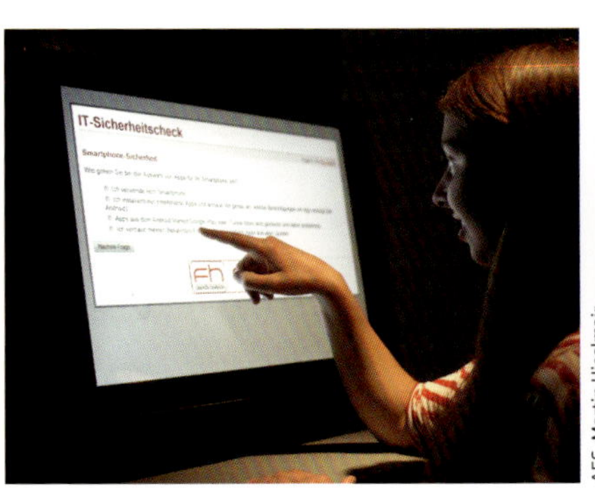

The Department of Secure Information Systems at the Upper Austria University of Applied Sciences' Hagenberg Campus has developed a security check that generates custom-tailored, practical suggestions for maximizing security in dealings with smartphones and notebooks, the internet, a Facebook account and Google. It starts by posing questions that establish how the particular user deals with these new media, and then gives individualized solutions to security issues.

Das Department Sichere Informationssysteme der FH OÖ in Hagenberg hat einen Sicherheits-Check entwickelt, mit dem maßgeschneiderte Tipps für den sicheren Umgang mit Smartphone, Notebook, Internet, Facebook und Google erstellt werden können. Hierbei wird zunächst durch mehrere Fragen der Umgang der TeilnehmerInnen mit den neuen Medien ermittelt, um ihnen dann individuelle Sicherheitshinweise mitzugeben.

Facebook Security
Sichere Informationssysteme FH OÖ

Facebook profiles governed by standard settings are poorly protected from the prying eyes of visiting undesirables. Those who trust these setting might, under certain circumstances, be in for unpleasant surprises. This installation lets visitors see who can access what information in an inadequately protected Facebook profile. Then, they can get hands-on experience with the settings that really do protect their profile

Facebook-Profile sind unter Standardeinstellungen nur schlecht vor unerwünschten MitleserInnen geschützt – wer auf diese Einstellungen vertraut, kann unter Umständen unangenehme Überraschungen erleben. An dieser Station kann jede/r erfahren, wer welche Informationen aus einem mangelhaft geschützten Facebook-Profil auslesen kann, und anschließend selbst ausprobieren, welche Einstellungen das Profil richtig absichern.

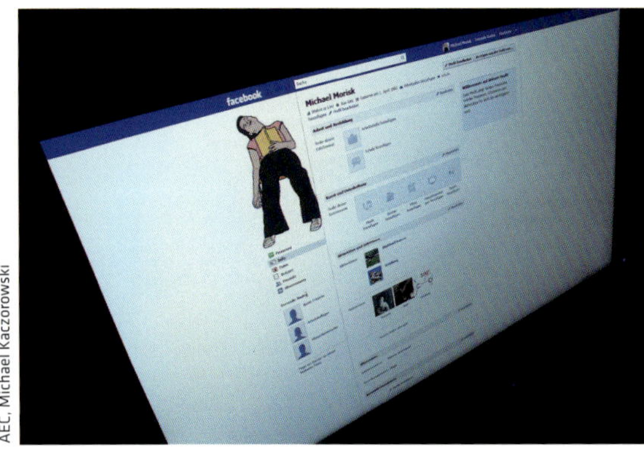

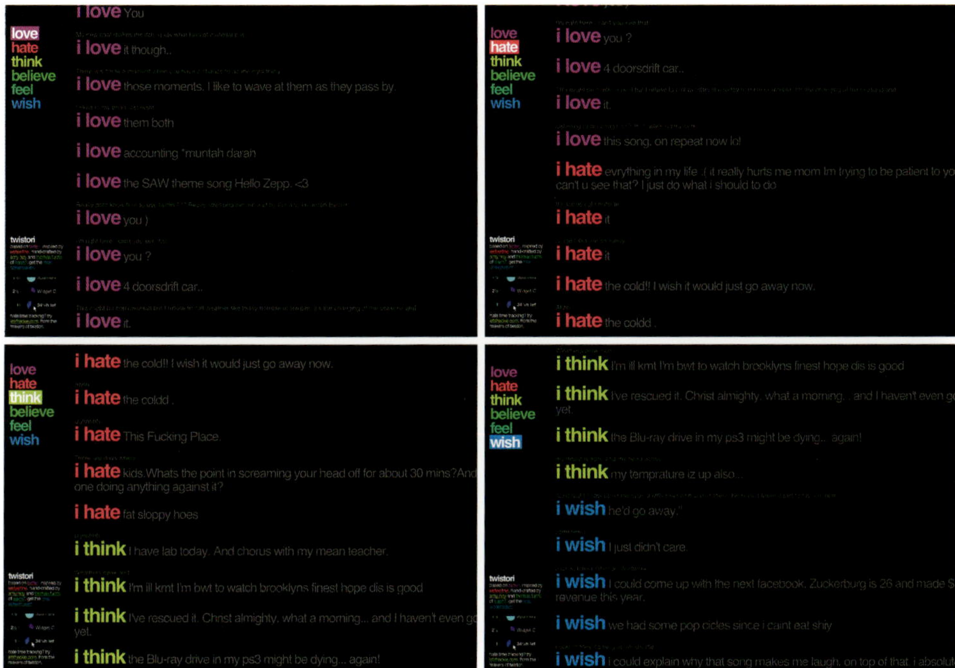

Twistori
Amy Hoy, Thomas Fuchs

I love the word "what if"—I hate being up so early—I think he maybe missed me a teeny bit ...—I believe my 30s will be better than my 20s—I feel pretty great starting off this week. I honestly think I'm finally on track to happiness & bliss!—I wish I could hug them and say bless you ...

Twistori is a very simple Twitter tool that gives you an impression of what people throughout the world love, hate, think, believe, feel and wish for. Thousands of Tweets are scanned in real time; those that contain such terms as love, hate or think are captured and displayed in the style of a LIVE Ticker.

I love the word "what if" – I hate being up so early – I think he may be missed me a teeny bit ... – I believe my 30s will be better than my 20s – I feel pretty great starting off this week. I honestly think I'm finally on track to happiness & bliss! – I wish I could hug them and say bless you ...

Twistori ist ein ganz einfaches Twitter-Tool, das einen Eindruck davon gibt, was Menschen in aller Welt lieben, hassen, denken, glauben, fühlen und sich wünschen. Tausende Tweets werden in Echtzeit gescannt und jene, die Begriffe wie love, hate oder think enthalten, eingesammelt und wie ein LIVE-Ticker aufgelistet.

http://twistori.com/#i_love

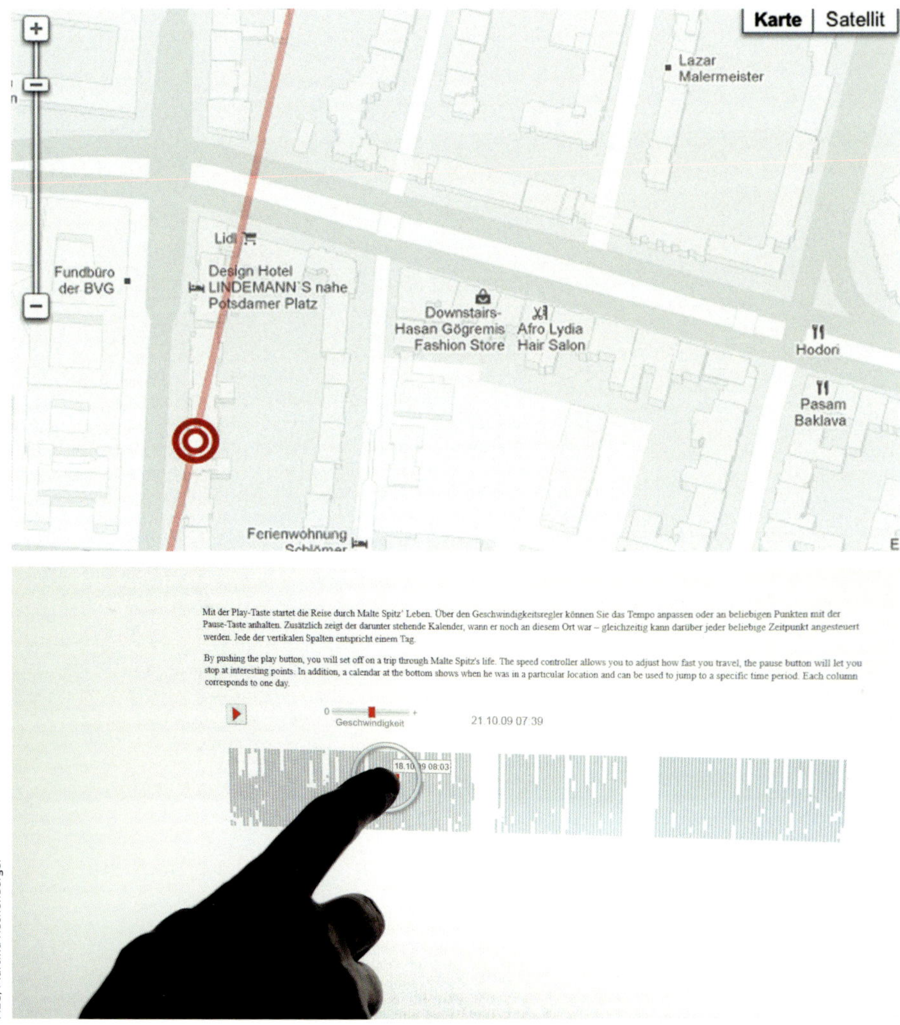

AEC, Martina Hechenberger

Handytracking
Malte Spitz, OpenDataCity, Zeit Online

Malte Spitz is a member of the national committee of Germany's Green Party and an outspoken opponent of telecommunications data retention. To show how far these legal provisions go to implement the permanent surveillance of respectable citizens not suspected of any crime, he sued to force T-Mobile to release the data about him that it had stored for the period August 2009 to February 2010. With the help of an interactive map developed by Opendatacity, these data were visualized and then published at *Zeit Online.* The result is an impressive graphic that provides highly detailed information about where Malte Spitz was, when and how long he was there, how often he called someone or was called by others, how many SMSs he wrote and how much time he spent online. Combined with his Tweets and blog entries, this data coalesces into a comprehensive picture of what Malte Spitz was up to.

Malte Spitz ist Mitglied des Bundesvorstands der Grünen in Deutschland und entschiedener Kritiker der Vorratsdatenspeicherung (VDS). Um zu zeigen, wie weit die permanente Überwachung unbescholtener BürgerInnen durch die VDS geht, klagte er T-Mobile auf Herausgabe der zwischen August 2009 und Februar 2010 über ihn gespeicherten Daten. Mithilfe einer von Opendatacity entwickelten interaktiven Karte ließ er diese Daten visualisieren und anschließend auf *Zeit Online* veröffentlichen. Ergebnis ist eine beeindruckende Grafik, die minutiös darüber Auskunft gibt, wann sich Malte Spitz wo aufhielt, wie lange er verweilte, wie oft er jemanden anrief, wie oft er angerufen wurde, wie viel SMS er schrieb und wie lange er im Netz war. Kombiniert mit seinen Tweets und Blogeinträgen, lässt sich sehr genau nachvollziehen, was Malte Spitz wann wo gemacht hat.

http://www.zeit.de/datenschutz/malte-spitz-vorratsdaten

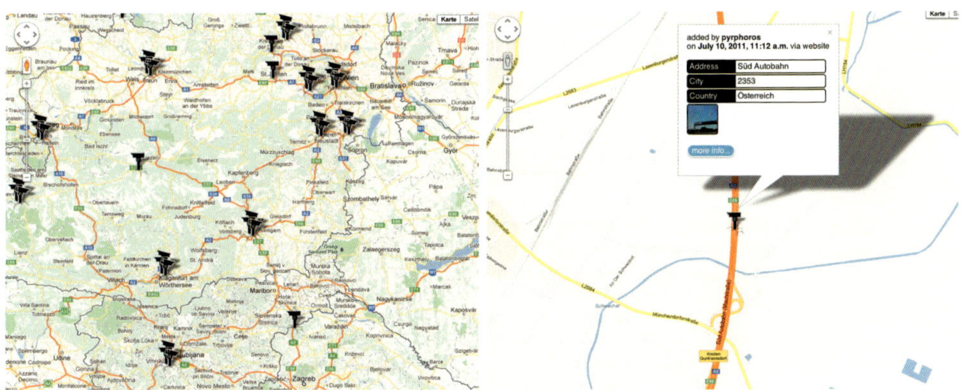

Surveillance Awareness Database (SAD)
Vienna University of Technology

The *Surveillance Awareness Database* is a social media project by Vienna University of Technology students Sarah Naber and Alexander Kraicsich that aims to show how widespread video surveillance of public spaces has become. The two undergrads launched a website to which users can upload photos of surveillance cameras including the installation's geographical coordinates. The result is a digital map showing the precise location and a picture of several hundred video cameras—including portions of the Linz video surveillance network.

Das Social-Media-Projekt *Surveillance Awareness Database* (SAD) der TU-Studierenden Sarah Naber und Alexander Kraicsich will zeigen, wie flächendeckend die Videoüberwachung des öffentlichen Raums mittlerweile fortgeschritten ist. Die beiden DiplomandInnen initiierten eine Online-Plattform, die dazu aufruft, Überwachungskameras vor Ort zu fotografieren und diese Bilder inklusive Geokoordinaten hochzuladen. Ergebnis ist eine digitale Map mit den Standorten und Bildern bereits mehrerer hundert Videokameras – auch Teile der Linzer Videoüberwachung werden hier abgebildet.

http://SADproject.tv

Sarah Naber, Alexander Kraicsich, Peter Purgathofer, Sylvia Purgathofer-Müller

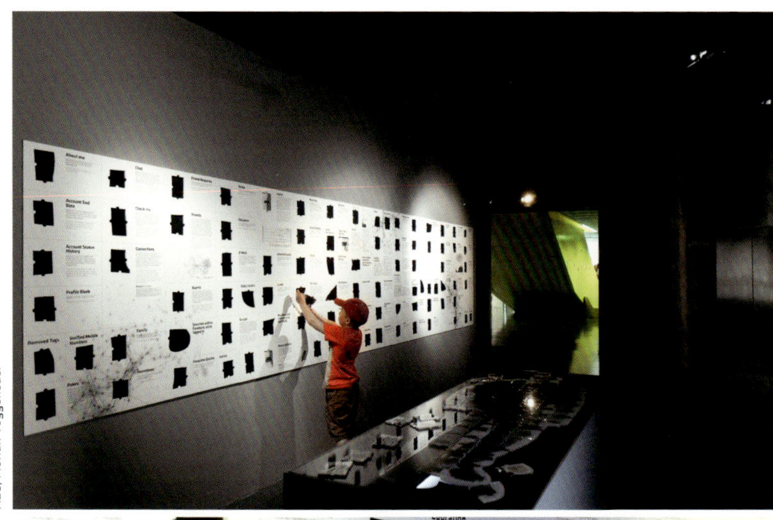

AEC, Florian Voggeneder

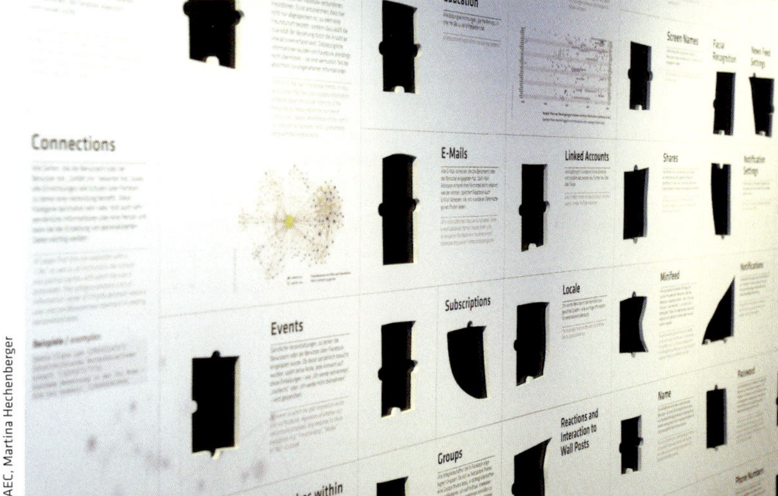

AEC, Martina Hechenberger

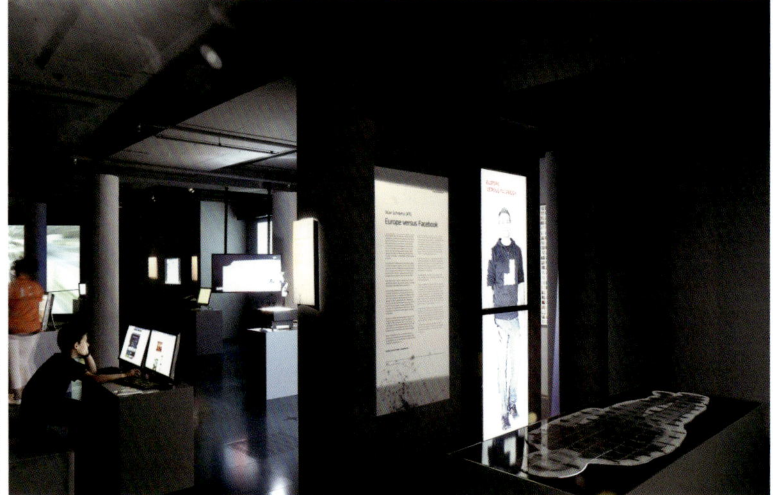

AEC, Florian Voggeneder

Europe vs. Facebook
Max Schrems, Ars Electronica Futurelab

With over 800 million users worldwide, the Facebook social networking service is one of the favorite meeting places online. Here, people can correspond with friends, contact business associates, get information about popular music groups, share pictures or join multi-player games—and all of it seemingly free of charge. Facebook isn't paid for in cash; instead, the price is revealing private and in some cases quite personal information. This data then gets processed and categorized so that target group-specific, personalized ad space on Facebook can be sold to companies with something to promote. Harvesting information in this way is legal in the USA; in Europe, however, Facebook violates existing data protection laws.

Austrian student Max Schrems is at the center of the *Europe versus Facebook* initiative that formed in August 2011. It demanded, pursuant to the EU's data protection law, that Facebook reveal all information it had gathered about Max Schrems. Inspection of the 1,200-page dossier Facebook released revealed that legal violations had indeed occurred and provided the grounds upon which the initiative filed numerous charges against Facebook.

A thorough and comprehensive analysis of all the categories in which Facebook stores data about individual users yields an extraordinarily detailed jigsaw puzzle composed of personal information that users willingly input themselves as well as what is gleaned behind the scenes by Facebook on its own.

The *Europe vs. Facebook* initiative confronts the world's largest social network with four primary demands: More transparency as far as the use of personal data is concerned; opt-in instead of opt-out, which means that users shouldn't have to act to prevent publication of their data but rather give their permission for what would, by default, be prohibited; genuine control over the user's own data, which friends have been able to reveal to Facebook up to now; as well as data minimization in order to prevent the accumulation over time of enormous quantities of digital rubbish. Moreover, *Europe vs. Facebook* finds it unacceptable that the social network stores certain data forever and withholds from users the possibility of expunging them.

Visitors of the Ars Electronica Center can put together the jigsaw puzzle depicting Max Schrems and discover what kind of data Facebook, an American corporation, has stored in its files about them.

http://europe-v-facebook.org/DE/de.html

Europe vs. Facebook
Max Schrems, Ars Electronica Futurelab

Mit weltweit über 800 Millionen TeilnehmerInnen zählt das soziale Netzwerk Facebook zu den beliebtesten Treffpunkten im Internet. Hier können sich Menschen mit Freunden unterhalten, sich mit Geschäftsleuten organisieren, Informationen über ihre Lieblingsmusik einholen, Bilder austauschen oder mit einem gemeinsamen Spiel ihre Zeit verbringen – und das alles scheinbar ganz umsonst. Bezahlt wird bei Facebook nicht mit Geld, sondern mit dem Preisgeben privater und teils sehr persönlicher Informationen. Diese werden weiterverarbeitet, in Gruppen zusammengefasst und die daraus erstellten Werbeflächen zielgruppengerecht und personalisiert an andere Unternehmen verkauft. Während in den USA das Sammeln dieser Daten rechtlich gedeckt ist, verstößt Facebook in Europa damit gegen geltendes Datenschutzrecht.

Rund um den österreichischen Studenten Max Schrems formierte sich im August 2011 die Initiative *Europe versus Facebook*. Unter Berufung auf das Datenschutzrecht der EU wurde die Herausgabe aller Daten eingefordert, die Facebook über Max Schrems gesammelt hatte. Bei der Durchsicht des 1.200 Seiten langen Dossiers kristallisierten sich nach und nach Rechtsverstöße heraus, die die Initiative zu mehreren Anzeigen gegen Facebook veranlasste.

Werden alle Datenkategorien aufgeschlüsselt, die Facebook über eine Person speichert, ergibt sich ein außerordentlich detailreiches Puzzle an personenbezogenen Informationen, die wissentlich von den TeilnehmerInnen eingegeben und auch von Facebook selbst im Hintergrund ermittelt wurden.

Die Initiative *Europe vs. Facebook* verlangt vor allem vier Dinge vom weltgrößten sozialen Netzwerk: Mehr Transparenz, was die Verwendung personenbezogener Daten angeht, Opt-In statt Opt-Out, sprich jede/r UserIn soll sich nicht gegen die Veröffentlichung von Daten aussprechen müssen, sondern sich dafür entscheiden können, echte Kontrolle über die eigenen Daten, die bislang auch von FreundInnen an Facebook weitergegeben werden, sowie Datensparsamkeit, um dem schier endlosen Datenmüll entgegenzuwirken, der sich über die Zeit ansammelt. Darüber hinaus stößt sich *Europe vs. Facebook* daran, dass das soziale Netzwerk manche Daten für immer und ewig speichert – das Löschen dieser Daten ist den UserInnen unmöglich.

Bei dieser Installation können BesucherInnen des Ars Electronica Center das Puzzle von Max Schrems zusammensetzen und entdecken, welche Daten das US-amerikanische Unternehmen Facebook tatsächlich über sie gespeichert hat.
http://europe-v-facebook.org/DE/de.html

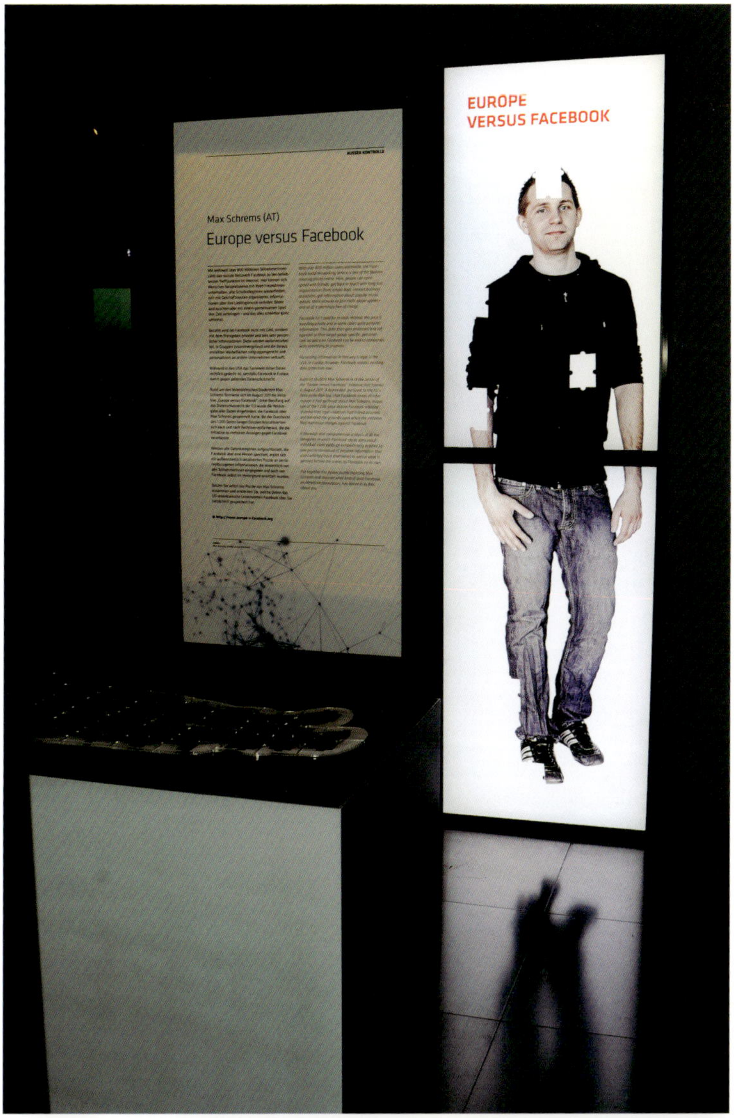

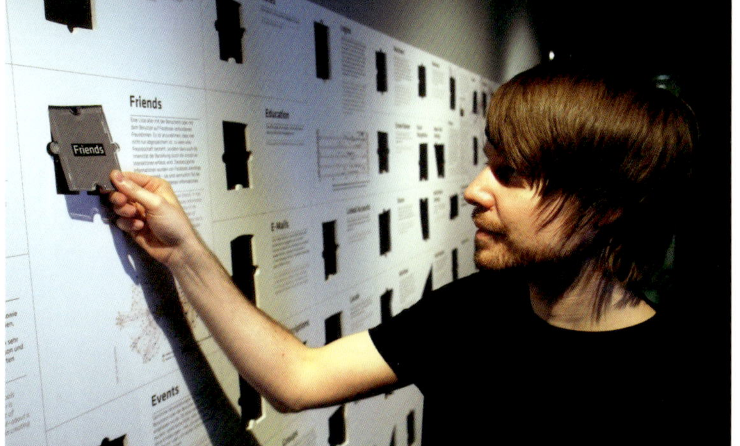

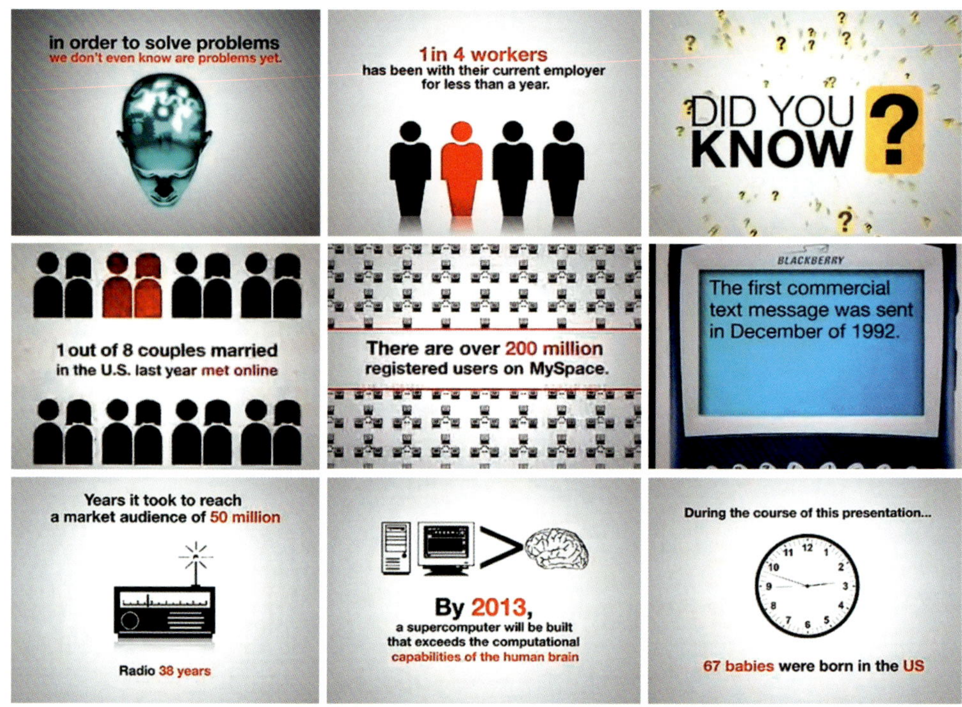

Did you know?

Karl Fisch, Scott McLeod, Jeff Brenman

Did you know? is an impressive video with a cool, clean, minimalist style. Its subject: the social, political and economic effects of accelerating technological development. All that's displayed on-screen are statistical statements that say something important about our constantly changing global reality—for instance, that China is about to become the country with the most English-speaking inhabitants, that the 10 jobs most in-demand in 2010 hadn't even existed six years before, and that if the MySpace social network were a country, it would be the world's fifth largest.

Did you know? ist ein ebenso reduziertes wie beeindruckendes Video rund um die sozialen, politischen und ökonomischen Auswirkungen der immer rasanteren technologischen Entwicklung. Eingeblendet werden ausschließlich statistische Kennzahlen unserer sich stetig verändernden globalisierten Realität, etwa, dass China bald jenes Land sein wird, in dem die meisten englischsprechenden Menschen leben, dass es die zehn begehrtesten Jobs des Jahres 2010 sechs Jahre zuvor noch nicht einmal gab oder dass das soziale Netzwerk MySpace, wäre es ein Land, das fünftgrößte der Welt wäre.
http://www.youtube.com/watch?v=cL9Wu2kWwSY

GoodMorning!
Jer Thorp

On the basis of more than 11,000 good-morning Tweets variously colored according to the time of day when they were sent, *GoodMorning!* presents a multihued visualization of the varying intensity of the use of Twitter in different parts of the world.

Anhand von mehr als 11.000, je nach Uhrzeit unterschiedlich eingefärbten „Guten Morgen"-Tweets veranschaulicht die Visualisierung *GoodMorning!* in welchen Teilen der Welt Twitter besonders intensiv genutzt wird.
http://blog.blprnt.com/blog/blprnt/goodmorning

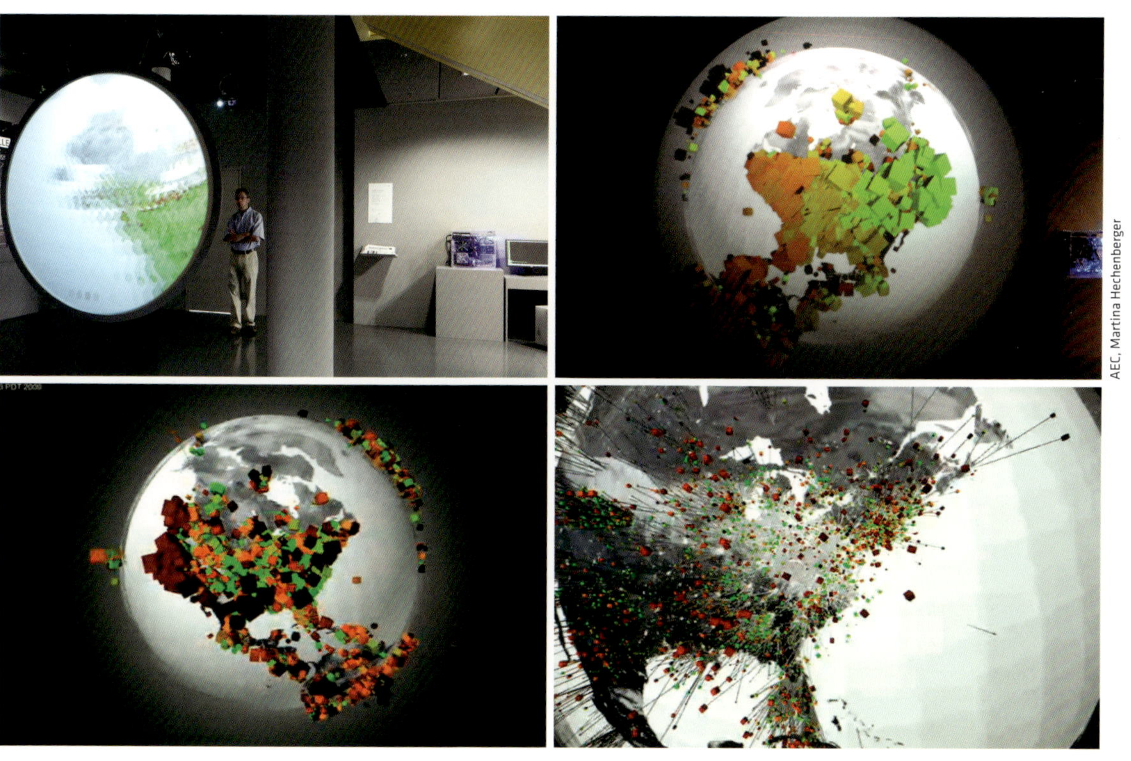

AEC, Martina Hechenberger

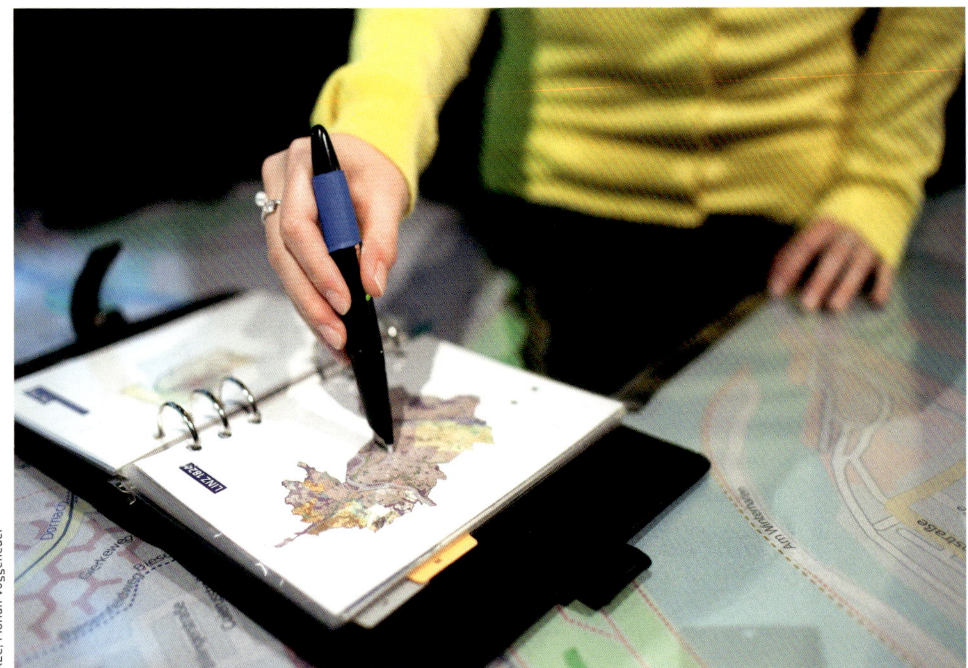

AEC, Florian Vogeneder

SimLinz
Ars Electronica Futurelab

Interlinking data and visualizing them bring out surprising realizations of interrelationships that seem to be hidden at first glance. *SimLinz*, the prototype of an interactive urban & geographical information system, uses selected data to enable users to follow the development of the City of Linz from the 1950s to the present. The walk-through databank makes it possible to experience complex and interrelated information in an intuitive way. To accomplish this, book and city map become an interactive surface; stylus and paper serve as the link between the computer and the projection.

Die Verknüpfung und Visualisierung von Daten ermöglicht überraschende Einblicke in Zusammenhänge, die sich auf den ersten Blick scheinbar verbergen. Als Prototyp für ein interaktives Stadt- und Geoinformationssystem bietet *SimLinz* die Möglichkeit, die Entwicklung der Stadt Linz anhand exemplarischer Daten seit den 1950er Jahren bis heute zu verfolgen. Die begehbare Datenbank macht komplexe und verbundene Informationen intuitiv erfahrbar. Buch und Stadtplan werden dabei zur interaktiven Oberfläche, Stift und Papier verbinden sich mit Computer und Projektion.

The City of Linz, Ars Electronica Futurelab, FMM, The Province of Upper Austria, Linz AG, Via Donau, OpenStreetMap

Linz Panorama
Ars Electronica Futurelab

Enjoy a panoramic view over the rooftops of Linz from multiple vantage points and then zoom in for an ultra-close-up look at the individuals captured in these photographs. 15 wide-angle shots, each with a resolution of up to 130,000 x 40,000 pixels and made up of nearly 300 individual exposures, offer a degree of sharpness that far surpasses what can be achieved with conventional digital cameras. Special software assures that the images—some with 20 gigabytes—are depicted smoothly from one zoom level to another.

Blicken Sie von mehreren Aussichtspunkten über die Dächer der Stadt Linz und begeben Sie sich in greifbare Nähe zu den auf den Fotografien abgebildeten Menschen. 15 Panoramabilder, die mit einer Auflösung von bis zu 130.000 x 40.000 Pixel aus beinahe 300 Einzelaufnahmen zusammengesetzt sind, bieten eine Detailschärfe, die die Möglichkeiten herkömmlicher Digitalkameras bei Weitem übertreffen. Eine spezielle Software sorgt dafür, dass die teilweise 20 Gigabyte großen Bilder auf den verschiedenen Zoomstufen flüssig dargestellt werden.

Panorambild: Norbert Artner

AEC, Martin Hieslmair

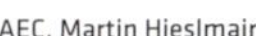

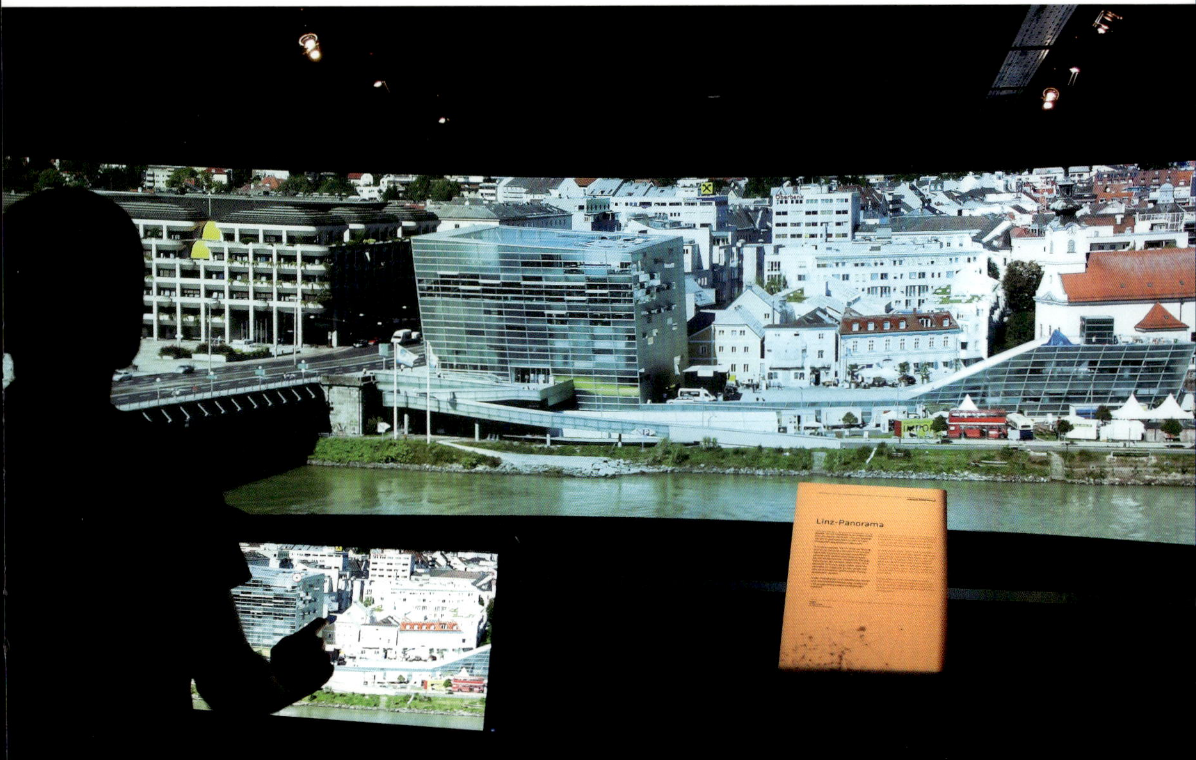

Telecommunications Data Retention

Facts

Telecommunications data retention (TDR) is an amendment to the Austrian telecommunications law (TKG) that was passed by the Lower House of the Austrian Parliament on April 29, 2011 and ratified by the Upper House on May 12, 2011. This amendment went into force on April 1, 2012 and provides the legal basis for storing for a period of six months data on the telecommunications activity of all Austrian citizens even in the absence of suspicion of the commission of a crime or without a court order. TDR is meant to help solve crimes or even prevent them from being committed.

TDR originated in the EU guideline 2006/24/EG that all member states of the European Union are required to implement on a national basis. Germany's Federal Constitutional Court found the original legislation to be unconstitutional because it could not be reconciled with the Constitution of the Federal Republic of Germany. Indeed, Austria delayed integrating the EU guideline into federal law but this failure to implement it led to the country being censured by the EU in July 2010. Numerous protests and initiatives that regarded the amendment as an abridgment of basic human rights were unable to prevent the amended law from going into effect.

What is being stored?

- IP addresses: Internet service providers are required to store both the exact time of day as well as the numerical address of a computer or smartphone that accesses the internet. Indeed, the IP address of a telecommunications device does not refer directly to a specific person. In the case of internet access via analog connection, however, the telephone number must be stored. Providers of internet telephony services (VoIP) are required to store the date, time of day and duration of every conversation as well as the contact data.
- Cell phones: All devices involved in a cell phone connection are registered by means of International Mobile Subscriber Identity (IMSI) and International Mobile Equipment Identity (IMEI). In addition to the date and time of day the call was made, the location label (Cell ID) is stored, whereby the location and duration of the call can be determined. The date, time of day and telephone numbers are stored whenever an SMS is sent.
- E-mails: Internet providers are required to store for six months details about e-mails such as the contact data they contain.

What is not being stored?

None of the cases described above has to do with storing content. TDR constitutes registering and storing the date, time of day and origin of the communication. Access to communication content will still call for a court order after April 1, 2012.

Who can get access to the data?

According to § 90 TKG, a court of law, a prosecutor's office and the police may request in writing information from a telecommunications service provider if the requested data are necessary to "investigate, establish the commission of and prosecute a crime (...) the severity of which justifies a court order in accordance with § 135 Abs 2a StPO"–i.e. an "intentionally committed offense punishable by imprisonment for more than one year." Thus, these data may not be used in civil lawsuits; the new guidelines pertain only to criminal proceedings.

Vorratsdatenspeicherung

Fakten

Die Vorratsdatenspeicherung (VDS) ist eine Novelle des österreichischen Telekommunikationsgesetzes, welche am 29. April 2011 im Nationalrat beschlossen und am 12. Mai 2011 vom Bundesrat bestätigt wurde. Diese Gesetzesänderung trat am 1. April 2012 in Kraft und schafft die rechtliche Grundlage, Telekommunikationsdaten aller NutzerInnen ohne einen Verdacht oder einen gerichtlichen Beschluss sechs Monate lang zu speichern. Die VDS soll dabei helfen, Straftaten aufzuklären oder gar im Vorfeld zu verhindern.

Ausgang der VDS ist die EU-Richtlinie 2006/24/EG aus dem Jahr 2006, die von allen Mitgliedsstaaten der Europäischen Union auf nationaler Basis umzusetzen ist. Das Bundesverfassungsgericht in Deutschland hat den ursprünglichen Gesetzesentwurf als verfassungswidrig eingestuft, da dieser nicht in Einklang mit dem deutschen Grundgesetz zu bringen war. Österreich zögerte zunächst mit der Einbindung der EU-Richtlinie ins nationale Gesetz und wurde deshalb im Juli 2010 wegen Nichtumsetzung von der EU verurteilt. Zahlreiche Proteste und Initiativen, die in der Gesetzesnovelle fundamentale Menschenrechte beschnitten sahen, konnten das Inkrafttreten nicht mehr verhindern.

Was wird gespeichert?

* IP-Adressen: Anbieter von Internet-Zugängen sind verpflichtet, sowohl den Zeitpunkt als auch die numerische Adresse des mit dem Internet verbundenen Computers oder Smartphones zu speichern. IP-Adressen von technischen Geräten weisen zwar nicht direkt auf eine konkrete Person hin, bei Internet-Verbindungen über einen analogen Anschluss muss jedoch auch die Telefonnummer gespeichert werden. Für Anbieter von Internet-Telefonie (Voice over IP, VoIP) ist die Aufzeichnung des Datums, der Uhrzeit, der Gesprächsdauer und der Kontaktdaten erforderlich.
* Mobiltelefone: Alle an einer Mobilfunkverbindung beteiligten Geräte werden mittels internationaler Mobilteilnehmerkennung (IMSI) und Gerätekennung (IMEI) erfasst. Neben Datum und Uhrzeit des Rufaufbaus wird auch die Standortkennung (Cell-ID) gespeichert, womit Ort und Zeitraum eines Telefonates bestimmt werden können. Datum, Uhrzeit und die Telefonnummern beim Versand von SMS werden ebenfalls gespeichert.
* E-Mails: Internetprovider sind verpflichtet, Details über E-Mails wie beispielsweise die darin enthaltenen Kontaktdaten sechs Monate lang zu speichern.

Was wird nicht gespeichert?

In keinem der beschriebenen Fälle werden Inhalte gespeichert. Die Vorratsdatenspeicherung umfasst das Aufzeichnen und Festhalten von Datum, Uhrzeit und Herkunft der Kommunikation. Für den Einblick in Inhalte ist auch nach dem 1. April 2012 ein gerichtlicher Beschluss notwendig.

Wer kann auf die Daten zugreifen?

Gerichte, Staatsanwaltschaften und die Kriminalpolizei dürfen laut § 90 TKG bei Kommunikationsanbietern schriftlich um Auskunft ansuchen, sofern die Daten „zur Ermittlung, Feststellung und Verfolgung von Straftaten" notwendig sind, „deren Schwere eine Anordnung nach § 135 Abs. 2a StPO rechtfertigt" – also bei einer „vorsätzlich begangenen Straftat, die mit mehr als einjähriger Freiheitsstrafe bedroht ist". In zivilrechtlichen Verfahren dürfen diese Daten somit nicht angewendet werden, die neuen Richtlinien betreffen ausschließlich strafrechtliche Prozesse.

Telecommunications Data Retention / Information Request
Vorratsdatenspeicherung / Auskunftsbegehren

Austrian citizens have the right to submit an information request to the Austrian Federal Ministry of the Interior, which is required to reveal what information about that person is stored in which databanks. Do you know which of the agency's files already contain traces you've left behind?

Österreichische StaatsbürgerInnen haben das Recht, ein Auskunftsbegehren an das Bundesministerium für Inneres zu stellen. Die Behörde ist verpflichtet, Auskunft darüber zu erteilen, welche Informationen über die betreffende Person in welchen Datenbanken gespeichert sind. Wissen Sie, in welchem dieser Verzeichnisse Sie bereits Spuren hinterlassen haben?

- Finanzbuchführung,
- Flugeinsatzevidenz,
- Protokollierung von Akten des Bundesministeriums für Inneres,
- Gleitzeiterfassung,
- Maschinenfehler- und Leitungsstörungsprotokoll,
- Inventar- und Materialbeschaffung sowie Verwaltung,
- Zentrale Wählerevidenz,
- Systemzugangskontrolle und Vergabe von Bedienerkennzeichen in der ADV,
- Versendung der Zeitschrift „Öffentliche Sicherheit",
- Automationsunterstützte Zutrittskontrolle,
- Zentrale Evidenz für Kraftfahrzeuge (Zentrales Kraftfahrzeugregister),
- Personeninformationen – Evidenthaltung von pass- und/oder waffenrechtlichen Informationen und/oder Gefährder-Informationen,
- Asylwerberinformationssystem,
- Modulares Wahlpaket 1993,
- Lokales Identitätsdokumentenregister (Lokale Evidenz zur Ausstellung von Dienstpässen und Evidenthaltung von Dienstpassdaten),
- Evidenthaltung der Ausbildungs- und Personaldaten der Bediensteten des GEK,
- Inventarisierung von literarischen Amtsbehelfen,
- Zentrale Europa-Wählerevidenz,
- Nationales Schengener Informationssystem (N.SIS),
- SIRENE Österreich (Supplementary Information Request at the National Entry),
- Manuelle Kartei des Chefärztlichen Dienstes für den Bereich der Bediensteten des Bundesministeriums für Inneres,
- Teilnahme am Informationsverbundsystem: Zentrales Fremdenregister,
- Zentrales Identitätsdokumentenregister (Zentrale Evidenz zur Ausstellung von Ausweisen und Evidenthaltung von Ausweisdaten),
- Evidenthaltung von ausgeschriebenen und widerrufenen Personenfahndungen,
- Teilnahme an einem Informationsverbundsystem: Kriminalpolizeilicher Aktenindex (KPA),
- Kulturgutfahndung,

- Zentrale Namensevidenz (ZNEV) des Erkennungsdienstes,
- Gleichsetzungstabelle gemäß § 16b Meldegesetz,
- Evidenthaltung von Aufnahmewerbern für den Exekutivdienst,
- Teilnahme am Informationsverbundsystem: Sicherheitsmonitor,
- Teilnahme am Informationsverbundsystem: Europol-Informationssystem (EIS),
- Teilnahme am grenzüberschreitenden Informationssystem Interpol – Automatic Search Facility for Stolen Motor Vehicles (ASF SMV),
- Teilnahme am grenzüberschreitenden Informationssystem Interpol – Automatic Search Facility for Stolen Travel Documents (ASF STD) und Automatic Search Facility for Stolen Administrative Documents (ASF SAD),
- Leistungszeiterfassung der Bediensteten des Bundesministeriums für Inneres für die Kosten- und Leistungsrechnung (BKLR),
- Videoüberwachung in Zugangsbereichen zu Amtsgebäuden des Bundesministeriums für Inneres und von speziellen Sicherheitszonen in diesen Amtsgebäuden für Zwecke des Eigentumsschutzes (Schutz des Eigentums und der Mitarbeiter und Organe des Auftraggebers) und des Verantwortungsschutzes (Schutz dritter Personen) mit ausschließlicher Auswertung in dem durch die Zweckbezeichnung definierten Anlassfall,
- Schuhspurenverwaltungs- und -suchprogramm (SchuVT),
- Teilnahme am Informationsverbundsystem: Evidenthaltung von Daten zu falschen und verfälschten Dokumenten, zum Gebrauch fremder Ausweise sowie zu Dokumenten, die als Beweismittel dienen,
- Administration der dienstgebergestützten Mahlzeitenverpflegung am Arbeitsplatz durch das Bundesministerium für Inneres,
- Teilnahme am Informationsverbundsystem: Einsatz-Protokoll-System (EPSweb),
- Evidenz zur Verwaltung und Mietabrechnung der vom Bundesministerium für Inneres genutzten Liegenschaften, Objekte und Räume (Immobiliendatenbank des BM.I),
- Teilnahme am Betreuungsinformationssystem über die Gewährleistung der vorübergehenden Grundversorgung für hilfs- und schutzbedürftige Fremde in Österreich (entsprechend der Grundversorgungsvereinbarung gemäß Art. 15a B-VG),
- Projektdatenbank für die vom BM.I verwalteten vier EU-Fonds des generellen Programms „Solidarität und Steuerung der Migrationsströme",
- Mobiltelefondatenkartenkostenanalyse- und Auswertungsprogramm betreffend die Mobiltelefonie der Bediensteten des Bundesministeriums für Inneres (Zentralleitung),
- Teilnahme am Informationsverbundsystem: Sachenfahndung – Evidenthaltung der Daten von nummerierten Sachen, die zur Fahndung ausgeschrieben wurden,
- Elektronisches Dateninformationssystem (EDIS).

This is a partial list compiled by ARGE DATEN to provide an impression as to which organizations already began gathering information even before the new telecommunications data retention provisions went into effect.
Dies ist eine unvollständige Liste, die von der ARGE DATEN erstellt wurde, um einen Eindruck davon zu vermitteln, welche Organisationen schon vor dem Inkrafttreten der Vorratsdatenspeicherung Daten erfasst haben.
Quelle: *www.argedaten.at*

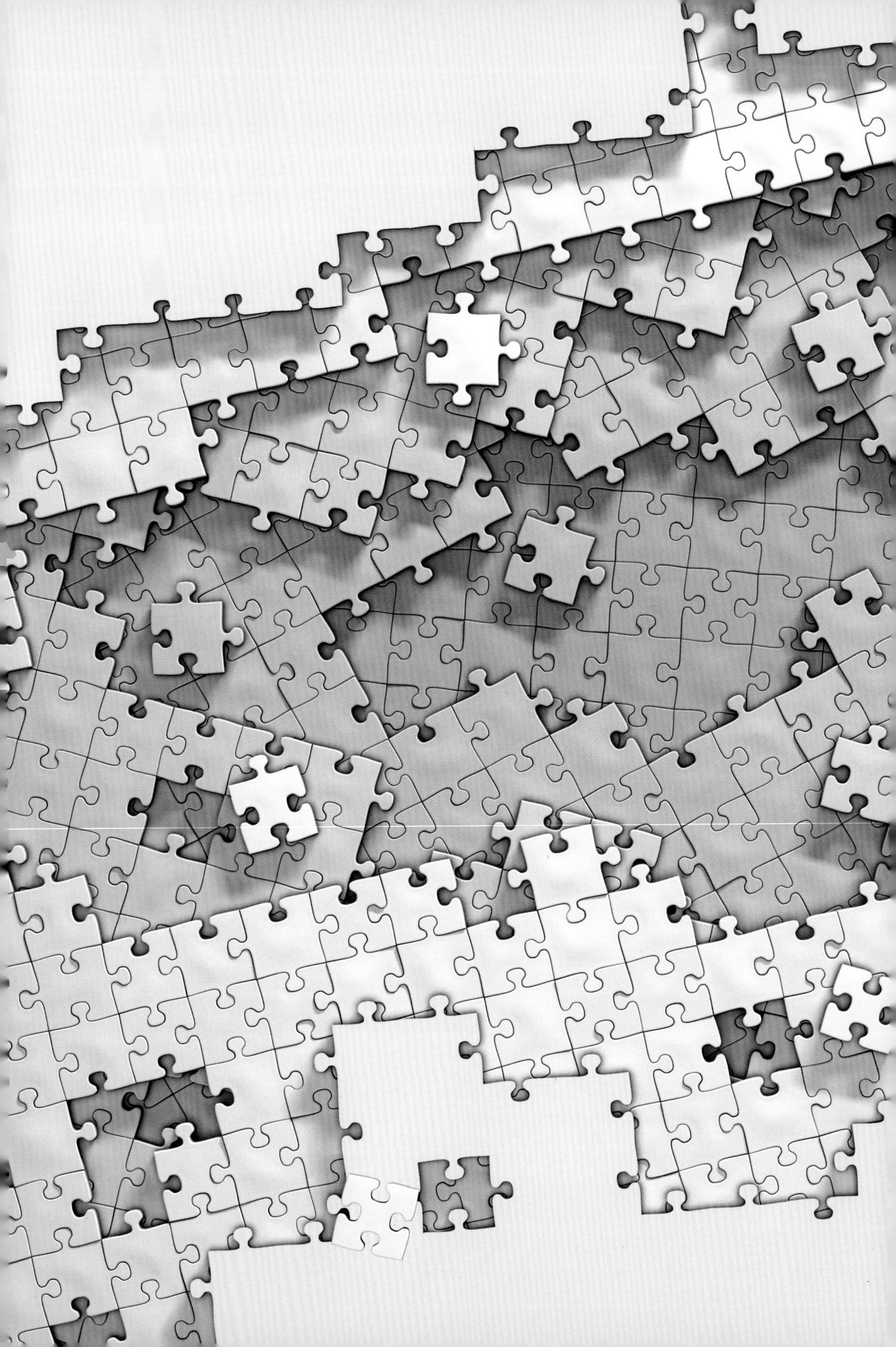

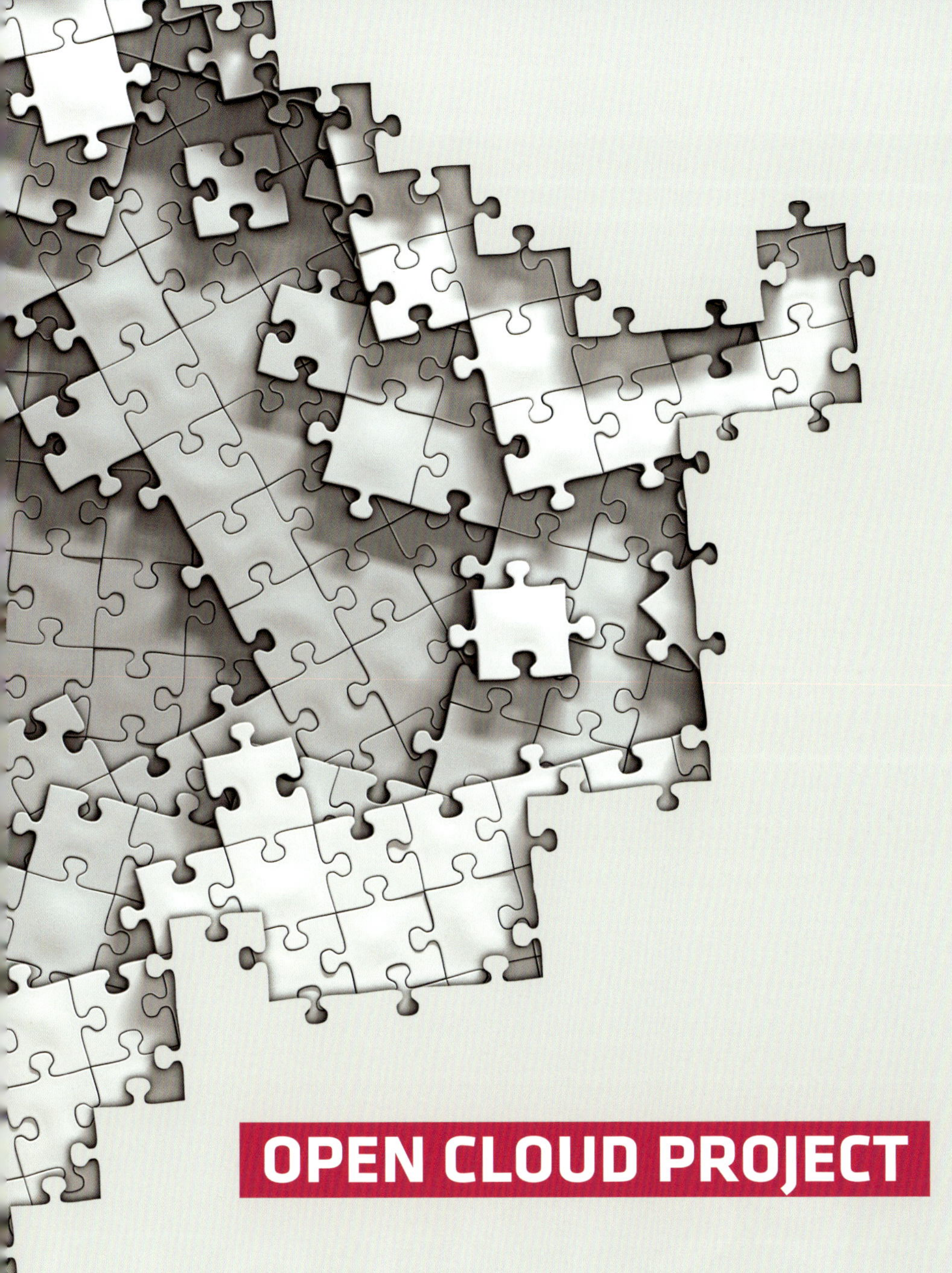

OPEN CLOUD PROJECT

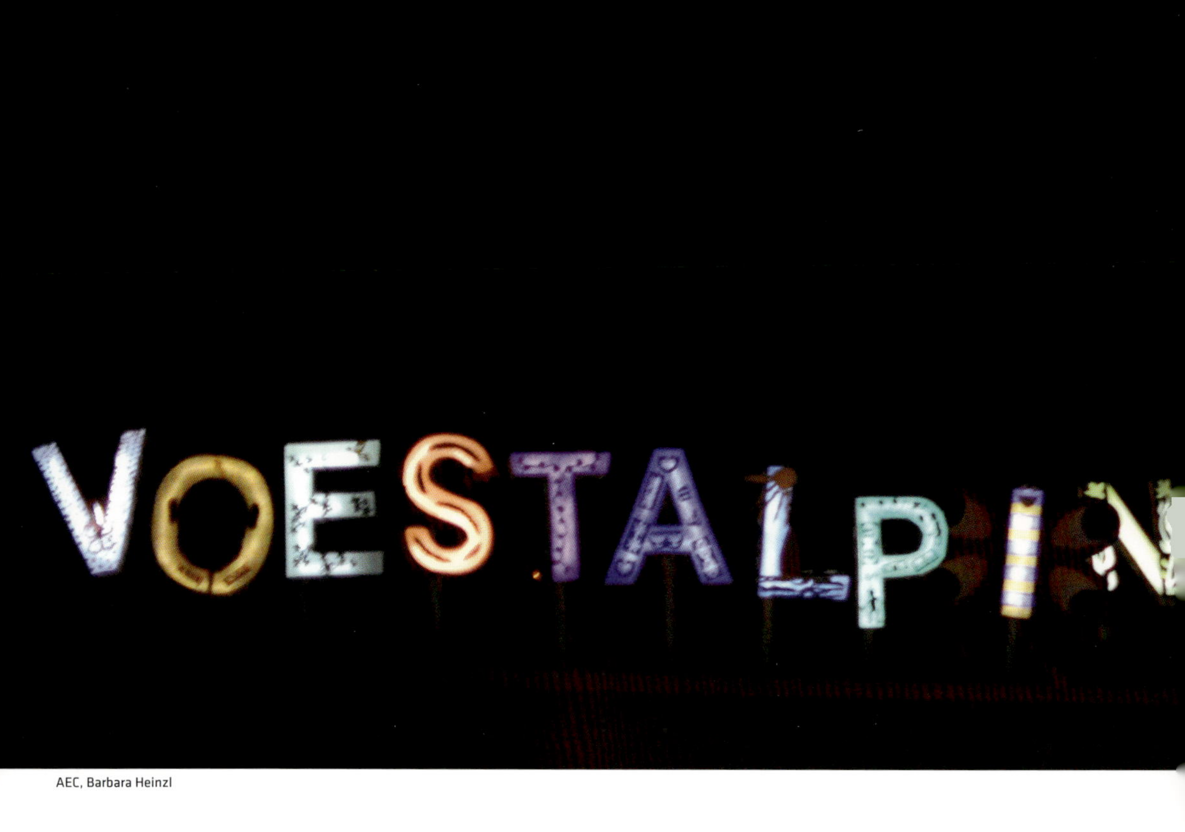

AEC, Barbara Heinzl

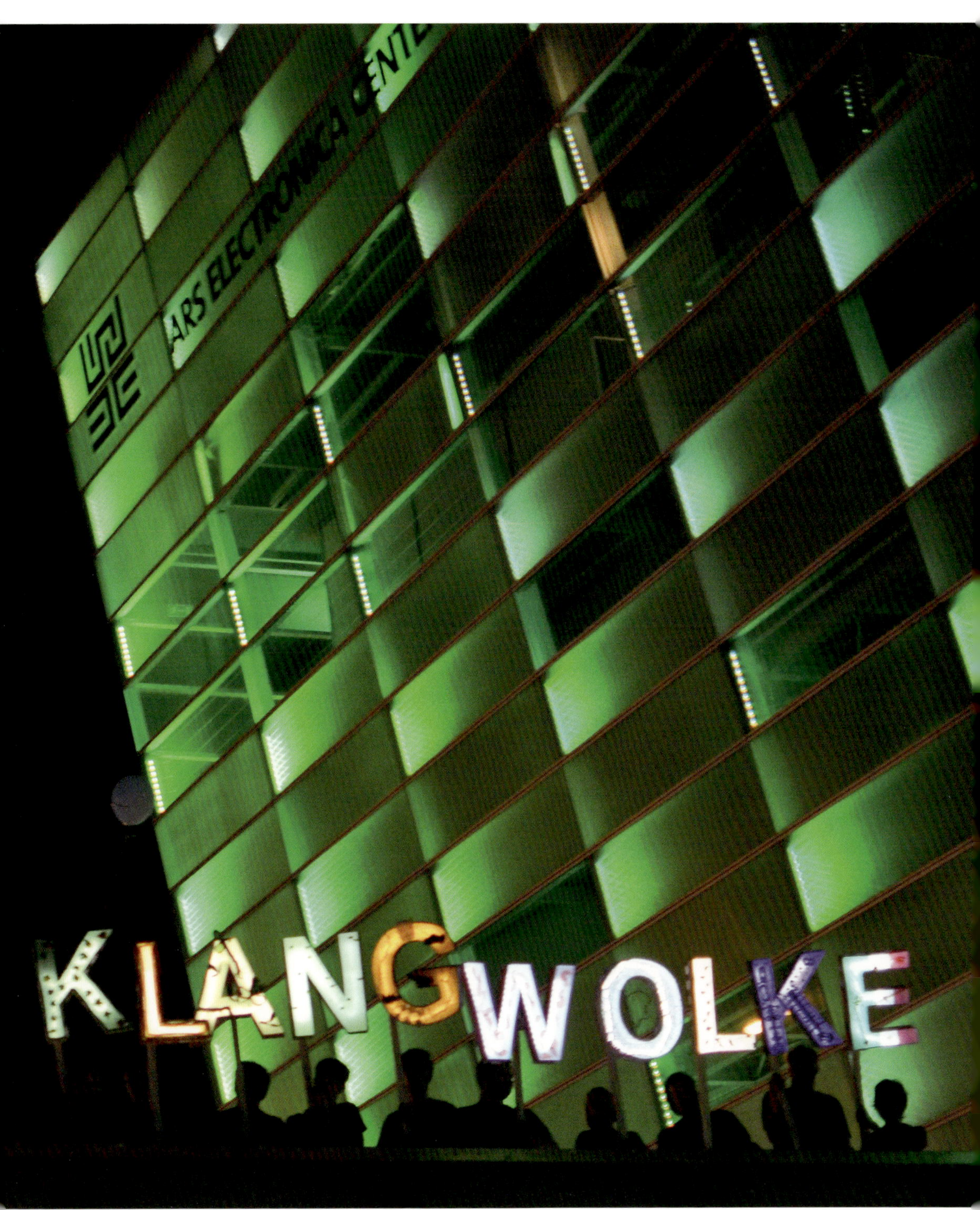

ARS ELECTRONICA CENTER
KLANGWOLKE

Gerfried Stocker

The Cloud in the Web
voestalpine Klangwolke 2012

This year, there's been quite a bit of talk about the now-legendary beginnings of the *Klangwolke* and the thinking that went into its launch. And for good reason—after all, a lot of what contributed to making it one of the most innovative and successful projects in the history of Ars Electronica Linz is, from a contemporary perspective, extraordinarily relevant once again. Back in the days when broadcasting and media, with the exception ham radio and CB, were strictly unidirectional information providers, and TV viewers—at least in Austria—had to be satisfied with a choice between the two channels offered by the state broadcasting company, the temporary opening of the mass medium radio for a broad-based participatory project was a daring venture indeed, but one that adumbrated in an utterly unpretentious way a future media reality that was difficult to imagine back then, but is now just normal everyday life. A reality in which media are open, multi-directionally interlinked, ubiquitous and mobile, and classic centers of power on the media landscape lie in ruins or in agony, their successors already going concerns.

Calling upon people to do something totally different with their radios—to use them not just as a receiver but as a transceiver to relay what they pick up and to propagate it into the public sphere—epitomizes the actual mission of the Klangwolke and its quality as a project. Thus, from its very inception, the *Klangwolke* wasn't just an open-air concert, though that in and of itself was utterly extraordinary too for that day and age, when you consider that this wasn't an appearance by a rock band but rather classical music that had been catapulted out of the confines of a concert hall and was being processed and visualized to boot, and by electronic artists no less! *Klangwolke* is, rather, an instrument of dialog with the inhabitants of a whole city, of an entire region, and an ingeniously conceived tool it has been for staging an encounter with the meaning of and challenges posed by a technology-driven future, but relocating it from the elitist circles of an art & science festival to the minds of the general public.

As popular as this event has been, perhaps its sociopolitical dimension is, in the final analysis, even greater than the impact of the many artistic performances. Thus, the *Klangwolke* is part of Ars Electronica's DNA, since, ultimately, the only way to fulfill the mission of this festival—to function as a platform for art, technology and society—is through the intentional interplay of experimental and popular approaches.

But what does it take to continue to cultivate this genetic substance after 33 years? How can it keep pace with what's gone down since, especially considering the fundamental change with respect to the conception of the public and private spheres we're witnessing, and in light of the equally deep-seated shift (that's already something taken completely for granted) in how media are used? Just consider the fact that everyone is now his/her own post & telegraph office, his/her own radio & TV studio, and the editor-in-chief of his/her own media universe.

This metamorphosis of our society has become common, everyday reality and nevertheless its effects and how they come about aren't any better understood than they were 33 years ago. And that's precisely what a *Klangwolke* has to be about in 2012, which is to say five years after the advent of the iPhone and Year 8 of the Age of Facebook.

A *Klangwolke* can't and shouldn't only have an interesting theme and spectacular effects. It should also always be a laboratory for the question of what the public sphere and participation in it entail. These basic principles have guided us in conceiving the 2012 *Klangwolke*.
It was clear from the very start that it couldn't be the opus magnum of an individual artist, and that the participation of the public had to go beyond mere special effects remote-controlled via cell phone. The aim was to shift essential design parameters into the collective sphere—that is, to put a part of the *Klangwolke* into the hands of the public, but also to derive the materials for a *Klangwolke* from the swarms of the cloud and thereby arrive at forms that symbolically express the realities of global networking. This is the spirit in which we launched the *Klangwolke ABC* and *Soundcloudminiature* projects that are ultimately nothing but artistically consistent updates of the legendary *radio-in-the-window action.* The decision not to commission a composer but rather to develop a soundtrack that was assembled—and not composed—out of resources available on the internet was another logical consequence. Open source and international cooperation in the development of technical effects have, in any case, long since become things that go without saying and even unavoidable realities if the objective is to master a certain level of complexity within a limited timeframe.
The *Klangwolke* has become a part of the identity of this city and its inhabitants; the level of recognition and approval it's accorded is extraordinarily high. It is totally exhilarating to experience how quickly you can motivate people to get actively involved in *Klangwolke* projects—all kinds of people: fire departments, clubs fostering traditional local customs, high-tech firms, government agencies, families and school classes.

Since the *Klangwolke* has always been a part of the Ars Electronica Festival, we're also taking this year's event as the occasion of a festival workshop. Subsumed under the heading *Open Cloud Project* will be a series of undertakings and events organized in conjunction with the *Klangwolke* that are likewise dedicated to coming up with a contemporary definition of "Art for All" and testing the viability of sound as a medium for artistic works in public spaces and networks. Among others *teardrops* by Rupert Huber in the cathedral of Linz and the *Mobile Ö1 Atelier* on Linz Main Square. Thus, the *Klangwolke* will be more than a one-hour show-event; it is itself becoming a network, an occasion and an event that is confronting the city and the people living in it over the course of months with issues having to do with shaping the future, and it has been enticing and encouraging people to think about these things and to get actively involved in them.
The 2012 *voestalpine Klangwolke* bears the name of our sponsor and partner, without whose support this production would simply have been impossible. It's being co-produced by thousands of people worldwide and implemented by a network of artists, technicians and organizers representing Ars Electronica and the Brucknerhaus. It will happen on Saturday evening, September 1, 2012, on the banks of the Danube, throughout the following week at various locations around town, and over the months that follow on the internet and at many regional venues throughout Upper Austria.

Gerfried Stocker

Die Wolke im Netz
voestalpine Klangwolke 2012

In diesem Jahr ist oft die Rede von den mittlerweile legendären Anfängen der *Klangwolke* und ihrem Gründungsgedanken. Aus gutem Grund, ist doch vieles von dem, was sie zu einem der innovativsten und erfolgreichsten Projekte in der Geschichte der Linzer Ars Electronica machte, gerade aus heutiger Sicht wieder hoch aktuell.

In einer Zeit, in der (von CB-Funkamateuren abgesehen) Rundfunk und Medien nur als unidirektionale Versorgungseinrichtungen existierten und man – zumindest in Österreich – gerade einmal zwischen zwei Programmen des staatlichen Fernsehens wählen konnte, war die temporäre Öffnung des Massenmediums Radio für ein breit angelegtes partizipatorisches Projekt mit Sicherheit eine gewagte Sache, die aber so in unprätentiöser Weise auf eine zukünftige Medienrealität verwies, die damals schwer vorstellbar war, aber heute ganz normal ist. Eine Realität in der Medien offen, multidirektional vernetzt, ubiquitär und mobil sind und klassische Machtzentren der Mediengesellschaft in Trümmern oder zumindest in Agonie liegen und durch andere, ganz neue ersetzt wurden.

Die Leute aufzufordern, mit ihren Radioempfangsgeräten etwas vollkommen anderes zu machen, sie nicht nur als *Receiver* (Empfänger), sondern auch als *Transceiver* einzusetzen, indem man das Empfangene weiterleitete und in den öffentlichen Raum hinaus schaltete, zeigt die eigentliche Aufgabe und Qualität des Projektes *Klangwolke*. *Klangwolke*, das hieß von Anfang an nicht bloß Open-Air-Konzert (obwohl selbst das für die damalige Zeit reichlich ungewöhnlich war, bedenkt man, dass hier nicht eine Rockband auftrat, sondern klassische Musik aus dem Konzertsaal rauskatapultiert und dabei noch von Elektronik-Künstlern verarbeitet und visualisiert wurde). *Klangwolke* ist vielmehr ein Instrument des Dialoges mit der Bevölkerung einer ganzen Stadt, einer ganzen Region, und sie war ein genial erdachtes Werkzeug, um die Auseinandersetzung mit den Themen und Herausforderungen einer technologiegetriebenen Zukunft aus den elitären Zirkeln eines Kunst- und Wissenschaftsfestivals in die Köpfe der breiten Bevölkerung zu tragen.

Damit hatte sie bei aller Popularität letztlich vielleicht sogar eine viel größere gesellschaftspolitische Dimension, als sie von vielen Kunstperformances erwirkt werden konnte. Die *Klangwolke* gehört somit zur DNA der Ars Electronica, da letztlich nur in dem gezielten Zusammenspiel von experimentellen und populären Zugängen die Mission des Festivals, eine Plattform für Kunst, Technologie und Gesellschaft zu sein, eingelöst werden kann.

Doch was heißt es, diese Erbsubstanz nach 33 Jahren weiter zu pflegen, wie kann sie mit dem Schritt halten, was sich seither getan hat, vor allem angesichts der grundlegenden Veränderung, die wir rund um die Begriffe des Öffentlichen bzw. des Privaten gerade erleben, angesichts der ebenso grundlegend anderen und bereits selbstverständlich gewordenen Nutzung der Medien? Denken wir nur daran, dass heute letztlich jede/r sein/ihr eigenes Post- und Telegrafenamt ist, dass jede/r sein/ihr eigenes Fernseh- und Rundfunkzentrum ist und jede/r selbst ChefredakteurIn seines eigenen Mediaversums.

Diese Mediamorphose unserer Gesellschaft ist selbstverständliche Realität geworden und dennoch mitnichten besser in ihren Wirkungen und Funktionen verstanden als vor 33 Jahren. Genau darum muss es in einer *Klangwolke* gehen, die im Jahr 2012 – oder sollte man sagen im Jahr 5 nach iPhone oder im Jahr 8 nach Facebook – stattfindet.

Eine *Klangwolke* kann und soll nicht nur ein interessantes Thema und aufregende Effekte haben, sie sollte immer auch ein Labor sein für die Frage nach dem, was Öffentlichkeit und Teilnahme an Öffentlichkeit anbelangt. Nach diesen Gesichtspunkten sind wir daran gegangen, die *Klangwolke* 2012 zu konzipieren.

Klar war von Anfang an, dass sie nicht das *Opus magnum* einer/s einzelnen Künstlers/in sein konnte und dass die Partizipation des Publikums schon über einen bloßen Fernsteuereffekt per Handy hinausgehen musste. Ziel war es, wesentliche Gestaltungsparameter in das Kollektiv zu verlagern, also dem Publikum einen Teil der *Klangwolke* in die Hand zu geben, die Materialien für eine *Klangwolke* aber auch aus den Schwärmen der Cloud heraus zu gewinnen und dabei Formen zu finden, die symbolisch die Realitäten der globalen Vernetzung zum Ausdruck bringen. So sind die Projekte *Klangwolken-ABC* und *Klangwolken-Miniaturen* entstanden, die letztlich die legendäre *Radio ins Fenster* Aktion nur konsequent in unsere Zeit weiterdenken. Aber auch die Entscheidung, keine/n Komponisten/in zu engagieren, sondern einen Soundtrack zu entwickeln, der aus über das Internet zugänglichen Ressourcen kombiniert statt komponiert wird, war eine logische Konsequenz. Open Source und internationale Kooperationen sind bei der Entwicklung technischer Effekte ja ohnedies längst schon selbstverständliche oder sogar unvermeidliche Realität, will man eine bestimmte Komplexität in begrenzter Zeit meistern.

Die *Klangwolke* ist zu einem Teil der Identität dieser Stadt und ihrer EinwohnerInnen geworden und trifft auf nahezu ungeteilte Zustimmung und Anerkennung. Es ist euphorisierend zu erleben, wie schnell man Menschen zur Teilnahme an *Klangwolken*-Projekten begeistern kann, seien es die Feuerwehren des Landes, brauchtumspflegende Vereine, High-Tech-Firmen, Amtsstellen oder Familien und Schulklassen.

Die *Klangwolke* war und ist aber immer auch Teil des Ars Electronica Festivals, und so nehmen wir die *Klangwolke* dieses Jahr auch zum Anlass für eine Festivalwerkstatt. Unter dem Schirm des *Open Cloud Project* werden eine Reihe von Projekten und Events organisiert, die sich rund um die *Klangwolke* ebenfalls den Fragestellungen nach einer zeitgemäßen Definition von „Kunst für alle" oder der Tragfähigkeit von Klang als Intermedium für künstlerisches Arbeiten in öffentlichen Räumen und Netzen widmen. Dazu gehören unter anderem *teardrops* von Rubert Huber im Linzer Dom sowie die Aktivitäten des *Mobilen Ö1 Ateliers*. Die *Klangwolke* wird damit mehr als ein einstündiges Show-Event: Sie wird selbst zu einem Netzwerk, einem Anlass und Ereignis, das die Stadt und ihre Einwohner über Monate mit Themenstellungen der Zukunftsgestaltung konfrontiert, sie verführt und dazu anregt darüber nachzudenken und sich selbst ein Stück weit einzubringen.

Die *voestalpine Klangwolke* 2012 – sie trägt den Namen des Sponsors und Partners, ohne dessen Unterstützung sie schlichtweg nicht möglich wäre – wird von tausenden Menschen weltweit mitgestaltet und von einem Netzwerk an KünstlerInnen, TechnikerInnen und OrganisatorInnen der Ars Electronica und des Brucknerhauses realisiert. Sie manifestiert sich am Samstag, den 1. September 2012, am Abend im Donauraum, die ganze darauffolgende Woche an verschiedenen Orten in der Stadt und über Monate hinweg im Internet und an vielen regionalen Außenstellen in ganz Oberösterreich.

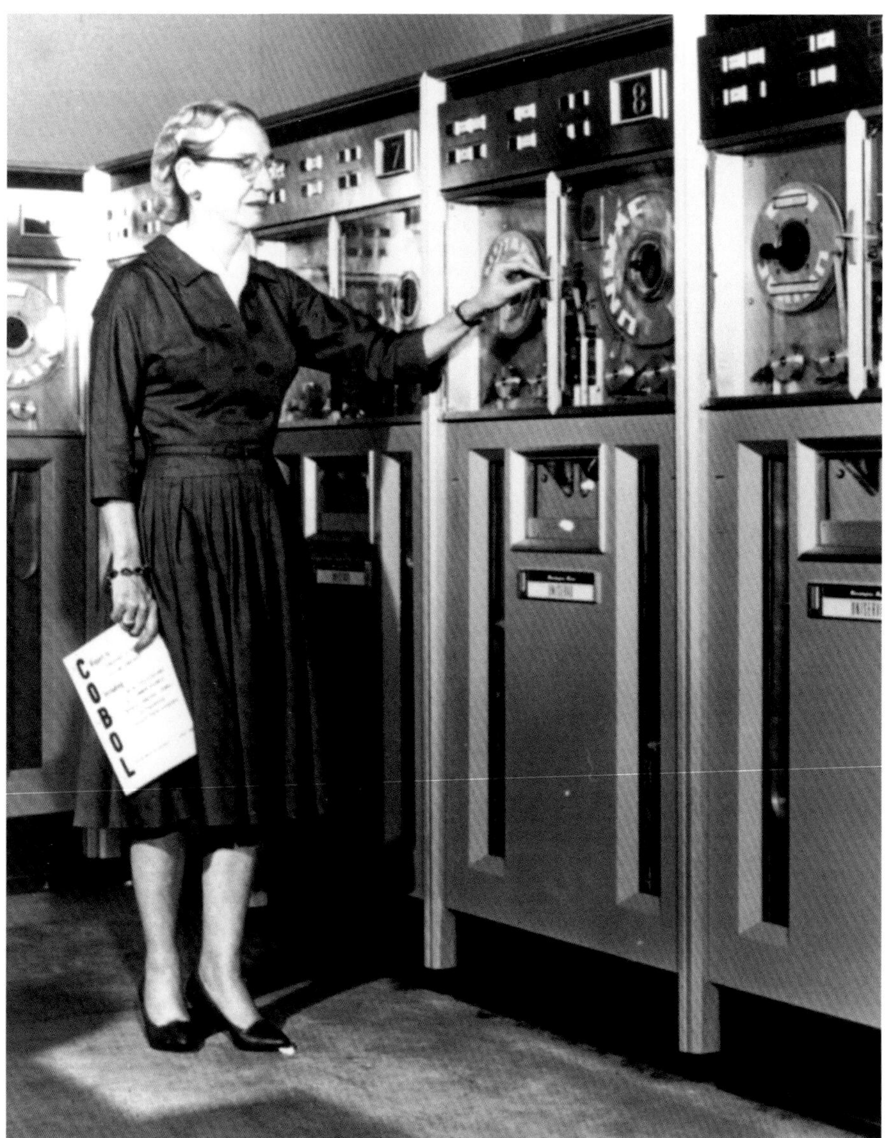

Computer scientist & programmer Grace M. Hopper (1906-92) at work on a UNIVAC mainframe in 1952
Die Computerwissenschaftlerin und Programmiererin Grace M. Hopper (1906–1992) bei der Arbeit
an einem UNIVAC-Mainframe, 1952

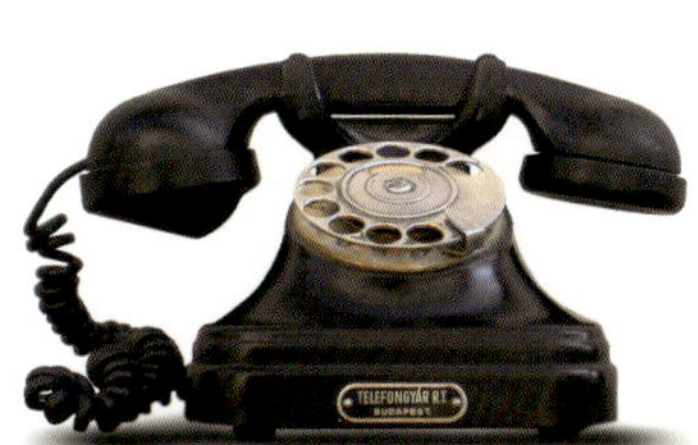 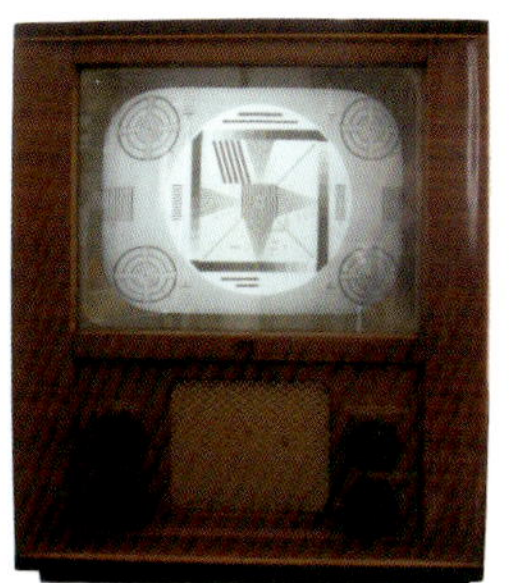 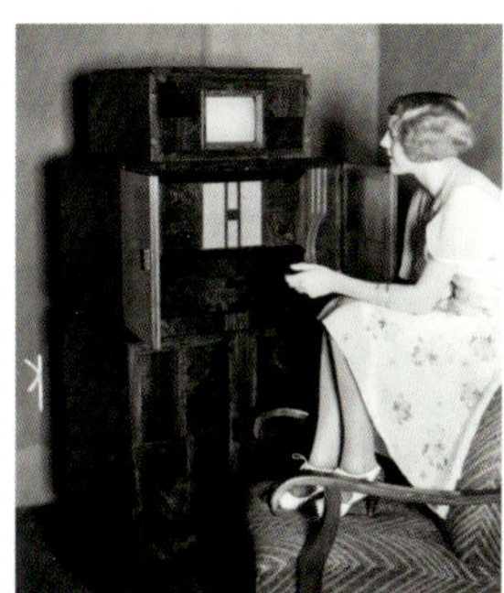

http://commons.wikimedia.org/wiki/File:Hungarian_Telephone_Factory_1937_Budapest.jpg
http://commons.wikimedia.org/wiki/File:SW_Testbild_auf_Philips_TD1410U.jpg?uselang=de
http://commons.wikimedia.org/wiki/File:Bundesarchiv_Bild_183-R26738,_Kombinierter_Fernseh-_und_Rundfunkempf%C3%A4nger.jpg

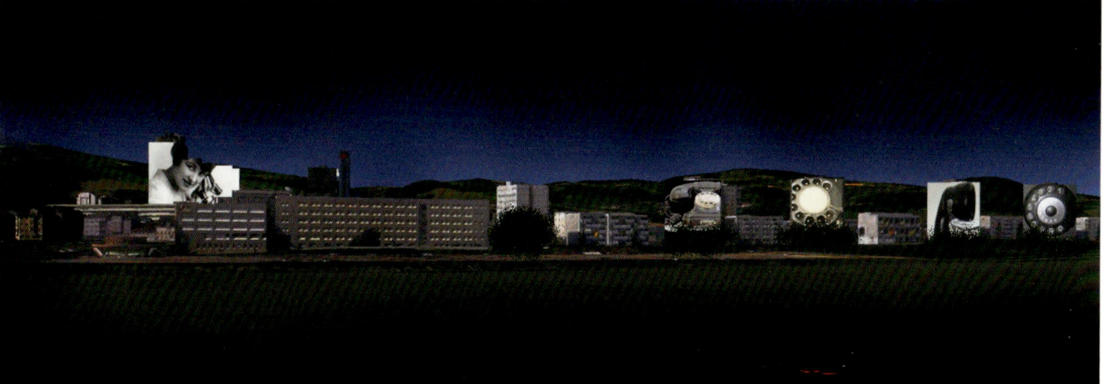

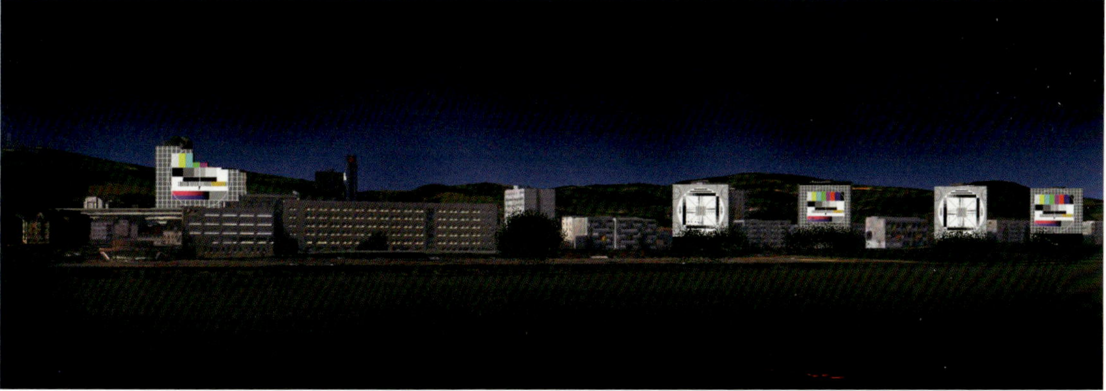

Projektionssimulation voestalpine Klangwolke 2012

Hannes Leopoldseder

A Step into the Future
The Linzer Klangwolke as a Cloud on the Internet

The 2012 *Klangwolke* is an account of the networking of our world. It recapitulates the key themes of Ars Electronica from 1979 to today, shows how new technologies have transformed our lives, and thus corresponds to "Art, Technology and Society," the overarching principle that has provided the Ars Electronica Festival's orientation for more than three decades now. "Culture for all," the postulate coined by Frankfurt cultural functionary Hilmar Hoffmann in the 1970s, was defined as a key element of Ars Electronica's mission in 1979, when the founders interpreted this above all as a mandate for audience participation. The 1979 Linzer Klangwolke as a "symphonic open-air featuring Bruckner's 8th" is still considered a pioneering initiative in fostering audience involvement.

How did Linz become a city of sound? In 1979, the following options were open to prospective *Klangwolke* audience members:

1. "Come to the musical main event in the Donaupark adjacent to the Brucknerhaus! Bruckner's Symphony Nr. 8 as a new auditory experience amidst a powerful multi-quadraphonic open-air extravaganza."
2. "Would you like to actively hear the Bruckner symphony electronically modified? You can do that at the peripheral sound stations in Pöstlingberg, Freinberg, Auhofgelände and Hummelhofpark."
3. "Make Linz a city of sound! On September 18 at 8:05 PM, tune your radio to ÖR and place it in an open window!"[1]

Plus, Linz taxi companies assured that every passenger transported during the broadcast would hear the *Klangwolke* on the cab's radio. At Linz's main train station, the *Klangwolke* resounded on Track 7. A hundred thousand people gathered in the park on the banks of the Danube to experience the first *Linzer Klangwolke;* several hundred made their way to the peripheral locations; thousands took part in the radio action.

The *Klangwolke* made a big splash in the media. The coverage in *Der Spiegel* was headlined "Swinging Toni": "In expectation of the Bruckner open-air, the grey industrial metropolis developed a case of Tuesday Night Fever."[2] The *Süddeutsche Zeitung* was especially enthralled by the idea of involving the entire city in this musical event: "The burghers enthusiastically participated. The 8th resounded from the speakers of the city's taxis and the radios of folks who didn't attend personally but did set up their radios on their windowsills."[3]

In the first 10 years, the *Klangwolke* actually did spread from Linz throughout Upper Austria. At the ORF – Austrian Broadcasting Company's Upper Austria Regional Studio, the executive producer of the radio action was Christine Schöpf, who is still, together with Gerfried Stocker, the Artistic Director of the Ars Electronica Festival. A special survey conducted in 1985 showed that 300,000 people in Upper Austria listened in on *Klangwolke* weekend that year, 130,000 in the Donaupark and 20,000 in their home towns. There was particularly strong response in Wels, Engelhartszell, Attnang-Puchheim, Bad Hall, Bad Kreuzen, Frankenburg, Fischlham, Hofkirchen an der Trattnach, Krenglbach, Lenzing, Unterach, Ried im Innkreis and Ulrichsberg. Everywhere: broadcasts al fresco, audience members seated or standing around a fire; in some places there were fireworks, slide shows and lots of other initiatives. *Radio-Klangwolke* in Klaus deserves special mention: on the local lake, the music was enhanced with light, fire and water. Approximately 5,000 people participated in this annual *Klauser Klangwolke.*

There's another remarkable detail about the year 1979. According to a survey, two-thirds of the attendees had never heard a Bruckner symphony concert. Following the first *Klangwolke,* sales of recorded classical music in Linz rose dramatically.[4]

In 1979 and the years that followed, the *Klangwolke* was Ars Electronica's booster rocket. *Musica Creativa* in 1980, the play-along concert on Linz's Main Square, was almost entirely oriented on audience participation. Walter Haupt's "carpet of sound" invited the public to engage in communicative music-making with homemade instruments. Prominent politicians and artists turned out with especially creative equipment. Bob Moog, the inventor of the synthesizer, strolled in amazement around the square, mingling with the musicians generating sounds with the most striking objects and devices.

Worldwide communication was at the heart of other Ars Electronica projects too—for example, *The World in 24 Hours,* a 1982 telecommunications project by Robert Adrian X that extended over an entire 24-hour period; *Van Gogh TV Europe* with Karel Dudesek on 3sat in 1989; and *Hotel Pompino* in 1990.

Three decades after its premiere, the 2012 *Klangwolke* is taking things to the next level. According to Ars Electronica Artistic Director Gerfried Stocker: "What I'm currently concentrating on is the *Klangwolken ABC* because human actions are what turn letters into words and messages. This gives rise to a wonderful transition from information space to social space, and it gives thousands of people the opportunity to really actively participate in the *Klangwolke*"[5]

Wolfgang Winkler, director of the Brucknerhaus: "There is a clear link between the 1979 *Klangwolke* and the 2012 *Klangwolke.* In 1979, *Radio in the Window* was the idea to take possession of space. Now, the internet is a very distinct link over 30 years. Space, then and now."[6]

The *Cloud in the Web* is not only a *Klangwolke* for all; it's also one "by all, for all." This is a new dimension in the highly diverse history of the *Klangwolke* that has presented itself year by year in correspondence to technological developments. Visitors to the 2012 *Klangwolke* can already get involved in the preparations and leave behind their distinctive marks with digital communiqués. Everyone is invited to participate in the *Klangwolke* on September 1 in the real world in the Donaupark, as well as to undertake creation and participation online. A step into the future.

1 Hannes Leopoldseder, *Linzer Klangwolke. Kunsterlebnis zwischen Himmel und Erde. Die Geschichte eines Markenzeichens,* edition Christian Brandstätter, Vienna 1988
2 Ibid
3 Ibid
4 Ibid
5 *www.youtube.voestalpineklangwolke*
6 Ibid

Hannes Leopoldseder

Ein Schritt in die Zukunft
Die Linzer Klangwolke als Wolke im Netz

Die *voestalpine Klangwolke* 2012 erzählt von der Vernetzung unserer Welt, sie erzählt von den Schlüsselthemen der Ars Electronica von 1979 bis heute, vom Wandel unseres Lebens durch neue Technologien, entsprechend den Leitthemen der Ars Electronica „Kunst – Technologie – Gesellschaft", die mehr als drei Jahrzehnte die Ausrichtung des Ars Electronica Festivals bestimmt haben.

„Kultur für alle", dieses vom Frankfurter Kulturdezernenten Hilmar Hoffmann in den 1970er Jahren geprägte Postulat, war bei der Gründung der Ars Electronica 1979 eine besondere Verpflichtung und wurde damals vor allem als Forderung nach der Mitwirkung des Publikums verstanden. Die Linzer Klangwolke 1979 als „Sinfonisches Open-Air mit Bruckners 8." gilt auch heute noch als Pionierprojekt für die Beteiligung des Publikums.

1979 – wie wird Linz zur Klangstadt? Für die Klangwolkenbesucher gibt es folgende Wahlmöglichkeiten:

1. „Kommen Sie zum zentralen Musikereignis in den Donaupark beim Brucknerhaus! Bruckners *Sinfonie Nr. 8* als neues Hörerlebnis in einer gewaltigen multiquadronfonischen Open-Air-Wiedergabe!"

2. „Wollen Sie aktiv die Brucknersinfonie elektronisch verändert hören? Das können Sie an den periphären Klangstationen: Pöstlingberg, Freinberg, Auhofgelände, Hummelhofpark."

3. „Machen Sie Linz zur Klangstadt! Schalten Sie am 18. September um 20.05 Uhr Ihr Radiogerät auf ÖR, und stellen Sie Ihr Gerät in das geöffnete Fenster!"[1]

Darüber hinaus haben die Linzer Taxis versichert, dass jeder Fahrgast, den sie während der Sendezeit befördern, im Radio die *Klangwolke* hören würde. Am Linzer Hauptbahnhof erklang die *Klangwolke* auf Gleis 7. Hunderttausend Menschen sind damals zur ersten *Linzer Klangwolke* in den Donaupark gepilgert. An den Außenstellen haben sich jeweils einige Hundert eingefunden, und an der Radioaktion beteiligten sich Tausende Menschen.

Das Medienecho auf die *Klangwolke* war gewaltig. *Der Spiegel* schrieb unter dem Titel „Swinging Toni": „In Erwartung von Bruckners-Open-Air geriet die graue Industriestadt in Tuesday Night Fever".[2] Die *Süddeutsche Zeitung* bewertete vor allem die Einbeziehung der ganzen Stadt in das musikalische Geschehen besonders positiv: „Die Bürger haben begeistert mitgemacht. Die Achte klang aus den Lautsprechern der Taxifahrer und der Bürger, die nicht selbst zur Donau gegangen waren. Sie hatten ihre Radioapparate ans Fenster gestellt."[3]

In den ersten zehn Jahren breitete sich tatsächlich die *Klangwolke* aus Linz über ganz Oberösterreich aus. Im ORF Landesstudio liefen für diese Radioaktion die Fäden bei Dr. Christine Schöpf zusammen, die nach wie vor gemeinsam mit Gerfried Stocker das künstlerische Direktorium des Ars Electronica Festivals bildet. 1985 ergab eine eigene Untersuchung, dass beim Klangwolken-Weekend jenes Jahres 300.000 Oberösterreicher die *Klangwolke* hörten: 150.000 im Radio, 130.000 im Donaupark und 20.000 in ihrem Heimatort. Besonders engagierte Städte und Märkte waren Wels, Engelhartszell, Attnang-Puchheim, Bad Hall, Bad Kreuzen, Frankenburg, Fischlham, Hofkirchen an der Trattnach, Krenglbach, Lenzing, Unterach, Ried im Innkreis, Ulrichsberg. Und viele andere. Überall: Übertragung ins Freie, Stehen oder Sitzen um ein Feuer, mancherorts ein Feuerwerk, Diaprojektionen, viele weitere Initiativen. Erwähnenswert ist die *Radio-Klangwolke* in Klaus: Auf dem Klauser See wurde die Musik durch Licht, Feuer und Wasser optisch aufbereitet. An dieser Klauser Klangwolke nahmen jährlich etwa 5.000 BesucherInnen teil.

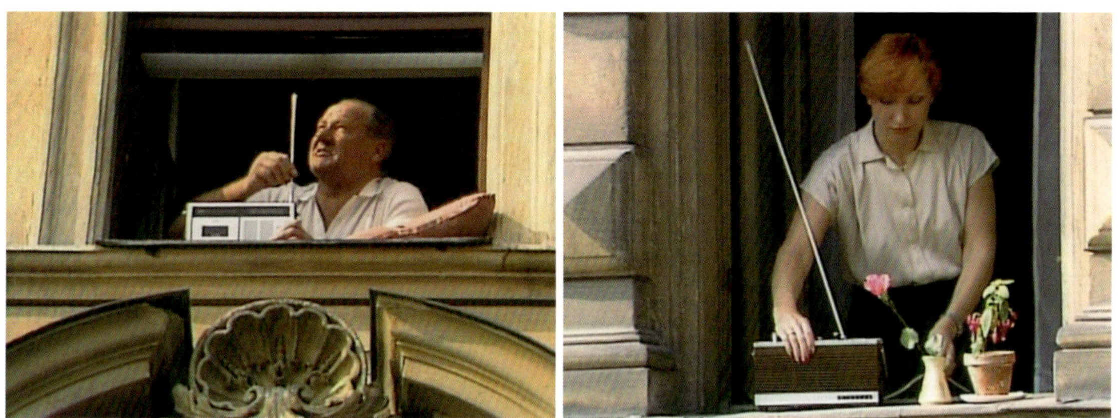

1979: "Make Linz a city of sound! On September 18 at 8:05 PM, tune your radio to ÖR and place it in an open window!"

1979: „Machen Sie Linz zur Klangstadt! Schalten Sie am 18. September um 20.05 Uhr Ihr Radiogerät auf ÖR, und stellen Sie Ihr Gerät in das geöffnete Fenster!"

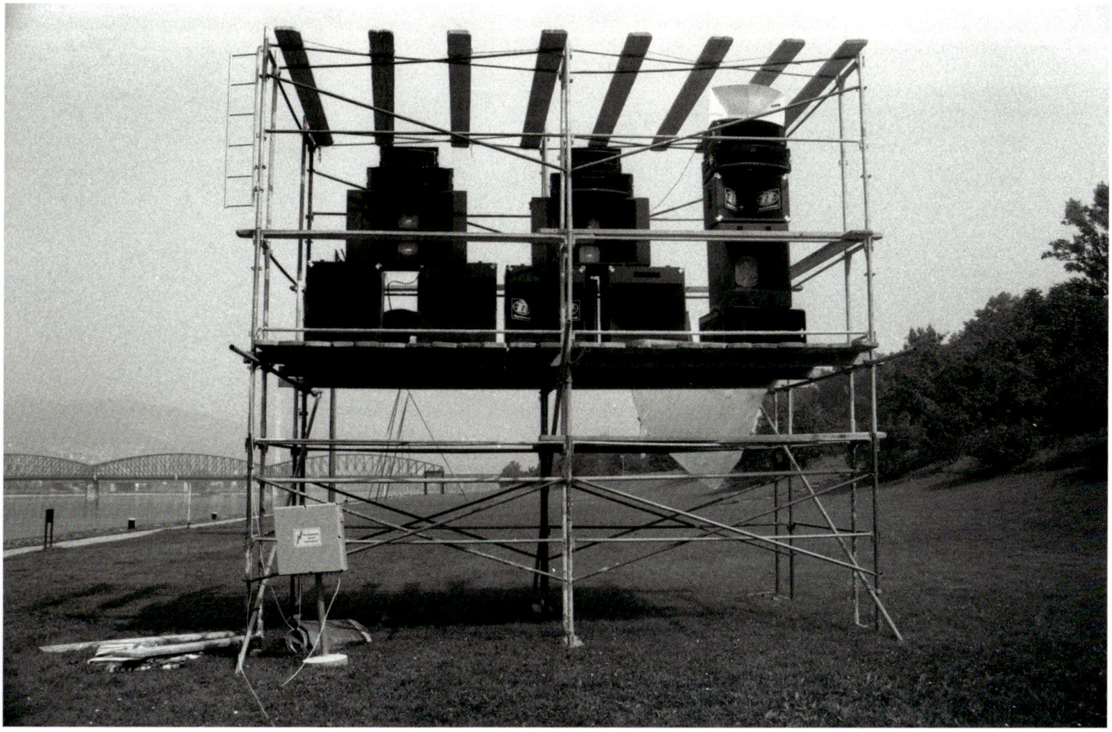

Linzer Donaupark, 1979

Bemerkenswert ist noch ein anderes Detail zum Jahr 1979: Zwei Drittel der Besucher, so das Ergebnis einer Umfrage, haben noch nie ein Konzert mit einer Bruckner-Sinfonie besucht. Nach der ersten Klangwolke hat sich der Umsatz der Tonträger mit klassischer Musik in Linz vervielfacht.[4]

Die *Klangwolke* wurde 1979 und in den folgenden Jahren zur Trägerrakete der Ars Electronica. 1980 war das Mach-Mit-Konzert *Musica Creativa* auf dem Linzer Hauptplatz fast ausschließlich auf die Partizipation des Publikums ausgerichtet. Zu einem Klangteppich von Walter Haupt wurde zu einem kommunikativen Musizieren mit selbst gebastelten Instrumenten eingeladen. Auch prominente PolitikerInnen und KünstlerInnen kamen mit besonders kreativen Instrumenten. Bob Moog, der Erfinder des Synthezisers, ging staunend über den Linzer Hauptplatz, drängte sich durch die vielen MusikerInnen, die oft mit auffälligen Gegenständen und Instrumenten Klänge erzeugten.

Um weltweite Kommunikation ging es aber auch bei anderen Projekten der Ars Electronica, zum Beispiel 1982 beim Projekt *Die Welt in 24 Stunden,* einem Telekommunikationsprojekt von Robert Adrian X, das sich über 24 Stunden erstreckte. 1989 setzte *Van Gogh TV Europe* mit Karel Dudesek mit einem europaweiten TV-Projekt auf 3sat einen weiteren Schritt, ebenso 1990 mit *Hotel Pompino.*

Drei Jahrzehnte nach der ersten *Klangwolke* setzt die *Klangwolke* 2012 wieder zu einem Sprung an. Gerfried Stocker, der künstlerische Leiter der Ars Electronica: „ Was mich derzeit am meisten beschäftigt, ist das Klangwolken-ABC, weil die Buchstaben durch die Aktionen von Menschen zu Wörtern und Botschaften werden. Damit entsteht ein wunderbarer Übergang vom Informationsraum zum sozialen Raum. Es gibt Tausenden Menschen die Gelegenheit, wirklich aktiv an der Klangwolke teilzunehmen".[5]

Wolfgang Winkler, Leiter des Brucknerhauses: „Es gibt eine deutliche Klammer zwischen der *Klangwolke* 1979 und der *Klangwolke* 2012. 1979 ist *Radio ins Fenster* erstmalig eine raumgreifende Idee. Jetzt ist das Internet eine ganz deutliche Klammer über 30 Jahre. Der Raum einst und jetzt."[6]

Die *Wolke im Netz* ist nicht nur eine *Klangwolke* für alle, sondern auch eine „von allen für alle": Dies ist eine neue Dimension in der abwechslungsreichen Geschichte der *Klangwolke,* die sich von Jahr zu Jahr entsprechend der technologischen Entwicklung präsentiert hat. Die Besucherinnen und Besucher der Klangwolke 2012 können sich bereits in die Vorbereitungen voll einklinken und mit digitalen Botschaften ihr eigenes Signum hinterlassen. Bei der *Klangwolke* selbst am 1. September steht ihnen die Mitwirkung in der Realwelt im Donaupark offen, ebenso die Kreation und Partizipation im Netz. Ein Schritt in die Zukunft.

1 Hannes Leopoldseder, *Linzer Klangwolke. Kunsterlebnis zwischen Himmel und Erde. Die Geschichte eines Markenzeichens,* edition Christian Brandstätter, Wien 1988
2 Ebenda
3 Ebenda
4 Ebenda
5 *www.youtube.voestalpineklangwolke*
6 Ebenda

Wolfgang Winkler

On a Tuesday Evening

Project, Backstage, Recollections

1979: Hannes Leopoldseder was looking for a link between Ars and Brucknerfest, two productions with contents as dissimilar as can be. He found it in Walter Haupt—genus: Bavarian; species: Münchner. A drummer in the Munich Opera Orchestra who paid a permanent substitute to sit in for him. But above all a composer and creative mind way beyond the composer cliché. He was a big fan of wide-open spaciousness even before he got to Linz. And, indeed, his *Music for a Landscape* was ultimately what established the tie-in to Linz. Hannes Leopoldseder and Walter Haupt, always accompanied by his organizational aide, muse, constant companion and future wife Rosi Nistler, thought intensively about a project in a public space and the *Linzer Klangwolke* was the outcome. As for myself, at this point, having just been recruited by Leopoldseder, my responsibilities at the ORF [Austrian Broadcasting Company] were strictly of an operational nature, though this quickly changed after the first *Klangwolke*. The discussions moderated by Hannes Leopoldseder between Haupt and me would provide enough material for a collection of anecdotes. But the work on the *Klangwolke* was clearly structured. Walter Haupt was the sound director in the Donaupark; the technical know-how and the development of the sound in the public space—quadraphonic in those days—was in the hands of the ORF's Upper Austria Regional Studio. I was the recording director, which is to say the one responsible for the musical details of the recording. The sound was fed via cables to loudspeakers outside and Walter Haupt was the sound director in Donaupark.

In this role during the 10 years of collaboration, he became a legend in Linz. Walter Haupt always stood in front of a lectern beside the container that housed the technical equipment in Donaupark and conducted the symphony. In going about this, he relayed what he wanted to my sound booth in the Brucknerhaus in a way that made a strong impression on the audience, who had no way of knowing that, due to the nature of the technology, these directives always came in too late. We output a sound from the Brucknerhaus and there was no way to modify it anymore.

So the performance—as far as Walter Haupt's role is concerned—was nothing more than show for the audience. The real work on the sound took place in the rehearsals in the days before the event. Thus, the *Klangwolke* had a realistic resemblance to the work of a conductor with an orchestra.

And so it began...

On a Tuesday evening, September 18, 1979, 19:59:30 o'clock, ORF Upper Austria Regional Studio. 30 seconds before the start of the *Linzer Klangwolke*. Direct broadcast via radio so that Linzers could put their radios out on their windowsills and receive the right music: Anton Bruckner's 8th Symphony performed by the Concertgebouw Orchestra Amsterdam conducted by Bernard Haitink.

Not live. Instead, in the studio, there was an 8-track tape from a record label. Four tracks were a conventional recording of the music, and four tracks, 5–8, were electronically modified as befitting Ars Electronica, a festival of electronic art. Only, who knew back then what Ars Electronica meant?

The desktop had just been born in America and the effort was being made to market this new device. Up to then, computers were mainframes, mostly operated by men in white lab coats who processed big reels of tape, the contents of which nobody understood anyway. That parameters of decisive importance for human existences were being stored on such tapes even then was not generally known. And how were you supposed to be able to think and work artistically with equipment like that?

Almost no one was aware then that efforts had long since gotten underway to utilize such computational machinery to replicate music—for instance, that of Johann Sebastian Bach. The results achieved in this connection by a certain Lejaren Hiller got an ambivalent reception. Lejaren Arthur Hiller (Februar 23, 1924, New York City – January 26, 1994, Buffalo NY) was an American composer who founded the experimental music studio at the University of Illinois at Urbana-Champaign in 1958. He composed, together with Leonard Isaacson, and produced the first significant computer music composition, the *Illiac Suite,* in 1957. Nevertheless, technology, art and music had been involved in a close interrelationship for a long time by then considering the work that John Cage, Pierre Schaeffer, Pierre Henry and others had already done.

So, it was 30 seconds before the big event. Everything was ready, all Linz had gathered at the Brucknerhaus eagerly awaiting the first strains of music. In the studio were sound engineer Franz Kiesl and little ol' me. Suddenly, Franz Kiesl asked me which tracks we really wanted to play now. This question at this point in time totally unnerved me. Everything had already been discussed and finalized. This final confirmation by Franz Kiesl threw me for a loop. After what seemed like an eternity, I said: 1-4! The broadcast and thus the *Klangwolke* began, and the two of us listened intently to the first notes: Bruckner or only almost Bruckner?

Bruckner resounded and the *Klangwolke* was born. There's no way of knowing how things would have turned out if, in those seconds before 8 PM, we had made the wrong decision.

Addendum, after 33 years of Linzer Klangwolken ...

The effort has been made throughout the intervening years to keep on striving to achieve the extraordinary. And this has more or less succeeded. Let us recall at this point in the proceedings director Hans Hoffer, Hubert Lepka and his machine-oriented productions and the fireworks *Klangwolke* of 2011 as proxies for many others. And let us not fail to mention the *Kinder-Klangwolken* that have been staged since 1998.

As I see it, this year's *Cloud in the Web* spans an arc back to the first *Klangwolke* in 1979. The idea then of people putting radios in their window to thus create a soundspace transcending the confines of Donaupark is being supplemented this year by presence online and thus given an apt contemporary update.

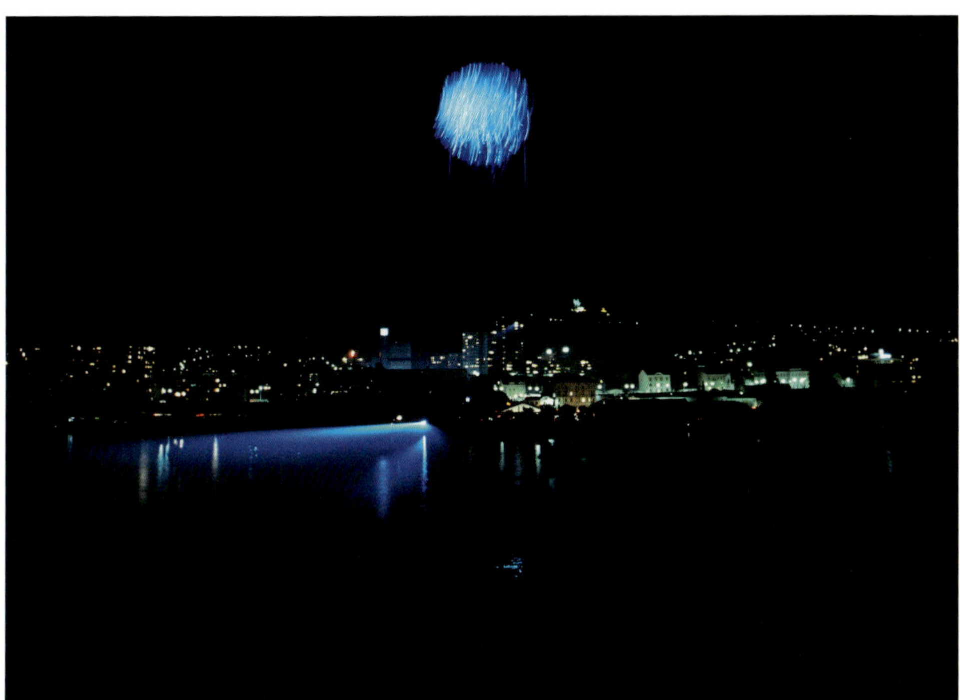

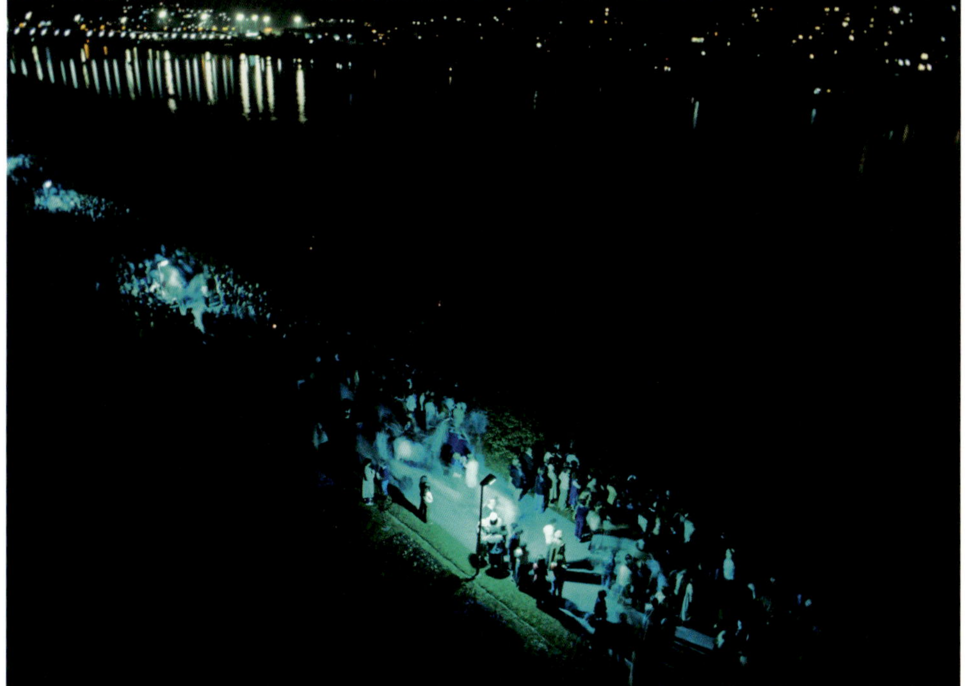

Linzer Klangwolke, 1979

Wolfgang Winkler

An einem Dienstagabend

Projekt, Backstage, Erinnerungen

1979: Hannes Leopoldseder suchte also eine Verbindung zweier so konträrer Inhalte wie Ars Electronica und Brucknerfest. Er fand sie in Walter Haupt, Bayer in der speziellen Abart der Münchner, Schlagzeuger des Münchner Opernorchesters, der sich einen ständigen Substituten bezahlte. Vor allem aber Komponist und kreativer Kopf jenseits des Klischees von Komponisten. Der offene Raum hatte es ihm schon vor Linz angetan. Seine *Musik für eine Landschaft* war es letztlich auch, die die Verbindung mit Linz herstellte. Hannes Leopoldseder und Walter Haupt, stets begleitet von seiner Organisationshilfe, Muse, ständigen Begleiterin und späteren Ehefrau Rosi Nistler, dachten also intensiv über ein Projekt im offenen Raum nach, und die Linzer *Klangwolke* war das Ergebnis. Zu diesem Zeitpunkt war ich selbst, gerade frisch von Leopoldseder für den ORF eingefangen, ausschließlich im operativen Bereich tätig, was sich nach der ersten *Klangwolke* sehr rasch änderte. Die Diskussionen unter der Leitung von Hannes Leopoldseder zwischen Haupt und mir würden wahrscheinlich leicht eine Anekdotensammlung füllen. Die Arbeit bei der Klangwolke war aber klar strukturiert. Walter Haupt war der Klangregisseur im Donaupark, das technische Know-how und die Entwicklung des Klanges im offenen Raum – damals über Quadrophonie – lag in den Händen des Landesstudios Oberösterreich. Ich selbst war der Aufnahmeleiter, also der, der für die musikalischen Details bei der Aufnahme zuständig war. Über Leitungen wurde dieser Klang zu den Lautsprechern im offenen Raum übertragen, und Walter Haupt war der Klangregisseur im Donaupark.

In dieser Rolle erlangte er in den zehn Jahren der Zusammenarbeit legendäre Berühmtheit in Linz. Walter Haupt stand immer am Container, in dem die Technik im Donaupark untergebracht war, vor einem Notenpult und dirigierte die Symphonie. Dabei sagte er in meiner Tonkammer im Brucknerhaus immer seine Wünsche sehr publikumswirksam durch. Das Publikum konnte aber nicht wissen, dass aufgrund der Technik solche Anweisungen letztlich immer zu spät kommen mussten. Wir schickten einen Klang aus dem Brucknerhaus hinaus, der von außen nicht mehr geändert werden konnte.

So war die Aufführung – die Sichtweise ist dabei auf Walter Haupt gerichtet – immer auch Show für das Publikum. Die wirkliche Arbeit am Klang geschah in den Proben in den Tagen vorher.

Die *Klangwolke* hatte so eine realistische Ähnlichkeit mit der Arbeit eines Dirigenten mit seinem Orchester.

Und so begann es ...

An einem Dienstagabend, 18. September 1979, 19:59:30, Studio Oberösterreich des ORF. 30 Sekunden vor dem Beginn der Linzer Klangwolke. Direkt übertragen über das Radio, damit die Linzer ihre Radios ins Fenster stellen können und die richtige Musik empfangen. Die *8. Symphonie* von Anton Bruckner, gespielt vom Concertgebouworchester Amsterdam unter der Leitung von Bernard Haitink.

Nicht live, sondern im Studio lag ein Acht-Spur-Band der Plattenfirma. Vier Spuren waren eine herkömmliche Aufnahme der Musik, vier Spuren, 5–8, waren vershattert, das heißt elektronisch verändert, wie es eigentlich einer Ars Electronica, einem Festival der elektronischen Kunst geziemt hätte. Nur, wer wusste damals schon, was Ars Electronica bedeutet?

Der Desktop wurde gerade in Amerika geboren, und man versuchte, dieses neue Gerät auf den Markt zu bringen. Computer waren bis dahin Großrechenanlagen, die von meist weiß gekleideten Männern bedient wurden, die wiederum große Bänder bearbeiteten, deren Inhalt ohnehin niemand verstand. Dass schon damals entscheidende Parameter menschlicher Existenz auf diesen Bändern gespeichert waren, war nicht Allgemeinwissen.

Und mit solchen Geräten sollte man auch künstlerisch denken und arbeiten können?

Es war fast niemandem bewusst, dass schon lange versucht wurde, mithilfe der Rechenanlagen die Musik, beispielsweise von Johann Sebastian Bach, nachzumachen. Die diesbezüglichen Resultate eines Lejaren Hiller waren zwiespältig. Lejaren Arthur Hiller (23. Februar 1924, New York City – 26. Januar 1994, Buffalo, New York) war ein amerikanischer Komponist, der 1958 das experimentelle Musikstudio an der University of Illinois in Urbana-Champaign gründete und die erste bedeutende Computer-Musik-Komposition, 1957 die *Illiac Suite,* mit Leonard Isaacson komponierte und technisch umsetzte. Technik, Kunst und Musik waren allerdings schon viel früher eine enge Beziehung eingegangen. Denken wir nur an John Cage, Pierre Schaeffer, Pierre Henry und andere mehr.

Es war also 30 Sekunden vor dem großen Ereignis. Alles war bereit, ganz Linz war beim Brucknerhaus versammelt und fieberte den ersten Tönen entgegen. Im Studio waren nur der Tonmeister Franz Kiesl und meine Wenigkeit. Plötzlich fragte mich Franz Kiesl, welche der Spuren wir nun wirklich spielen sollten. Diese Frage zu diesem Zeitpunkt brachte mich doch aus der Fassung. Es war alles besprochen und vereinbart. Diese letzte Rückversicherung Franz Kiesls brachte mich ins Stottern. Nach schier endlosen Sekunden sagte ich: 1–4! Die Sendung und damit die Klangwolke begann, und wir beide hörten gespannt auf die ersten Töne, Bruckner oder nur fast Bruckner?

Es erklang Bruckner, und damit war die Klangwolke geboren. Nicht auszudenken, wie die Geschichte verlaufen wäre, hätten wir in den Sekunden vor 20 Uhr die falsche Entscheidung getroffen.

Ergänzung nach 33 Jahren Linzer Klangwolken ...

Es wurde in all den Jahren immer wieder versucht, die Linie des Außergewöhnlichen beizubehalten. Das ist mehr oder minder gelungen. Erinnert sei an dieser Stelle an Hans Hoffer als Regisseur, an Hubert Lepka und seine maschinenorientierten Inszenierungen und an die Feuerwerksklangwolke 2011 nur als Beispiel für viele andere Klangwolken. Hinzu kamen noch die Kinder-Klangwolken seit 1998.

Mit der diesjährigen *Wolke im Netz* ist für mich ein Bogen zur ersten *Klangwolke* 1979 gegeben. Die Idee damals, die Radios ins Fenster zu stellen und damit einen Klangraum, der über den Donaupark hinausgeht, zu schaffen, wird heuer durch den Internet-Raum ergänzt und auch zeitgemäß abgeschlossen.

The Cloud in the Web—Storyline

The *Cloud in the Web* is a story about the web that interlinks the whole world—about how it came to be and how it's changing our lives.

Episode 1: Recalling the Pioneers

As is so often the case these days, this story too begins with discoveries and inventions: first and foremost, electricity, a force of nature that humankind learned to master and employ for its own purposes.

The initial episode is a tribute to the researchers and pioneers of the past: Luigi Galvani, Maxwell, Edison, Marconi and, of course, the mysterious Nikola Tesla. The two giant spools of the Tesla Orchestra (USA) are mounted on a ship sailing up the Danube. Accompanied by the opening bars of *Also sprach Zarathustra*, a performer tames the seven-meter-long lightning bolts that assault his body shielded within a chainmail suit that functions like a Faraday cage—a scene symbolic of humankind's ceaseless urge to subjugate nature.

In the final chord of the Zarathustra theme, drummers mix in, the pounding of their mighty beats triggering brilliant salvos from powerful spotlights, but as the music ebbs so does the blitz of bolts and beams of illumination. Only the subtly glowing mood of the full-moon night that just fell over Linz's riverside Donaupark fills the air, and the music segues into the larghetto of Frédéric Chopin's *Piano Concerto No. 1 in E minor, Op. 11.*

Power plants and electricity grids were built worldwide to henceforth power the machines in the factories, bring light to the streets and houses, and turn night into day.

The triumphant takeover of electrical power as the basis of our modern infrastructure is the theme of this scene. From the first note of the piano and with each note that follows, the lights of downtown buildings and streets are switched on. Each tone illuminates another building. The lights seem to adhere to the fingers of the pianist whose notes let there be light in buildings on up into the chain of hills north of Linz.

The poetic atmosphere of the piano concerto is abruptly terminated by alarming sounds and a driving rhythm. Suddenly, the flashing blue lights of emergency vehicles are visible in the hills that form the northern horizon—first at a few isolated locations; then spreading out like wildfire, to the accompaniment of increasingly dynamic music. Hundreds of fire trucks are the stars of this dramatic scene staged in conjunction with a large-scale regional disaster preparedness exercise. The tempest of blue light swells in the direction of the city, towards Donaupark, leaping across streets and over buildings, their lighting as well beginning to flicker in time to the music's driving beat. The whole northern half of town is in motion. The network has blanketed the city.

Episode 2: Telecommunications—The World Gets Smaller

But motors and light bulbs weren't all that changed the world then. News too was converted into electronic signals and dispatched around the globe. People could exchange ideas instantaneously over tremendous distances, and later even converse with one another by telephone. The world became smaller and telecommunications turned into a very big business.

Morse code characters dah-dit in the background, their staccato beat dictating the flashing of the spotlights. Voices chime in, reading messages aloud in phonetic alphabets, both English (Alfa, Bravo, Charlie) and German (Anton, Berta, Cäsar). Here, for the first time, the 5,000 illuminated letters come into play. Controlled by a radio network, they blink to the exact rhythm of these communiqués and thereby symbolize the transition from an internet that serves the purpose of exchanging data and information to our modern-day Web2.0 that has become a social space in which communication and connectedness top people's agendas.

Episode 3: From the Network of Computers to the Network of Human Beings

Arrayed along the riverbank are people in LED suits that, under the cloak of darkness, make them appear to be cyborgs. With illuminated pennants, they send signals using the international flag alphabet. Following a "Babylonian chaos" in which the languages and messages blend and interweave to the point of incomprehensibility, groups of people coalesce with their letters and form legible words, sentences and messages. Like a procession along the riverbank, they're a ticker displaying a live crawl text. Rowboats with letters and words on board float past on the current; model airplanes converted into flying letters inscribe the airspace above them. The musical leitmotiv of the film *Brazil* surfaces at this point to bring in an allusion to the conflict between the system and the individual, the central theme of the Digital Information Age.

Episode 4: A New Era of Entertainment

Then the mass media entered our homes—the radio into the kitchen, the telephone into the hall, the TV into the living room.

A sound collage of original gramophone recordings made in the early days of radio and television (Roosevelt, Chamberlain, Heinz Conrads, Caruso, et al.) is accompanied by historical images of old telephones, radio receivers and TV test patterns projected onto the façades of the high-rises on the north bank of the Danube.
The color schemes of the old-fashioned test patterns spread out across the skyline, symbolizing the inexorable proliferation of mass media and the determinative role of television.

Episode 5: Triumph of the Computer

Computers were as big as clothes closets and filled entire floors of buildings when, in 1969, the first four processors were hooked up into what would eventually be the internet. When NASA was going about getting Neil Armstrong to the Moon and back that same year, the computing power they had at their disposal didn't amount to the capabilities of a typical cell phone today. No one had an inkling of the developments this had launched.

This scene interconnects space exploration and the advent of the computer as examples of the spirit of inquiry and discovery that has driven humankind since time immemorial. We begin with close-ups of old mainframe computers projected onto the high-rises in the background, which thereby come to resemble gigantic central processing units. They're succeeded by animated graphic imagery of the Earth as seen from the Moon. Projected onto a 30-meter screen suspended by two cranes aboard a barge in the middle of the Danube are time-lapse images of Earth taken from the International Space Station (ISS). This scene is not accompanied by techno-electronic sounds, but rather a piece that suggests traditional Austrian folk music—vocal harmonies and acoustic guitars emotionally underscoring the breathtaking beauty of our planet seen from outer space and making the point that technology doesn't arise on its own, that it's always ultimately the manifestation of human yearnings and visions. This scene culminates in a live remote hook-up with the ISS and a message of greetings delivered to Linz from out in the cosmos.

Episode 6: The Robots Make Their Entrance

Along with the computer came the robots. And the fear of them. The fear that they'll take over our jobs and that they could someday even rule over us.

Appearing in the heavens is a swarm of drones—50 quadrocopters as autonomously flying pixel-points of light forming an oversized eye. Meanwhile, in the background, the high-rise façades display images of military drones with their gun-sights locked on target. They're the demons of modern technology with their countless possibilities of deployment, not for the benefit of humankind, but for purposes of surveillance and oppression.
With abrupt, heavily resounding drumbeats and *Carmina Burana*-like choral chants, two giant industrial robots that have been slumbering on the riverbank awake. With gaudy spotlights they scan their surroundings, dazzling the audience in their glare. A squadron of military helicopters flies in at low altitude from the east and takes up position threateningly close to the crowd. Noise and wind from the rotor blades dredge up apocalyptic associations now.
Barging into this scene and taking up position directly in front of the onlookers are 10 hydraulic lifts. They ascend, each with a person atop its platform: traditional Alpine Apperschnalzer cracking their whips that, according to ancient custom, have the power to drive out the demons of winter. Here, they symbolize overcoming the fear of high-tech hardware's supremacy, the battle of human versus machine. Each of the lashes' miniature sonic booms is registered electronically and flashes on the powerful searchlight mounted on each hydraulic lift. They shoot columns of light into the night sky, expressions of the hope that human reason will prevail.
And triumph it does. The music turns mellow, the harsh, gaudy lights are toned down, and the robots' movements become elegant and gentle. They rise up, their heads in the night sky, firing 20-meter-high fountains of water illuminated by spotlights. To the rhythm of the music, they seem to amuse themselves with the jets of water. Brief staccatos and wide-ranging figures arc through the air, a most aesthetic interplay of light, water and gravity.

Episode 7: We Are the Web

The internet isn't just a network of computers anymore. It's a network of people. It's our playground and our marketplace; a setting for encounter and exchange; our way to have our say. We are the people. We are the Web. We are the 99 %.

The swarm of robots appears aloft for a demonstration of what it's capable of. Never before has such a large number of quadrocopters banded together into a squadron of autonomous, interactive aircraft that can move about freely in space as a 3D graphic system. In addition to being a masterful technical achievement in its own right, it symbolizes crowds, swarms and communities, the beacons of hope for an open, participative social model and for the opportunities of each individual to have a say in the way things are and to network with others. To the strains of Rupert Huber's version of *The Beautiful Blue Danube* in which waltz time swings and sways with dub beats, the drones swoop down over Europe's great river. Mixed in with the music are soundbites recorded at various locations worldwide amidst Arab Spring and Occupy demonstrations. The projections display impressive statistics elaborating on the global dimensions of digital networking—imparting an optimistic view of its positive potential, as a down-payment on and vote of confidence in the visions of a better future.

Episode 8: Network Europe

Watercourses are this planet's oldest networks and still constitute its most vital arteries. The waters of the Danube link up 115 million people in 14 countries into a huge ecological and cultural network. And precisely because the technical means of these times can instantaneously transport us to any place on Earth whenever we want, we can't lose sight of the real physical setting in which we actually live our lives. Europe's future is in a strong network of ideas and human beings, a network open to ALL. Whether or not we master the challenge inherent in this is up to each and every one of us.

Japanese artists contributed the featured design element of the final episode: 50,000 blue LED balls that have been charged with solar energy. Floating down the Danube, they represent the wishes and hopes of all men and women living along the river. On their way, they encounter people in boats moving against the current, and bathe the river and its banks in a shimmering blue haze. A peaceful concluding mood that, at the last minute, is shattered when all the emergency vehicles that, in the meantime, have made their way down from the hills, turn on their blue lights and sirens. An open end, situated between hope and a state of alarm symbolic of Europe's current situation.

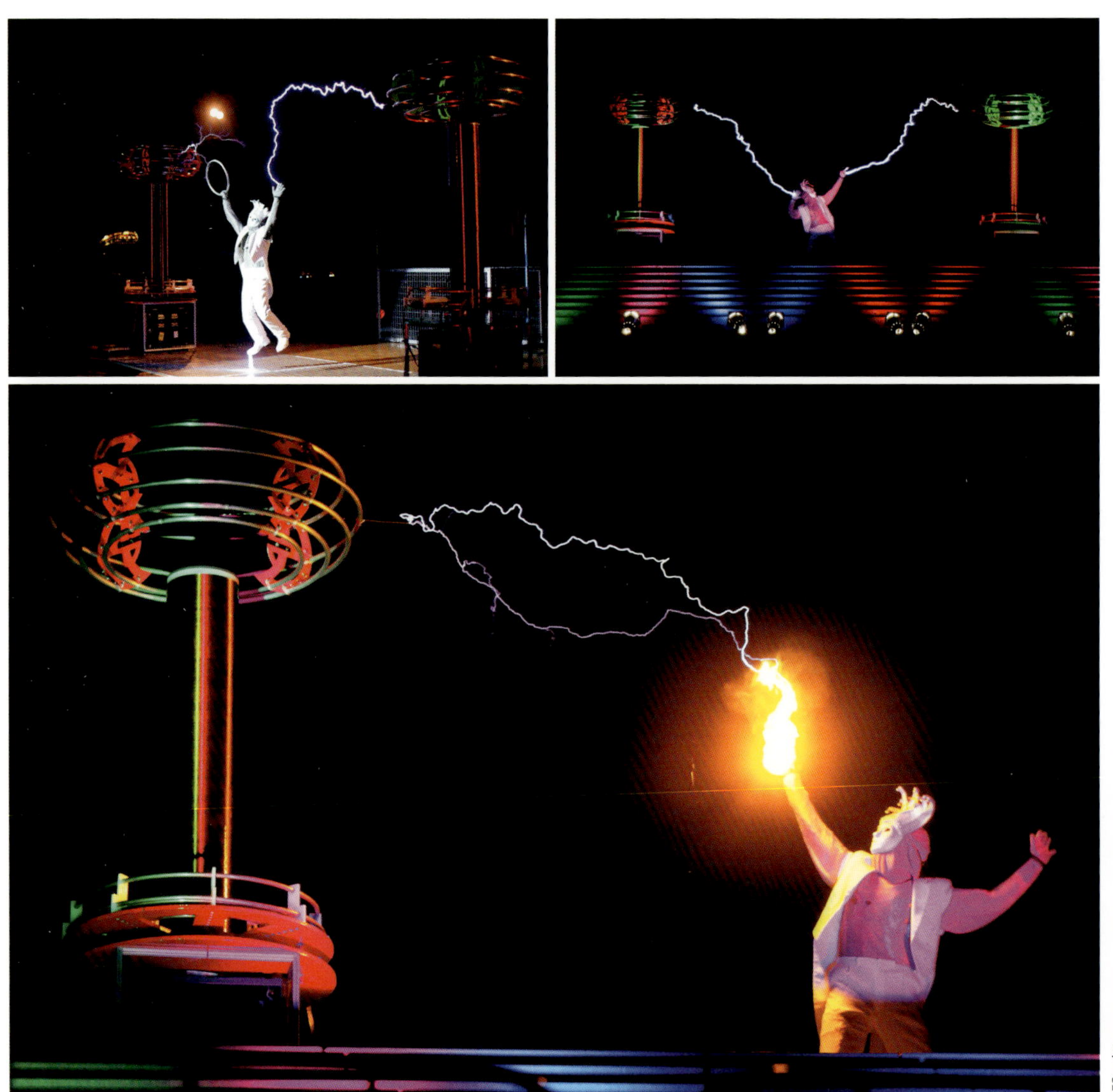

The Tesla Orchestra

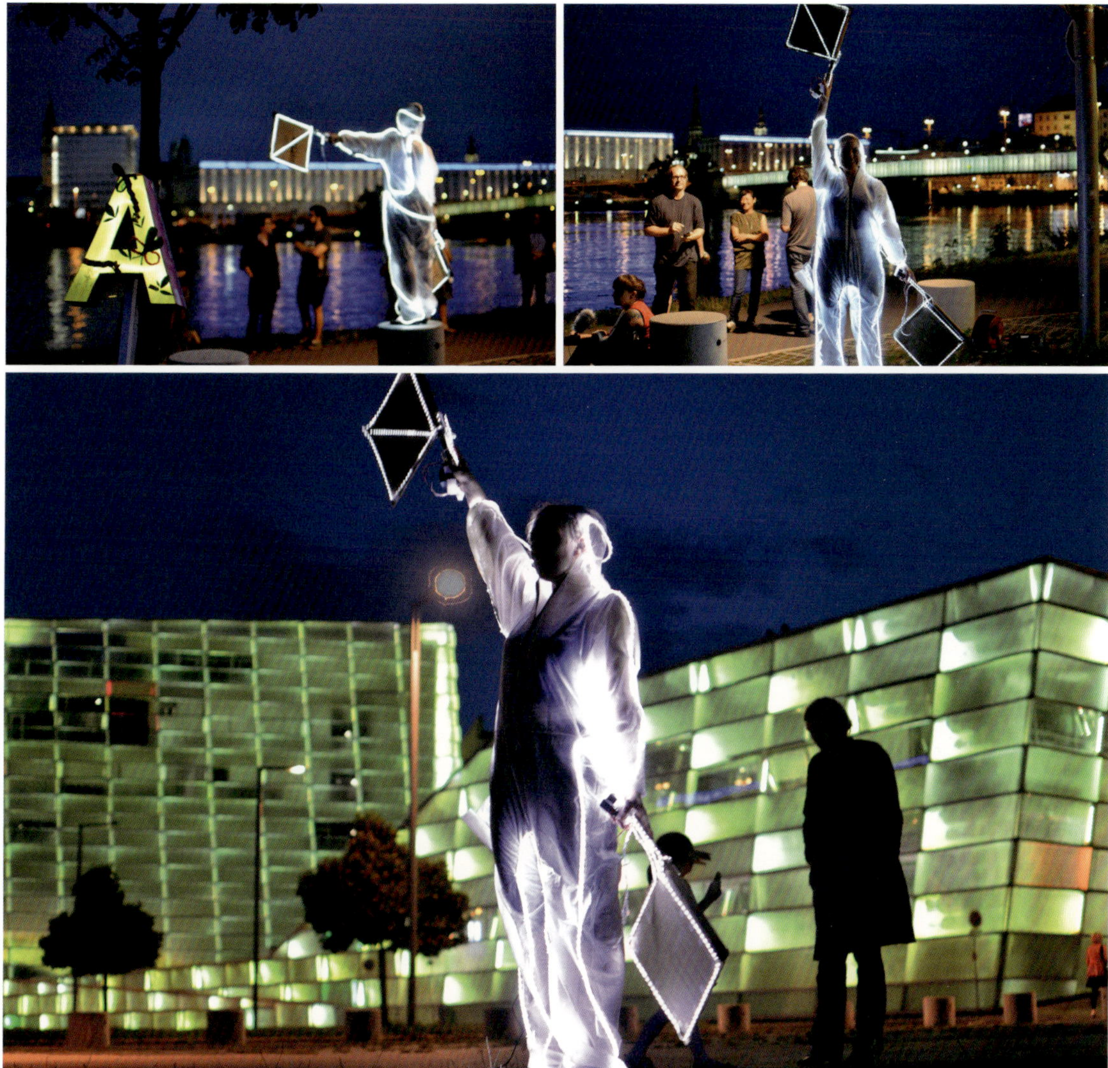

The LED suits undergo initial testing / Erste Tests der LED Anzüge

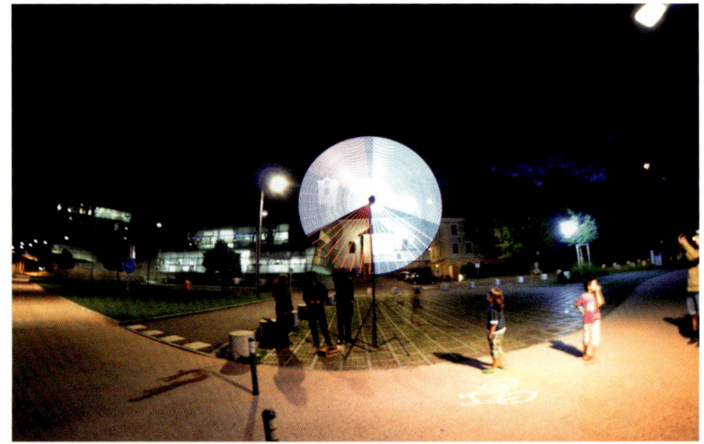

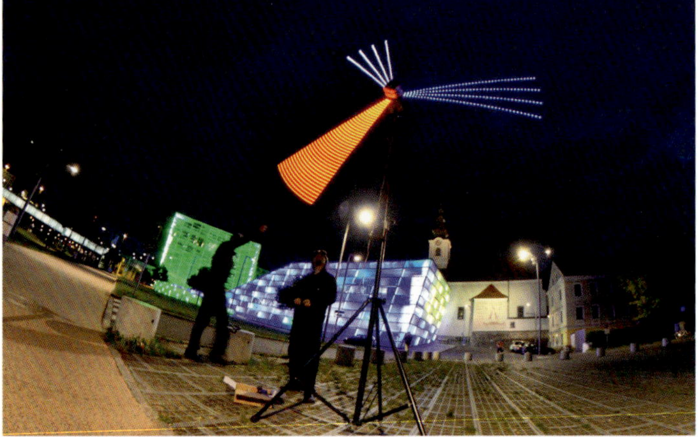

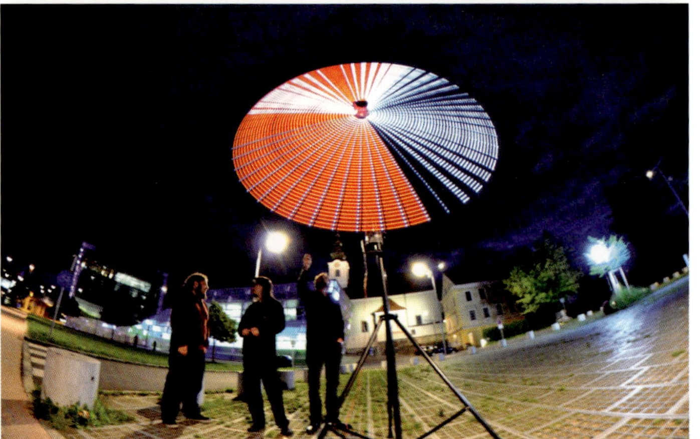

Test of various light effects / Test diverser Lichteffekte

AEC, Barbara Heinzl

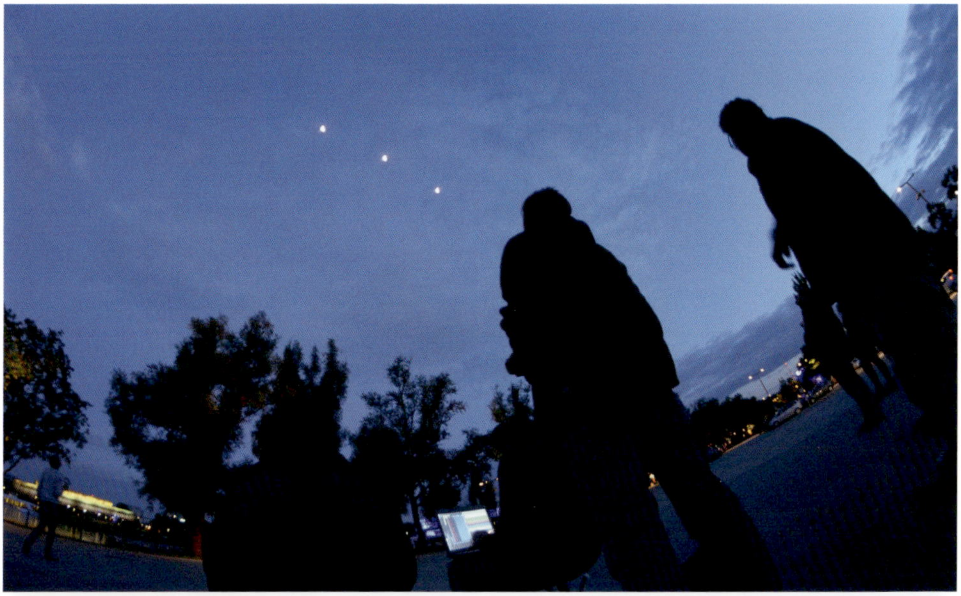

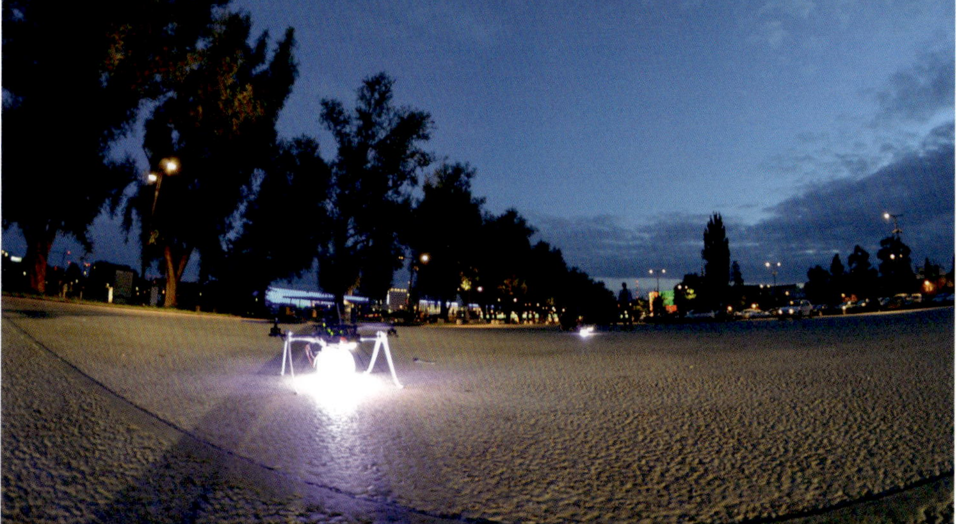

First test flights by the drones: Three Spaxels aloft! / Erste Flugversuche der Drohnen – drei Spaxel am Himmel!

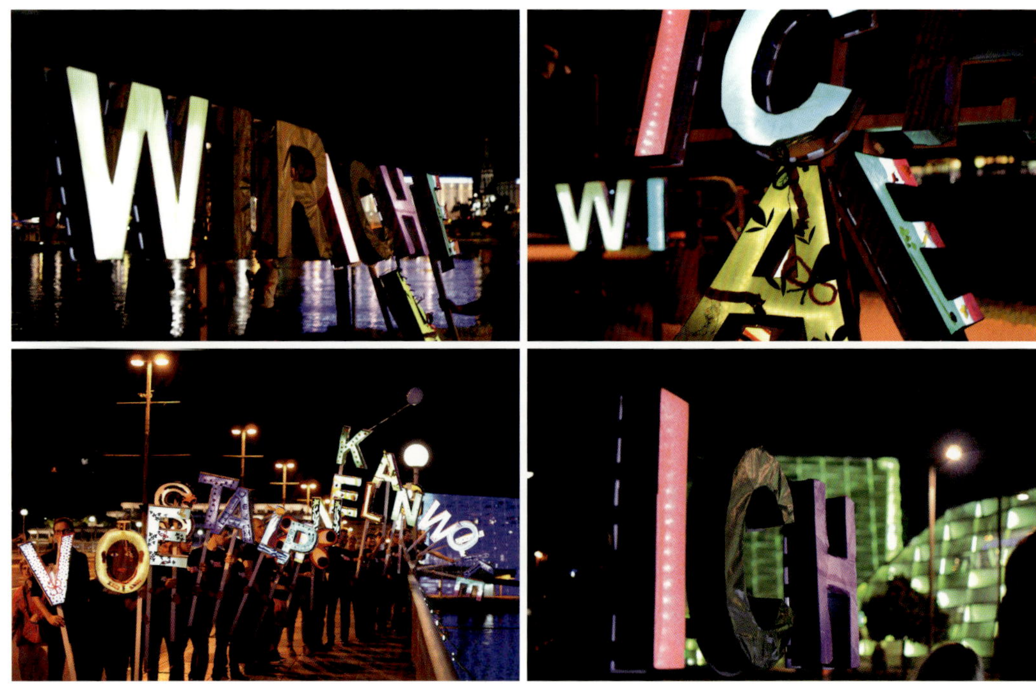

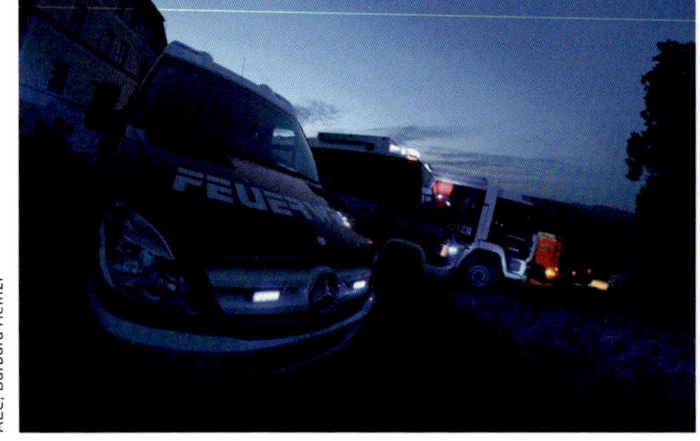

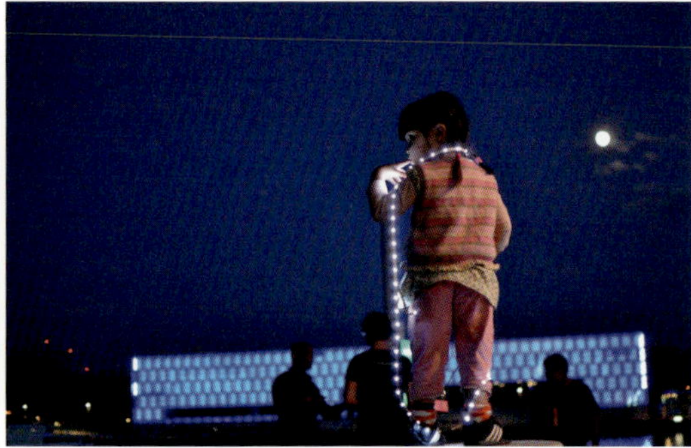

AEC, Barbara Heinzl

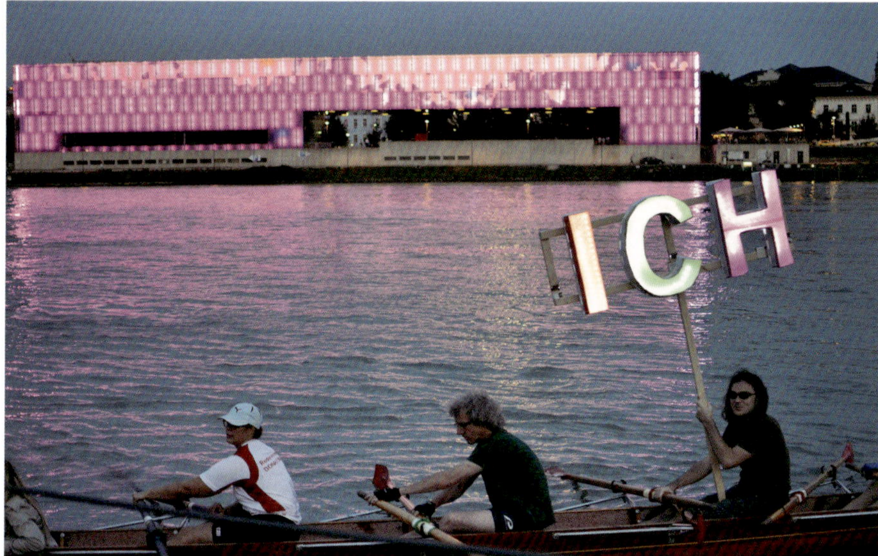

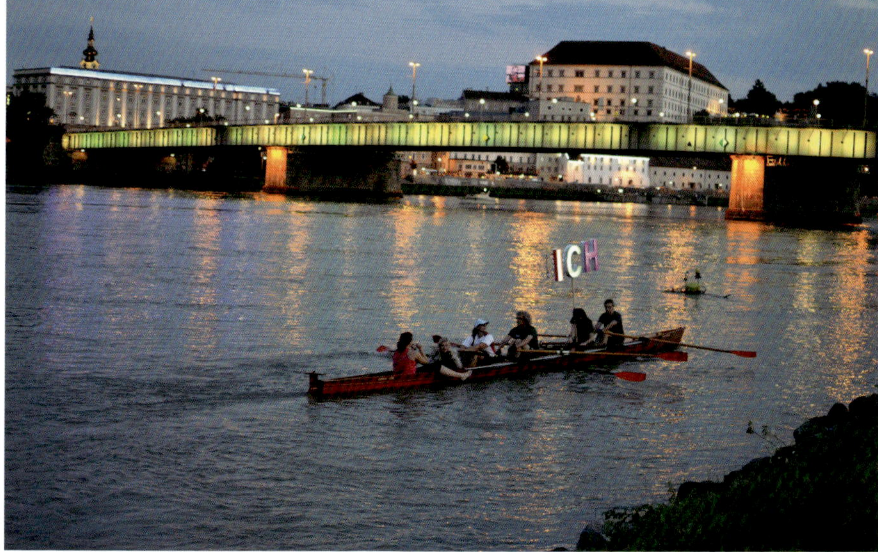

AEC, Barbara Heinzl

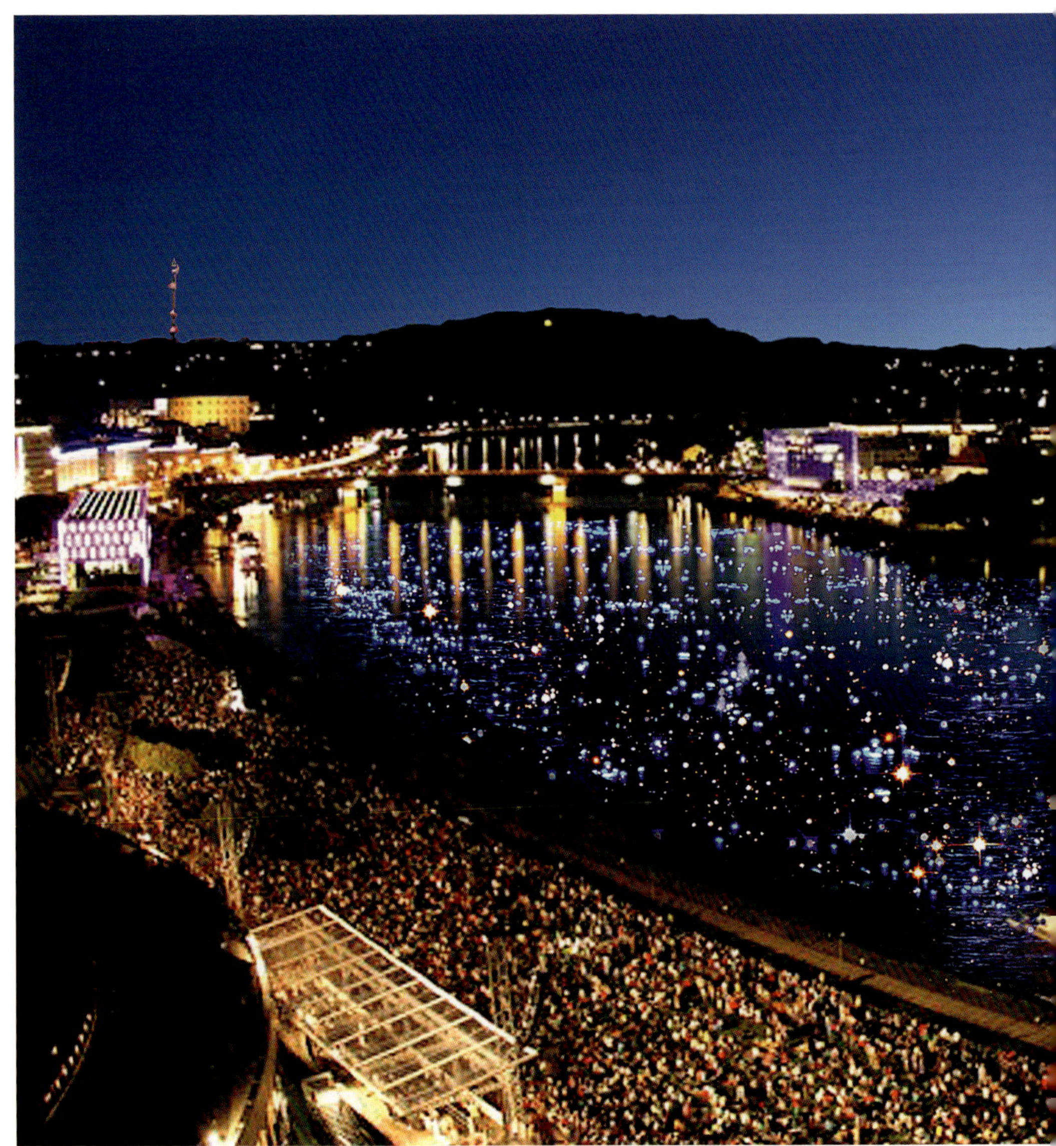

Simulation of the Amanogawa project (by Yoshihiro Harano) on the Danube in Linz
Simulation des Amanogawa Projekts (von Yoshihiro Harano) auf der Donau in Linz

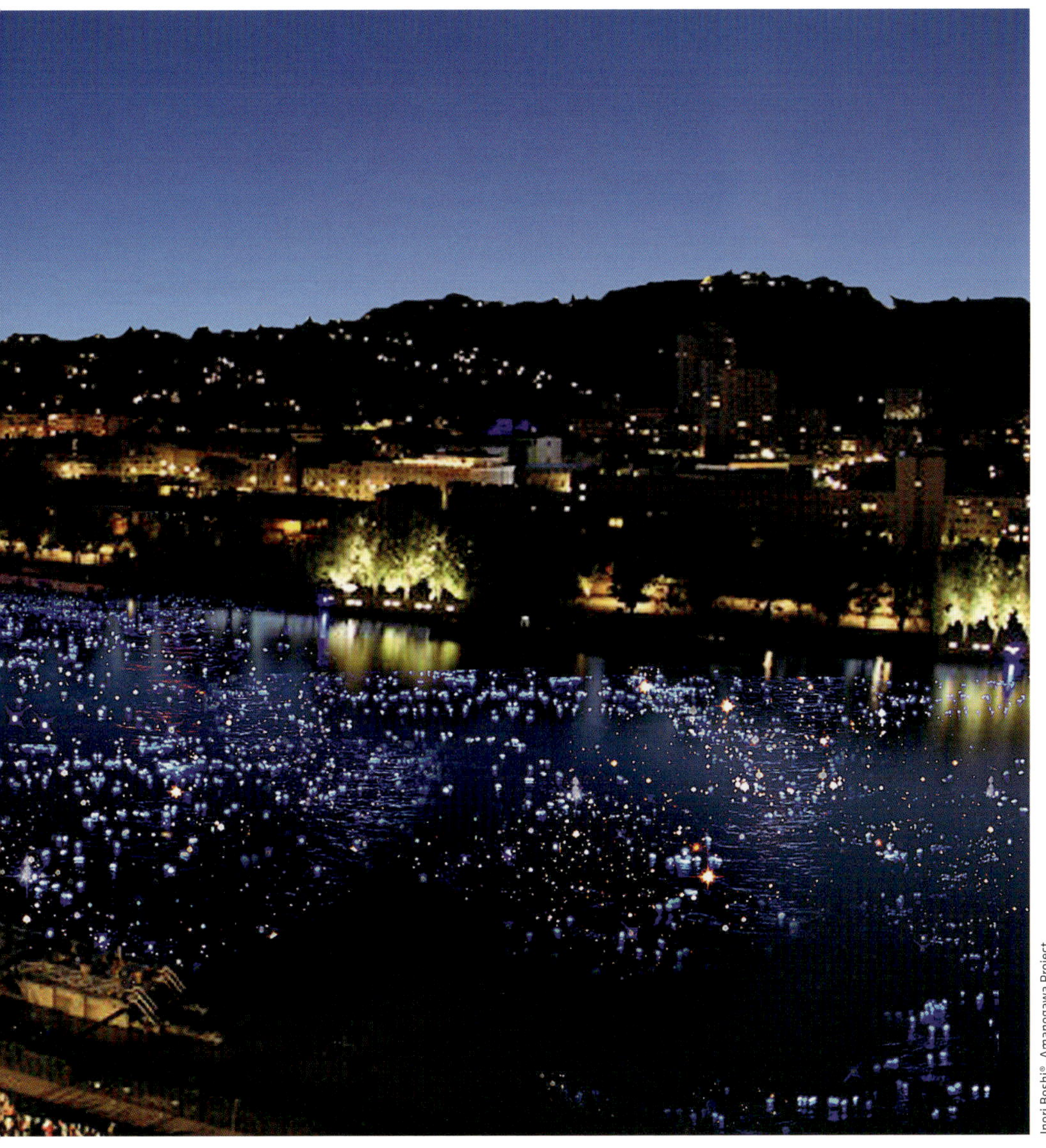

Inori Boshi®, Amanogawa Project

Die Wolke im Netz – Storyline

Die *Wolke im Netz* ist eine Geschichte über die weltweite Vernetzung, darüber, wie sie entstanden ist und wie sie unser Leben verändert.

Episode 1 – Referenz an die Pioniere

Wie so oft in unserer Zeit stehen auch am Anfang dieser Geschichte Entdeckungen und Erfindungen. Elektrizität, eine Naturgewalt, die der Mensch lernte zu beherrschen und für seine Zwecke einzusetzen.

Die erste Episode ist eine Hommage an die Forscher und Pioniere der frühen Tage: Luigi Galvani, Maxwell, Edison, Marconi und natürlich den geheimnisumwobenen Nikola Tesla. Die zwei großen Spulen des US-amerikanischen Tesla Orchestras werden, auf einem Schiff montiert, die Donau hinauffahren. Ein Performer wird zu den Klängen von *Also sprach Zarathustra* die über sieben Meter langen Blitzen bändigen, die in seinen von einem Kettenanzug, der wie ein Faradayscher Käfig funktioniert, geschützten Körper einschlagen – Symbol für den immerwährenden Drang des Menschen, die Natur zu beherrschen.
In den Schlussakkord des *Zarathustra*-Themas mischen sich Trommler, deren Schläge Lichtsalven von starken Scheinwerfern auslösen, doch mit der Musik klingen auch alle Blitze und Scheinwerfer aus. Nur die Lichtstimmung der gerade angebrochenen Vollmondnacht liegt über dem Donaupark, und die Musik geht über in den Anfang des Larghetto von Frédéric Chopins 1. *Klavierkonzert op. 11.*

Weltweit entstanden Kraftwerke und Stromnetze, trieben fortan die Maschinen in den Fabriken, brachten Licht in die Straßen und Häuser und ließen die Nacht zum Tag werden.

Der Siegeszug des elektrischen Stroms als Basis unserer modernen Infrastruktur ist das Thema dieser Szene: Mit dem ersten Ton des Klaviers werden nun Ton für Ton Gebäude- und Straßenbeleuchtung der Stadt geschaltet. Jeder Ton erleuchtet ein weiteres Gebäude, die Lichter scheinen an den Fingern des Pianisten zu kleben, der mit seinen Tönen Gebäude bis in die Hügelketten nördlich von Linz schaltet.
Die poetische Stimmung des Klavierkonzerts wird unvermittelt durch alarmierende Sounds und einen treibenden Rhythmus abgebrochen. Plötzlich tauchen in den Hügelketten am Horizont Blaulichter von Einsatzfahrzeugen auf. Erst an wenigen Orten, um sich dann mit der zunehmenden Dynamik der Musik wie ein Flächenbrand auszubreiten. Hunderte Einsatzfahrzeuge der Feuerwehr gestalten diesen Teil im Rahmen einer überregionalen Koordinationsübung. Das Blaulichtgewitter breitet sich Richtung Stadt, in Richtung Donaupark aus und springt über auf Straßen und Gebäudebeleuchtungen, die nun ebenfalls im peitschenden Rhythmus der Musik zu flackern beginnen, die ganze nördliche Hälfte der Stadt ist in Bewegung. Das Netzwerk hat die Stadt überzogen.

Episode 2 – Telekommunikation – Die Welt wird kleiner

Doch nicht nur Motoren und Glühbirnen veränderten damals die Welt, auch Nachrichten wurden in elektrische Signale umgewandelt und um den ganzen Globus verschickt. Menschen konnten sich blitzschnell über große Entfernungen austauschen, später sogar miteinander telefonieren. Die Welt wurde kleiner und Telekommunikation zum ganz großen Geschäft.

Morsezeichen erklingen im Hintergrund und steuern in ihrem Takt die Scheinwerfer, dazu kommen Stimmen, die Nachrichten im englischen und deutschen Buchstabieralphabet vorlesen: Hier kommen zum ersten Mal die 5.000 Leuchtbuchstaben zum Einsatz, sie blinken, über ein Funknetz gesteuert, exakt im Rhythmus dieser Botschaften und symbolisieren den Übergang vom Internet, das dem Austausch von Daten und Informationen diente, zum Web 2.0 unserer Tage, das zu einem sozialen Raum geworden ist, in dem es primär um Kommunikation und Verbundenheit geht.

Episode 3 – vom Netzwerk der Computer zum Netzwerk der Menschen

An den Ufern stehen Menschen in LED-Anzügen, die sie im Dunkeln wie Cyborgs aussehen lassen, und signalisieren mit leuchtenden Fahnen das internationalen Flaggenalphabet. Nach einem „babylonischen Chaos", in dem sich Sprachen und Nachrichten zur Unverständlichkeit verdichten und überlagern, formieren sich Menschengruppen mit ihren Buchstaben und bilden lesbare Worte, Sätze und Botschaften. Wie Paraden laufen sie nun als „Laufschriften" das Donauufer entlang, Ruderboote mit Buchstaben und Worten an Bord schwimmen auf dem Fluss vorbei, und zu Buchstaben umgebaute Modellflugzeuge ziehen ihre Bahnen.
Musikalisch taucht hier das Leitmotiv des Films *Brazil* auf und verweist auf den Konflikt von System und Individuum als einem zentralen Thema des digitalen Informationszeitalters.

Episode 4 – eine neue Ära der Unterhaltung

Dann kamen die Massenmedien in unsere Wohnungen, das Radio in die Küche, das Telefon in den Flur, der Fernseher ins Wohnzimmer.

Eine Soundcollage aus Originalaufnahmen der ersten Grammophone der frühen Jahre von Rundfunk und Fernsehen (Roosevelt, Chamberlain, Heinz Conrads, Caruso …) wird begleitet von historischen Bildern alter Telefone, Radiogeräte und TV-Testbildern, die auf die Fassaden der Hochhäuser am Nordufer der Donau projiziert werden.
Die Farbmuster der alten Testbilder breiten sich über die ganze Skyline aus und symbolisieren das unaufhaltsame Vordringen der Massenmedien und die bestimmende Rolle des Fernsehens.

Episode 5 – Siegeszug der Computer

Computer waren noch groß wie Schränke, die ganze Stockwerke füllten, als 1969 die ersten vier Rechner des späteren Internet verbunden wurden, und um im gleichen Jahr Neil Armstrong zum Mond zu bringen, hatte die NASA weniger Rechnerleistung zur Verfügung, als heute in jedem durchschnittlichen Handy steckt. Niemand konnte ahnen, welche Entwicklung damit begonnen hatte.

In dieser Szene werden Weltraumfahrt und der Siegeszug der Computer miteinander verbunden, als Beispiele für den Forscher- und Entdeckergeist, der die Menschheit immer wieder antreibt. Zu Beginn werden Close-Ups von alten Mainframe-Computern auf die Hochhäuser im Hintergrund projiziert, die damit wie gigantische Rechneranlagen aussehen. Später werden sie von Bildanimationen der Erde vom Mond aus gesehen abgelöst. Auf einer 30 Meter großen Leinwand, die von zwei Kränen auf einem Lastenschiff in der Mitte der Donau gehalten wird, werden von der ISS Zeitrafferaufnahmen der Erde projiziert. Die Musik dieser Szene ist nicht technoid-elektronisch, sondern ein an Volksmusik angelehntes Stück mit mehrstimmigem Gesang und akustischen Gitarren, das die berührende Schönheit unseres von außen gesehenen Planeten emotional überhöht – ein Hinweis darauf, dass Technik nicht aus sich heraus entsteht, sondern letztlich immer auch Ausdruck menschlicher Sehnsüchte und Visionen ist. In dieser Szene kommt es zu einer Live-Schaltung zur ISS mit einer kurzen Grußbotschaft aus dem Weltall nach Linz.

Episode 6 – Auftritt der Roboter

Mit dem Computer kamen die Roboter – und die Angst vor ihnen. Die Angst, dass sie uns die Arbeit wegnehmen und einst sogar beherrschen könnten.

Am Himmel erscheint der Drohnenschwarm, 50 Quadrocopter als autonom fliegende Licht- und Bildpunkte stellen ein überdimensionales Auge dar, während im Hintergrund auf den Hochhäusern Bilder von militärischen Drohnen gezeigt werden, die mit ihrem Fadenkreuz Ziele ins Visier nehmen: Dämonen der modernen Technologie mit ihren unzähligen Möglichkeiten, sie nicht zum Wohl der Menschen, sondern zu Überwachung und Unterdrückung einzusetzen.

Mit scharfen, wuchtigen Trommelschlägen und *Carmina Burana*-artigen Chorsätzen erwachen zwei am Ufer aufgestellte große Industrieroboter zum Leben. Mit grellen Suchscheinwerfern durchmessen sie ihre Umgebung, blenden das Publikum. Vom Osten her kommen mehrere Militärhubschrauber im Tiefflug und nehmen bedrohlich nahe vor dem Publikum ihre Position ein. Lärm und Wind von den Rotorblättern sorgen für beklemmende Momente.

In diese Szene hinein fahren knapp vor dem Publikum zehn Hebebühnen mit Personen hoch: Apperschnalzer, die einem alten Brauchtum zufolge mit ihrem Peitschenknall die Dämonen des Winters vertreiben – hier als Symbol gegen die Furcht vor einer Dominanz der technischen Apparate, für den Kampf von Mensch und Maschine. Jeder Peitschenknall wird elektronisch abgenommen und schaltet mächtige Suchscheinwerfer, die von den Hebebühnen aus in den Himmel leuchten und die Hoffnung zum Ausdruck bringen, dass die Vernunft des Menschen siegen wird.

Und natürlich siegt sie, die Musik wird sanft, die grellen Lichtstimmungen weichen sanften, warmen Farben, und die Bewegungen der Roboter werden elegant und geschmeidig. Sie richten sich auf, mit ihren Köpfen in den Nachthimmel, und jagen 20 Meter hohe, von Scheinwerfern bestrahlte Wasserfontänen in die Luft. Im Rhythmus der Musik beginnen sie nun mit den Wasserstrahlen zu spielen, kurze Staccatos und weit ausholende Figuren werden in die Luft geschleudert, ein ästhetisches Spiel mit Licht, Wasser und Schwerkraft.

Episode 7 – Wir sind das Netz

Das Internet ist heute nicht mehr bloß ein Netzwerk von Computern, es ist ein Netzwerk von Menschen, es ist unser Spielplatz, unser Marktplatz, ein Ort für Begegnung und Austausch, unser Weg, uns eine Stimme zu verschaffen: Wir sind das Volk – wir sind das Netz – wir sind die 99 Prozent.

Der Schwarm der Roboter erscheint am Himmel und zeigt, was er drauf hat. Noch nie zuvor wurde eine so große Zahl von Quadrocoptern zu einem Schwarm autonom aufeinander reagierender Fluggeräte verbunden, der sich als 3D-Bildsystem frei im Raum bewegen kann. Nicht nur eine technische Meisterleistung für sich, sondern Symbol für Crowds, Swarms, Communities, die Hoffnungsträger für offene und partizipatorische Gesellschaftsmodelle, für die Möglichkeiten jedes Einzelnen, sich eine Stimme zu verschaffen und sich zu vernetzen. Zu den Klängen eines von Rupert Huber eingespielten Donauwalzers, in dem sich Walzertakt und Dub-Beats verbinden, fegen die Drohnen über die Donau. In die Musik mischen sich O-Töne vom Arabischen Frühling und von *Occupy*-Demonstrationen auf der ganzen Welt. Auf den Projektionen sind eindrucksvolle Statistiken über die weltweite Dimension der digitalen Vernetzung zu sehen: eine optimistische Sicht auf die positiven Potenziale, als Vertrauensvorschuss in die Visionen einer besseren Zukunft.

Episode 8 – Netzwerk Europa

Wasserwege sind die ältesten Netzwerke dieses Planeten und nach wie vor seine wichtigsten Lebensadern. Das Wasser der Donau verbindet 115 Millionen Menschen in 14 Ländern und ist ein riesiges ökologisches und kulturelles Netzwerk. Und gerade weil wir mit den technischen Mitteln unserer Zeit in jedem Moment an jedem Ort der Welt sein können, dürfen wir unsere realen Lebensräume nicht aus den Augen verlieren. Die Zukunft Europas liegt in einem starken und für ALLE offenen Netzwerk von Ideen und Menschen – ob wir die Herausforderung meistern, liegt an uns allen.

50.000 mit Solarenergie aufgeladene, schwimmende, blaue LED-Kugeln sind das zentrale Gestaltungselement der letzten Episode. Sie sind ein Beitrag japanischer KünstlerInnen, und wenn sie die Donau hinunterschwimmen, repräsentieren sie die Wünsche und Hoffnungen aller Menschen, die entlang der Donau leben. Auf ihrem Weg begegnen sie Menschen, die ihnen in Booten flussaufwärts entgegenkommen, und tauchen den Fluss und seine Ufer in einen blauen Schimmer. Eine friedvolle Schlussstimmung, die im letzten Moment kippt, wenn alle Feuerwehrfahrzeuge, die mittlerweile von den Hügeln herunter gekommen sind, ihre Blaulichter und ihre Sirenen einschalten. Ein offenes Ende zwischen Hoffnung und Alarmzustand als Symbol für die aktuelle Situation Europas.

Horst Hörtner

Klangwolke
Research & Development

Brainstorms and input from colleagues and acquaintances are always the first concrete leads—after all, participatory projects have to get started somewhere. But a concept all by itself doesn't make a project take wing. What I'm talking about here is the idea of the drone swarm that I had initially formulated in 2011. Great idea to be sure—but why hadn't anybody ever done it before?

Some checking around took us to the Swiss Federal Institute of Technology in Zurich and lots of other research groups including the University of Pennsylvania's GRASP Lab. We contacted all leading experts—at least the civilian ones—in the field of unmanned aerial vehicles (UAVs), the technical term used to refer to the model airplanes and helicopters commonly known as drones. And we did indeed find out why there hasn't yet been a swarm of drones in use outdoors. A swarm of 50 UAVs maneuvering inside a building is a tough but ultimately doable job. The GRASP Lab attracted a lot of attention in January 2012 with an autonomous indoor swarm of 20 UAVs. Indoors, it's possible to utilize an extremely precise external tracking system (i.e. additional infrastructure is used for exact positioning). Outdoors, you're either forced to use very inexact GPS or you're confronted with skyrocketing positioning costs. The idea of putting a big swarm of UAVs in the air outdoors simply seemed too risky in light of the short timeframe until September 2012 and the plethora of unknowns. We were told: "An autonomous swarm flying outdoors is not in the realm of possibilities—not in this length of time, not with this budget."

Nevertheless, the idea that was ultimately to be implemented had considerably less to do with aerial robotics—to say nothing of autonomous swarms—than was initially assumed. For me, art's primary mission is to confront and come to terms with semantic interrelationships and their effects. So it just might be due to the Futurelab's artistic know-how that semantic interrelationships were brought out here that did not immediately occur to other experts. This initial situation—one that literally cried out for a transdisciplinary approach—developed into what was both a creative-artistic as well as a technical challenge for authorities in a diverse array of fields. Upon closer inspection, it became clear that this would indeed represent a further evolutionary step in the field of aerial robotics, but that the revolutionary potential here was above all in the area of computer graphics.

The assignment as initially formulated—drones performing coordinated aerial maneuvers outdoors—became a totally subordinated task, to a certain extent a precondition for the actual matter at hand: ceasing to conceive of pixels—short for picture elements, the dots that make up an electronic image—in a two-dimensional, physically specified matrix, but rather making the pixel matrix itself dynamic and thus making the pixels' physical position with respect to each other flexible. That is the original consideration upon which this idea is based. Suddenly, there's the theoretical possibility of conceiving a matrix of picture elements made up of matrix points that are movable in six degrees of flexibility. We've coined the term spaxel (an acronym for space picture element) to refer to pixels of a matrix freely definable in space.[1]

At this point, the focus of fundamental research suddenly shifts away from the disciplines of mechatronics and aeronautics to computer graphics. For the *Klangwolke,* a degree of resolution of 50 pixels (that is, spaxels or drones) is pretty bad, to be sure. Nevertheless, it's still not out of the question that, over the course of developing the UAVs further, we could reach a point at which we would have displays with several thousand or hundreds of thousands of spaxels at our disposal. What an exciting prospect—just imagine the capability of virtually simulating a large building without having to have recourse to a monitor screen! The simulation is airborne on site, and walking through this virtual reality doesn't even require a simulation environment. Holo-Deck? Science fiction? It's here and now!

But it was the recognition of this semantic interrelationship that ultimately convinced us to embark on this daring technical venture—a joint venture, actually, since this endeavor called for associates such as UAV manufacturer Ascending Technologies and a thoroughly experienced team of artists, researchers and developers from the Ars Electronica Futurelab's staff.

The technical challenge isn't a matter of getting drones to fly autonomously; the whole point is creating visual compositions in space, in an urban space.

This undertaking—one in which, at the time this text is being written, utter failure still has to be considered a potential outcome—morphed the problem into a matter of feasibility. As a technical "proof of concept," it is sufficient to successfully draw letters of the alphabet, simple patterns and 3D objects in midair—whether autonomously navigated, executed via automated, external control, or as light & motion sequences preprogrammed to the UAVs (referred to as videos in the two-dimensional realm). Any means of expression is deployed legitimately (from a scholarly perspective) as long as the objective is clearly formulated: spaxel.

From here on in, our point of concentration with respect to controlling the drones/UAVs was in the area of applied research—or actually, applied development, and thus well within the realm of doability. The fundamental research took place in computer graphics, which meant, as anybody familiar with the Futurelab well knows, that we were on our home turf! The prototype—the so-called proof of concept in computer graphics—is defined as an instrument for investigation in art, especially in conjunction with testing this new technology's suitability as a means of artistic expression.

As a festival dedicated to art, technology and society, Ars Electronica proceeds in this way because experience has repeatedly shown that projects situated at the nexus of these three realms and characterized by a high degree of relevance in all three of them have consistently been among those projects that have really been worth the effort in numerous respects. Accordingly, these spaxels/drones, after having successfully undergone trial by ordeal at this year's *voestalpine Klangwolke*, will become regularly deployable infrastructure in conjunction with scientific assignments primarily having to do with computer graphics, and will also be available for various types of artistic projects.

Participation as Tool

When a project is conceived as a participatory endeavor and thus invites international involvement on a massive scale, then a logical consequence of this is to integrate members of the public on as broad a basis as possible into the entire technical development process too. Approaches such as open source, Creative Commons and open hardware constitute the point of departure of these considerations.

Every concept begins with the search for suitable open-source tools, and the work done on every task we are commissioned to carry out ought to result in open structures. Processing, Super Collider, Arduino gcc, OSC, rtpMIDI are only a few of the tools that come into play. We don't always succeed in using open-source tools; all too often, we're confronted by proprietary hardware. When problematic issues make it impossible to comply with our basic principle—for instance, a few of the chips built into receiver devices used in the illuminated letters constructed for the

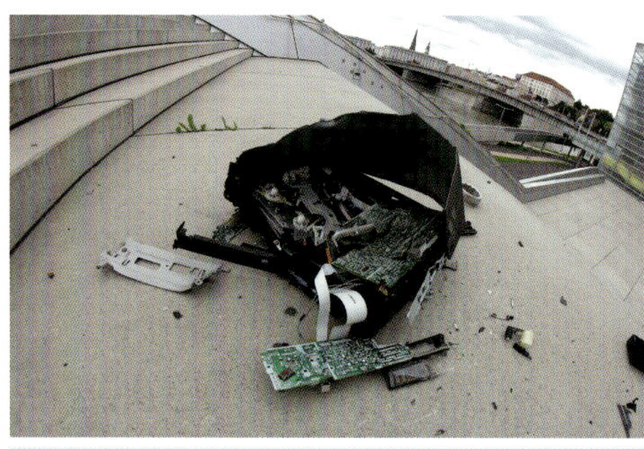
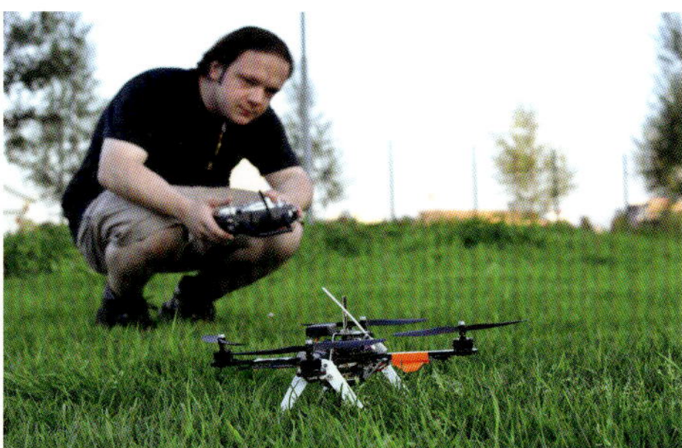
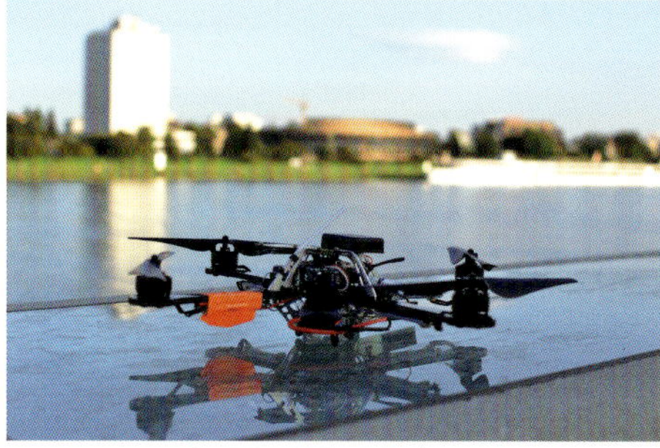
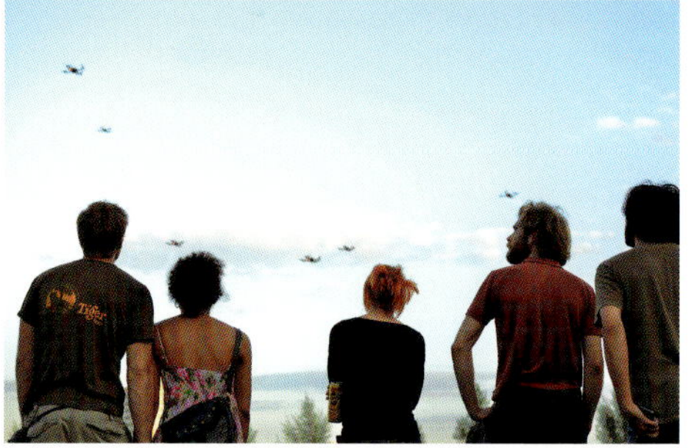

UAV-Unmanned Arial Vehicles / Drohnen

AEC, Barbara Heinzl

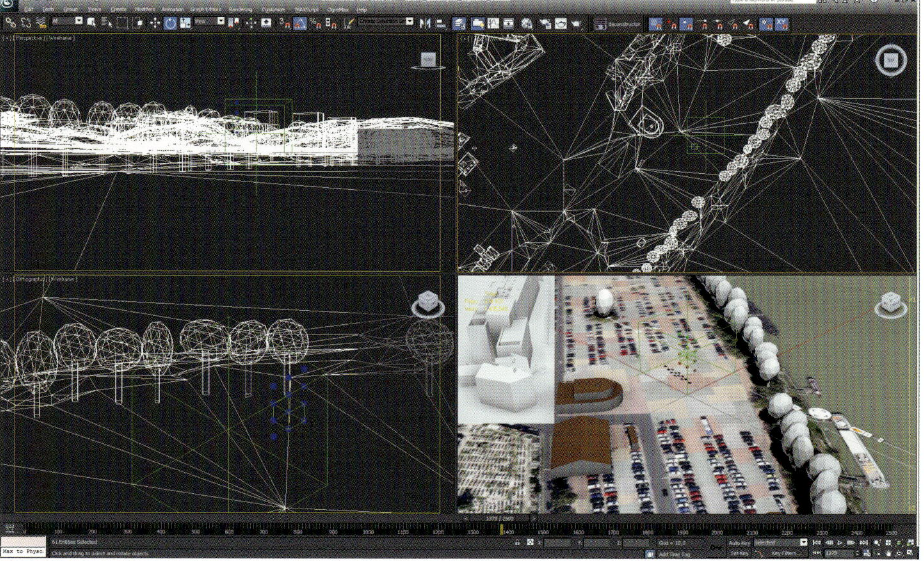

AEC, Andreas Jalsovec

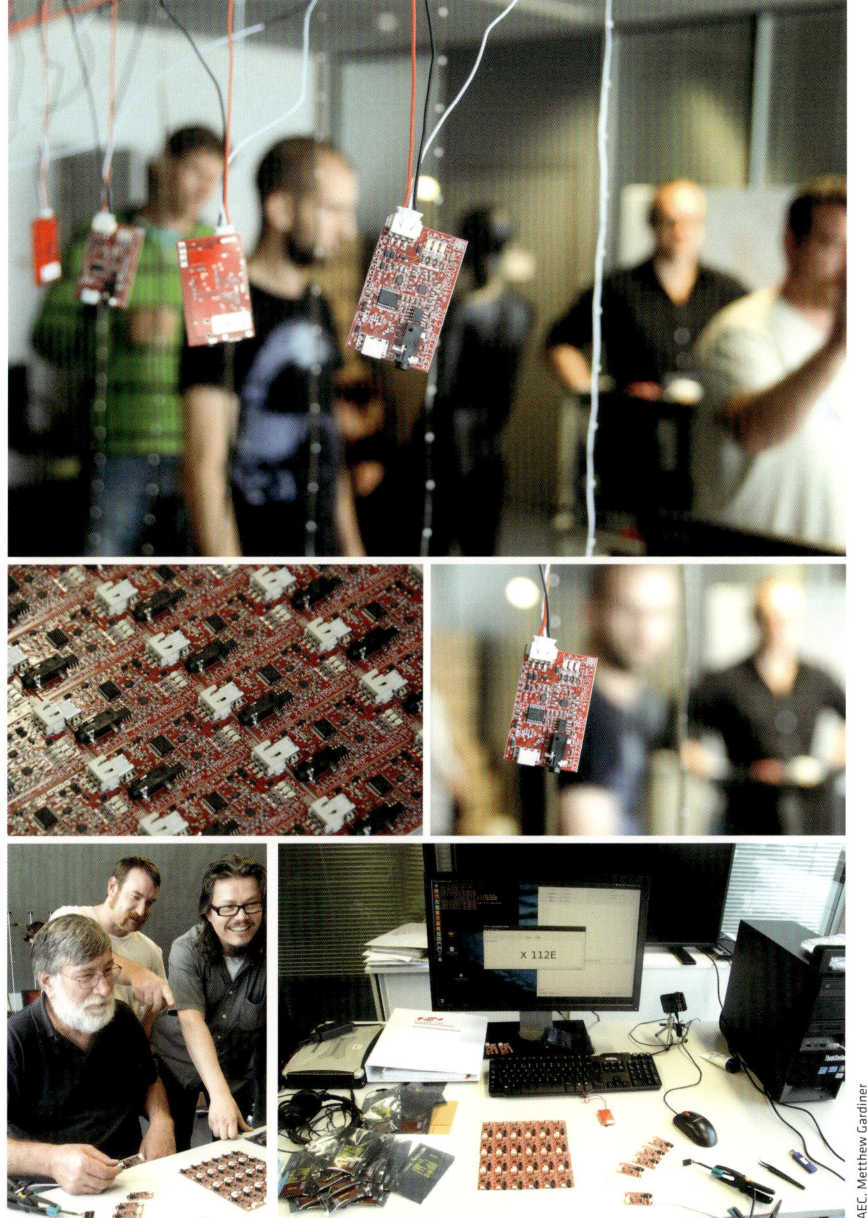

The printed circuit boards for the illuminated letters—planned in Australia, built in Upper Austria, and successfully tested at the Ars Electronica Futurelab / Die Platinen für die Leuchtbuchstaben – geplant in Australien, gebaut in Oberösterreich und erfolgreich getestet im Ars Electronica Futurelab

AEC, Metthew Gardiner

voestalpine Klangwolke—we at least release the schematic diagram, so that anyone will be able to use the solutions we've come up with and everybody will have the opportunity to carry on where the *Klangwolke* crew left off.

The crew—at the time of this writing still dispersed over four continents prior to converging on the Futurelab a few days before the event—is working on the hardware, the components of which are currently in transit. The individual elements are being shipped from China, South Korea, Japan and the USA to Regau, Upper Austria, where they'll be assembled according to construction plans from Australia to make up thousands of receivers. The illuminated letters being built by our many workshop participants will be connected to the internet via these receivers and thereby respond to control signals from the transmitter set up in Donaupark.

1   See Hörtner, H., Gardiner, M., Haring, R., Lindinger, C. (2012). *Spaxels, Pixels in Space. A Novel Mode of Spatial Display.* Proceedings by SIGMAP

Horst Hörtner

Klangwolke
Research & Development

Ideen aus dem nahen Umfeld sind immer die ersten greifbaren Anstöße – auch Partizipationsprojekte finden irgendwo ihren Ausgangspunkt. Eine Idee allein macht jedoch noch kein Projekt. Ich meine damit die Idee des Drohnenschwarms, die ich zum ersten Mal 2011 formuliert hatte. Schöne Idee, sicher – aber warum hat das bisher noch niemand gemacht?

Recherchen führten uns über die ETH Zürich und unzählige andere Forschungsgruppen bis hin zum GRASP Lab der University of Pennsylvania. Wir kontaktierten alle ausgewiesenen Experten, zumindest des zivilen Forschungsumfeldes von „UAVs". Die Abkürzung „UAV" steht für „Unmanned Arial Vehicles", wie die fachlich korrekte Bezeichnung der im Deutschen flapsig „Drohnen" genannten Modell-Flieger bzw. Modell-Hubschrauber lautet.

So erfuhren wir, warum es bislang noch keinen Drohnenschwarm im Outdoor-Bereich gegeben hat. Indoor sei ein Schwarm mit fünfzig UAVs schwierig, aber durchaus machbar. Das GRASP Lab hat im Jänner 2012 mit einem autonomen Indoor-Schwarm aus zwanzig UAVs großes Aufsehen erregt. Indoor – im Gebäudeinneren – ist der Einsatz eines sehr genauen, externen Trackings durchaus möglich (d. h. es wird eine zusätzliche Infrastruktur zur genauen Positionsbestimmung verwendet). Outdoor – im freien Gelände – ist man entweder mit sehr ungenauem GPS oder enorm hohen Kosten für die Positionsbestimmung konfrontiert. Die Idee, einen großen Schwarm im Freien fliegen zu lassen, schien einfach zu verwegen, wenn man die kurze Zeitspanne bis September 2012 und die vielen Unbekannten bedachte. „Ein autonom fliegender Schwarm outdoor", hieß es, sei „unmachbar! Nicht in der Zeit, nicht mit diesen Budgets."

Die umzusetzende Idee hat aber tatsächlich wesentlich weniger mit Flugrobotik – oder gar mit autonomen Schwärmen zu tun –, als es auf den ersten Blick scheint. Ich unterstelle der Kunst, sich in besonderem Maß mit Bedeutungszusammenhängen und mit der Wirkung dieser Zusammenhänge auseinanderzusetzen. Es mag also auf das künstlerische Know-how des Futurelab zurückzuführen sein, dass sich hier Bedeutungszusammenhänge aufdrängten, die anderen Expertisen nicht sofort zugänglich waren. Diese Ausgangslage, die geradezu nach einer transdisziplinären Arbeitsweise verlangte, entwickelte sich zu einer sowohl kreativ-künstlerischen als auch technischen Herausforderung für Autoritäten unterschiedlichster Bereiche. Bei genauerem Hinsehen wird klar, dass es sich zwar um einen weiteren evolutionären Schritt der Flugrobotik handelt, dass aber das revolutionäre Potenzial hier vor allem im Bereich der Computergrafik liegt.

Die anfangs gestellte Aufgabe – Drohnen koordiniert durch die Luft im Freien zu bewegen – wird dadurch zu einer völlig untergeordneten Task; gewissermaßen zur Voraussetzung für das eigentliche Anliegen: Die bislang bildgebenden Punkte – „Pixel" (Kurzform für „Picture Element") – nicht in einer zweidimensionalen, physikalisch festgeschriebenen Matrix zu denken, sondern die Matrix der Bildpunkte selbst dynamisch und damit in ihrer physikalischen Position zueinander verhandelbar zu machen, das ist die ursprüngliche Überlegung, die dieser Idee zugrunde liegt. Plötzlich gibt es die theoretische Möglichkeit, eine Matrix von Bildpunkten aus in sechs Freiheitsgraden beweglichen „Matrizen-Punkten" zu denken. Wir haben diese Bildpunkte einer im Raum frei definierbaren Matrix „Spaxel" (Kurzform für „Space Picture Element") genannt.[1]

Ab hier verschiebt sich der Fokus der Grundlagenforschung plötzlich weg von der Disziplin der Mechatronik und Aeronautik hin zur Computergrafik. Die Auflösung von fünfzig Pixel (bzw. Spaxel oder Drohnen) der Klangwolke ist zweifelsohne denkbar schlecht. Dennoch ist nicht auszuschließen, dass wir im Laufe der Weiterentwicklung der UAVs schon bald über Displays mit mehreren tausend oder hunderttausend Spaxel verfügen werden. Welch eine Aussicht, wenn man sich vorstellt, ein riesiges Gebäude virtuell simulieren zu können, ohne dabei auf einen Bildschirm zurückgreifen zu müssen. Die Simulation steht vor Ort in der Luft, und man kann diese virtuelle Realität sogar ohne Simulationsumfeld durchschreiten. HoloDeck? Science-Fiction? Sicher, heute noch!

Das Erkennen dieses Bedeutungszusammenhanges aber war es, das uns zur Überzeugung brachte, dieses technische Wagnis einzugehen. Die geeigneten Partner vorausgesetzt – wie zum Beispiel Ascending Technologies als Hersteller der UAVs – und das in vielen Projekten erprobte KünstlerInnen-, Forschungs- und Entwicklungsteam des Ars Electronica Futurelab.

Die technische Herausforderung liegt nicht darin, Drohnen autonom fliegen zu lassen – es geht darum, Bildkompositionen im Raum zu erstellen bzw. in den urbanen Raum zu stellen.

Dieses Unterfangen, das zum Zeitpunkt der Entstehung dieses Textes auch das Scheitern als möglichen Ausgang ins Kalkül ziehen muss, verlagert die Problemstellung hin zum Machbaren. Als ein technisches „Proof of Concept" reicht es, wenn es gelingt, Schriftzeichen, einfache Muster und 3D-Objekte in den Himmel zu zeichnen. Ob autonom gesteuert, ob über automatisierte, externe Steuerung realisiert oder über im Vorfeld auf den UAVs gespeicherte Licht- und Bewegungssequenzen (im zweidimensionalen Bereich als Videos bezeichnet). Jedes Mittel zum Ausdruck ist (wissenschaftlich) korrekt eingesetzt, solange das Ziel klar formuliert ist: Spaxel.

Unsere Konzentration bezüglich der Steuerung der Drohnen oder UAVs liegt von hier an im Bereich der angewandten Forschung – eher noch der angewandten Entwicklung, also im durchaus machbaren Rahmen. Die Grundlagenforschung passiert in der Computergrafik. Wer das

Futurelab kennt, weiß: ein Heimspiel! Der Prototyp bzw. der „Proof of Concept" der Computergrafik versteht sich als Untersuchungsinstrumentarium der Kunst – speziell im Hinblick auf die Untersuchung dieser neuartigen Technologie, auf ihre Tauglichkeit als Medium künstlerischen Ausdrucks.

Die Ars Electronica als ein Festival für Kunst, Technologie und Gesellschaft geht diesen Weg, weil ihre Vergangenheit schon zu oft gezeigt hat, dass ein Projekt, das im Nexus dieser drei Bereiche stattfindet und von hoher Relevanz in allen drei Bereichen gekennzeichnet ist, stets zu jenen Projekten gehört, das in vielerlei Hinsicht den Einsatz lohnt. So werden diese Spaxels bzw. Drohnen, die bei der *voestalpine Klangwolke* ihre Bewährungsprobe antreten werden, im Anschluss daran als permanent bespielbare Infrastruktur sowohl für wissenschaftliche Aufgaben, die sich vorrangig mit Computergrafik beschäftigen, als auch für künstlerische Projekte unterschiedlichster Ausrichtungen zur Verfügung stehen.

Partizipation als Werkzeug

Wenn ein Projekt als Partizipationsprojekt konzipiert und somit offen ist für eine internationale Beteiligung im großen Stil, dann ist die Einbindung einer möglichst breiten Öffentlichkeit auch in den gesamten technischen Entwicklungsprozess eine logische Konsequenz. Ansätze wie Open Source, Creative Commons und Open Hardware stellen den Ausgangspunkt der Überlegungen dar.

Jedes Konzept beginnt mit der Suche nach den geeigneten Open-Source-Werkzeugen. Jede Auftragsentwicklung zielt im Ergebnis auf offene Strukturen. Processing, Super Collider, Arduino gcc, OSC, rtpMIDI sind die nur einige der Werkzeuge, die zum Einsatz kommen. Nicht immer gelingt uns der Einsatz von Open-Source-Tools, zu oft stoßen wir auf proprietäre Hardware. Bei Problemstellungen, die diese wesentliche Anforderung nicht erfüllen, wie zum Beispiel einige der Chips, die in den Empfangs-Devices der bei *voestalpine Klangwolke* eingesetzten Leuchtbuchstaben verbaut werden, legen wir zumindest den Bauplan offen: Jede(r) soll die gefundenen Lösungen einsetzen können, jede(r) soll die Möglichkeit erhalten, dort weiter zu machen, wo das Klangwolken-Team aufhört.

Das Team – zur Zeit der Texterstellung noch auf vier Kontinenten verteilt, um sich wenige Tage vor der Aufführung im Futurelab zu treffen – arbeitet an Hardware, deren Bestandteile sich gerade auf dem Transportweg befinden. Die Einzelteile werden aus China, Südkorea, Japan und den USA nach Regau in Oberösterreich geliefert, wo sie nach Konstruktionsplänen aus Australien verbaut und zu tausenden Empfängern gefertigt werden. Die von den vielen Workshop-TeilnehmerInnen gebauten Leuchtbuchstaben werden über diese Empfänger mit dem Internet verbunden und reagieren so auf die Steuerimpulse des Senders im Donaupark.

---

1 siehe dazu: Hörtner, H., Gardiner, M., Haring, R., Lindinger, C. (2012). *Spaxels, Pixels in Space. A Novel Mode of Spatial Display.* Proceedings by SIGMAP

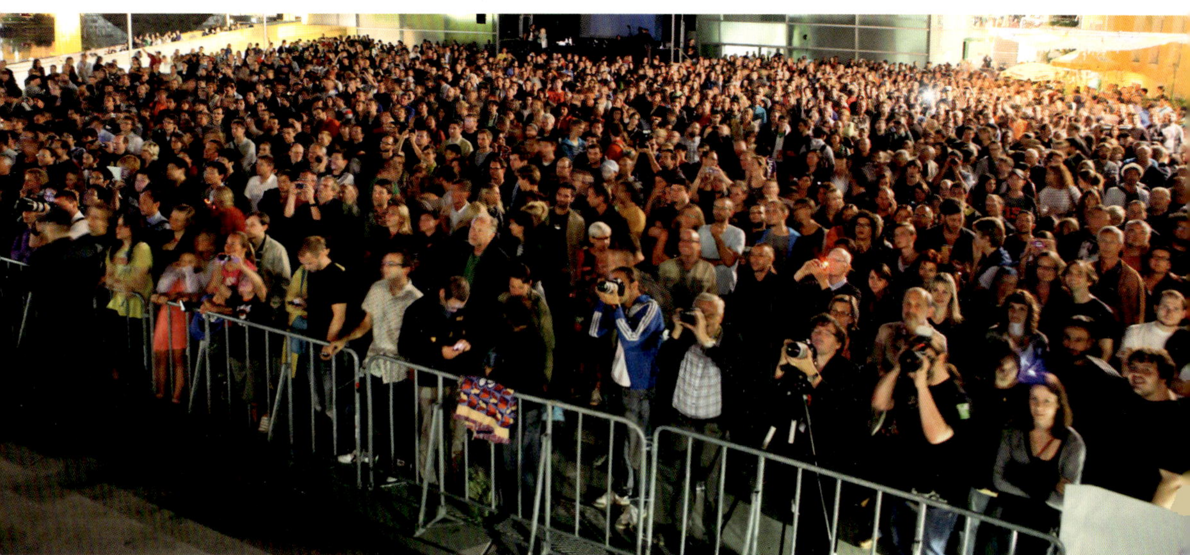

AEC, rubra

The World's Most Extensive Snapshot

voestalpine Klangwolke visitors—the more, the merrier—are going to simultaneously photograph one another. All of these individual portraits depicting the group at a single moment will be brought together via the *voestalpine Klangwolke* website and then worked up into a gigapixel picture collage that will go on display in the Ars Electronica Center as well as the *Linz Changes* pavilion at the Urfahr Fair in October. The world's largest gigapixel image taken by multiple cameras thus poses yet another technical and substantive challenge to the *voestalpine Klangwolke* participants' collective.

Die umfangreichste Momentaufnahme der Welt

Es werden (möglichst) alle Besucher und Besucherinnen der *voestalpine Klangwolke* im selben Moment ein Foto voneinander machen. Alle Einzelaufnahmen dieses Moments werden über die Webseite der *voestalpine Klangwolke* gesammelt, danach als Gigapixel-Bild-Collage aufbereitet und im Ars Electronica Center, sowie im *Linz Verändert*-Pavillon am Urfahraner Jahrmarkt im Oktober zugänglich gemacht. Das größte, von unterschiedlichen Einzelkameras produzierte Gigapixelbild der Welt, wartet als weitere technische und inhaltliche Herausforderung auf das Kollektiv der TeilnehmerInnen der *voestalpine Klangwolke*.

241

Hideaki Ogawa, Emiko Ogawa

Klangwolken ABC

In 1979, the history of Ars Electronica was initiated. It was also the time of the very first *Klangwolke*. At this groundbreaking event, the citizens of Linz tuned in to the same radio channel, and all of Linz was covered with a carpet of sound. One huge soundscape was created through this participatory process.

Today, in 2012, information technology allows information to circulate freely, while social media enable people to connect to each other in new forms that are not defined through any traditional framework. On the one hand, they serve as triggers to stage demonstrations against anachronistic ideas and politics; on the other hand, global disasters such as the Fukushima nuclear accident seem like a warning to today's technology-based society. All these developments and events related to information, governance and media inspire basic questions about the very nature of the individual in modern society: What is the individual? What is a nation? What is information? In this context, what role does the written word, the written character play in the world? Google is only one example for the power of characters in today's global village, as an information retrieving system entirely based upon characters. In addition, we communicate with each other using character-based services, such as e-mail, Twitter and Facebook. We rely more on characters to get in touch with each other than ever before—and we are more in touch with characters themselves than ever before.

Considering this idea of audience participation in the context of social media, the *Klangwolken ABC* was initiated as a social participation project, focusing on "character" in the age of networks, constituting one of the core programs at the *voestalpine Klangwolke* 2012. People create their own characters to interact with radio frequencies at the event—a huge galaxy of characters meeting at the Danube shoreline.

In *Klangwolken ABC* workshops, people construct their own alphabet characters and add a receiver and LED kit to link to the *Klangwolken* event itself. They select a character, assemble it, and personalize it in creative ways. Literally, every single person/character creates a unique character. The character created in the workshop is recorded in an image database and becomes part of the *Klangwolke Font*. In addition, the participants join CharakterBook, an online service that works like a micro-facebook, enabling people to browse for other characters created by other participants, to create messages, and to take social action. The individual characters created by the participants become words or messages through communicating and collaborating with each other. In the *Klangwolken ABC*, we collect messages as combinations of characters with characters—people with people.

The characters created for the *Klangwolken ABC* are used to hack all kinds of text information in the media as well as in the cities themselves. All information written in dryly-formatted letters can be replaced by democratic and colorful representations. A variety of information, such as the signage in the city of Linz, news information about the city and texts at the Ars Electronica Festival 2012, has been reconfigured through the Klangwolken Font.

On the day of the *Klangwolken* event, *Klangwolken ABC Parades* will take place in the city of Linz. Additionally, a multitude of characters will gather along the Danube River at sunset. Maybe a full message will be displayed, maybe only single characters will be seen—but similar to 1979, when people tuned in to the same radio frequency, a universe of characters will interact with a radio frequency at the Donaupark. Responding to sound, to radio signals for individual characters and messages in groups, the LEDs will light up. At first, it may seem like an expression of information society deluged by characters. However, suddenly strong messages will pop up in this space.

Thus, *Klangwolken ABC* not only shows mere character information, but also leads to actual tangible actions by people; moreover, people create their own shared "now".

Considering the history of characters, Shizuka Shirakawa, who wrote Kanji (Chinese characters in Japanese), said: "Kanji is an ideogram; its shape tells us the concept and way of life of people of the era when Chinese characters were established. Each single character, while still keeping the primal form, seems to want to talk well with its own identity."[2] A character was a magic container to contain the culture and the story of the world. The alphabet seems to have an innate intention for democracy. In an alphabet, the individual letter hardly makes sense. Only when it "meets" other alphabet characters, is new meaning created. A character is always looking for other characters. It can't hide the essential desire to associate with others. What happens if we create an additional meaning—like an ideogram—for individual alphabet characters?

The *Klangwolken ABC* shows a new form of characters. All the characters created in the workshops are full of creativity and ideas—they represent a whole cosmos created by people. Each character mirrors their individual preferences, cultural backgrounds, construction techniques and ways of thinking.

Interestingly, when we express text information, such as news and tweets, through the Klangwolke Font, the expression gap between normal typeface and colorful characters makes it seem as though the new characters attempt to reveal a hidden intention behind the information. Again, what is information? *Klangwolken ABC* expresses a primordial form of information, through two processes—by matching the creator of the character to the sender of the information and by collecting the emotional desire in the physical place of the *Klangwolke* event.

The topic of the character as a magic container will be investigated in-depth during a special exhibition at the AEC in 2012. This exhibition will explore the following questions, among others: How did this *Klangwolken ABC* provoke social intervention? What is the character essentially? How has the world been recorded with the magic container? How do people interact with the different forms of magic container with developing technologies, and what do we want to convey by using the magic container as human beings?

Finally, the *Klangwolke Font* is going to be an Open Font and this new culture originating in the *voestalpine Klangwolke* 2012 will continue to convey the mood of the era, as a symbol for action in the real world.

1 *http://www.aec.at/klangwolke/participate/soundcloud-abc*
2 Shizuka Shirakawa: Kanji, Iwanami Shinsho, 1970

ABC Werkstatt
ab 2. Juni
Ars Electronica Center

Radioempfänger abholen
ab 13. Aug.
Ars Electronica Center

KLANGWOLKE!
1. Sept. 2012
Donaupark

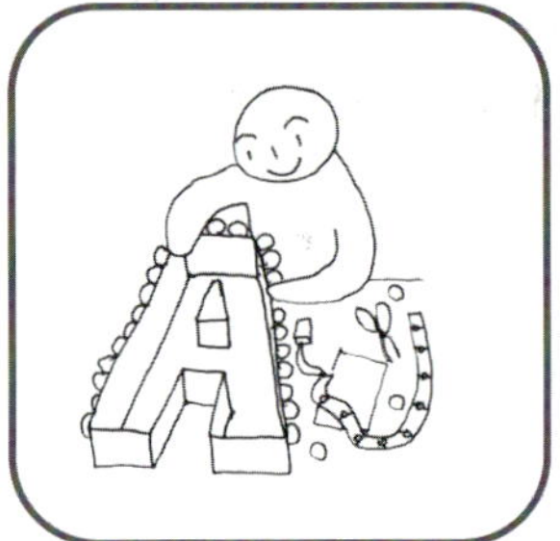
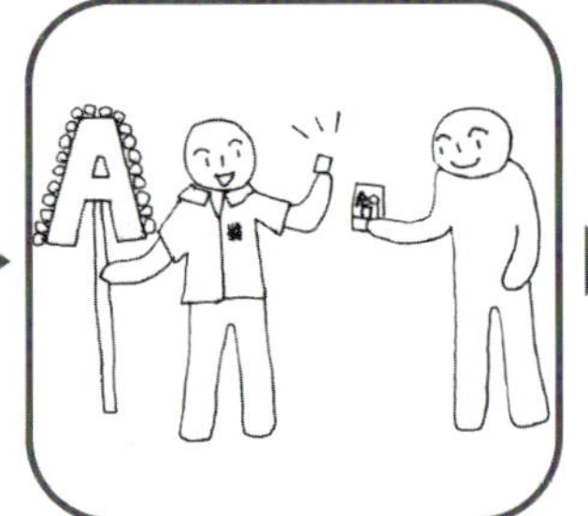
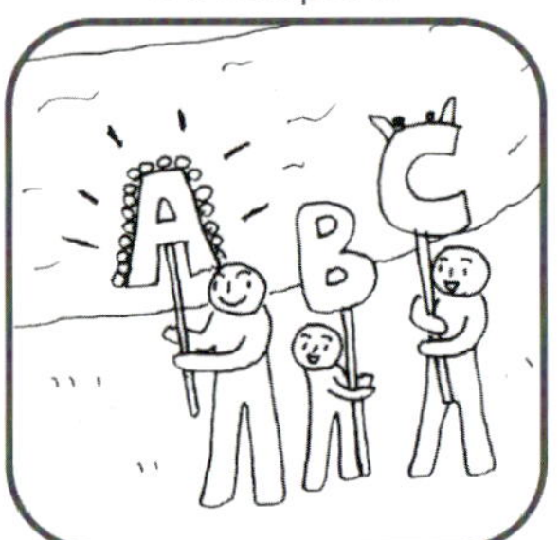

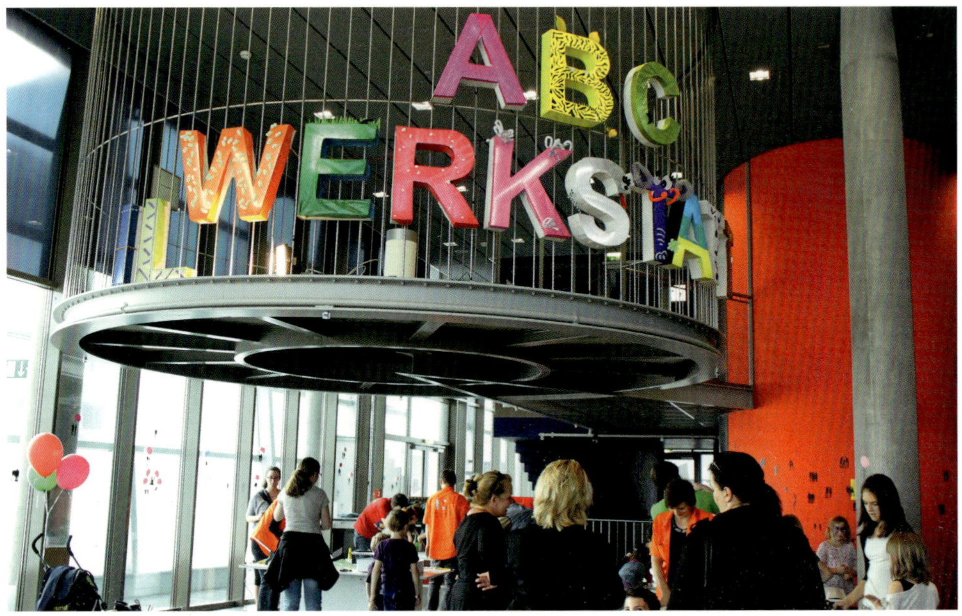

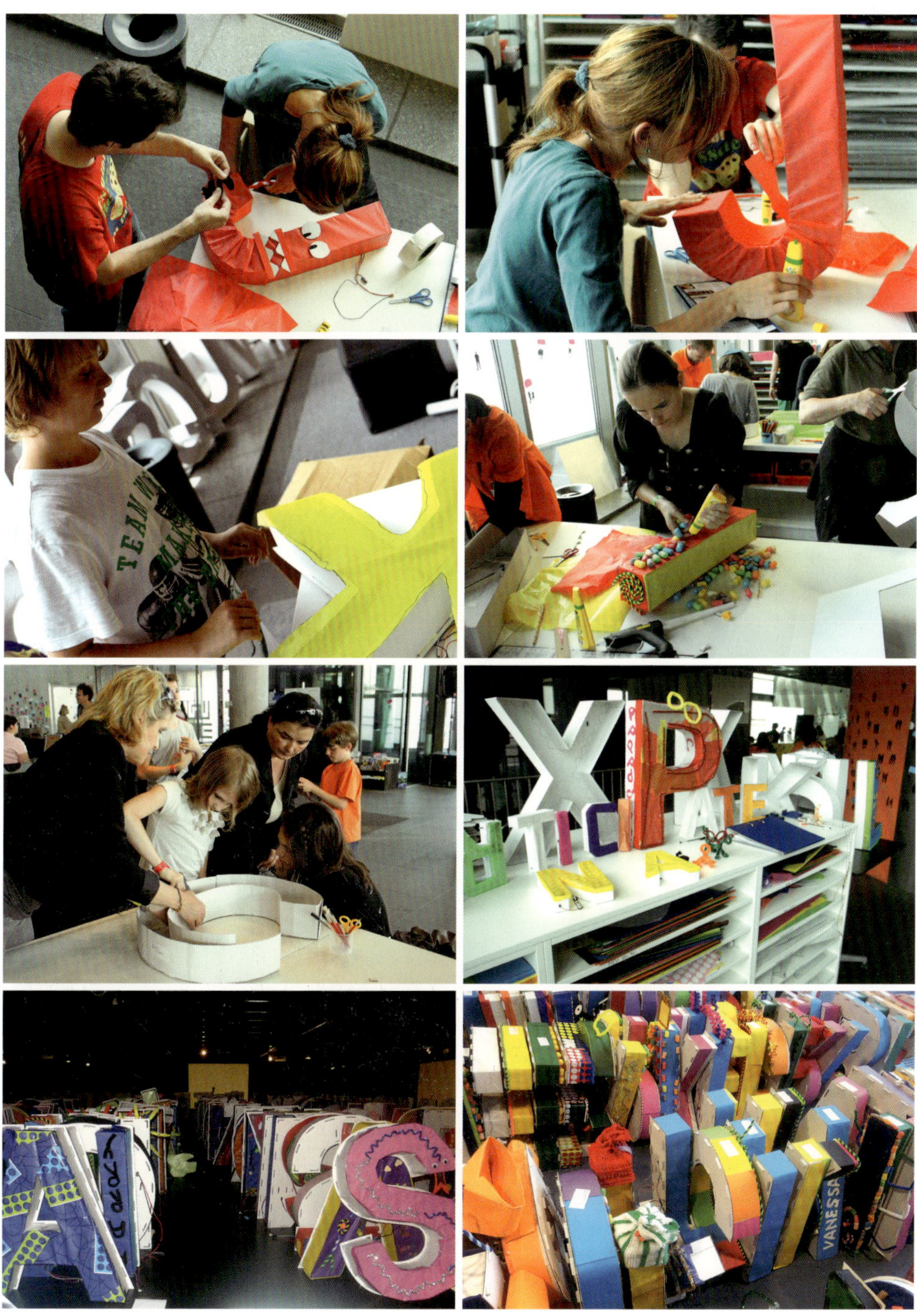

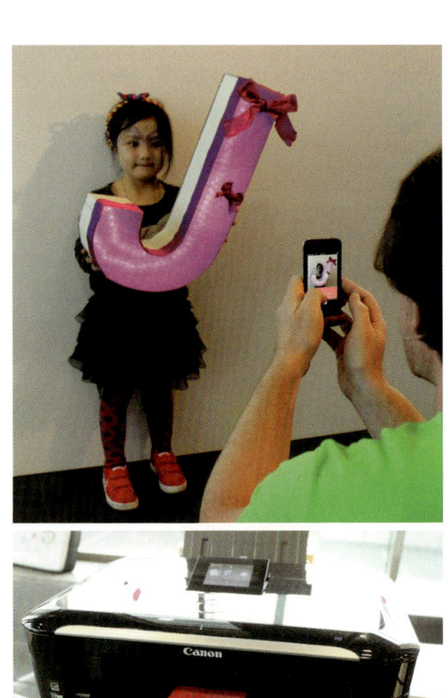

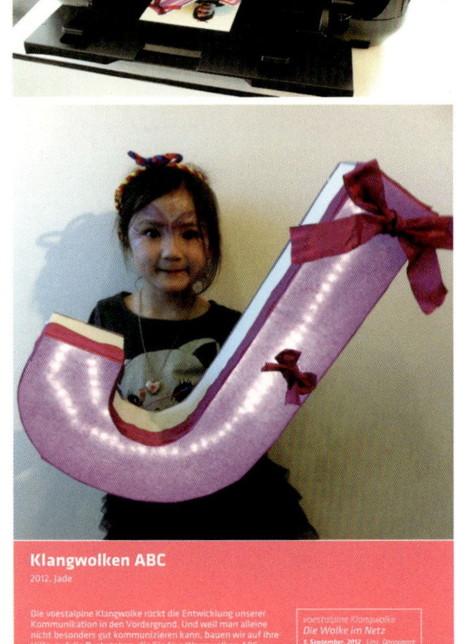

Klangwolken ABC
2012, Jade

Die voestalpine Klangwolke rückt die Entwicklung unserer
Kommunikation in den Vordergrund. Und weil man alleine
nicht besonders gut kommunizieren kann, bauen wir auf ihre
Hilfe, auf die Buchstaben, die Sie fürs Klangwolken ABC
basteln. In Workshops im Ars Electronica Center, aber auch
von zu Hause aus. Werden Sie Teil der Klangwolke!

voestalpine Klangwolke
Die Wolke im Netz
1. September, 2012 Linz, Donaupark
www.aec.at/klangwolke

ARS ELECTRONICA

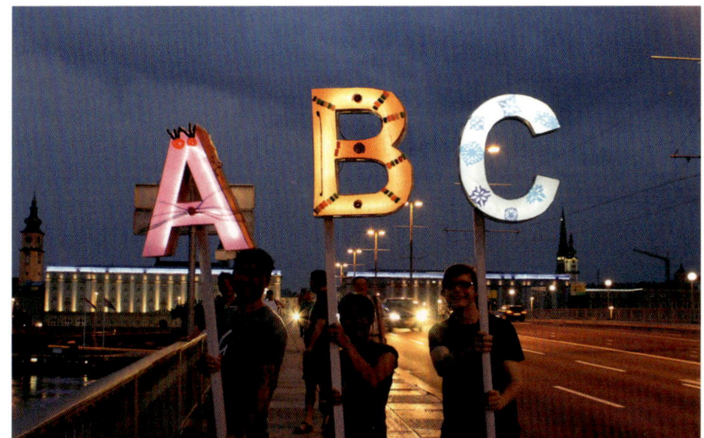

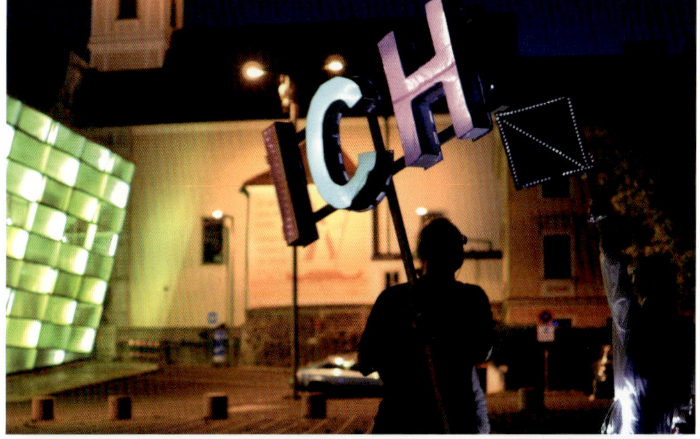

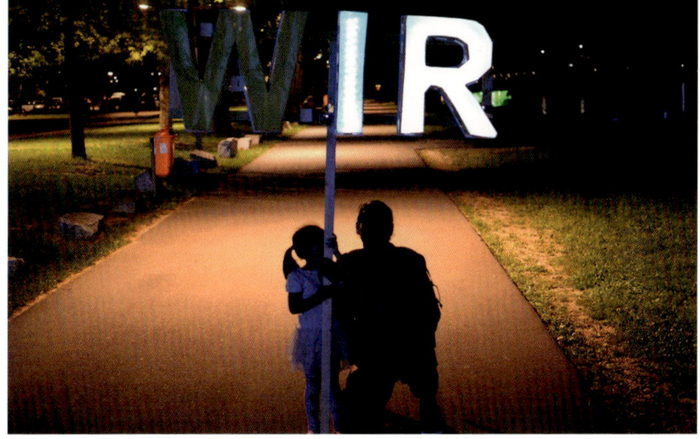

AEC, Barbara Heinzl

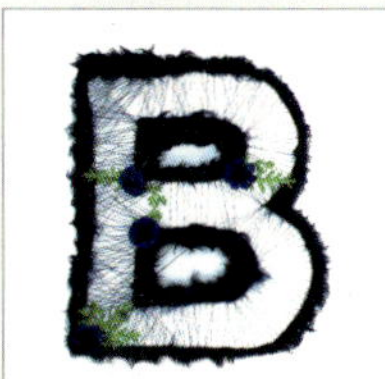 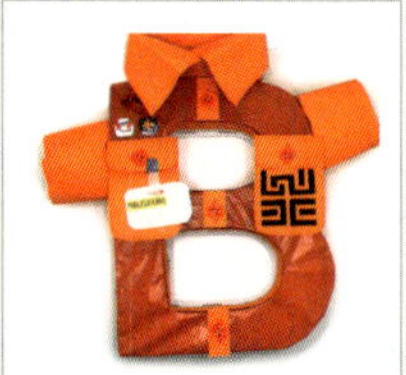 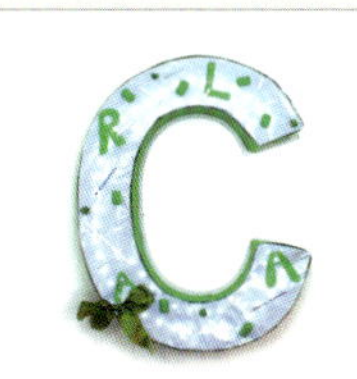 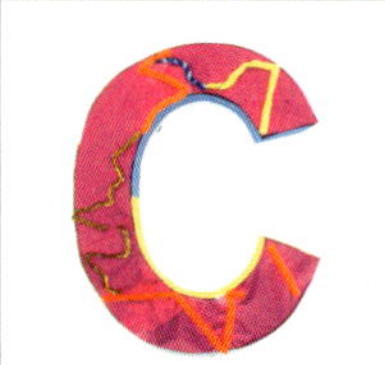
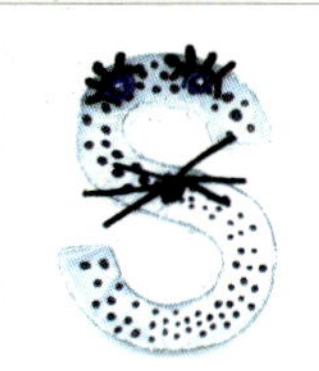 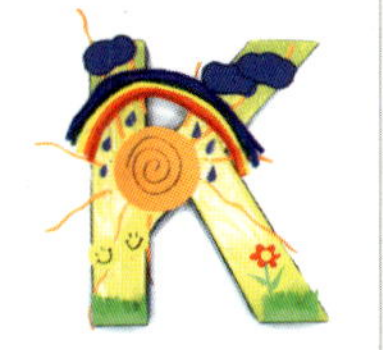 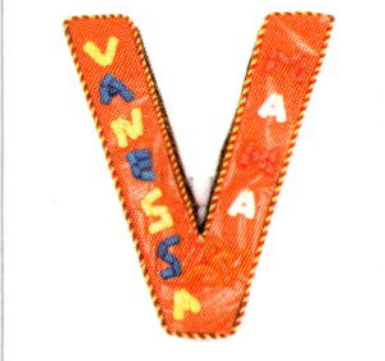 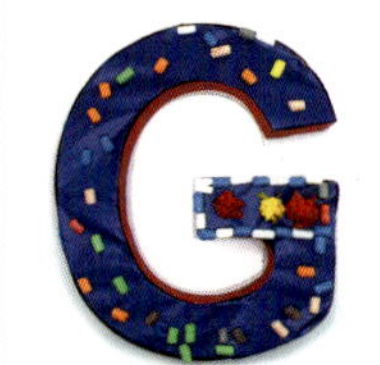
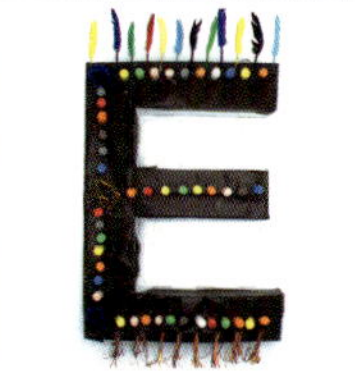 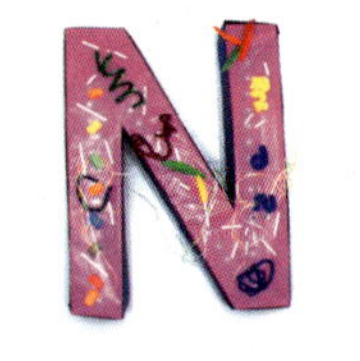 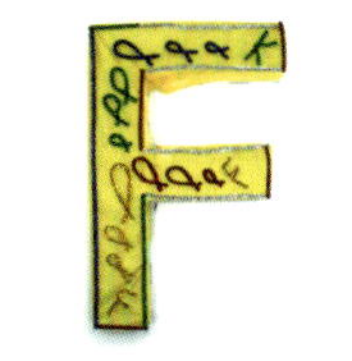 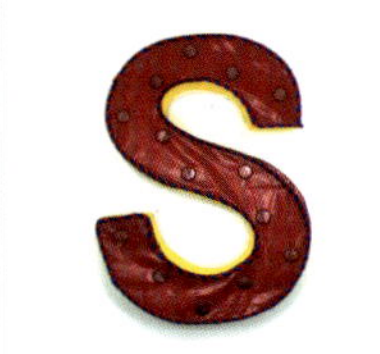
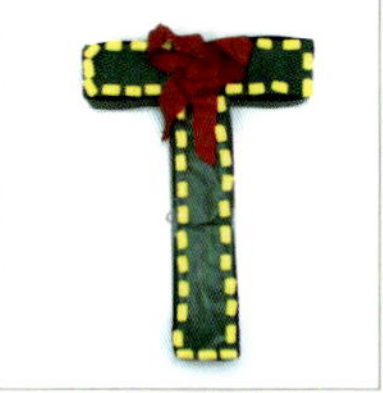 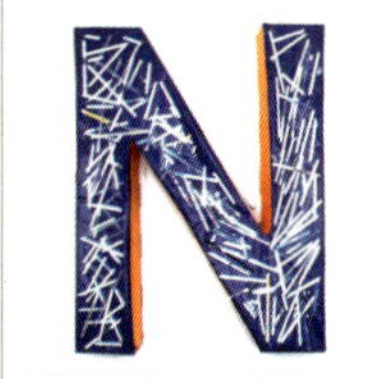 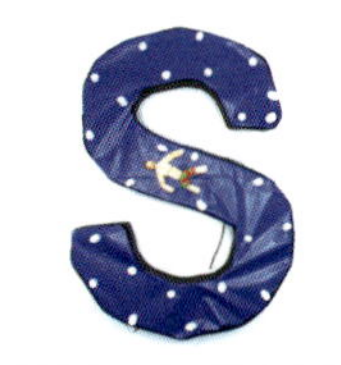 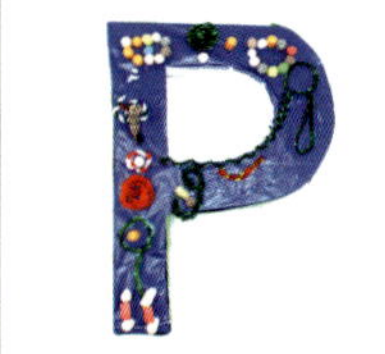
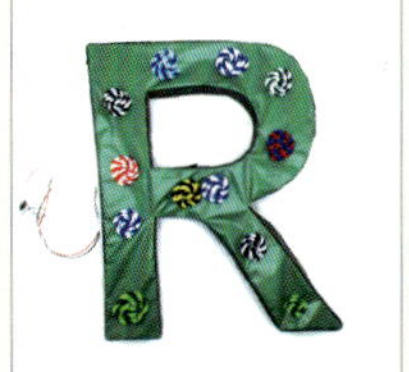 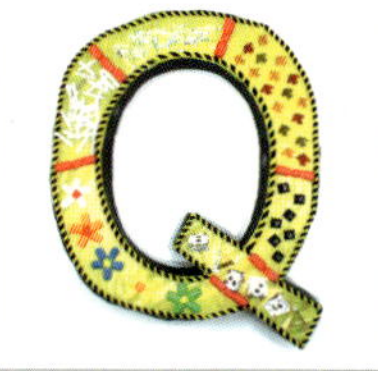 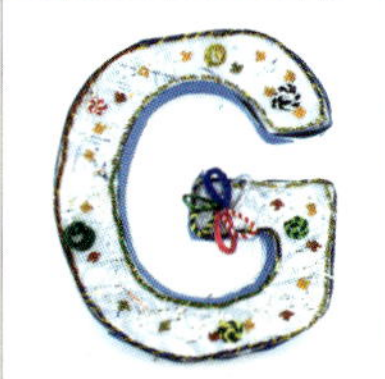 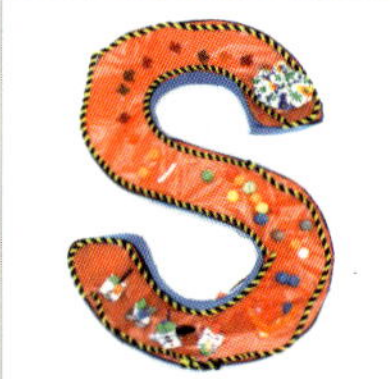
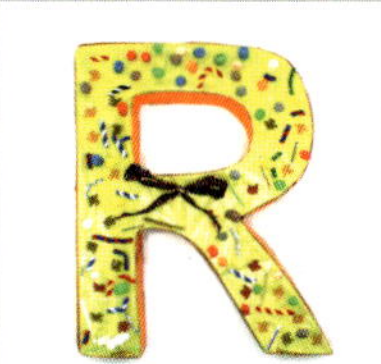 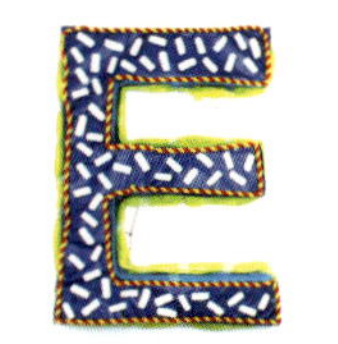 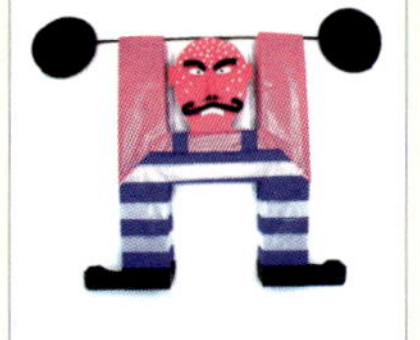 
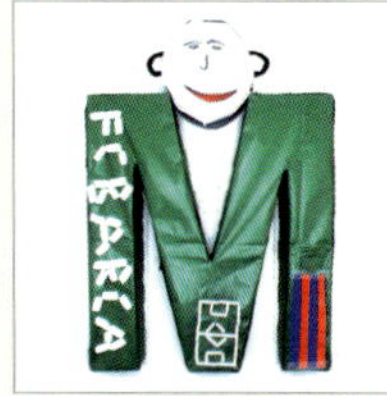 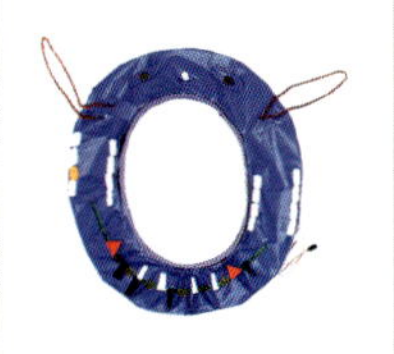  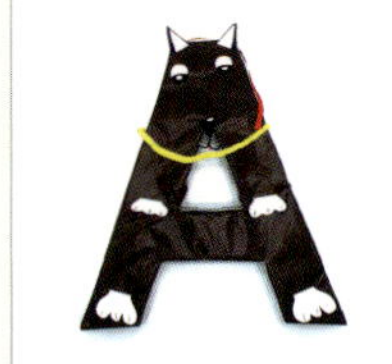

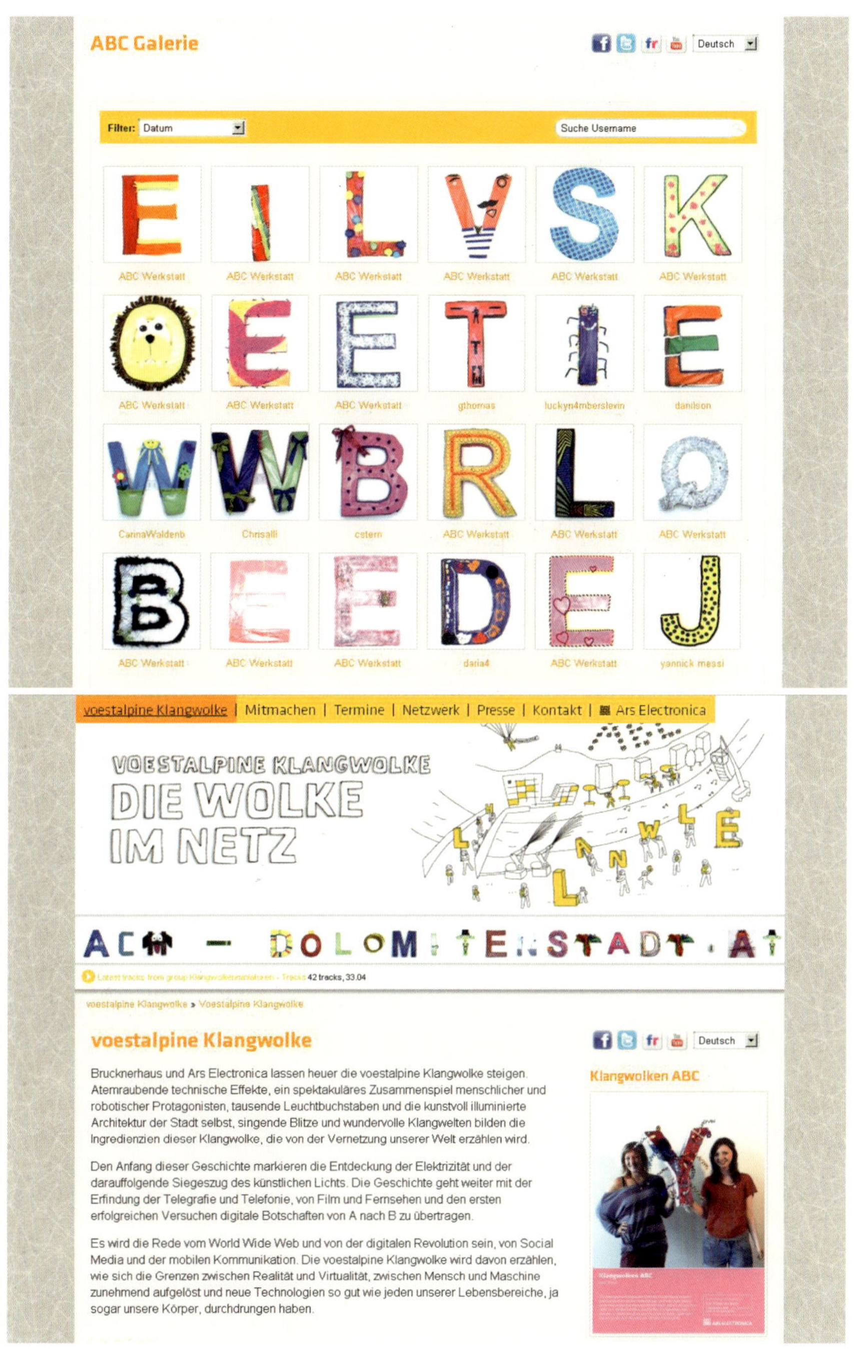

voestalpine Klangwolke

Brucknerhaus und Ars Electronica lassen heuer die voestalpine Klangwolke steigen. Atemraubende technische Effekte, ein spektakuläres Zusammenspiel menschlicher und robotischer Protagonisten, tausende Leuchtbuchstaben und die kunstvoll illuminierte Architektur der Stadt selbst, singende Blitze und wundervolle Klangwelten bilden die Ingredienzien dieser Klangwolke, die von der Vernetzung unserer Welt erzählen wird.

Den Anfang dieser Geschichte markieren die Entdeckung der Elektrizität und der darauffolgende Siegeszug des künstlichen Lichts. Die Geschichte geht weiter mit der Erfindung der Telegrafie und Telefonie, von Film und Fernsehen und den ersten erfolgreichen Versuchen digitale Botschaften von A nach B zu übertragen.

Es wird die Rede vom World Wide Web und von der digitalen Revolution sein, von Social Media und der mobilen Kommunikation. Die voestalpine Klangwolke wird davon erzählen, wie sich die Grenzen zwischen Realität und Virtualität, zwischen Mensch und Maschine zunehmend aufgelöst und neue Technologien so gut wie jeden unserer Lebensbereiche, ja sogar unsere Körper, durchdrungen haben.

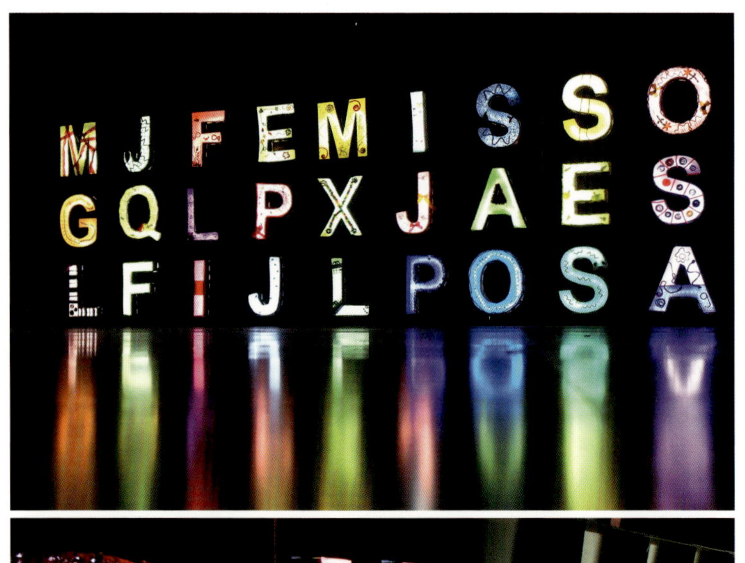

M J F E M I S S O S O
G Q L P X J A E S E S
F I J L P O S A

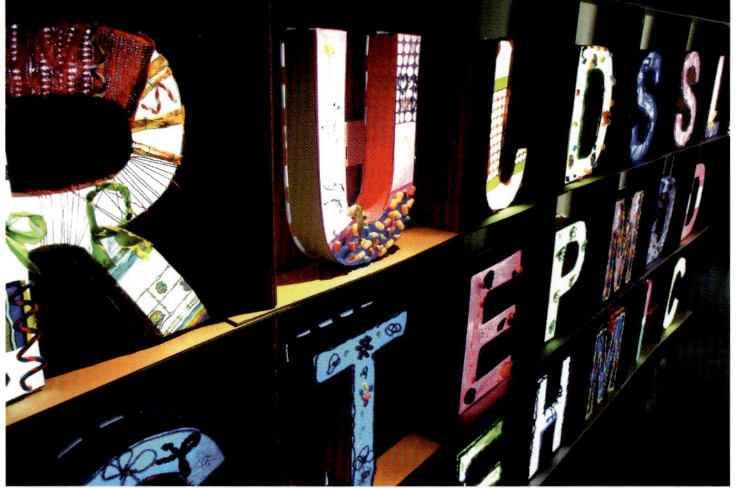

R U L D S S
R E P M D D
T E H M L C

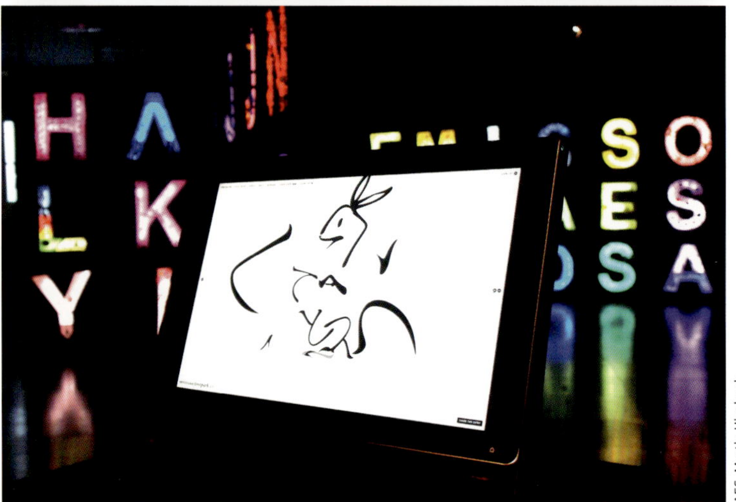

H A S O
L K E S
Y O S A

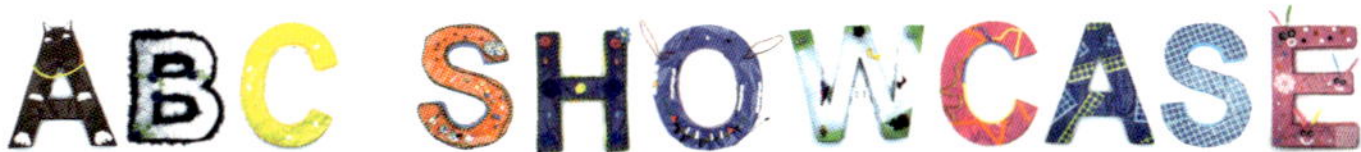

Ars Electronica Center
1.8.2012 – 31.10.2012

Visitors to the Ars Electronica Center and people from Linz and the surrounding region have been designing countless elaborately decorated illuminated letters that will play a starring role in the voestalpine Klangwolke. The artistry and craftsmanship will continue right up to the big show on September 1, 2012. The best of them as well as other works on the subject of letters will be on display in the ABC Showcase at the Ars Electronica Center.

Unzählige, aufwendig gestaltete Leuchtbuchstaben wurden im Vorfeld der voestalpine Klangwolke bereits von den BesucherInnen des Ars Electronica Center und den EinwohnerInnen von Linz und Oberösterreich gestaltet – und das Basteln geht bis zur Klangwolke am 1. September 2012 noch munter weiter. Ein Best-Of der Buchstaben wird neben anderen Arbeiten zum Thema Buchstaben im ABC-Showcase des Ars Electronica Center präsentiert.

Exquisite Clock (2010)
João Henrique Wilbert

Famous Books – Treasures of the Bavarian State Library (2010)
Bayerische Staatsbibliothek

Fontpark 2.0 (2008)
Yugo Nakamura, Morisawa Inc.

Motiongraphic (2012)
Sebastian Neitsch

The Alphabet 2 (2012)
Alessandro Novelli, Andrea Gendusa, Mario Arcadu, Giulia Arantxa Novelli

TypeDrawing (2005)
Hansol Huh

Digitale Schriften (2011)
Höhere Graphische Bundes-Lehr- und Versuchsanstalt Wien: Regina Hochmeister, Marianne Korec, Tanja Lenk, Jessica Maierhofer, Petra Sedlaszek , Bernhard Stegbauer, Jakob Stubner, Katarina Udel

Hideaki Ogawa, Emiko Ogawa

Klangwolken-ABC

Die Geschichte der Ars Electronica begann 1979. In diesem Jahr fand auch die allererste Klangwolke statt, bei der unzählige Bürger der Stadt Linz dasselbe Radioprogramm einstellten und ganz Linz in eine Klangwolke gehüllt war. Durch diesen partizipatorischen Prozess entstand eine riesige, sich über die ganze Stadt ausbreitende Klanglandschaft.

Heute, 2012, gewährleistet die Informationstechnologie die freie Zirkulation von Informationen, und Social Media ermöglichen den Menschen, sich miteinander in neuen Formen, die durch keine traditionellen Paradigmen definiert sind, in Verbindung zu setzen. Einerseits sind diese neuen Medien Impulsgeber, um beispielsweise Demonstrationen gegen anachronistische Ideen und politische Systeme zu organisieren, andererseits scheinen globale Katastrophen wie der GAU von Fukushima eine Warnung vor der Technologiegläubigkeit der heutigen Gesellschaft zu sein. All diese Entwicklungen und Ereignisse, die mit Information, Herrschaft und Medien in Beziehung stehen, werfen grundlegende Fragen über die Rolle und Stellung des Individuums in der modernen Gesellschaft auf: Was ist das Individuum? Was ist eine Nation? Was ist Information?

Welche Rolle spielt in diesem Zusammenhang das geschriebene Wort, der geschriebene Buchstabe in der Welt? Google – als ein zur Gänze auf Buchstaben beruhendes Informationssuchsystem – ist ein Beispiel für die Macht der Buchstaben im globalen Dorf der Gegenwart. Außerdem kommunizieren wir miteinander vorwiegend über buchstabenbasierte Dienste wie E-Mail, Twitter und Facebook. Um miteinander in Kontakt zu treten, sind wir mehr denn je auf Buch-staben angewiesen – und wir sind auch mit den Schriftzeichen selbst mehr in Berührung als je zuvor.

Diese Idee der Partizipation des Publikums im Kontext von Social Media aufgreifend, wurde das *Klangwolken-ABC* als Projekt gesellschaftlicher Partizipation ins Leben gerufen. Es fokussiert auf Schriftzeichen im Zeitalter der Netzwerke und ist eines der Hauptprojekte bei der *voestalpine Klangwolke* 2012. Jeder gestaltet seinen eigenen Buchstaben, mit dem er später bei der Veranstaltung mit den Radiofrequenzen in Interaktion tritt – erwartet werden Scharen von Buchstaben, die sich am Ufer der Donau versammeln.

In den *Klangwolken-ABC*-Workshops basteln die Teilnehmer ihre eigenen Buchstaben und bestücken sie mit Empfängern und LEDs, um sich mit der Klangwolke in Verbindung setzen zu können. Sie wählen einen Buchstaben aus, bauen ihn zusammen und gestalten ihn individuell. In jedem einzelnen Buchstaben kommt buchstäblich ein bestimmter Charakter zum Ausdruck. Die Buchstaben werden dann in einer Bilddatenbank gespeichert, aus der sich der so entstandene Font der Klangwolkenschrift speist. Darüber hinaus wirken die Teilnehmer am *CharakterBook* mit, einem Onlinedienst, der wie ein Mini-Facebook funktioniert und die Suche nach den Buchstaben anderer Teilnehmer ermöglicht, um Botschaften zu entwickeln und gesellschaftliche Aktionen zu initiieren. Kommunikation und Kooperation verbinden die einzelnen Buchstaben der Teilnehmer zu Wörtern oder Botschaften. Im *Klangwolken-ABC* sammeln wir Botschaften, die Kombinationen unterschiedlicher Ausdrucksformen sind – die für Verbindungen von Menschen mit Menschen stehen.[1]

Die für das *Klangwolken ABC* hergestellten Buchstaben werden dazu verwendet, alle möglichen Informationen, die den Medien oder auch den Städten selbst zu entnehmen sind, zu „hacken". Sämtliche Informationen, die in nüchternen schwarzen Buchstaben geschrieben sind, können durch demokratische, farbenfrohe Darstellungen ersetzt werden. Eine Vielzahl von Informationen, wie etwa die Beschilderung in der Stadt Linz, Nachrichtenberichte über die Stadt und Texte des Ars Electronica Festival 2012, wurden mit der Klangwolkenschrift neu gestaltet. Am Tag der Klangwolke werden in Linz *Klangwolken-ABC*-Paraden stattfinden. Außerdem wird sich eine große Gruppe von

Buchstaben bei Sonnenuntergang an der Donau versammeln. Vielleicht wird dabei eine vollständige Botschaft verbreitet, vielleicht treten auch nur einzelne Buchstaben hervor – im Unterschied zu 1979, als die Menschen dieselbe Radiofrequenz einstellten, wird diesmal die Welt der Buchstaben mit einer Radiofrequenz beim Donaupark in Interaktion treten. LEDs werden als Reaktion auf bestimmte Klänge bzw. auf Radiosignale für einzelne Buchstaben oder Botschaften aufleuchten. Zuerst mag dies wie eine Manifestation der von Buchstaben überschwemmten Informationsgesellschaft wirken, dann jedoch werden starke Botschaften auftauchen und für sich im Raum stehen. Im *Klangwolken-ABC* kommt nicht nur die Persönlichkeit der Buchstabenkonstrukteure zum Ausdruck, es führt auch zu konkreten Aktionen der Beteiligten, die gemeinsam ihr Hier und Jetzt gestalten.

Shizuka Shirakawa, der in Kanji (japanische Bezeichnung für chinesische Schriftzeichen) schrieb, sagte über die Geschichte der Buchstaben: „Kanji ist ein Ideogramm; seine Form beschreibt uns die Vorstellung und Lebensweise der Menschen in der Zeit, als die chinesischen Schriftzeichen eingeführt wurden. Jeder einzelne Buchstabe scheint eine eigene Identität zu haben und aus ihr heraus sprechen zu wollen, während er seine ursprüngliche Form beibehält."[2] Ein Buchstabe war ein magisches Medium, ein Reservoir, in dem die Kultur und die Geschichte der Welt aufbewahrt wurden. Dem Alphabet scheint eine Tendenz zu demokratischen Strukturen immanent zu sein. Der einzelne Buchstabe eines Alphabets ergibt kaum Sinn. Nur wenn er auf andere Buchstaben des Alphabets trifft, entsteht Bedeutung. Ein Buchstabe ist immer auf der Suche nach anderen Buchstaben. Er kann sein Bestreben, sich mit anderen zu verbinden, nicht verleugnen. Was geschieht, wenn wir – einem Ideogramm vergleichbar – für einzelne Buchstaben des Alphabets eine zusätzliche Bedeutung generieren?

Das *Klangwolken-ABC* zeigt eine neue Art von Buchstaben. Alle in den Workshops konstruierten Buchstaben sind voller Kreativität und Ideen – sie repräsentieren einen von Menschen geschaffenen Kosmos. Jedes Schriftzeichen spiegelt die individuellen Vorlieben der Mitwirkenden, ihren kulturellen Hintergrund, ihre Denkweise und auch die Konstruktionstechniken wider.

Wenn wir Textinformationen wie News und Tweets mit der Klangwolkenschrift verfassen, erweckt die Diskrepanz zwischen einer normalen Schrifttype und den bunten Buchstaben interessanterweise den Eindruck, als würden Letztere versuchen, eine hinter der Information verborgene Intention aufzudecken. Wieder stellt sich die Frage: Was ist eigentlich Information? Das *Klangwolken-ABC* repräsentiert eine sehr ursprüngliche Form der Information. Dies gelingt mithilfe von zwei Prozessen: indem der Buchstabenschöpfer und der Informationsübermittler in einen Dialog treten sowie durch Rezeption der emotionalen Sehnsucht an dem physischen Ort, an dem die Klangwolke stattfindet.

Das Thema des Buchstabens als magisches Medium wird noch 2012 im Ars Electronica Center in einer Sonderausstellung eingehend behandelt. Diese Ausstellung wird sich u. a. mit folgenden Fragen auseinandersetzen: Wie löste dieses *Klangwolken-ABC* gesellschaftliche Interventionen aus? Was ist überhaupt ein Buchstabe? Wie wurde die Welt mit diesem magischen Medium aufgezeichnet? Wie interagieren Menschen mit den verschiedenen Formen des Mediums im Rahmen der sich neu entwickelnden Technologien und was wollen wir vermitteln, wenn wir es verwenden? Abschließend bleibt noch zu erwähnen, dass die Klangwolkenschrift ein Open-Source-Font sein wird und dass diese neue Kultur, die von der *voestalpine Klangwolke* 2012 ausgeht, auch weiterhin die Stimmung der Zeit vermitteln wird – symbolhaft für reales Handeln in der Wirklichkeit.

Aus dem Englischen von Martina Bauer

1   *http://www.aec.at/klangwolke/participate/soundcloud-abc/*
2   Shizuka Shirakawa: Kanji, Iwanami Shinsho, 1970

Soundcloud Miniatures—Picnic in the Cloud

The *voestalpine Klangwolke* is taking advantage of the fact that it's never been as easy to produce music as it is today. That's why as many people as possible ought to take advantage of this chance to make their very own personal mark on how the sound cloud sounds. In going about this, it's of absolutely no importance whether they contribute sound textures, rhythms they discover in urban or rural settings, or songs they've composed themselves. Everywhere you go, inspiration awaits. And just like people now photograph their breakfast, their menu or their cats without giving it a second thought, they ought to discover their ears as recording devices too, which, with the help of digital aids, can impart totally new impressions of the world in which we live. The point: sharing, turning other people on to cool stuff, listening and experiencing together.

The Ars Electronica Center's *SoundLab* was set up especially for the *voestalpine Klangwolke*. In this open sound studio, users can get hands-on experience with recording, digitizing, processing and producing sounds. The *SoundLab* is also the setting of workshops in which Marco Palewicz, a teacher at the Linz School of Music, skillfully demonstrates the extensive but at the same time extraordinarily user-friendly processing capabilities of modern DAWs (Digital Audio Work-stations). Workshop participants learn to play software synths, program beats, combine loops and samples from the internet into new creations, collect the ambient noise of the cityscape, the countryside or even voestalpine's plant grounds, and weave them together into sound carpets.

All of these sounds—which can be produced not only in the AEC's *SoundLab* but also at home or on the go—can be submitted as *soundcloud miniatures* to *www.soundcloud.com* and thus become part of a sound pool made available to others.

And this sound pool will also provide the raw material for Marco Palewicz to compose the sound track for an episode of the *voestalpine Klangwolke* on September 1.

On September 2, the *soundcloud miniatures* will finally get to star in a show of their own. At *Picnic in the Cloud* they'll be the stuff of live performances, sound experiments and remixes forming a soundtrack that delivers a behind-the-scenes look at the *voestalpine Klangwolke*. Throughout the day, visitors will be able to examine, close-up and at their leisure, all the ingre-dients that went into the previous evening's spectacle. Towards sundown, there'll be live remixes with *soundcloud miniatures* serving as the performance's source, and Austrian radio station FM4 will broadcast a musical lineup custom-tailored to the occasion.

During the time leading up to the Festival and the *Klangwolke,* FM4 will be calling upon listeners to think about things they've always wanted to say (or hear said) really, really loud. And FM4 will be offering them the chance to make this dream come true using what is possibly Austria's most powerful PA system. Listeners are invited to submit brief communiqués—perhaps a poem, the sounds of someone's life or a favorite tune. The FM4 crew will put this material together into a one-hour show in the style of their prizewinning FM4 Shortcuts, which will then be broadcast live and simultaneously given back to the cloud.

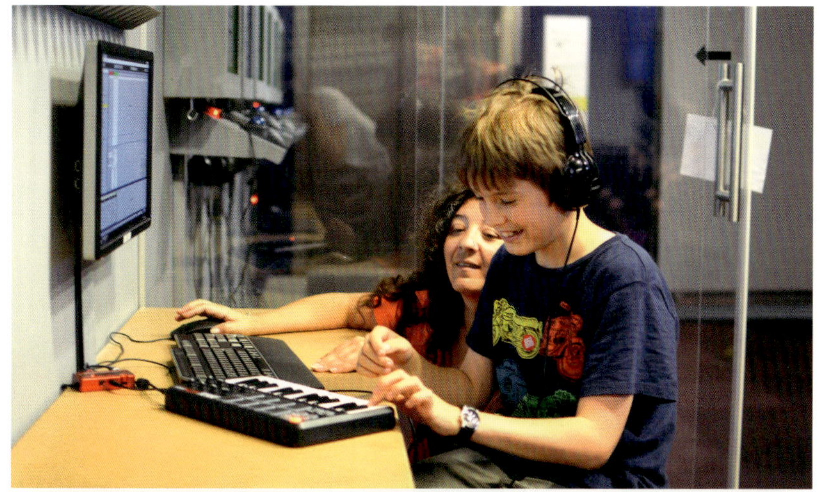

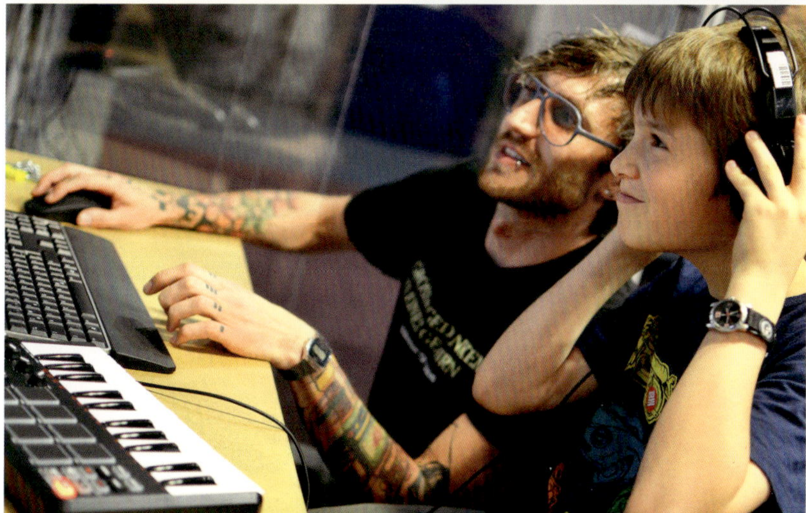

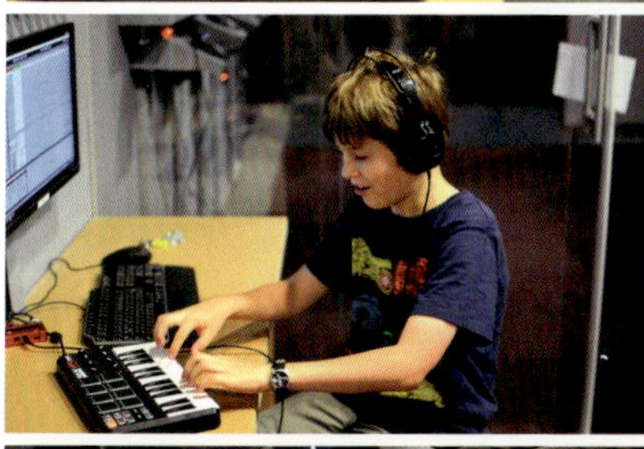

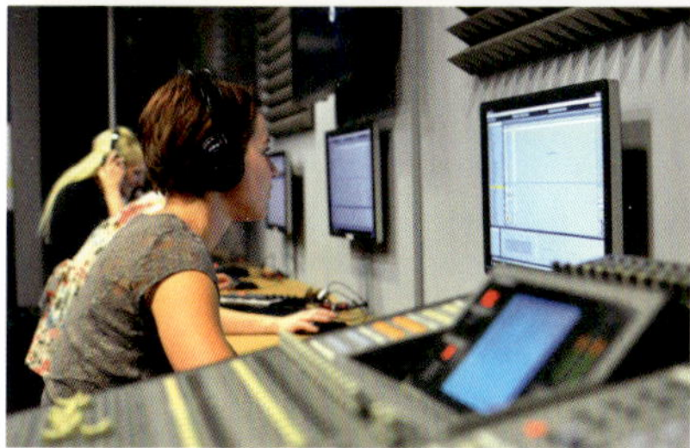

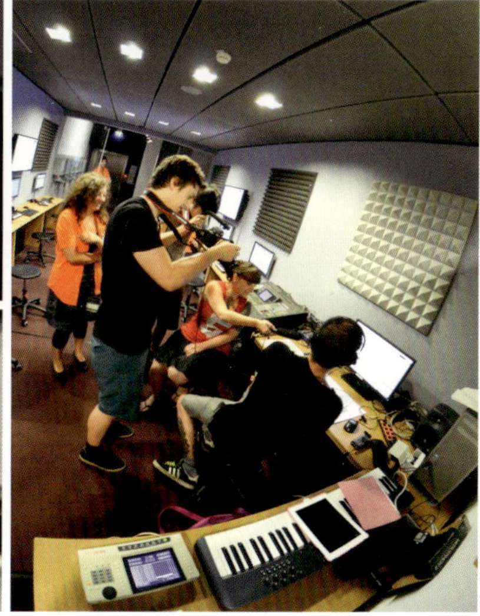

Ars Electronica Center, *SoundLab*

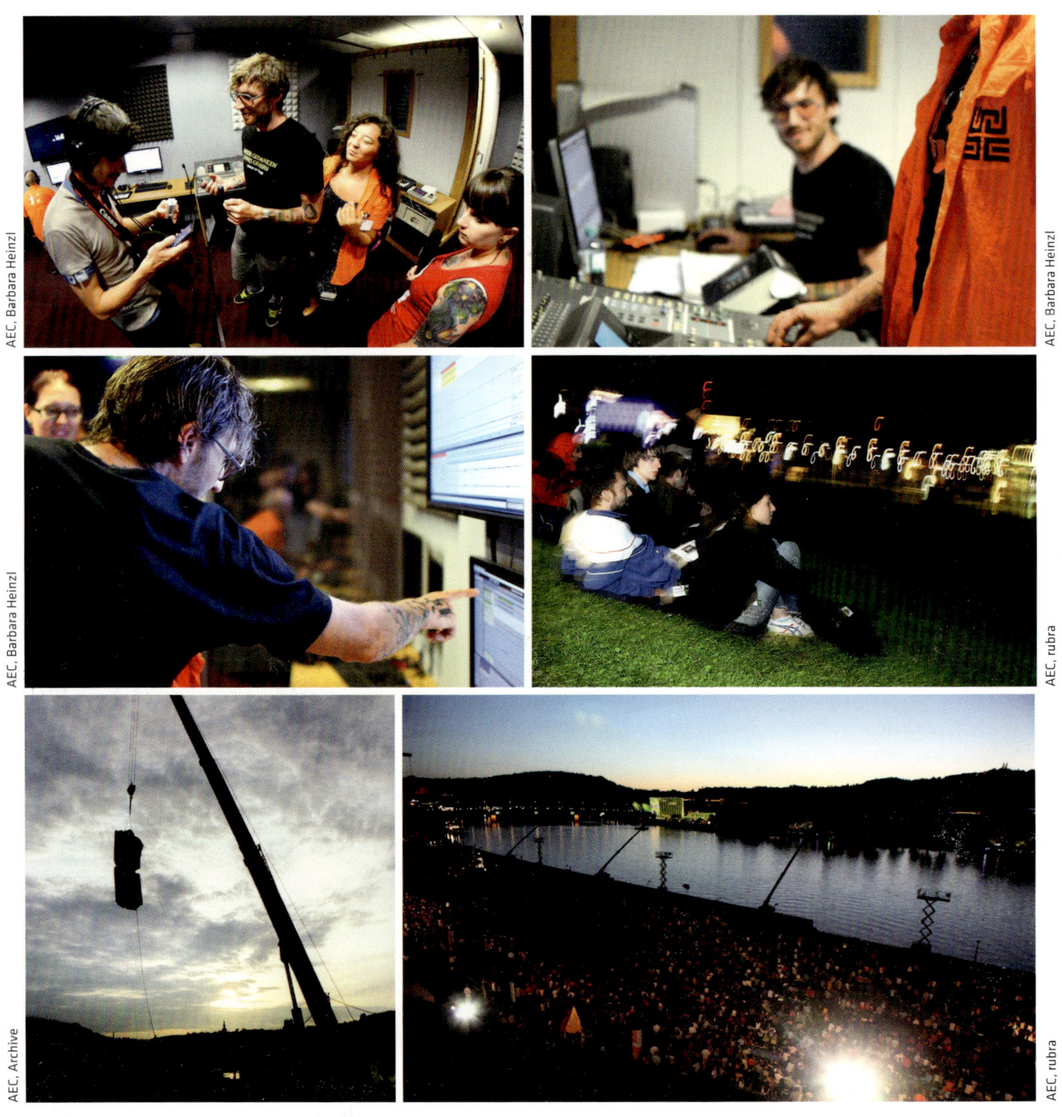
AEC, Barbara Heinzl
AEC, Barbara Heinzl
AEC, Barbara Heinzl
AEC, rubra
AEC, Archive
AEC, rubra

Klangwolken-Miniaturen – Picknick in der Wolke

Die *voestalpine Klangwolke* macht sich zu Nutzen, dass es wahrscheinlich nie so leicht war, Musik zu produzieren, wie es heute der Fall ist. Deswegen sollen so viele Menschen wie möglich die Chance nutzen und ihren ganz persönlichen Eindruck vermitteln, wie eine Klangwolke zu klingen hat. Dabei ist es egal, um welche Art Klang es sich handelt, ob es Soundtexturen sind, Rhythmen, die sich in der Stadt oder Natur wiederfinden, oder um selbst geschriebene Musik. Die Inspiration wartet hinter jeder Ecke, und so wie es mittlerweile gang und gäbe ist, sein Frühstück, seine Speisekarte oder seine Katze zu fotografieren, sollen die Ohren als Aufzeichnungsgeräte entdeckt werden, die mit Hilfe von digitalen Helfern ganz neue Eindrücke der Welt, in der wir leben, vermitteln können. Es geht ums Teilen, ums Vermitteln und um das gemeinsame Zuhören und Erleben.

Im Ars Electronica Center wurde speziell für die *voestalpine Klangwolke* das *SoundLab* eingerichtet, ein offenes Tonstudio, in dem vermittelt wird, wie der Prozess der Aufnahme, Digitalisierung, Bearbeitung und Produktion von Klang abläuft. Im *SoundLab* werden unter der Leitung von Marco Palewicz, Lehrender an der Musikschule Linz, Workshops abgehalten, in denen vermittelt wird, wie umfangreich und gleichzeitig zugänglich die Bearbeitungsmöglichkeiten von modernen DAWs (Digital Audio Workstations) sind. Es werden Softwaresynths gespielt, Beats programmiert, Loops und Samples aus dem Netz zu immer wieder neuen Geschöpfen kombiniert, aber auch Umgebungsgeräusche in der Stadt, der Natur oder auch auf dem Gelände der voestalpine gesammelt und zu Klangteppichen zusammengewoben.

All diese Sounds, die nicht nur im *SoundLab* des AEC, sondern auch zu Hause oder unterwegs entstehen können, werden als Klangwolken-Miniaturen über *www.soundcloud.com* eingereicht und stehen ihrerseits wieder als Soundpool für andere zur Verfügung. Auf diesen Soundpool greift Marco Palewicz zurück, um den Soundtrack einer Episode der *voestalpine Klangwolke* am 1. September zu komponieren.

Am 2. September stehen die *Klangwolken-Miniaturen* endgültig im Zentrum der Aufmerksamkeit, beim *Picknick in der Wolke* werden aus ihnen Live-Performances, Klangspiele und immer wieder neue Remixes. Die *Klangwolken-Miniaturen* bilden den Soundtrack zu einem Blick hinter die Kulissen der *voestalpine Klangwolke*. Untertags können die Zutaten, die am Vorabend Teil des Spektakels waren, in Ruhe und aus der Nähe angeschaut und untersucht werden, gegen Abend geht es dann mit Live Remixes, die den Miniaturenpool der *Klangwolke* als Quelle für ihre Performance hernehmen, und mit einem eigens abgestimmten Programm von FM4 so richtig zur Sache.

Im Vorfeld des Ars Electronica Festivals und der *Klangwolke* fordert FM4 seine Hörer dazu auf, sich zu überlegen, was sie schon immer einmal so richtig laut sagen bzw. hören wollten, und stellt ihnen dafür einen Slot auf der wahrscheinlich stärksten Open-Air-PA Österreichs in Aussicht. Die Leute können kurze (Wort-)Beiträge, (Gedichte, Sounds aus ihrem Leben, Lieblingssongs) schicken. FM4 stellt aus diesem Material eine ca. einstündige Sendung im Stil der preisgekrönten FM4 Shortcuts zusammen. Die Sendung wird zeitgleich im Radioprogramm gespielt, aber auch wieder an die Cloud zurückgegeben.

Text: Michael Kaczorowski

Yoshihiro Harano

The Amanogawa Project

Throughout history streams and rivers have been a source of benefit and well-being for the countries they flow through.

The *Amanogawa Project* (Milky Way Project) focuses on creating new attractions for whole waterfront areas. This project offers great opportunities for people to enjoy the allure of streams and rivers and to experience special lighting effects on the surface of the water.

By introducing artificial light to the natural stream or river, we incorporate people's everyday lives into the surroundings and create a temporary cultural landscape. We can reflect on the past history and memories of the stream or river and on cultural and economic influences at work on the water front. When we create a special stage on the water surface, the Milky Way emerges.

As we make a wish on the stars in the night sky, LED-based light balls (Japanese: Inori Boshi— いのり星®) float off people's hands onto the water surface. This is the moment when the surface of the river turns into the Milky Way. The river is no longer the water we take for granted in our daily lives. Instead, we start to reflect on how fast the river flows, and we discover other faces of the river, which are normally hidden below the surface.

LED-based light balls (Inori Boshi®) play an important role as the key device that connects the river and the people. Inori Boshis are hydrophilic, special communication tools, which light up when they come into contact with water. Each ball is 8.5 cm in diameter. Very high sensitive solar panels attached to each ball generate enough electricity to light the LED, and the surplus energy is stored within the ball. Natural energy is renewed and circulates and the balls can be reused indefinitely, which reduces the environmental impact of the project.

We also see this project as our nation's way of sending a message to people all over the world following the disastrous earthquake in 2011.

Our Milky Way Project has been implemented in various urban rivers and lakes and can be introduced to, and enhance, communities all over the world.

For the *voestalpine Klangwolke* in Linz, panoptic productions are created, encompassing the whole city with the focus on the Danube, a 2,850 km-long international waterway that connects Western Europe and the Black Sea. The history and the memories of the Danube contain the history of Europe itself. The eternal flow of time and space connects our Past, Present and Future along the river.

We will float Light Balls (Inori Boshi®) on one part of the Danube, so that festival visitors can discover a new aspect of the river from a different perspective. Incandescent blue light from the "Prayer Stars" symbolically full of people's wishes will illuminate the Danube and create a one-off Milky Way in Linz.

Text: Tomofumi Okada

(Inori Boshi®) is a patent of the *Amanogawa Project* and is a registered trade mark.
Solar panels, rechargeable batteries and LEDs are provided by Panasonic.

Creator: Yoshihiro Harano
Creative director: Tomofumi Okada
Project manager: Koichiro Mikuriya

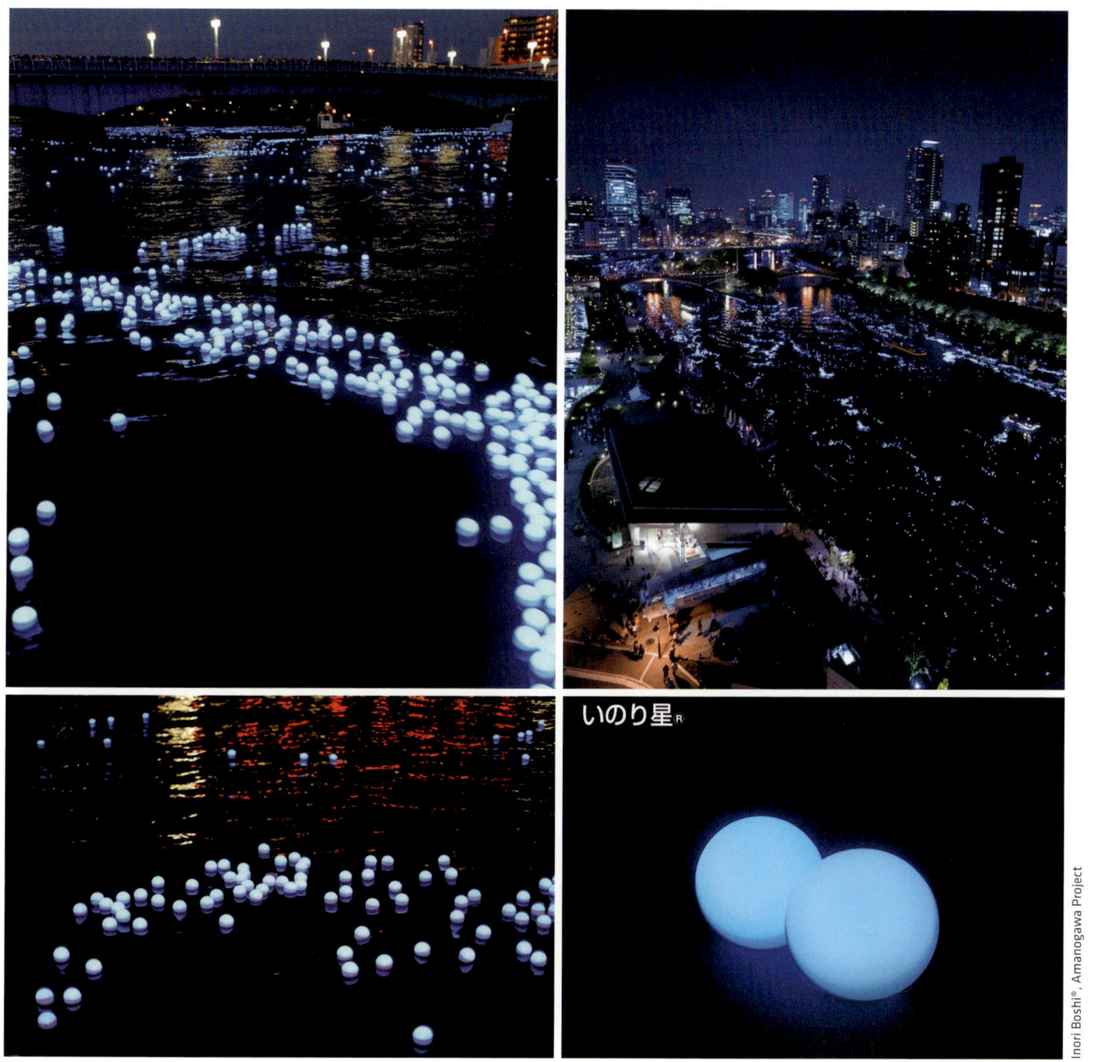

Inori Boshi®, Amanogawa Project

Yoshihiro Harano

Das Amanogawa Projekt

Flüsse waren seit jeher ein Segen für die Landstriche, die sie durchströmen, und haben ihnen stets Glück und Wohlstand gebracht.

Das *Amanogawa Project* (Milchstraßenprojekt) erhöht die Strahlkraft ganzer Stadtviertel, indem es mit Lichteffekten auf den sie durchfließenden Gewässern die Lust darauf weckt, sie neu zu entdecken. Durch die Verbindung künstlicher Lichtquellen mit der natürlichen Bewegung des Flusses wird die Aufmerksamkeit der Menschen für ihre alltägliche Lebenswelt neu belebt. Es entsteht eine temporäre Kulturlandschaft, deren Anblick dazu anregen kann, den mit dem Fluss verknüpften Erinnerungen und historischen Ereignissen nachzusinnen oder die Einflüsse der an seinen Ufern stattfindenden kulturellen und wirtschaftlichen Aktivitäten zu überdenken.

Wir verwandeln den Wasserweg für eine Nacht in die Milchstraße. Wie die Wünsche, die wir normalerweise an die Sterne am Himmel richten, übergeben wir dem Fluss symbolisch sogenannte „Gebetssterne" (japanisch: inori-boshi – いのり星®) in Form von LED-Leuchtkugeln. Mit einem Mal ist der Fluss nicht mehr nur ein Fluss, den wir im Alltag längst nicht mehr beachten, sondern wir nehmen seine Fließgeschwindigkeit und andere, üblicherweise unter seiner Oberfläche verborgene Aspekte wahr.

Für die Verbindung zwischen Fluss und Mensch spielen die Leuchtkugeln (inori-boshi®) eine bedeutende Rolle. Sie sind hydrophile Kommunikationsmittel, die aufleuchten, sobald sie mit dem Wasser in Berührung kommen. Die Leuchtkugeln haben einen Durchmesser von 8,5 cm und sind mit hoch empfindlichen Solarmodulen ausgestattet, die genügend Strom erzeugen, um die LEDs zum Leuchten zu bringen, während der überschüssige Strom in der Kugel gespeichert wird. Die Kugeln arbeiten also mit erneuerbarer Energie und werden auch selbst immer wieder verwendet, sodass das Projekt nicht umweltbelastend ist.

Darüber hinaus betrachten wir das Projekt als unsere Art, nach den verheerenden Erdbeben in unserem Land eine Botschaft an die Menschen in aller Welt zu senden. Unser Milchstraßenprojekt wurde in mehreren urbanen Fluss- und Seenlandschaften mit der bereits nächsten Leuchtkugelgeneration realisiert. Es ist auf alle möglichen lokalen Situationen übertragbar und wird doch jedesmal ein einmaliges Ereignis sein.

Bei der *voestalpine Klangwolke* in Linz wird in einem panoptischen Ansatz die gesamte Stadt rund um die Donau einbezogen. Der 2.850 km lange, Westeuropa mit dem Schwarzen Meer verbindende Fluss ist mit Erinnerungen behaftet, in denen sich die gesamte Geschichte Europas spiegelt. In seinem ewigen Strom von Raum und Zeit verbindet der Fluss Vergangenheit, Gegenwart und Zukunft.

Die Leuchtkugeln (inori-boshi®), die wir auf einem Teil der Donau aussetzen, sollen den Klangwolkenbesuchern neue Aspekte des Flusses erschließen und ihn mit anderen Augen sehen lassen. Die symbolisch mit den Wünschen der BesucherInnen und BewohnerInnen von Linz versehenen Leuchtkugeln werden die Donau in ein strahlend blaues Licht tauchen und eine einmalige „Linzer Milchstraße" entstehen lassen.

Text: Tomofumi Okada   Aus dem Englischen von Wilfried Prantner

Martin Honzik

A Klangwolke by All, for All

… just when all seems dark as night, from somewhere shines a ray of light …

What does it mean to produce a Klangwolke "by all, for all"? First of all, it means taking this mission seriously. Not degrading it to some kind of publicity stunt or paying mere lip service to it, but rather really considering whether and how such an ambitious undertaking can even be pulled off. That means, regardless of which strategies you subsequently pursue, the first thing you have to do is open things up, inward and outward. Inward, when it's a matter of conception and content; outward, because you have to line up as many partners as you can. All those who collaborate on such a project have to be particularly flexible because ideas have to be, of necessity, jointly developed, revised, tossed out, reconceived and, finally, implemented. The fact that there does exist an entity that moderates the interaction and provides direction is something that is necessarily so and doesn't have to be kept a big, dark secret—though it is crucial to point out that there's a big difference between moderating and dictating.

It's a privilege to produce the *voestalpine Klangwolke–The Cloud in the Web* simply because the *Klangwolke* has attained the status of an institution here. An incomparable event that after more than 30 years still attracts 100,000 enthralled, enthused viewers. The *Klangwolke* is simply one of the greatest stages that a producer of artistic & cultural events can have placed at his/her disposal. Being offered the opportunity to collaborate on such an event, to be able to have direct input into its design, is enough to fire anybody up. Regardless of whom we initially approached— an aquatic sports association, a model airplane club, a fire department, music schools, the apprentice training facility at a steel mill, crane manufacturers, shipyards or the Austrian Army— and offered the chance to work on the *Klangwolke*, it was never just one door that opened, but always two or three. Because, after all, a refusal to get involved would have been unthinkable anyway. But the response was just the opposite—immediately, new ideas were born as to how the respective contributions to the *voestalpine Klangwolke* could be staged in a way that would be even more exciting, more spectacular, in a word: better, than what we had initially imagined. For us, this was a really wonderful experience, but at the same time one that wasn't always simple, since with each step away from the area of our own maximum familiarity and expertise, we ceded a modicum of control. Because, let's face it, the ultimate form that the contributions of the aquatic athletes, passenger pigeon breeders, and mounted, whip-cracking Aperschnalzer would or could ultimately take was, from this point on, to a very considerable extent out of our hands. Our job became one of laying out our cards—putting our basic conceptions and expectations on the table—then adapting them with the respective experts and finally trusting that this theory would also be doable in actual practice. For art & culture producers, sitting down with rowers in a boathouse, meeting with the fire chief at his headquarters and attending a planning session with the Aperschnalzer amidst a high Alpine meadow was, as can be imagined, a thoroughly new experience. And at the same time a quintessential aspect of living up to our claim to be producing a *Klangwolke by all*.

Producing a *Klangwolke by all* then entails arranging all these contributions in a way that each becomes a part of a coherent narrative. A story that has to do with the audience's life experiences. Not a fictive account, but one that animates people to consider what they've just seen because it has to do with the world and the times in which we all live. In it, opportunities and risks are discussed, as are past and (possible) future developments that have had and will continue to have a direct influence on our society.

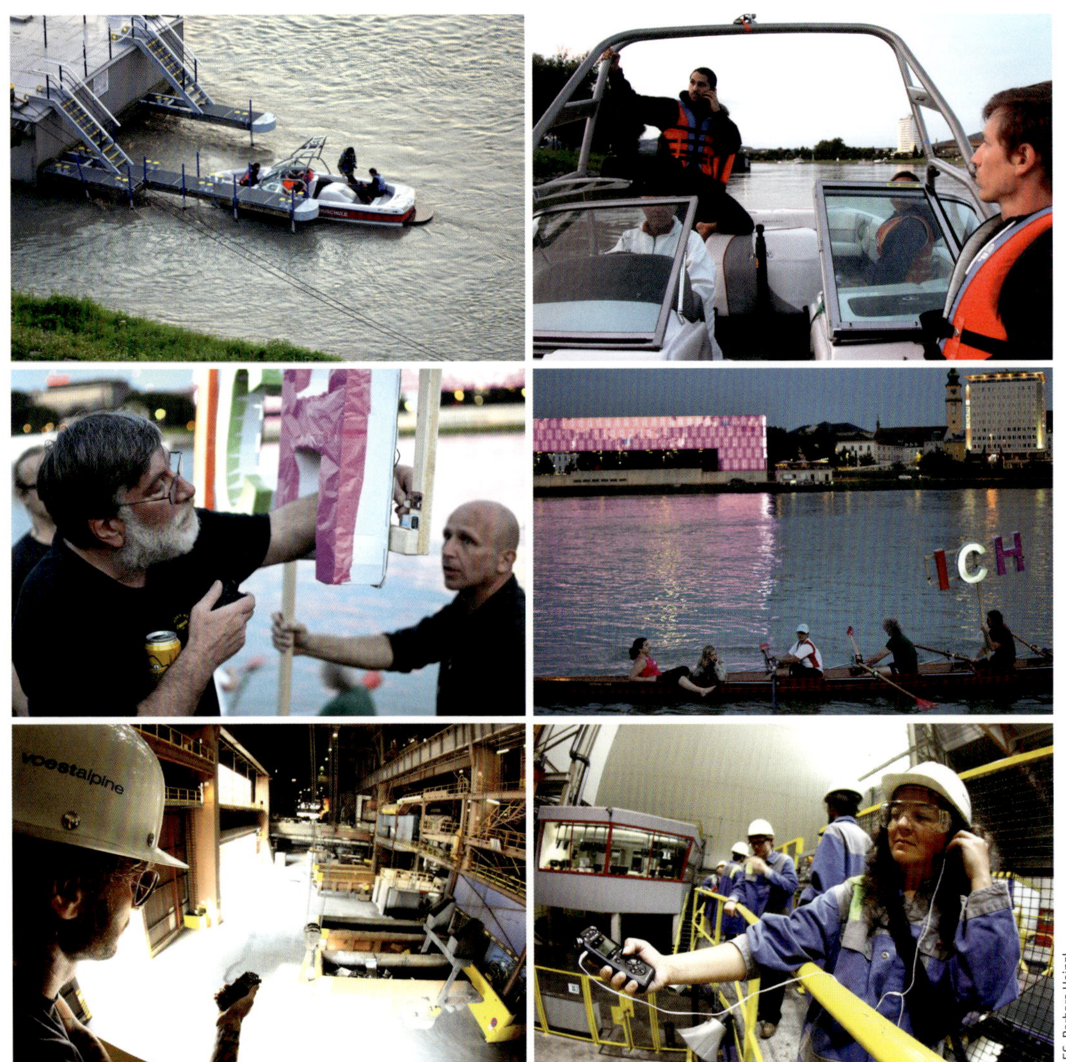

Klangwolken rehearsals

… wenn du denkst, es geht nicht mehr, kommt von irgendwo ein Lichtlein her …

Was es heißt, eine Klangwolke „von allen für alle" zu machen? Erstmal, diesen Anspruch ernst zu nehmen. Nicht zum Marketinggag oder Lippenbekenntnis zu degradieren, sondern sich zu überlegen, ob und wie ein derart ambitioniertes Vorhaben überhaupt umgesetzt werden kann. Ganz egal, welche Strategien man im Weiteren dann verfolgt, bedeutet es zuerst, das Vorhaben zu öffnen, nach innen und nach außen. Nach innen, wenn es um Konzeption und Inhalte geht; nach außen, weil möglichst viele Partner eingebunden werden sollen. Alle, die an einem solchen Projekt mitwirken, müssen überdurchschnittlich flexibel sein, weil Ideen gemeinsam entwickelt, abgeändert, verworfen, neu entwickelt und schließlich umgesetzt werden wollen und müssen. Dass es dabei eine lenkende, moderierende Einheit gibt und geben muss, soll deshalb nicht unter den Teppich gekehrt werden, wobei zwischen „moderieren" und „vorgeben" dennoch ein großer Unterschied besteht.

Die *voestalpine Klangwolke – die Wolke im Netz* zu gestalten ist ein Privileg. Ganz einfach deshalb, weil die *Klangwolke* hierzulande eine Institution ist. Ein unvergleichlicher Event, der seit inzwischen mehr als 30 Jahren immer wieder aufs Neue 100.000 Menschen anlockt, in den Bann zieht und begeistert. Die *Klangwolke* ist schlicht und einfach eine der größten Bühnen, die es für Kunst- und Kulturschaffende überhaupt gibt. Besteht die Möglichkeit, an einem solchen Event mitzuwirken, ja, ihn mitgestalten zu können, ist so gut wie Jede und Jeder sofort Feuer und Flamme. Ganz egal, mit wem wir im Vorfeld gesprochen haben – ob wir uns mit dem Wassersportverein, dem Modellflugclub oder der Feuerwehr, mit den Musikschulen oder der voestalpine-Lehrwerkstätte, mit Kranherstellern, Schiffsbauern und dem österreichischen Bundesheer getroffen haben – und eine Zusammenarbeit im Rahmen der *Klangwolke* angeboten haben, immer ist nicht nur eine, sondern sind gleich zwei bis drei Türen aufgegangen. Weil ein Nicht-Mitmachen sowieso undenkbar war, ja, im Gegenteil, sofort neue Ideen geboren wurden, wie der jeweilige Beitrag zur *voestalpine Klangwolke* noch spannender, spektakulärer, kurz: besser ausfallen würde, als wir uns das gedacht hätten – eine wirklich tolle Erfahrung für uns, die zugleich aber nicht immer ganz einfach war, weil mit jedem Schritt weg von unserem ureigensten Feld natürlich auch Kontrolle verlorenging. Denn wie der Beitrag der Wassersportler, Brieftaubenzüchter oder berittenen Aperschnalzern letztlich genau ausfallen würde, lag nur noch sehr begrenzt in unserer Hand. Uns oblag es lediglich, unsere grundsätzlichen Vorstellungen und Erwartungen auf den Tisch zu legen, diese dann gemeinsam mit den ExpertInnen zu adaptieren und anschließend darauf zu vertrauen, dass diese Theorie in der Praxis auch wirklich umsetzbar sein wird. Dass Kunst- und Kulturproduzenten dabei mit Ruderern im Bootshaus zusammensaßen, sich mit dem Feuerwehrkommandanten in deren Leitstelle trafen oder auf der Alm mit den Aperschnalzern Pläne schmiedeten, war eine durchaus neue Erfahrung für uns. Und zugleich das Einlösen unseres eigenen Anspruchs, eine *Klangwolke von allen* zu machen.

Eine *Klangwolke* für alle zu machen heißt dann, alle diese Beiträge so zu arrangieren, dass sie Teil einer zusammenhängenden Geschichte werden. Einer Geschichte, die mit der Lebenswelt und den Erfahrungen des Publikums zu tun hat. Keine fiktive Story, sondern eine, die zum Nachdenken anregt, weil sie von der Welt und der Zeit handelt, in der wir alle leben. Chancen und Risiken werden dabei ebenso thematisiert wie vergangene und (mögliche) zukünftige Entwicklungen, die unmittelbaren Einfluss auf unsere Gesellschaft hatten und haben werden.

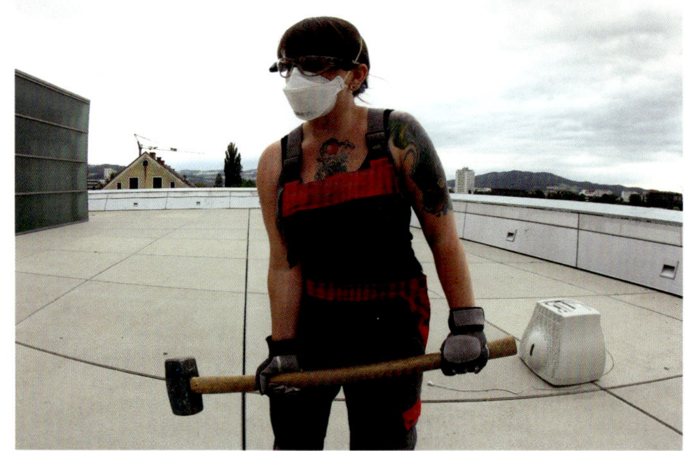

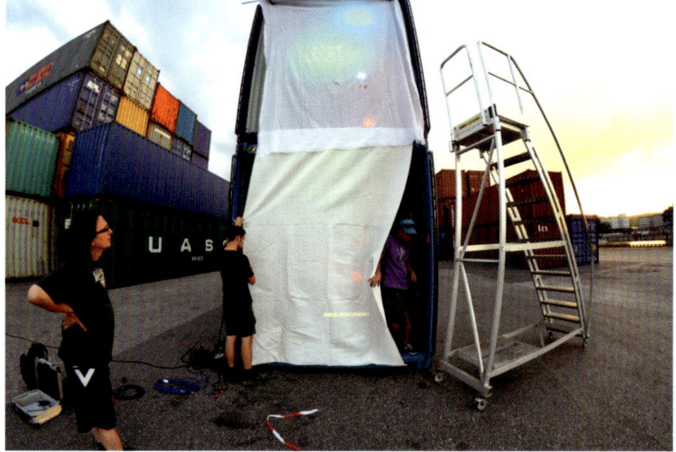

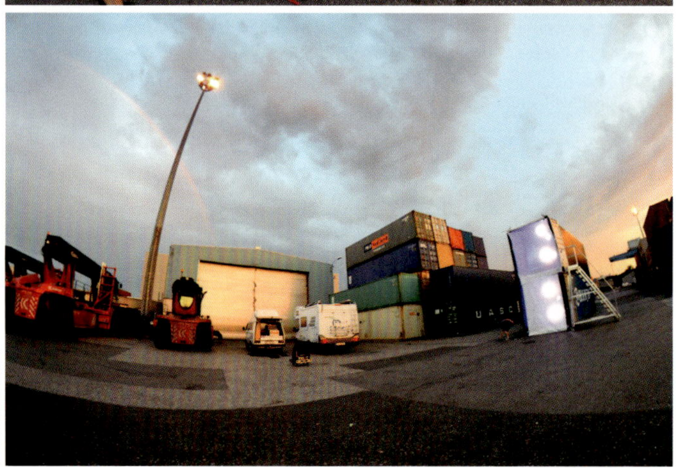

AEC, Barbara Heinzl

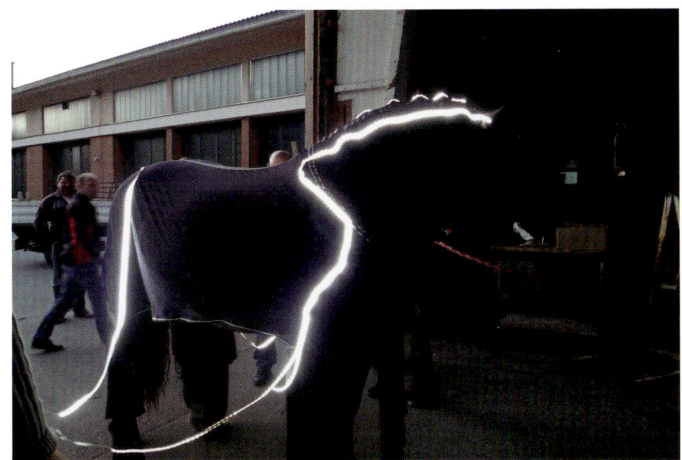

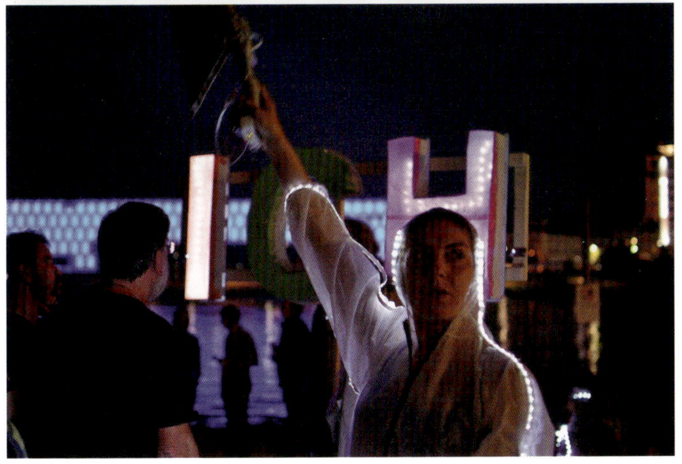

Gerhard Kürner

Digital Media
The Change is the Challenge

" When it comes to an undertaking like the 2012 Klangwolke *The Cloud in the Web* that's all about networking and collaboration, a sponsoring partnership too just has to entail active participation. voestalpine doesn't sign on as sponsor of a major event like the Klangwolke and then simply sit back and watch; we pitch in wherever we can.
The Cloud in the Web is a perfect fit in our corporate culture, since we're made up of more than 360 mid-size companies worldwide. You could say that voestalpine spans the globe like a cloud, and we intensively take advantage of the digital opportunities afforded by the cloud in our R&D and our cooperative projects. "

Gerhard Kürner, Director of Corporate Communications, voestalpine

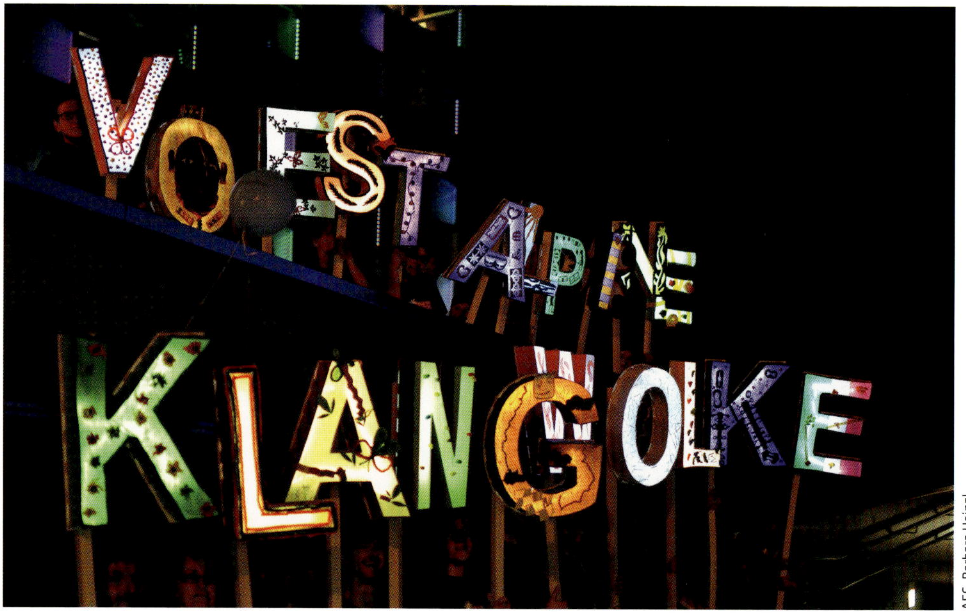

AEC, Barbara Heinzl

266

How and why voestalpine uses social media

Digital technologies have often been the driving and accelerating forces behind significant changes in recent years and have brought forth promising innovations, ideas and impetus from social life, the political arena and the world of business. We're now living in the Social Media Age. Technology alone isn't the point anymore; the relationship factor is the key. Now, extensive social constructs are recreated online. People, with their complete identity, their personality and their experiences, and companies too, can no longer avoid "socialization" on the Web. The future will be powerfully influenced by a new currency, so-called digital social capital, and people, companies and media will be measured according to the form in which they set up and maintain relationships online. For companies and their communication, it is very important to keep up with changes in the use of media. This way of seeing things and readiness to go along with new developments help to build a strong following around the company's brand. voestalpine has been on the Social Web for four years now with various activities design to provide information, foster communication and intensify interaction with all essential target groups. In going about this, the corporate website *www.voestalpine.com* and the corporate blog *www.voestalpine.com/blog* are the sources of content fed to leading social media platforms including Facebook (also the setting of a separate new page dedicated to employment opportunities: voestalpine Karriere), Twitter, XING, LinkedIn, Flickr, Youtube, and Slideshare. We have also developed a Social Media Manual that provides staff guidelines (in seven languages) on how to act in conjunction with professional activities on the Social Web.

Ultimately, the internet, like classic media, is a carrier medium of messages, but with one specific, defining characteristic. The rapid-fire dialog (in contrast to print media outlets' "letter-to-the-editor" culture) calls for a much more concerted process of engaging with and adapting to the people with whom we're communicating. Senders and recipients of these messages have to find a shared carrier frequency. In order to achieve the objective of this communication, you have to develop content that is custom-tailored to the medium and the user, content that isn't just consumed but rather disseminated and recommended as well. On the basis of this content, a valuable process of positioning can take place. As a result, a company increases its digital social capital and builds up sustainable relationships with its target groups.

Gerhard Kürner

Digitale Medien
Die Herausforderung liegt im Wandel

„ Bei einem Vorhaben wie der Klangwolke 2012 *Die Wolke im Netz,* bei dem sich alles um Vernetzung und Zusammenarbeit dreht, muss auch eine Sponsoring-Partnerschaft aktives Mitwirken beinhalten. Die voestalpine sponsert ein Großevent wie die Klangwolke nicht einfach und lehnt sich dann zurück, sondern sie arbeitet mit, an allen Ecken und Enden. *Die Wolke im Netz* passt hervorragend zu unserem Unternehmen, da wir weltweit mehr als 360 mittelständische Unternehmen haben, die voestalpine sich sozusagen wie eine Wolke rund um die Welt spannt und wir bei Forschung, Entwicklung und Zusammenarbeit die digitalen Möglichkeiten sehr intensiv nutzen. “

Gerhard Kürner, Leiter der Konzernkommunikation der voestalpine

Wie und warum die voestalpine Social Media nutzt

Digitale Technologien waren in den vergangenen Jahren oftmals Treiber und Beschleuniger von bedeutenden Veränderungen und brachten entscheidende Innovationen, Ideen und Impulse aus Gesellschaft, Politik und Wirtschaft hervor. Mittlerweile sind wir im Social-Media-Zeitalter angekommen, und es geht nicht mehr um die reine Technologie, sondern um den Beziehungs-Faktor. Heute werden umfangreiche soziale Konstrukte im Netz abgebildet, Menschen mit ihrer kompletten Identität, ihrer Persönlichkeit und ihren Erfahrungen, aber auch Unternehmen können sich der „Sozialisierung" im Web nicht mehr entziehen. Die Zukunft wird stark von einer neuen Währung, dem „digitalen Sozialkapital", beeinflusst, und Menschen, Unternehmen und Medien werden daran gemessen, in welcher Form sie Beziehungen im Web aufbauen und pflegen.

Für Unternehmen und deren Kommunikation ist es sehr wichtig, auf den Wandel der Mediennutzung einzugehen. Dieses Verständnis und die Bereitschaft, neue Entwicklungen mitzutragen, helfen, eine starke Community rund um die eigene Marke zu versammeln. Seit vier Jahren ist die voestalpine im Social Web vertreten und setzt seither verschiedene Aktivitäten um Information, Kommunikation und Interaktion mit allen wesentlichen Zielgruppen aufzubauen. Dabei werden, von der Corporate Website *www.voestalpine.com* und dem Corporate Blog *www.voestalpine.com/blog* ausgehend, die wichtigsten Social-Media-Plattformen bespielt – u. a. Facebook (seit kurzem zusätzlich mit einem eigenen Auftritt rund um die Arbeitswelt: voestalpine Karriere), Twitter, XING, LinkedIn, Flickr, Youtube, Slideshare. Weiters wurde für die Mitarbeiter das „Social Media Manual" entwickelt, das in sieben Sprachen Handlungsempfehlungen für die beruflichen Aktivitäten im Social Web gibt.

Letztendlich ist das Internet – wie die klassischen Medien auch – „Trägermedium" von Botschaften, mit einem Spezifika: Aufgrund des schnellen Dialogs (im Gegensatz zur „Leserbrief-Kultur" im Printbereich) erfordert es vielmehr, sich in der Kommunikation auf sein Gegenüber einzustellen. Sender und Empfänger müssen eine gemeinsame „Trägerfrequenz" finden. Um das Ziel der Kommunikation zu erreichen, benötigt es Inhalte, die auf Medium und Nutzer abgestimmt sind und dadurch nicht nur konsumiert, sondern auch weiterverteilt und empfohlen werden. Und auf Basis dieser Inhalte kann sich eine wertvolle Positionierung entwickeln: Ein Unternehmen erhöht das digitale Sozialkapital und baut langfristig tragfähige Beziehungen zu seinen Zielgruppen auf.

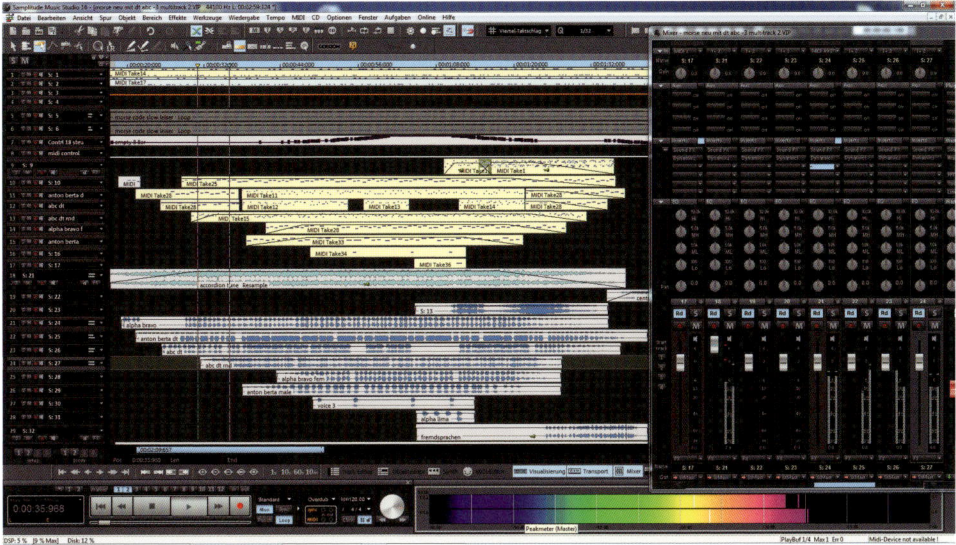

Michael Kaczorowski

Making Music in the 21st Century

Depending on whom you talk to, you get quite a wide range of responses when the conversation turns to the subject of music and the internet. Many people hold the opinion that the internet's job when it comes to music is the same as it is with information dissemination: the internet enables lots of artists to get their music heard. Access to audiences becomes more open, more democratic, thus putting an end to the time when the only way to reach enthusiasts was via middlemen like record labels and distributors. Blogs, online magazines, Twitter, Soundcloud and Facebook are a few of the multipliers that enable up-and-coming artists and musicians just getting started to not have to be excluded from the public sphere as they go about nurturing their artistry. Especially in the case of music that targets specialized tastes, the internet offers a huge selection of distribution and performance possibilities.

The music industry is singing the blues about the new rules of the game. Their executives missed the boat when it was time to develop new business models, and they're now in a state of innovation panic as their revenues decline. Don't invite the internet and the music industry to the same party; they'll make a scene!

Of course, these two positions have been simplistically rendered. It's precisely because a vastly larger quantity of music is now available anytime, anywhere that the influence exerted by those wielding classical marketing techniques might now be greater than it ever was. Nowadays, to attract even a little bit of attention, you have to scream really, really loud. And the music industry is still good at that. How this stalemate will be played out in the coming years remains a matter of great interest that will surely be associated with unpleasant answers.

But what do the artists actually do? They profit not only from the new tools that enable them to make a name for themselves, but also from the ever-greater creative possibilities. More and more people are involved in digitizing all possible sounds and making them available for free. What used to be a laborious, demanding exercise is now literally a matter of a couple of mouse clicks. Genre borders are becoming blurred because musical resources across the entire spectrum are pretty much constantly available, and music from throughout the world and of the most diverse types and styles is constantly being sampled, disassembled, rearranged and recombined. Millions of components offer millions of possibilities for millions of people for whom it's never been as easy to produce music as it is today.

Music isn't a finite cosmos in which only the gifted are entitled to a backstage pass. Music and sounds enwrap all of us every day, and make such strong impressions on our perceptions that most people have already forgotten to trust their ears. The *voestalpine Klangwolke* calls upon the public to get actively involved, to record what they perceive, to mix together whatever they feel belongs together, and to not let themselves be told what art is and is not. The barrier that's been shoved into place between music makers and consumers ought to be torn down so that every sound enjoys equal rights to be heard. There's no right or wrong here.

It used to be that writing and performing music was quite an elaborate undertaking. And if you wanted to immortalize the music for posterity, you had to possess extensive knowledge of musical notation or you had to take the time to teach your compositions to other people. Of course, the invention of sound recording obviated this problem, so that today serious music is practically the only genre in which musical notation is still used as the basis for composition. But musical notation isn't all that belonged in the tool box of a serious artist—there was also harmonics, to say nothing of inspiration, talent and imagination. Writing a piece of music often demanded considerable mental exertion. After all, the emotions had to be first gotten down on paper before they could finally be made to resound. And the composer was often left entirely to his/her own devices. The external influences were what one heard, what one perceived, what one had perhaps read somewhere, and the composer ultimately processed these influences.

For centuries, performing music depended on instruments and people who had mastered them. Sound recording broke with this tradition by making it possible to reproduce music anytime and anywhere, always in exactly the same way—no interpretation, no falsification, no variation. Hit PLAY and the music plays.

The fact that it didn't take too long for somebody to attempt to take advantage of the new possibilities, not only for reproducing music, but also for composing and producing, it is attributable to human curiosity. At first inextricably bound to big, expensive sound studios, the artists of *musique concrète* laid the foundation for the kind of music we are familiar with today—and not only from the Pop charts. The re-contextualization of previously recorded material, cutting, rearranging and composing, launched a paradigm shift in music production. All of a sudden, the skills that were called for differed completely from what had been necessary just a few years before. Everything changed, abruptly.

Today, we're experiencing the impact that these developments have had on music. Nobody has to know the slightest thing about harmony and dissonance, thirds, fifths and final cadences to be able to "write" music. The influences are no longer abstract inspirations and intuitions; they're right there, right in front of your nose, waiting to be used, to be made into new music. Regardless of whether they're saved to your own hard drive or available in the endless expanses of the internet, the Digital Revolution makes access to samples, loops and one-shots simpler than ever before. On the software side, there have been significant developments too. Today's digital audio workstations (DAW) are a quantum leap beyond what was available in 2000 as far as capabilities and convenient, efficiency-enhancing features are concerned. And then there are the ever-more-comprehensive software tools and plug-ins like Melodyne and Autotune that have, since their advent, made such a powerful impact on our perceptive faculties.

What does all this mean for the artist?

People who create music have been brought closer together by the internet whether they like it or not. It's hardly possible any more for someone to say that he/she really creates music totally independently. As soon as you begin to rely on digital tools, you're building on the work of others. Regardless of whether this is a matter of presets on software synthesizers, preprogrammed beats on diverse software drum computers or, in the clearest possible case, samples and loops of other people's work, as soon as you have recourse to this easily accessible material, you're actually no longer composing music; you're combining someone else's intellectual property into a new work. No value judgment will be forthcoming here; nevertheless, this represents yet another significant incursion in musical culture. Ultimately, many people who create music don't even know anymore where the material they use comes from. Needless to say, you know where you downloaded or purchased it, but you have little or no idea who's actually behind it. The point is the sound, the tone, the effect; it's no longer a matter of whom it comes from or who gets the creative credit for it. Many pieces of music produced in the modern way are no longer compositional efforts in the classic sense, but rather a more or less appealing new combination of previously existing components, rhythms, melodies and sounds.

Michael Kaczorowski

Musikmachen im 21. Jahrhundert

Abhängig davon, mit wem man sich zum Thema Internet und Musik unterhält, bekommt man ein ziemlich breites Spektrum an Antworten. Es gibt viele, die die Meinung vertreten, dass das Internet auch für den Bereich Musik dieselbe Funktion übernimmt wie für die Informationsvermittlung: Das Internet erlaubt es einer Vielzahl von Künstlerinnen und Künstlern, ihrer Musik Gehör zu verschaffen, der Zugang zum Publikum wird offener, demokratischer, vorbei sind die Zeiten, wo man nur über Mittelsmänner wie Labels oder Plattenfirmen den Zugang zu Interessierten schaffen konnte. Blogs, Onlinemagazine, Twitter, Soundcloud, Facebook und ähnliche sind die Multiplikatoren, die es aufstrebenden KünstlerInnen oder MusikerInnen, die noch am Anfang ihrer Karrieren stehen, ermöglichen, ihre Kunst nicht unter Ausschluss der Öffentlichkeit zu produzieren. Vor allem Musik für speziellere Geschmäcker sieht im Internet einen riesigen Pool an Vertriebs-, aber auch Auftrittsmöglichkeiten.

Die alteingesessene Musikindustrie seufzt unter den neuen Spielregeln, hat den Zeitpunkt verpasst, neue Geschäftsmodelle zu entwickeln, und befindet sich in einem Zustand der Innovationspanik, die Umsätze sind weggebrochen. Dicke Freunde sind das Internet und die Musikindustrie nicht.

Natürlich sind diese zwei Positionen vereinfacht dargestellt. Gerade dadurch, dass eine ungleich größere Menge an Musik immer und überall zur Verfügung steht, ist der Einfluss, den klassische Marketingmaßnahmen ausüben, womöglich so groß wie schon lange nicht mehr. Um im großen Pool Aufmerksamkeit auf sich zu ziehen, muss man laut schreien. Das kann die Musikindustrie immer noch gut. Wie sich diese Pattstellung in den nächsten Jahren auflösen wird, ist eine äußerst spannende Frage, die mit unangenehmen Antworten verbunden sein wird.

Aber was machen eigentlich die Künstlerinnen und Künstler? Die profitieren nicht nur von neuen Werkzeugen, um ihren Namen unters Volk zu bringen, sondern auch von immer größeren kreativen Möglichkeiten. Immer mehr Leute beschäftigen sich damit, alle möglichen Sounds zu digitalisieren und gratis zur Verfügung zu stellen. Was früher mühsamst in Kleinarbeit erledigt werden musste, ist heute sprichwörtlich einen Mausklick entfernt. Genregrenzen verschwimmen, weil verschiedenste Musikressourcen quasi immer verfügbar sind, und Musik aus aller Welt, aus unterschiedlichsten Musikrichtungen wird immer wieder aufs Neue zusammengesetzt, auseinandergenommen, neu arrangiert, neu kombiniert. Millionen Baublöcke bieten Millionen Möglichkeiten für Millionen von Leuten, für die es noch nie so leicht war wie heute, Musik zu produzieren.

Musik ist kein geschlossener Kosmos, der nur von Talentierten betreten werden kann. Musik und Klang ist etwas, das uns alle täglich umschließt, und unsere Wahrnehmung so stark prägt, dass die meisten schon darauf vergessen haben, ihren Ohren zu vertrauen. Die *voestalpine Klangwolke* fordert das Publikum heraus, sich zu beteiligen, das aufzuzeichnen, was man wahrnimmt, zu mischen, was für sie zusammengehört, und sich nicht sagen zu lassen, was Kunst ist und was nicht. Die Barriere, die sich zwischen die Musizierenden und die Konsumierenden geschoben hat, soll niedergerissen werden, so dass jeder Sound dasselbe Recht hat, gehört zu werden. Denn es gibt hier kein richtig oder falsch.

Früher war das Schreiben und Aufführen von Musik eine durchaus aufwändige Tätigkeit: Wollte man Musik für die Nachwelt verewigen, musste man über profunde Kenntnisse in Notensatz verfügen, oder man musste sich die Zeit nehmen, die eigenen Kompositionen anderen Leuten beizubringen. Durch die Erfindung der Tonaufzeichnung ist dieses Problem freilich gelöst, der Notensatz als Kompositionsgrundlage ist heute praktisch nur noch in der ernsten Musik erhalten. Doch nicht nur Notensatz gehörte zum Werkzeugkasten eines ernstzunehmenden Künstlers, sondern unter anderem auch Harmonielehre, von Inspiration, Talent und Vorstellung einmal abgesehen. Das Schreiben eines Musikstückes verlangte oftmals nach umfangreicher Denkarbeit, die Emotionen mussten zunächst zu Papier gebracht werden, um sie schließlich erklingen zu lassen. Und der Komponist bzw. die Komponistin, sie waren oftmals alleine auf sich gestellt, die Einflüsse von außen waren das, was man hörte, was man wahrgenommen, was man womöglich irgendwo gelesen hat, und diese Einflüsse wurden schließlich verarbeitet.

Jahrhundertelang war das Aufführen von Musik abhängig von Instrumenten und von Menschen, die die Instrumente beherrschen. Die Tonaufzeichnung brach mit dieser Tradition, sie ermöglichte es, Musik immer, überall und jederzeit zu reproduzieren, immer auf dieselbe Art und Weise. Keine Interpretation, keine Verfälschung, keine Abwandlung. Play, und die Musik spielt.

Dass es nicht allzu lange gedauert hat, bis die Ersten versuchten, die neuen Möglichkeiten nicht nur zum Reproduzieren, sondern zum Komponieren und Produzieren zu verwenden, ist der menschlichen Neugier geschuldet. Zunächst an riesige und teure Tonstudios gebunden, legten KünstlerInnen der *musique concrète* die Grundlage für die Art von Musik, die wir heute nicht nur aus den Charts der Popularmusik kennen. Die Verfremdung von aufgezeichnetem Material, das Schneiden, das Neuarrangieren und Komponieren läutete einen Paradigmenwechsel in der Musikproduktion ein. Auf einmal waren gänzlich andere Fertigkeiten verlangt als noch wenige Jahre zuvor, und es wurde auf einmal alles anders.

Heute erleben wir den Einfluss, den diese Entwicklungen auf Musik gehabt haben. Niemand muss auch nur einen Hauch über Harmonie und Dissonanz, Terzen, Quinten, Schlusskadenzen oder ähnliches wissen, um Musik „schreiben" zu können. Die Einflüsse sind nicht mehr abstrakte

Eingebungen, sie warten direkt vor der eigenen Nase darauf, eingesetzt zu werden, zu neuer Musik gemacht zu werden. Egal, ob auf der eigenen Festplatte oder in den endlosen Weiten des Internet, durch die digitale Revolution ist der Zugang zu Samples, Loops oder One-Shots so einfach wie nie zuvor. Auch auf Seiten der Software gab es bedeutsame Entwicklungen, die heutigen DAWs (Digital Audio Workstation) sind sogar mit jenen aus dem Jahr 2000 herum kaum noch zu vergleichen, was Leistungsfähigkeit und Werkzeuge, die den Workflow vereinfachen, angeht. Von immer umfangreicheren Softwareinstrumenten oder Plug-Ins wie Melodyne oder Autotune, die unsere Wahrnehmung mittlerweile stark verändert haben, ganz zu schweigen.

Was bedeutet das alles für Musikschaffende?

Die Musikschaffenden sind durch das Netz zusammengerückt, freiwillig oder nicht. Es ist kaum noch möglich, davon zu sprechen, dass man Musik wirklich komplett allein gemacht hat. Sobald man sich auf digitale Werkzeuge verlässt, baut man auf der Arbeit von anderen auf. Egal, ob es sich um Presets von Softwaresynthesizern, vorprogrammierten Beats aus diversen Softwaredrumcomputern oder ganz konkret um Samples oder Loops von anderen handelt: Sobald man auf dieses leicht zugängliche Material zurückgreift, ist man eigentlich nicht mehr kompositorisch tätig, sondern kombiniert das geistige Eigentum anderer zu einem neuen Werk. Eine Wertung soll an dieser Stelle nicht abgegeben werden, doch handelt es sich auch hier wiederum um einen bedeutenden Einschnitt in die Musikkultur, schließlich weiß man als Musikschaffender in vielen Fällen schlicht nicht, woher das Material kommt, das man verwendet. Natürlich, man weiß, wo man es heruntergeladen oder gekauft hat, aber man weiß kaum mehr, wer tatsächlich dahintersteht. Es geht um den Sound, es geht um den Ton, es geht um den Effekt, es geht nicht mehr darum, von wem er stammt, wer kreativ für diesen Sound verantwortlich ist. Ein modern produziertes Musikstück ist oftmals keine kompositorische Anstrengung im klassischen Sinn mehr, sondern eine mehr oder minder gelungene, neue Kombination aus vorhanden Bausteinen, Rhythmen, Melodien und Klängen.

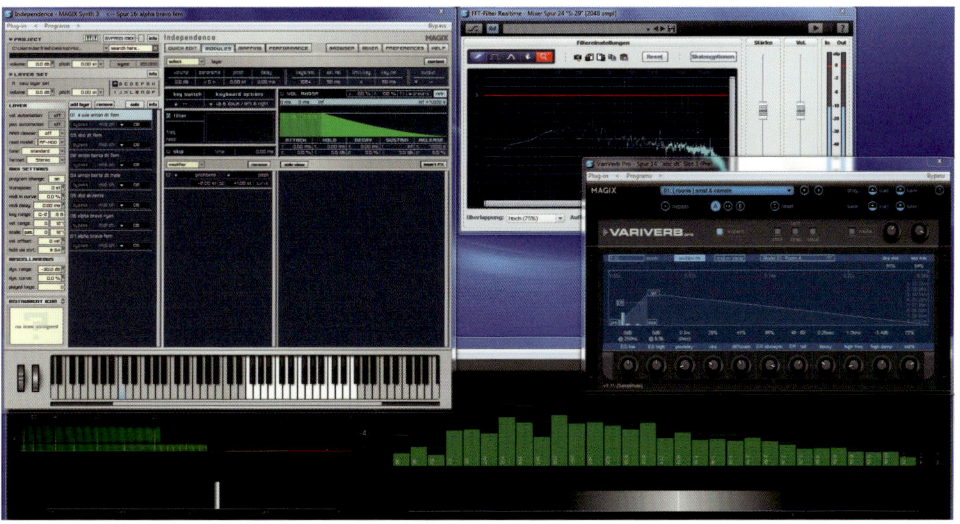

Rupert Huber

teardrops

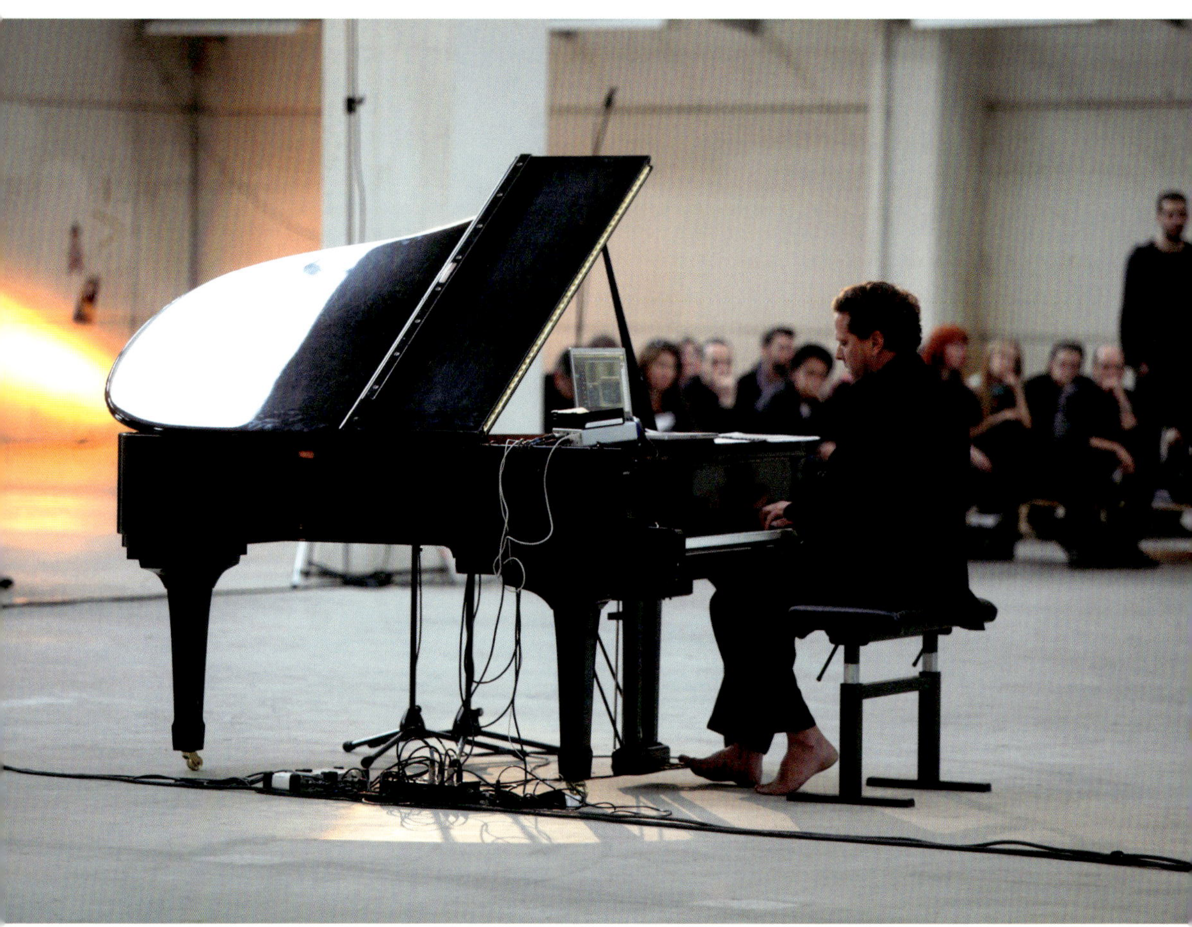

Ars Electronica 2010, Rubert Huber

music installation and concert
for piano, noise gates, sonic feeds and church organ

by
rupert huber

2 pm to 12 midnight
concert: 11 pm to 12 midnight

like tears, re-contextualized and original piano sounds descend in the church interior, move about in a procession and seek to escape the force of gravity. breaks and disruptions, like the chiming of church bells, mark the time.
whether the tears flow out of
hope
desperation
joy
mourning
is irrelevant.

concert: the piano's striking force triggers, by means of noise gates (audio effect: sound below a preset volume level is suppressed), filtered electronic real-time re-contextualizations of the sounds of the piano.
they become interwoven with each other and with the sound structures of the installation, which consist of piano tones, effect loops and re-contextualized piano sounds, and send the musical drops off as if in a procession through the church.

the sound's movement in the space, the being-reset back to a purportedly original state, the non-existence of an alternative in reality;
among the piano, its electronic extension and the church organ, there exists a direct causal relationship: imitation and counter-movement are two parameters to which the two scales upon which the tonal space is based correspond.

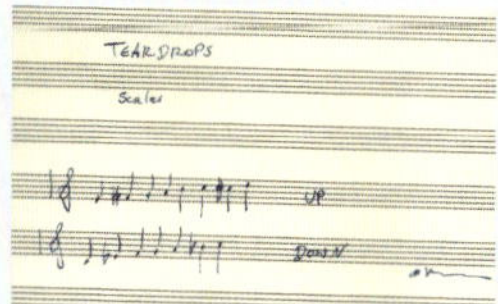

the scales dovetail tonally and spatially over the course of the composition.

the phenomenon of gravity is juxtaposed to both the up-and-down movements of the sounds themselves and the spatial patterns of motion.

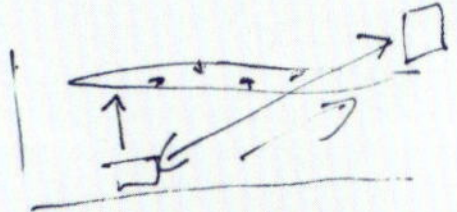

teardrops fall throughout the day beginning at 2 pm; the sound installation is then simultaneously the cantus firmus in concert.
the concert for piano, noise gates, nine loudspeakers and church organ arises from the installation like a person awaking from slumber—whereby the force juxtaposed to gravity is the conscious part of the composition, the lying-asleep its subconscious element.
The "conscious" segment ends at midnight; there ensues descent back into the unconsciousness that had acoustically dominated the church since 2 pm.

4 terms name the locations at which the sound is made audible:
hope
desperation
joy
mourning
thus hope morphs into joy at times, mourning concludes as joy ....

teardrops is a composition by rupert huber
music installation and concert produced and realized by rupert huber

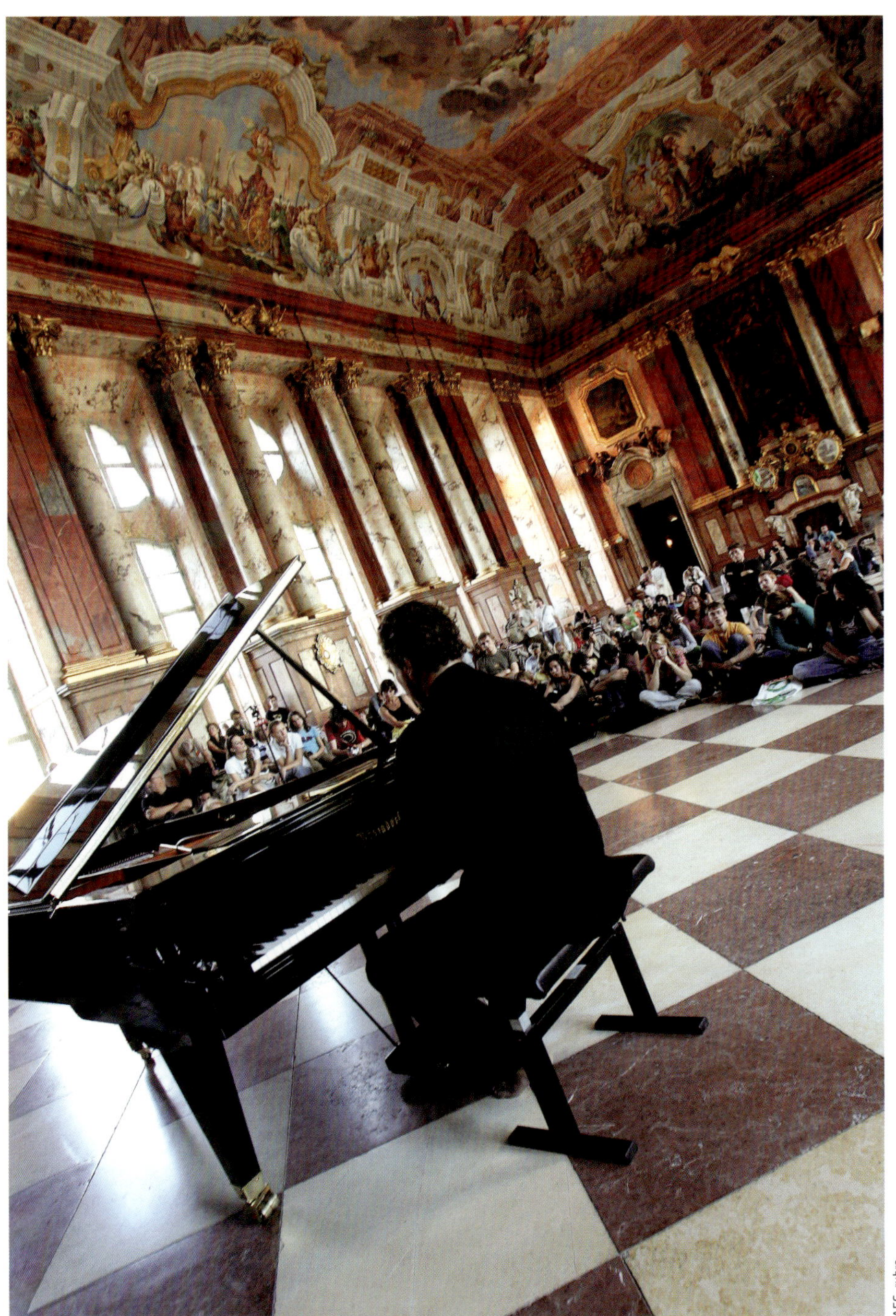

Ars Electronica 2006, Rubert Huber

musikinstallation und konzert
für klavier, noise gates, sonische zuspielungen und kirchenorgel

von
rupert huber

14 bis 24 uhr
konzert 23 bis 24 uhr

wie tränen fallen im kirchenraum verfremdete und originale klaviertöne; wandern in einer
prozession herum und versuchen, der schwerkraft zu entfliehen. brüche und störungen
markieren wie kirchenglocken die zeit.
ob die tränen aus
hoffnung
verzweiflung
freude
trauer
fließen, ist unerheblich.

konzert: die anschlagstärke des klaviers löst durch noise gates (audio-effekt: klang unterhalb
einer festgelegten lautstärke wird unterdrückt) gefilterte elektronische echtzeit-verfremdungen
des pianoklanges aus.
sie verschränken sich ineinander und mit den klangstrukturen der installation, die aus
klaviertönen, effektschleifen und verfremdungen von pianoklängen besteht und die
musikalischen tropfen wie in einer prozession durch die kirche schickt.

die bewegung des klanges im raum, das zurückgeworfen-werden auf ein angeblich
ursprüngliches, die nichtexistenz einer alternative in der realität;
zwischen klavier, seiner elektronischen erweiterung und der kirchenorgel besteht eine direkte
kausale beziehung: imitation und gegenbewegung sind zwei parameter, denen die dem
tonalen raum zugrundeliegenden 2 skalen entsprechen.

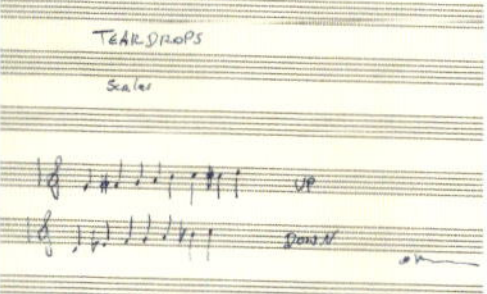

die skalen verschränken sich im laufe der komposition tonal und räumlich.

dem phänomen der schwerkraft werden die auf- und abbewegungen der klänge an sich und
die räumlichen bewegungsmuster entgegengehalten .

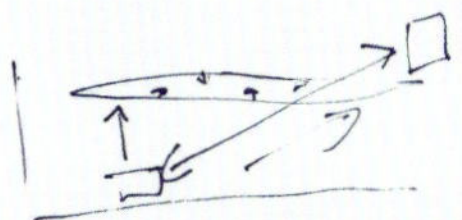

teardrops fallen den ganzen tag ab 14 uhr, die klanginstallation ist dann gleichzeitig
der cantus firmus im konzert.
das konzert für klavier, noise gates, 9 lautsprecher und kirchenorgel erhebt sich aus der
installation wie ein mensch, der aus dem schlaf erwacht. die im zuge dessen der schwerkraft
entgegengehaltene kraft als bewusster, das im-schlaf-liegen als unbewusster teil der
komposition.
der „bewusste" teil endet um mitternacht und sinkt zurück in das unbewusste, das schon seit
14 uhr die kirche klanglich dominiert.

4 begriffe benennen die orte der klangwiedergabe:
hoffnung
verzweiflung
freude
trauer
so geht mitunter hoffnung in freude über, trauer endet als freude ....

teardrops ist eine komposition von rupert huber,
musikinstallation und konzert produziert und aufgeführt von rupert huber

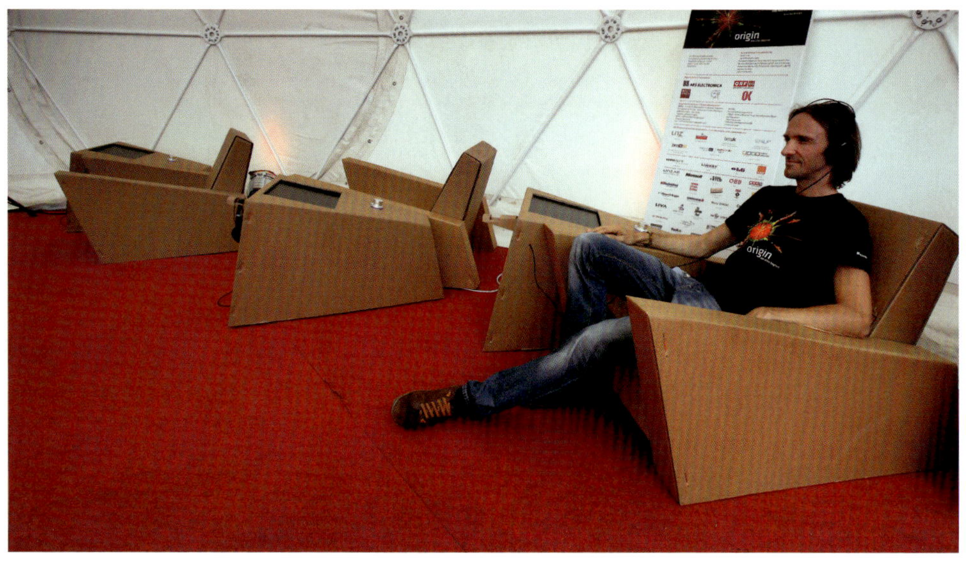

The Mobile Ö1 Atelier

At this year's Ars Electronica Festival THE BIG PICTURE, the Austrian Broadcasting Company's radio station Ö1 and Ars Electronica will be featuring projects and installations having to do with auditory influences in public spaces. What do urban spaces have to offer our ears? Every city has its own acoustic stories to tell, just like every room speaks and an audible event intonates. Topography, architecture, history, economic and social structures and dynamics—all of them can be heard.

In the city, sounds are omnipresent. They specify spaces, situations and identities. They strongly influence us as individuals. In the *Mobile Ö1 Atelier* Peter Cusack and Sam Auinger will join students at the UdK–Berlin University of the Arts in an investigation of Linz's Main Square and its immediate surroundings. Prior to and during the festival, they'll be working on an interactive audio map. The aim of this artistic research project is to get a better understanding of urban soundscapes.

The *Mobile Ö1 Atelier* is staging encounters by youngsters and grown-ups alike with the soundscape that surrounds us in everyday life. And in this connection, of course, the *voestalpine Klangwolke* is playing a special role. Anyone can get actively involved in this year's extravaganza. In special workshops in the *Mobile Ö1 Atelier,* you can create your own illuminated letters for the *Klangwolke ABC* and then equip them with LEDs and a receiver.

Once again this year, the *Mobile Ö1 Atelier* is hosting workshops and speeches in conjunction with u19 – CREATE YOUR WORLD, the Future Festival of the Next Generation. In our proving ground dedicated to the world of tomorrow, you can develop ideas and concepts, run experiments and analyze the results. Detailed coverage will be provided by young reporters from the Ö1 Kinderuni.

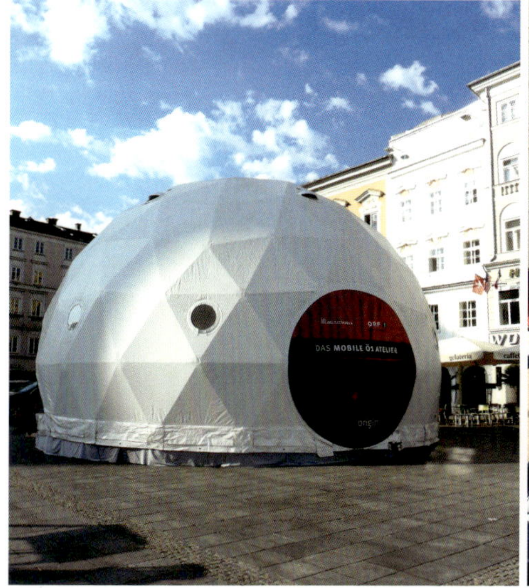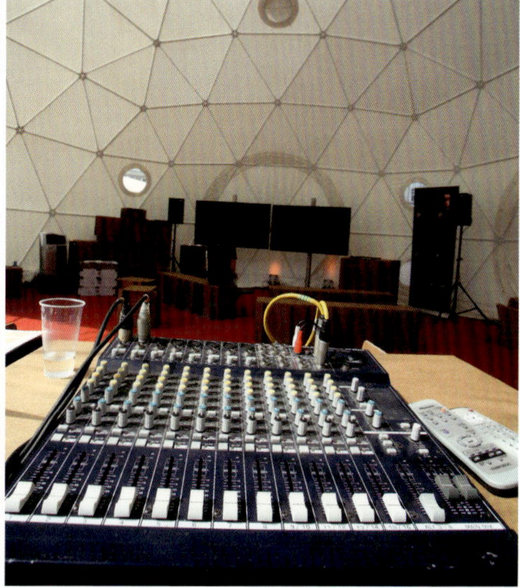

AEC, rubra

Das Mobile Ö1 Atelier

Radio Österreich 1 und Ars Electronica präsentieren beim diesjährigen Ars Electronica Festival THE BIG PICTURE Projekte und Installationen, die sich mit den auditiven Einflüssen im öffentlichen Raum beschäftigen. Was haben urbane Räume unseren Sinnen zu bieten? Jede Stadt erzählt ihre auditive Geschichte, so wie jeder Raum spricht und ein Klangereignis färbt. Topografie, Architektur, Geschichte, ökonomische und soziale Struktur und Dynamik – all das lässt sich hören.

Klänge in der Stadt sind allgegenwärtig. Sie bestimmen Räume, Situationen und Identitäten. Als Individuen beeinflussen sie uns maßgeblich. Im *Mobilen Ö1 Atelier* untersuchen Peter Cusack und Sam Auinger gemeinsam mit StudentInnen der UdK Berlin den Linzer Hauptplatz und sein näheres Umfeld. Es wird im Vorfeld und während des Festivals eine interaktive Audio-Karte erarbeitet. Das künstlerische Forschungsprojekt produziert Diskursmaterial zum Verständnis von urbanen Klanglandschaften.

Das *Mobile Ö1 Atelier* ermöglicht Kindern und Erwachsenen die Begegnung und Auseinandersetzung mit der Klanglandschaft, die uns tagtäglich in unserem Umfeld umgibt. Dabei spielt natürlich auch die *voestalpine Klangwolke* eine besondere Rolle: Jede und jeder kann Teil dieses Kunstprojekts werden: In eigenen Workshops im *Mobilen Ö1 Atelier* können Sie Ihren persönlichen Leuchtbuchstaben für das *Klangwolken-ABC* gestalten und mit LEDs und Empfänger bestücken lassen.

Auch u19 – CREATE YOUR WORLD, das Zukunftsfestival der nächsten Generation, ist wieder mit Workshops und Vorträgen im *Mobilen Ö1 Atelier* zu Gast. Hier werden Ideen und Konzepte entwickelt, Experimente ausprobiert und darüber nachgedacht, wie die Welt von morgen aussehen könnte. Die jungen ReporterInnen der Ö1-Kinderuni werden darüber berichten.

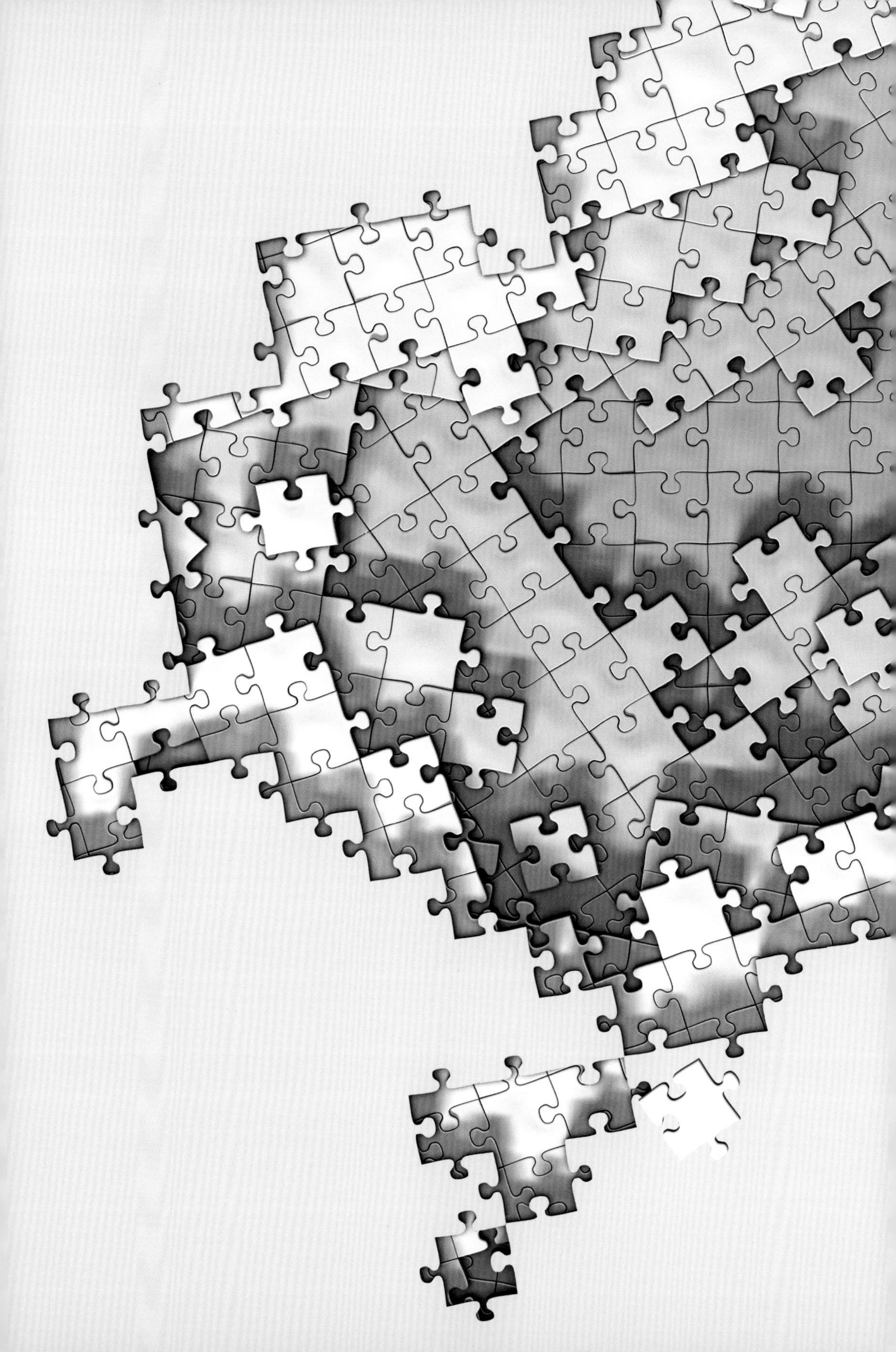

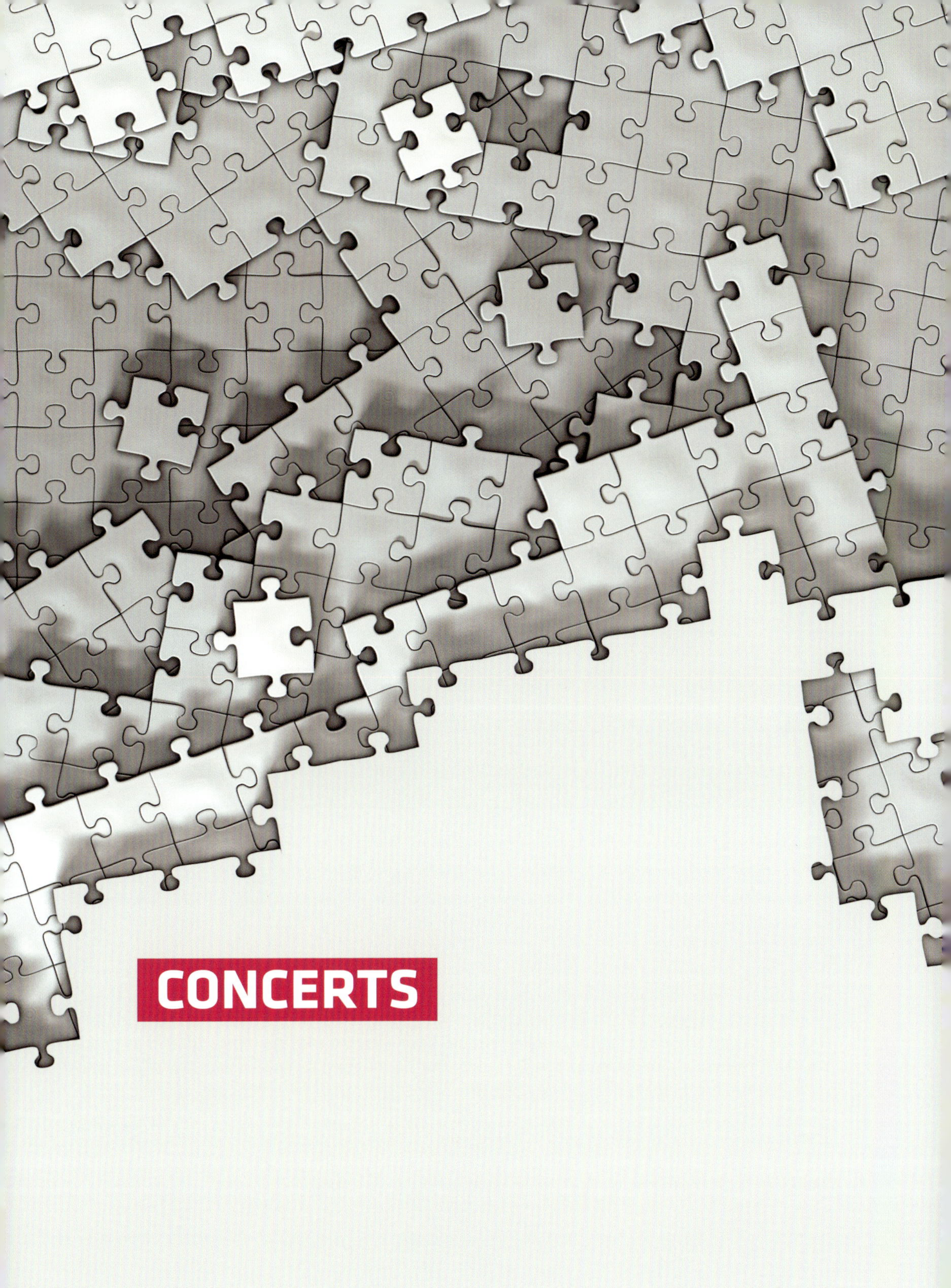
CONCERTS

Resonant Bridges
Die Große Konzertnacht

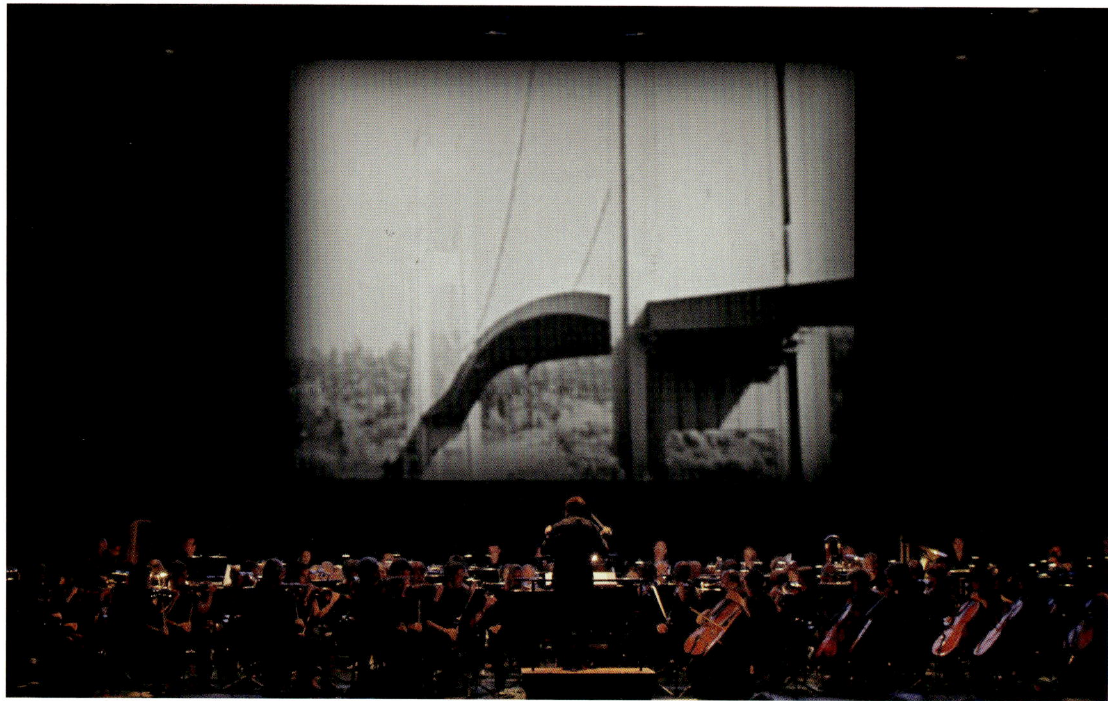

Resonance phenomena and the building of bridges both literal and figurative have been recurring themes in the lineup of this concert series that has been staged for 10 years now in cooperation with Brucknerhaus Linz and the Bruckner Orchestra. This is a collaborative undertaking set at the nexus of orchestral music and digital sounds/live electronics, one of the defining features of which is that all the works played by the orchestra are simultaneously visualized. The point is also to discover and develop new musical spaces, interpretations and aesthetic modes of implementation. In light of the festival theme, THE BIG PICTURE, the *Big Concert Night* is taking the opportunity to take a more wide-ranging look at things, one that peers beyond the purview of habitual confines and the boundaries of specialized disciplines and regards a modern, globally networked world whose social and political events are reflected by the musical offerings.

The *Resonant Bridges* evening concert is an encounter with old masters and new virtuosos. Thematically as well, the lineup interweaves opposites, juxtaposing the venerability of the Buddhist worldview with the recent revolutionary events of the Arab Spring.

Resonanzphenomäne und Brückenschläge im eigentlichen und im symbolischen Sinn ziehen sich durch das Programm der nunmehr bereits seit zehn Jahren stattfindenden Konzert-Kooperation mit dem Brucknerhaus Linz und dem Bruckner Orchester Linz. Eine Kooperation, die sich im Spannungsfeld zwischen Orchestermusik und digitalen Klängen bzw. Live-Elektronik befindet und nicht zuletzt dadurch auszeichnet, dass alle vom Orchester gespielten Werke auch visualisiert werden. Ziel ist es, damit auch neue musikalische Räume, Interpretationen und ästhetische Umsetzungen zu entwickeln und zu entdecken. Im Widerschein des Festival-Themas THE BIG PICTURE erlaubt die *Große Konzertnacht* einen offeneren Blickwinkel, der über Gewohnheiten und Fachdisziplinen hinausblicken lässt und eine moderne, global vernetzte Welt abbildet, deren soziale und politische Ereignisse sich in den musikalischen Darbietungen wiederfinden. Der Konzertabend *Resonant Bridges* bringt uns alte Meister und neue Virtuosen näher. Auch thematisch verweben sich die Gegensätze: das Ehrwürdige der buddhistischen Lebensanschauung steht dem Revolutionären des allzu aktuellen Arabischen Frühlings gegenüber.

Tiefdruckgebiet
HEAVYLISTENING (Carl Schilde / Anselm Venezian Nehls)

The evening begins on the open terrace of the Lentos Art Museum with a musical offering of a very different sort. Berlin's HEAVYLISTENING duo presents *Tiefdruckgebiet* (low pressure area) featuring rides pimped-out with massive subwoofers.
Each automobile corresponds to an instrument; its driver, the instrumentalist. The low-frequency sounds the subwoofers blast are pure sine waves between approximately 25 and 50 Hz, the simplest possible vibrations. The frequencies of these tones are attuned to the resonance characteristics of the performance venue as well as the participating autos.
The sound produced by a single car is nothing special. But as soon as the sine waves of several autos overlap and are reflected by the building façades, physical effects such as beat frequencies, amplifications and cancellations result. Complex rhythms at the low end of the human hearing range emerge. Speaking becomes difficult; the air seems to liquefy.
Due to the influence exerted by architecture, interpreters and traffic, *Tiefdruckgebiet* (low pressure area) sounds different at every location and to each listener. The duration of the performance also depends on the particular concert venue.[1]

Der Abend beginnt im Freiraum des Lentos Kunstmuseum mit einer Musikdarbietung der etwas anderen Art: Die Berliner Gruppe HEAVYLISTENING bringt in *Tiefdruckgebiet* mit massiven Subwoofern getunte Autos zum Klingen. Diese erzeugen ein körperlich spürbares Wellenfeld sich gegenseitig modulierender Subbass-Schwingungen in den Straßen der Stadt. Jedes Auto entspricht einem Instrument, sein Fahrer dem Instrumentalisten. Die über die Subwoofer abgespielten tieffrequenten Klänge sind reine Sinustöne zwischen ca. 25 und 50Hz, die einfachsten vorstellbaren Schwingungen. Diese Töne sind in ihren Frequenzen sowohl auf die Resonanzen des Aufführungsortes als auch auf die der teilnehmenden Autos abgestimmt. Jedes Auto für sich klingt unspektakulär. Sobald sich die Sinustöne mehrerer Autos jedoch überlagern und von den Hauswänden reflektiert werden, kommt es zu physikalischen Effekten wie Schwebungen, Verstärkungen und Auslöschungen – komplexe Rhythmen an der unteren Grenze des menschlichen Hörvermögens entstehen. Das Sprechen fällt schwer, die Luft scheint sich zu verflüssigen. Aufgrund des Einflusses von Architektur, Interpreten und Verkehr klingt *Tiefdruckgebiet* an jedem Ort und für jeden Zuhörer anders. Auch die Länge der Aufführung richtet sich nach dem Ort des Konzertes.[1]

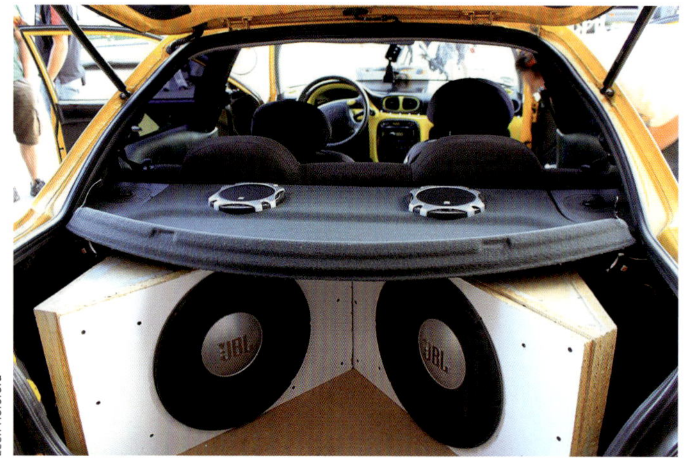

1 *Tiefdruckgebiet* premiered at 48 Stunden Neukölln 2011, a festival in Berlin, where it was honored with the 1st Art Prize. Of eight subwoofers, only five survived the concert. Its presentation at Ars Electronica 2012 will be the second performance of *Tiefdruckgebiet*. For it, the composition is being specially adapted to Linz's architectural facts and circumstances. / *Tiefdruckgebiet* wurde im Rahmen von 48 Stunden Neukölln 2011 in Berlin uraufgeführt und mit dem 1. Kunstpreis des Festivals ausgezeichnet. Von acht Subwoofern überstanden nur fünf das Konzert. *Tiefdruckgebiet* wird bei der Ars Electronica 2012 zum zweiten Mal aufgeführt und die Komposition speziell auf die architektonischen Gegebenheiten der Stadt Linz angepasst.

Songs of Milarepa
Philip Glass

Performed by Bruckner Orchester Linz / Dennis Russell Davies
Visualization by Tom Lorenz / ambientartlab, Michael Mayr

The evening continues with Philip Glass' *Songs of Milarepa*, three lieder based on poems by Milarepa, an 11th-century Tibetan poet, yogi and ascetic. Born a Jew, Glass has been involved with Buddhism since the 1970s. He arranges these texts in his typical hypnotic-repetitive style. *Songs of Milarepa* were originally created as orchestral lieder; they have now been reworked for piano and baritone. The visualization is by Tom Lorenz and Michael Mayr.

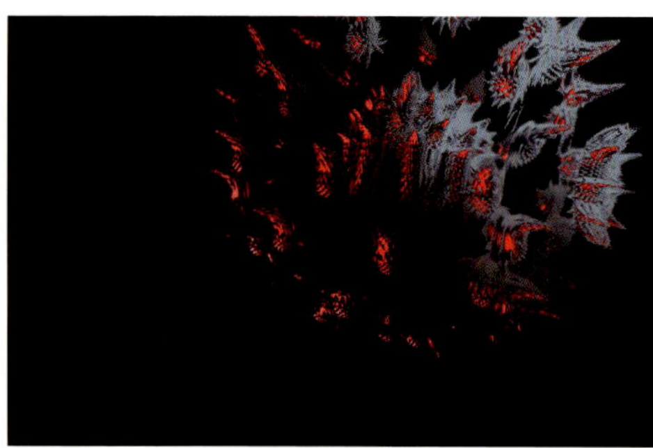
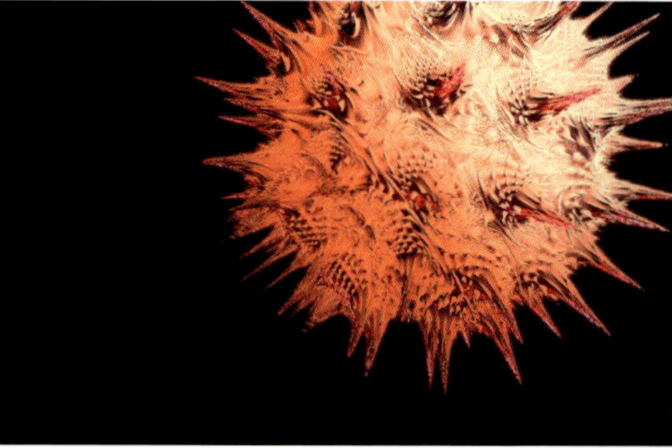

Michael Mayr

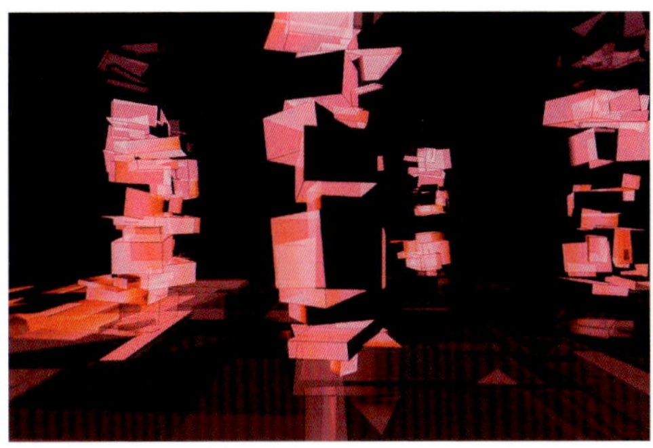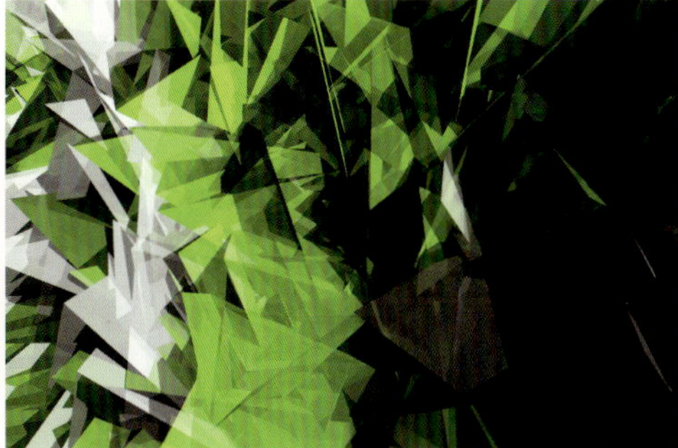

Tom Lorenz / ambientartlab

Fortgesetzt wird der Abend dann mit Philip Glass' *Songs of Milarepa*, drei Liedern, die auf Gedichten des im 11. Jahrhundert lebenden tibetanischen Poeten, Yogi und Asketen Milarepa beruhen. Glass, ursprünglich aus der jüdischen Tradition stammend, beschäftigt sich seit den 1970er Jahren mit dem Buddhismus und arrangiert diese Texte in seinem so typisch hypnotisch-repetitiven Stil. Die *Songs of Milarepa* wurden ursprünglich als Orchesterlieder verfasst und nun für Klavier und Bariton umgearbeitet. Für die Visualisierung verantwortlichen zeichnen Tom Lorenz / ambientartlab und Michael Mayr.

Echoes of the Miraculous
Johannes Berauer

Performed by Bruckner Orchester Linz / Dennis Russell Davies
Visualization by Leonardo / Backlab Collective

Johannes Berauer wrote *Echoes of the Miraculous* in spring 2011, a time of political upheaval that he perceived as oppressive and unsatisfactory. Nevertheless, in spite of it all, he opted for a positive composition that rejects all logical objections to the coming of better times, and is meant to evoke an ingenuous, childlike view of the world. Berauer's tonal vocabulary is strongly influenced by jazz—the piece's most important chords consist of two triads separated by a major seventh. The tender ambiguity of this sound pervades the space like a question. The main theme of the composition is variously elaborated in four sequences. In the final part, rhythmic patterns come to predominate and lead to a fun, playful finale. The visual accompaniment is provided by Leonardo from Backlab Collective.

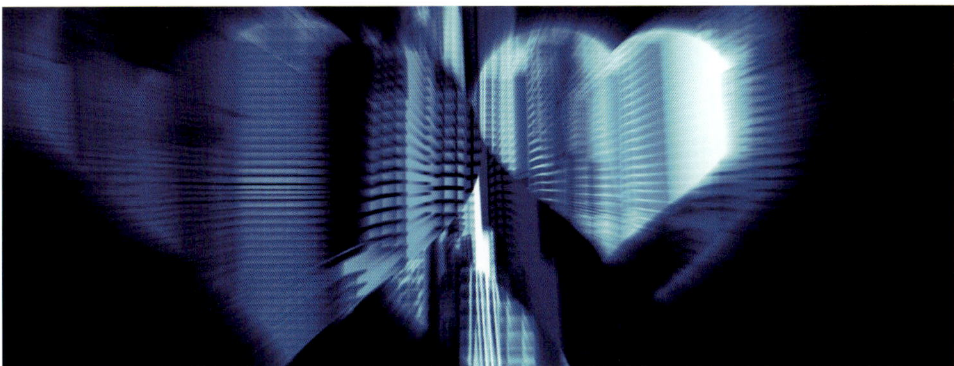

Leonardo / Backlab Collective

285

Johannes Berauer schrieb *Echoes of the Miraculous* im Frühjahr 2011, einer Phase der politischen Umwälzung, die er selbst als bedrückend und unbefriedigend empfand. Wie zum Trotz entschied er sich für eine positive Komposition, die alle logischen Einwände gegen eine bessere Zukunft zurückweist und an eine unbefangene, kindliche Sicht der Welt erinnern soll. Berauers Tonsprache ist stark vom Jazz beeinflusst – der wichtigste Akkord des Stücks besteht aus zwei Dreiklängen im Abstand einer großen Septime. Die zarte Ambiguität dieses Klangs hängt als Frage im Raum. Das Hauptthema der Komposition wird in vier Abschnitten unterschiedlich verarbeitet. Im letzten Teil erlangen rhythmische Patterns die Oberhand und führen in ein kindlich verspieltes Finale. Die visuelle Umsetzung liefert Leonardo vom Backlab Collective.

Ima Koko
Misato Mochizuki

Performed by Bruckner Orchester Linz / Dennis Russell Davies
Visualization by Conny Zenk

In her composition *Ima Koko* (Japanese: Here and Now), Misato Mochizuki confronts the development of consciousness, conceptions of diversity, and shared origins. In accordance with the teachings of Buddhism that the cosmos is contained in a mote of dust and eternity in the blink of an eye, the Here and Now is a moment that extends into endlessness, a point on the spiral of incessant time, a projection onto the present. The piece begins with the striking of a gong, the repetition of which, by stretching time and space, gradually reveals the individual parts almost as if the person beholding it could place an individual note under a magnifying glass and enlarge it to the point at which particles and waves of matter become visible. The role of the electronics is to accompany the sound extension by expansion and spatialization as well as through modification of the musical coloration. Conny Zenk did the visualization of this piece.

Misato Mochizuki setzt sich in ihrer Komposition *Ima Koko* (japanisch für „Hier und Jetzt") mit der Entwicklung des Bewusstseins auseinander, mit Vorstellungen von Vielfalt und gemeinsamem Ursprung. Der Lehre des Buddhismus folgend, dass der Kosmos in einem Staubkorn und die Ewigkeit in einem Augenblick enthalten sind, ist das Hier und Jetzt ein sich ins Unendliche ausdehnender Augenblick, ein Punkt auf der Spirale der fortwährenden Zeit, eine Projektion auf die Gegenwart. Das Stück beginnt mit einem Gongschlag, dessen Wiederholung durch Dehnung von Zeit und Raum allmählich die Einzelteile offenbart, als könnte man den Ton unter die Lupe nehmen, bis die Partikel und Wellen der Materie zu erkennen sind. Die Rolle der Elektronik besteht darin, die Klangstrecken durch Erweiterung und Verräumlichung, aber auch durch Veränderung der musikalischen Färbung zu begleiten. Die Visualisierung zu diesem Stück stammt von Conny Zenk.

Conny Zenk

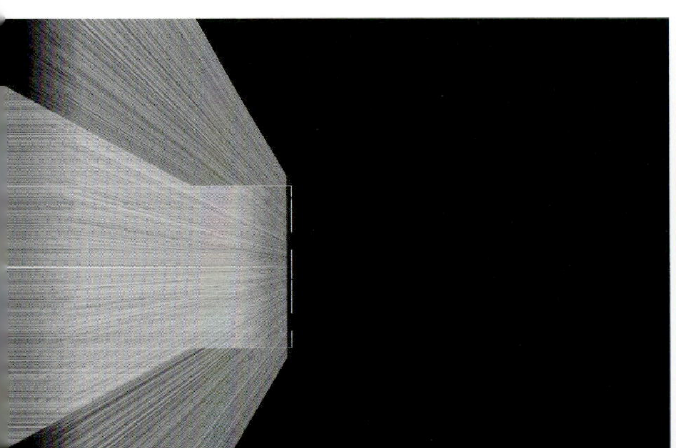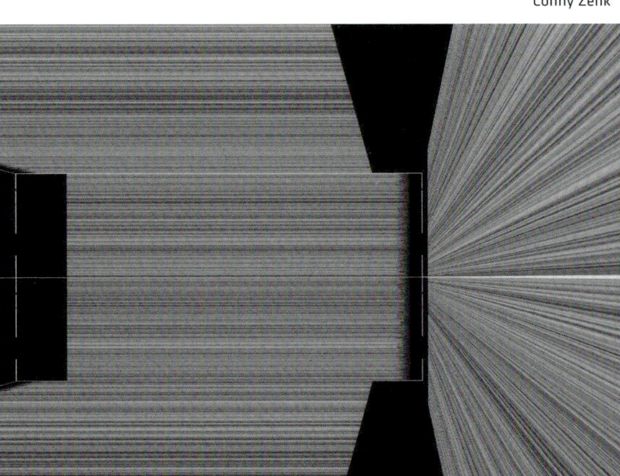

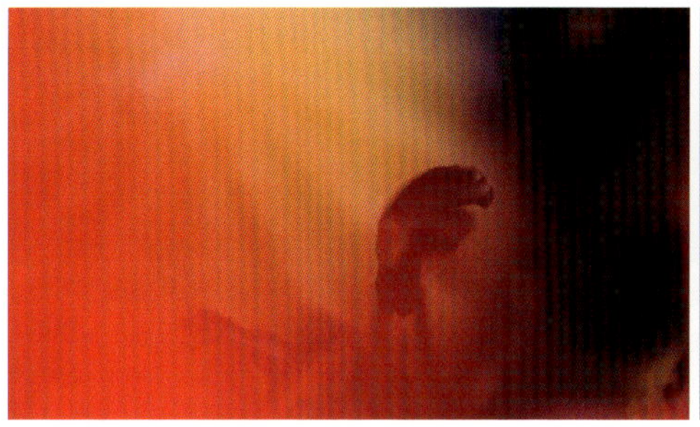

Anna Bertsch [annablume]

Etappe
Amr Okba

Performed by Bruckner Orchester Linz / Dennis Russell Davies
Visualization by Anna Bertsch [annablume]

Amr Okba's work *Etappe* is an effort to come to terms with the Arab Spring. With "Day of Rage – January 25, 2011" as his point of departure, Okba considers the uprising against the brittle, unresponsive regime in musical terms. The daily grind is a matter of survival, of keeping from being worn down by incessant oppression. This rhythm is then acoustically put to an end when the inner voice cries out for rebellion against the prevailing system, a voice that thousands follow on that day. Nevertheless, the uprising represents only a single stage, and Okba still regards the ending as open. The visualization accompanying this work is by Austrian artist Anna Bertsch [annablume].

Amr Okba nähert sich in seinem Werk *Etappe* dem Arabischen Frühling an. Den „Tag des Zorns" – den 25. Jänner 2011 – als Ausgangspunkt nehmend, denkt Okba musikalisch über das Aufbegehren gegen das erstarrte Regime nach. Der Rhythmus des Regimes und der Alltagstrott drücken sich im Streben nach dem täglichen Überleben aus. Dieser Rhythmus wird aber akustisch gebrochen, als die innere Stimme zu einem Aufstand gegen das vorherrschende System ruft, deren Stimme an jenem Tag Abertausende folgen. Dennoch kann der Aufstand nur eine Etappe sein, das Ende sieht Okba als immer noch offen. Die Visualisierung dazu kommt von der österreichischen Künstlerin Anna Bertsch [annablume].

Piano Solo of the Soundtrack *Merry Christmas, Mr. Lawrence*
Ryuichi Sakamoto

Jazz Study, Triple Paced (First Version) I&II
John Cage

Performed by Japanese pianist Maki Namekawa
Visualization by Candaş Şişman / NOHlab / Plato Media Lab

An intimate experiential space will be the setting for Japanese pianist Maki Namekawa's performance of the works of two visionary composers who are also considered great thinkers. Her concert marks Ryuchi Sakamoto's 60th birthday and the 100th anniversary of John Cage's birth. The visualizations that Candaş Şişman and the crew at NOHlab / Plato Media Lab developed for the Ars Electronica Center's Deep Space that gets visitors right up close to the projection walls can be expected to work in a surprising new way in the wide open space of the Hall.

Einen intimen Erlebnisraum widmet die japanische Pianistin Maki Namekawa den Werken zweier visionärer Komponisten, die auch als große Denker gelten dürfen. Mit ihren Klavierrezitationen gratuliert sie Ryuchi Sakamoto zum 60. und John Cage zum 100. Geburtstag. Die für den Deep Space des Ars Electroncia Center, mit seiner fast intimen Nähe zu den Projektonswänden entwickelten Visualisierungen von Candaş Şişman und dem Team von NOHlab / Plato Media Lab kommen im großen offenen Saal des Brucknerhauses auf überraschend neue Weise zur Wirkung.

The City / Five Years Older by Dirk Koy / Equipo
Countdown by Céline Desrumaux
Unnamed Soundsculpture by Daniel Franke, Cédric Kiefer

Serving as intermezzi between the orchestral pieces are three works of animation from the Prix Ars Electronica. Two of them are visual interpretations of pieces of music: In *Countdown*, Céline Desrumaux tells her story to the music of Apparat; *The City* by Dirk Koy / Equipo was made as a music video for the band Five Years Older. *Unnamed Soundsculpture* by Daniel Franke and Cédric Kiefer features an impressive symbiosis of dance, computer animation and sounds from Machinefabriek's piece *Kreukeltape.*

Als Intermezzi zu den Orchesterstücken kommen drei Animationen aus dem Prix Ars Electronica zum Einsatz. Zwei davon sind visuelle Interpretationen von Musikstücken: Céline Desrumaux erzählt ihre Geschichte *Countdown* zur Musik von Apparat, und *The City* von Dirk Koy / Equipo ist als Musikvideo für die Band Fives Years Older entstanden. In *Unnamed Soundsculpture* von Daniel Franke und Cédric Kiefer kommt es zu einer überzeugenden Symbiose von Tanz, Computeranimation und den Sounds von Machinefabrieks Musikstück *Kreukeltape.*

This is a Recorded Message by Jean-Thomas Bédard

In the spirit of the festival theme, the selected short film is a work from 1973 and thus a time before there were PCs and cell phones. Canadian filmmaker Jean-Thomas Bédard and composer Alain Clavier created a montage of hundreds of advertising images and newspaper photos from this time. *This is a Recorded Message* presents a consumers' view of the world as reflected in the mass media.

Ganz im Zeichen des Festivalthemas steht die Wahl eines Kurzfilms aus dem Jahr 1973, einer Zeit also, noch bevor es PCs und Handies gab. Der kanadische Filmemacher Jean-Thomas Bédard und der Komponist Alain Clavier haben für *This is a Recorded Message* hunderte von Werbesujets und Zeitungsfotos montiert und bringen uns das massenmediale Konsum-Weltbild dieser Zeit in Erinnerung.

Ö1 Kunstradio: G.X. Jupitter-Larsen

Rounding things out is a performance by G.X. Jupitter-Larsen, a radio artist and author from Los Angeles who's collaborating with Ö1-Kunstradio on the occasion of the 25th anniversary of this radio art program that's unique the world over.

Den Abschluss bildet eine Performance von G.X. Jupitter-Larsen, Radiokünstler und Autor aus Los Angeles – Teil einer Kooperation mit dem Ö1-Kunstradio anlässlich des 25-jährigen Bestehens dieses weltweit einmaligen Radio-Kunst-Programms.

Resonant Bridges is the latest step in the successful collaboration of the Bruckner Orchestra Linz under Dennis Russell Davies, the Brucknerhaus Linz and Ars Electronica. Their aim is to test innovative ways of combining music and new visual forms of expression. Curators: Dennis Russell Davies, Wolfgang Winkler, Heribert Schröder, Gerfried Stocker

Deep Space Music

An encounter of sound and image, music and computer animation in the Ars Electronica Center's extraordinary projection space—300 m² of high-definition visuals in a setting custom-made for real-time interaction and 3D experiences, a space conducive to intensity and intimacy on the part of artist and audience member alike. In Deep Space, Japanese pianist Maki Namekawa and visualization artist Candaş Şişman with the NOHlab / Plato Media Lab crew are collaboratively staging a concert of supreme musical as well as visual artistry.

Begegnung von Klang und Bild, Musik und Computeranimation im außergewöhnlichen Projektionsraum des Ars Electronica Center, der mit seiner 300 Quadratmeter großen Projektionsfläche gleichzeitig Interaktion und 3D-Erlebnis ermöglicht. Ein für Künstler und Publikum intensiver und intimer Erlebnisraum. Die japanische Pianistin Maki Namekawa und der Visualisierer Candaş Şişman mit dem Team von NOHlab / Plato Media Lab gestalten ein musikalisch wie visuell anspruchsvolles Konzert im Deep Space.

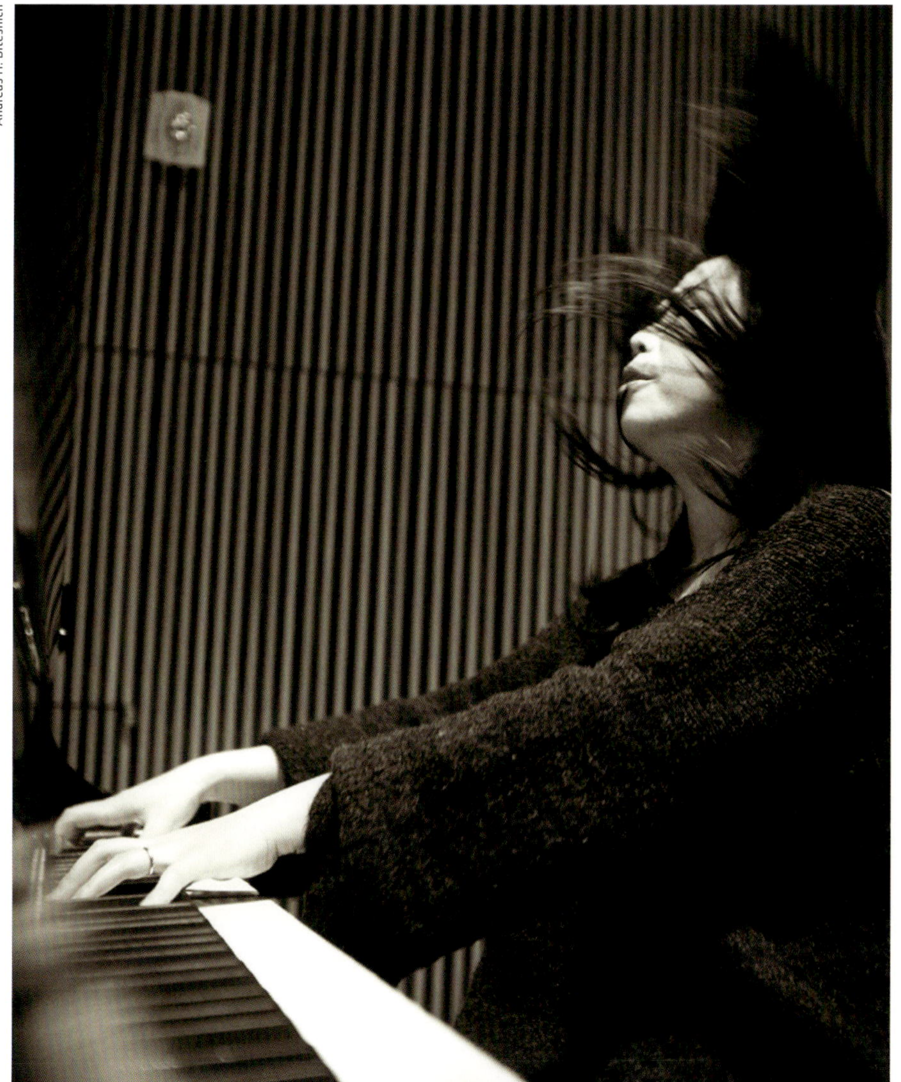

Andreas H. Bitesnich

Fom the film Merry Christmas, Mr. Lawrence
Ryuichi Sakamoto (*1952)
Merry Christmas, Mr. Lawrence–The Fight–A Hearty Breakfast–Last Regards

Ryuichi Sakamoto, the Japanese composer and artist, is celebrating his 60th birthday this year. He works in various musical genres including classical, avant-garde pop (YMO-Yellow-MagicOrchestra) and jazz, and has several film sound tracks to his credit (including *The Last Emperor* directed by Bernardo Bertolucci). In 2005, his composition was the year's most popular ringtone for Finnish cell phone maker Nokia. He is also a supporter of the Sayonara Nuclear Power Plants campaign that responded to the Fukushima catastrophe by organizing demonstrations and collecting signatures calling for a nuclear-free Japan. *Merry Christmas, Mr. Lawrence* is a 1983 film by Japanese director Nagisa Oshima. The original Japanese title means "Merry Christmas on the battlefield." Ryuichi Sakamoto composed the hauntingly moving soundtrack. There is a piano solo version of this music as a suite.

Ryuichi Sakamoto, der japanische Komponist und Künstler, feiert in diesem Jahr seinen sechzigsten Geburtstag. Er bewegt sich in verschiedenen musikalischen Genres wie Klassik, Avantgarde-Pop (YMO-YellowMagicOrchestra) oder Jazz und hat einige Filmmusiken komponiert (u. a. *Der letzte Kaiser* unter der Regie von Bernardo Bertolucci). Für den finnischen Mobiltelefonhersteller Nokia komponierte er die im Jahr 2005 beliebtesten Klingel- und Signaltöne für das Handy. Außerdem unterstützt er die Kampagne *„Atomkraft, Sayonara!"*, die nach der Nuklearkatastrophe von Fukushima mit Demonstrationen und einer Unterschriftensammlung zum Atomausstieg Japans aufgerufen hat. 1983 entstand der Film *Merry Christmas, Mr. Lawrence* unter dem japanischen Regisseur Nagisa Oshima. Der japanische Originaltitel bedeutet auf Deutsch „Fröhliche Weihnachten auf dem Schlachtfeld" und Ryuichi Sakamoto komponierte die Filmmusik dazu. Von dieser Musik gibt es eine Klavier-Solofassung als Suite.

Visuals: Candaş Şişman, Deniz Kader / NOHlab / Plato Media Lab

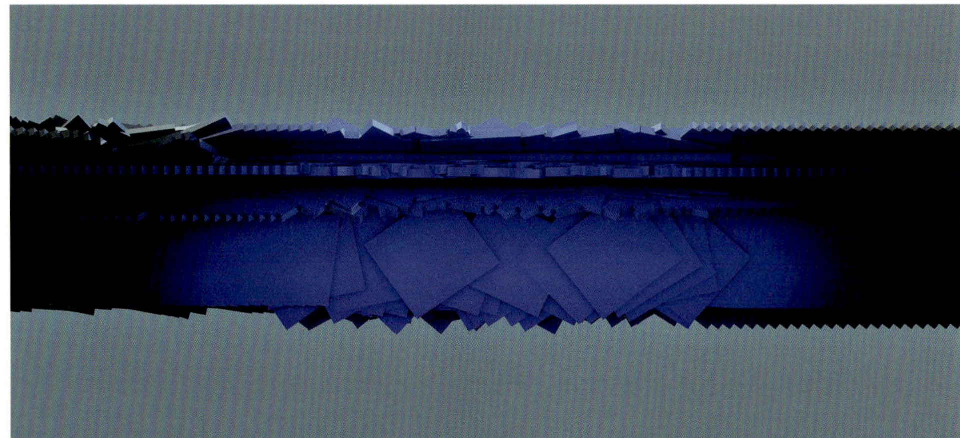

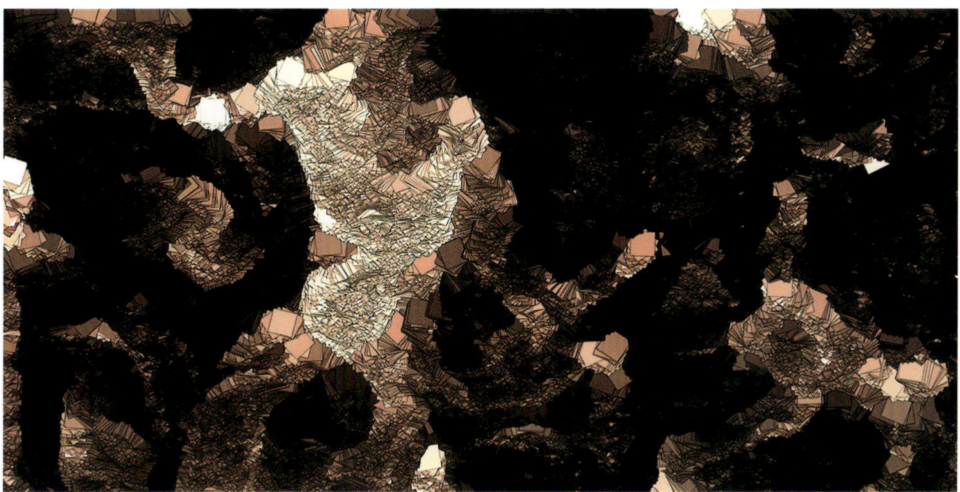

Visuals: Candaş Şişman, Deniz Kader / NOHlab / Plato Media Lab

Jazz Study
John Cage (1912–1992)
Triple-Paced (First Version) I & II

American composer/artist John Cage would have celebrated his 100th birthday this year. He was the central figure in the Happening movement that emerged in the late 1950s. Once, in a hotel after a concert late at night when all the restaurants were closed, my husband Dennis Russell Davies got to enjoy a macrobiotic meal of brown rice and mushrooms prepared by Cage himself, which, in my opinion, says a lot about his character. The composition I'll play in *Deep Space Music* is a quintessentially classic solo work for a piano that gets by without any metal nails between its sides, but isn't a toy piano either. The sound gets across Cage's philosophy—his serenity, the wild intensity of minimalist materials. One can just imagine the wonderful smile on his face as he collected mushrooms that had suddenly just sprung up out of the earth. This simplicity fascinated him, and this simplicity is also what he strove for in his music.

Der amerikanische Komponist und Künstler John Cage würde 2012 seinen hundertsten Geburtstag feiern. Er war die Schlüsselfigur der gegen Ende der 1950er Jahre entstandenen „Happening-Bewegung". Mein Mann Dennis Russell Davies hat einmal nach einem Konzert, als kein Restaurant mehr geöffnet hatte, im Hotel mit Cage dessen selbst gekochte makrobiotische Mahlzeit – braunen Reis und Pilze – gegessen, was meiner Meinung nach viel über seinen Charakter aussagt. Die Komposition, die ich bei *Deep Space Music* spiele, ist ein sehr klassisches Klavier-Solowerk – es kommt ganz ohne Metallnägel zwischen den Klavierseiten aus und ist auch kein Toy-Piano. Der Klang transportiert Cages Philosophie – seine Gelassenheit, die wilde Intensität minimaler Materialien. Man kann sich sein wunderbares Lächeln beim Sammeln der Pilze vorstellen, die wie aus dem Nichts der Erde kommend plötzlich da sind. Diese Einfachheit hat ihn fasziniert - und diese Einfachheit strebt er auch in seiner Musik an.

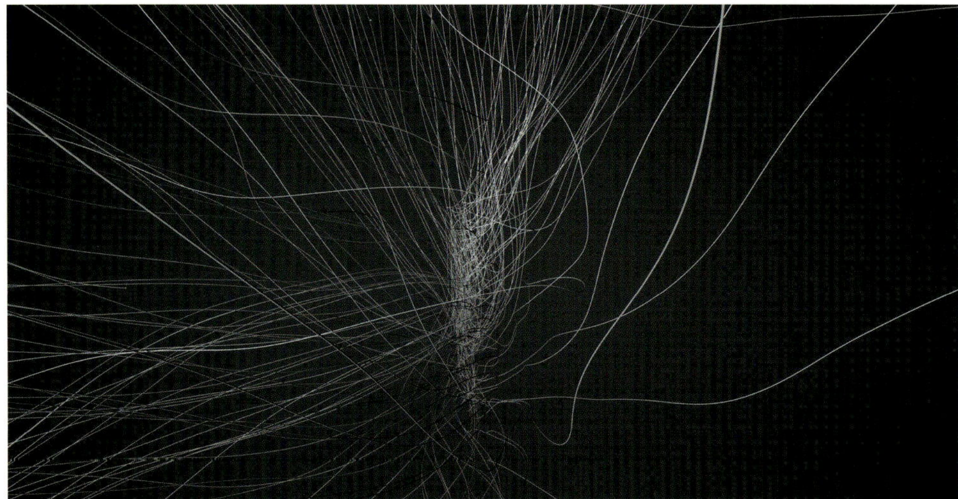

Visuals: Candaş Şişman, Deniz Kader / NOHlab / Plato Media Lab

From *The Hours*
Philip Glass (*1937)

The Poet Acts
Morning passages

Philip Glass turned 75 this year. He is a good friend whom I often meet on a purely social basis. His daily Qigong training and his Tibetan Buddhist faith create a place of serenity for him that provides a welcome respite from everyday life. For me, it's wondrous how he has managed over the years to take very similar minimalistic phrases and create so many compositions out of them. His tonal conceptions and the use of a wide array of instruments always bring forth unexpected sound experiences in his works. In *Deep Space Music* I'll play his piano solo suite from the film *The Hours*. From his very first note, he creates a mental world that seems totally removed from the present.

Philip Glass ist heuer 75 Jahre alt geworden. Er ist ein guter Freund und ich begegne ihm auch oft ganz privat. Sein tägliches Qigong-Training und sein tibetisch-buddhistischer Glauben schaffen für ihn einen Ort der Ruhe, wo er Abstand vom Alltag findet. Für mich ist es ein Wunder, wie er seit Jahren immer wieder ganz ähnliche minimalistische Phrasen hernimmt und daraus so viele Kompositionen schafft. Seine Klangvorstellungen und der Einsatz verschiedener Instrumente führen Stück für Stück zu immer unerwarteteren Klangerlebnissen. Bei *Deep Space Music* spiele ich seine Klavier-Solosuite aus dem Film *The Hours*. Er erschafft gleich mit dem ersten Ton eine mentale Welt, die von der Gegenwart entrückt wirkt.

Text: Maki Namekawa

During the creation process of this project, we made up a system with two contradicting rules. The first rule is: we want to let the performer improvise just as she feels like doing, so the system has to be real-time processed. The second rule, on the other hand, is to make the visuals look as if the design was made just for that song, so we had to study the song in detail and create a set of possibilities with it. To make these two rules work together, we designed a new player that works like a DJ. All visuals are pre-designed but their timing changes depending on the speed improvisation. Also, there are some layers that blend into each other and are close to the music when an unexpected improvisation happens. We aim to achieve a real-time feeling combined with the quality of pre-design.

Zwei sich widersprechende Regeln bestimmten den Schaffensprozess dieses Projekts. Die erste Regel lautete: Die Ausführende soll völlig frei improvisieren können, weshalb das System alles in Echtzeit verarbeiten muss. Die zweite Regel dagegen besagte: Die Visuals sollen wie explizit für diesen Song gemacht wirken. Daher mussten wir ihn bis ins Kleinste analysieren und verschiedene Möglichkeiten für jedes Detail generieren. Damit diese beiden Regeln auch wirklich zusammen funktionieren, haben wir einen neuen Player entwickelt, der wie ein DJ arbeitet. Alle Visuals sind fertig gestaltet, doch ihr Timing ändert sich mit dem Tempo der Improvisation. Zusätzlich überlagern sich mehrere Layer, sodass die Bilder auch bei unerwarteten Improvisationen ganz nah an der Musik bleiben. Das Projekt soll das Gefühl einer Echtzeitanwendung und die Qualität vorgefertigter Elemente miteinander vereinen.

Text: Candaş Şişman

NOHlab–Art Direction / Visuals: Candaş Şişman, Deniz Kader
Plato Media Lab Team–Technical direction / Interaction design
Team Supervisor: Bager Akbay; Coding & Support: Ismail Kasarci, Osman Koc, Zeynep Ozkazanc, Zeynep Nal, Senem Umut, Güliz Turan, Mehmet Kalaman

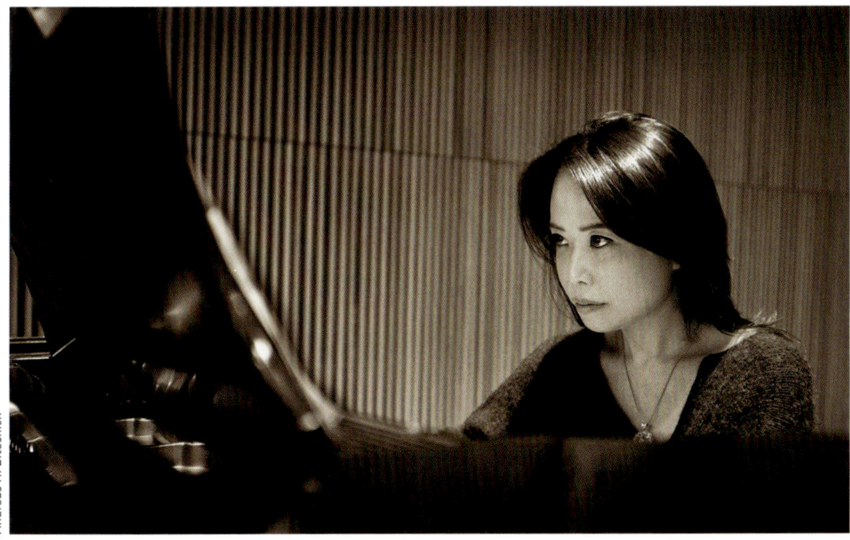

Andreas H. Bitesnich

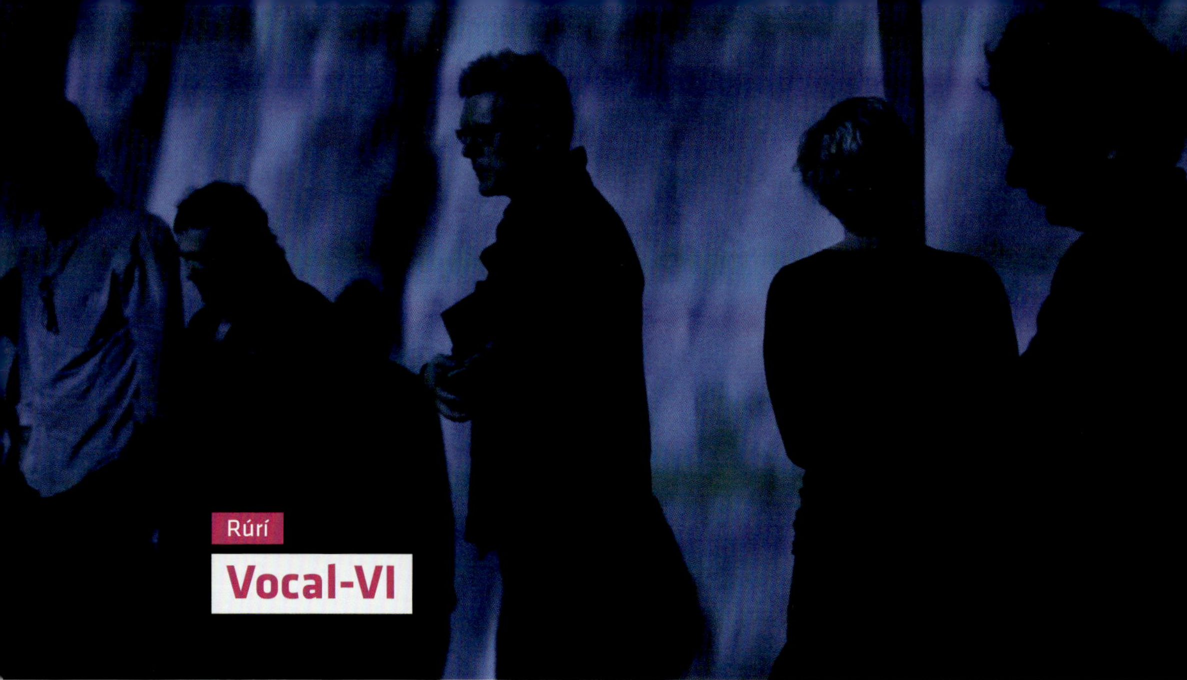

María Rún Jóhannsdóttir

Rúrí, one of the Nordic lands' leading artists, has over three decades of intensive creativity to her credit. Her works are inquiries into the great cosmic and terrestrial interrelationships. "For me, art is philosophy," says Rúrí, who has committed herself to a life lived intentionally and to interacting responsibly with nature.

Rúrí has been active since the early 1990s as a member of the Experiment Environment artists' group, first and foremost in Scandinavia. Her first permanent work in a public space was *Rainbow* (1991) at the international airport in Keflavík, but this piece too is based on the concept of the ephemeral and the threatened—after all, a rainbow is not at all consummate and final. This gigantic steel-and-glass sculpture is related to two prior works that deal with the same motif. For a 16-millimeter film, a rainbow fashioned of hand-colored linen attached to a 17-meter-tall bamboo pole was set ablaze (1983); another one formed out of salt was exposed to the elements until it vanished (1985).

In Iceland, a rainbow—like a waterfall—is a frequently seen and always spectacular phenomenon, one that interweaves sensory stimuli with mythical potential. The rainbow stands for transience and transcendence; waterfalls, on the other hand, constitute an enduring, powerful presence. But it is precisely this impression that Rúrí calls into question in an ongoing series of works she launched in the early 21st century. With the presentation of *Archive – Endangered Waters* at the 2003 Venice Biennale, Rúrí confronted the international public with a sensitive issue: the destruction of her homeland's natural environment through the construction of gigantic hydroelectric dams. In doing so, her attention was focused on water with its factual, symbolic and spiritual significance for all the world's nations and cultures. For her visual-acoustic work *Archive,* she created portraits of threatened waterfalls in both photographic images as well as sound and presented them in a multimedia installation. In subsequent works as well, Rúrí juxtaposes the enormous power of cascading water to a formal fragility that alludes to the endangerment of this vital resource. *Vocal-VI,* a video performance conceived especially for Ars Electronica Center's Deep Space, is to be understood in this context too.

http://www.ruri.is

294

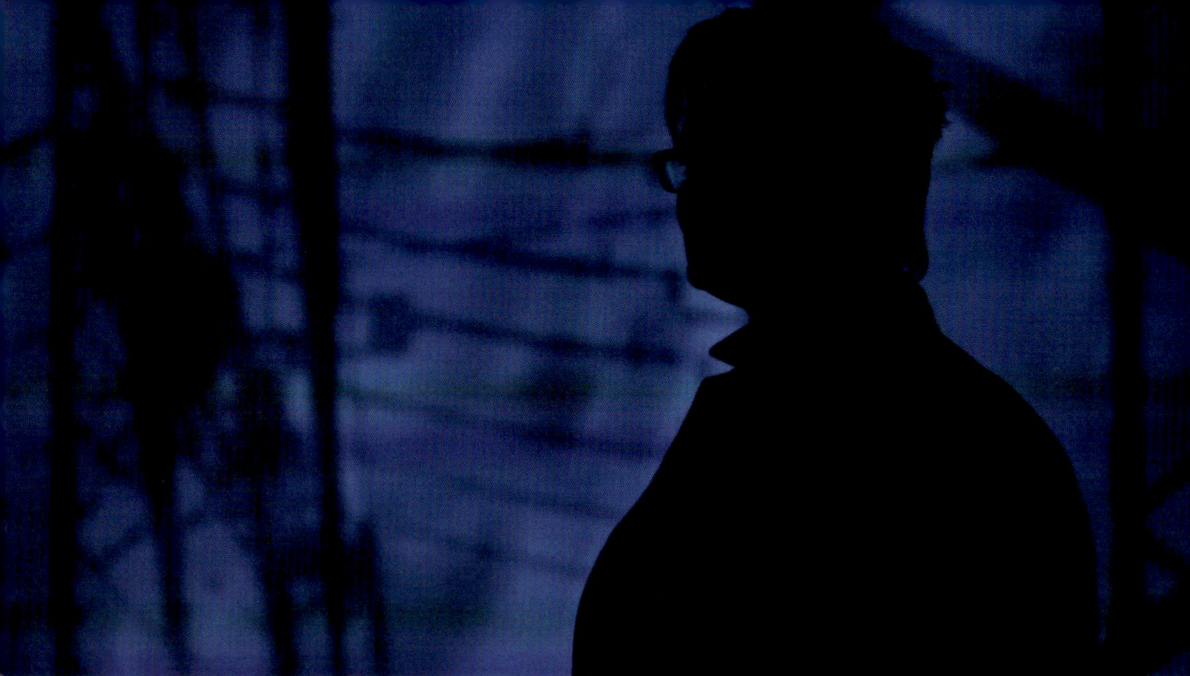

Rúrí zählt mit über drei Jahrzehnten intensivem Schaffen zu den führenden Künstlerinnen der nordischen Länder. Ihre Arbeiten hinterfragen die großen kosmischen und irdischen Zusammenhänge. „Kunst ist für mich Philosophie", sagt Rúrí, die sich für ein bewusstes Leben und den verantwortungsbewussten Umgang mit der Natur einsetzt.

Im Rahmen der Künstlergruppierung „Experiment Environment" war Rúrí seit den frühen 1990er Jahren vor allem im skandinavischen Raum aktiv. Zu dieser Zeit entstand mit *Rainbow* (1991) am Internationalen Flughafen in Keflavík ihr erstes permanentes Werk im öffentlichen Raum. Doch auch dieser Arbeit liegt das Konzept des Ephemeren und Bedrohten zugrunde, denn der Regenbogen ist nicht vollkommen. Verwandt ist diese gigantische Stahl- und Glasskulptur mit zwei vorangegangenen Arbeiten, die sich mit dem gleichen Motiv befassen: Für einen 16-mm-Film wurde ein Regenbogen aus handgefärbtem Leinen, der an einer 17 Meter hohen Bambusstange in die Luft ragte, in Brand gesetzt (1983), ein anderer in Salz geformt und der Witterung so lange ausgesetzt, bis er verschwand (1985).

Der Regenbogen ist wie der Wasserfall ein in Island häufiges und immer spektakuläres Phänomen, bei dem sich sinnliche Reize mit mythischem Potenzial verknüpfen. Steht der Regenbogen für das Ephemere und Transzendente, so sind die Wasserfälle von dauerhafter, kraftvoller Präsenz. Genau diesen Eindruck relativiert Rúrí in einer Anfang des 21. Jahrhunderts beginnenden und sich bis heute fortsetzenden Werkreihe. Mit der Präsentation ihres *Archive – Endangered Waters* auf der Venedig Biennale 2003 hat Rúrí der Weltöffentlichkeit ein sensibles Thema vor Augen geführt: Die Vernichtung der Natur ihres Heimatlandes durch den Bau überdimensionierter Staudämme. Ihr Hauptaugenmerk lag dabei auf dem Wasser mit seiner faktischen, symbolischen und spirituellen Bedeutung für alle Nationen und Kulturen der Welt. Für das visuell-akustische *Archive* porträtierte sie bedrohte Wasserfälle, sowohl in fotografischem Bild wie in Sound und präsentierte diese in einer multimedialen Installation. Auch in sich anschließenden Arbeiten setzt Rúrí der gewaltigen Kraft der Wassermassen eine formale Fragilität entgegen, die auf die Bedrohung der lebensnotwendigen Ressource hinweist. In diesen Kontext fällt auch die eigens für den Deep Space des Ars Electronica Center konzipierte Videoperformance *Vocal-VI.*
http://www.ruri.is

Text: Christian Schoen

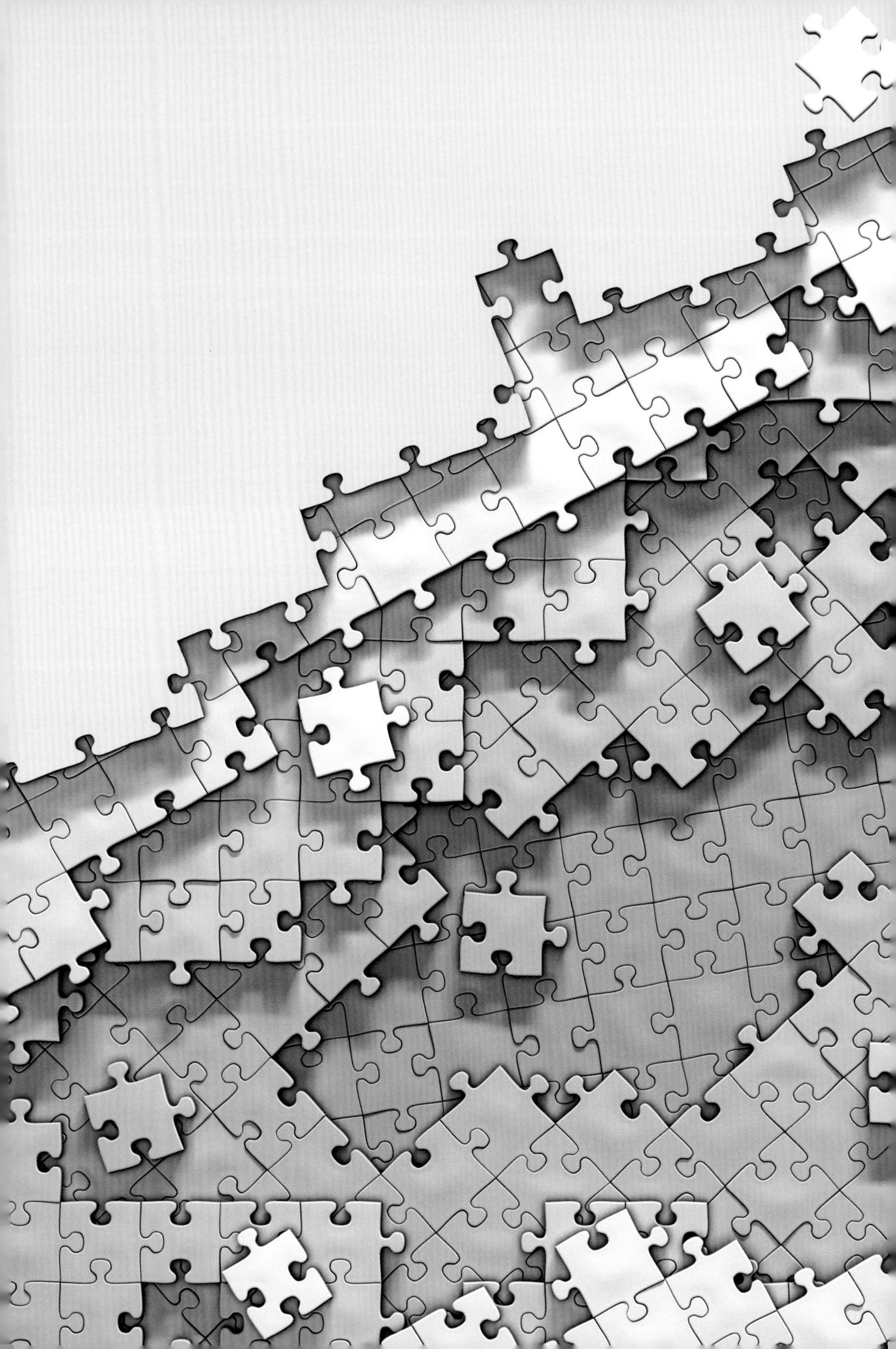

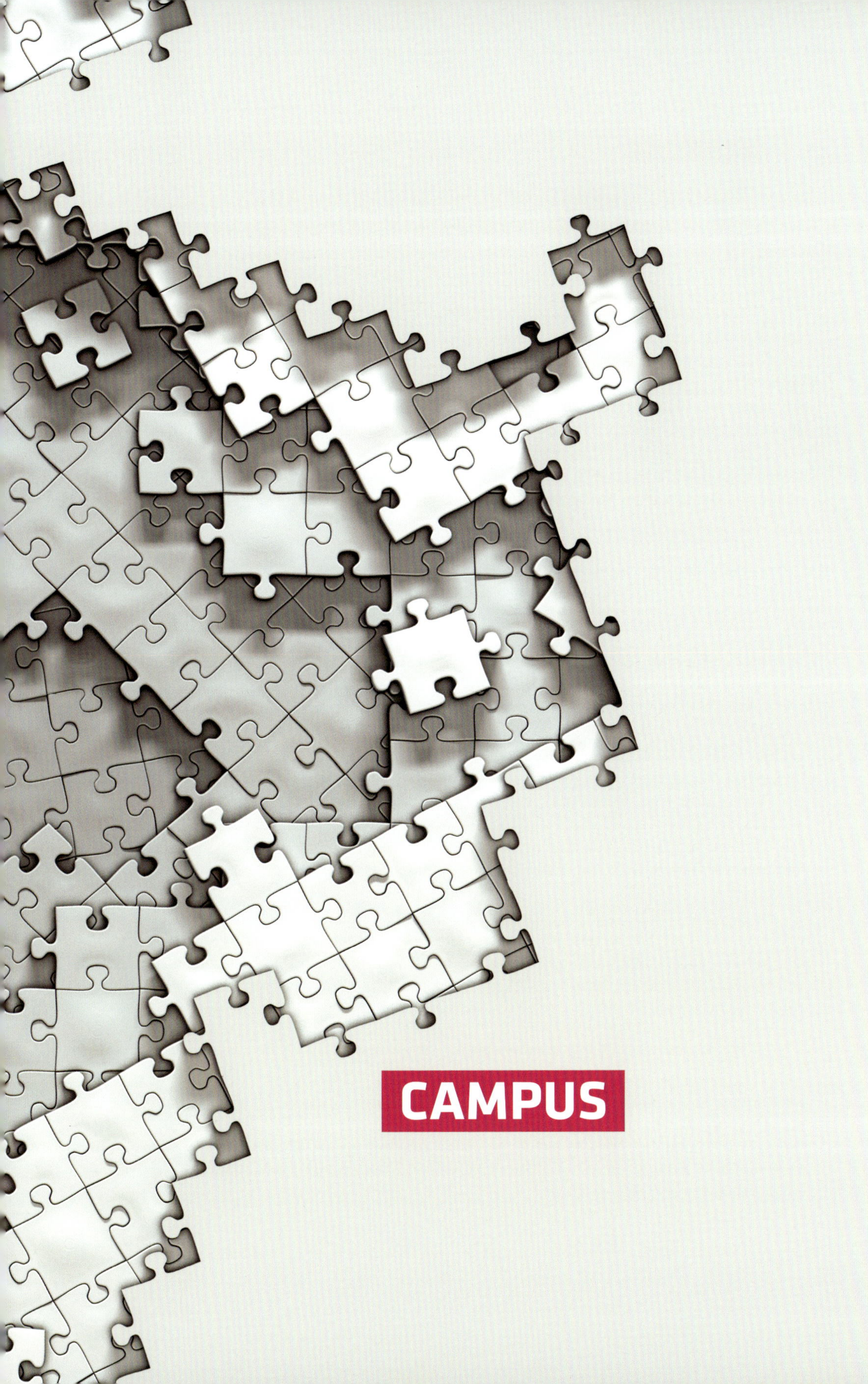
CAMPUS

Sabine Sanio

Sound Studies and Auditory Culture
Berlin University of the Arts—The Sound Studies Master's Program

The *Sound Studies* master's program is producing this year's Campus at Ars Electronica. This is a great opportunity for a relatively new program to present current and former students' work to a large audience and to acquaint visitors with what this field is all about.

In the media, at concerts and in clubs, we are constantly confronted by artificial domains of sound & imagery, the suggestive power of which is attributable not least of all to modern audio technology. Nevertheless, concepts for the design of our auditory urban culture are still in a formative stage. And the question that arises is whether it would be possible for us to comprehensively design everyday life to an extent that is already the case in the media. But before this question can be answered, society has to be sustainably sensitized to auditory experience and phenomena.

Towards a Culture of Hearing

Many people still persistently neglect the auditory dimension of our world, though all of us are intimately aware of sound and the language of things, and attuned to noises' eloquence—they not only aid us in orientation; they make our world a lively place and endow it with spatial depth.

The theory of auditory culture emphasizes this issue, in that it conceives of auditory phenomena as constituting an integral part of our reality, a dimension in its own right. It focuses on hearing and thereby shifts perspective from an object of perception to a process of perceiving. Accordingly, the classical idea of the reception of a musical work represents only one particular instance. The center of attention is occupied by perception as such, the subject matter of psychoacoustics and perception psychology. Phenomenology, on the other hand, deals with the complex perceptual situations encountered in everyday life, whereby auditory orientation inevitably occurs in interaction with the other senses, especially the eyes, motor functions and the corporeal experience of the whole person. Ultimately, hearing has to be conceived in conjunction with the other forms of human expression to which it constantly reacts—from the voice and speech all the way to musical expressions.

On the basis of this theoretical approach, the *Sound Studies* master's program deals with the entire spectrum of sounds and noises produced by our modern culture. This shifts the focus to cultural life, which brings out novel insights into the functions of our auditory faculties. But establishing the realm of hearing as a cultural sphere in its own right also calls for criteria and categories of perception and design of our acoustic environment.

The *Sound Studies* Master's Program

Following a multiyear start-up phase, the *Sound Studies* master's program at the UdK–Berlin University of the Arts was launched in 2006. Situated at the nexus of art and science, theory and practice, this project-oriented program of study offers a curriculum that includes both theoretical scholarship as well as courses in art and design. Its trademark: acquiring practical skills, working independently on projects entailing art or applied science, and encounters with related theoretical considerations.

The program was expanded in 2012 to include two required courses: Theory and History of Auditory Culture and Hearing Competence. In Hearing Competence students train their ability to assess and describe the spectral and spatial characteristics of a sound, and, if need be, to modify them. There are five electives: Experimental Sound Design deals with sound art and similar phenomena at the interface of music and graphic art. The opportunity to go more deeply into the theoretical-scholarly aspects of this field is offered by the course Auditory Culture: Research, whereas Auditory Design, Auditory Media Design and Auditory Architecture are application-oriented.

Auditory Design considers sound from the perspective of function and includes, in addition to sound branding and interaction design, the auditory design of functional spaces. Auditory Architecture expands the design possibilities available to architects, urban planners and landscape architects by providing them with a basis for using acoustic experiences as the point of departure of design work. Auditory Media Design deals with the complex interrelationship between the tools of audio technology and the results to be achieved with them, with particular emphasis on the possibilities of producing sounds and structures in real time and the resulting implications for performance and composition.

All of these courses impart skills and insights in order to make the framework conditions in film, advertising, product design and urban planning productive for the design of auditory culture. At the same time, though, they formulate programmatic positions. Whoever offers an exclusively auditory approach for design, media design or architecture needs a concept that goes beyond strictly auditory considerations, that reflects the fundamentals of this field as well as the changes that come about as soon as hearing is taken into account. Accordingly, these courses convey to students not only fundamental insights into the central aspects, various manifestations and elements of auditory culture; they also impart the empirical foundation of auditory theory that places these various areas into an overall context and puts forth comprehensive criteria of auditory experience and design.

Lebensräume—Sound Studies at the 2012 Ars Electronica Festival

The theme of Sound Studies' showcase at this year's Ars Electronica is *Lebensräume* (Habitats). In addition to an exhibition of the same name featuring works by current undergrads and alumni, there's a presentation of the Auditory Architecture Research Unit's *Klangumwelten Ernst-Reuter-Platz* research project. The *Lebensräume* theme focuses attention on hearing in various experiential spaces and situations. This broad spectrum of constellations and interactions leads almost inevitably to an inquiry into how the way we experience acoustic phenomena affects our conception of the reality of life. Implicitly, the concept of *Lebensräume* thus also reflects the phenomenological concept of *Lebenswelt* (the world we live in)—instead of interpreting the intuitive experience of everyday life as an expression of a particular conception of reality, the experience itself is taken seriously here and, in its entire diversity, made accessible to the senses. Speeches at Kepler Salon and afo architekturforum oberösterreich as well as a series of projects, events and performances in urban spaces round out the lineup of presentations Sound Studies is staging at Ars Electronica.

lebensraeume.soundstudies.info
www.udk-berlin.de/soundstudies

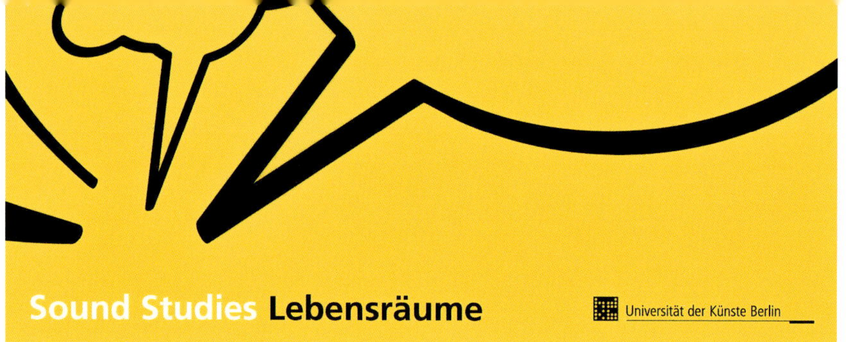

Sabine Sanio

Sound Studies und die Kultur des Auditiven
Universität der Künste Berlin – Masterstudiengang Sound Studies

Der Masterstudiengang *Sound Studies* ist 2012 Campus-Partner der Ars Electronica – für den noch jungen Studiengang eine gute Gelegenheit, sich vor einem größeren Publikum mit eigenen Arbeiten zu präsentieren und seinen Gegenstandsbereich anschaulich zu machen.
In den Medien, in Konzerten und Clubs geraten wir heute ständig in künstliche Klang- und Bildwelten, deren suggestive Kraft sich nicht zuletzt moderner Audiotechnik verdankt. Demgegenüber stehen Konzepte zur Gestaltung unserer auditiven urbanen Kultur noch ganz am Anfang, und es fragt sich, ob wir uns im Alltag eine ähnlich umfassende Gestaltung wie in den Medien wünschen können. Doch bevor diese Frage geklärt werden kann, muss zunächst eine nachhaltige Sensibilisierung für das Auditive erfolgen.

Auf dem Weg zu einer Kultur des Hörens

Bis heute wird die Dimension des Hörens gerne vernachlässigt, dabei wissen wir alle um den Klang und die Sprache der Dinge, um die Beredsamkeit der Geräusche – sie helfen uns nicht allein bei der Orientierung, sie machen unsere Welt lebendig und verleihen ihr räumliche Tiefe. Die Theorie auditiver Kultur verleiht diesem Thema Nachdruck, indem sie das Auditive als eigenständige Dimension unserer Wirklichkeit begreift. Sie stellt das Hören in den Mittelpunkt und bewirkt damit einen Wechsel der Perspektive vom Wahrnehmungsgegenstand zum Wahrnehmenden. Die klassische Idee musikalischer Werkrezeption stellt dabei nur einen Sonderfall dar. Im Zentrum steht die Wahrnehmung als solche, die in Psychoakustik und Wahrnehmungspsychologie Thema ist, während die Phänomenologie sich mit den komplexen Wahrnehmungssituationen des Alltags befasst: Dort erfolgt die hörende Orientierung stets in Interaktion mit den anderen Sinnen, besonders mit dem Auge sowie mit der Motorik und der körperlichen Erfahrung der gesamten Person. Schließlich muss das Hören zusammengedacht werden mit den menschlichen Ausdrucksformen, auf die es ständig reagiert, angefangen mit Stimme und Sprechen bis hin zur musikalischen Betätigung. Auf der Grundlage dieser Theorieansätze befasst sich der Masterstudiengang *Sound Studies* mit dem ganzen Spektrum der Klänge und Geräusche unserer modernen Kultur. Damit verschiebt sich der Blickwinkel auf das kulturelle Leben, was neue Einsichten in die Funktionen des Auditiven eröffnet. Um jedoch die Sphäre des Hörens als eigenständigen Bereich unserer Kultur zu etablieren, benötigt man auch Kriterien und Kategorien der Wahrnehmung und Gestaltung unserer klingenden Umwelt.

Der Masterstudiengang Sound Studies

Nach einer mehrjährigen Gründungsphase wurde der Masterstudiengang *Sound Studies* 2006 an der Universität der Künste Berlin eröffnet. Angesiedelt im Spannungsfeld von Kunst und Wissenschaft, Theorie und Praxis verbindet dieser als Projektstudium angelegte Studiengang theoretisch-wissenschaftliche und künstlerisch-gestalterische Lehrangebote. Zu seinen

Markenzeichen gehört die Kombination aus Erlernen praktischer Fähigkeiten, Entwerfen eigener praktischer oder künstlerischer Projekte und Auseinandersetzung mit entsprechenden Theorieansätzen. Seit der Erweiterung 2012 gibt es zwei Pflichtfächer: Theorie und Geschichte auditiver Kultur und Kompetenz des Hörens. In der Kompetenz des Hörens trainieren die Studierenden ihre Fähigkeit, spektrale und räumliche Eigenschaften eines Klangereignisses einzuschätzen, zu beschreiben und gegebenenfalls zu verändern. Fünf Wahlpflichtfächer kommen hinzu: Die Experimentelle Klanggestaltung widmet sich der Klangkunst und ähnlicher Phänomene im Grenzbereich von Musik und Bildender Kunst. Die Möglichkeit zur Vertiefung der theoretisch-wissenschaftlichen Auseinandersetzung bietet das Fach Auditive Kultur: Recherche. Demgegenüber sind die Fächer Auditives Design, Auditive Mediengestaltung und Auditive Architektur anwendungsbezogen konzipiert. Das Auditive Design betrachtet Klang aus der Perspektive der Funktion und umfasst neben Sound Branding und Interaction Design auch die auditive Gestaltung funktionaler Räume. Die Auditive Architektur hingegen erweitert die Gestaltungsmöglichkeiten der Gebäude-, Stadt- und Landschaftsplanung, indem sie die hörende Erfahrung zum Ausgangspunkt für die Entwurfsarbeit nimmt. Die Auditive Mediengestaltung schließlich beschäftigt sich mit den komplexen Wechselwirkungen zwischen Werkzeugen der Audiotechnik und den damit zu erzielenden Resultaten, mit besonderem Schwerpunkt auf den Möglichkeiten der Erzeugung von Klang und Struktur in Echtzeit und den sich daraus ergebenden Implikationen für Performance und Komposition. Alle diese Fächer vermitteln Fähigkeiten und Kenntnisse, um die Rahmenbedingungen in Film, Werbung, Produktdesign und Stadtplanung für die Gestaltung der auditiven Kultur produktiv zu machen. Zugleich formulieren sie jedoch programmatische Positionen: Wer für Design, Mediengestaltung oder Architektur einen ausschließlich auditiven Zugang anbietet, benötigt ein über die Problematik des Auditiven hinausweisendes Konzept, das die Grundlagen des Fachs ebenso reflektiert wie die Veränderungen, die sich ergeben, sobald man das Hören einbezieht. Insofern vermitteln diese Fächer den Studierenden nicht allein grundlegende Kenntnisse über zentrale Aspekte, Erscheinungsweisen und Elemente der auditiven Kultur, sie liefern auch das empirische Fundament für eine Theorie des Auditiven, die die unterschiedlichen Bereiche in einen Gesamtzusammenhang rückt und übergreifende Kriterien auditiver Erfahrung und Gestaltung entwirft.

Lebensräume – Sound Studies bei Ars Electronica 2012

Die *Sound Studies* präsentieren sich beim Ars Electronica Festival mit dem Thema „Lebensräume". Gezeigt wird neben der gleichnamigen Ausstellung mit Arbeiten aktueller und ehemaliger Studierender auch das von der Auditory Architecture Research Unit realisierte Forschungsprojekt *Klangumwelten Ernst-Reuter-Platz.*

Das Thema „Lebensräume" lenkt die Aufmerksamkeit auf das Hören in unterschiedlichsten Erfahrungsräumen und -situationen. Dieses breite Spektrum an Konstellationen und Interaktionen führt fast zwangsläufig zu der Frage, auf welche Weise die Hörerfahrung unsere Vorstellung von der Lebenswirklichkeit prägt. Implizit reflektiert der Begriff der Lebensräume damit auch das phänomenologische Konzept der Lebenswelt – statt die intuitive, alltägliche Erfahrung als Ausdruck einer bestimmten Wirklichkeitsvorstellung zu interpretieren, wird hier diese Erfahrung selbst ernst genommen und in ihrer Vielfalt erfahrbar gemacht.

Vorträge im Kepler Salon und im afo architekturforum oberösterreich sowie eine Reihe mit Projekten, Events und Performances im urbanen Raum runden den Auftritt der *Sound Studies* bei der diesjährigen Ars Electronica ab.

lebensraeume.soundstudies.info
www.udk-berlin.de/soundstudies

Sam Auinger

Lebensräume
The Exhibition of the Sound Studies Master's Program

Lebensräume is a hybrid: simultaneously an exhibition and a showcase spotlighting the UdK–Berlin University of the Arts' new *Sound Studies* master's program. A jury selected the best works from among submissions by current and former *Sound Studies* students. As artistic director, my job is to curate and produce the exhibition with the support of Georg Spehr. *Lebensräume* subsumes three themes: The Urban Lebensraum; Space, Resonance, Atmosphere; and Participation: Actions and Performances. Visitors are invited to get acquainted with *Sound Studies* by partaking of, thinking about, listening to and participating in this exhibition.

The Urban Lebensraum

Five artistic R&D projects focusing on five Berlin neighborhoods—*Fehrbelliner Platz, Siemensstadt, Kurfürstendamm, Prenzlauer Berg* and *Fasanenplatz*—scrutinize the complex interrelationship among history, politics, city planning and architecture with their manifold interactions of social and economic forces. Audio miniatures custom-tailored to each neighborhood respond to two hearing-related questions: "How do we experience the cityscape?" and "What do our urban neighborhoods have to offer our senses?" Thus, the approach they take to understanding these places covers a broad spectrum.
Another artistic inquiry into an urban neighborhood will actually take place during the festival. British artist Peter Cusack, the inventor of so-called *sonic journalism,* and some students currently enrolled in the program will do auditory research on Linz's Main Square. Their findings and results will be made public on a daily basis in the exhibition and online.

Lebensräume ist ein Hybrid: zugleich Ausstellung und Präsentation des jungen Masterstudiengangs *Sound Studies* der UdK Berlin. Eine Jury traf eine Auswahl der besten Arbeiten aus den Bewerbungen von ehemaligen und aktuellen Studierenden der *Sound Studies.* Als künstlerischer Leiter kam mir die Aufgabe zu, die Realisierung der Ausstellung mit der Unterstützung von Georg Spehr kuratorisch zu betreuen. Thematisch gliedert sich die Ausstellung *Lebensräume* in drei Bereiche: Der urbane Lebensraum; Raum, Resonanz, Atmosphäre; Partizipation: Aktionen und Performances. BesucherInnen sind eingeladen, studierend, betrachtend, hörend und sich beteiligend *Sound Studies* kennen zu lernen.

Der urbane Lebensraum

Fünf künstlerische Stadtteilforschungsprojekte in Berlin - *Fehrbelliner Platz, Siemensstadt, Kurfürstendamm, Prenzlauer Berg* und *Fasanenplatz* - gehen dem komplexen Zusammenhang von Geschichte, Politik, Stadtplanung und Architektur mit ihrem vielfältigen Beziehungsgeflecht aus sozialen und ökonomischen Interaktionen nach. Zu jedem untersuchten Quartier fragt eine Reihe von Audiominiaturen auditiv/hörend: „Wie erleben wir Stadt?" und: „Was haben unsere städtischen Quartiere unseren Sinnen zu bieten?" und spannen so ein breites Spektrum an möglichen Verständniszugängen.
In einem weiteren künstlerischen Stadtteilforschungsprojekt widmen sich während des Festivals aktuell Studierende des Studiengangs unter Leitung des britischen Künstlers Peter Cusack, dem Erfinder des *sonic journalism,* auditiv dem Linzer Hauptplatz. Täglich werden die aktuellen Ergebnisse in der Ausstellung sowie im Netz veröffentlicht.

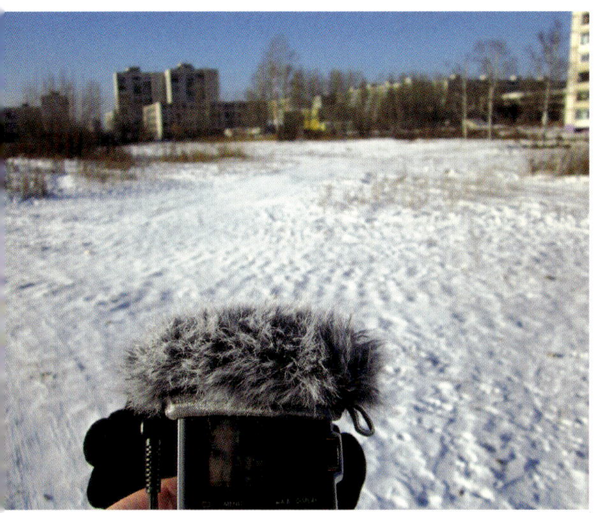

Johannes Kiersch

Methodisch verwandt ist die Masterarbeit von Johannes Kiersch, *Auf Wiedersehen, geliebte Mutter – Sibirien und der Ferne Osten erwarten uns!* Seine Klangreise führte Kiersch in den Fernen Osten Russlands, nach Wladiwostok, Komsomolsk am Amur und auf die Baikal-Amur-Magistrale. Seine zwischen Simulation und Realität, Stille und Lärm changierende Klang-collage kombiniert Zwischentöne aus sowjetischer Vergangenheit und russischer Gegenwart, aus verlassenen Fabriken und von chinesischen Märkten, aus einem ehemaligen Straflager und einem Rohstoffexporthafen.

Methodologically related is the master's thesis by Johannes Kiersch, *Auf Wiedersehen, geliebte Mutter – Sibirien und der Ferne Osten erwarten uns!* His tonal journey took him to far eastern Russia: Vladivostok, Komsomolsk on the Amur and the Baikal-Amur railway line. His auditory collage fluctuating between simulation and reality, silence and noise, combines multifaceted, nuanced sounds from the Soviet past and the Russian present, from abandoned factories and Chinese bazaars, from a former prison camp and a port for the transshipment of outbound raw materials.

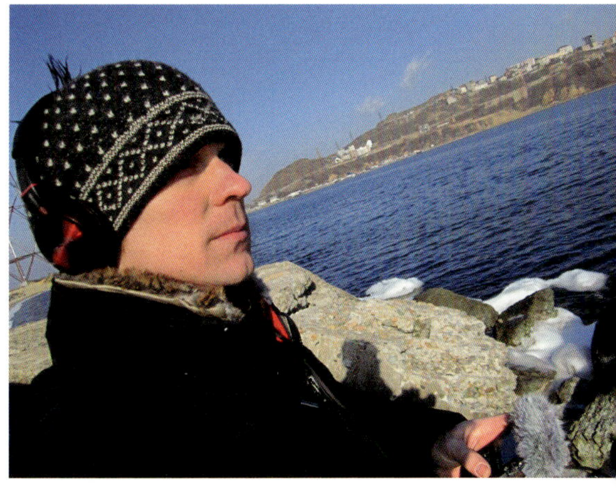

Johannes Kiersch

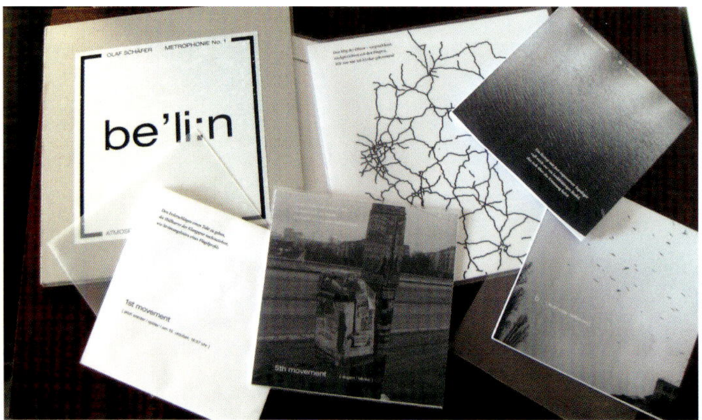

Olaf Schäfer

[be,li:n]–Atmosphäre eines Klanggeflechts (Metrophonie No.1, 2008), Olaf Schäfer's master's thesis, is part of a larger-scale research effort into methods of representing sounds in architectural structures and urban ensembles. Its programmatic neologism—a portmanteau of metropolis and polyphony—stands for the synthesis of a cityscape and its soundscape.

The theme of artist Marco Montiel-Soto's *strudel between contradiction y confusión* is his transitory life commuting between Maracaibo and Berlin. Contradiction, place, image, home and French curator Nicolas Bourriaud's concept of "radicant" frame the discourse in this work.

Die Masterarbeit *[be,li:n] – Atmosphäre eines Klanggeflechts (Metrophonie No.1, 2008)* von Olaf Schäfer ist Teil einer größer angelegten Erforschung der Darstellbarkeit von Klängen im architektonischen und urbanen Gefüge. Ihr programmatischer Neologismus, zusammengesetzt aus „Metropole" und „Polyphonie", benennt die Synthese der Stadt mit ihren Klängen.

Der Künstler Marco Montiel-Soto macht in *strudel between contradiction y confusión* sein transitorisches Leben zwischen Maracaibo (Venezuela) und Berlin (Deutschland) zum Thema. Begriffe wie Contradiction, Place, Image, Home etc. bilden zusammen mit dem künstlerischen Konzept des „Radikant" von Nicholas Bourriaud den Diskursrahmen für diese Arbeit.

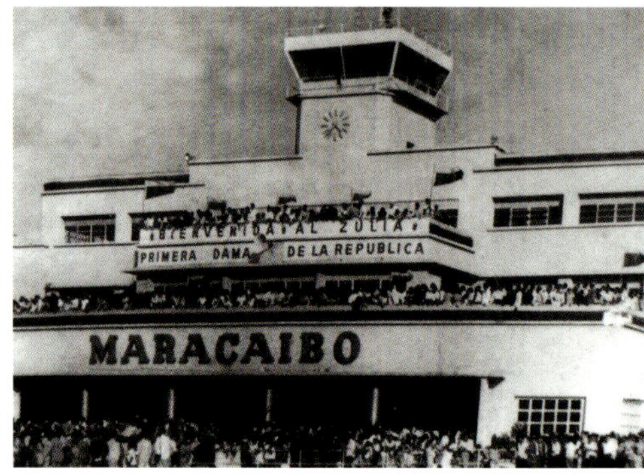

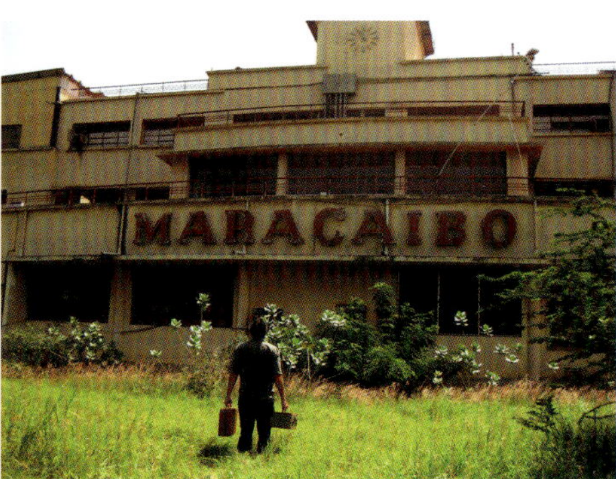

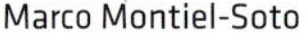

Marco Montiel-Soto

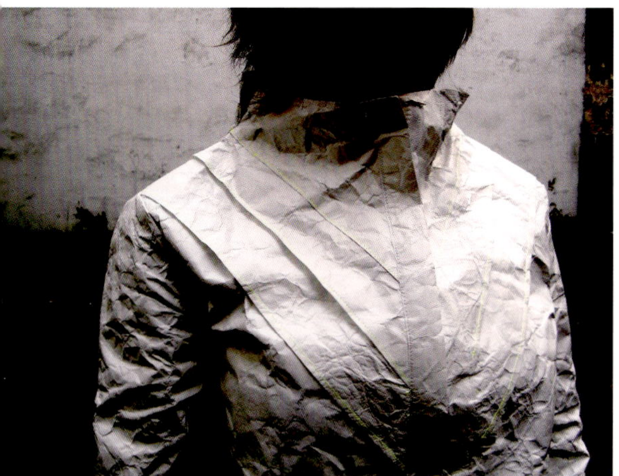

Pheline Binz

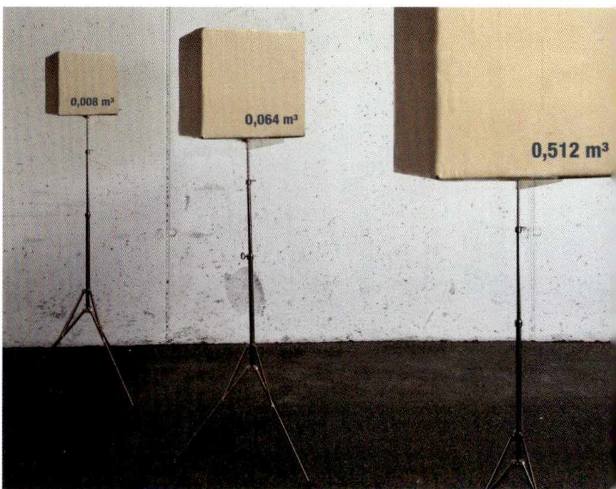

Robert Schwarz

Space, Resonance, Atmosphere

This theme subsumes various aspects and characteristics of space—resonance, materiality and vibration, phenomena having to do with perception and atmosphere, as well as the sonification and communication of extrasensory magnitudes.

The subject of *Enhance Your Presence (EYP)* by Pheline Binz and *Sonic Suit* by Satoshi Morita is people—men and women in the clothes they wear and the places they inhabit, how they move and communicate, experience space and time. Pheline Binz's sound jacket makes possible nonverbal interpersonal communication as well as human-machine interaction via sound. Satoshi Morita's *Sonic Suit* stimulates the receptors of the skin with vibro-tactile sound vibrations of corresponding frequency and intensity.

Robert Schwarz was inspired by one of Robert Musil's texts to develop a physical model for acoustic thinking about space and freedom. He elaborates on it in *Ein Fliegenpapier – Gelenkte Aleatorik (0,008 m³ : 0,064 m³ : 0,512 m³).*

Raum, Resonanz, Atmosphäre

Dieses Themenfeld handelt von unterschiedlichen Aspekten und Eigenschaften des Raums, angefangen mit Resonanz, Materialität und Schwingung über Phänomene der Wahrnehmung und der Atmosphäre bis hin zur Sonifikation und Kommunikation des für Menschen nicht Wahrnehmbaren.

Enhance Your Presence (EYP) von Pheline Binz und *Sonic Suit* von Satoshi Morita thematisieren den „bekleideten Menschen" in seinen Lebenswelten, wie er sich bewegt, kommuniziert, Raum und Zeit erfährt. Die Klang-Jacke von Pheline Binz ermöglicht non-verbale Kommunikation zwischen Menschen sowie eine Mensch-Maschine-Interaktion über Sound. Satoshi Moritas *Sonic Suit* hingegen stimuliert die Rezeptoren der Haut durch vibrotaktile Schallschwingungen entsprechender Frequenz und Intensität.

Inspiriert von einem Text von Robert Musil entwickelt Robert Schwarz in *Ein Fliegenpapier – Gelenkte Aleatorik (0,008 m³ : 0,064 m³ : 0,512 m³)* ein physikalisches Modell für akustische Gedanken über Raum und Freiheit.

Prägung by Harald Christ shows the work process as a system for depicting sound. The installation integrates several system components. A performance consists of a programmed pneumatic-powered machine—originally a façade printer that normally works with paintballs—"playing" a metallic resonance board by firing projectiles at it from a distance. Based on graphic templates, the stiff membrane of the board undergoes a plastic transformation—the deformation of the material makes the continuous intervention in the resonance characteristics of the thin metal membrane visible.

Steffen Martin's *Clownzeichner* takes a playful approach to the sensory interrelationship of seeing and hearing. "Clownzeichner is almost a readymade. It consists of an active loudspeaker and three felt-tip pens that are moved by the acoustic energy of musical compositions. The idea of a written music as silent eye-music brought me to this inquiry into the boundaries between the categories of our perception: What is added to the sound when it's visualized and what is taken away from it?"

Prägung von Harald Christ zeigt den Werkprozess als klangbildnerisches System. Die Installation bezieht mehrere Systemkomponenten mit ein. In einer Performance „bespielt" eine programmierte, pneumatisch arbeitende Maschine – ursprünglich ein Fassadendrucker, der sonst mit Farbkugeln arbeitet – ein Resonanzblech aus der Distanz mit Projektilen. Nach grafischer Vorlage wird die starre Membran des Blechs plastisch transformiert, die Materialumformung macht den kontinuierlichen Eingriff in die Resonanzeigenschaften der dünnen Blechmembran sichtbar.

Steffen Martins *Clownzeichner* geht spielerisch dem Wahrnehmungszusammenhang von Sehen und Hören nach. „Der Clownzeichner ist fast ein Readymade, bestehend aus einem Aktivlautsprecher und drei Filzschreibern, die durch die akustische Energie musikalischer Kompositionen angetrieben werden. Die Idee einer geschriebenen Musik als stiller Augenmusik brachte mich zur Frage nach den Grenzen zwischen den Kategorien unserer Wahrnehmung: Was wird dem Klang hinzugefügt, wenn er visualisiert wird, und was wird ihm genommen?"

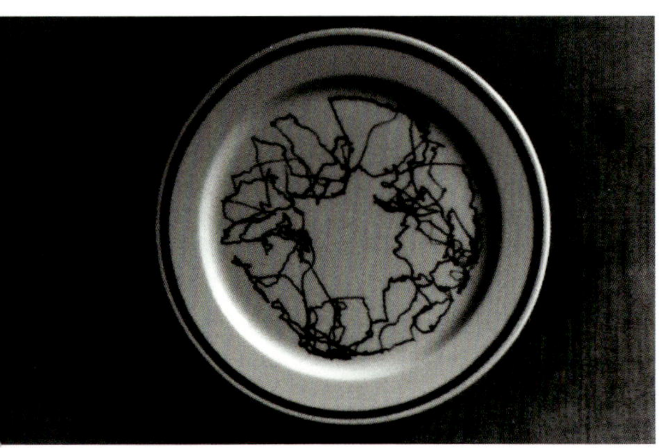

Steffen Martin

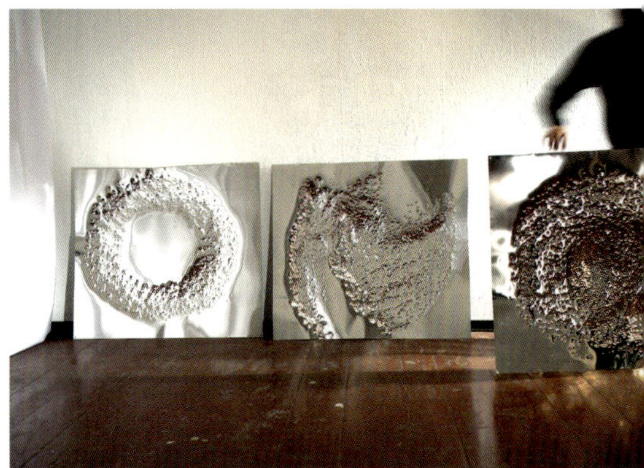

Harald Christ

Feld III by Julius Stahl shows sound as movement between the visible and the audible. The installation consists of a movie screen on which 1,400 wires have been mounted. Pure tone glissandi make the wires resonate in very low, inaudible frequencies, whereby the resonations are visible as "stationary waves" along the individual wires. Minimal differences in the lengths of the wires bring forth modulations of the frequencies and engender visually perceptible movements that are propagated over the entire wave field—a self-contained mobile micro-polyphony.

Korinsky, a group of artists, produced *Digi.flat 90-12,* a wall-mounted work consisting of flat-bed scanners that demonstrates a complex aesthetic phenomenon. The scanners remain recognizable as such, though, upon closer scrutiny, viewers see the rhythmic movement of the devices' fluorescent tubes. Phase shift prevents repetition. Observation over an extended period gives rise to a meditative effect that's enhanced by the sounds of the scanners and the wave movements that suggest lamps moving back and forth in a confined space.

Feld III von Julius Stahl zeigt den Klang als Bewegung zwischen Sichtbarem und Hörbarem. Die Installation besteht aus einer mit 1400 Drähten bestückten Leinwand. Die Drähte werden über Sinuston-Glissandi in sehr tiefen, nicht hörbaren Frequenzen zur Resonation gebracht. Die Resonationen sind als „stehende Wellen" entlang der einzelnen Drähte sichtbar. Minimale Unterschiede in der Länge der Drähte lassen Modulationen der Frequenzen hervortreten und gestalten visuell erfahrbare Bewegungen, die über das gesamt Wellenfeld verlaufen – eine in sich bewegte Mikropolyphonie.

Digi.flat 90-12 der Künstlergruppe Korinsky, eine aus Flachbettscannern gefügte Wandarbeit, demonstriert ein komplexes ästhetisches Phänomen. Die Scanner bleiben als solche erkennbar, doch bei genauer Betrachtung wird die rhythmische Bewegung der Leuchtröhren der Geräte sichtbar. Phasenverschiebung verhindert Wiederholung. Bei längerer Beobachtung entsteht eine meditative Wirkung, unterstützt durch die Klänge der Scanner und Wellenbewegungen, die die in einem begrenzten Raum hin- und herfahrenden Lampen andeuten.

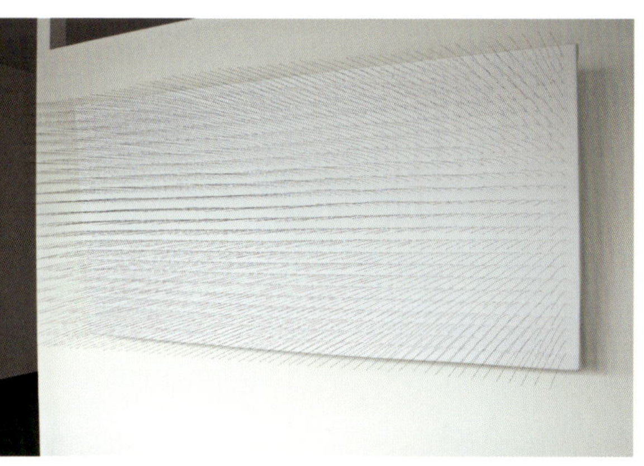

Julius Stahl

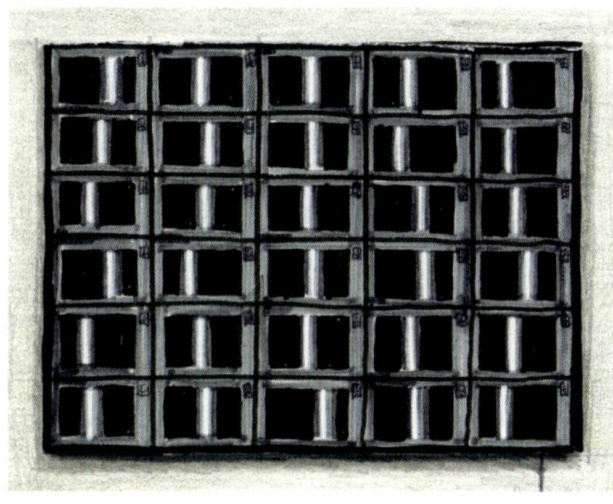

Korinsky

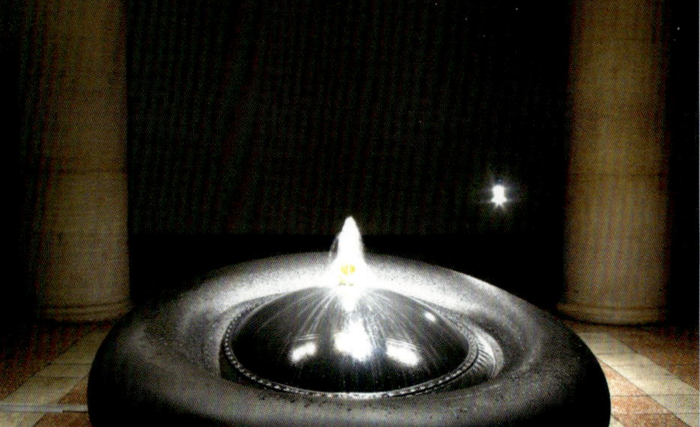

Johannes Steininger

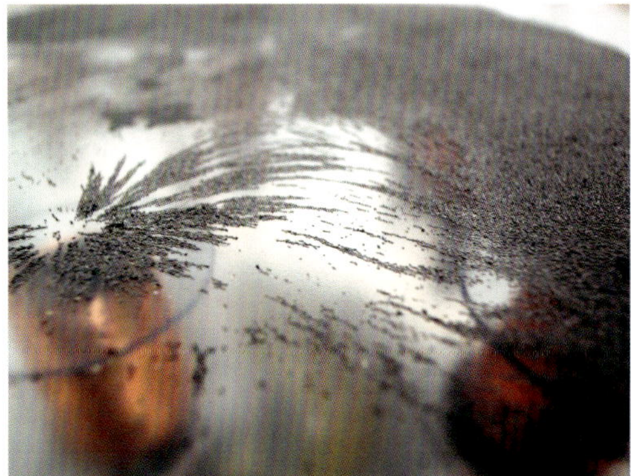
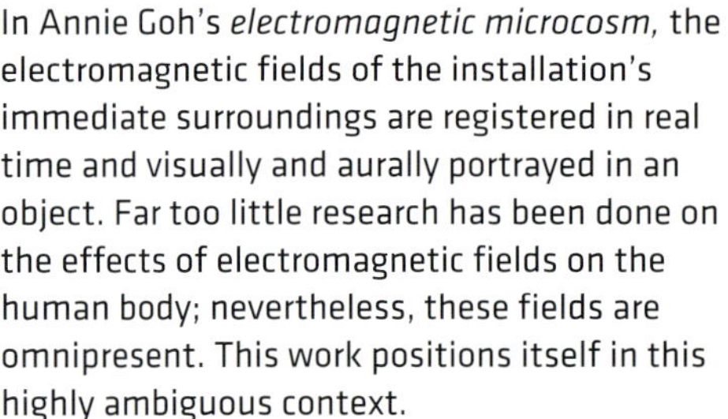

Annie Goh

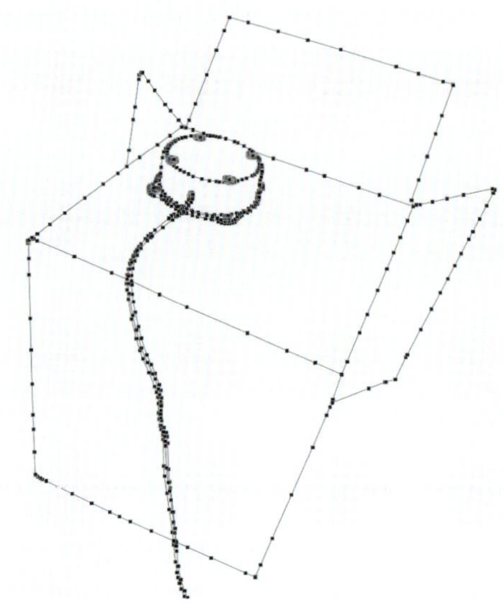

Alois Späth

In Annie Goh's *electromagnetic microcosm*, the electromagnetic fields of the installation's immediate surroundings are registered in real time and visually and aurally portrayed in an object. Far too little research has been done on the effects of electromagnetic fields on the human body; nevertheless, these fields are omnipresent. This work positions itself in this highly ambiguous context.

Alois Späth's *Panharmonicon 2* is an offbeat sort of jukebox that inquires into loudspeakers. A DVD player uses transducers to play the Styrofoam and cardboard that it came packed in.

Johannes Steininger's *auditive atmosphaeren-konstruktion 2012* actively determines auditory atmospheric qualities. The preexisting tonal atmosphere that is intrinsic to the nature of the particular physical space—involved as fundamental form in the auditory perception of space by both ears—is atmospherically amplified in this way.

In Annie Gohs *electromagnetic microcosm* werden elektromagnetische Felder der näheren Umgebung in Echtzeit übertragen und in einem Objekt visuell und auditiv abgebildet. Die Auswirkungen elektromagnetischer Umgebungen auf den menschlichen Körper sind kaum erschöpfend erforscht, jedoch sind elektromagnetische Felder omnipräsent. Die Arbeit positioniert sich in diesem mehrdeutigen Kontext.

Alois Späth diskutiert in seinem *Panharmonicon 2,* einem eigenwilligen Musikautomat, die Lautsprecherfrage. Ein DVD-Spieler bespielt mittels Transducern sein Verpackungsmaterial, Styropor und Pappkarton.

Johannes Steiningers *auditive atmosphaeren-konstruktion 2012* bestimmt aktiv auditive atmosphärische Qualitäten – die vorgefundene wesenseigene Geräuschatmosphäre der Räumlichkeit, als Grundform in die hörende Raumwahrnehmung mit beiden Ohren involviert, wird auf diese Weise atmosphärisch überhöht.

Two very personal and poetic installations—
Breathing Room by Elen Flügge and *Ampere* by
Frauke Schmidt—deal with individual perception
and perception of self in sound and space.

The façade of the Linz Art University's building on
the Main Square will be the setting of two works
of art: Thomas Wochnik's *Rauschgold* will mark
the entrance to the Campus exhibition with
audible and visible signs; Daisuke Ishida's
installation *Vordergrundgeräusche 2012*

Die sehr persönlichen und poetischen Installatio-
nen von Elen Flügge – *Breathing Room* – und
Frauke Schmidt – *Ampere* – thematisieren
Eigen- und Selbstwahrnehmung in Klang und
Raum.

Zwei künstlerische Arbeiten bespielen die
Fassade des Linzer Kunst-Uni-Gebäudes. Thomas
Wochnik markiert mit dem hör- und sichtbaren
Zeichen *Rauschgold* den Zugangsbereich zur
Campus-Ausstellung, während Daisuke Ishidas

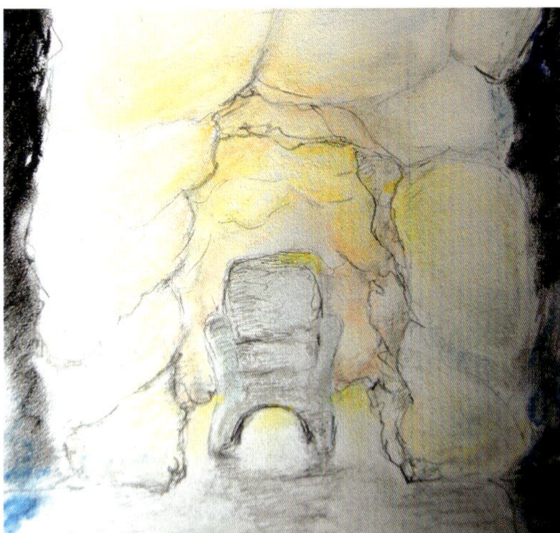

Elen Flügge

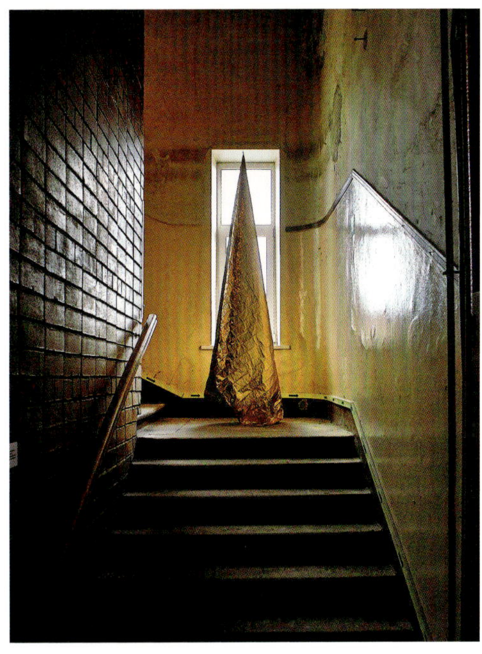

Thomas Wochnik

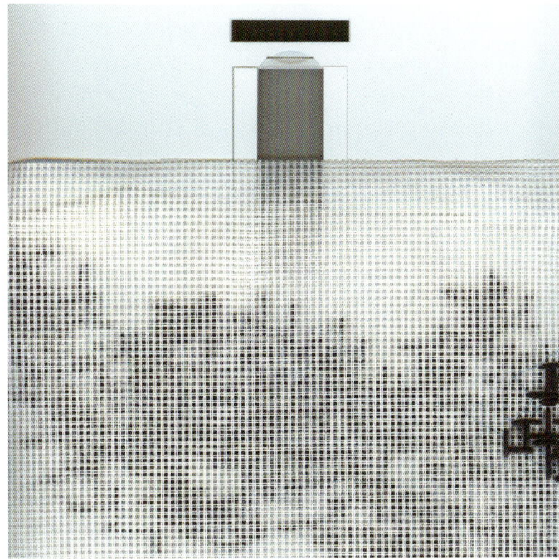

Frauke Schmidt

establishes an interactive, observable relationship with the site's ambient noise. "It is the entity of the surrounding sound in the north of Brückenkopfgebäude in Linz and its sound pressure level visualized via the building illumination as a volume unit meter. The light beams prominently draw attention to the existence of the background noise and its dynamic variance. As a result, background noise may become foreground noise."

Installation *Vordergrundgeräusche 2012* eine interaktiv beobachtbare Beziehung zum Umgebungsklang herstellt. „It is the entity of the surrounding sound in the north of Brückenkopfgebäude in Linz and its sound pressure level visualized via the building illumination as a volume unit meter. The light beams bring attention to the existence of the background noise and its dynamic variance prominently. In result, background noise may become foreground noise."

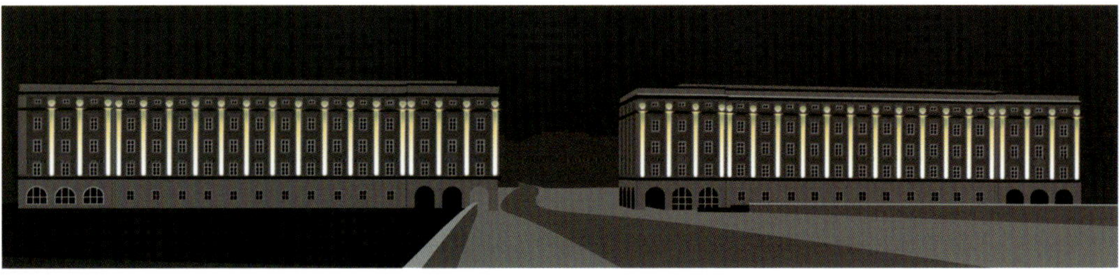

Daisuke Ishida

In the *Campus Laboratory,* current Sound Studies undergrads together with Prof. Alberto de Campo and students in his Generative Kunst / Computational Art class will be developing interventions in public, urban and medial spaces. In the lab, they'll be designing site-specific works that constitute artistic reflections of particular settings within the Linz cityscape as well as treatments of hot topics such as gentrification processes. They'll also be re-conceptualizing habitats by modeling communications processes used by deep-sea creatures *(Varia Zoosystematica Profundorum)* and in virtual spaces interlinking short local chains of causation into long multi-local chain reactions *(The Ways Things May Go).*

Im *Campus Labor* entwickeln vor Ort Studierende von *Sound Studies* gemeinsam mit Prof. Alberto de Campo und Studierenden seiner Klasse Generative Kunst / Computational Art Arbeiten zur konkreten Intervention im öffentlichen, urbanen und medialen Raum. Im Labor entwerfen sie ortsspezifische Arbeiten, die konkrete urbane Lebensräume in Linz künstlerisch reflektieren und auch aktuelle Themen wie z. B. Gentrifikationsprozesse einbeziehen. Außerdem erdenken sie Lebensräume neu, indem sie Kommunikationsprozesse bei Tiefsee-Kreaturen modellieren *(Varia Zoosystematica Profundorum)* oder in virtuellen Räumen lokale kurze Kausalketten zu langen multilokalen Kettenreaktionen vernetzen *(The Ways Things May Go).*

**Studierende der Sound Studies
und der Klasse Generative Kunst /
Computational Art, Alberto de Campo**
Emilia Rosaria Badalà
Max Baginski
Kyan Bayani
Anna Maria Bogner

Constantin Engelmann
Klaus Hamlescher
Sascha Hanse
Sonja Heyer
Dominik Hildebrand Marques Lopes
Sara Hildebrand Marques Lopes
Philipp Klein

Martin Lutz
Thomas Meier
Conrad Rodenberg
Eva Pedroza
Elisa Storelli
Marcus Thomas
Michel Wähling

Participation:
Actions and Performances

There will be a performance of *HVL001-Tiefdruckgebiet – das mobile Subbass-Konzert*, a project by the group HEAVYLISTENING aka Anselm Venezian Nehls and Carl Schilde, one of the prizewinners in the 2012 Prix Ars Electronica's Digital Musics & Sound Art category *(#tweetscapes)*. On the streets of Linz, rides pimped out with massive subwoofers will be generating a physically palpable wave-field of reciprocally modulating sub-bass vibes. The architecture on site, audience members, pedestrians who just happen to pass by, and the local traffic situation are the variables that make *Tiefdruckgebiet* sound different at each location and to each listener. Julius Stahl's site-specific installation *Transitions* will provide festivalgoers with a wireless headset system to enable them to exchange aural impressions and thus tune in to each other's auditory perspective. In the paradoxical situation of perception divided in multiple respects, new and unexpected points of view emerge.

Partizipation:
Aktionen und Performances

Zur Aufführung kommt das Projekt *HVL001-Tiefdruckgebiet – das mobile Subbass-Konzert* der Gruppe HEAVYLISTENING aka Anselm Venezian Nehls und Carl Schilde, einer der Preisträger in der Kategorie Digital Musics & Sound Art des Prix Ars Electronica 2012 *(#tweetscapes)*. In den Straßen von Linz erzeugen mit massiven Subwoofern getunte Autos ein körperlich spürbares Wellenfeld sich gegenseitig modulierender Subbass-Schwingungen. Die Architektur vor Ort, das Publikum, zufällige Passanten und der Verkehr lassen *Tiefdruckgebiet* an jedem Ort und für jeden Zuhörer anders klingen.
In Julius Stahls ortsspezifischer Installation *Transitions* können Besucher während des Festivals über ein drahtloses Mikrophon- und Kopfhörersystem ihre auditive Wahrnehmung tauschen und so die auditive Perspektive des anderen einnehmen. In der paradoxen Situation einer in mehrfacher Hinsicht geteilten Wahrnehmung entstehen neue, unerhörte Perspektiven.

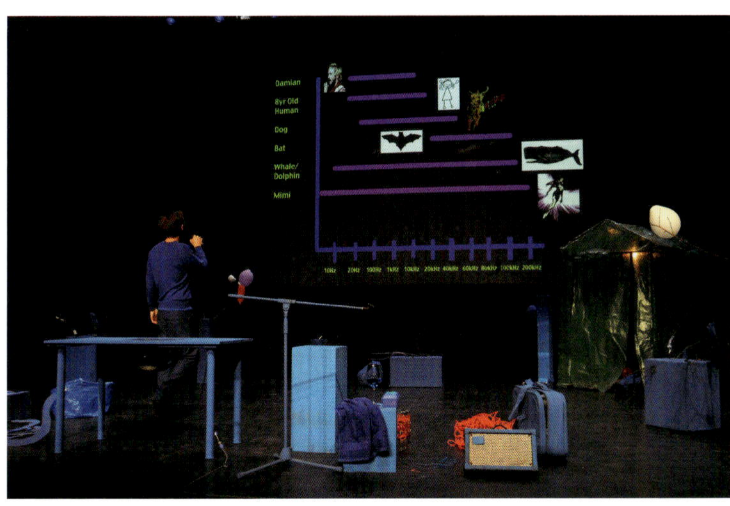

Damian Rebgetz

The theatrical performance *VOICE BOX (that thing in your throat)* by and starring Damian Rebgetz with sidemen Thomas Koch and Alexander Sieber deals on extremely personal terms with (one's perception of) one's own voice: "This lecture/performance is an encounter with the materiality of the voice's sound. Inspired by his first singing teacher's stories about Enrico Caruso's ability to shatter crystal hitting high notes with his powerful tenor voice, Damian Rebgetz asks: 'What would it be like to make things, bodies or buildings move with the sound of your voice?'"
Finally, auditory guided tours will encourage group members to think with their ears.

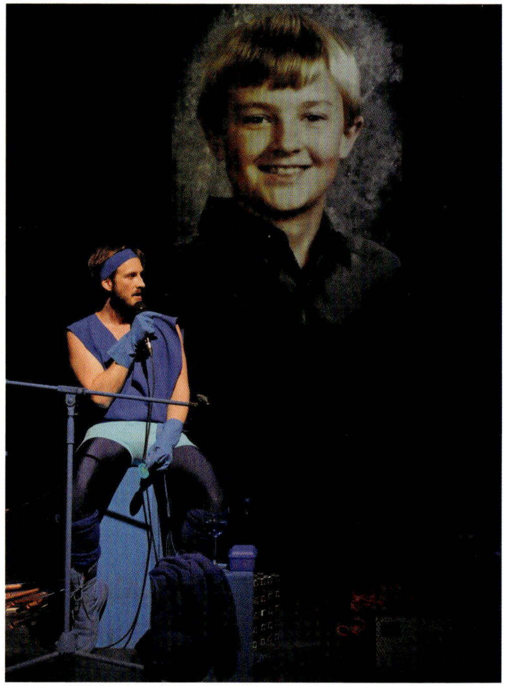

Damian Rebgetz

Artistic directors: Sam Auinger, Georg Spehr
Organization: Silvia Keller, Katrin Emler, Andrea Riedel
Technology/exhibition construction: Dany Scheffler, Cecile Bouchier
Archive: Martin Supper, Frauke Schmidt, Carsten Meier
Graphics: Peter Prautzsch
Text editor: Sabine Sanio

With support of Linz Art University, Kepler Salon, Tabakfabrik Linz, The German Academic Exchange Service (DAAD), afo architekturforum oberösterreich

Special thanks to Hannes Baumgartner, Mirko Behrens, Ingrid Beirer, Regula Corsten, Hannes Franks, Wolfgang Galler, Robert Henke, Yukio King, Marcel Kloppenburg, Edi Scholz, Caroline Siegers, Gerd Thaller, Andre Zogholy and B7 Fahrradzentrum

Die Theaterperformance *VOICE BOX (that thing in your throat)* von und mit Damian Rebgetz mit Unterstützung von Thomas Koch und Alexander Sieber setzt sich auf sehr persönliche Art und Weise mit (der Eigenwahrnehmung der) Stimme auseinander: „Diese Lecture Performance befasst sich mit der Materialität des Klangs der Stimme. Inspiriert von Erzählungen seines ersten Gesangslehrers über Enrico Carusos Fähigkeit, mit seinem hohen Tenor-Es Kristall zum Springen zu bringen, fragt Damian Rebgetz: ‚Wie wäre es, Dinge, Körper und Gebäude mit dem Klang deiner Stimme zu bewegen?'"
In geführten Hörspaziergängen werden die Besucher zum Denken mit den Ohren angeregt.

Alex Arteaga

Klangumwelt Ernst-Reuter-Platz
Exhibition developed by the Auditory Research Unit

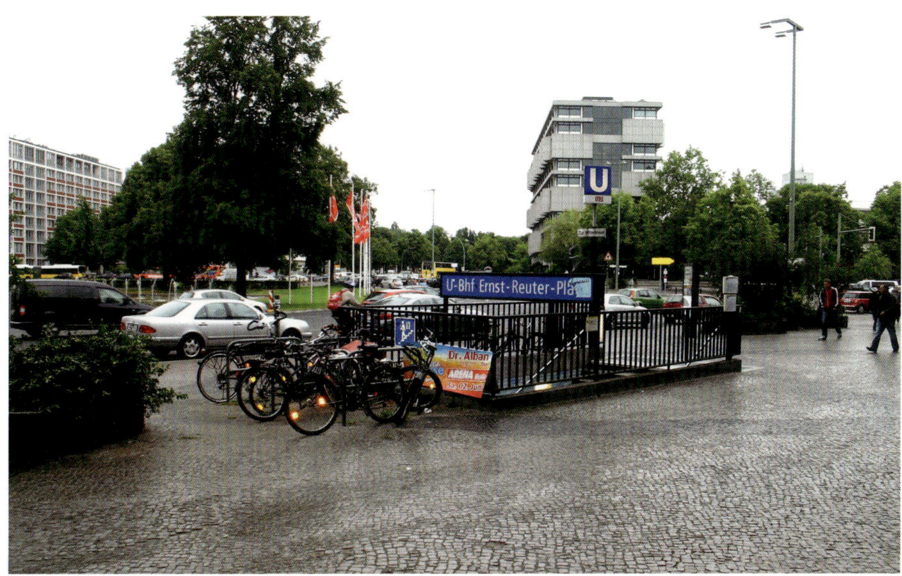

Klangumwelt Ernst-Reuter-Platz is the first exhibition to showcase auditory-architectural design. It presents all the approaches to and suggestions for the architectural transformation of Ernst-Reuter-Platz, a square in Berlin, that were developed by the Auditory Architecture Research Unit *www.auditive-architektur.de.*

Auditory architecture is a new discipline. Its practitioners design architecture on the basis of the auditory experience it engenders. Implicit in this reorientation of the point of departure of architectural design is a reinterpretation of the entire design process. The perceived space—i.e. space as an aesthetic experience—occupies the focal point of this process; accordingly, its objective is the configuration of the framework conditions of perception. Auditory architecture is not object-oriented, but rather process-oriented. The point of the design is not creating architectural objects; instead, architectural objects establish the conditions of aesthetic experience (see the essay "Auditive Architektur. Einführung in eine neue Disziplin" at *www.kunsttexte.de/auditive_perspektiven).*

On the basis of systematic research on the dynamic structure of Ernst-Reuter-Platz as an acoustic environment conducted over the course of a year by Annette Matthias and Thomas Kusitzky, the unit's staff came up with a design that fulfills the project's goal: the transformation of the square from a space that optimizes the flow of vehicular traffic and plays up this arrangement as emblematic of a modern metropolis, into a habitat that serves as the City of Berlin's interface with the campus of the Technical University and the UdK–University of the Arts. Bernhard Hermkes' 1955 design is an archetype of the urban planning & mobility paradigms of that historical period; as such, it's protected by architectural preservation provisions. The Auditory Architecture Research Unit's design makes possible the necessary readaptation of the square without thereby curtailing the presence of the original design. The new design envisions Ernst-Reuter-Platz as a setting for diverse activities: people passing through (with the aim of integrating the flows of motorists as well as pedestrians and cyclists) and those pausing here for purposes of relaxing, socializing and communicating. The implementation of the paradigm shift in the conceptualization of everyday life in the big city through the use of auditory architectural means attests to the social transformation potential of operative aesthetic thinking.

Just as auditory-architectural design calls essential aspects of the design process into question, exhibiting the design constitutes a challenge too. The processual and relational approach of auditory architecture is at odds with the traditional function of an exhibition: putting objects on display. Here, the aim is to enable exhibition visitors to take an experience-based approach to the transformation of the auditory dimension of Ernst-Reuter-Platz and the cityscape's reconfiguration on that basis. Without completely dispensing with the explanation and depiction of these changes by means of written and visual elements, the focus of the presentation is on directly encountering auditory evidence. Detailed background information will be provided by Alex Arteaga's speech *Auditory Architecture. Towards an architecture of embodiment* at afo architektur forum oberösterreich, and by themed tours of the exhibition itself.

The design and the exhibition are the work of Alex Arteaga, Anna Bogner, Frédérik Eyl, Harald Fugmann, Gunnar Green, Boris Hassenstein, Thomas Koch, Thomas Kusitzky, Dominik Schumacher, Willy Sengewald, Alexander Teichmann and Hans-Peter Tennhardt.

The *Klangumwelt Ernst-Reuter-Platz* project has received funding from the BBSR–Federal Institute for Research on Building, Urban Affairs and Spatial Development's Building the Future research initiative.

Alex Arteaga

Klangumwelt Ernst-Reuter-Platz
Ausstellung entwickelt von der Auditory Architecture Research Unit

In der Ausstellung *Klangumwelt Ernst-Reuter-Platz* wird zum ersten Mal ein auditiv-architektonischer Entwurf präsentiert. Gezeigt werden alle Ansätze und Vorschläge zur architektonischen Transformation des Berliner Ernst-Reuter-Platzes, die in der Auditory Architecture Research Unit *(www.auditive-architektur.de)* entwickelt wurden.

Die Auditive Architektur ist eine neue Disziplin, deren Ziel darin besteht, Architektur ausgehend von der auditiven Erfahrung zu entwerfen. Diese neue Bestimmung des Ausgangspunktes architektonischen Designs impliziert eine Umdeutung des gesamten Entwurfsprozesses. Der erlebte Raum, d. h. der Raum als ästhetische Erfahrung, bildet den Fokus dieses Prozesses und die Gestaltung von Rahmenbedingungen des Wahrnehmens dementsprechend sein Ziel. Die Auditive Architektur ist nicht objekt-, sondern prozessorientiert. Die architektonischen Objekte sind nicht der Gegenstand des Entwerfens, vielmehr bilden sie Bedingungen ästhetischer Erfahrung (siehe dazu den Aufsatz „Auditive Architektur. Einführung in eine neue Disziplin" unter *www.kunsttexte.de/auditive_perspektiven)*.

Aufbauend auf einem Jahr systematischer Erforschung der dynamischen Struktur des Ernst-Reuter-Platzes als Klangumwelt durch Annette Matthias und Thomas Kusitzky wurde ein Entwurf konzipiert, welcher das Ziel dieses Projektes erfüllt: die Transformation des Platzes von einem Raum, der den Autoverkehr optimiert und diesen als Symbol einer modernen Stadt inszeniert, in einen Lebensraum, der als Schnittstelle zwischen der Stadt, dem Campus der Technischen Universität und der Universität der Künste Berlin fungiert. Der Entwurf von Bernhard Hermkes aus dem Jahr 1955 verkörpert exemplarisch das Stadt- und Mobilitätsparadigma dieser Epoche und steht aus diesem Grund unter Denkmalschutz. Der Entwurf der Auditory Architecture Research Unit ermöglicht die nötige Umfunktionalisierung des Platzes, ohne die Präsenz des ursprünglichen Designs einzuschränken. Diesem Entwurf folgend wird der Ernst-Reuter-Platz ein Ort vielfältiger Aktivitäten: Transit – nicht nur auto-, sondern auch fußgänger- und fahrradgerecht –, Aufenthalt, Erholung und Entspannung sowie Austausch und Kommunikation. Die Implementierung des Paradigmenwechsels in die Konzeption des Lebens in der Stadt mit auditiv-architektonischen Mitteln beweist das gesellschaftliche Transformationspotenzial operativen ästhetischen Denkens.

Ebenso wie das auditiv-architektonische Entwerfen zentrale Aspekte des Designprozesses in Frage stellt, ist auch das Ausstellen des Entwurfs eine Herausforderung. Der prozessuale und relationale Ansatz der Auditiven Architektur konterkariert die traditionelle Funktion des Ausstellens: das Zeigen von Objekten. Im Gegensatz dazu wird ein erfahrungsbasierter Zugang zur Transformation der auditiven Dimension des Ernst-Reuter-Platzes und zur darauf basierenden Umdeutung des urbanen Raums ermöglicht. Ohne die Erklärung und Darstellung dieser Veränderungen durch sprachliche und visuelle Elemente auszuschließen, liegt der Fokus der Präsentation auf ihrer Erschließung als auditive Evidenz. Die Ausstellung wird durch den Vortrag von Alex Arteaga *Auditory Architecture. Towards an architecture of embodiment* im afo architektur forum oberösterreich sowie thematische Führungen kontextualisiert.

Entwurf und Ausstellung wurden von Alex Arteaga, Anna Bogner, Frédérik Eyl, Harald Fugmann, Gunnar Green, Boris Hassenstein, Thomas Koch, Thomas Kusitzky, Dominik Schumacher, Willy Sengewald, Alexander Teichmann und Hans-Peter Tennhardt realisiert.

Das Projekt *Klangumwelt Ernst-Reuter-Platz* wurde im Rahmen der Forschungsinitiative Zukunft Bau des Bundesinstitutes für Bau-, Stadt- und Raumforschung (BBSR) gefördert.

Interface Cuisine
Interface Cultures at Ars Electronica 2012

The relation that can be drawn between the process of art making and *cuisine* is not so far-fetched. Numerous artists have made connections between food, cooking and art. Haute cuisine is seen as an artform itself, where high quality ingredients, innovative arrangements, a strong sense of improvisation and a high level of creativity lead to dishes that can be experienced as art works.

Interface Cuisine is the umbrella term that covers this year's Interface Cultures exhibition. The title was chosen because the art-making process is similar to the cooking process. Cooking and art production both fuse chosen ingredients, brewing and forming them into creations that are inspired and informed by the familiar and the exotic. The manifold cultures represented at Interface Cultures are the ingredients that the students use for the mold of their creations. Members of the Interface Cultures master study program at the University of Art and Design come from very different cultures and countries. Every student brings his/her own cultural background, tradition, education, experience and creative sensitivity. Working together leads to a vibrant cultural mash-up, a fusion and infusion of cultures where novel connections emerge, creative mutations form and novel interface solutions are created and invented. The resulting projects surprise and challenge, they let us participate, and they create their own cultural languages, where the whole is more than the sum of it parts.

Es ist nicht so weit hergeholt, Kunstschaffen und Haute Cuisine zueinander in Bezug zu setzen – zahlreiche Künstler haben Parallelen zwischen Essen, Kochen und Kunst gezogen. Die Haute Cuisine versteht sich als Kunstform, die qualitativ hochwertige Zutaten, innovative Zusammenstellungen sowie ein hohes Maß an Improvisation und Kreativität zu Gerichten verschmelzen lässt, die durchaus künstlerischen Ansprüchen genügen.

Die diesjährige Ausstellung des Linzer Studiengangs Interface Cultures trägt den Titel *Interface Cuisine,* der durch die Verbindungslinien zwischen Kunst und Kochen inspiriert wurde. Kochen und Kunstschaffen nehmen ausgesuchte Zutaten, mixen und vermengen sie zu Kreationen, die sowohl vertraut als auch exotisch geprägt sind. Die verschiedenen im Studiengang vertretenen Kulturen sind die Zutaten, die den Studierenden als Gussform für ihre Werke dienen. Die Studierenden im Masterstudium Interface Cultures an der Universität für künstlerische und industrielle Gestaltung in Linz stammen aus verschiedenen Ländern und Kulturen. Sie sind von der eigenen kulturellen Herkunft, Tradition, Bildung, Erfahrung und künstlerischen Sensibilität geprägt. Durch den Austausch mit anderen entsteht ein dynamisches kulturelles Mashup; es kommt zu einer Verschmelzung und Vermengung der Kulturen, aus der unerwartete Verbindungen, schöpferische Mutationen und neuartige Interface-Lösungen hervorgehen. Die daraus entstehenden Projekte verblüffen und fordern die Betrachter heraus; sie erlauben Teilhabe und schaffen ihre eigene kulturell determinierte Sprache, deren Ganzes mehr als die Summe aller Teile ist.

Aus dem Englischen von Sonja Pöllabauer

Faculty: Christa Sommerer, Laurent Mignonneau, Martin Kaltenbrunner, Michaela Ortner, Marlene Hochrieser, Georg Russegger; Lecturers: Gebhart Sengmüller, Andreas Weixler, Sabine Seymour, Tiago Martins, Mahir Yavuz, Times Up, Hideyaki Ogawa, Christopher Lindinger, Daniel Hug, Chris Ziegler, Margarete Jahrmann, Alexander Wilhelm, Stefano Vanotti, Johannes Grenzfurthner, Ulrich Andel, Christian Guetzer

Misawa Daichi

Transparent Sculpture: Passages
Sound installation

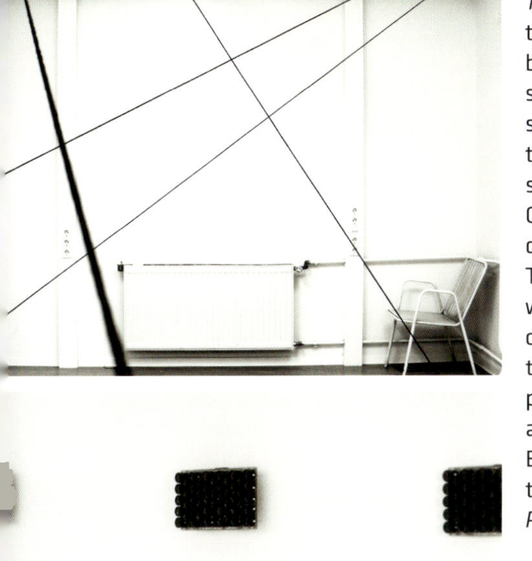

Transparent Sculpture: Passages is a sound installation that includes sweet spots from the focal points between multiple directional speakers. These can send sound to the limited listening area. These sweet spots, which are deployed in the installation, imply the existence of sonic structures: a transparent sculpture.

Compositions from field recordings of passages in different areas are used as a motif for the sculpture. They include the ambience of languages, songs, weather conditions and people. The different areas correspond to the Western and the Eastern part of the world. The ambience is a cultural and musical product that represents the aesthetics of a certain area.

By walking through and searching for the sculpture, the visitor experiences the *Transparent Sculpture: Passages*.

whoun (a.k.a. Juan Cedenilla)

230312:QRmovie

230312:QRmovie is an interactive installation that shows a movie made up of QR codes. The user watches how the image of a QR is transformed becoming a new image. By using a mobile phone, electronic tablet or other device for QR reading, the user can access the hyperlinks that allow him to watch the hyperlinked film in small fragments of very short duration.

A hyperlink is a reference to data, leads us from one place to another, makes us jump in space to continue reading or gives extra information about the events. It is introduced as something non-linear in the reading. But a movie is linear; one frame is always followed by another. The frames are spatially ordered, so that the viewer sees the first frame, then the second, then the third etc. *230312: QRmovie* compares and contrasts the concepts "linear" and "non-linear", and transforms the non-linearity of the hyperlinks into something linear like a movie.

Alberto Boem

Poetry in Form of Movement
Interactive sound installation

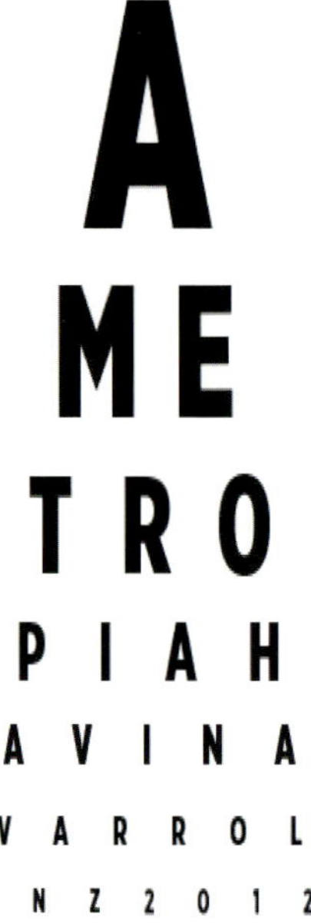

The Italian poet Giorgio Caproni said that poets are like miners who dig into the world to find a universal meaning.
In this installation visitors are invited to explore a virtual mine of sounds and words to create a personal and intimate meaning and experience.
The system presented here, which links orality and gestural performance, is an invisible and impalpable auditory interface for performing real-time sound poetry through body interaction.
The environment is composed of a video sensor, which detects the movement of every part of the users' body, and four speakers that display the sound created and controlled in real-time by the users. The sound space consists of an archive of prerecorded poetry that the users can modify and modulate through active participation with their body.
Through the exploration of the different correspondence between body and space, the users are able to create their own new sound poetry compositions.
Take it seriously, or just do it for fun!

Havi Navarro

Ametropia

Ametropia is an interactive video installation in which a text is displayed following eye chart rules. The font size scales according to the distance between the participant and the text. When the reader goes for a closer look, the onto-types become smaller. Any wish to fully read the text, will remain unsatisfied. Playing with sensory expectation, *Ametropia* aims to create a moment of reflection in the participant's approach to art.

Peter Eszes, OS Kantine
Budapest Farmers Hack

This project aims to initiate the use of unused gardens and to provide environmental data and give feedback to the users. In order to do this we are using open source technology to build sensors that are connected to the internet and provide 24-hour data. From the sensors the user will get data about the humidity, the temperature and the amount of light. Alarms are triggered if the humidity or the temperature is too low or too high. Additional data from the users (amount of crops, amount of work etc.) about each and every garden will provide information about the history, data

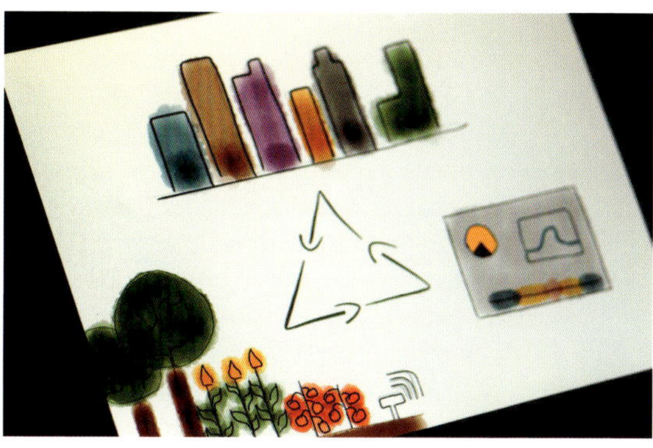

visualization and which crops will grow well. By using social networks we will connect people who would like to have a garden with people who have an unused garden. The collected data will be used to pick the right garden.

Veronika Krenn
Made with Love

Knitting used to conjure up a romantic image. A woman sitting by the fireside, her hands constantly moving up and down. With the act of knitting we followed our natural instincts, making warm and comfortable things for those we love. In the 1930s home-knitted clothes represented a social status. Wearing a sweater showed that the man is already taken, earns enough money that the woman can stay at home and knit and that she loves and cares about him. Industrialization, knitting machines, the increasing wool price and feminist attitudes worked together to turn knitting into an unrespectable hobby.

Can we transfer the romantic image to machine knitting?

Hugging is a form of physical intimacy. It indicates familiarity, love or friendship, a romantic exchange–just like knitting for someone. The interactive knitting installation *Made with Love* encourages visitors to hug the person next to them, to get the knitting mill to knit.

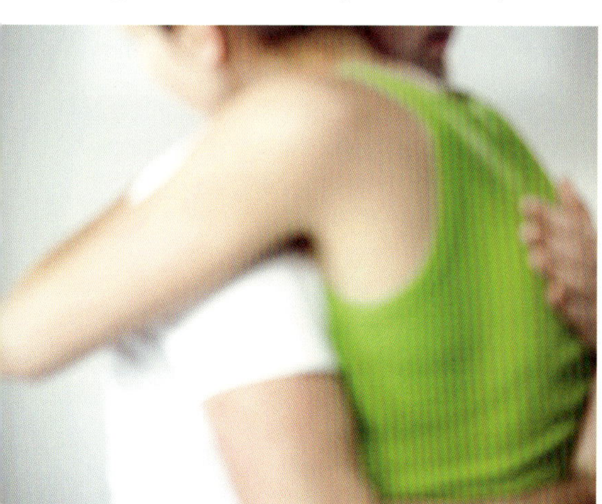

Sarah Wimmer

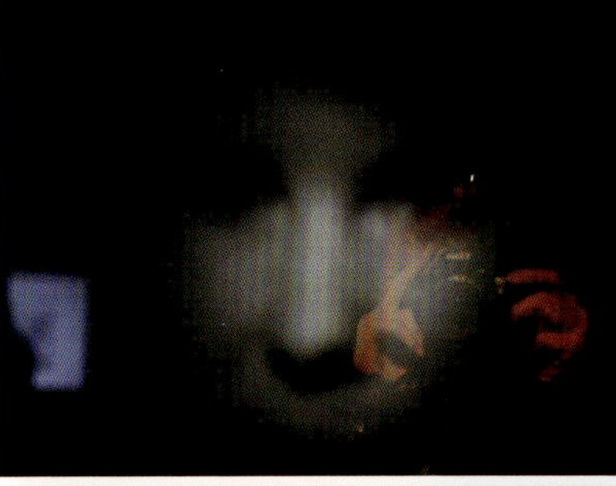

Maša Jazbec
Monolith
Interactive installation

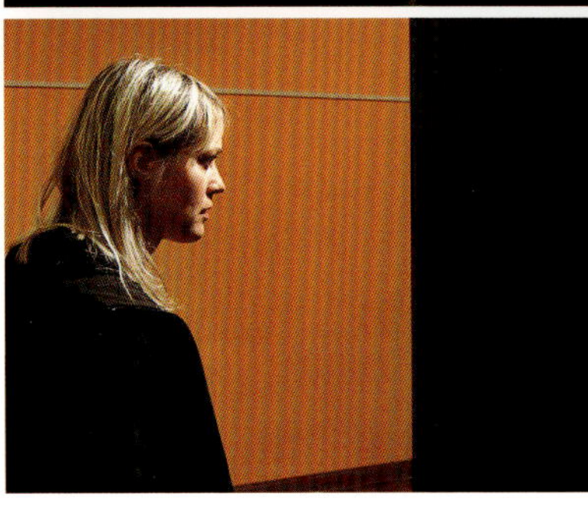

Participants are the subject of the *Monolith.* When we are confronted with the *Monolith,* questions arise about ourselves, our origin and about where evolution is leading us in the near future. New technologies culturally mutate our perception of the human body from a naturally self-regulating system to an artificially controlled and electronically transformed object. The installation reflects the relationship between the human, the screen and the virtual world. It presents digital technology as an invasion that has changed our culture, our existence and our perception of the world. When we enter the space of the *Monolith,* our image is absorbed and transformed into a digital entity, floating into the next evolutionary step. On the one hand we are confronted with the fact that human thoughts and life are being transformed by something inhuman. On the other hand evolution refers not only to a physical form, but also to a transformation of consciousness and humanity. Entry into the virtual reality is happening in real time, and we are in two worlds simultaneously. It is only the awareness that moves into the virtual world while the body remains in the real world and time.

Sound support: Ulrich Brandstätter

Oliver Kellow
Synchronisis
Interactive device

Synchronisis provides a meditative environment in which two participants can experience harmony by matching the breathing patterns of one another. The breathing apparatus provides feedback not from the individual, but by comparing the relative states of the two participants. Once in a reflexive pattern, the equilibrium becomes self-sustaining—a shared, intimate experience.

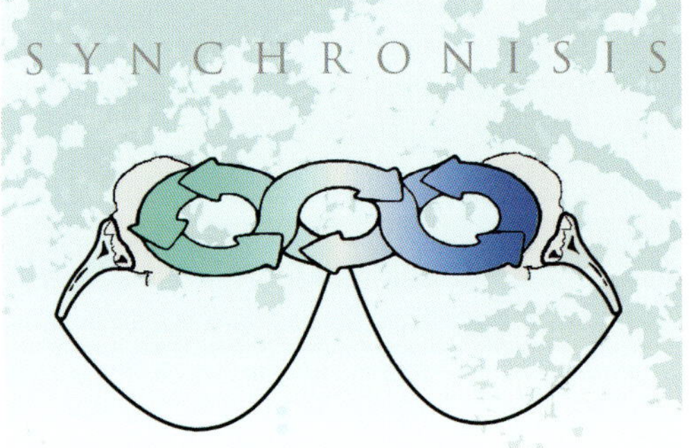

If the patterns are in sync, the lights pulse slowly together. Likewise, the sound slowly harmonizes to a throbbing pulse caused by natural harmonic resonance—closely matched waveforms of similar structure.

The act of sharing breath is both a symbolic and a corporeal experience that is often found in mythology, spiritual texts and literature. It is often accredited as an ethereal agent representing the passage of soul or of an "essence". Imposing conscious control on autonomous functions is also common practice in concentration and meditation exercises.

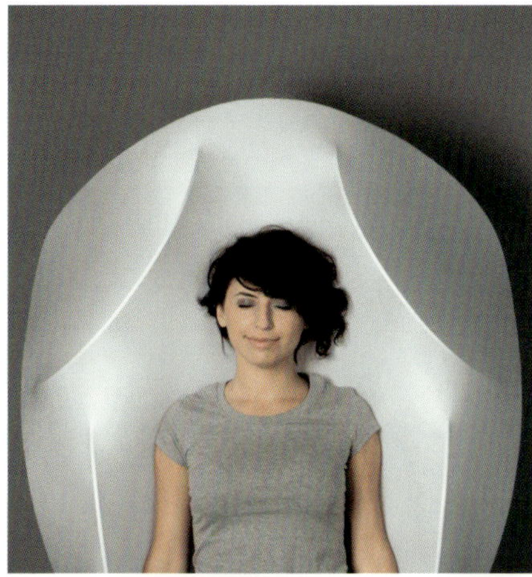

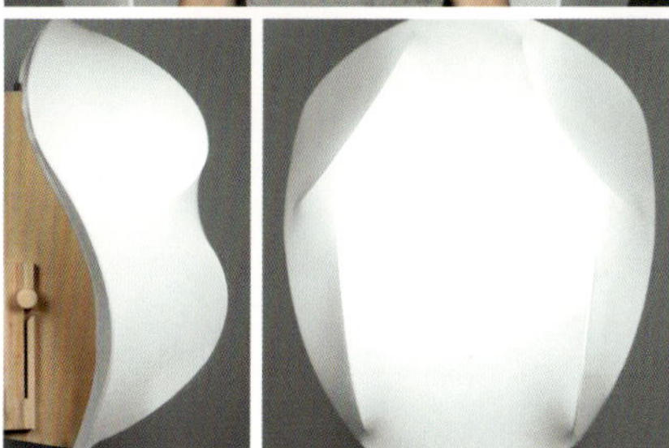

Justyna Zubrycka
Mórimo
Tactile sound aesthetic experience

The project aims to provide a platform for musical expression, with an emphasis on tactile properties of sound. In addition to being heard, the human body can perceive sounds also as haptic sensations, from subtle vibrations to shaking. *Mórimo* is a womb-like interface, that allows you to experience this phenomena as a sensuous aesthetic composition. The listener is immersed in acoustic waves with various frequencies, mostly at the edge of hearing.

This project was developed in the Interface Cultures program at The University of Art and Design Linz, and finalized as a diploma project at the Industrial Design Department, Academy of Fine Arts in Cracow.

Music: Miron Grzegorkiewicz (How How)

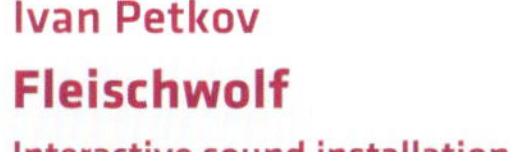

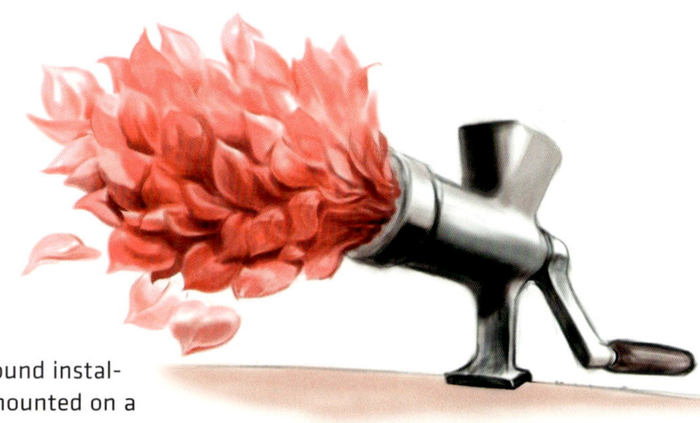

Ivan Petkov
Fleischwolf
Interactive sound installation

Fleischwolf is an interactive sound installation in the form of a meat grinder mounted on a massive wooden table. Turning the crank causes the machine to emit a sound that initially resembles a very deep bass voice. When the crank is turned more vigorously and faster, the characteristics of the sound change too. At a certain speed, a baby's scream is recognizable, but due to the construction of the meat grinder, it's hard to maintain this sound. So whether this scream is audible at all depends on the installation visitors.

This work is an experiment in the context of media psychology and interactive art. Although it consists of very specific, interconnected elements, the message it conveys is determined by the experiences and backgrounds of each individual visitor.

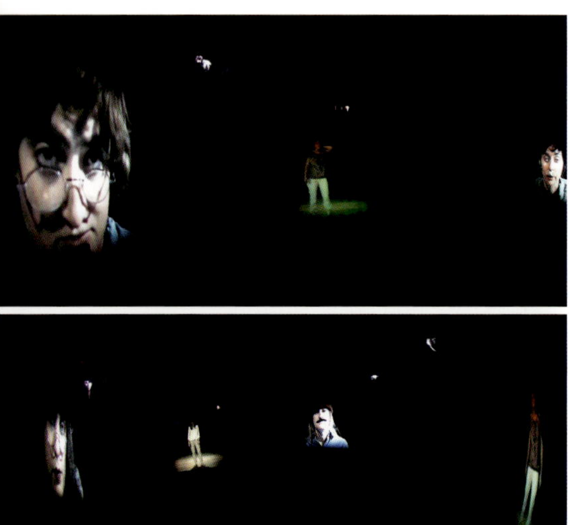

Lenka Klimešová, Maja Štefančíková
Error Stage in Five Layers
Video installation, 2011

The installation consists of four videos, which surround the visitors and communicate with them. The videos evoke a kind of theatrical scene, inspired by Aristotelian tragedy, in which the spectator finds himself/herself part of the cross-point communication. The authors have chosen a theatrical environment as a metaphor of the art scene: looking for a place at the scene in terms of authorship constitution and casting the roles–including the role of the spectator, the role of the director / the author and the role of the critic / the curator. The visitor's catharsis, if any, is the final effect of the artwork, the spectator's ability to perceive, enjoy and reflect the artwork. The main protagonists are the authors themselves, who comment on the process of creation and, at the same time, confront the superconscious voices that unsettle their self-confidence and creativity. The full shot and the close up are used to distinguish between the ego and superego confrontation.
Curator: Eva Filová

Jaak Kaevats, Onur Sönmez
Jason Shoe

Sharing quantified personal data has become a common ritual of contemporary life. Inherent human activities such as running, sleeping or eating are reduced to distilled sensory data represented by kilometers, hours or calories and shared on social networks. The *Jason Shoe* experiment is carried out using a bottle of water equipped with a servo as an actuator, simulating the patterns of real human running, to deceive the widely used Nike+ running sensor. The setup produces a tweaked and adjusted alternate reality as there is no actual running involved. By finding new ways of exploiting already existing sensory interfaces, we attempt to find new thresholds of reality and investigate their interaction within the existing cultural context.

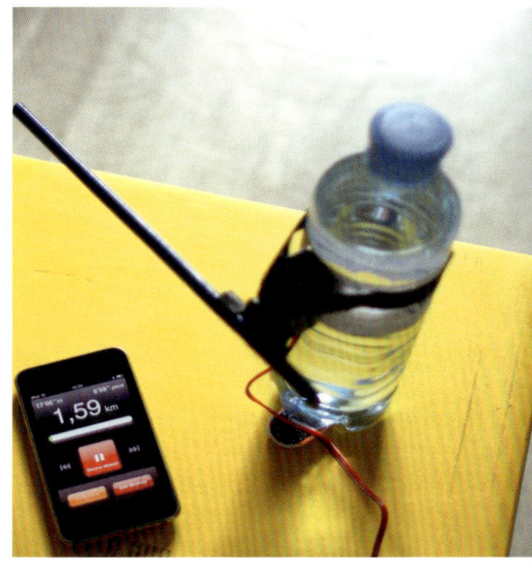

The reality is unconvincing without measured and published evidence. Noone questions the accuracy of the alternate reality as long as the objective quality of the measurement is guaranteed by a commonly accepted value system.

Onur Sönmez & Roswitha Angerer
How Do You Do?

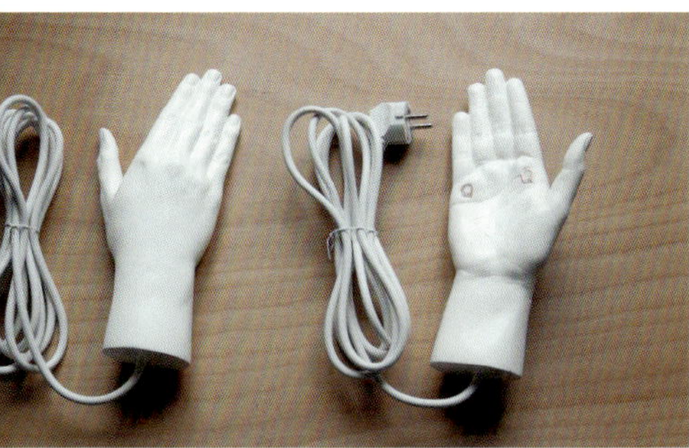

"Living, naturally, is never easy. You continue making the gestures commanded by existence for many reasons, the first of which is habit. Dying voluntarily implies that you have recognized, even instinctively, the ridiculous character of that habit, the absence of any profound reason for living, the insane character of that daily agitation and the uselessness of suffering." (Albert Camus–The Myth of Sisyphus)

What if you have a simple, utilitarian device, e.g.your kettle, with a reminder function that makes you question the very essence of your existence and, according to your answer, proposes a gesture, a polite way out.

The hand proposes an unpredictable life-changing experience, from possible death to a simple burn on your hand, from arrhythmic heart palpitations to violent muscle contractions.

Cèsar Escudero Andaluz
File_món

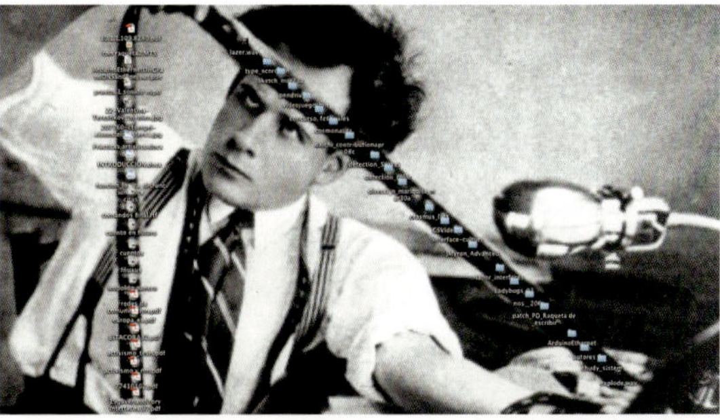

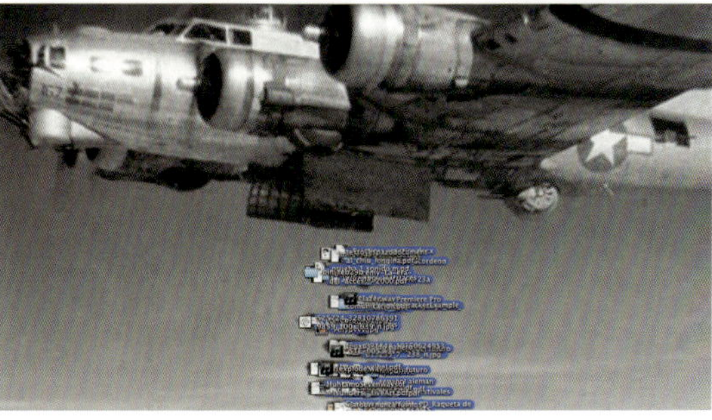

To talk about the image is to talk about meaningful surfaces, interpretable maps that represent the world. The technical reproduction of these images is presented to us today as simple pieces of the visible, shown by means of screens via television and internet in a continuous and unstoppable flow. Our position as a spectator puts us in a sea of information and disinformation, that causes rejection on the one hand, on the other hand alienation and conformity. This project works between this insensitivity to the representation and the predisposition to believe nothing we see. *File_món* is a series of images generated on the computer desktop through the distribution of icons and files arranged over images, which are downloaded from the internet and set as wallpaper. The computer screen is used as a canvas for a critical collage. It appraises the potential of creating new images on the computer without using any image authoring software.

Nina Mengin
You got the power
Airflow-controlled video installation

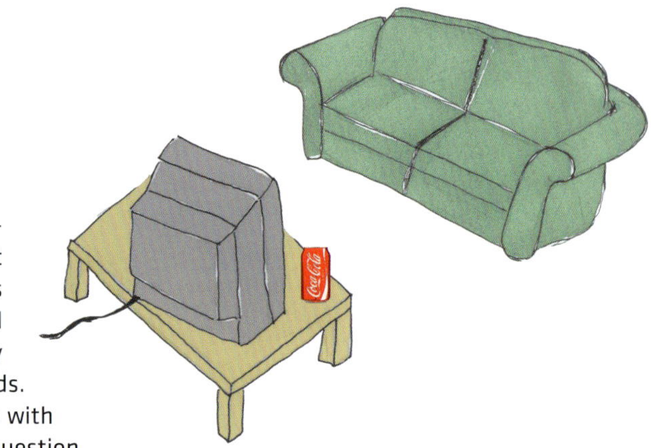

Water is one of the most important natural resources we have. Without it humankind is unable to survive. Water is also an important resource for global industries. Companies like Coca-Cola buy water resources for their production needs. The installation *You got the power* deals with the preservation of nature and poses the question whether believing in your own ability and possibility to change things is like believing in fairytales. The installation consists of a couch, a television showing a video, a Coca-Cola can and a straw as an interaction device.

Marie Polakova & Chiara Esposito
EYEVERSE
Installation

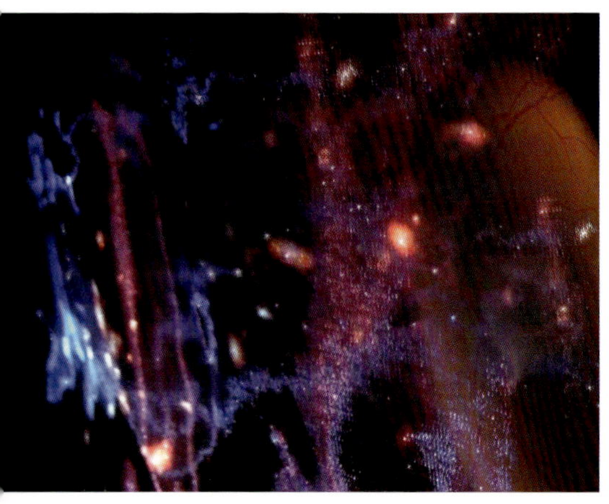

Eyeverse is a parallel universe. Its starry skies are generated on the basis of angiography photographs, reflecting pathological changes in the eyes affected by Proliferative Diabetic Retinopathy.

Eyeverse is a dynamic and changing environment. The final form into which it will evolve is unknown, and so is its duration. It is bound up with the life of one of its authors and the medical condition of her eyes–circumstances impossible to foresee.

At the exhibition visitors are invited to experience multidimensional, changing space and celestial formations of *Eyeverse,* as well as the medical images from which these originated, thus underlining the core thought of this artwork, which is *transformation.* Each of us has this power as individuals–the power to transform our fears. The power to turn tears into flawless, shimmering diamonds. The power to turn our deepest nightmares into beautiful smiles, images, forms or words, which might inspire others. Or to just simply make the world a more beautiful place and to let go of our fears.

Fabrizio Lamoncha
Poo Printer
Hybrid artwork

A common idiosyncratic habit of all birds is their inevitable punk nature to shit over our most precious belongings.
This is an experiment with a group of male zebra finches. The author/captor, who has a *1984* Big Brother kind of role, provides the implementation guidelines for transforming this countercultural attitude into a marketable artsy product. The observation of this group of non-breeding birds in captivity and the experimentation with induced behaviors has been rigorously documented for this task. This project investigates in a hybrid, artistic and scientific framework the physiological, mechanical and social dynamics of birds in captivity in a simulated factory chain environment. The result is the *Poo Printer*, an analog generative typography printer that uses the bird poo as the particle substance in order to slowly generate the Latin alphabet characters over a large paper roll.

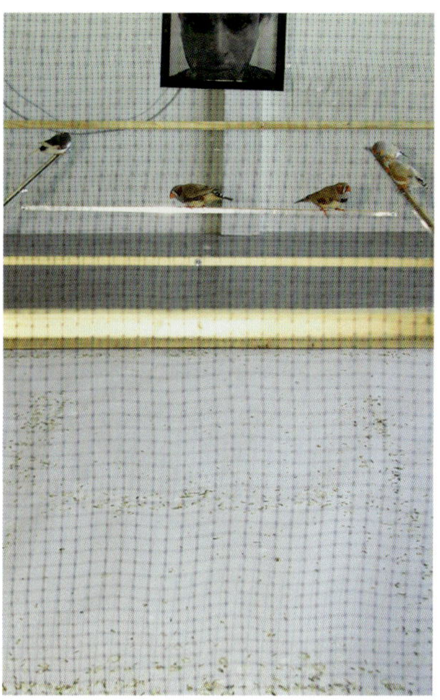

Andrea Suter
magic circle
Video piece, 2012

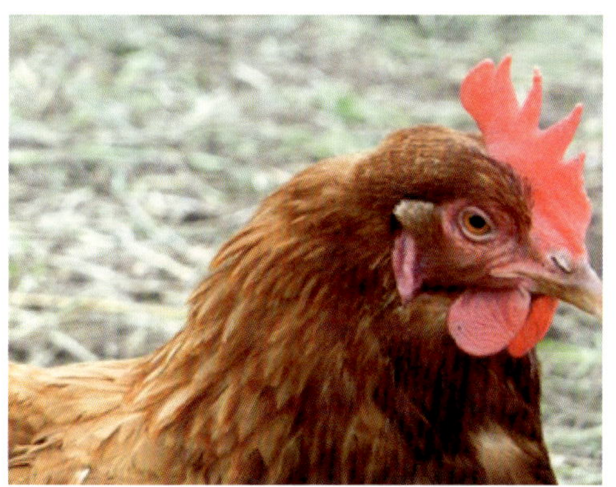

The *magic circle* "theory" is used within game development. It represents the idea of a magic circle, which a participant is supposedly unable to leave. The theory comes from an old wives' tale about a chicken that is unable to leave the circle that is drawn around it.
The video piece by Andrea Suter tests the truth of the legend.

Media Art vs. Art Media

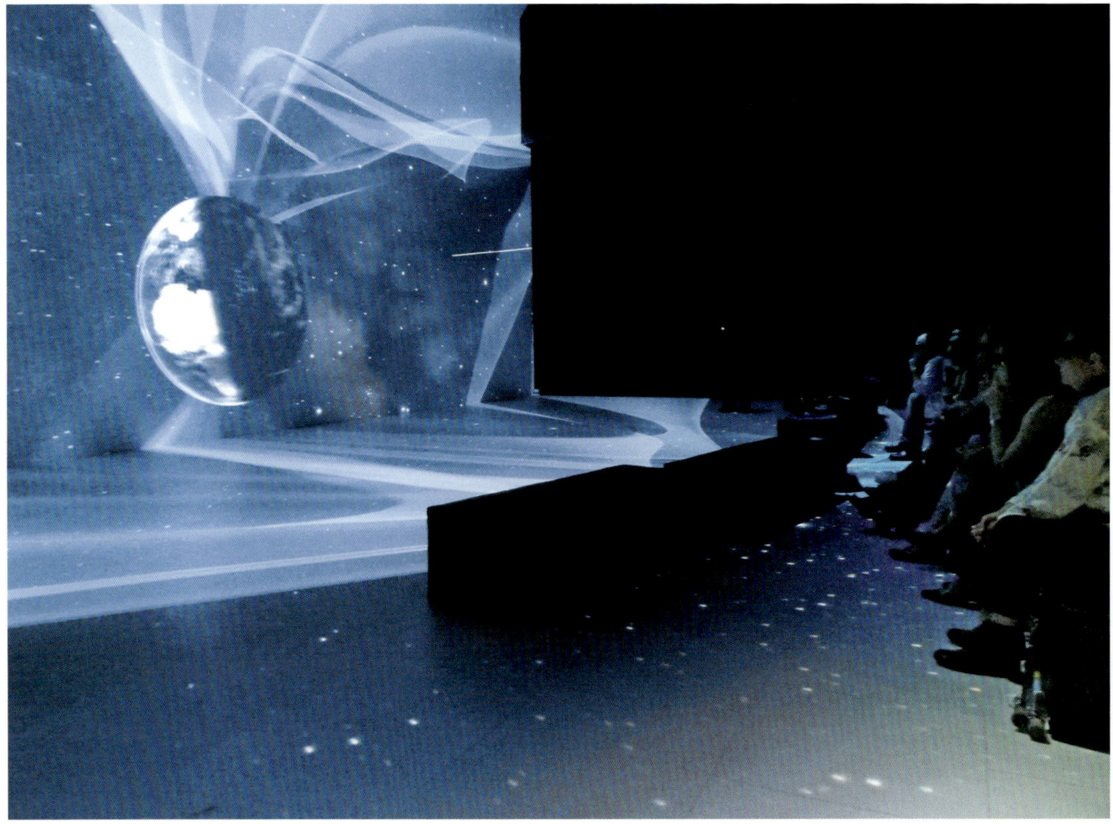

Ars Electronica Center, Deep Space: *Uniview*

Theory and Practice of Mediating the Public's Encounters with Media-based & Science-based Art

In light of numerous current exhibitions in museums and other such spaces, one could legitimately ask, in concurrence with insights of science theoretician Paul Feyerabend[1], where science ends and art begins, or where art ends and science begins. The recent advent of media-based or science-based art forms has updated this hypothesis formulated by Feyerabend in the 1970s with reference to scientific methods. At the *dOCUMENTA (13)* in 2012, Kristina Buch, holder of a degree in biology, planted a little garden for rare butterfly species, and Pierre Huyghe cordially invited a swarm of bees to make themselves at home in the head of a figurative sculpture. And even a year before (he took part in) *dOCUMENTA (13),* quantum physicist Anton Zeilinger and his entire crew of laboratory and personal assistants were showcased by an exhibition in Linz at the 2011 Ars Electronica Festival, which has featured, for the last 33 years in addition to works of media art and sound art, physical and biological phenomena at the nexus of science and art, and at which the laboratory itself has come to be an object most coveted by exhibition curators whose reconnoiterings along the border where art and science meet can no longer even be adequately described as exhibitions because quantum particles, human beings, and (live) butterflies and bees can hardly be subsumed by the generally accepted understanding of objects as the stuff of which an exhibition traditionally consists.

But what ultimately comes to be put on exhibit when objects and, accordingly, works are redefined in this way? Or would a better formulation be: of what does the performance consist? Don't these conceptual shifts also modify the conditions of possible presentations, and, due to the time-based nature and performativity of more and more works of art, doesn't the process of conceiving exhibitions have to move increasingly in the direction of performance practices (such as those used by concert impresarios)? Or, in the area of science-related presentations, wouldn't it be preferable to seek performative elements and their presentation possibilities beyond the documentary realm?

During a guided tour highlighting selected installations at the 2012 Ars Electronica Festival, *Media Art vs. Art Media* will address questions related to these issues, and, in doing so, will also methodologically scrutinize the history of museology as a history of the confrontation with objects. Attributed object discourses have changed considerably over the course of recent decades along with the above-described development in the arts, with the influence of various scientific disciplines on museological research and, by no means of least importance, due to the resulting increase in the number of objects of relevance to museums or that might conceivably be exhibited in them. In this methodological sense as well, *Media Art vs. Art Media* will examine the extent to which existing museological concepts of objects and authenticity are (still) suitable for the analysis of novel objects of media-based and science-based art, which ways of presenting and mediating the public's encounter with such objects are called for, and how the forms of displaying such objects and the curatorial process of dealing with them are to be categorized within the context of the museum's mission.

http://www.museum-joanneum.at/museumsakademie

Museological tour of the exhibitions in cooperation with the Museumsakademie Joanneum Graz
Concept: Gunther Reisinger, Bettina Habsburg-Lothringen

1   Paul Feyerabend, *Wider den Methodenzwang* (Against Method), Frankfurt/Main 1976

MedienKunst vs. KunstMedien

Theorie und Praxis des Vermittelns medien- und wissenschaftsbasierter Kunst

Mit dem Wissenschaftstheoretiker Paul Feyerabend[1] gedacht , könnte man in aktuellen musealen und ausstellenden Kontexten vielfach die Frage stellen, wo Wissenschaft endet und Kunst beginnt oder: wo Kunst endet und Wissenschaft beginnt. Speziell hinsichtlich medien- oder wissenschaftsbasierter Kunstformen erfährt diese von Feyerabend in Bezug auf wissenschaftliche Methoden bereits in den 1970er Jahren formulierte These seit einiger Zeit eine Aktualisierung: Bei der *dOCUMENTA (13)* pflanzt Kristina Buch 2012 als diplomierte Biologin ein Gärtchen für seltene Schmetterlingsarten oder lässt Pierre Huyghe einen Bienenschwarm gezielt auf dem Kopf einer figurativen Plastik nisten. Und bereits ein Jahr vor (seiner Teilnahme bei) der *dOCUMENTA (13)* war mit Anton Zeilinger ein Quantenphysiker samt seines experimentellen und personell assistierenden Umfelds bei der Ars Electronica 2011 in Linz ausgestellt, wo im Rahmen des Festivals neben medien- und klangkünstlerischen Arbeiten seit nunmehr 33 Jahren auch physikalische oder biologische Phänomene an der Schnittstelle zur Kunst gezeigt werden oder das Labor selbst zum Objekt der museal-ausstellenden Begierde wurde – allesamt Grenzgänge zwischen Wissenschaft und Kunst und als Ausstellungen nicht mehr adäquat zu beschreiben, weil Quantenteilchen, Menschen oder (lebende) Schmetterlinge und Bienen kaum in das gängige Verständnis von Objekten (als traditionelle Grundlagen einer Ausstellung) fallen. Was gelangt bei derartig geänderten Objekt- und damit Werkbegrifflichkeiten letztlich aber zur Ausstellung? Oder sollte man besser formulieren: zur Aufführung? Ändern sich durch diese Begriffsverschiebungen nicht auch die Bedingungen möglicher Präsentationen, und müsste aufgrund der Zeitbasiertheit und Performativität bei immer mehr künstlerischen Arbeiten nicht in Richtung Aufführungspraxen (wie in der Musik) gedacht werden? Oder könnte man im Bereich der wissenschaftsnahen Präsentationen nach dem performativen Element und dessen Präsentationsmöglichkeiten abseits des Dokumentarischen suchen?
Im Rahmen eines geführten Rundgangs durch ausgewählte Stationen des Ars Electronica Festival 2012 widmet sich die Veranstaltung *MedienKunst vs. KunstMedien* diesbezüglichen Fragen und versucht damit auch, die Geschichte der Museologie als eine Geschichte der Auseinandersetzung mit dem Objekt auf den methodischen Prüfstand zu stellen. Zugeordnete Objektdiskurse haben sich im Verlauf der letzten Jahrzehnte mit der beschriebenen Entwicklung der Künste, mit dem Einfluss verschiedener wissenschaftlicher Disziplinen auf die museologische Forschung und nicht zuletzt aufgrund einer daraus resultierenden Zunahme museumsrelevanter bzw. musealisierbarer Objekte stark verändert. Auch in diesem methodischen Sinn prüft die

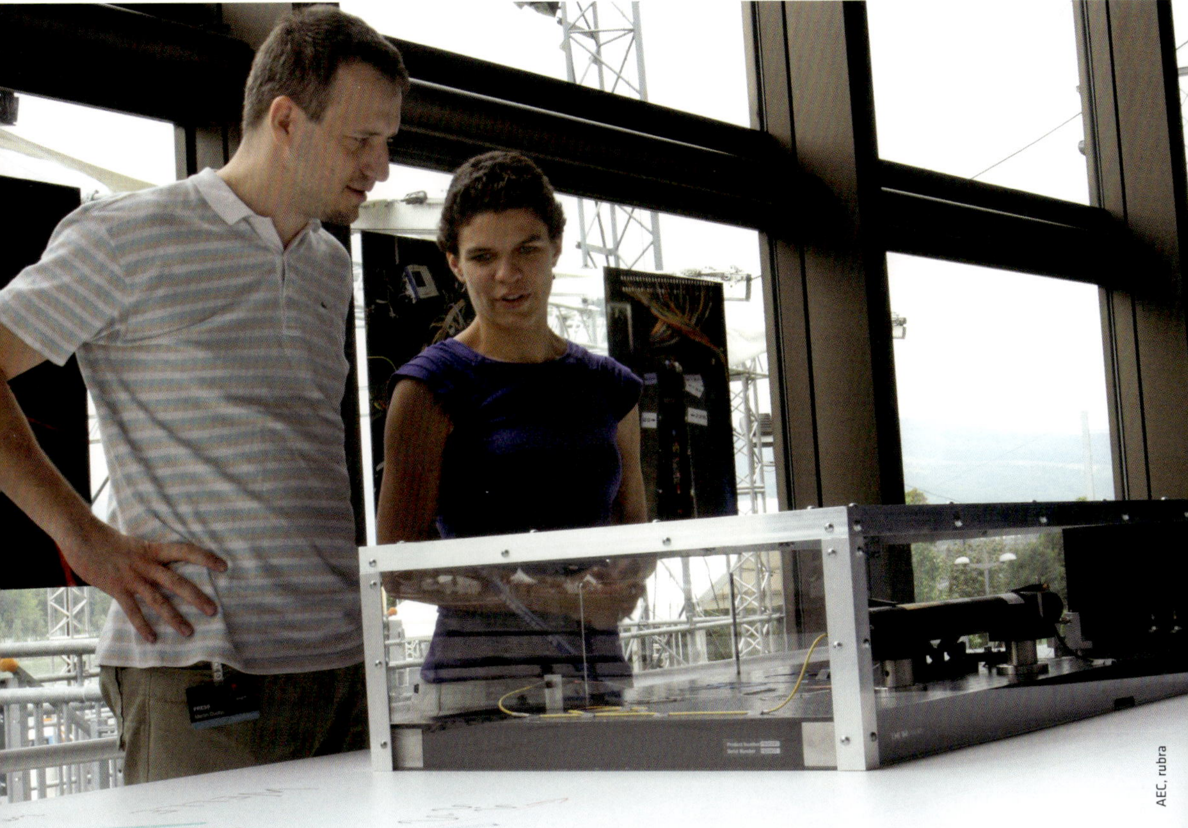

Ars Electronica 2011: *Demonstrationsexperimente Quantenphysik* by CoQuS – Vienna Doctoral Program on Complex Quantum Systems.

Veranstaltung, wie weit existierende museologische Objekt- und Authentizitätsbegriffe (noch) geeignet sind, neuartige Objekte der medien- und wissenschaftsbasierten Kunst zu analysieren, welche Art und Weise der Präsentation und Vermittlung diese nahelegen und wie die Formen des Zeigens und der kuratorischen Auseinandersetzungen im Kontext musealer Ausrichtung und Darstellung einzuordnen sind.

Text: Gunther Reisinger, Bettina Habsburg-Lothringen

1   Paul Feyerabend, *Wider den Methodenzwang*. Frankfurt/Main 1976

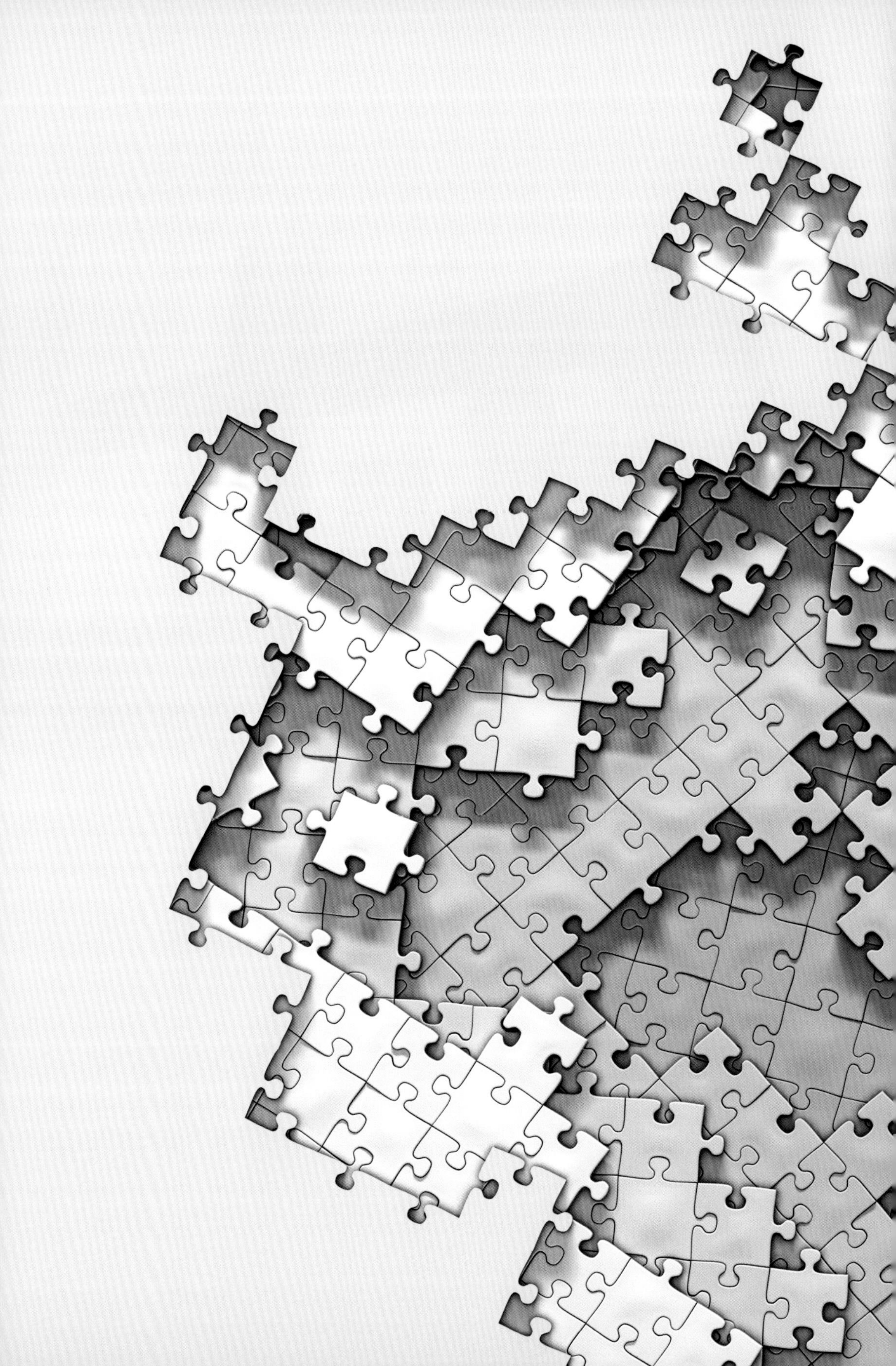

ARS ELECTRONICA ANIMATION FESTIVAL 2012

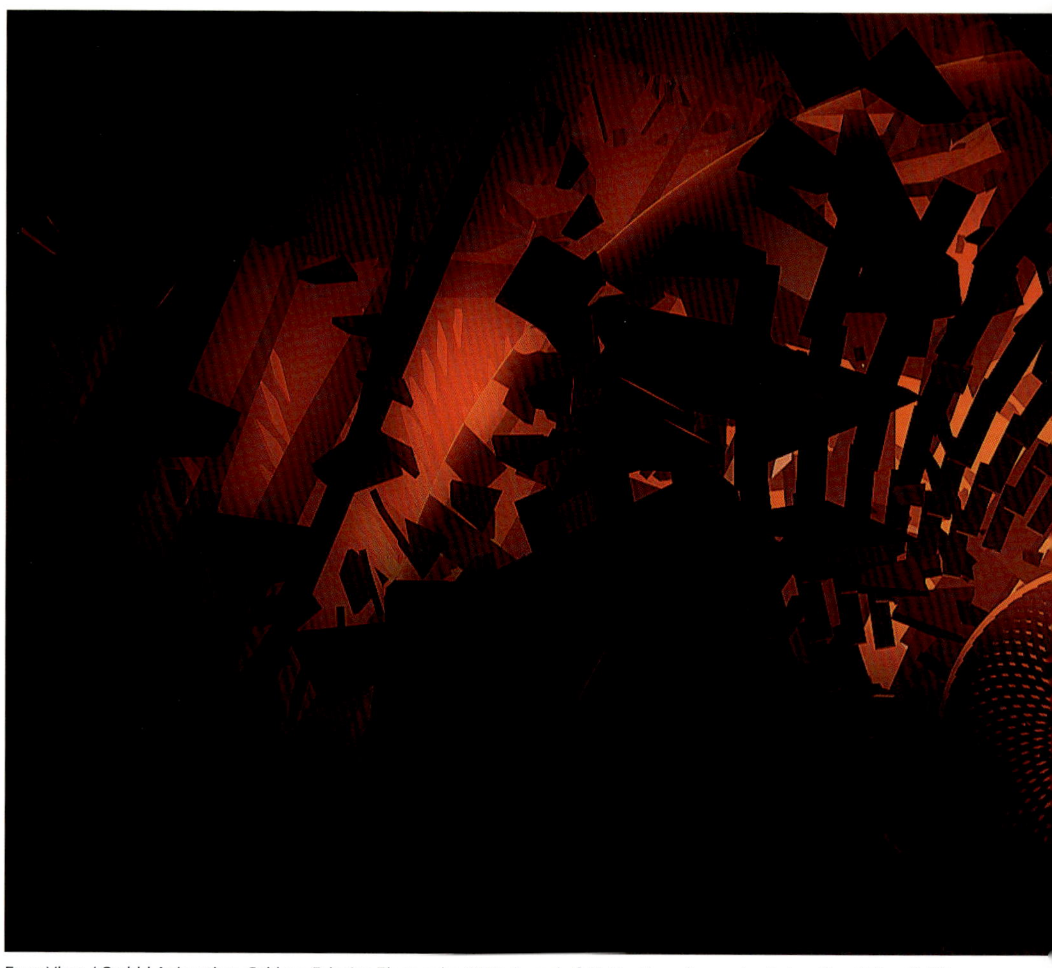

Evan Viera / Orchid Animation: *Caldera*, Prix Ars Electronica 2012, Award of Distinction, Computer Animation / Film / VFX

Ars Electronica
Animation Festival 2012

A photographer temporarily confined to a wheelchair stares out his rear window observing the neighbors, and becomes convinced one of them has committed a murder. A 1954 cinematic masterpiece directed by Alfred Hitchcock and starring Grace Kelly and James Stewart is the point of departure of this work by Jeff Desom, a filmmaker from Luxemburg. A local bar had commissioned him to produce visual material for a big-screen projector installed there. His idea: digitally recreate the film set—the rear courtyard scene of the original—and let some of the windows of the apartments across the way serve as displays showing excerpts from the original film distilled down to a 20-minute loop. Jeff Desom's work has been honored with the 2012 Golden Nica grand prize in the Prix Ars Electronica's Computer Animation category.

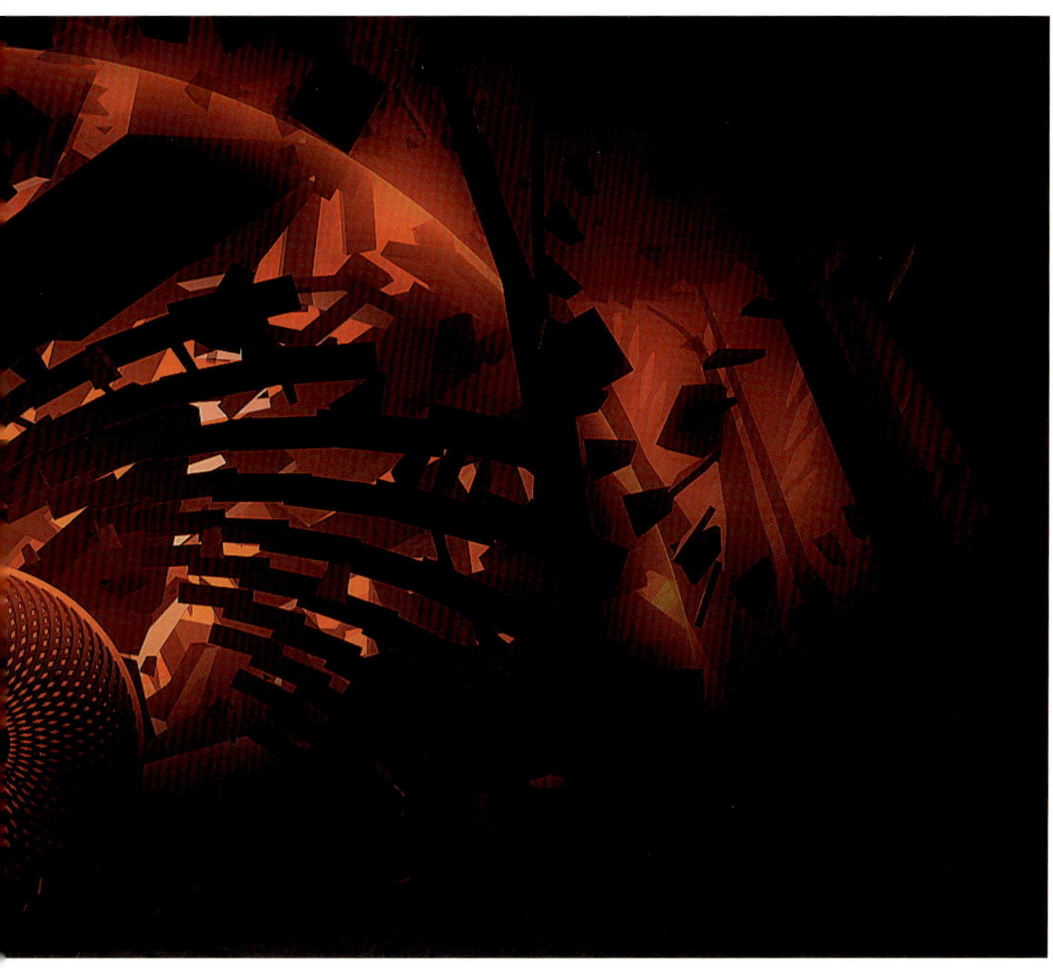

A young girl who's addicted to pills and on the verge of careening out of control resolves to get a grip on her screwed-up life. In a strange underwater world, she encounters what might be a liberating side of human existence. The narrative captivates viewers with simple, touchingly beautiful digital images that work as if by suggestion. *Caldera* by Evan Viera has been singled out for recognition with an Award of Distinction in the 2012 Prix Ars Electronica's Computer Animation category.

An Air Force astronaut lands on a strange planet, where he encounters a previously unknown humanoid species. The ape-like creatures are far superior to humans, and possibly possess the key to saving Earth. For the outstanding special effects they produced under the direction of F/X specialist Tim Burton, New Zealand-based WETA Company garnered the second Award of Distinction bestowed in the 2012 Prix Ars Electronica's Computer Animation category.

The Prix Ars Electronica's prizes aren't meant "only" to recognize the year's outstanding achievements in the competition's seven categories; they also aim to spotlight emerging trends and point the way to the future.

In this spirit, *Rear Window Loop* exemplifies a movement that has been apparent in the digital world in recent years and even a bit longer in works by experimental filmmakers: using so-called found footage—visual material shot for other purposes—to compose new sequences. But this film—if it can even be called that, which is precisely the point here—is emblematic of a trend towards breaking through limits and crossover synergies that have become increasingly pervasive in this genre. Is *Rear Window Loop* simply a film and thus a screen-based work? Or an installation? Exuberant playfulness with available material? Or is it just Jeff Desom's homage to Hitchcock's masterful classic? All questions are admissible; an authoritative answer can come from the artist alone.

Caldera exemplifies another trend that has been developing steadily in recent years—the short film that demands competence in storytelling and screenwriting, one in which the filmmaker and storyteller take advantage of the possibilities and tools of computer animation in responding to the challenges to their imagination. But this work also stands for a trend that manifested itself clearly among submissions to this year's Prix Ars Electronica: the marked prevalence of stories that dwell on the dark side of life and crises in the lives of individual people. The Animation Festival has dedicated an entire program to this phenomenon.

Last but not least: *Rise of the Planet of the Apes.* Since the 1980s, productions by the major F/X studios have been driving technical development and trailblazing in uncharted territory. Practically every new film writes a new chapter in the history of technological progress. In this account, *Rise of the Planet of the Apes* truly stands out. One of the jurors who is herself an expert in the F/X field said: "I know of no other film that leaves the audience so completely unaware that they're watching special effects."

The Ars Electronica Animation Festival is a compilation from among the 610 submissions to the 2012 competition. Approximately 100 excerpts provide an overview of what filmmakers around the world have been up to lately.

Nine programs have been distilled from this year's entries. There's also a lineup of works from the Japanese Media Festival as well as a best-of selection from the 2012 CREATE YOUR WORLD category for Austrian youngsters age 19 and under. With a total of 11 one-hour programs, the Ars Electronica Animation Festival is an up-to-the-minute showcase of what's happening in the commercial arena, the halls of academia, and artists' ateliers.

Ars Electronica Animation Festival curated by: Christine Schöpf, Jürgen Hagler

Ein vorübergehend an den Rollstuhl gefesselter Fotograf spioniert vom Hinterhoffenster seine Nachbarn aus, denn er ist überzeugt, dass einer von ihnen einen Mord begangen hat. Ein filmisches Meisterwerk von Alfred Hitchcock aus dem Jahr 1954 mit Starbesetzung – Grace Kelly und James Stewart – liefert dem luxemburgischen Filmemacher Jeff Desom den Stoff. Er hat den Auftrag, für eine luxemburgische Bar visuelles Material für dort installierte Breitbildprojektoren zu produzieren. Er baut dafür digital das Szenario: den Hinterhof als Ort des Originals, und in den diversen Fenstern des digitalen Szenarios laufen Ausschnitte aus dem Originalfilm, verknappt zu einem 20-minütigen Loop. Jeff Desom bekommt dafür die Goldene Nica, den Hauptpreis, in der Kategorie Computeranimation / VFX / Film des Prix Ars Electronica 2012.

Ein junges Mädchen, tablettenabhängig und dementsprechend im Ausnahmezustand, nimmt ihr fehlgeleitetes Leben in die Hand: In einer fremden Unterwasserwelt begegnet sie einer – möglicherweise – befreienden Seite des Lebens. In einfachen und berührend schönen digitalen Bildern wird der Zuseher suggestiv von der Erzählung eingenommen – *Caldera* von Evan Viera ist eine Auszeichnung in der Kategorie Computeranimation / VFX / Film des Prix Ars Electronica 2012.

Ein Airforce-Astronaut landet auf einem fremden Planeten und begegnet dort einer unbekannten Spezies von Humanoiden: den Menschen weit überlegenen Affen, die möglicherweise den Schlüssel dafür besitzen, wie die Erde zu retten sei. Für die Special Effects unter der Regie des F/X Spezialisten Tim Burton erhält die neuseeländische Weta Digital die zweite Auszeichnung in der Kategorie des Prix Ars Electronica Computeranimation / VFX / Film 2012.

Die Preise des Prix Ars Electronica wollen nicht „nur" alljährlich Bestleistungen in den insgesamt sieben Wettbewerbskategorien auszeichnen, sondern sie wollen auch richtungsweisend und trendformulierend sein.

So steht *Rear Window Loop* für eine in den letzten Jahren sichtbare Bewegung in der digitalen Welt, die der Experimentalfilm bereits länger kennt: Found Footage, also vorhandenes Bild/Rohmaterial, wird verwendet, um daraus neue Einheiten zu komponieren. Aber der Film – ist es ein solcher? – steht, und das ist wohl der entscheidendere Ansatz, für einen Trend zur Grenzüberschreitung, der sich in diesem Genre zunehmend breit macht. Ist *Rear Window Loop* einfach ein Film und damit eine screen-basierte Arbeit? Oder eine Installation? Das lustvolle Spiel mit vorhandenem Material? Oder ist es einfach nur eine Referenz, die Jeff Desom dem Großmeister Hitchcock erweist? Alle Fragen sind zulässig, eine schlüssige Antwort darauf kann nur der Künstler selbst geben.

Caldera steht für den seit einigen Jahren sich stetig entwickelnden Trend zum Kurzfilm, der Kompetenz im Storytelling und Drehbuchschreiben erfordert und mit den Möglichkeiten und Werkzeugen der Computeranimation die Fantasie der Filmemacher und Geschichtenerzähler herausfordert. Diese Arbeit steht aber auch für einen Trend, der sich in diesem Jahr des Prix Ars Electronica sehr deutlich abzeichnet: für den Trend zu Geschichten, die die Schattenseiten des Lebens oder Ausnahmezustände der menschlichen Existenz thematisieren – wir haben diesem Kapitel ein eigenes Programm im Animationsfestival gewidmet.

Last but not least, *Planet der Affen: Prevolution.* Seit den 1980er Jahren haben die Produktionen der großen F/X-Studios die technische Entwicklung vorangetrieben und Neuland erobert. Mit fast jedem Film ist ein großes Stück an technologischer Entwicklung geschrieben worden, und dafür ist *Planet der Affen: Prevolution.* ein besonderes Beispiel. Wie sagt eine Jurorin und selbst Spezialistin für F/X-Produktion: „Ich kenne keinen anderen Film, wo man F/X so vergisst wie hier."

Das Ars Electronica Animation Festival ist eine Kompilation aus den insgesamt 610 Einreichungen in diesem Jahr und gibt mit rund hundert Filmausschnitten einen Überblick über internationale Positionen und Sichtweisen.

Neun Programme wurden aus den Einreichungen destilliert. Dazu kommen das Programm des Japanese Media Festival sowie das Programm von u19 – CREATE YOUR WORLD als Best-of der Leistungen unter 19-Jähriger in Österreich. Mit seinen insgesamt elf einstündigen Programmen ist das Ars Electronica Animation Festival ein aktueller Showcase für Produktionen aus dem kommerziellen Bereich ebenso wie aus der akademischen Welt und aus Künstlerateliers.

Text: Christine Schöpf, Jürgen Hagler
Ars Electronica Animation Festival kuratiert von: Christine Schöpf, Jürgen Hagler

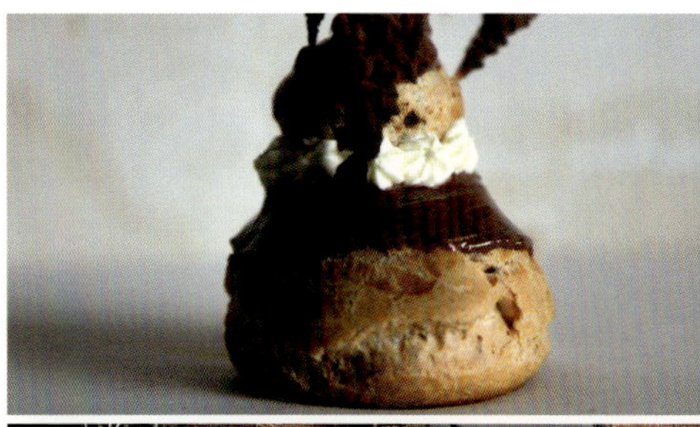
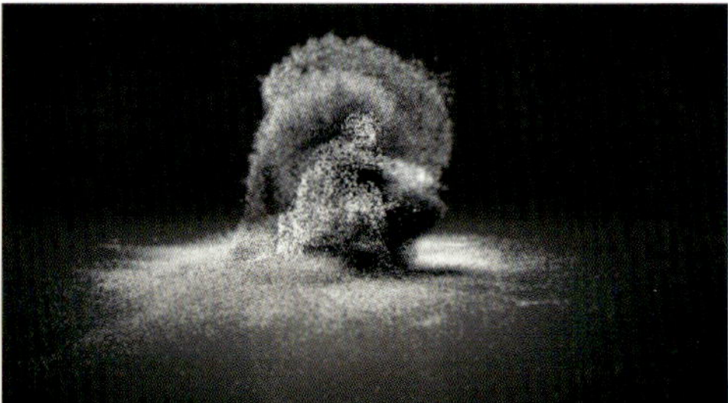
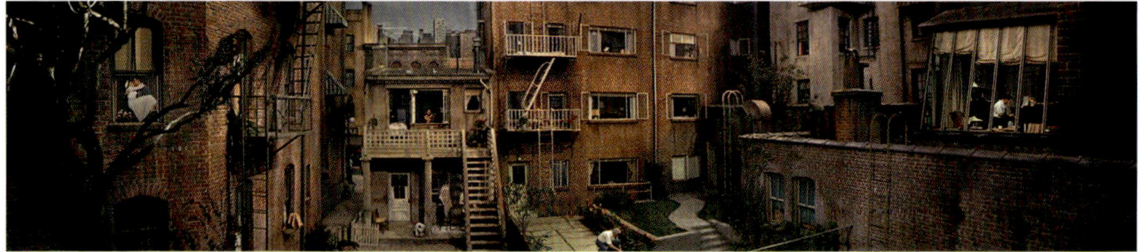

Artfilm

Experimental arrays and semi-abstract visual takes make up this program. What they all have in common is their highly artistic mode of expression. Investigations with found footage, visual ramifications, works that take a "Let's go from reality to abstract" approach (and vice-versa) make up the *Artfilm* program.

Versuchsanordnungen und semiabstrakte visuelle Beispiele sind der Stoff für dieses Programm – ihnen gemeinsam ist der dahinter stehende künstlerische Gestus. Experimente mit Found Footage, visuelle Verästelungen, das „Let's-go from reality to abstract" und umgekehrt bestimmen das Programm *Artfilm*.

About Music

Music videos, discussions of music, demonstrations of how many ways music can come about—all of these approaches are found here. Keep in mind: they're all about music, each in its own key.

Musikvideos, über Musik diskutieren und zeigen, wie Musik auch entstehen kann – das alles sind die Ansätze, die dieses Programm ausmachen. Wohlgemerkt: Es geht immer um Musik, nur die Positionen dazu sind verschieden.

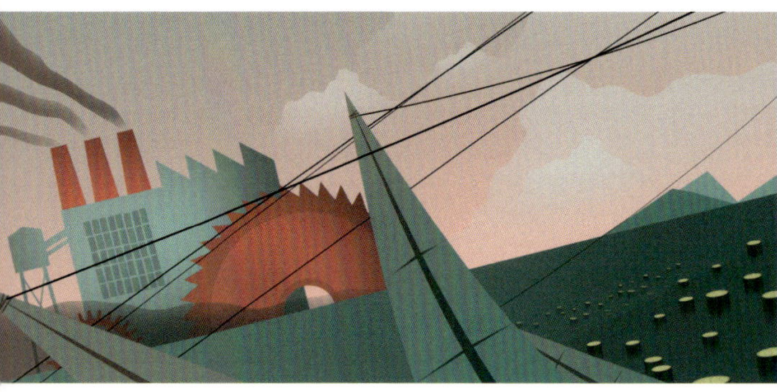
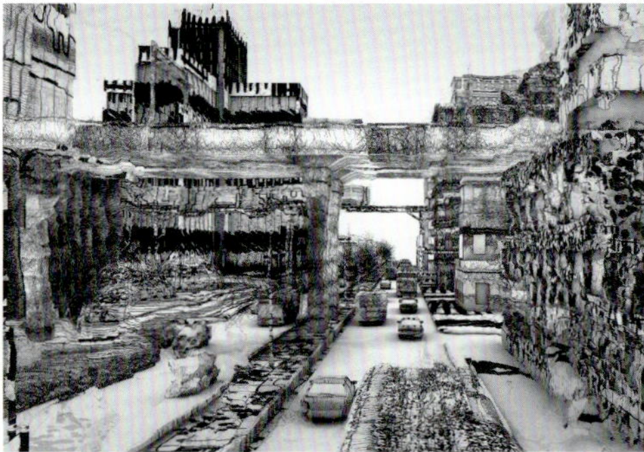

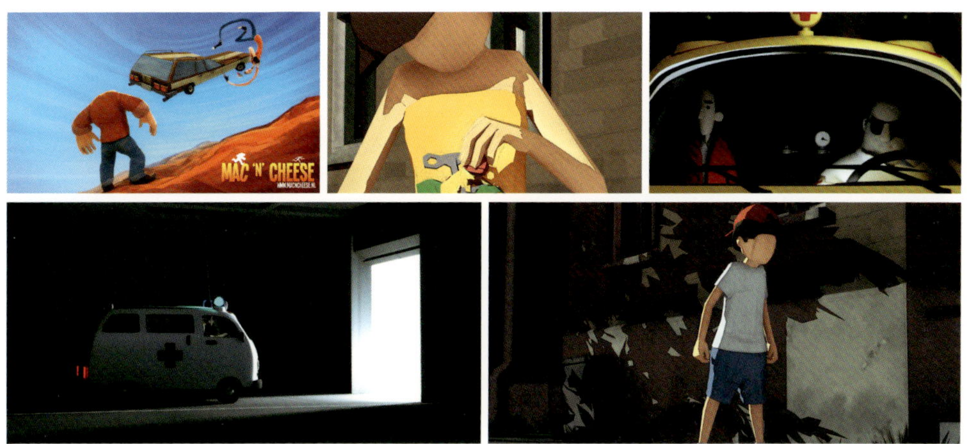

Inner Spaces

Times in which some force majeur determines the course of human events, circumstances that completely invert our so-called normal surroundings—these in particular have reared their (ugly) heads at the Prix Ars Electronica this year. Subtly told tales that urge those who confront them to reflect about their own lives.

Menschliche Ausnahmezustände, das Auf-den-Kopf-Stellen der „normalen" uns umgebenden Welt sind Themen, die uns in diesem Jahr des Prix Ars Electronica besonders aufgefallen sind. Subtil erzählte Filme, die zum Nachdenken über sich selbst anregen.

Visual Effects

Feature films by major Hollywood studios, computer games and commercials have long been treating viewers to a taste of the repertoire of visual effects specialists. Regardless of our overall rating of the final product, each one contains a high concentration of creativity and know-how. This program is an excursion through today's world of possibilities.

Spielfilme großer Hollywood-Firmen, Gaming und Werbung führen uns seit Jahren das Repertoire der großen Macher vor Augen. Wie immer wir zu den Produkten stehen – in jeder Neuproduktion ist ein enormes Maß an Neuentwicklung und Know-how verpackt. Lassen Sie sich mit diesem Programm in die Welt des Machbaren entführen.

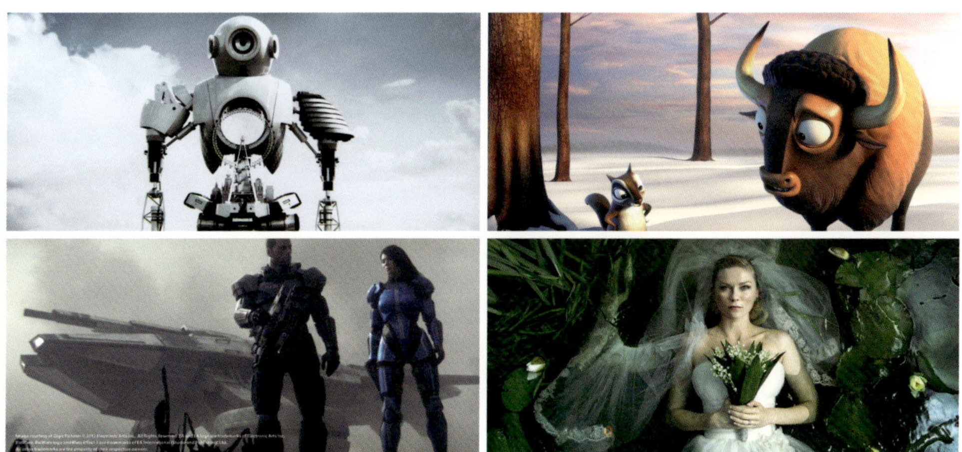

Comedy

A big party for (gay) flamingos, a farm with inflated cows, grubs that overrun gardens, a detective story with a positive conclusion—stories to which laughter is the only appropriate response.

Eine Big-Party für (schwule) Flamingos, eine Farm mit aufgeblasenen Kühen, Engerlinge, die in Gärten einfallen, Kriminalstory mit positivem Ausgang – es sind allesamt ziemlich komische Geschichten, die zum Lachen auffordern!

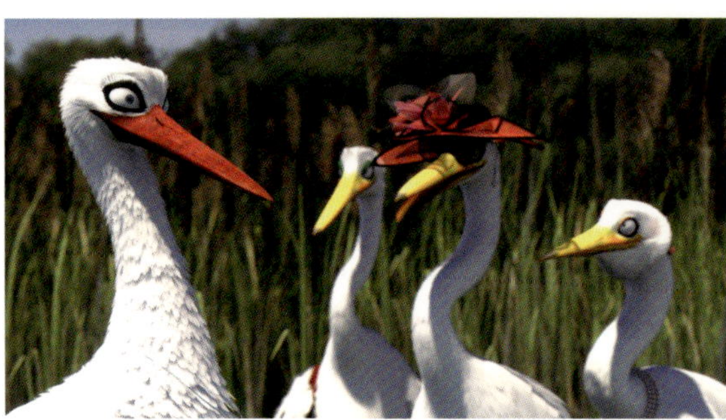 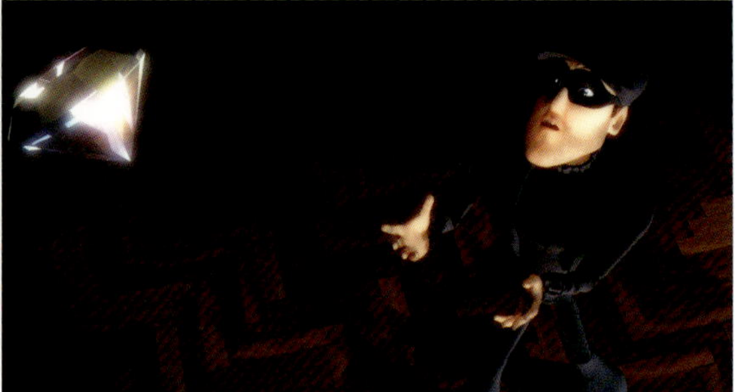

Position & Message

Nuclear waste disposal; events in pre-World War II Austria that culminated in civil war and are generally swept under the carpet nowadays; historical footage of the Warsaw Ghetto; a horror-filled story from the Middle Ages—this program is full of films with a statement to make.

Atommüllentsorgung, die in den Bürgerkrieg mündende, normalerweise ausgeblendete Geschichte Österreichs vor dem Zweiten Weltkrieg, Minutenausschnitte aus dem Warschauer Ghetto oder eine grausame Geschichte aus dem Mittelalter – Filme, die Positionen einnehmen, in ein Programm gepackt.

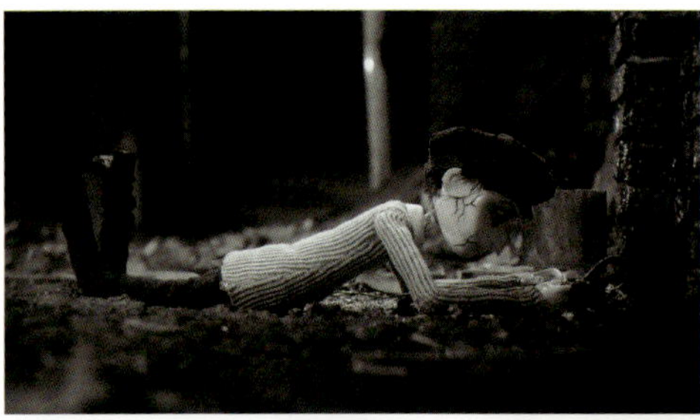 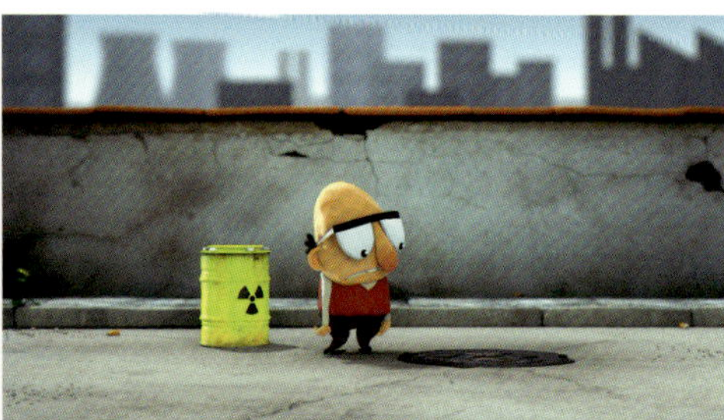

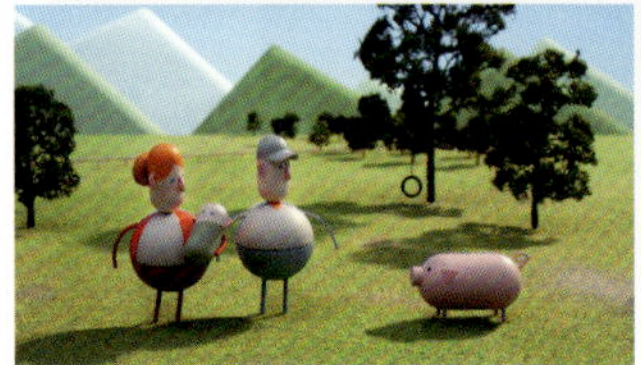 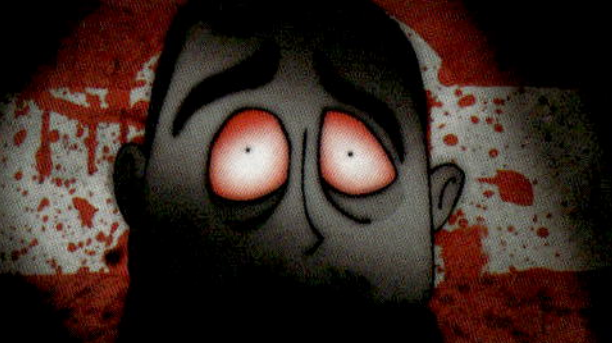 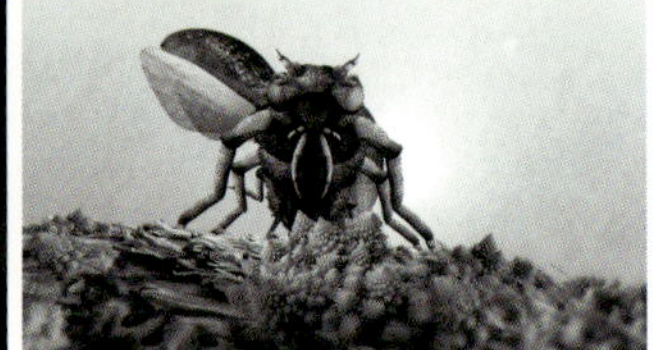

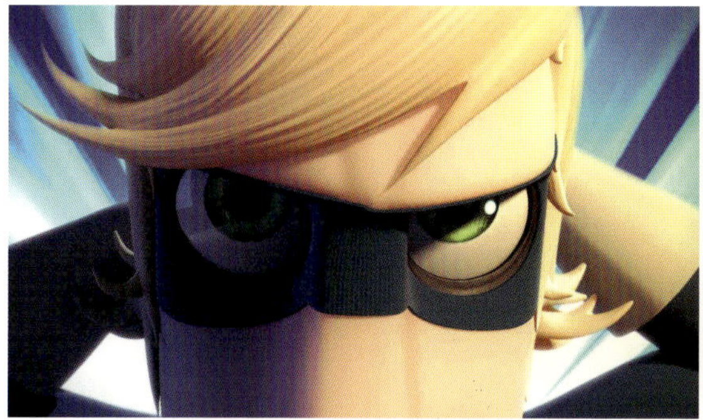
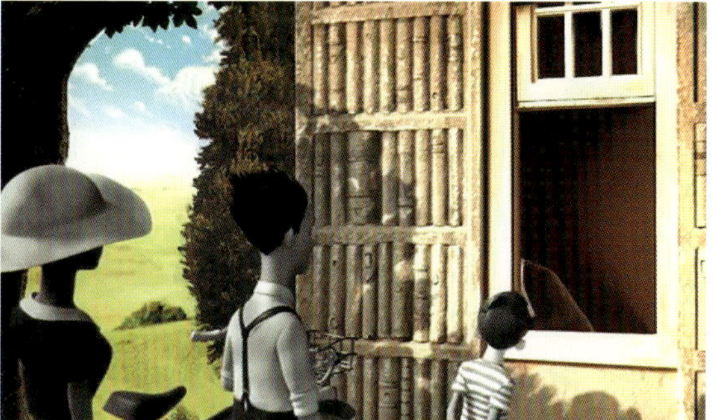

Narration

Poetically beautiful but also bizarrely told tales—each one a masterpiece in its own right. Get carried away by the fantastic world of flying books. Or marvel at the experiences of a brick from a warehouse at some port somewhere.

Poetisch schön, aber auch skurril erzählte Geschichten: Jeder Film ist für sich ein Meisterwerk! Lassen Sie sich von der fantastischen Welt der Flying Books ebenso faszinieren wie von den Erlebnissen eines Ziegels aus einer Lagerhalle am Hafen von irgendwo!

Late Nite

This stuff is definitely not for young audiences or those who lack nerves of steel! It's a collection of horrors that could (almost) only have been brought to the screen by computer animators.

Dieses Programm ist definitiv nicht für Jugendliche und nur etwas für starke Nerven! Eine Sammlung schauderhafter Geschichten, die (fast) nur über Computeranimation visualisiert werden können!

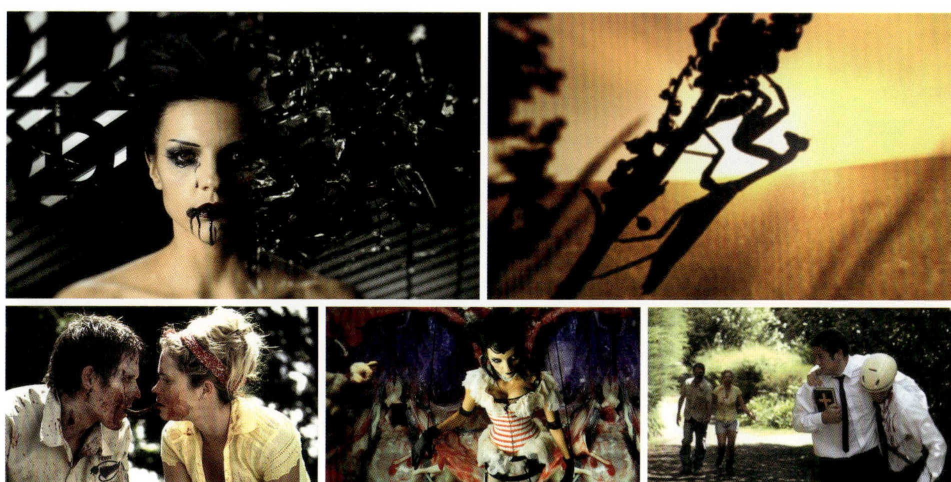

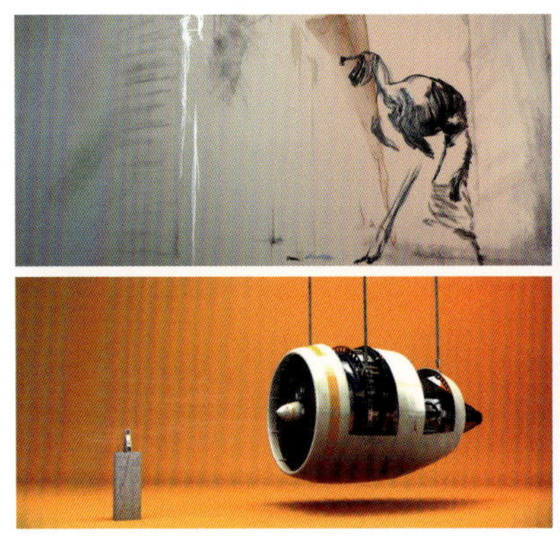
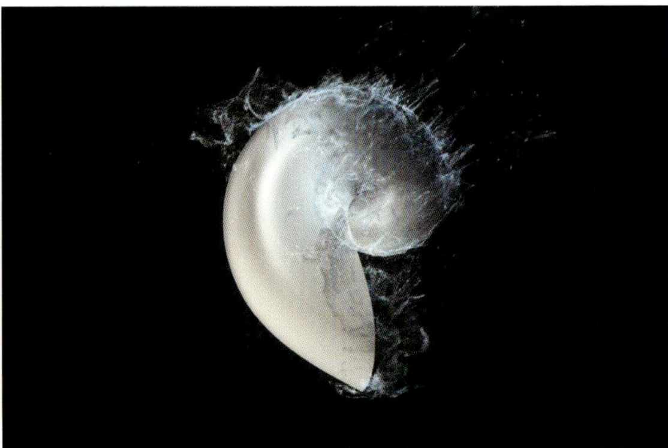

Motion & Graphics

Each individual image a work of art in and of itself? Here, dynamic meets visual—as a teaser, a façade installation, a short narrative film or a surreal physics experiment.

Jedes Einzelbild ein Kunstwerk für sich? In diesem Programm treffen Bewegung und Grafik zusammen: als Teaser, als Fassadeninstallation, als narrativer Kurzfilm oder als surreal-physikalisches Experiment.

Japan Media Arts Festival Selection

Visual imaginativeness and unconventional narrative forms characterize animation made in Japan. This program shows various kinds of Japanese animation from the latest Japan Media Arts Festival, which is the hybrid festival that focuses on Japanese pop culture phenomena such as animation, manga, games and media arts. The Japan Media Arts Festival is an annual contest for 4 divisions of Art, Entertainment, Animation and Manga.

Ideenreichtum und unkonventionelle Erzählformen sind charakteristisch für japanische Trickfilme. Das hier vorgestellte Programm ist eine Retrospektive verschiedener japanischer Animationsfilme, die bereits im Rahmen des letzten Japan Media Arts Festival vorgestellt wurden, einem hybriden Festival der japanischen Pop-Kultur, das neben Medienkunst auch Trickfilme, Mangas und Spiele zeigt. Das Japan Media Arts Festival ist ein jährlich ausgeschriebener Contest in den Bereichen Kunst, Unterhaltung, Animation und Manga.

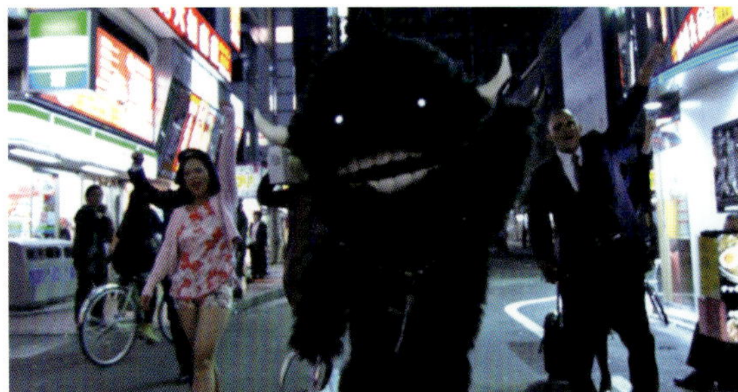
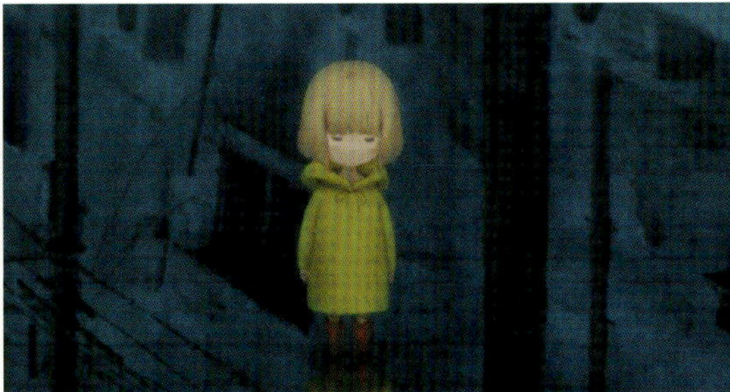

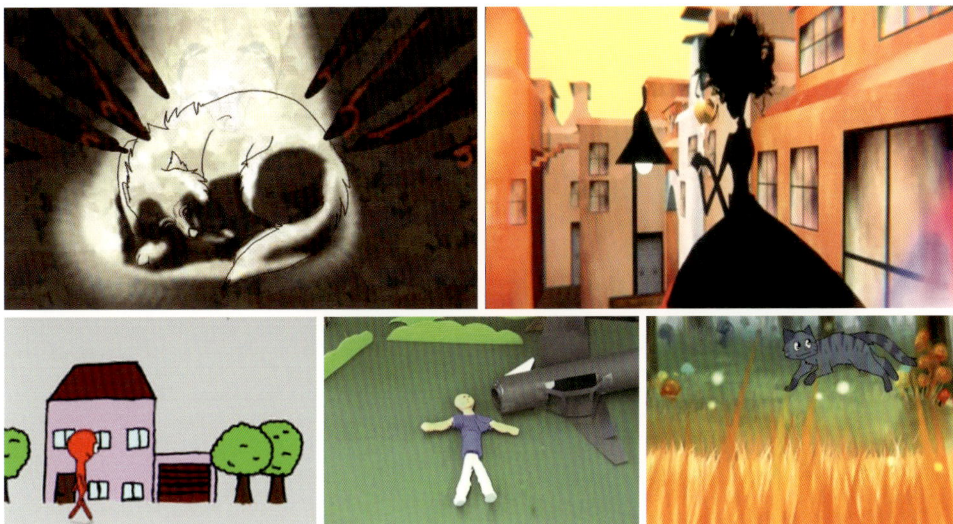

Young Animations

Witty, off-beat, subtle, tragic and serious animated work produced by young filmmakers will be screened during the Festival Ars Electronica. Every year, gifted young filmmakers submit their movies to u19 – CREATE YOUR WORLD (Austria), bugnplay (Switzerland), MB21 (Germany) and C3<19 (Hungary). The greatest hits will be featured in young animations.

Witzige, schräge, subtile, tragische und ernste Animationen, von jungen Menschen produziert, werden im Rahmen des Ars Electronica Festivals gezeigt. Jedes Jahr reichen begabte FilmemacherInnen ihre Animationen bei u19 – CREATE YOUR WORLD (Österreich), bugnplay (Schweiz), MB21 (Deutschland) und C3<19 (Ungarn) ein. Die besten davon werden in den Young Animations gezeigt.

media literacy award [mla]

With "Utilize | Understand | Create" as its watchwords, the media literacy award [mla] has been honoring the best media projects at European schools for over 10 years now. This competition is one of Europe's most important initiatives to foster media competence and was itself singled out for recognition with the prestigious Comenius Medal. The Ars Electronica Animation Festival will screen a selection of the best animated films and videos submitted for mla prize consideration.

Unter dem Motto „Anwenden | Verstehen | Gestalten" prämiert der media literacy award [mla] seit mehr als 10 Jahren die besten Medienprojekte an europäischen Schulen. Der Wettbewerb zählt damit zu den wichtigsten Medienkompetenz-Initiativen in Europa und wurde dafür mit der renommierten Comenius-Medaille ausgezeichnet. Im Rahmen des Ars Electronica Animation Festivals wird eine Auswahl der besten beim mla eingereichten Animationen und Videos gezeigt.

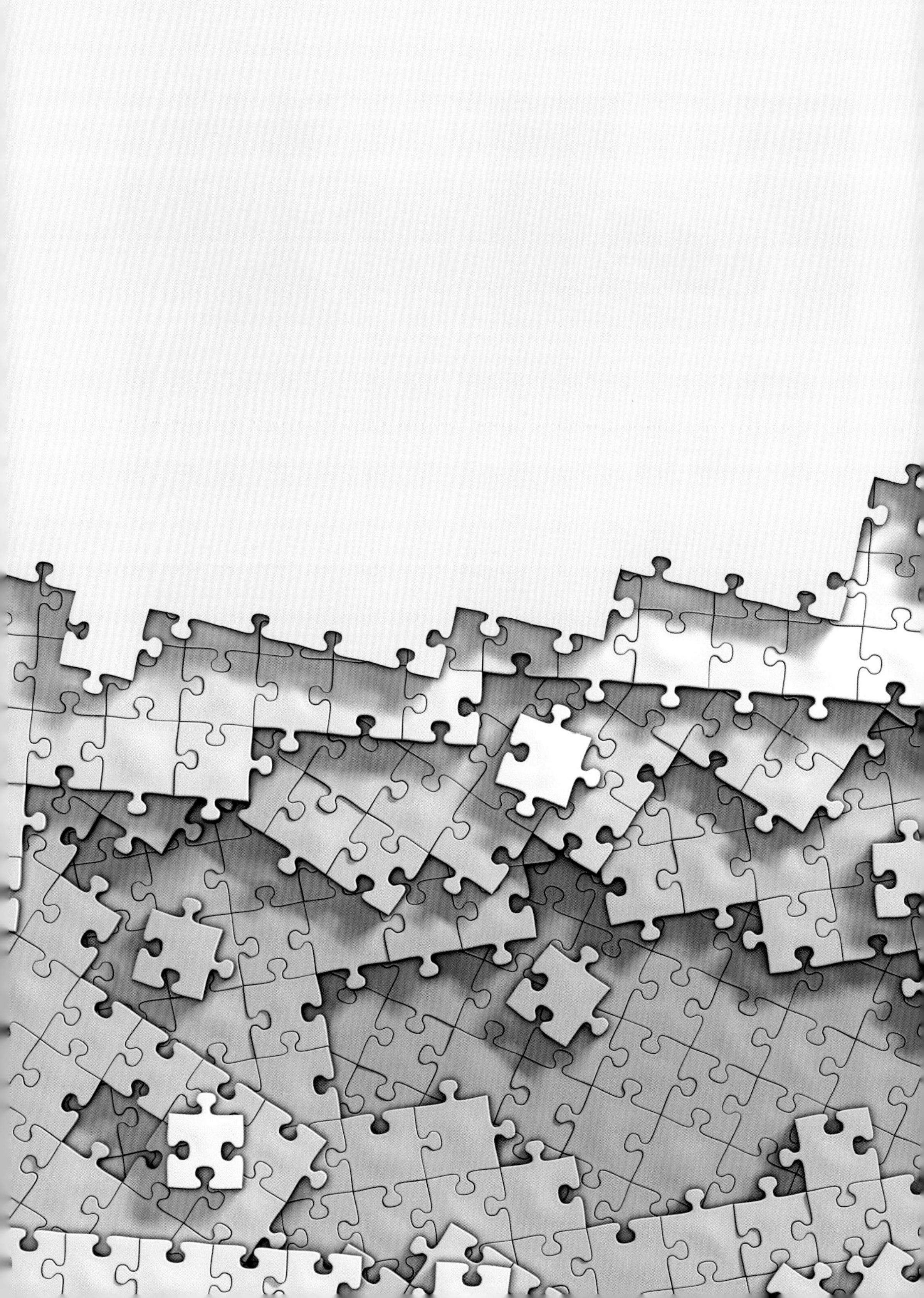

ARS ELECTRONICA
FUTURELAB

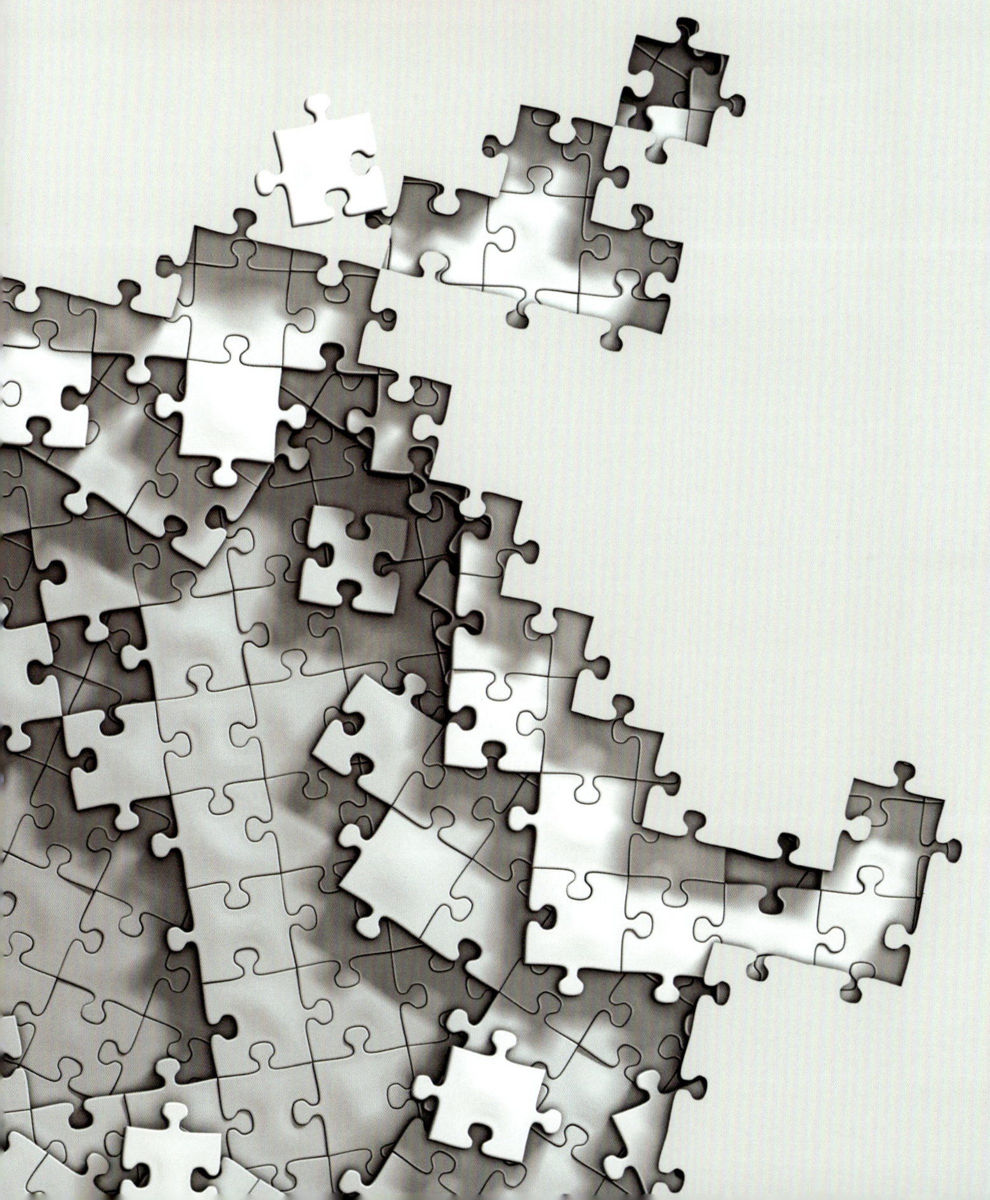

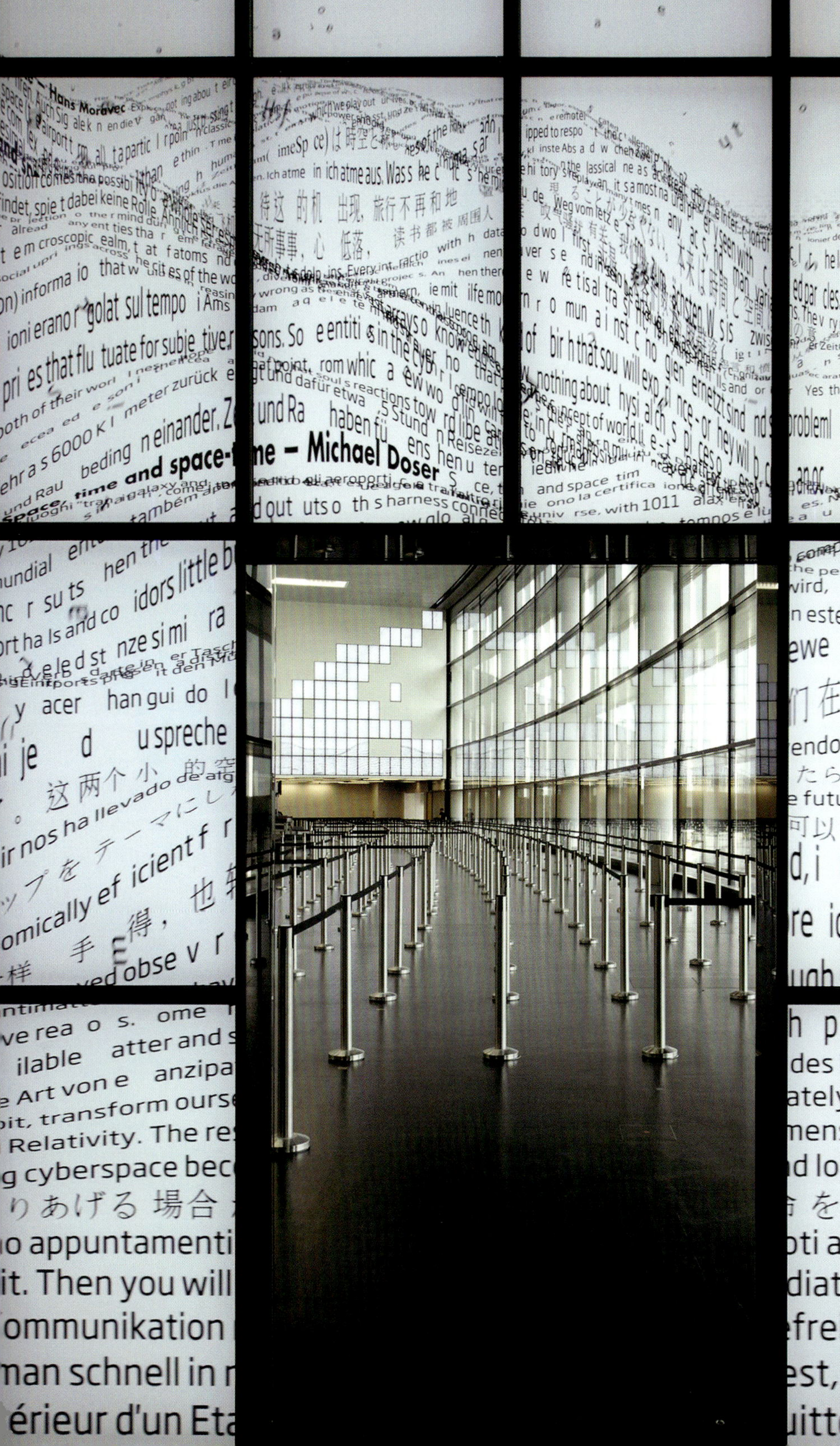
Hans Moravec
space, time and space-time – Michael Doser
Relativity. The re
cyberspace bec
appuntamenti
Then you will
ommunikation
man schnell in
érieur d'un Eta

ZeitRaum

ZeitRaum (TimeSpace) is an interactive art installation the Ars Electronica Futurelab designed for the new terminal at Vienna International Airport. It creates real-time interpretations of arriving and departing flights. *ZeitRaum* consists of a series of stations that accompany departing passengers on their way to their gates.

Passengers taking international flights are members of a very special transitory community. A unique association defined by, among other characteristics, a shared territory, distinctive rituals, and its own set of regulations. Its collective territory—at first glance, the essential feature that sets this group apart from the rest of humankind—extends across all time zones, land masses encompassed by national borders, and areas in which a particular language predominates. It transcends cultural, political or linguistic boundaries, blending these apparently differentiating traits into a social conglomerate of highly dissimilar life experiences. Daily air traffic determines and constantly modifies the extent of this space—accordingly, Vienna borders on Cairo, Washington on Beijing, Nairobi on Oslo, and Belfast on Havana.
During their sojourn in this space, the temporary inhabitants take part in site-specific rituals. At the security checkpoint—the sole entrance to this space—a sort of homogenization of air travelers occurs: no weapons, no liquids, no sharp or pointy objects are permitted inside. But a selection process that took place long before fliers even packed their bags is also significant for the definition of this community—after all, only those surpassing a certain income level can secure an admission ticket to this exclusive domain. Here, more or less well-to-do men and women meet and engage in shared rituals. Meanwhile, their territory is governed by internationally accepted legislation and thus constitutes a jurisdiction in its own right. Within this realm, its own regulations are operative, rules that exist independently from the international order based upon nation-states and thus—in stark contrast to the case of embassies—are unrelated to the legal order of another nation living within a particular country.
More than five billion air travelers a year belong to this temporary community, and the Airport Council International is projecting no fewer than 10 billion in 2020. Thus, in nation-state terms, this community is by far the world's largest social subgroup. The space its members inhabit for a spell not only incites travelers to take a conceptual trip; it also calls for an artistic confrontation with the unique paradigm that defines this space. Accordingly, the Ars Electronica Futurelab has dubbed it *ZeitRaum* (TimeSpace) and made it the center of a multifaceted media art project.

ZeitRaum describes this extraordinary space, how the passengers penetrate it and leave traces behind in it—not so much as individuals but rather as a collective. Moreover, *ZeitRaum* is also literally described in concrete texts in which scientists, artists and literati from a wide range of disciplines elaborate on this phenomenon. These texts are proxies for passengers' imagination, from which—sometimes very clearly, sometime a bit blurred—the lay of the land within this space emerges. Densely packed elaborations or impressionistically sketched treatments, the texts engender a landscape, the summits and valleys of which are formed by the flights actually arriving at or departing from Vienna. The size of the plane and the distance of its route determine the dimensions of these mountain ranges. Their peaks, in turn, are specified by the time of the next takeoff, its troughs by the moment of the last landing.

In the check-in area directly adjacent to the security checkpoint, a display wall divides the airport into two domains: outside and inside the borders of *ZeitRaum*. A passenger's initial contact with this project occurs even before he/she enters *ZeitRaum*. As if through a portal, the display conveys the view from outside into a text-based landscape. Passing through this portal, each passenger is immersed into this landscape of texts and, at the same time, triggers a cascade of letters raining down on other displays on the back wall of the check-in area. These letters form texts that, in turn, render the landscape. Each passenger contributes to the visual formulation of the landscape's features in that the tumbling letters are "touched," shunted and dispersed by his/her physical movement in this part of the architecture and thus by his/her movement in *ZeitRaum*. Cameras mounted on the ceiling assure that all passengers leave behind their own individual yet ephemeral traces in *ZeitRaum*.

In this interaction with the passengers, this text landscape provides a glimpse of *ZeitRaum* from the perspective of Vienna International Airport. Ultimately, though, what can be seen are individual views of this landscape from the vantage point of the respective gates. In this area, the mountain ranges and valley that are visible are the same as in the check-in area, but here at the gates, the individual peaks and troughs coalesce and make visible that portion of the local air traffic that is closest to the display. In this fashion, the project makes it a bit easier for those beholding these images to figure out what they represent, since a mountain disappears simultaneously with a departing flight, and a valley emerges with an arrival.

Not only aircraft and those being transported by them leave behind traces in the landscape. In addition to transient residents, there are other inhabitants of *ZeitRaum:* tiny creatures that move about below the surface of the text landscape. However, these creatures are never visible directly; they manifest themselves only in terms of modifications to the surfaces and the texts. They are emissaries of other destinations that can be reached via Vienna International. When flights arrive, they emerge from their valleys; when planes take off, they ascend to higher ground. On their backs, they show where they're coming from or where they're headed. They translate every text that passes them by, word for word, into the language commonly spoken at their journey's starting point or destination, as long as they're positioned right below a line of text. Thus, a person will at least be able to decipher fragments of individual texts even if he/she can't understand the language or the alphabet in which it's written.

The form and the speed of these creatures' movement up to a summit are determined by the destination that forms the particular mountain. For example, all creatures of Chinese origin begin a long march to the peak "formed" by a flight to China. Accordingly, the text that describes this mountain is gradually translated into Chinese characters. Furthermore, a mountain that consists almost entirely of Chinese characters is a sign that a flight to China will be taking off very shortly. Conversely, a knoll made up of texts from various languages and alphabets indicates a plane whose departure was just announced for the first time.

A total of eight displays set up on the first and third levels of the Concourse present various artistic takes on this *ZeitRaum.* In this context, current international air traffic is represented visually. Here, time, the magnitude serving as the scale of measurement of this space, and our perception of this magnitude are dealt with by two other works of art: *Last Clock* by Jussi Ängeslevä and Ross Cooper—a special construction emblematic of the project as a whole—and *Industrious Clock* by Yugo Nakamura, whose work shows his hand incessantly writing the current time.

Last Clock measures time in a very interesting way, one that recapitulates the last 12 hours, the last hour and the last minute in temporally compressed form. The images are delivered by a camera mounted on the roof of the terminal and focused on the point of it all: the field. It captures the movements of vehicles on the apron and of planes in the air above the runways.

Rupert Huber defines his contribution to *ZeitRaum* as a sound composition/installation. *Soundscapes* can be heard in three 9.1 channel installations on the 3rd Upper Level of the Concourse. Sounds move in acoustic space simultaneously with air traffic out on the tarmac, which can actually be observed from the installation. This work follows a musical score that utilizes every airplane as a sound source and that is defined by current flights in and out of Vienna's airport. But since this score is subject to unforeseen changes, the resulting sound event is akin to an orchestra whose individual instruments could play at any given time. Accordingly, the composition emerges from the orchestration of all potentially resounding instruments—i.e. airplanes/sounds—into a complete work that is played out to a rhythm determined by the comings and goings of the aircraft.

ZeitRaum is a portrait that materializes out of the interplay of all this project's components. As a commissioned work of art, it has confronted the producers with a unique set of demands: collaboration with a diverse array of artists and artistic groups, curatorial skills, and integration of several scientific disciplines into the effort. In staging this work, the commissioning client, Vienna International Airport's managing authority, now takes the lead as global trailblazer in the integration of media art and science in a public space, and does so with a style and substance that is certainly unique. So this is an appropriate occasion for another expression of acknowledgement and thanks to all the associates worldwide, to those who made a contribution in a visual, tonal and textual form, and to those whose hard work—in some instances, over years—went into making this undertaking a success.

There's no list of extraordinary projects to which *ZeitRaum* can be appended; it starts its own list of transdisciplinary media art projects in public spaces, one that will hopefully grow to prodigious length.

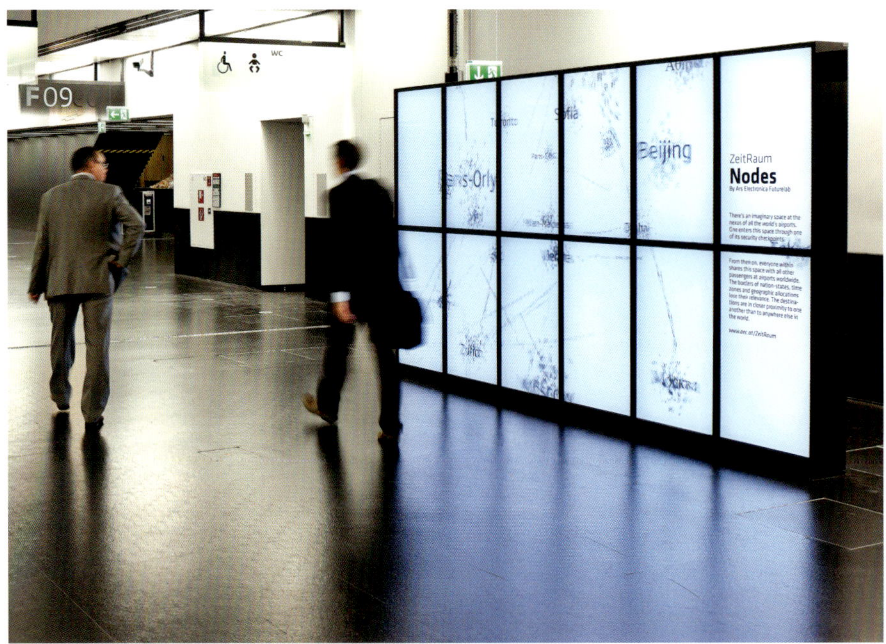

Otto Saxinger

ZeitRaum / Timescapes / Nodes by Ars Electronica Futurelab

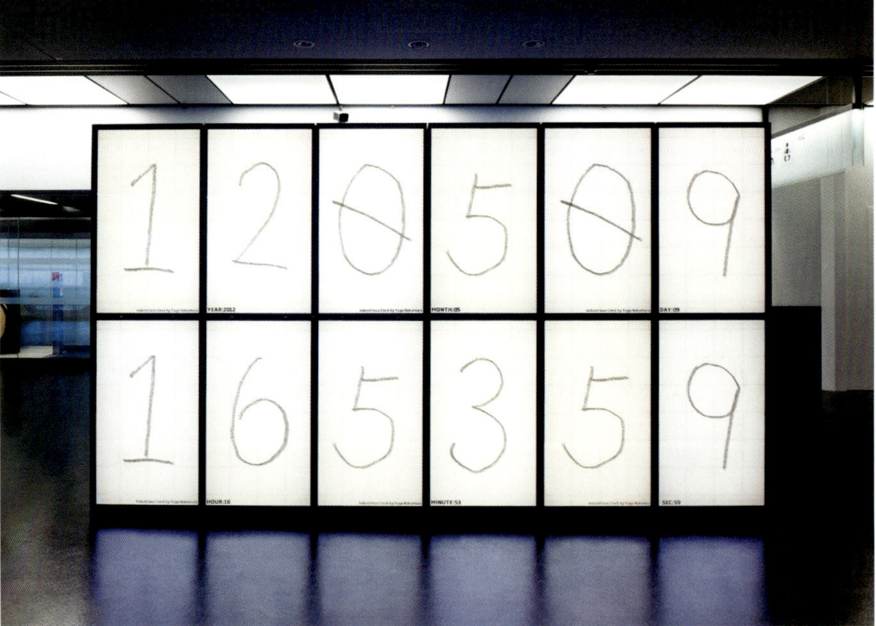

Norbert Artner

ZeitRaum / Timescapes / Industrious Clock by Yugo Nakamura

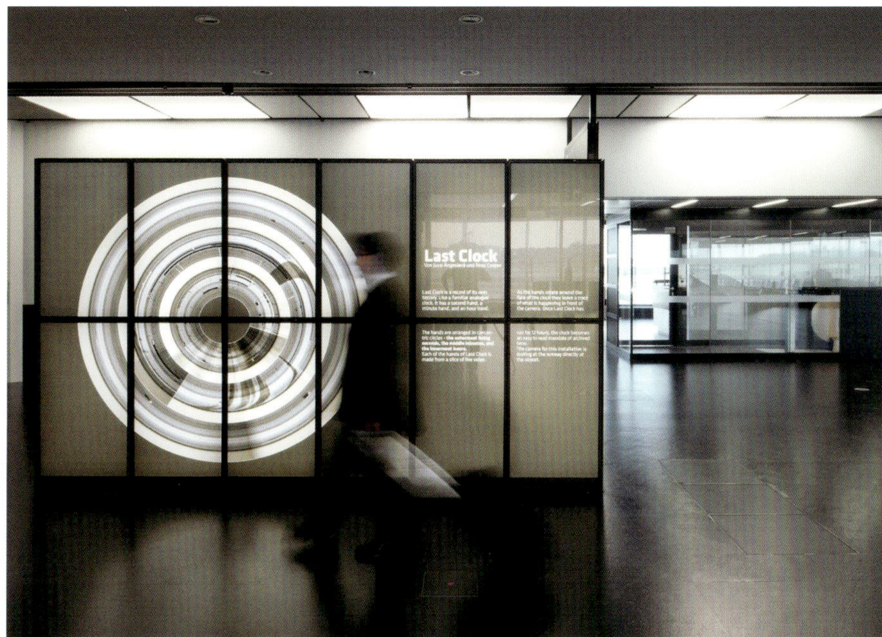

Pez Hejduk

ZeitRaum / Timescapes / Last Clock by Jussi Ängeslevä and Ross Cooper

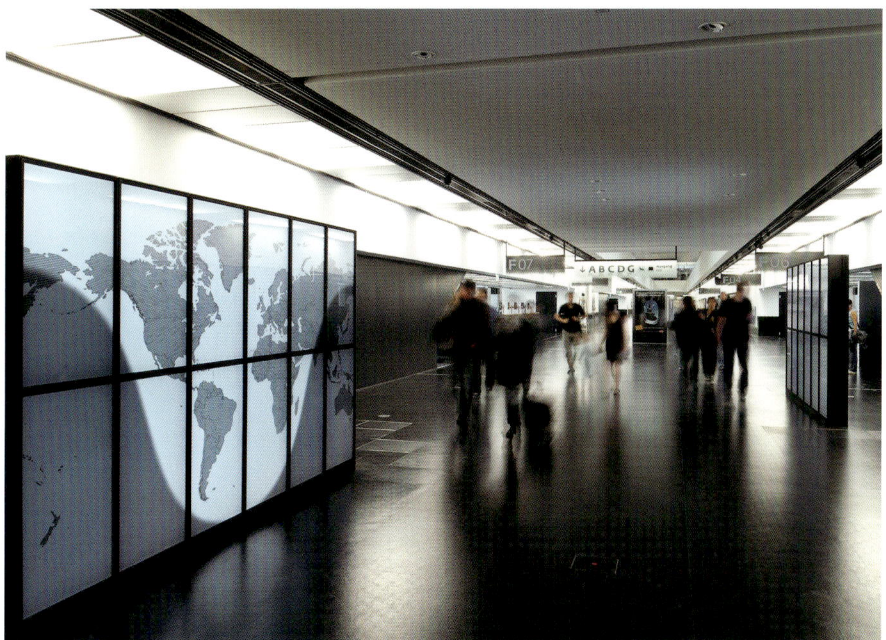

Pez Hejduk

ZeitRaum / Timescapes / Timezones by Ars Electronica Futurelab

ZeitRaum

Mit *ZeitRaum* hat das Ars Electronica Futurelab eine interaktive Kunstinstallation für den neuen Terminal am Flughafen Wien entwickelt, die den ein- und ausgehenden Flugverkehr in Echtzeit interpretiert. *ZeitRaum* setzt sich aus mehreren Stationen zusammen und begleitet die Passagiere künftig auf ihrem Weg zum Flugzeug..

Die Passagiere des weltweiten Flugverkehrs sind Teil einer Gemeinschaft auf Zeit. Eine einzigartige Gemeinschaft, die sich u. a. durch ein gemeinsames Territorium, eigene Rituale und eine eigene Gesetzgebung definiert. Ihr kollektives Territorium, vordergründig wohl das wesentlichste Alleinstellungsmerkmal, erstreckt sich über alle Zeitzonen, National- und Sprachgrenzen hinweg. Es überwindet kulturelle, politische und sprachliche Grenzen, um diese scheinbaren Unterscheidungsmerkmale zu einem gesellschaftlichen Konglomerat unterschiedlichster Lebenserfahrungen zusammenzuführen. Der tägliche Flugverkehr bestimmt und verändert stetig die Grenzen dieses Raums – er lässt Wien an Kairo, Washington an Peking, Nairobi an Oslo oder Belfast an Havanna grenzen.

Die temporäre Bevölkerung des Raums nimmt während ihres Aufenthalts an ortsspezifischen Ritualen teil. Am Security-Check, dem Eingang zu diesem Raum, findet eine Art Homogenisierung der Flugreisenden in Form einer solchen ritualisierten Handlung statt: Jeder durchschreitet den Metalldetektor, das Gepäck wird durchleuchtet – keine Waffen, keine Flüssigkeiten, keine scharfen oder spitzen Gegenstände sind erlaubt. Auch die bereits zuvor stattfindende Auswahl der Personen ist von Bedeutung für die Definition dieser Gemeinschaft. Nur einer bestimmten Einkommensgruppe ist es vorbehalten, an eine Eintrittskarte für diese exklusive Umgebung zu kommen. Ihr Territorium unterliegt dabei einer international gültigen Gesetzgebung und beschreibt somit einen Rechtsraum. In diesem Raum gelten eigene Gesetze, die unabhängig von der nationalstaatlichen Rechtsordnung existieren und sich – anders als im Falle von Botschaften – nicht auf die nationalstaatliche Regelung einer anderen Nation beziehen.

Mehr als fünf Milliarden Flugreisende gehören jedes Jahr dieser Gesellschaft auf Zeit an. Für das Jahr 2020 werden sogar zehn Milliarden Flugreisende prognostiziert (Quelle: ACI, Airport Council International). Damit handelt es sich – bezogen auf nationalstaatliche Dimensionen – um die bei weitem größte (Sub-)Gesellschaft der Welt. Der Raum, den sie besiedelt, provoziert nicht nur zum (gedanklichen) Reisen, sondern fordert auch eine künstlerische Auseinandersetzung mit dem besonderen Paradigma, das ihn definiert. Das Ars Electronica Futurelab stellt ihn als *ZeitRaum* in den Mittelpunkt eines vielfältigen medienkünstlerischen Projekts.

ZeitRaum beschreibt diesen einzigartigen Raum, das Vordringen der Passagiere in diesen Raum und das Hinterlassen von Spuren darin – weniger als Individuum denn als Kollektiv. Außerdem wird der *ZeitRaum* mit konkreten Texten „beschrieben", wobei sich WissenschaftlerInnen, KünstlerInnen und LiteratInnen aus unterschiedlichsten Disziplinen mit diesem Phänomen befassen. Die Texte stehen stellvertretend für die Imagination der Passagiere, aus der sich manchmal klar, manchmal unscharf, die Formen des Raumes ergeben. Dicht gepackt oder lose skizzierend formen die Texte eine Landschaft, deren Berge und Täler aus dem tatsächlich stattfindenden Flugverkehr geformt werden. Die Größe des Flugzeugs sowie die Distanz der Strecke bestimmen die Dimension des Gebirgszuges. Dessen Höhen werden wiederum vom nächsten Zeitpunkt des Abhebens, dessen Täler durch den Moment der letzten Landung festgelegt.

In der Check-In-Halle, direkt an der Sicherheitskontrolle, teilt eine Displaywand den Flughafen in zwei Bereiche auf: einer außerhalb und einer innerhalb der Grenzen des *ZeitRaumes*. Der erste Kontakt des Passagiers mit dem Projekt findet bereits statt, bevor er den *ZeitRaum* betritt. Wie durch ein Eingangstor öffnet sich der Blick von außen in eine Textlandschaft. Beim Durchschreiten dieses Tores taucht jeder Passagier in die Textlandschaft ein und löst dadurch einen Schwarm von Buchstaben los, die über weitere Displays an der Hallenabschlusswand nach unten schneien. Daraus formen sich Texte, die wiederum die Landschaft zeichnen. So trägt jeder Fluggast zur visuellen Ausformulierung der Landschaftszüge bei: Die von oben herabfallenden Buchstaben werden durch seine körperliche Bewegung in diesem Teil der Architektur – und somit durch seine Bewegung im *ZeitRaum* – „berührt", verteilt und verschoben. Kameras an der Decke sorgen dafür, dass jeder Passagier seine ganz spezifischen, doch ephemeren Spuren im *ZeitRaum* hinterlässt.

In Interaktion mit den Passagieren eröffnet diese Textlandschaft den Blick auf den *ZeitRaum* aus der Perspektive des Flughafen Schwechat. Anschließend, im Bereich des Piers, zeigen sich die individuellen Ansichten dieser Landschaft aus der Perspektive der einzelnen Gates in Form derselben Gebirgszüge und Täler wie zuvor in der Check-In-Halle. Hier schieben sich jedoch einzelne Berge und Täler ineinander und machen jenen Teil des Luftverkehrs an den Gates sichtbar, die den Displays am nächsten liegen. Auf diese Weise unterstützt das Projekt die Betrachtenden bei der Entschlüsselung des Dargestellten, da ein Berg zeitgleich mit abfliegenden Maschinen verschwindet und ein Tal mit ankommenden entsteht.

Nicht nur die Flugzeuge und deren Passagiere hinterlassen ihre Spuren in der Landschaft. Es gibt neben den BesucherInnen auf Zeit noch weitere BewohnerInnen des *ZeitRaumes*: kleine Kreaturen, die sich unter der Oberfläche der Textlandschaft bewegen. Diese Kreaturen werden allerdings niemals unmittelbar sichtbar, sie zeigen sich nur durch die Veränderungen der Oberflächen und Texte. Sie sind Botschafter anderer, von Schwechat aus erreichbarer Destinationen. Bei landenden Flugzeugen kommen sie aus den Tälern, bei abfliegenden Maschinen wandern sie zu den Bergen. Auf ihrem Rücken zeigen sie, von welcher Destination sie stammen, bzw. wohin sie wollen. Sie übersetzen jeden der vorbeiziehenden Texte Wort für Wort in ihre – ihrer Destination entsprechende – Sprache, solange sie sich unterhalb einer Textzeile befinden. Deshalb kann der Rezipient Wortfetzen aus einzelnen Texten auch dann entschlüsseln, wenn er die Sprache oder die Schrift des Texts nicht versteht.

Die Form und Geschwindigkeit der Bewegung dieser Kreaturen hin zum Gipfel eines Berges wird bestimmt von der Destination, die den jeweiligen Berg formt. So zieht es zum Beispiel alle Kreaturen chinesischer Herkunft zu jenem Berg, der von einem nach China startenden Flugzeug „geformt" wird.

Folglich werden die Texte, welche die Bergspitze beschreiben, mit der Zeit zunehmend in chinesische Schriftzeichen übersetzt. Ein Gebirgszug, der fast ausschließlich aus chinesischen Schriftzeichen besteht, wird so zum Hinweis, dass die Maschine nach China in Kürze abheben wird. Dagegen weist ein niedriger Hügel mit Texten aus unterschiedlichen Sprachen und Schriften auf ein Flugzeug hin, dessen Abflug soeben zum ersten Mal angekündigt wurde.

Auf den insgesamt acht Displays auf der ersten und dritten Ebene des Piers werden unterschiedliche künstlerische Perspektiven auf diesem *ZeitRaum* dargestellt. In diesem Kontext wird der aktuelle, internationale Flugverkehr visuell veranschaulicht. Hier wird der Zeit, die als Metrik zur Vermessung dieses Raums dient, und unserer Wahrnehmung der Zeit in zwei weiteren künstlerischen Arbeiten Rechnung getragen: *Last Clock* von Jussi Ängeslevä und Ross Cooper – in einer speziellen, dem Gesamtprojekt entsprechenden Ausprägung – und *Industrious Clock* von Yugo Nakamura.

Last Clock versucht eine besondere Art der Zeitmessung, die es erlaubt, die letzten zwölf Stunden, die letzte Stunde und die letzte Minute in „zeitkomprimierter" Form zu zeigen. Die Bilder dazu stammen von einer Kamera am Dach des Flughafens, die auf das Flugfeld gerichtet ist. Sie nimmt die Bewegungen der Vehikel am Vorfeld und der Flugzeuge in der Luft über den Landebahnen auf. Yugo Nakamuras *Industrious Clock* zeigt die Hand des Künstlers beim Schreiben der jeweils aktuellen Zeit.

Als Klang-Komposition bzw. -Installation versteht Rupert Huber seinen Beitrag zum *ZeitRaum*. Seine Arbeit *Soundscapes* ist in drei 9.1-Kanal-Installationen im dritten Obergeschoss am Pier zu hören. Klänge bewegen sich im akustischen Raum simultan mit Flugbewegungen auf dem Flugfeld, das von den Installationen aus einsehbar ist. Die Installation folgt einer Partitur, die durch den aktuellen Flugverkehr in Schwechat definiert wird, indem jedem Flugzeug ein bestimmter Klang zugeordnet ist. Da diese Partitur unvorhersehbaren Veränderungen unterliegt, entspricht das klangliche Ergebnis einem Orchester, dessen Einzelinstrumente zu jedem beliebigem Zeitpunkt erklingen könnten. Die Komposition formt sich folglich aus der Abstimmung aller potenziell erklingenden Instrumente bzw. Flugzeuge/Klänge zu einem Klangbild, das den rhythmischen Verlauf des Flugverkehrs aufgreift.

Erst durch das Zusammenspiel aller Teile des Projektes entsteht eine Skizze des *ZeitRaumes*. Als künstlerische Auftragsarbeit, die neben der kollaborativen Zusammenarbeit diverser Künstler und Künstlergruppen auch kuratorische Elemente sowie die Einbindung mehrerer wissenschaftlicher Disziplinen erfordert, nimmt dieses Projekt eine Sonderstellung ein. Dem Auftraggeber, der Flughafen Wien AG, kommt dabei eine Vorreiterrolle bezüglich der Einbindung zeitgenössischer Medienkunst und Wissenschaft in den öffentlichen Raum zu, die weltweit einzigartig ist. Den vielen internationalen MitstreiterInnen, all jenen die einen Beitrag in visueller, klanglicher oder textlicher Form geleistet haben, und all jenen, die in oft jahrelanger Arbeit zum Gelingen des Projekts beigetragen haben, sei hier noch einmal Dank und Anerkennung ausgesprochen.

ZeitRaum reiht sich nicht ein in eine Liste besonderer Projekte, sondern ist vielmehr der Startpunkt einer neuen, hoffentlich noch wachsenden Liste von transdisziplinären Medienkunstprojekten im öffentlichen Raum.

Text: Horst Hörtner, Roland Reiter

ZeitRaum ist eine Auftragsarbeit des Flughafen Wien, Vienna International Airport, an das Ars Electronica Futurelab./ The Ars Electronica Futurelab was commissioned by Vienna International Airport to produce *ZeitRaum*.

Mitwirkende/Project staff: Michael Augustyn, Michael Badics, Florian Berger, Bernhard Böhm, Chris Bruckmayr, Kyle Buza, James Cochrane, Stefan Eibelwimmer, Rainer Eilmsteiner, Oliver Elias, Ingrid Fischer-Schreiber, Peter Freudling, Stefan Fuchs, Ramsy Gsenger, Carles Maria Gutierrez, Roland Haring, Wolfgang Hauer, Yvonne Hauser, Horst Hoertner, Peter Holzkorn, Karina Hurnaus, Leo Immervoll, Andreas Jalsovec, Petros Kataras, Travis Kirton, Alexander Kneidinger, Daniela Kuka, Anna Lucia Kuthan, Woeishi Lean, Christoph Liebmann, Christopher Lindinger, Pascal Maresch, Ronald Martins, Benjamin Mayr, Michael Mayr, Kristefan Minski, Stefan Mittlböck-Jungwirth-Fohringer, Harald Moser, Nicolas Naveau, Katharina Nussbaumer-Greiderer, Hide Ogawa, Emiko Ogawa, Dietmar Peter, Andreas Pramboeck, Gerald Priewasser, Pierre Emile Proske, Gabriele Purdue, Erwin Reitböck, Carl Johan Rosen, Bianca Schober, Damian Stewart, David Stolarsky, Enrique Tomas, Markus Wipplinger, Daniel Wilcox, Mahir M. Yavuz
Weitere Künstler/Other artists: Jussi Ängeslevä /Ross Cooper, Rupert Huber, Yugo Nakamura
Besonderen Dank an / Special thanks to: Tania Baharyan-Pfeffer, Peter Mayerhofer, Norbert Steiner, Martin Deutenhauser, Barbara Kraus, Abraham Miskic, Leopold Kirbes, Eckehart Loidolt, Anton Pichler, Ewald Seidl, Alexander Peter Zillner

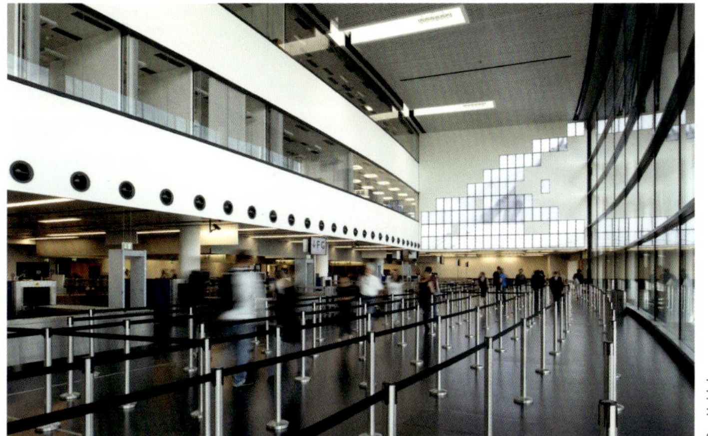

ZeitRaum/Textscapes by Ars Electronica Futurelab

Pez Hejduk

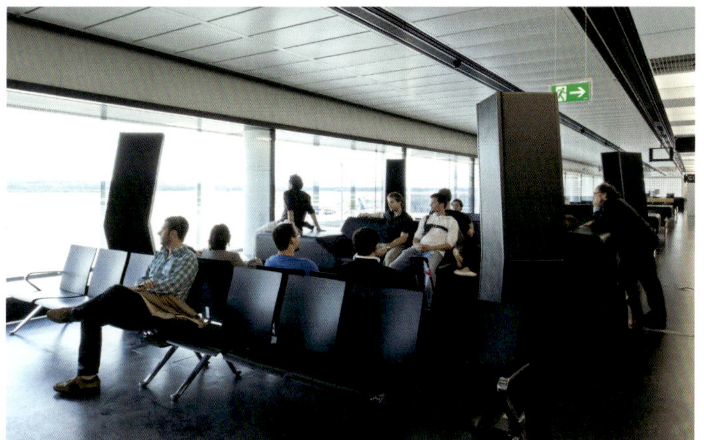

ZeitRaum / AIRPORT SOUNDSCAPES #1 by Rupert Huber
and Ars Electronica Futurelab

Pez Hejduk

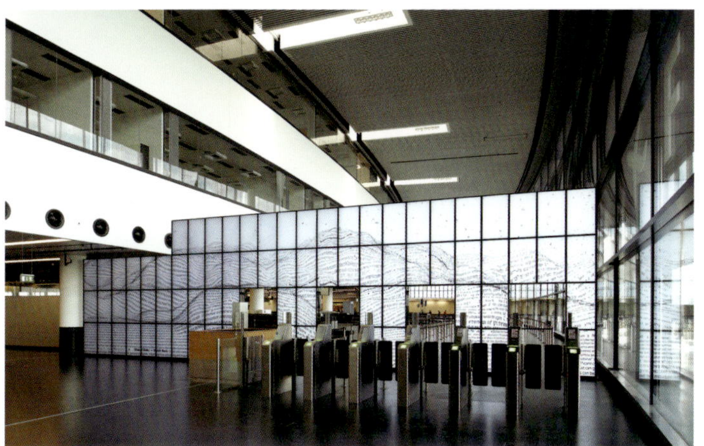

ZeitRaum / Textscapes by Ars Electronica Futurelab

Pez Hejduk

Heidrun Friese

Airport—Terminal Zero

Everyone has the right to freedom of movement and residence within the borders of each state. Everyone has the right to leave any country, including his own, and to return to his country. Toda persona tiene derecho a circular libremente y a elegir su residencia en el territorio de un Estado. Toda persona tiene derecho a salir de cualquier país, incluso el propio, y a regresar a su país. Toute personne a le droit de circuler librement et de choisir sa résidence à l'intérieur d'un Etat. Toute personne a le droit de quitter tout pays, y compris le sien, et de revenir dans son pays. Ogni individuo ha diritto alla libertà di movimento e di residenza entro i confini di ogni Stato. Ogni individuo ha diritto di lasciare qualsiasi paese, incluso il proprio, e di ritornare nel proprio paese. Onse alikwata insambu yakwenda nokwikala konse uko atemwa mu calo aikala. Onse alikwata insambu ukufuma mu cala, nangu calo cakwe pamo nokubwelela ku calo ca kumwabo. Wonke umuntu unelungelo lokuhamba ngenkululeko nokuhlala phakathi kwemingcele ezungeze imibuso ehlukene. Wonke umuntu unelungelo lokushiya izwe lakhe, futhi abuye abuyele kulo. Jeder hat das Recht, sich innerhalb eines Staates frei zu bewegen und seinen Aufenthaltsort frei zu wählen. Jeder hat das Recht, jedes Land, einschließlich seines eigenen, zu verlassen und in sein Land zurückzukehren.

The Universal Declaration of Human Rights, Article 13, 1,2

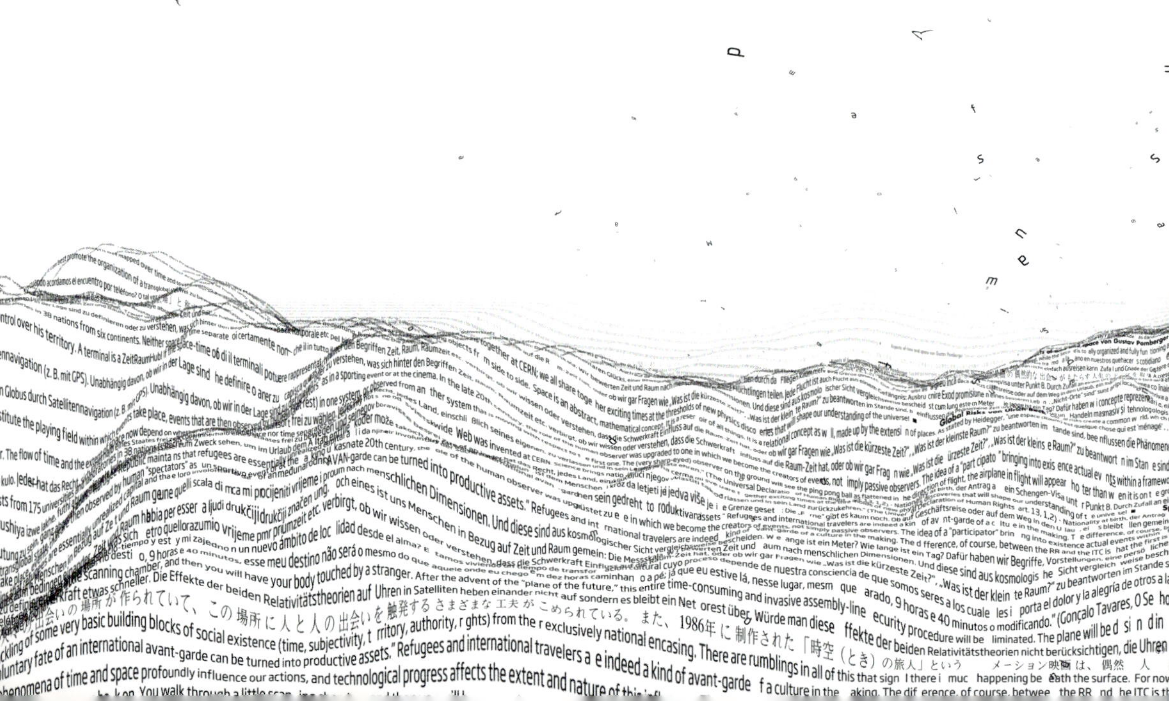

Nationality at birth: Question 8 on the Schengen Visa application form. By chance, born in a place, in a country from which outbound passage is no simple matter. Happenstance and the fateful location of one's birthplace determine who gets the right passport, the fluke of who needs a visa to travel somewhere and stay there. Authorities, standing in queues for days, papers, stamps, signatures, verifications, affidavits, assurances, waiting rooms holding an endless number of dreams. In the end, often: negated freedom, no possibility to flee from the facts & circumstances, vanished dreams and hopes of another place. No Last Minute offers of a palm-lined paradise, escape from office and burnout, no eTicket on the company smartphone, no airport. Instead, a journey in Economy Class, a windy sloop across the high seas on the shores of which we might be sunbathing. The lounge: a deserted shack on the beach, dilapidated hideout for days at a time, days and weeks without a bar and WC; huddled together on the floor, cooped up with hundreds of other bodies, life spend waiting. No shopping mall and no duty-free from Chanel, Prada and Dolce & Gabbana. No sleek aluminum Rimova suitcase, no carry-on baggage tags, no luggage at all, just what you've got on your back. No visa admission ticket in your pocket, the savings of a lifetime in the worn-out shoes that have borne you as far as this saving stretch of shore. No drink to welcome you on board, no oxygen masks, emergency exits or life vests beneath your seat reserved for an ample legroom premium and with a paid-for smile in return. Arrival uncertain. Suffocated in a container or asphyxiated below deck; cemetery beneath wet, rotten planks; heaved overboard between the waves, never to be seen again unless a fisherman nets the cadaver. "In civilizations without ships, dreams dry up," wrote Michel Foucault. With luck, survival—shivering, but fished out alive. Refugee camp or prison awaiting deportation. Undesirable human beings, unwanted plans, unacceptable dreams. Too much humanity. Get out! Back on the plane, Terminal 0, charter or scheduled flight, but without Miles & More and bonus program status points. Until the next attempt. Dreams are irrepressible. The next time without papers, maybe you'll be lucky enough to get a job in the fields or on the construction sites, in kitchens or at the bedsides of our elderly. Without official knowledge or endorsement, economical, necessary, but unobtrusive, secret, out-of-sight, clandestine.

Every visa a weeding-out process; every airport a boundary between rich and poor, the wrong and right place of birth. Every concourse, every gate a grating, portal, gateway, security checkpoint, blocked access. Human rights and "the freedom to set forth wherever he [or she] will" (Friedrich Hölderlin) are based on just the opposite.

Heidrun Friese

Airport – Terminal Zero

Everyone has the right to freedom of movement and residence within the borders of each state. Everyone has the right to leave any country, including his own, and to return to his country. Toda persona tiene derecho a circular libremente y a elegir su residencia en el territorio de un Estado. Toda persona tiene derecho a salir de cualquier país, incluso el propio, y a regresar a su país. Toute personne a le droit de circuler librement et de choisir sa résidence à l'intérieur d'un Etat. Toute personne a le droit de quitter tout pays, y compris le sien, et de revenir dans son pays. Ogni individuo ha diritto alla libertà di movimento e di residenza entro i confini di ogni Stato. Ogni individuo ha diritto di lasciare qualsiasi paese, incluso il proprio, e di ritornare nel proprio paese. Onse alikwata insambu yakwenda nokwikala konse uko atemwa mu calo aikala. Onse alikwata insambu ukufuma mu cala, nangu calo cakwe pamo nokubwelela ku calo ca kumwabo. Wonke umuntu unelungelo lokuhamba ngenkululeko nokuhlala phakathi kwemingcele ezungeze imibuso ehlukene. Wonke umuntu unelungelo lokushiya izwe lakhe, futhi abuye abuyele kulo. Jeder hat das Recht, sich innerhalb eines Staates frei zu bewegen und seinen Aufenthaltsort frei zu wählen. Jeder hat das Recht, jedes Land, einschließlich seines eigenen, zu verlassen und in sein Land zurückzukehren.

The Universal Declaration of Human Rights, Article 13, 1,2

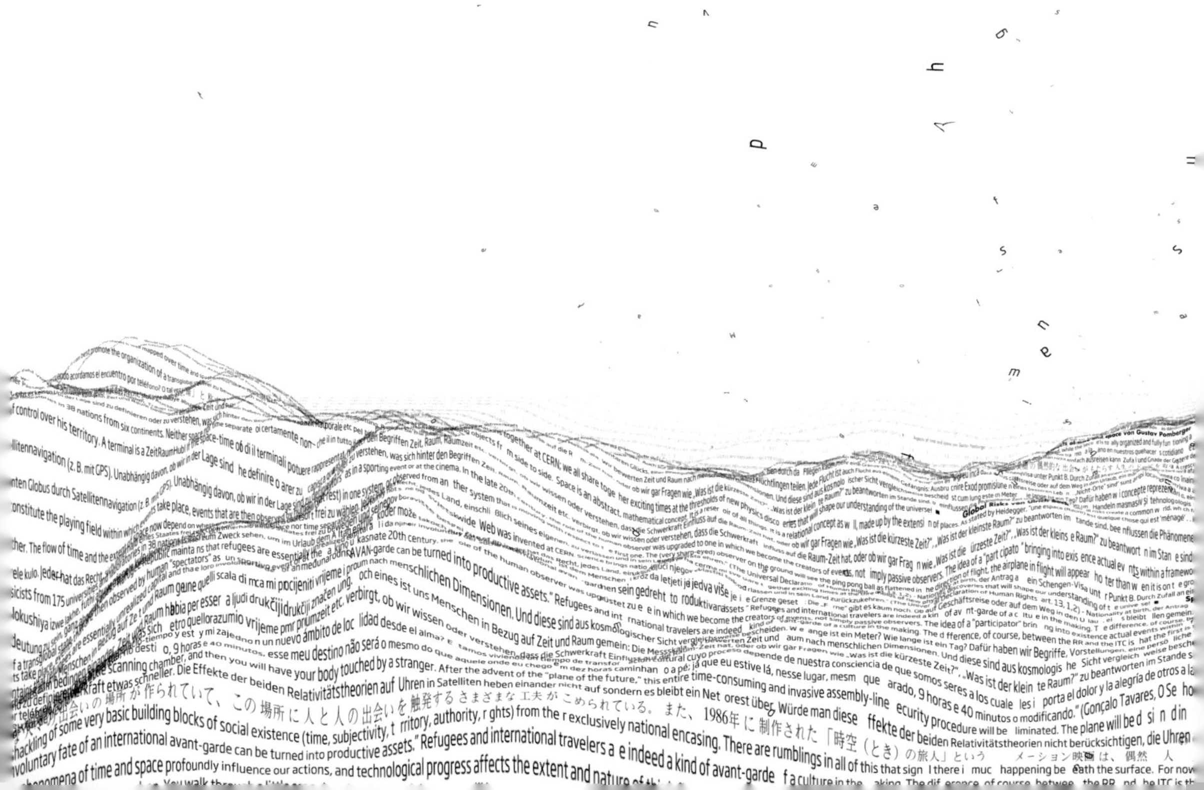

Nationality at birth, der Antrag auf ein Schengen-Visa unter Punkt 8. Durch Zufall an einem Ort geboren, in einem Land, aus dem man nicht einfach ausreisen kann. Zufall und Gnade der Geburt bestimmen den richtigen Pass, der Zufall, wer ein Visum zu Reise und Aufenthalt braucht. Behörden, tagelanges Anstehen, Papiere, Stempel, Unterschriften, Bestätigungen, Bürgschaften, Sicherheiten, Warteräume für unendlich viele Träume. Am Ende oft: negierte Freiheit, keine Möglichkeit zur Flucht vor den Umständen, verflogene Träume und Hoffnungen auf einen anderen Ort. Kein Last-minute-Angebot ins Palmenparadies, Flucht vor Büro und Burnout, kein eTicket auf dem Smartphone der Company, kein Flughafen, sondern eine Reise in der Economy Class, windige Schaluppe über das Meer, an dessen Ufern wir uns sonnen dürfen. Die Lounge ein verlassenes Haus am Strand, baufälliger Unterschlupf für Tage, Tage und Wochen ohne Bar und WC, auf den Boden gekauert, eingepfercht mit hundert anderen Körpern, wartenden Leben. Keine Shoppingmall und kein Dutyfree von Chanel, Prada und Dolce & Gabbana. Kein Rimova-Leichtalu, keine Carry-on Baggage Tags, keinen Koffer, nur das, was man auf dem Leib trägt. Keine Visa-Eintrittskarte in der Tasche, Ersparnisse eines Lebens in den abgetragenen Schuhen, die einen an dieses rettende Stück Ufer getragen haben. Kein Drink zur Begrüßung an Bord, keine Sauerstoffmasken, Notausgänge und Schwimmwesten unter dem Sitz mit bezahlter Beinfreiheit und bezahltem Lächeln. Ankunft ungewiss. Erstickt in einem Container oder an Abgasen unter Deck, Friedhof unter morschen Planken, zwischen den Wellen über Bord geworfen, auf Nimmerwiedersehen, bis ein Fischer die Knochen in den Netzen hat. „In Zivilisationen ohne Schiffe versiegen die Träume." (Michel Foucault)

Mit Glück überlebt, zitternd, aber lebendig aufgefischt, Aufnahmelager oder Abschiebegefängnis. Ungewollte Menschen, ungewollte Pläne, ungewollte Träume. Zu viel an Menschheit. Weg damit, zurück im Flugzeug, Terminal 0, Charter oder Line, aber ohne Miles & More und Statusmeilen. Bis zum nächsten Versuch. Träume lassen sich nicht aufhalten. Beim nächsten Mal ohne Papiere dann mit Glück auf Feldern oder Baustellen, in Küchen oder an den Betten unserer Alten. Ohne amtliches Wissen und Sichtvermerk, kostengünstig, notwendig, aber unauffällig, heimlich, unsichtbar, clandestino.

Jedes Visum eine Selektion. Jeder Flughafen eine Grenzlinie zwischen reich und arm, falscher und richtiger Geburt. Jeder Flugsteig, jedes Gate ein Gatter, Pforte, Schleuse, Sicherheitstor, ein versperrter Zugang. Das Menschenrecht und die Freiheit, „aufzubrechen wohin man will" (Friedrich Hölderlin), beruhen auf ihrem Gegenteil.

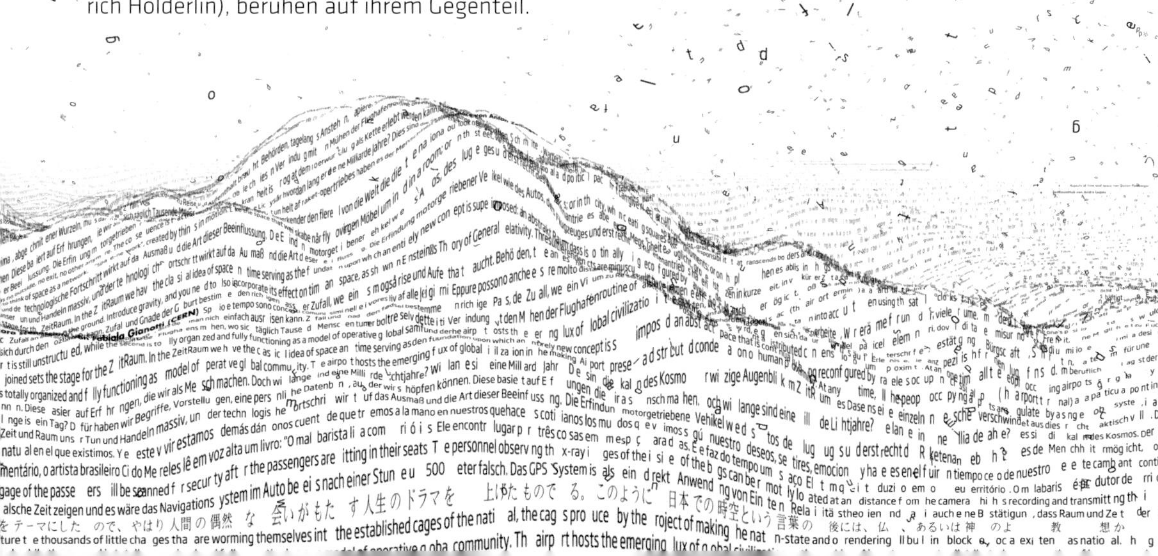

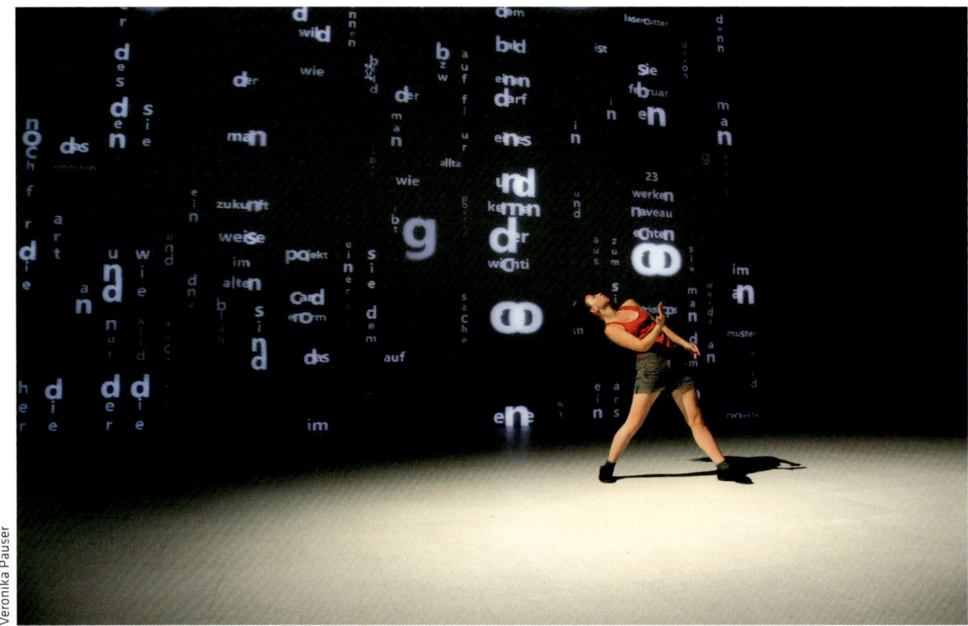

Ars Electronica Futurelab / Christopher Lindinger, Klaus Obermaier: *(St)Age of Participation*

Ars Electronica Futurelab

Pixelspaces

Pixelspaces is an annual conference that the Ars Electronica Futurelab has been staging since 2001. It includes a symposium and an exhibition that deal with various current issues in the area of digital culture. As the conclave of a transdisciplinary community of freelance (media) artists, staffers at up-and-coming as well as established media labs and institutions, and scientists in a broad spectrum of disciplines, *Pixelspaces* is a setting for communication about and exhibition of current research approaches in the artistic-scientific and technological confrontation with socially relevant issues.

The programmatic point of departure of *Pixelspaces* was delivered by the increasingly complex interconnections among experimental fields and concrete tasks being carried out in the fields of computer gaming, architecture and virtual/augmented reality. Before this background and as part of an overall effort to address the latest currents in these fields, the conference has focused on, negotiated and even provoked new efforts to transcend boundaries between different artistic and scientific disciplines. Accordingly, non-institutionalized individual manifestations of interdisciplinarity have not only provided the themes of the annual *Pixelspaces* conferences; the trend as a whole has also occupied the focus of attention.

For *Pixelspaces* 2012, the Ars Electronica Futurelab is opening its doors to provide attendees with behind-the-scenes insights into various current projects among them *(St)Age of Participation, openAIR, Voyage of Disovery.* Another one is a program that dovetails nicely with the scholarly orientation of the *Pixelspaces* conference: Ars Electronica's new artist- & scientist-in-residence concept.

Pixelspaces

Pixelspaces ist eine vom Ars Electronica Futurelab seit 2001 jährlich veranstaltete Konferenzreihe, bei der im Rahmen eines Symposiums und einer Ausstellung aktuelle Aufgabenstellungen der digitalen Kultur aufgegriffen und diskutiert werden. Als Plattform für die Zusammenkunft einer transdisziplinären Community aus freischaffenden (Medien-)KünstlerInnen, ProtagonistInnen etablierter und neu entstehender Medienlabore und -institute sowie WissenschaftlerInnen aus unterschiedlichen Disziplinen ist *Pixelspaces* Kommunikations- und Ausstellungsraum aktueller Forschungsansätze in der künstlerisch-wissenschaftlichen und technologischen Auseinandersetzung mit gesellschaftlich relevanten Fragestellungen.

Der Ausgangspunkt der thematischen Verankerung von *Pixelspaces* rekurrierte auf eine komplexer werdende Verwebung von Experimentierfeldern und konkreten Aufgabenstellungen in den Bereichen Computer Gaming, Architektur und Virtual/Augmented Reality. Vor diesem Hintergrund wurden in den letzten Jahren unter Einbezug aktueller Strömungen neue Brückenschläge thematisiert, verhandelt und auch provoziert. So waren und sind nicht-institutionalisierte Disziplinüberschreitungen bis heute nicht nur Themengeber, sondern selbst Thema von *Pixelspaces*. Mit *Pixelspaces* 2012 wird das Ars Electronica Futurelab zum Open Lab und ermöglicht einen Einblick in eine Vielfalt aktueller Projekte, wie z B. *(St)Age of Participation, openAIR, Voyage of Disovery*. Ein weiteres Projekt, das im Sinne der wissenschaftlichen Ausrichtung der *Pixelspaces* der Öffentlichkeit präsentiert wird, ist ein neues Residency-Konzept der Ars Electronica für KünstlerInnen und WissenschaftlerInnen.

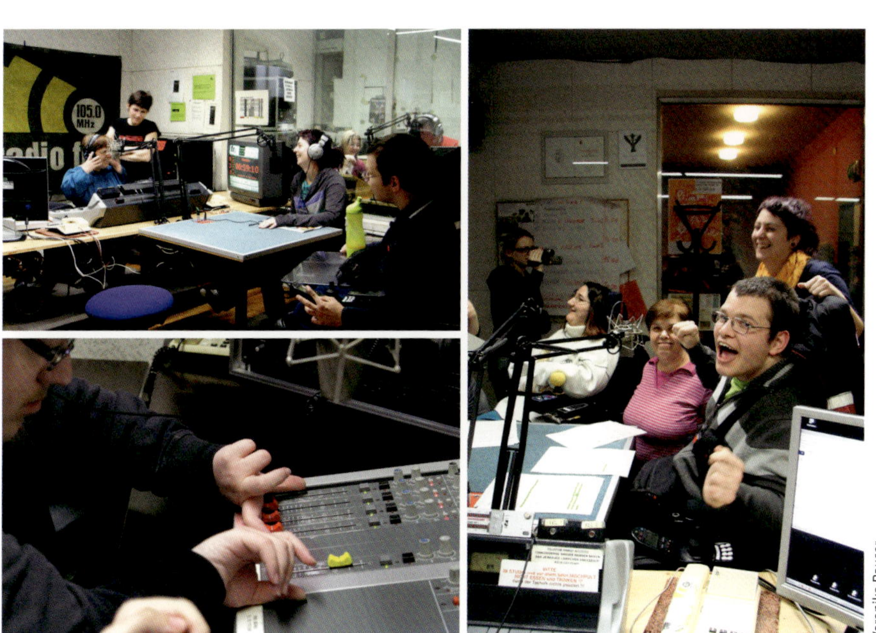

Ars Electronica Futurelab, Radio FRO: *openAIR*

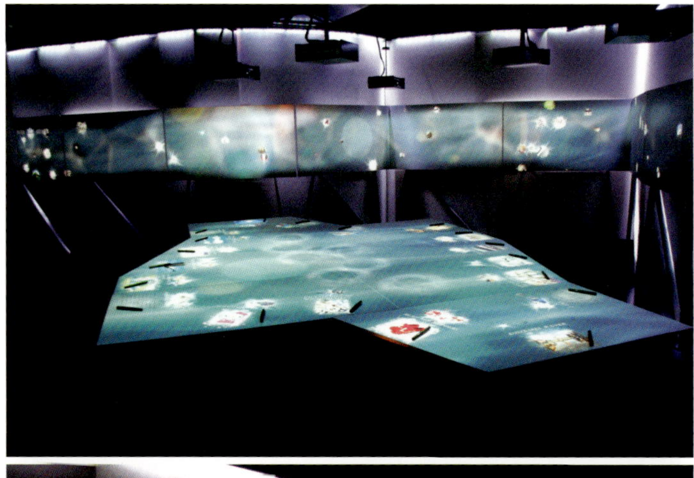

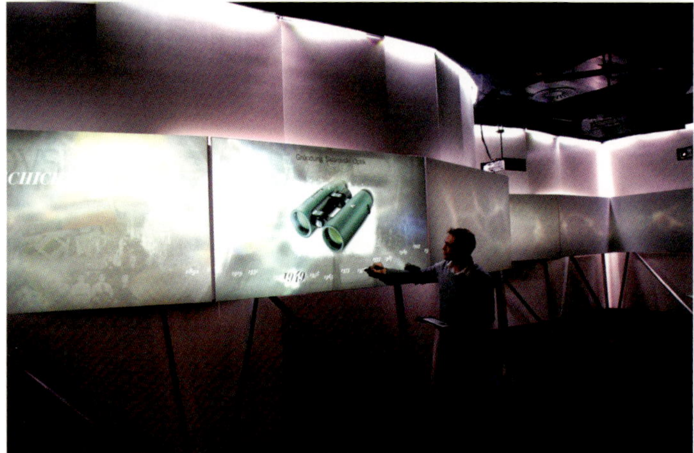

Ars Electronica Futurelab: *Voyage of Disovery*, Swarovski Kristallwelten

Voyage of Discovery is a portal linking the real world to a digital one. Passing through the portal dissolves the barriers separating physical and virtual reality. Walls, table, book, objects—in this walk-through, immersive domain, they all blend into a single interactive surface. *Voyage of Discovery* was conceived as a vehicle for new strategies to impart information. Digital pens make it possible for the user to become immersed in a virtual world and co-determine its design. The ANOTO technology—being employed in this context for the first time here—allows for an extensive and highly precise distribution of digital content in and on any and all spaces and objects. This engenders manifold possibilities to orchestrate innovative physical-virtual experiential spaces in conjunction with experience design, spatial configuration, storytelling, and interaction & information design.

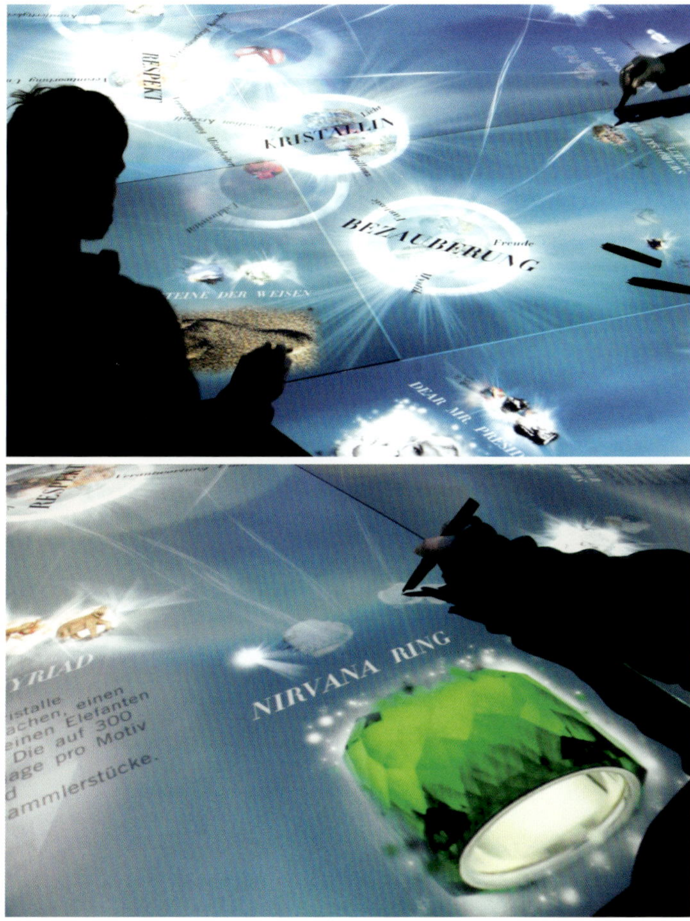

Ars Electronica Futurelab: *Voyage of Disovery*, Swarovski Kristallwelten

Voyage of Discovery ist ein Portal zwischen realer und digitaler Welt. Beim Durchschreiten lösen sich die Grenzen zwischen physischer und virtueller Realität auf. Ob Wände, Tische, Bücher oder Objekte, an diesem begehbaren immersiven Ort verschmilzt alles zu einer einzigen interaktiven Oberfläche. *Voyage of Discovery* wurde als ein Vehikel für neue Vermittlungsstrategien konzipiert. Mithilfe von digitalen Stiften können die User in die virtuelle Welt eintauchen und sich an ihrer Ausgestaltung beteiligen. Die in diesem Kontext bislang erstmals eingesetzte ANOTO-Technologie erlaubt eine großflächige und punktgenaue Verteilung von Inhalten in und an jeglichen Räumen und Objekten. Dadurch eröffnen sich vielfältige Chancen für die Ausformulierung neuartiger physisch-virtueller Erlebnisräume in Bezug auf Experience Design, Gestaltung, Storytelling, Interaktions- und Informationsdesign.

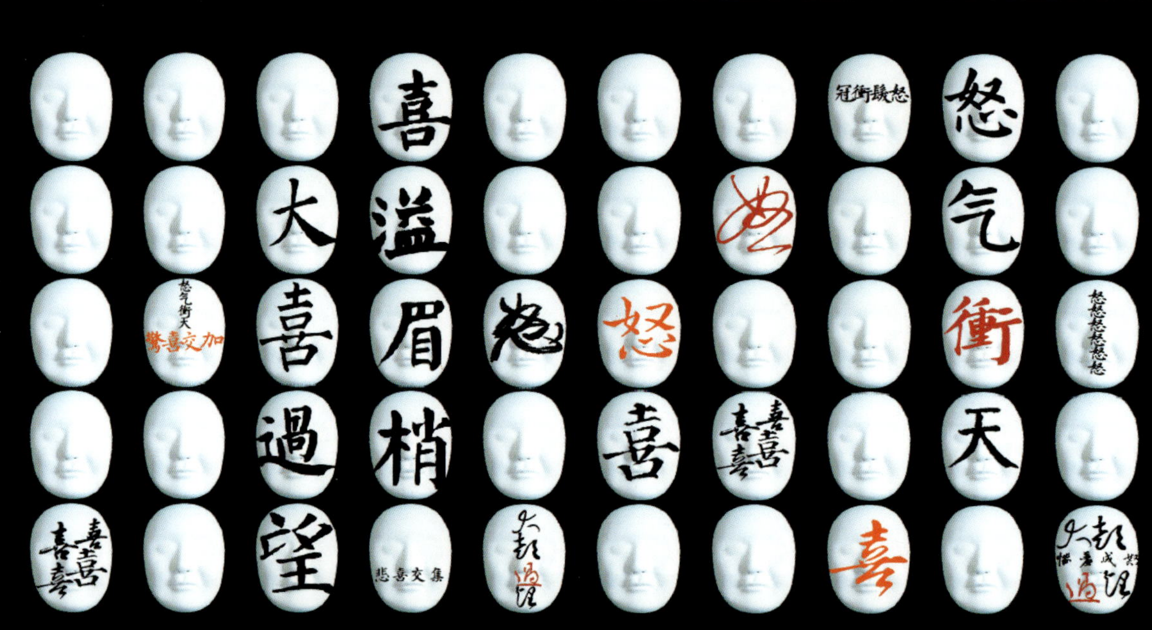

Shi Zheng, Tang Xiaodan: *Calligraphy Masks*

Futurelab.Academy

Ars Electronica Futurelab.Academy was created to support students from international partner universities to realize innovative projects in the field of media art. The format's unique features contain the Ars Electronica Futurelab's expertise and the possibility to participate in the world's most renowned festival for art, technology and society—the Ars Electronica Festival. Selected team members from the Ars Electronica Futurelab conduct workshops and seminars, which are open for a group of students. The topics of these lectures will be determined jointly beforehand, with the partner institutions being able to select from a variety of workshop topics. During the lectures, the students develop artistic concepts together with the lecturer from the Ars Electronica Futurelab, which are to be realized in the course of the semester. Most questions regarding content and technology should already be answered during this time. However, also during the realization process, the Ars Electronica Futurelab provides its expertise via phone conferences and Q&A sessions. Finally, the students' artworks are assessed by the university professor together with the Ars Electronica Futurelab, with the aim of presenting the best works in a special exhibition at the Ars Electronica Festival. Therefore, the students have the opportunity to go through the whole process of artistic creation—from finding an idea to producing the exhibition together with an internationally experienced team.

Futurelab.Academy's first workshop series took place at the China Academy of Art, the first art school in China, as well as the leading institution in the research and education of new media art in the country. Its former New Media Art Department had nurtured a new generation of new media artists in China. The School of Intermedia Art at the Academy, newly founded in 2010, combines the former New Media Art Department with other units, including the graduate program in Contemporary Art and Social Thought, thus establishing a full-scale media arts program that covers different directions in the field, with each of its five Labs having its own area of emphasis. The Ars Electronica Futurelab workshop series at the China Academy of Art was initiated by Dajuin Yao, sound artist, art historian, and Director of Open Media Lab at the Academy. Both institutions jointly developed a thematic direction for the workshop series that focuses on the interface between traditional culture and media technology. Roland Haring, Co-Director of Research and Innovation at Futurelab led the first workshop. Haring gave a thorough explanation of media art production principles and intermediate programming skills for interactive art. The workshop also invited a guest speaker, Lu Dadong, a young calligrapher and famous rock group leader, to give a demonstration and talk on the basics of Chinese calligraphy, which provided much background information as well as inspiration. Although being the place of origin of Chinese calligraphy, with neighboring countries such as Japan and Korea extending its area and application, China now faces a serious crisis with the 3,000 year old writing system and the art of writing. First of all, traditional cultural elements, of which calligraphy is but a small part, are conspicuously absent in everyday life in China; and this break with past is particularly severe for the young generation. Only a small elite circle of mostly older people now practises Calligraphy in China. Even more detrimental is the prevalence of writing by keyboard inputting on computers and cell phones, which has virtually all but replaced handwriting in reality. And the continuation of the Chinese character production mechanism, which relies on not only visual recognition and memory, but more on physical, motor memory of writing out each stroke of a character in sequence by hand, is facing a serious crisis—without the latter, the former will become increasingly difficult. Further complications are caused by the fact that Chinese calligraphy is done in the traditional, non-simplified script form, which most Chinese people in the Mainland today cannot fully comprehend. It is within this context of the alienation and disconnection of the young Chinese with their own past that this workshop proves to be all the more interesting and important. In this workshop, the students are given an opportunity to research on and re-think about a topic that usually falls outside their targets of new media artistic concerns—Chinese calligraphy and the writing system in general. They have to confront their own cultural heritage, as well as looking for its possibilities of extension with the help of technology and the various new media. It also stimulates the young artists to ponder on the question whether they need their own identity in the present globalization of new media art.

Therefore, the workshop has initiated several art projects that are now works-in-progress. At least some of them will be shown at the Ars Electronica Festival 2012. For instance, Xiong Zhen-kai's *Cubelligraphy* proposes a 4-meter cube made up with dozens of layers of thin gauze, forming a space that the audience can walk in and out of freely. Audio-visual work showing animated calligraphy is projected from the two sides of the cube, thus forming a quasi-solid space of immersive environment of digital calligraphy filled with light and shadows and sound.

Inspired by the ancient Chinese "concrete poem" piece *Poem in a Plate,* Shi Zheng and Tang Xiaodan's *Concrete Poetry* is a video projected onto a series of raised 3-dimensional models on a wall. The video content are a series of concrete poems using Chinese characters related to all types of emotions in animation, and is accompanied by the sound of human voice expressing the corresponding emotions, such as anger, sadness, hatred, love, etc. Video is also central to Wang Zhipeng's *Eternity,* where a single Chinese character (yong, meaning "eternity") in calligraphy form is turned into a fractal image animation in which there is no beginning and no end. Everything is in a state of constant flux and scale is symbolically relative. The work is shown with three separate vertically projected videos on the wall. The fractals are audio-visual in format, i.e., animations with soundtrack composed with the Chinese pronunciation of the word "eternity" and environmental sounds.

With *Calliscope,* Luo Hang, Yan Weidan and Qiu Linru are developing a periscope or helmet, with video screen installed inside, which is worn by the viewer, who uses a glove controller or pointing device to view a 3D, virtual reality-type, representation of the earliest forms of Chinese characters related to agriculture. The control interface is designed in the form of a Rubik's Cube, in which different Chinese character animations reside, and the viewer can choose to zoom in/go into each cubic cell to experience the 3D pictographic rendering of the ancient pictographs. Another 3D-visualization is proposed by Shen Bijun, Pan Ying and Ma Bin's project *Hexagram Field.* Here, a chart of Chinese divination hexagrams is projected from the top to the floor. The visitor's position on this chart interacts with the projection of 3D graphics on the wall, which are particle animations of the different Chinese characters in various writing styles, showing how each pictograph evolved in history, but still understandable across cultural differences.

Inspired by the Tibetan prayer wheel, Tan Lijie and Qu Qianwen's work *Living Outside of Time* is made up of small wooden wheels inscribed with calligraphy, which in turn form a large, suspended prayer wheel. The visitor can easily turn the small wheels from outside or inside the large wheel structure, which triggers multi-channel sound resulting in a religious atmosphere, and at the same time the double-layered central pillar emits lights via the calligraphic carvings from the center of the wheel.

With some of the resulting works presented in the Festival within such a short period of time, we look forward to more Futurelab workshops that tackle other aspects of art, culture, and technology at China Academy of Art and other international partner universities in the future.

Text: Dajuin Yao, Horst Hörtner, Roland Haring, Roland Reiter

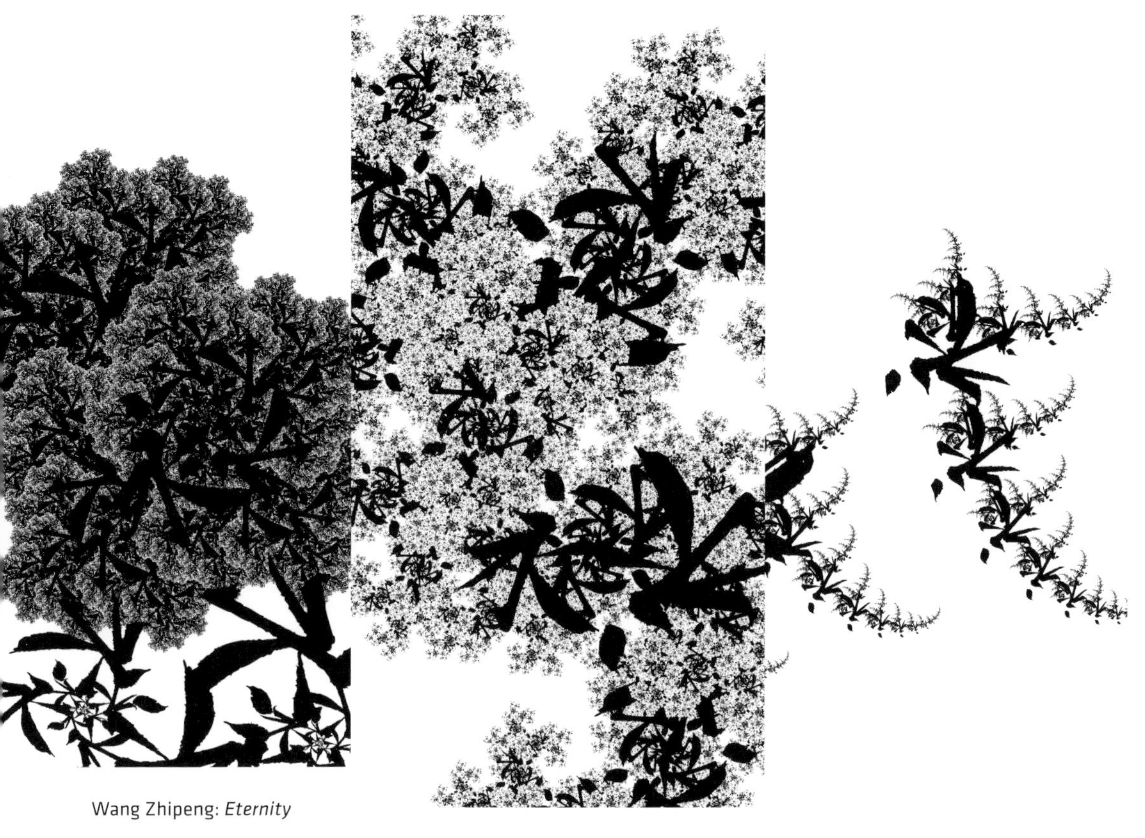

Wang Zhipeng: *Eternity*

Futurelab.Academy

Die Ars Electronica Futurelab.Academy wurde gegründet, um Studierenden internationaler Partneruniversitäten bei der Realisierung innovativer Projekte im Bereich Medienkunst zu unterstützen. Das Format zeichnet sich dadurch aus, dass die Teilnehmer nicht nur die Möglichkeit haben, auf die Expertise des Ars Electronica Futurelab zurückzugreifen, sondern auch am renommiertesten Festival für Kunst, Technologie und Gesellschaft – der Ars Electronica – teilzunehmen.

Ausgewählte Teammitglieder des Ars Electronica Futurelab leiten Workshops und Seminare für je eine Studentengruppe. Die Themen dieser Lectures werden vorher gemeinsam festgelegt, wobei die Partnerinstitutionen aus einer Vielzahl von Themen wählen können.

Während der Lectures entwickeln die Studierenden gemeinsam mit dem Vortragenden vom Ars Electronica Futurelab künstlerische Konzepte, die im Lauf des Semesters verwirklicht werden sollen. Die meisten inhaltlichen und technischen Fragen sollten in dieser Zeit geklärt werden. In der Realisierungphase leistet das Futurelab auch per Telefonkonferenz und in Q&A-Sessions Unterstützung. Abschließend werden die Arbeiten der Studierenden von ihrem Universitätsprofessor und dem Ars Electronica Futurelab bewertet, und die besten Arbeiten werden in einer Sonderausstellung beim Ars Electronica Festival präsentiert. Die Studierenden haben daher die

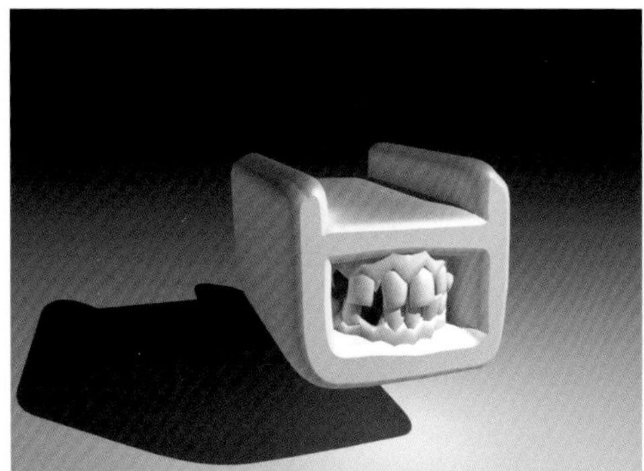

Luo Hang, Yan Weidan, Qiu Linru: *Calliscope*

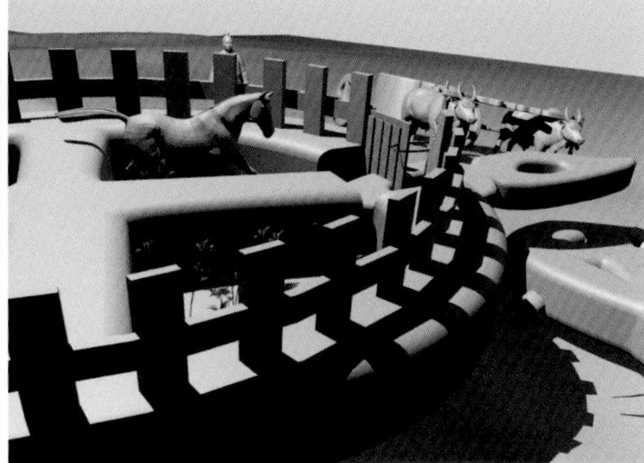

Luo Hang, Yan Weidan, Qiu Linru: *Calliscope*

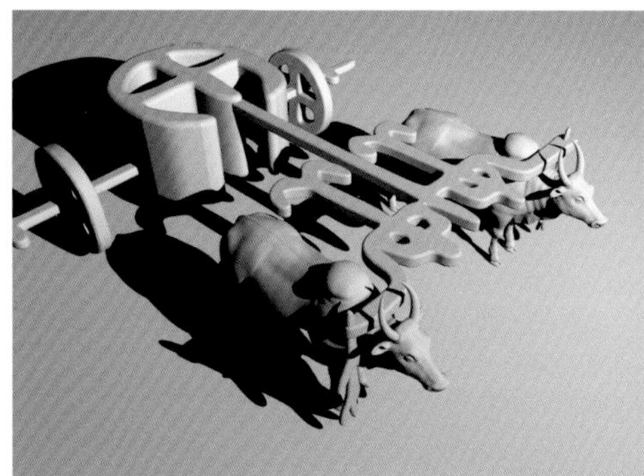

Luo Hang, Yan Weidan, Qiu Linru: *Calliscope*

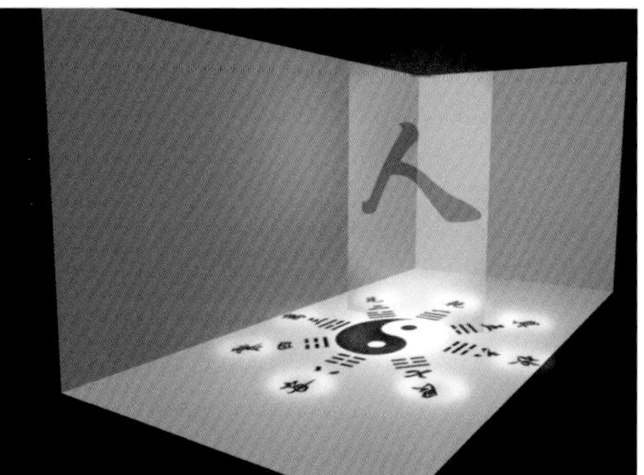

Shen Bijun, Pan Ying, Ma Bin: *Hexagram Field*

Gelegenheit, den gesamten Prozess künstlerischen Schaffens zu durchlaufen – von der Ideenfindung bis zur gemeinsamen Gestaltung der Ausstellung mit einem international erfahrenen Team.

Die erste Workshopreihe der Futurelab.Academy fand an der China Academy of Art statt, der einflussreichsten Kunsthochschule und führenden Forschungs- und Bildungsinstitution für neue Medienkunst des Landes. Das frühere New Media Art Department hat eine neue Generation von MedienkünstlerInnen in China hervorgebracht. Die 2010 neu gegründete School of Intermedia Art an der China Academy of Art vereint unter einem Dach das ehemalige New Media Art Department sowie andere Einheiten, etwa ein Graduiertenprogramm für die Studienrichtung Contemporary Art and Social Thought, und begründete damit ein umfassendes Medienkunstprogramm, das unterschiedliche Richtungen auf dem Gebiet abdeckt, da jedes der fünf Labors seinen eigenen Schwerpunkt hat. Die Ars Electronica Futurelab Workshopreihe an der China Academy of Art wurde von dem Klangkünstler, Kunsthistoriker und Leiter des Open Media Lab der Akademie, Dajuin Yao, initiiert. Gemeinsam haben die beiden Institutionen eine thematische Ausrichtung für die Workshopreihe entwickelt, die die Schnittstelle von traditioneller

Kultur und Medientechnologie ins Blickfeld rückt. Den ersten Workshop leitete Roland Haring, Co-Director der Research and Innovation Group am Futurelab. Haring erläuterte ausführlich die Prinzipien der Medienkunstproduktion und die erforderlichen Programmierkenntnisse für interaktive Kunst. Auch ein Gastredner – Lu Dadong, ein junger Kalligraf und Bandleader einer bekannten Rockgruppe – war eingeladen, die alte Kunst der chinesischen Kalligrafie vorzuführen und über ihre Grundlagen zu sprechen. In seinem inspirierenden Vortrag erhielten die Teilnehmer interessante Hintergrundinformationen.

Obwohl die Kalligrafie ihren Ursprung in China hat und sich von dort aus in Japan und Korea verbreitete, wo sie auch eine Erweiterung erfuhr, sieht sich das Land heute mit einer ernsthaften Krise der 3.000 Jahre alten Schreibkunst konfrontiert. Ein Grund dafür ist, dass traditionelle kulturelle Praktiken, von denen die Kalligrafie nur ein kleiner Teil ist, im chinesischen Alltag auffallend wenig präsent sind; dieser Bruch mit der Vergangenheit ist vor allem bei der jungen Generation zu beobachten. Die Kalligrafie wird heute von einem kleinen elitären Kreis meist älterer Personen praktiziert. Noch nachteiliger wirkt sich das Tippen auf Computer- oder Mobiltelefontastaturen aus, das das Handschriftliche so gut wie ersetzt hat. Und die Fortdauer der chinesischen Schriftbildproduktion, die nicht nur auf dem visuellem Erkennen und dem Gedächtnis beruht, sondern vielmehr noch auf dem physisch-motorischen Gedächtnis, in dem die Ausführung jedes Strichs eines Schriftzeichens abrufbar sein soll, ist ernsthaft gefährdet – ohne Letzteres wird auch Ersteres zunehmend schwieriger. Weitere Komplikationen ergeben sich durch die Tatsache, dass die chinesische Kalligrafie in der traditionellen, nicht vereinfachten Schrift geschrieben wird, die die meisten in der VR China lebenden Chinesen heute nicht mehr beherrschen. In diesem Kontext der Entfremdung und Distanzierung junger Chinesen von ihrer eigenen Vergangenheit ist dieser Workshop besonders interessant und wichtig. Die Studenten haben hier die Gelegenheit, über Themen zu forschen und nachzudenken, die im Zuge ihrer Beschäftigung mit neuen Medien häufig vernachlässigt werden: die chinesische Kalligrafie und das Schreiben im Allgemeinen. Sie müssen sich mit ihrem eigenen kulturellen Erbe auseinandersetzen und nach Erweiterungsmöglichkeiten desselben mit Hilfe von Technologie und verschiedenen neuen Medien suchen. Darüber hinaus werden die jungen KünstlerInnen angeregt, sich mit der Frage auseinanderzusetzen, ob sie angesichts der gegenwärtigen Globalisierung der neuen Medienkunst überhaupt eine eigene Identität brauchen.

Der Workshop hat mehrere Kunstprojekte initiiert, die nun bereits im Produktionsprozess sind. Zumindest einige davon sollen beim Ars Electronica Festival 2012 gezeigt werden, etwa Xiong Zhenkais *Cubelligraphy*, ein vier Meter großer Würfel aus Dutzenden Lagen hauchdünnen Gewebes, der einen Raum bildet, der vom Publikum nach Belieben betreten werden kann. Eine audiovisuelle Arbeit, die animierte Kalligrafie zeigt, wird auf zwei Seiten des Würfels projiziert und schafft einen amorphen Raum, ein immersives Environment, das den Betrachter in die Welt der digitalen Kalligrafie eintauchen lässt, die von Licht, Schatten und Klängen erfüllt ist.

Das chinesische Gedicht „Poem in a Plate" im Stil konkreter Poesie inspirierte Shi Zheng und Tang Xiaodan zu einer Umsetzung konkreter Poesie als Videoprojektion auf eine Reihe von erhöhten dreidimensionalen Modellen auf einer Wand. Das Video zeigt eine Reihe visueller Gedichte, bei denen animierte chinesische Schriftzeichen für verschiedenste Emotionen, wie Zorn, Traurigkeit, Hass, Liebe etc. stehen; dazu ist eine Stimme zu hören, die den entsprechenden Emotionen Ausdruck verleiht.

Ein Video steht auch im Zentrum von Wang Zhipengs Arbeit *Eternity,* bei der ein einzelnes chinesisches Schriftzeichen *(yong,* in der Bedeutung von „Ewigkeit") in eine Fraktalanimation verwandelt wird, die weder Anfang noch Ende kennt. Alles befindet sich in ständiger Bewegung und der Maßstab ist nur symbolisch zu verstehen. Die Arbeit wird in drei vertikal projizierten Videos auf der Wand gezeigt. Die Fraktale sind audiovisuell, d. h. Animationen mit Soundtrack, wobei die Komposition aus der chinesischen Aussprache des Wortes „Ewigkeit" und Umgebungsgeräuschen besteht.

Calliscope ist ein von Luo Hang, Yan Weidan und Qiu Linru entwickeltes Periskop bzw. ein Helm, in den ein Videomonitor installiert ist. Der Betrachter trägt diesen Helm und steuert mit einem Handschuh oder einer Zeigevorrichtung eine virtuelle 3D-Darstellung der frühesten Formen chinesischer Buchstaben, die sich auf Landwirtschaft bezogen. Die Steuerung hat die Form eines Zauberwürfels, in den verschiedene Animationen chinesischer Buchstaben integriert sind. Der Betrachter kann jede dieser kubischen Zellen heranzoomen und eine piktografische 3D-Wiedergabe der alten Bildzeichen betrachten. Eine weitere 3D-Visualisierung präsentieren Shen Bijun, Pan Ying und Ma Bin mit ihrem Projekt *Hexagram Field.* Hier wird ein Diagramm mit chinesischen Weissagungshexagrammen von der Decke auf den Boden projiziert. Die Position des Besuchers auf dieser Grafik interagiert mit der Projektion der 3D-Grafiken an der Wand, die Animationen verschiedener chinesischer Schriftzeichen in verschiedenen Schreibstilen sind und die Entwicklung der Bildzeichen im Lauf der Zeit zeigen, die trotz der kulturellen Unterschiede nach wie vor verständlich sind.

Tan Lijies und Qu Qianwen wurden für ihre Arbeit *Living Outside of Time* von tibetischen Gebetsmühlen inspiriert. Die Arbeit besteht aus kleinen Holzwalzen mit kalligrafischen Inschriften, die ihrerseits eine große, frei hängende Gebetsmühle bilden. Die BesucherInnen können die kleinen Walzen von außer- oder innerhalb der Installation leicht in Schwingung versetzen, wodurch ein Mehr-kanalton ausgelöst wird, der eine religiöse Stimmung erzeugt, während gleichzeitig die zentrale Säule durch die kalligrafischen Gravuren aus dem Zentrum des Rades Licht ausstrahlt. Wir freuen uns auf die Präsentation einiger der in so kurzer Zeit entstandenen, hier beschriebenen Arbeiten beim Festival sowie auf weitere Futurelab Workshops, bei denen andere Aspekte von Kunst, Kultur und Technologie an der China Academy of Art und anderen internationalen Partneruniversitäten in der Zukunft aufgegriffen werden.

Text: Dajuin Yao, Horst Hörtner, Roland Haring, Roland Reiter

Aus dem Englischen von Martina Bauer

Ars Electronica Solutions / CMoDA

GeoCity Beijing

GeoCity Beijing is an information visualization study project for "GeoCity Smart City", the main exhibition curated by CMoDA (China Millennium Monument Museum of Digital Arts) for Beijing Design Week 2012, in collaboration with Ars Electronica and Tsinghua University, Beijing. Beijing, the fast growing mega city, inevitably spawns outrageous urban issues. The migration workers versus the static household and the social security system, the increasing number of private cars on the road versus the old capital's closed traffic network, the public transportation system that lacks service design, the downgraded air quality after the 2008 Olympics, a city with ubiquitous macro infrastructure, but no micro walkable area. How can we modify and transform the old concrete jungle to host the new urban mobility movement via digital intervention?

The theme of Beijing Municipality's action plan from the last to the current 5-year period has evolved from Digital Beijing to Smart Beijing. The Digital Beijing initiative makes the mega city become a tera-data generator. In the era of Big Data with the social media boom and the internet, data quality has gone beyond traditional taxonomy and structure, while data quantity is exploding. How can we map the various geo, spatial, social and urban data, and then curate them according to point of interests to get instant insights into the urban issues? The answer lies in the city's own data mine.

Data visualization, mentioned by the Global Agenda Councils Reports 2011–2012, is a supporting tool to map the world as a complex system. It's a powerful stomach to digest tons of data. For example, millions of pieces of data can be processed and translated into 30 seconds of 3D animation, zipping the decades into a single moment.

GeoCity Beijing is the point of departure to provide a holistic way to view and understand complex urban issues via data visualization. It studies Beijing's urban mobility via mapping population, transportation, telecommunication, green and social data and future simulation into one dynamic dashboard portal to facilitate interdisciplinary research and communication for city operators and urban planners, leading to collaborative innovation in city development. It also allows the public easy access to the open data of the city.

The GeoCity model was developed by Ars Electronica Futurelab. *GeoCity Beijing* is the model's first Asian application after Linz and Berlin and is a collaboration of Ars Electronica Solutions, CMoDA CoINNO Lab and the Information Art and Design Department of Tsinghua University, Beijing.

Text: Yang Lei

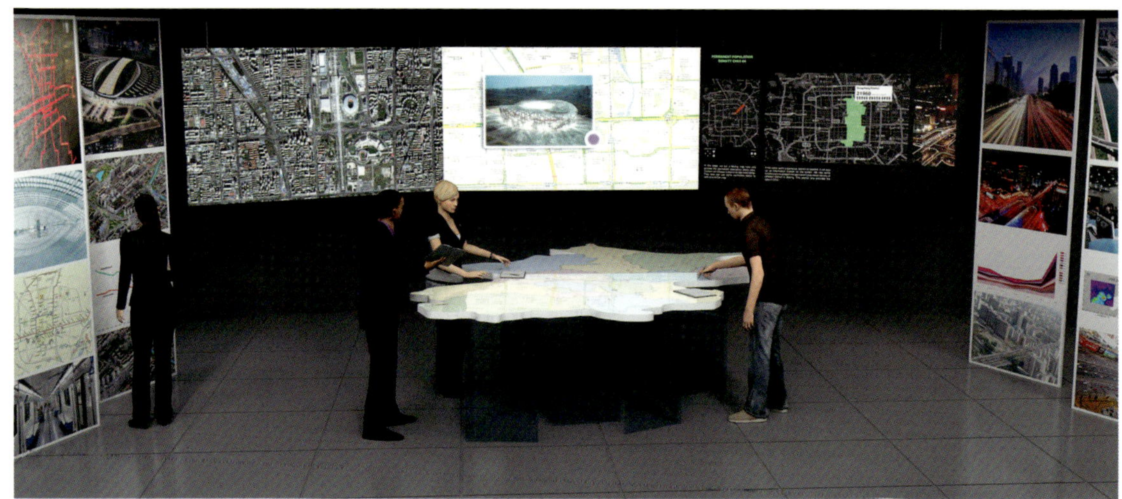

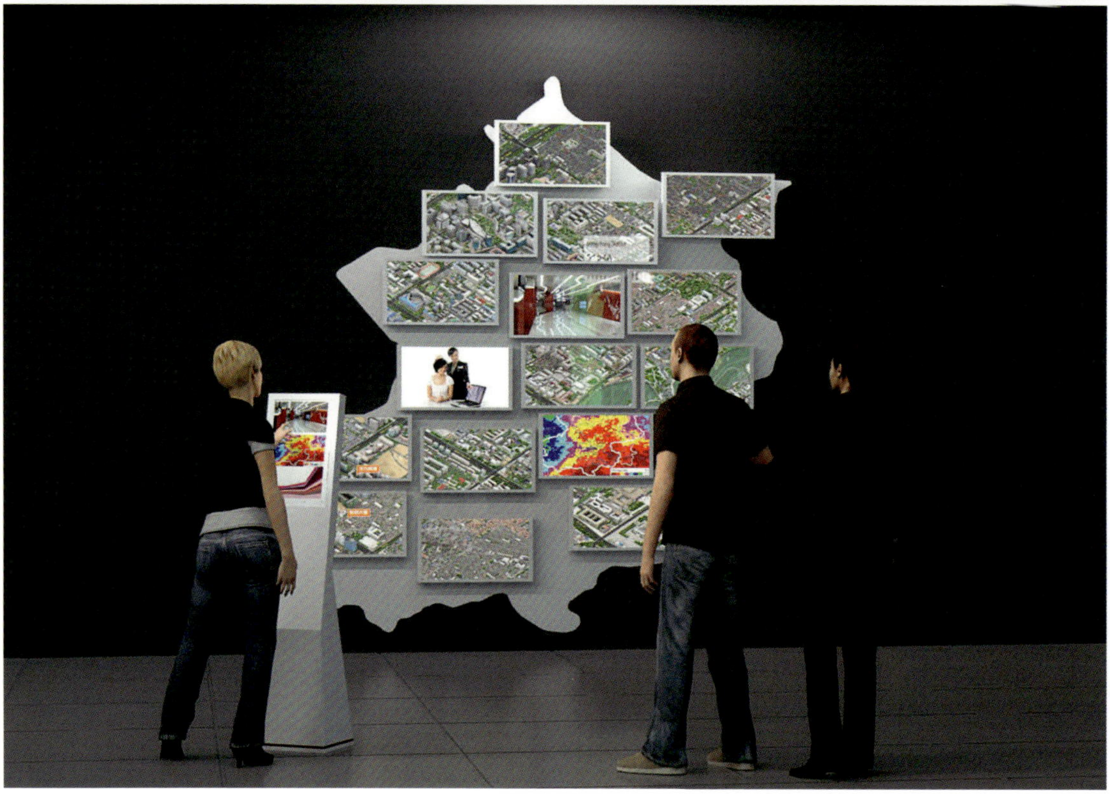

GeoCity Beijing

GeoCity Beijing, ein Forschungsprojekt zur Informationsvisualisierung, wird im Rahmen von *GeoCity Smart City* präsentiert, der Hauptausstellung der *Beijing Design Week 2012.* Die Ausstellung wird vom China Millennium Monument Museum of Digital Arts (CMoDA) in Zusammenarbeit mit Ars Electronica und der Universität Tsinghua (Peking) kuratiert.

Peking, eine rasant wachsende Megacity, sieht sich mit den massiven Folgen der Urbanisierung konfrontiert. Arbeitsmigration versus unflexiblem Haushaltsregistrierungs- und Sozialversicherungssystem; die Zunahme des motorisierten Individualverkehrs im Kontrast zum geschlossen Verkehrnetz der alten Hauptstadt; die fehlende Serviceorientierung im öffentlichen Verkehr; die schlechte Luftqualität nach den Olympischen Spielen 2008; die ausufernde Makroinfrastruktur ohne ausreichenden Ausbau der Infrastruktur für Fußgänger auf der Mikroebene. Die zentrale Frage lautet: Wie können wir den alten Betondschungel durch digitale Interventionen an neue Formen der urbanen Mobilität anpassen?

Der Fünfjahres-Aktionsplan der Pekinger Stadtregierung hat sich vom *Digital Beijing* zum *Smart Beijing* entwickelt. Die *Digital Beijing*-Initiative lässt die Megacity Peking zum Super-Datengenerator werden. Im Zeitalter der Datenexplosion dank Sozialer Medien und des Internet hat sich die Datenbeschaffenheit über traditionelle Taxonomien und Strukturen hinweggesetzt, während die Datenmenge gigantische Ausmaße annimmt. Wie können die verschiedenen Geo-, räumlichen, sozialen und stadtbezogenen Daten abgebildet und schwerpunktmäßig in einer Ausstellung präsentiert werden, um einen unmittelbaren Einblick in Aspekte der Urbanisierung zu liefern? Das Heben der Datenschätze der Stadt liefert die Antwort darauf.

Die Berichte des *Global Agenda Councils*-Netzwerks (2011–2012) beschreiben Datenvisualisierung als Möglichkeit zur Darstellung unserer Welt als komplexes soziales System. Man kann die Datenvisualisierung als Magen mit enormem Fassungsvermögen betrachten, der in der Lage ist, Tonnen von Daten zu verdauen. Millionen Daten können so beispielsweise in 30-Sekunden-3D-Animationen umgewandelt und Jahrzehnte in einen kurzen Moment verpackt werden.

GeoCity Beijing liefert mittels Datenvisualisierung neue und umfassende Einsichten in vielschichtige Fragen der Urbanisierung. Durch die Visualisierung diverser Daten (Bevölkerungs-, Verkehrs-, Telekommunikations-, Umwelt-, Sozial- und Simulationsdaten) in einem dynamischen Dashboard-Portal kann die urbane Mobilität in Peking abgebildet werden. Das wiederum ermöglicht interdisziplinäre Forschung und Kommunikation zwischen der Stadtverwaltung und Städteplanern sowie eine gemeinsame Erarbeitung von Innovationspotenzialen in der Stadtentwicklung. Auch die Bewohner können so leicht auf frei zugängliche städtische Daten zugreifen.

Das *GeoCity*-Modell wurde vom Ars Electronica Futurelab entwickelt. Mit *GeoCity Beijing* wird das Modell nach Linz und Berlin erstmals in einer asiatischen Stadt umgesetzt. Es handelt sich um eine Zusammenarbeit zwischen Ars Electronica Solutions, CMoDA CoINNO Lab und dem Information Art and Design Department der Universität Tsinghua in Peking.

Aus dem Englischen von Sonja Pöllabauer

Ars Electronica Futurelab / The OHMI Trust

The OHMI Ars Electronica Competition

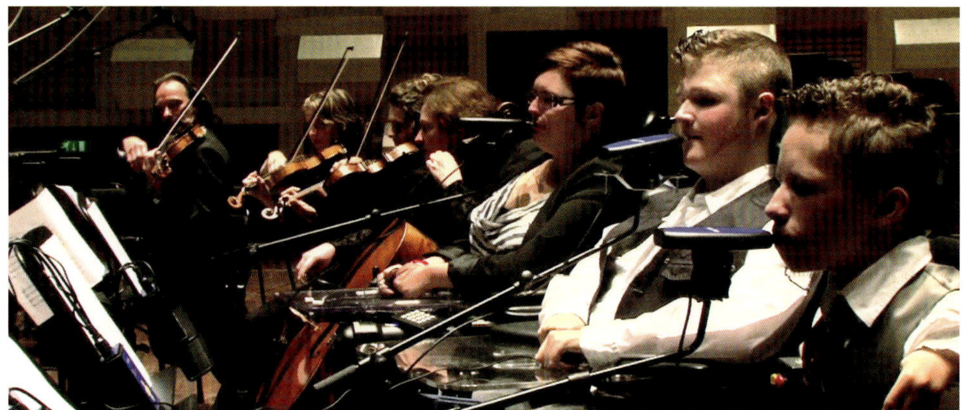

Three disabled musicians, Christian Gouweleeuw, Karin van Dijk and Glen Nugteren play Magic Flutes (designed by Ruud van der Wel) together with Ebred Reijnen, Loortje van den Brink, Maartje van Rheeden and Carla Schrijner of the Rotterdam Philharmonic Orchestra. *)

This unique competition was launched at the 2011 Ars Electronica Festival and is now attracting entries from throughout the world. The challenge is to create musical instruments for the disabled that can allow them to participate fully in music making.

Music fills our world. It is on billions of CDs, iPods, films, TV and radio stations, played live and recorded in countless concert halls, clubs, shops, even lifts, and, of course, in our homes. In nearly every instance that music is played on instruments that need two highly functioning hands and arms. If you have even a slight disability in one hand or arm you will be excluded. Through the creation or adaption of instruments, we can open-up the potential for undifferentiated participation for everyone in musical life.

The competition rules can be found on the online entry forms at *ohmi.aec.at.* The challenge to create instruments that can replicate the characteristics of an orchestral instrument is a hard one, but the entries received so far suggest it is a challenge that can be met. The first judging will be in 2013, for which entries can be submitted up to June 30th 2013.

Text: Stephen Hetherington

*) The video, recorded at the Concert Hall de Doelen, Rotterdam, can be seen at *http://vimeo.com/44395359*

Dieser einzigartige Wettbewerb wurde beim Ars Electronica Festival 2011 ins Leben gerufen und verzeichnet nun Einreichungen aus der ganzen Welt. Die Aufgabe besteht in der Entwicklung eines Musikinstruments, das Behinderten ermöglicht, uneingeschränkt am Musikleben teilzunehmen.

Unsere Welt ist von Musik erfüllt. Man findet sie auf Milliarden von CDs, iPods, in Filmen, bei TV- und Radiostationen, sie wird in unzähligen Konzerthäusern, Clubs, Geschäften, sogar in Lifts und natürlich zu Hause live gespielt oder aufgenommen. Fast immer wird diese Musik auf Instrumenten gemacht, die zwei voll funktionsfähige Hände und Arme bedingen. Ist auch nur eine Hand oder ein Arm leicht beeinträchtigt, wird man aus dem Kreis der Musiker ausgeschlossen. Mit der Entwicklung oder Adaptierung von Instrumenten wird nun jedem die uneingeschränkte Teilnahme am Musikleben eröffnet.

Die Teilnahmebedingungen sowie das Online-Anmeldeformular findet man auf *http://ohmi. aec.at.* Ein Instrument zu entwickeln, das die Charakteristika eines klassischen Instruments aufweist, ist natürlich eine schwierige Herausforderung, aber die bisherigen Einreichungen lassen erwarten, dass sie zu bewältigen ist. Die erste Bewertung, für die Projekte bis zum 30. Juni 2013 eingereicht werden können, findet 2013 statt.

Aus dem Englischen von Michael Kaufmann

The OHMI Trust *(www.ohmi.org.uk)* was formed by Stephen Hetherington and Martin Dyke in 2011 in response to Stephen's attempts to find a musical instrument his hemiplegic daughter could play at school. The trust's main object is to find, then teach, musical instruments for the disabled. In addition to Ars Electronica, the OHMI Trust collaborates with the City of Birmingham Symphony Orchestra, HemiHelp, and Drake Music.
The OHMI Trust is supported by generous financial contributions from numerous individuals, and from CHK Charities, The Limoges Trust, The Austin and Pilkington Trust, and the D'Oyle Carte Charitable Trust.

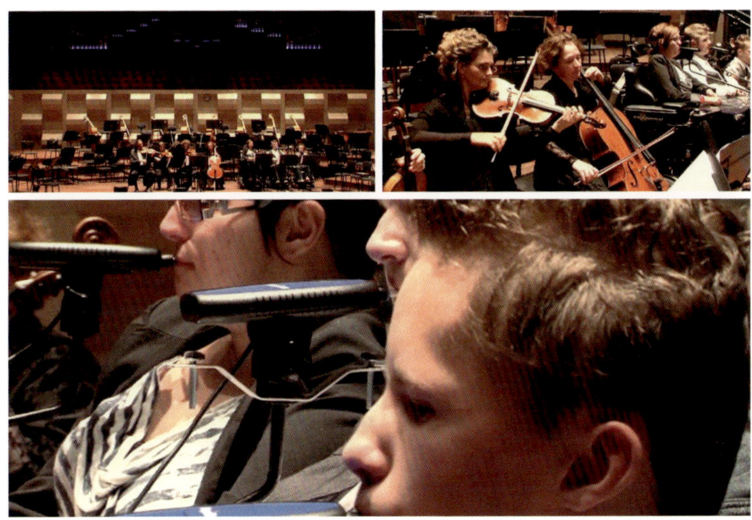

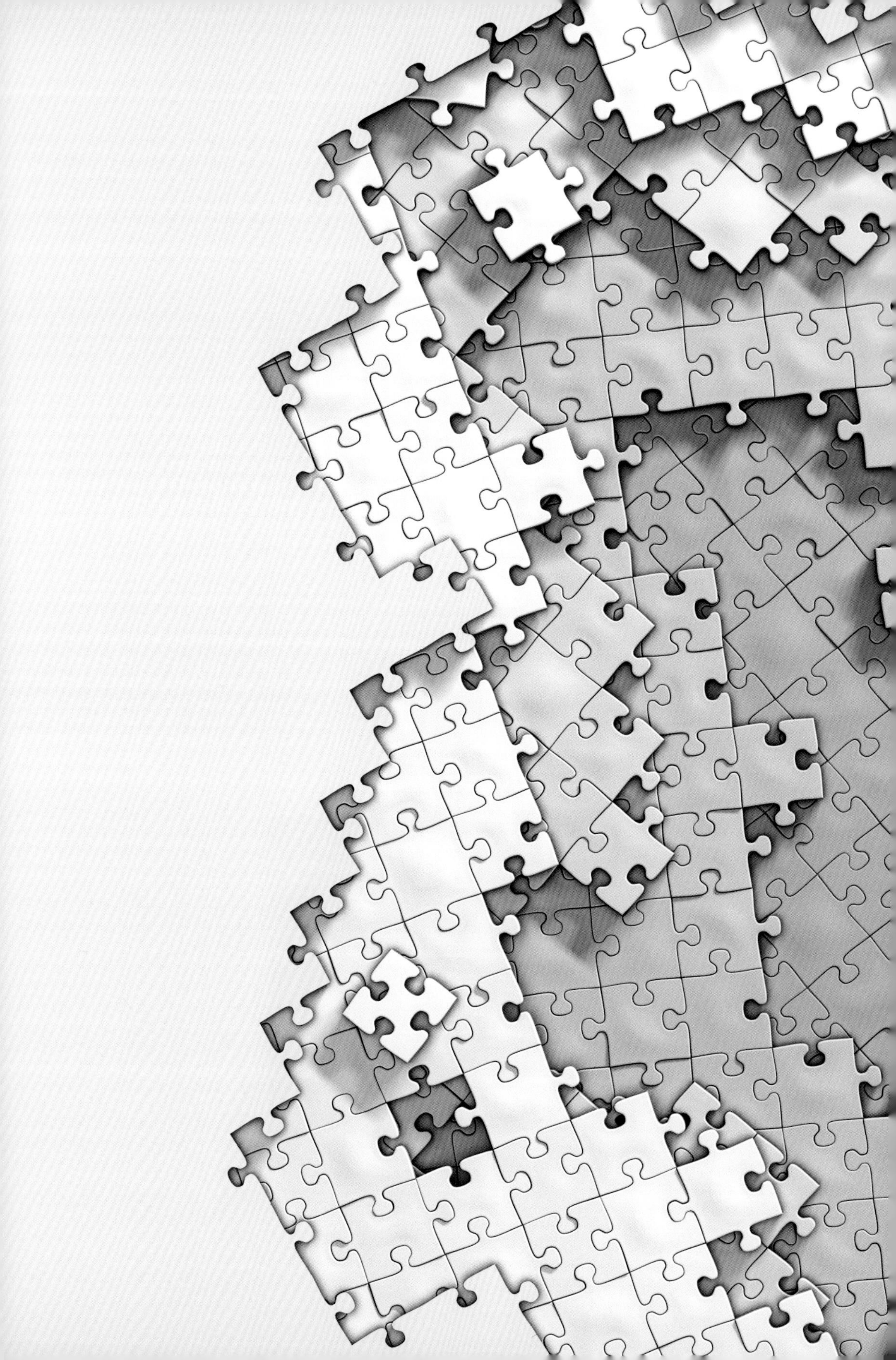

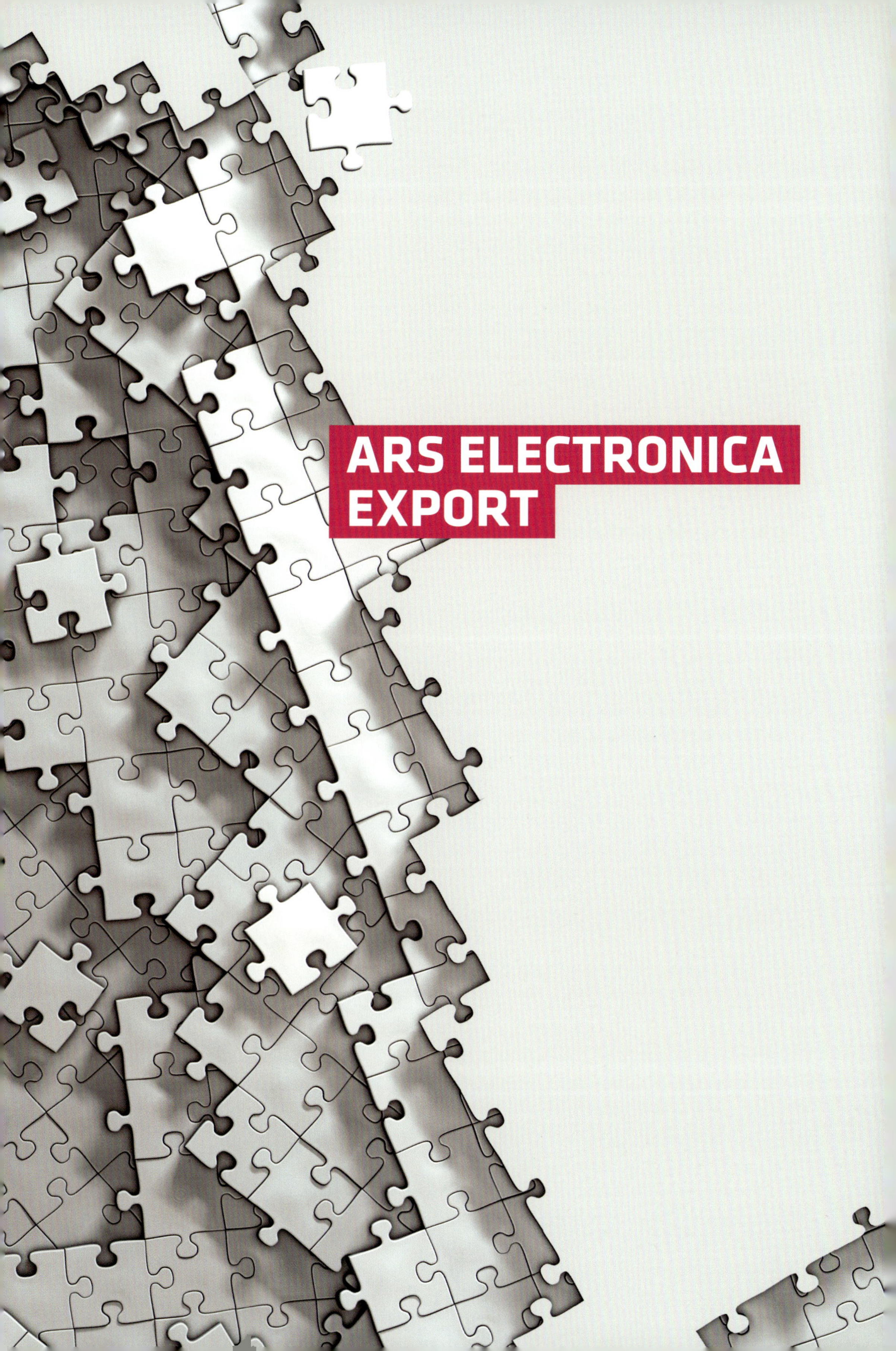
ARS ELECTRONICA
EXPORT

Ars Electronica Export
External Exhibitions 2011/2012

Since 2004 in response to strong international demand, Ars Electronica has developed numerous exhibitions jointly with partner institutions all over the world. Each and every exhibition was customized for the particular venue and staged in collaboration with the host institution.

Seit dem Jahr 2004 hat Ars Electronica aufgrund der hohen internationalen Nachfrage gemeinsam mit internationalen Partnern zahlreiche Ausstellungen entwickelt. Jede einzelne dieser Ausstellungen wurde speziell für den Ort und gemeinsam mit den gastgebenden Institutionen zusammengestellt.

Among the latest international exhibition projects are:
Zu den jüngsten internationalen Ausstellungsprojekten zählen:

Poetry of Motion
BREEZÉ BREEZÉ Shoppingmall Osaka
Osaka, 10.12. – 18.12.2011

Poetry of Motion is Ars Electronica's latest showcase of excellence in media art. The BREEZÉ BREEZÉ Mall and the shoppers who frequent it will be part of an experiment in which Ars Electronica stages six selected artistic approaches to examining how media art can enrich the flow of everyday life. This project was initiated by Kansai Telecasting Corporation and is being produced with the support of the Austrian Cultural Forum in Tokyo.

Unter dem Titel *Poetry of Motion* präsentierte Ars Electronica ausgewählte Medienkunst. Die BREEZÉ BREEZÉ Shoppingmall mit ihrem Publikum wird zum Ort des Experiments, und Ars Electronica untersucht mithilfe sechs ausgewählter künstlerischer Positionen, wie Medienkunst den Strom des Alltags anreichern kann. Dieses Projekt wurde initiert von Kansai Telecasting Corporation und wird unterstützt vom österreichischen Kulturforum in Tokio.

tour en l'air (1998), Ursula Neugebauer
Exquisite Clock (2009), João Wilbert (FABRICA)
Heartbeat Picnic (2010), Junji Watanabe, Yui Kawaguchi, Kyosuke Sakakura, Hideyuki Ando
Shadowgram (2010), Ars Electronica Futurelab: Roland Haring, Hideaki Ogawa, Christopher Lindinger, Emiko Ogawa, Matthew Gardiner and David Stolarsky:
Innocence (2010), Ars Electronica Futurelab: Katharina Nussbaumer, Hideaki Ogawa, Andreas Jalsovec, Christoph Liebmann, Erwin Reitböck, Michael Mayr, Stefan Hehr
Ars Wild Card (2011), Ars Electronica: Hideaki Ogawa, Emiko Ogawa, Manuela Naveau

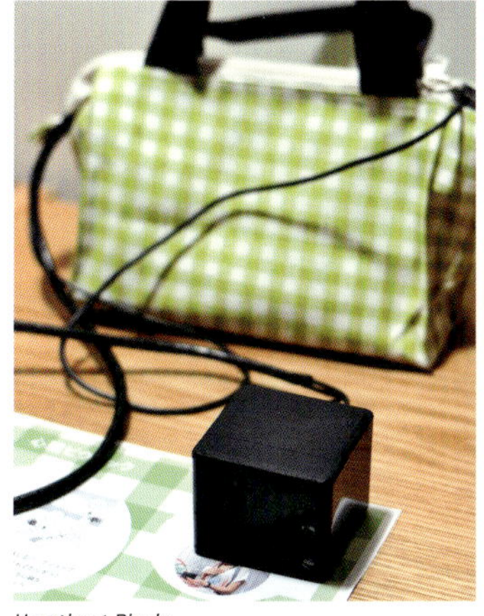

Heartbeat Picnic

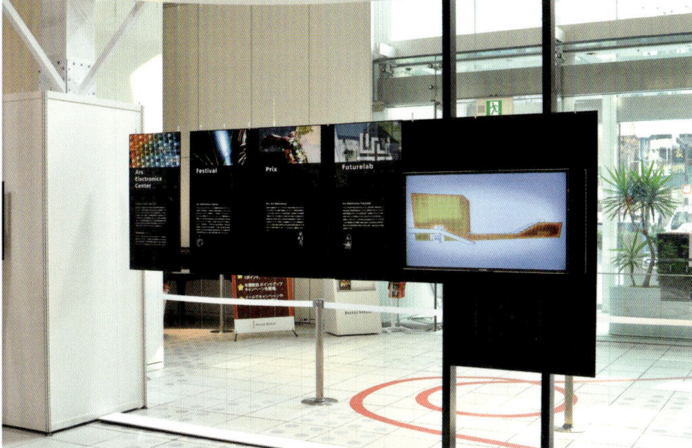

Information Screen

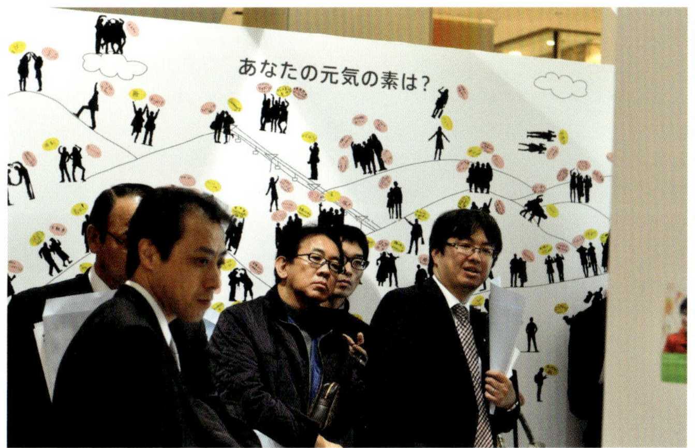

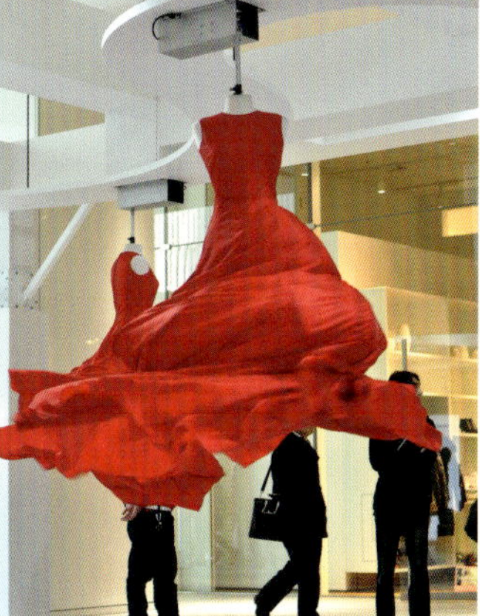

tour en l'air

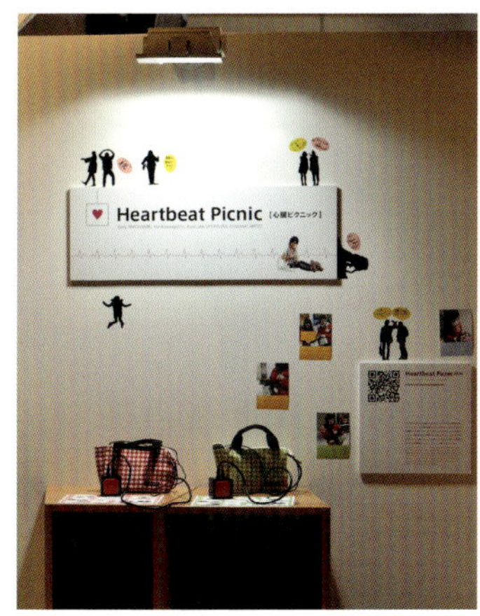
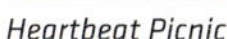

Heartbeat Picnic

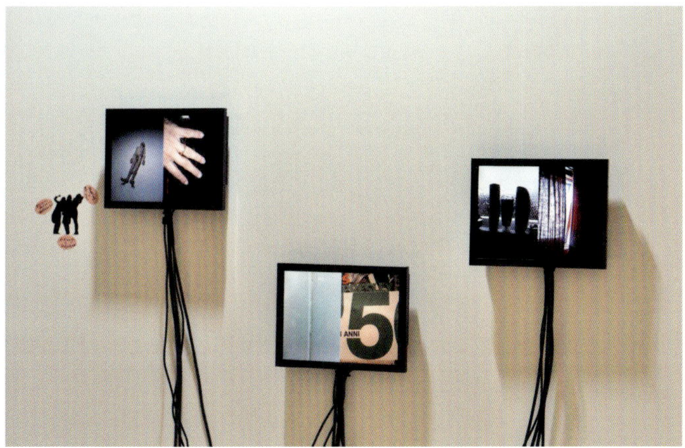

Exquisite Clock

Ars Wild Card Workshop
Tokyo Great Creativity 2012 – The Revolution of the Geniuses
Tokyo, 17.02. – 19.02.2012

Ars Electronica collects Tokyo's creativity with *Ars Wild Card* (iPhone Application). Creative "matters", "things", "works", "experiments" , "places" and etc ... Please let us know Tokyo`s creativity of today from your point of view. *Ars Wild Card* is part of the following events

Ars Electronica fragte nach der Kreativität Tokios mittels *Ars Wild Card* (iPhone-Applikation). Diese wurde bei folgenden drei Ausstellungen als Workshop eingesetzt:

http://gyre-omotesando.com/; www.idd.tamabi.ac.jp/art/misconversion/; www.cgarts.or.jp/scg/
Organized by: CG-Arts; supported by KTV (Kansai Telecasting Corporation)

Ars Wild Card

Ars Wild Card is an iPhone application developed by Ars Electronica Linz as a participative workshop tool for exhibitions and interventions in public spaces. This application and QR codes assigned to each exhibited project make it possible to generate content about the works on display in a frame with which installation visitors can photograph the works and comment on them right on site. The application also permits personal impressions to be collected via online sharing at the website *http://awc.aec.at/*. Plus, there's the option of posting the substantively framed and commented images on all popular social media sites. At the exhibition venue, *Ars Wild Cards* printed out as postcards constitute a constantly growing collection of snapshots of the exhibition taken by visitors on site or via online participation. Visitors can also take printed-out *Ars Wild Card* postcards home with them.

Ars Wild Card ist eine iPhone-Applikation, die als partizipatives Workshop-Tool für Ausstellungen und Interventionen im öffentlichen Raum von Ars Electronica Linz entwickelt wurde. Mittels der Applikation und QR-Codes pro ausgestelltem Projekt werden Inhalte zu den Arbeiten in einem Rahmen generiert, mit dem man die Arbeiten fotografieren und auch direkt vor Ort kommentieren kann. Die Applikation erlaubt zusätzlich, dass die persönlichen Eindrücke via Online-Sharing auf der Website *http://awc.aec.at/* gesammelt werden. Optional gibt es auch die Möglichkeit, dass die inhaltlich gerahmten und kommentierten Bilder auf alle gängigen Social-Media Plattformen gestellt werden können. Am Ort der Ausstellung bilden die ausgedruckten *Ars Wild Cards* als Postkarten eine ständig anwachsende Momentaufnahme der Ausstellung durch die BesucherInnen oder per Online-Partizipation. Ausgedruckte *Ars Wild Card*-Postkarten können auch von den BesucherInnen mit nach Hause genommen werden.

Idea and concept: Hideaki Ogawa, Emiko Ogawa, Manuela Naveau (Ars Electronica)
Software development: Memetics GmbH
Design: Stefan Eibelwimmer

Ars Wild Card debuted at *Poetry of Motion*, an exhibition produced by Ars Electronica Linz in collaboration with KTV (Kansai Telecasting Corporation) that ran December 10–18, 2011 in Osaka, Japan, followed by many other presentations among them in South Korea at the Sunset Janghang Festival July 14–22, 2012.

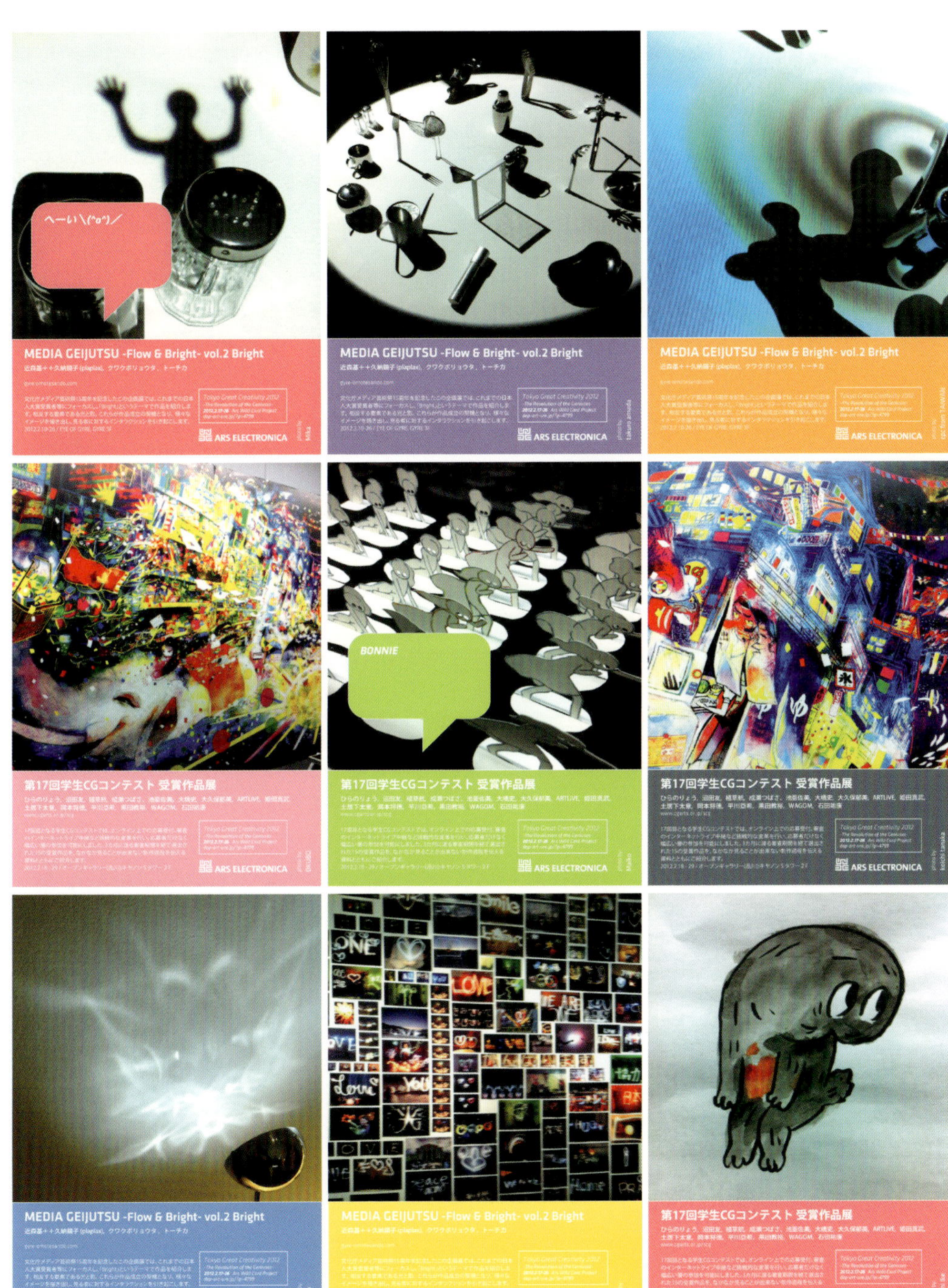

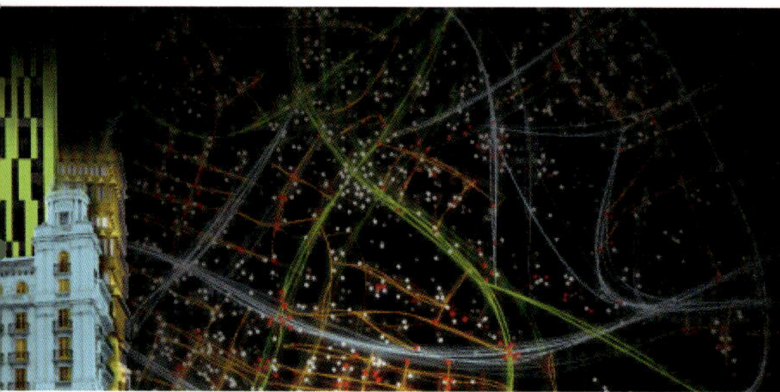

www.paseoproject.eu

PASEO PROJECT – New creative models to experience the city
Saragossa, 27./28.03.2012 and 26./27.06.2012

Zaragoza City of Knowledge (Zaragoza ciudad del conocimiento) has got assistance from Ars Electronica, as the Spanish foundation launches its *PASEO PROJECT,* an effort to jointly seek creative new ideas for communication in and with a city. At a symposium that used Ars Electronica and its impact on Linz as a best-practice example, participants had the opportunity to consider other interesting models developed by artists and creative engineers as interventions in a real or virtual cityscape. The event also served as the setting for the debut of an idea platform designed to collect new artistic projects and bundle local creativity involving the interplay of art and technology, and of a city and its citizens. In a workshop that was set for the end of June, the project ideas had been presented to a diversified array of individuals from Zaragoza and three of the most outstanding projects had been singled out for recognition.

Die spanische Stiftung *Saragossa Stadt des Wissens (Zaragoza ciudad del conocimiento)* startete mit Unterstützung von Ars Electronica in Saragossa das Programm *PASEO PROJECT,* um sich gemeinsam auf die Suche nach neuen kreativen Ideen der Kommunikation in und mit einer Stadt zu machen. Am Beispiel der Ars Electronica und ihren Einfluss auf Linz wurden in Form eines Symposiums weitere interessante Modelle vorgestellt, die von KünstlerInnen und kreativen TechnologInnen als Intervention für einen realen oder virtuellen Stadtraum erarbeitet wurden. Die Veranstaltung wurde auch genutzt, um erstmals eine Ideenplattform zur Sammlung von neuen künstlerischen Projekten zu eröffnen und um lokale Kreativität im Zusammenspiel zwischen Kunst und Technologie, einer Stadt und ihren BürgerInnen zu bündeln. In einem Workshop Ende Juni trafen die Projektideen auf unterschiedliche Personen aus Saragossa, und drei der herausragendsten Projekte wurden prämiert.

Supported by österreichisches Kulturforum, Madrid

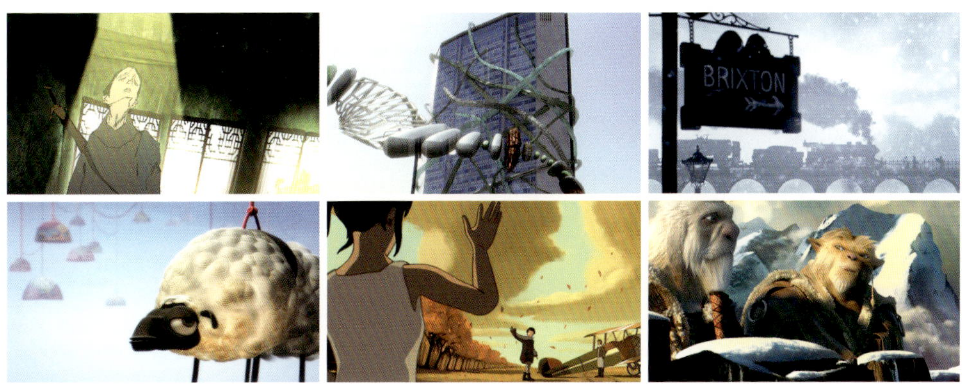

Ars Electronica Animation Festival – On Tour

The *Ars Electronica Animation Festival 2011* screens a selection of outstanding films submitted to the Prix Ars Electronica 2011. These 120 visual highlights have been divided into 12 lineups. In collaboration with the Austrian Ministry of European and International Affairs a Blu Ray have been developed by the Ars Electronica Futurelab, which has been sent to all Austrian cultural forums and embassies worldwide. The Ars Electronica Animation Festival 2011 has been presented:

Das Programm des *Ars Electronica Animation Festival 2011* ist eine Selektion der besten beim Prix Ars Electronica 2011 eingereichten Arbeiten in der Kategorie Computer Animation / Film / Visual Effects. Es bietet ca. 120 ausgewählte visuelle Highlights, gegliedert in 12 Programmschienen. Gemeinsam mit dem Bundesministerium für europäische und internationale Angelegenheiten wurde vom Ars Electronica Futurelab eine Blu Ray erarbeitet, die an alle österreichischen Kulturforen und Botschaften versendet wurde. Das Ars Electronica Animation Festival 2011 wurde gezeigt:

24.01.2012	United Kingdom, Austrian Cultural Forum London
22.04.2012	Yemen, *Earth Day*, National Science Museum Yemen
18.–20.05.2012	Greece, New Codes*/ Athens Video Art Festival 2012
18.–30.05.2012	Russia, Perm Museum, Perm
25.05.2012	Israel, Holon Mediatheque
01.06.2012	Russia, World Music Festivals Dikaja Mjata
	http://www.mintmusic.ru/Moscow
26.05.2012	United Kingdom, OHMI Trust at CBSO Centre in Berkley
	Street, Birmingham
06.06.2012	France, Le Cube Paris / Screening Marathon
06.–18.07.2012	Iran, Second Tehran Annual Digital Art Exhibition@Mohsen Gallery
14.–22.07.2012	South Korea, Sunset Janghang Festival, Seochon-gun
27.09.–04.11.2012	Germany, Donumenta, Regensburg
28.09.–06.10.2012	China, Beijing Design Week

Athens International Film Festival, Internationales Kulturfestival *Cervantino*, Guanajuato, Mexico; National Maritime Museum, Greenwich.
Further presentations in Katowice, Beijing, Sao Paulo, Buenos Aires, Tallinn, Marseille and Tokyo are in discussion.

Ars Electronica – Impuls und Bewegung
Automobilforum Unter den Linden der Volkswagen AG
Berlin, 11. Juli bis 2.September 2012

Following the two very successful shows *Poetry of Motion* in 2010, and *What Machines Dream of* in 2011, Ars Electronica was invited back for another guest appearance at Automobilforum Unter den Linden in Berlin. The exhibition produced in cooperation with Volkswagen AG was entitled *Impetus and Movement.* It featured 19 works by 11 internationally renowned artists and Ars Electronica Futurelab staffers.

In this third exhibition staged jointly by Ars Electronica and Volkswagen, the spotlight was focused on a balancing act between absolute self-determination and utter disenfranchisement. In it, the urban space as an extreme example of a living situation that is as real as it is elaborately construed is conceived as a laboratory for the development and testing of innovative strategies and approaches. Prizewinning works of art open up extraordinary spheres of association that range from philosophical reflection to the pursuit of self-awareness in real-world settings.

Nach der erfolgreichen Schau *Poesie der Bewegung* sowie *Wovon Maschinen träumen* in den vergangenen beiden Jahren war Ars Electronica erneut zu Gast im Berliner Automobilforum Unter den Linden. In Kooperation mit der Volkswagen AG wurde diesmal die Ausstellung *Impuls und Bewegung* gezeigt. Achtzehn Werke von einundzwanzig international renommierten KünstlerInnen wurden dabei präsentiert.

Im Mittelpunkt des dritten gemeinsamen Ausstellungsprojekts von Ars Electronica und Volkswagen AG steht der Balanceakt zwischen Selbstbestimmtheit und Entmündigung. Der urbane Raum als ein extremes Beispiel einer ebenso realen wie konstruierten Lebenssituation wird dabei als ein Laboratorium zur Entwicklung und Erprobung innovativer Strategien und Herangehensweisen gedacht. Preisgekrönte künstlerische Arbeiten eröffnen hier einmalige Assoziationsräume, die von der philosophischen Betrachtung bis zur gelebten Selbsterfahrung reichen.

Floor, Cantoni/Crescenti
Particles, Daito Manabe & Motoi Ishibashi
Ser y durar, Democracia
In Your Hands, Dash Macdonald
Save yourself!!!, Hideyuki Ando, Tomofumi Yoshida, Junji Watanabe
CabBoots, Martin Frey
The Tenth Sentiment, Ryota Kuwakubo
Transitions, Julius Stahl
Acoustic Octahedral Geometry, Daisuke Ishida
Inter-Discommunication Machine, Kazuhiko Hachiya
Home Made Rollercoaster, John Ivers
Melonia Shoes, Naim Josefi
The Grand Rapids Lipdub, Status Creative
This too shall pass & Needing/Getting, OK Go
Techno Jeep, Julian Smith
Tipp-Kicker, Joseph Herscher
The Page Turner, Joseph Herscher
Parcour Videos, Red Bull

The tenth sentiment

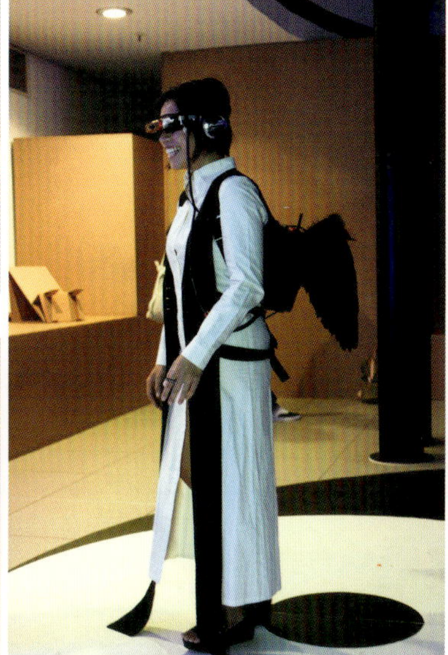

Inter-DisCommunication machine

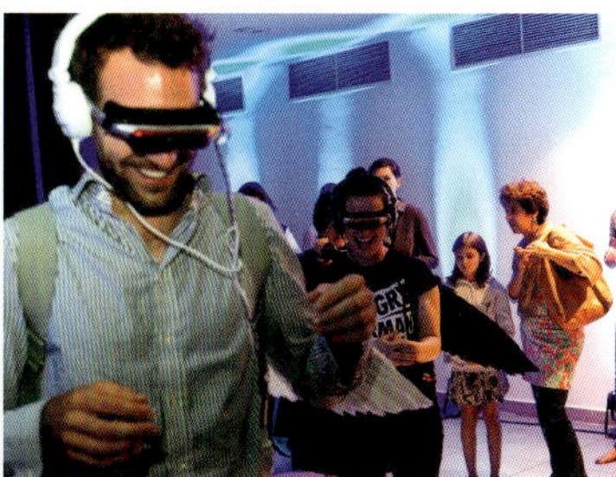

Inter-Discommunication machine

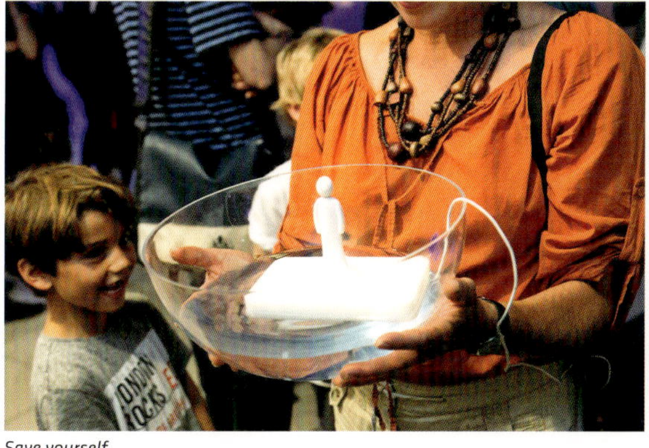

Floor

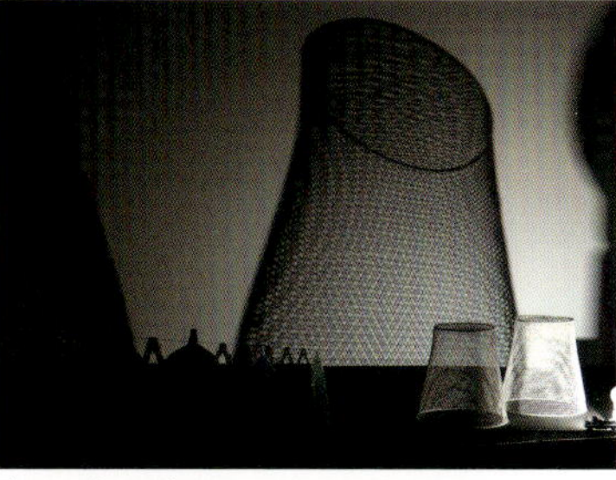

The tenth sentiment

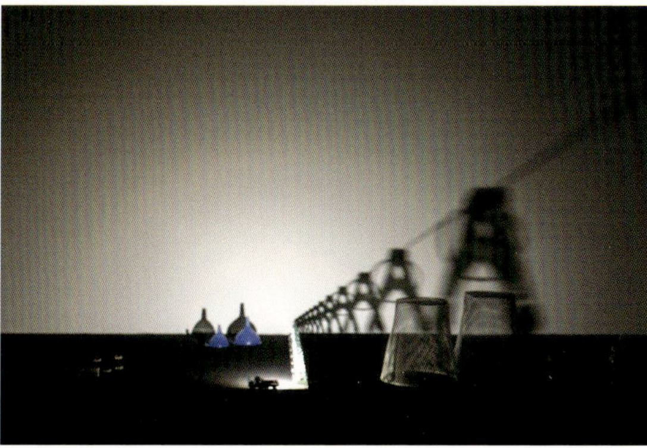

Save yourself

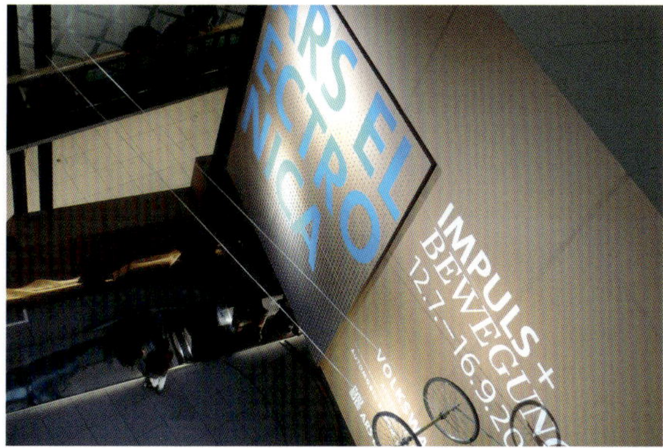

The tenth sentiment

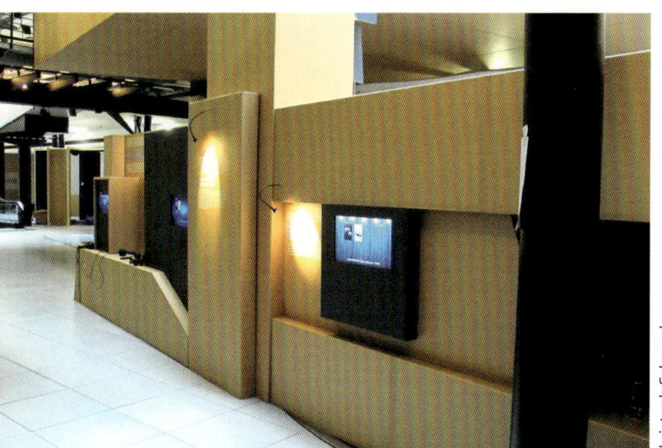

Tipp-Kicker

Architecture: PappLab and Anytime Architekten

Christoph Schemel

Impetus and Movement

The city is unequalled by any of humankind's other habitats as a manifestation of our modern world's complexity. It evokes the many social, cultural and ethnic conflicts that cut across our society, as well as the feeling of a common bond among its inhabitants. Millions of people live and work together in metropolises, cognizant that nowhere else on earth do people exist in such close proximity and nevertheless have so many options to pursue their own individual lives and lifestyles.

None of our other habitats, in order to make peaceful coexistence possible at all, necessitates such a complex composition of how human beings live together—a set of rules that circumscribes every aspect of our lives but at the same time opens up behavioral latitude to the greatest extent possible. One that defines itself as a commitment to every person's right of self-determination, but that also demarcates clear boundaries. However, this container, so to speak, that is the sum of all conceivable compromises must never be capped and sealed; it has to be understood as an ongoing process that is made to keep moving by applying one new impetus after another. If that doesn't occur or does to an insufficient extent, resistance arises.

That such disobedience can develop a dynamism all its own is demonstrated by a trendy sport named parkour. Back in the 1990s, young people in certain Paris suburbs began to take a totally new approach to making their predominantly steel, concrete and glass environment their own. They declared conventional sidewalks to be off-limits and set off on their own paths—routes that always had to lead from Point A to Point B as quickly and directly as possible. In going about this, the traceurs ("trailblazers") acrobatically overcome seemingly insurmountable barriers. In addition to intentionally disregarding prevailing rules, the traceurs highly esteem not damaging their surroundings. Parkour stands for responsible, independent behavior that is freed from regulations and that shows respect for the environment and for other human beings. Now, 20 years after it was invented, Parkour has long since ceased to be a youth movement in the banlieue; it's a trendy urban sport that's being promoted by the PR agencies of an international soft drink manufacturer.

A completely different strategy of attaining one's objective is celebrated by American artist Joseph Herscher. He designs and builds giant machines to perform very specific tasks, whereby the jobs are generally rather simple matters whereas the devices to do them are about as complex as can be. Herscher's contrivances are usually powered by tiny balls that, once they're set in motion, collide with various obstacles and, in doing so, invariably trigger new motion. Impetus is followed by movement is followed by impetus is followed by movement.

Whether speedy and direct like a traceur or as circuitous and slow as Herscher, the path is the actual objective in both cases. As playful and effortless, as unfailing as these two seem to be in arriving at their respective destinations, a trifle is all it takes to send either of them careening out of equilibrium. And that's also exactly what it is about them that enthralls us. Hovering above every act of surmounting an impediment, no matter how elegantly accomplished, is the possibility of failing in grandiose fashion.

Impuls und Bewegung

Wie kein anderer Lebensraum ist die Stadt Sinnbild für die Komplexität unserer modernen Welt. Sie steht für die vielen sozialen, kulturellen und ethnischen Konflikte quer durch unsere Gesellschaft ebenso wie für das Zusammengehörigkeitsgefühl ihrer EinwohnerInnen.

Millionen Menschen leben und arbeiten in der Stadt zusammen, im Bewusstsein, nirgendwo sonst so beengt zu sein und doch nirgendwo sonst so viele Möglichkeiten zur individuellen Lebensgestaltung vorzufinden.

Kein anderer unserer Lebensräume erfordert eine derart komplexe Komposition des Zusammenlebens, um ein friedliches Miteinander überhaupt erst zu ermöglichen. Ein Regelwerk, das jeden unserer Lebensbereiche erfasst, gleichzeitig aber größtmöglichen Handlungsspielraum eröffnet. Eines, das sich als Bekenntnis zum selbstbestimmten Handeln aller versteht, das aber auch klare Grenzen aufzeigt. Diese Summe aller denkbaren Kompromisse darf aber, als Gefäß betrachtet, niemals einer Deckelung unterworfen sein, sondern muss als ein Prozess verstanden und durch neue Impulse in ständiger Bewegung gehalten werden. Passiert das nicht oder in zu geringem Ausmaß, regt sich Widerstand.

Dass solcher Ungehorsam seine ganz eigene Dynamik entfalten kann, zeigt die Trendsportart Parkour. Es waren die 1990er Jahre, in denen Jugendliche in den Pariser Vororten damit begannen, sich ihre aus Stahl, Beton und Glas gestaltete Umwelt auf völlig neue Weise anzueignen. Sie erklärten herkömmliche Wege zum Tabu und schlugen ihre eigenen Pfade ein, Pfade, die immer so schnell und so direkt wie möglich von A nach B führen müssen. In akrobatischer Manier überwinden die „Traceurs" (das sind die, „die den Weg ebnen") dabei vermeintlich unüberwindbare Hindernisse. Neben dem ganz bewussten Missachten des Gebotenen legen die Traceurs Wert darauf, ihre Umgebung nicht zu schädigen. Parkour steht für ein von Vorschriften emanzipiertes, eigenverantwortliches Handeln, das Respekt und Achtung für Umwelt und Mitmenschen impliziert. 20 Jahre nach seiner Erfindung ist Parkour längst keine Jugendbewegung in den Banlieues mehr, sondern eine urbane Trendsportart, die von den PR-Agenturen eines weltweit agierenden Getränkeherstellers rasant in Szene gesetzt wird.

Eine völlig andere Strategie des Ans-Ziel-Gelangens zelebriert der US-Künstler Joseph Herscher. Er entwirft und baut riesige Maschinen, um ganz bestimmte Aufgaben zu erledigen. Wobei diese Aufgaben stets einfach, die Maschinen dagegen so komplex wie nur möglich ausfallen. Angetrieben werden Herschers Apparaturen meist von kleinen Kugeln, die, einmal in Bewegung versetzt, mit verschiedenen Hindernissen kollidieren und dabei immer wieder neue Bewegung auslösen. Auf Impuls folgt Bewegung folgt Impuls folgt Bewegung.

Ob so direkt und schnell wie der Traceur oder so umständlich und langsam wie Herscher, der Weg ist bei beiden das eigentliche Ziel. So spielerisch und leicht, ja, so unbeirrbar beide scheinbar an ihr Ziel gelangen, es genügt da wie dort eine Kleinigkeit, um alles aus dem Gleichgewicht zu bringen. Und genau das ist es auch, das uns da wie dort in den Bann zieht. Dass über jedem noch so eleganten Überwinden des nächsten Hindernisses stets die Möglichkeit des grandiosen Scheiterns schwebt.

This exhibition was produced jointly by Ars Electronica and Volkswagen Aktiengesellschaft
Automobil Forum Unter den Linden, Konzernforum Berlin; director: Cornelia Schneider
Curators: Martin Honzik, Gerfried Stocker / Ars Electronica Linz
Ars Electronica Production Crew: head of production: Michael Lettner; technical management:
Karl Julian Schmidinger; project management: Miriam Schmeikal
Ars Electronica Production Team Berlin: assembly crew: Johannes Ramsl, Martin Haselsteiner, Alexander Böhmler
Carpenter: Martin Kneidinger
Architecture: Anytime Architekten – Jürgen Haller, Christoph Weidinger, *http://any-time.net*
PappLab: Wodo Gratt, Inga Hehn, Martin Flotzinger, Christoph Stadler, Thomas Latzel

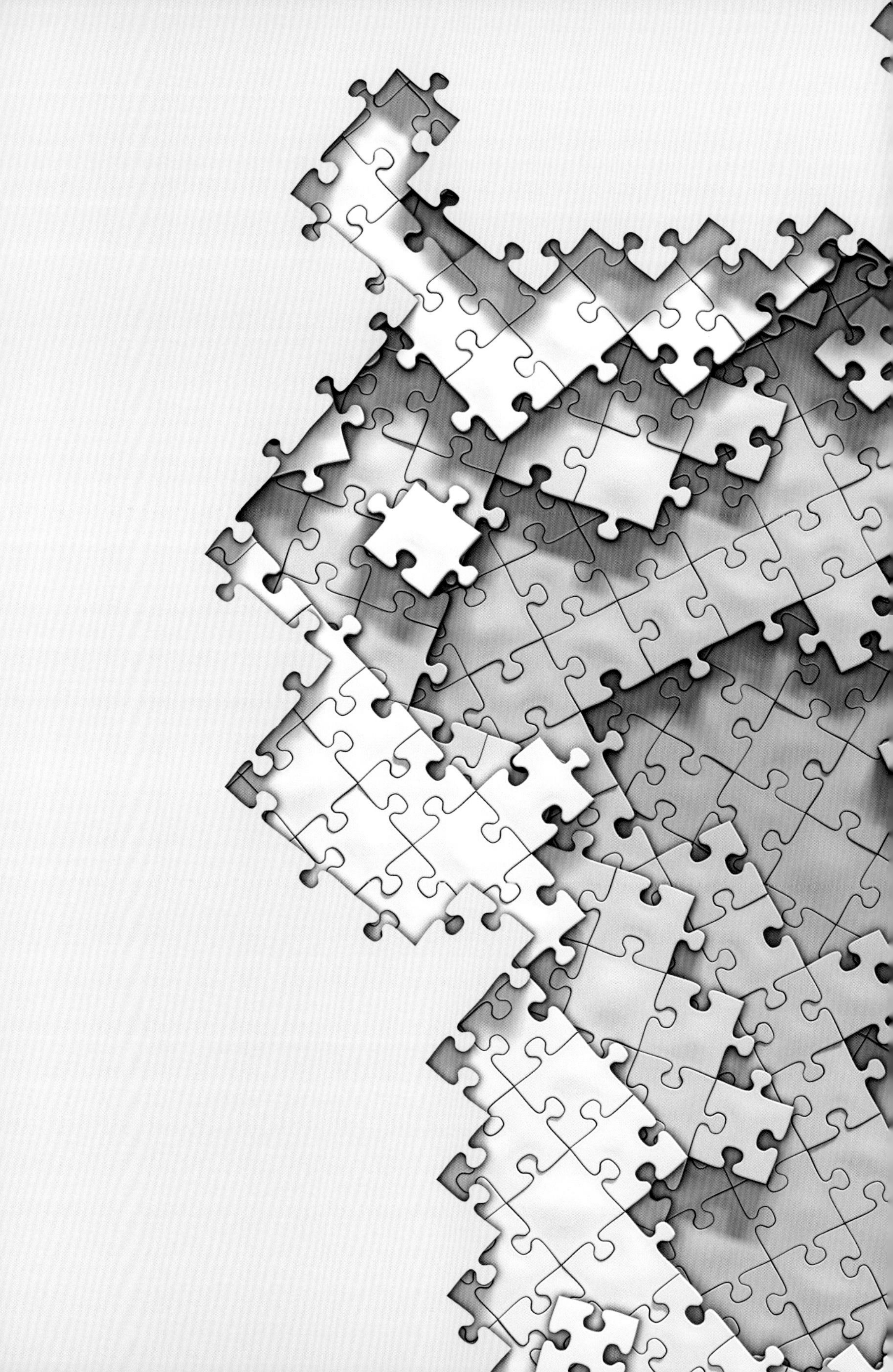

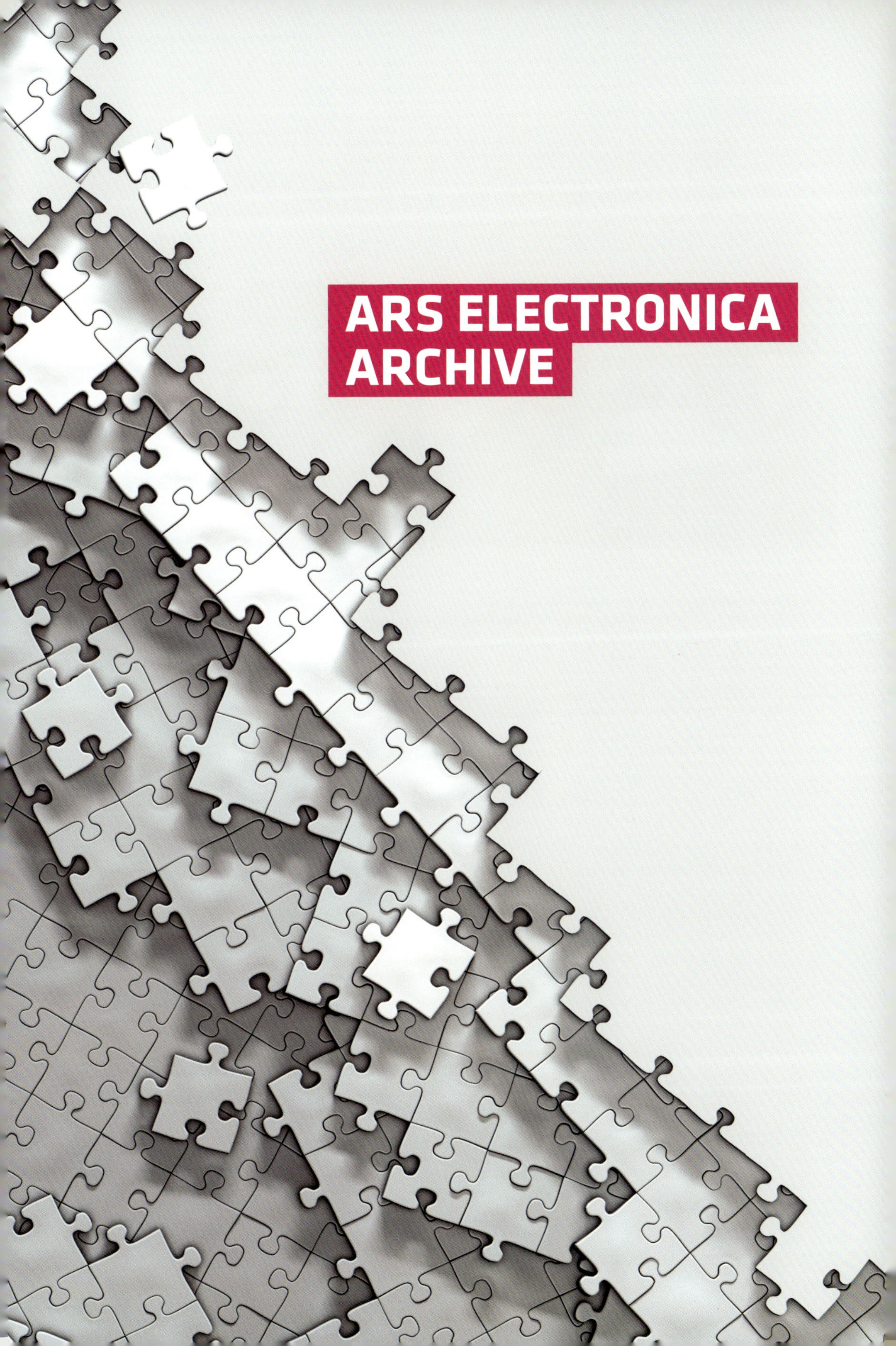

ARS ELECTRONICA
ARCHIVE

Martina Hechenberger, Theresa Schubert-Minski

The Ars Electronica Archive

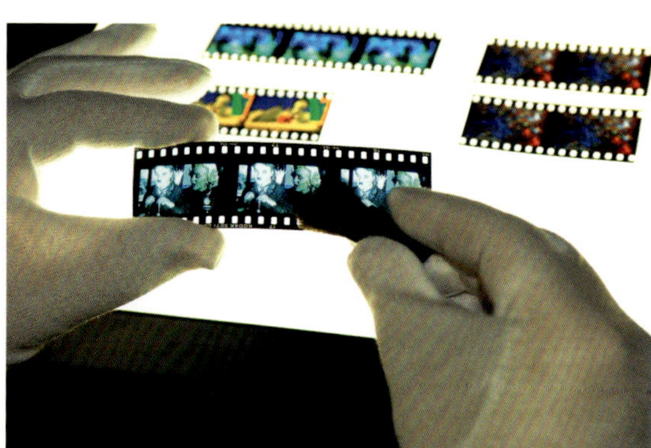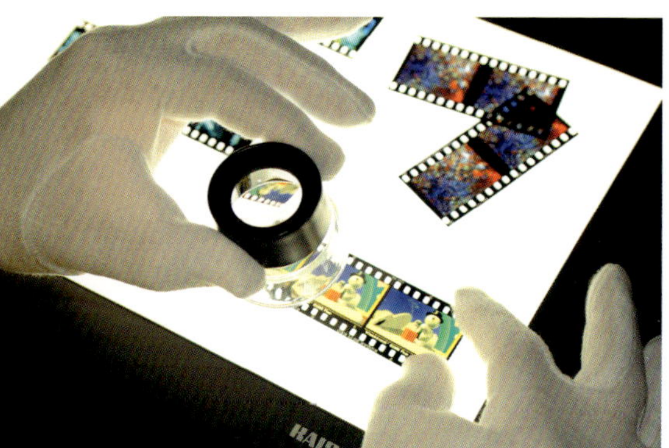

Ars Electronica's archive contains a diverse assemblage of artistic works and documentation of projects, exhibitions and activities over a timeframe of more than 30 years in the wide-ranging international field of media art. The broad substantive spectrum of the content is matched by its tremendous diversity of physical and digital formats, which constitutes a substantial challenge for the archivist. Whereas there are proven methods for conserving physical objects, long-term archiving of digital data still raises countless issues.

Digitization Processes and a Living Archive

The archiving of project documentation as well as, somewhat later, submissions for Prix Ars Electronica prize consideration, began at a very early stage. Thanks to the involvement of the ORF – Austrian Broadcasting Company's Upper Austria Regional Studio, much of the program staged in the early years was recorded and professionally archived, which established the basis for the tremendous number of media documents to come.

In 1995 in conjunction with the construction of the Ars Electronica Center – Museum of the Future, work also began on a permanent Ars Electronica website. As part of this effort, selected catalog texts and photos of projects were put online for the first time.

The complete digitization of all catalogs published to date was done in 1999, which made both texts and images in their original page layout as well as text-only versions available on the internet. Since 1999, all new publications have been put online shortly after having appeared in printed form.

During the period 2005-08, the Ludwig Boltzmann Institute Media.Art.Research founded jointly with Linz Art University and Linz's Lentos Art Museum worked out the basic principles for systematically archiving and providing access to all of Ars Electronica's holdings.

During the construction of the new Ars Electronica Center in 2008, the most comprehensive digitization and archiving project since the 1990s was launched by Ars Electronica to specifically and centrally inventory and digitize material. Ars Electronica's archive has been reconfigured and developed both digitally and physically.

Following several digitization projects and migrations of older data logs, now all entries to the Prix Ars Electronica of a current year are also automatically transferred to the archive as they are submitted. Digital photographs are archived directly and, via an interface, made public on social media sites. The archive has thus been brought to life! It no longer just conserves glimpses of bygone days; it's constantly being updated with new material. It's a direct repository of all newly published photos including their metadata, and thereby makes them (re)searchable. The ongoing, prompt input of data and media by staff members makes it possible to conserve important information.

Additional work has been done on further material from the history of Ars Electronica in conjunction with Austrian and international research projects. Museum subsidies from the Austrian Federal Ministry of Education, Art and Culture have made it possible to physically conserve various collections of analog photographs, to inventory and digitize them, and add them to the research databank. Digitising Contemporary Art, a three-year project being carried out in cooperation with 25 European partner institutions and funded by the European Union, is producing high-quality digital reproductions as well as strategies for long-term archiving. The Ars Electronica Archive is making a substantial contribution to this project by creating approximately 2,600 digital objects (including metadata) documenting Prix Ars Electronica prizewinners and making this material available. This content, which includes much audiovisual material about the projects, can also be accessed via the *www.archive.aec.at* online portal. Some of this information is being conveyed by Austria's Kulturpool to Europeana *www.europeana.eu* to thereby become a part of Europe's largest online art collection.

In conjunction with this year's Ars Electronica Festival THE BIG PICTURE the Ars Electronica Archive is going online with a new look and expanded multimedia content and makes its contents publicly accessible. A multi-touch table provides guests with a look at the festival's fascinating history. Additional terminals offer a convenient way to browse through all the online holdings.

Enduring eternally ...

Aside from legal issues, long-term digital archiving is the biggest problem facing archives today. This has to do with the obsolescence of data types, formats, software and databanks as well as the hardware and operating systems necessary to run them. No universal solution has yet been developed to assure the future readability of files and metadata. Furthermore, the time intervals between launches of significant technical innovations have become shorter and shorter over the last decade, which makes it ever harder to predict the future and to define archiving standards. But despite these imponderables, what practical strategies can a media archive elaborate to guarantee data security at least over the medium term?

In the meantime, Ars Electronica has internally developed a reliable solution that encompasses storage, backup and data control. All data are saved to a second storage medium and incrementally backed up on a daily basis. Following completion of this process, automated watchdog software verifies the checksums and other metadata with respect to their identity and modifications, if any. Constant auditing and ongoing development of archiving standards is nevertheless indispensible and an essential part of quality management.

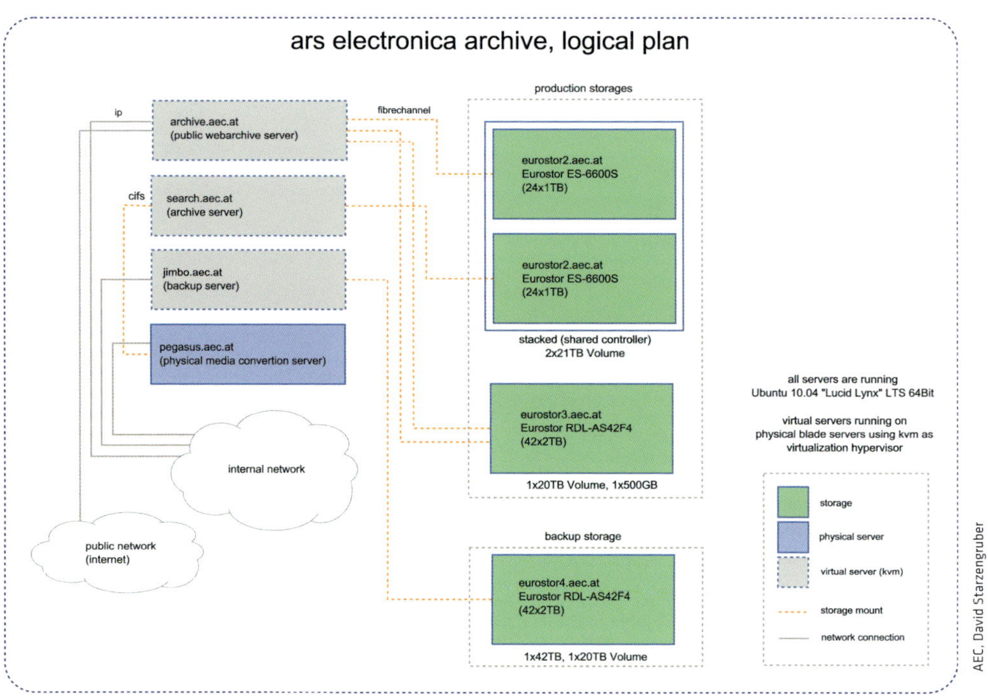

Das Archiv der Ars Electronica enthält eine vielfältige Mischung an künstlerischen Arbeiten sowie Dokumentationen von Projekten, Ausstellungen und Aktivitäten im breiten Feld der internationalen Medienkunst über einen Zeitraum von über 30 Jahren. Die Bandbreite der Inhalte spiegelt sich auch in der Vielfalt der physischen und digitalen Formate wieder und gibt die Herausforderung an das Archiv vor. Während es bei der Archivierung physischer Objekte verifizierte Methoden gibt, wirft die Langzeitarchivierung digitaler Daten immer noch eine Unmenge an Fragen auf.

Digitalisierungsprozesse und ein lebendes Archiv

Die Archivierung von Projektdokumentationen und später auch die der Einreichungen zum Prix Ars Electronica hat bereits sehr früh begonnen. Durch die Beteiligung des ORF wurde schon in den Anfangsjahren sehr viel an Programm aufgezeichnet und professionell archiviert und damit der Grundstein für die überaus große Zahl an Mediendokumenten gelegt.

1995 begann man im Zuge der Errichtung des Ars Electronica Center – Museum der Zukunft, auch eine eigene permanente Website für Ars Electronica aufzubauen. Dabei wurden zum ersten Mal ausgewählte Katalogtexte und Fotos von Projekten online gestellt.

1999 folgte die komplette Digitalisierung aller bislang erschienenen Festivalkataloge, die sowohl mit Text und Bildern im Seitenlayout als auch als reine Textversionen im Internet zugänglich gemacht wurden. Ab 1999 wurden die jeweils neuen Publikationen bereits kurz nach ihrem Erscheinen ins Netz gestellt.

In den Jahren 2005 bis 2008 wurden über das gemeinsam mit der Kunstuniversität Linz und dem Lentos Kunstmuseum Linz gegründete Ludwig Boltzmann Institut Medien.Kunst.Forschung. wichtige Grundlagen für die systematische Archivierung und Erschließung des gesamten Bestands erarbeitet.

Im Zuge des Neubaus des Ars Electronica Center wurde 2008 das bisher umfangreichste Digitalisierungs- und Archivierungsprojekt von Ars Electronica seit den 1990er Jahren gestartet, um gezielt und zentral Material zu inventarisieren und digitalisieren. Das Archiv der Ars Electronica wurde neu aufgebaut und entwickelt, sowohl digital als auch physisch.

Nach diversen Digitalisierungsprojekten und Migrationen älterer Datenstämme können heute auch die gesamten Einreichungen zum Prix Ars Electronica eines laufenden Jahres automatisch ins Archiv überführt werden. Digitale Fotografien werden direkt im Archiv angelegt und über eine Schnittstelle auf Social-Media-Plattformen publiziert. Das Archiv wurde damit zum Leben erweckt und bildet nicht mehr nur längst Vergangenes ab sondern wird laufend mit neuem Material aktualisiert. Es bewahrt direkt alle neu veröffentlichten Fotos inklusive ihrer Metadaten und macht diese somit wieder recherchierbar. Die laufende und zeitnahe Eingabe von Daten und Medien durch MitarbeiterInnen gewährleistet, dass wichtige Informationen erhalten bleiben.

Im Rahmen von nationalen und internationalen Forschungsprojekten konnten weitere Bestände aus der Geschichte der Ars Electronica aufgearbeitet werden: Durch die Museumsförderung des BMUKK wurden verschiedene Sammlungen von analogen Fotografien physisch konserviert, inventarisiert, digitalisiert und der Recherchedatenbank hinzugefügt. Im Rahmen des dreijährigen von der EU geförderten Kooperationsprojekts DCA (Digitising Contemporary Art) entstehen qualitativ hochwertige digitale Reproduktionen und Strategien zur Langzeitarchivierung in Zusammenarbeit mit 25 europäischen Partnern. Das Archiv der Ars Electronica leistet durch die Digitalisierung und Bereitstellung von rund 2.600 Digitalisaten mit Metadaten von Preisträgern des Prix Ars Electronica einen substanziellen Beitrag zu diesem Projekt. Diese Inhalte sind auch über das Online-Portal *www.archive.aec.at* erreichbar und beinhalten eine Vielzahl an audiovisuellen Materialien zu den Projekten. Ein Teil dieser Informationen wird über die österreichische Plattform Kulturpool auch an Europeana *www.europeana.eu* übermittelt und reiht sich dort in die größte europäische Online-Kunstsammlung.

Mit dem diesjährigen Ars Electronica Festival THE BIG PICTURE geht das Ars Electronica Archiv im neuen Look und multimedial online und öffnet sich aus diesem Anlass den Besuchern. An einem Multitouch-Table kann die Festivalgeschichte entdeckt werden, zusätzliche Terminals laden zum Browsen durch den gesamten Online-Bestand ein.

Ewig währt …

Die digitale Langzeitarchivierung ist neben den rechtlichen Fragestellungen eines der größten Probleme, mit dem sich Archive konfrontiert sehen. Dies betrifft die Veraltung von Datentypen, Formaten, Software und Datenbanken sowie der nötigen Hardware und Betriebssysteme. Für die Gewährleistung der Lesbarkeit von Dateien und Metadaten in der Zukunft gibt es bisher noch keine allgemeingültige Lösung. So haben sich auch die Zeitabstände, in denen technische Innovationen auf den Markt kommen, in den letzten zehn Jahren immer mehr verkürzt, was es zusätzlich erschwert, Prognosen für die Zukunft zu treffen und Archivstandards festzulegen. Aber welche praktikablen Strategien kann ein Medienarchiv trotz dieser Unwägbarkeiten erarbeiten, um zumindest eine mittelfristige Datensicherheit zu garantieren?

Innerhalb der Ars Electronica wurde mittlerweile eine zuverlässige Lösung entwickelt, die Storage, Backup und Datenkontrolle umfasst. Alle Daten befinden sich auf einem zweiten Storage und werden täglich inkrementell gesichert. Nach Abschluss dieses Prozesses überprüft eine automatisierte Watchdog-Software die Prüfsummen und weitere Metadaten der Dateien auf Identität und eventuelle Veränderungen. Eine ständige Prüfung und Weiterentwicklung der Archivierungsstandards ist trotzdem unerlässlich und Teil des Qualitätsmanagements.

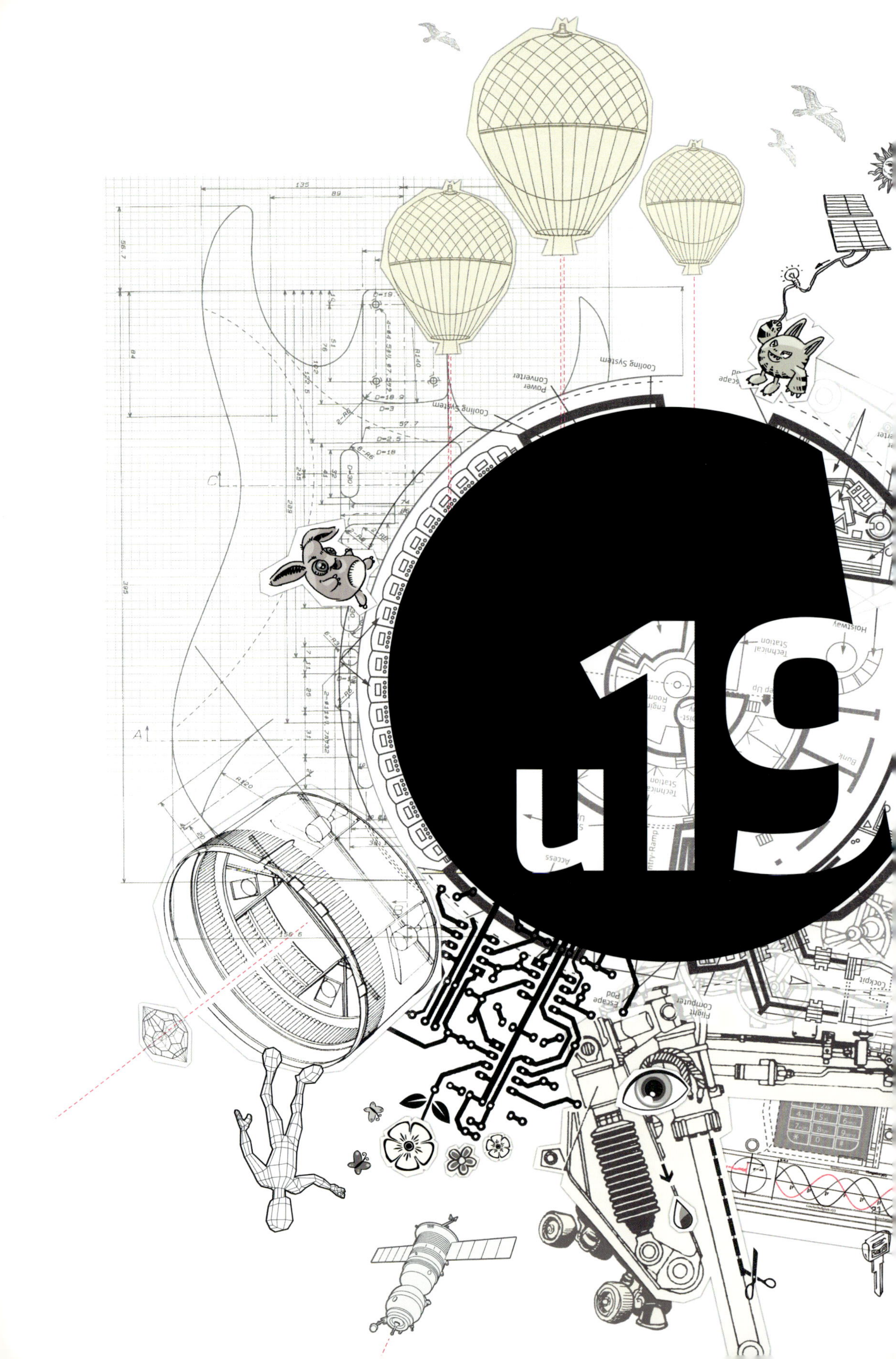

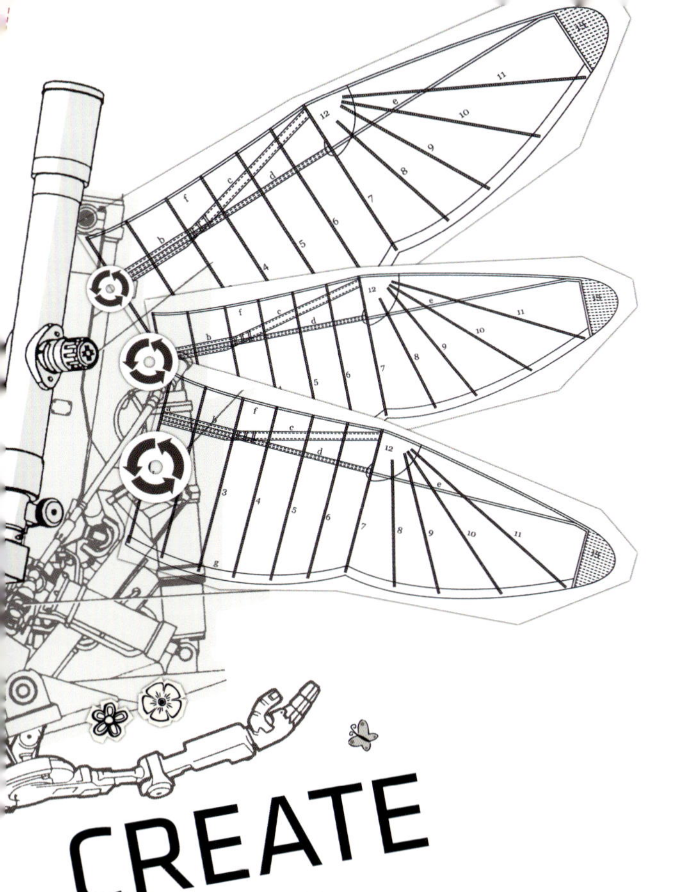

CREATE
YOUR
WORLD

ZUKUNFTSFESTIVAL DER NÄCHSTEN GENERATION

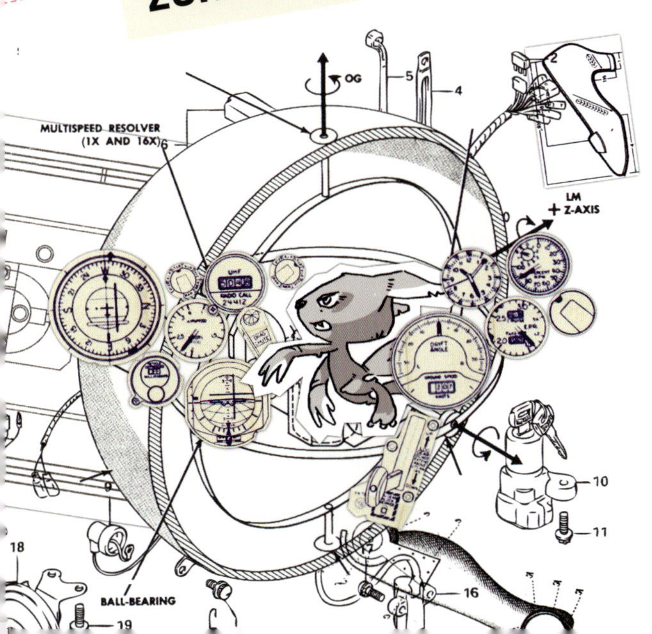

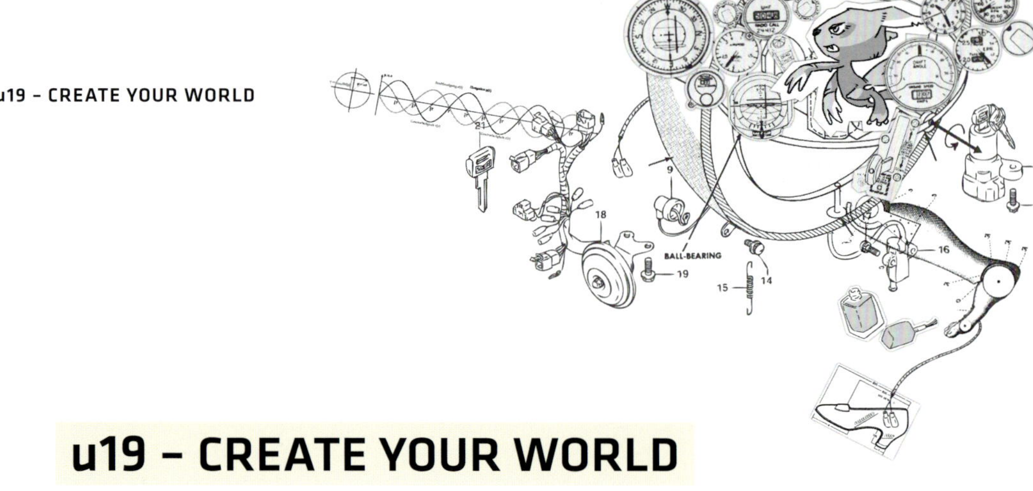

u19 - CREATE YOUR WORLD

u19 - CREATE YOUR WORLD reaches out to kids and young people who want to have a lot more say about the world in which they're going to be spending their future and seeks to encourage youngsters to develop their own ideas and visions, to present them to others and to try them out.
The formats designed to make it happen include an annual nationwide idea competition, the Future Festival of the Next Generation also held annually, a lineup of tours and workshops offered throughout the year, as well as programs custom-tailored to specific types of schools and all different grades.

u19 - CREATE YOUR WORLD is a joint experiment by youngsters and partners from art and culture, educational and scholarly institutions, government agencies and the private sector.
They're collaboratively developing and implementing all u19 - CREATE YOUR WORLD activities.

u19 - CREATE YOUR WORLD richtet sich an Kinder und Jugendliche, die bei der Gestaltung ihrer Zukunft mehr als nur ein Wörtchen mitreden wollen, und will junge Menschen dazu ermutigen, ihre eigenen Ideen und Visionen zu entwickeln, zu präsentieren und auf die Probe zu stellen.
Die Formate dafür umfassen einen jährlich österreichweit ausgeschriebenen Ideenwettbewerb, ein ebenfalls jährliches stattfindendes Zukunftsfestival der nächsten Generation, ein ganzjähriges Führungs- und Workshop-Angebot sowie eigens für unterschiedliche Schultypen und -stufen entwickelte Programme.

u19 - CREATE YOUR WORLD ist ein gemeinsames Experiment von Kindern und Jugendlichen und Partnern aus Kunst und Kultur, Bildung und Wissenschaft, Politik und Wirtschaft. Gemeinsam entwickeln und realisieren sie alle Aktivitäten von u19 - CREATE YOUR WORLD.

Patron / Ehrenschutz: Margit Fischer, Vorsitzende des Vereins Science Center Netzwerk / Chairwoman of the Science Center Network Association, Dr. Claudia Schmied, Bundesministerin für Unterricht, Kunst und Kultur / Austrian Federal Minister of Education, Art and Culture

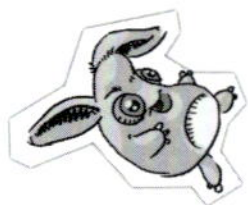

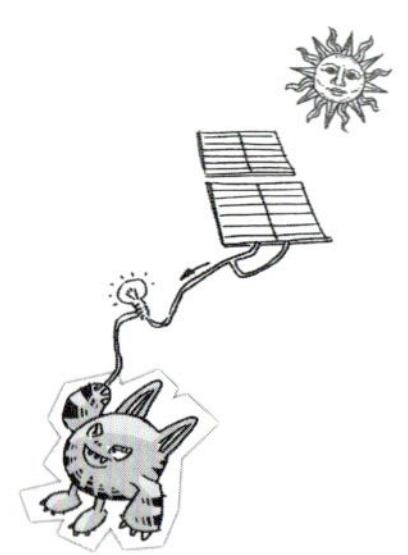

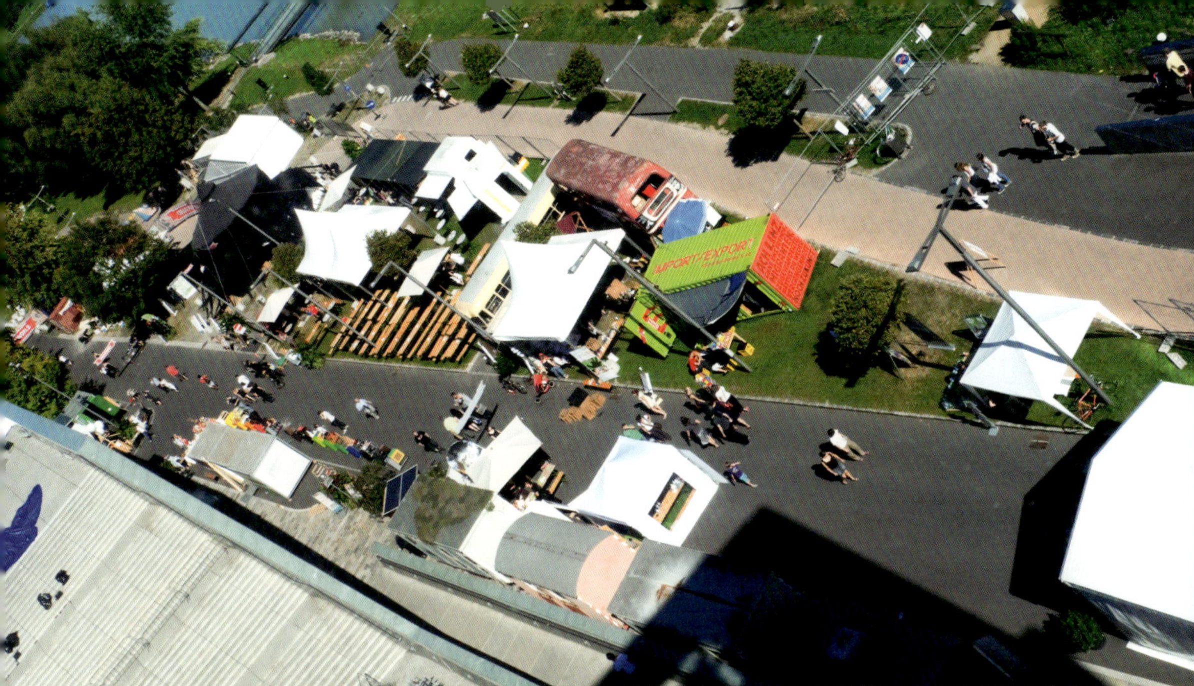

The following projects are being conducted in conjunction with the 2012
u19 – CREATE YOUR WORLD – Future Festival of the Next Generation
Beim diesjährigen u19 CREATE YOUR WORLD – Zukunftsfestival der nächsten Generation
sind folgende Projekte beteiligt:

u19 – CREATE YOUR WORLD EXHIBITIONS

Bescheidene Helden – TrägerInnen des Alternativen Nobelpreises
Katharina Mouratidi (DE)

Biologische Abbaubarkeit und Verwendung bzw. Fermentation von Biopolymeren in Biogasanlagen
Verena Haderer, Bernhard Mayr /HTL Innviertel-Nord Andorf (AT)
Anerkennungspreis Science, Jugend Innovativ 2012

Game Corner: Apart, Night Mary & Valory
Studierende der Fachhochschule Hagenberg (AT)

First Aid Live
Stephan Stadlmair, Oliver Prexl, Anant Sangar/ HTBLuVA Salzburg (AT)
Sonderpreis idea.goes.app, Jugend Innovativ 2012

Intelligente Steuerung elektrischer Geräte zur besseren Nutzung alternativer Energien
Lukas Bernhofer (AT)
Sonderpreis Klimaschutz, Jugend Innovativ 2012

media literacy award
Bundesministerium für Unterricht, Kunst und Kultur (AT)

WHATCHADO?
Ali Mahlodji WHATCHADO (AT)

[the next idea] Exhibition

qaul.net – tools for the next revolution
Christoph Wachter, Mathias Jud (CH)
http://www.qaul.net

DESIGNING ZERO – ENERGY BUILDING COMPONENTS WITH SMART THERMOBIMETAL
Doris Sung (US) / DOSU Studio Architecture and University of Southern California

Matopy
Sam Jewell (UK)
http://getaudioweb.com

u19 Exhibition

state of revolution
Agnes Aistleitner (AT) / HBLA für Künstlerische Gestaltung, Linz

BioBookCover
BG/BRG Stainach (AT)
www.biobookcover.at

Bin Baum mit 2 Stämmen
Stephan Friedl, Asya Serimoglu, Anita Simic, Daniel Wieczorek, Lorena Zorkic (Radio Poly, PTS 3, Wien / AT)
radiopoly.wordpress.com

Zukunftswürfel
Kindergarten Auwiesenstraße 60 (AT)

Balancing Robot
Christian Grill, Magdalena Kranjec, Sonja Stankovic, Maximilian Tabelander, Sasa Vasiljkovic (NMS-Telfs-Dr.-Aloys-Weissenbach / AT)

iTanky
Felix Krause (AT)
itanky.com

Weltrekord für eine bessere Welt
BG/BORG Kirchdorf

Das Superhirn
BG Wasagasse (AT)

Fragment Planet
Simon Stix (AT)
www.indiedb.com/games/fragment-planet

Impressive Title (Paradise)
Michaela Gehmayr, Laura Kaltenbrunner (AT)

RiffGrabber
Alin Kalam, Peter Paikl, Wolfgang
Schneiderbauer, Manmeet Singh, Christian Sorko
(HTL Ottakring / AT)
www.riffgrabber.at

handsome
Felix Brandstetter, Gregor Eckmayr, Valentina
Heinisch, William Mikulaschek, Anna Neubauer,
Killian Sochor (C.LOUD / AT)

ConnectIn(g)
Dino Grgic, Robin von Mendel, Franz Reinstadler,
Magnus Reinstadler (BORG Gastein / AT)

Quadrocopter
Lukas Pfeifhofer, Tanja Roschanz
(HTL Mössingerstraße Klagenfurt / AT)
quadrocopter.drseus.eu

Flat Water Bottle / Evolution of Animation
Michael Schmidl (AT)

Young Animations

PC Orchestra (C3 <19 / HU) – Levente Szabo

Monsterfauchen (mb21 / DE) – Richard Forstmann

Ich rette die Welt (u19 – CREATE YOUR WORLD) –
Christina Lampl, Julia Schmid, Katharina Ulbing,
Patricia Ulbing

Water Drop (C3 <19 / HU) – Gabor Kozma

Worst Case Scenario Desaster (u19 – CREATE YOUR
WORLD) - Johanna Führlinger

A City is Blooming Up (u19 – CREATE YOUR
WORLD) - Georg Adelmann, Markus Bratusek,
Daniel Meissl, Claudia Ofner, Dominik Pfeifer,
Anja Ponsold, Christoph Teni, Leopold Wagner

Wien wächst (u19 – CREATE YOUR WORLD) –
Simon Casetti, Valentin Gensthaler, Stefan Reuter,
Franziska Weber

Ferenderinator (mb21 / DE) – Carl-Humann-
Grundschule

Evolution of Animation (u19 – CREATE YOUR
WORLD) - Michael Schmidl

Flat Water Bottle (u19 – CREATE YOUR WORLD) -
Michael Schmidl

Connect(I)ng (u19 – CREATE YOUR WORLD) - Dino
Grgic, Robin von Mendel, Franz Reinstadler,
Magnus Reinstadler

3-7-4 (mb21 / DE) – Maximilian Niclas Heinemann,
Hauke Thiessen, Lars Thiessen

handsome (u19 – CREATE YOUR WORLD) – Felix
Brandstetter, Gregor Eckmayr, Valentina Heinisch,
William Mikulaschek, Anna Neubauer, Killian
Sochor

Milchmädchen (mb21 / DE) – Kathrin Kuhnert

Il Mago (bugnplay / CH) – Lauro Silini
robodrama (u19 – CREATE YOUR WORLD) –
Christian Henninger

Der kleine Mann auf dem Mond
(bugnplay / CH) - David Hornik, Julian Scheiben

Creation Story (C3 <19 / HU) – Animcsop Team

Mirror Tale (C3 <19 / HU) – Vanessa Tunde Cseh

Impressive Title (Paradise) (u19 – CREATE YOUR
WORLD) - Michaela Gehmayr, Laura Kaltenbrunner

Der schlaue Fuchs (bugnplay / CH) – Ricardo
Böhringer, Fabiola Günther, Mario Günther

Swans in the Water (C3 <19 / HU) – Judit Banhelyi

Lost in the Jungle (bugnplay / CH) – Florian Pittet

ABC-Werkstatt
Ars Electronica

Akkurace
Lehrlingswerkstatt BRP-Powertrain / AT)

BioBookCover
Gerald Baumann, Aaron Ebner, Roland Lemmerer
(BRG Stainach / AT)

Blog Lab
Erli Grünzweil

Budapest Farmers Hack
Interface Cultures (AT), OS Kantine (HU), Peter
Eszes (HU)

Campus Labor: Varia Zoosystematica Profundorum
Alberto de Campo (AT/DE) und 16 TeilnehmerInnen
der Klasse Generative Kunst/Computational Art der
Universität der Künste Berlin (DE)

C.loud Jugendredaktion
C.loud TV, C.loud FM (AT)

Create Your Adventure Game
Almuth Frommhold, Jana Leinweber, Kirsten
Mascher, Daniel Seitz (Medienkulturzentrum
Dresden / DE)

Create Your Region Camp – Ideenschleuder
Ars Electronica, Leaderregionen
Oberösterreich (AT)

create your scene – Mach (d)eine Szene!
Abteilungen Bildnerische Erziehung und
Mediengestaltung der Kunstuniversität Linz (AT)

**Die Zukunft liegt in unseren Händen –
Erneuerbare Energien**
Youth Future Project (DE)

Erste Hilfe – Do You Know How?
Rotes Kreuz (AT)

Fahrradfit-Werkstatt
B7 Fahrradzentrum (AT)

**Get.ideas: Kreativitätstechniken für die eigene
Projektidee**
Jugend-Umwelt-Plattform JUMP (AT),
Klimabündnis OÖ (AT)

Happylab – Vienna Fab Lab goes Linz
INNOC – Österreichische Gesellschaft für
innovative Computerwissenschaften (AT)

OTELO Menschen-Kraft-Werk
OTELO Offenes Technologielabor (AT)

papplab
Tom Latzel (AT), Inga Hehn (AT), Christoph Stadler
(AT), Motz Flotzinger (AT), Stefan Füreder (AT),
Wodo Gratt (AT)

Planet Under Pressure
ScienceCenter-Netzwerk (AT)

QiwiDrone – Quadrocopter
Tanja Roschanz (AT), Lukas Pfeifhofer (AT)

Sound Lab
Ars Electronica Center

SWITCH
Ars Electronica Futurelab, Elekit Japan Co., LTD (JP)

u19 mobil
Ars Electronica

Virtual Radio
FAB Jugend Virtual Office (AT)

VolxTV: Ein Lichtkunst-DIY-Workshop
Jördis Drawe, Uwe Schüler (Kulturgüter-
Schuppen / DE)

Wearable Music
Andrea Rosales (CO), Juan Tirado, Gian María
Troiano and Nina Valkanova (Interactive Technolo-
gies Group am Information and Communication
Technologies Department der Universitat Pompeu
Fabra / ES)

Die fahrende Zuckerwattemaschine
BRG Schloss Traunsee, Gmunden (AT)

Nähküche
Felicitas Egger (AT)

schnittBOGEN
Michaela Hudecová Königshofer, schnittBogen –
Offene Werkstatt für Textil | Mode | Design (AT)

u19 – CREATE YOUR WORLD – EVENTS

Warm-Up
Tom Pohl (AT)

Show Down
Tom Pohl (AT)

Klangwolke ABC Parade
Tom Pohl (AT)

Bilden Medien!?
Pädagogische Hochschule OÖ (AT)

Create Your Region – Inselhüpfen
Ars Electronica, Leaderregionen
Oberösterreich (AT)

dorf tv. open house
Dorf TV (AT)

missing character
Clara Hirschmanner (AT)

MOHUBS
OTELO Offenes Technologielabor (AT)

Kukusch_Kultursuppe
Verein Kukusch_Kunst und Kultur an Schulen /AT)
in Zusammenarbeit mit Alenka Maly (AT)

Limelight
Jeremiah Diephuis (US), Gerald Hauzenberger,
Wolfgang Hochleitner, Rene Ksuz, Michael Lankes,
Thomas Peintner, Madgalena Soukup
(Fachhochschule Hagenberg / AT)

KiJA-Musical Meine Rechte – Deine Rechte
Kinder- und Jugendanwaltschaft OÖ (AT),
Gruppe Traumfänger – Theater mit Seele (AT)

Prix Forum u19
Prix Ars Electronica

NoPET
Jasmin Kaufmann, Robin Kaufmann, Timon
Kaufmann (CH)

Informatika Labor
Dávid Cserich, Dániel Kiss (HU)

Stress Ops
Tom Creutz, Richard Forstmann, Lynn Hoff,
Moritz Röber (DE)

u19 Ceremony
Prix Ars Electronica

Wendepunkt. Ändere deine Richtung!
Podiumsgespräch – ExpertInnenfrühstück –
Kunstwerkstatt
Rotes Kreuz (AT)

Impressions u19 – CREATE YOUR WORLD – Future Festival of the Next Generation 2011

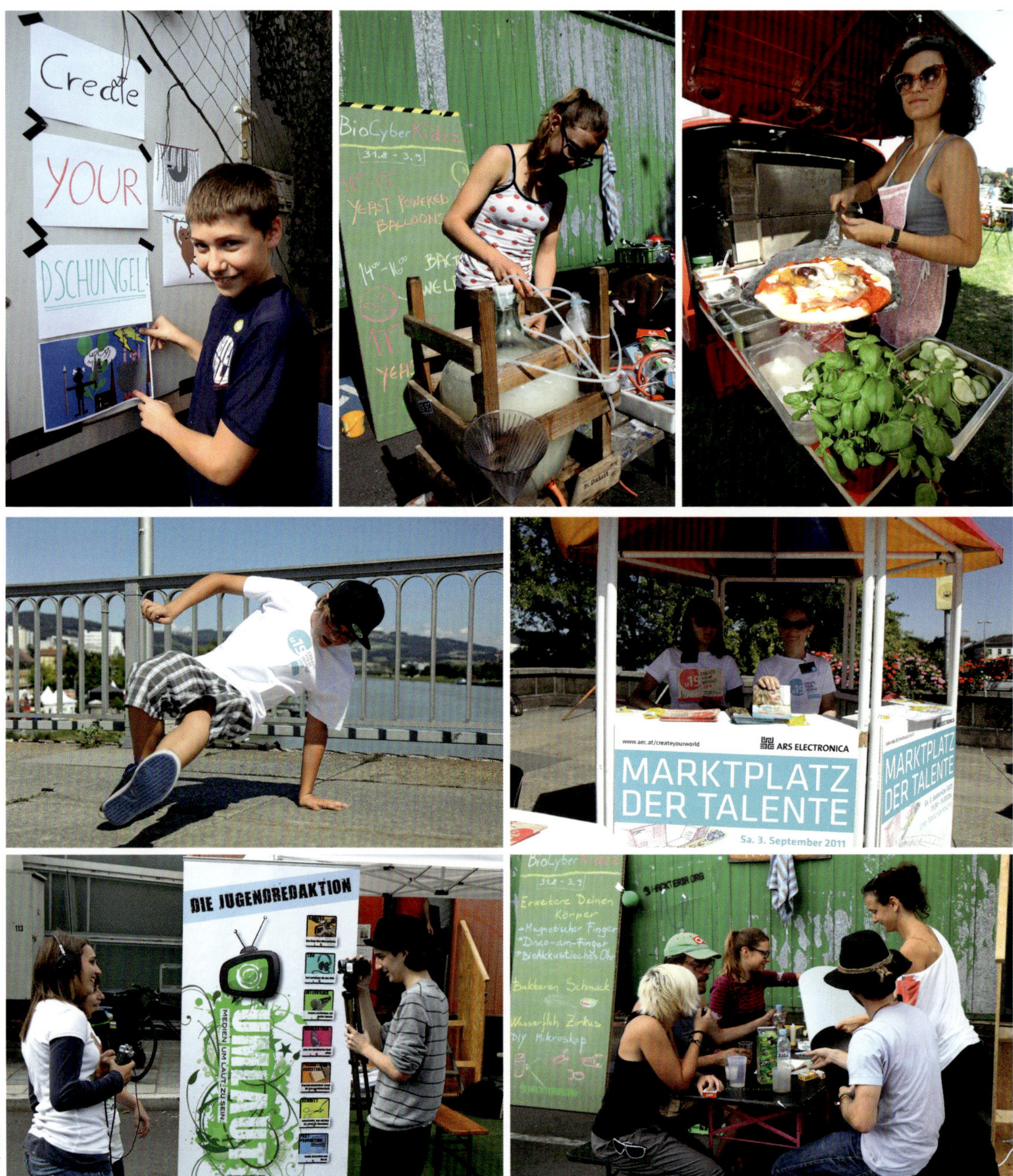

AEC, rubra

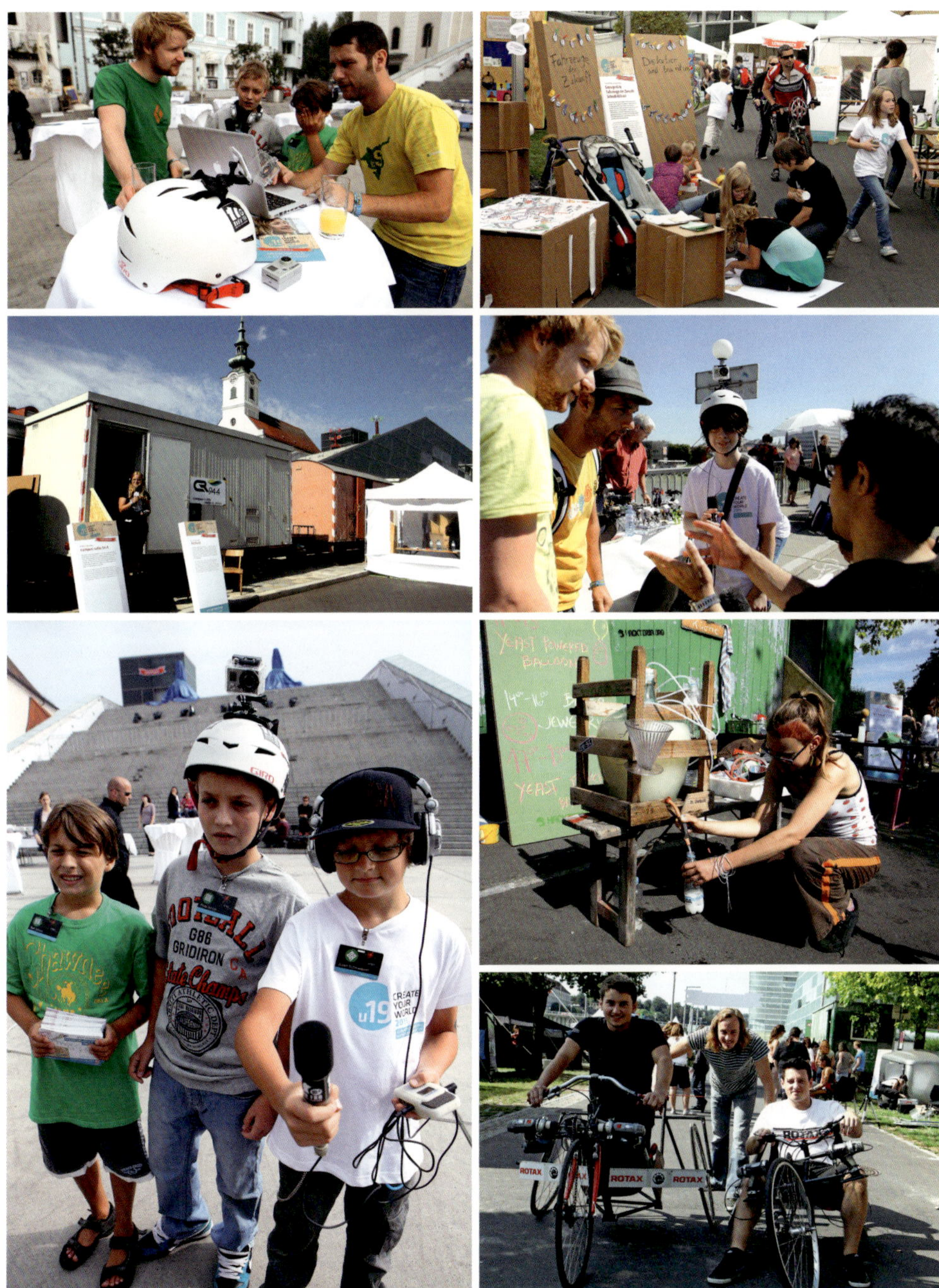

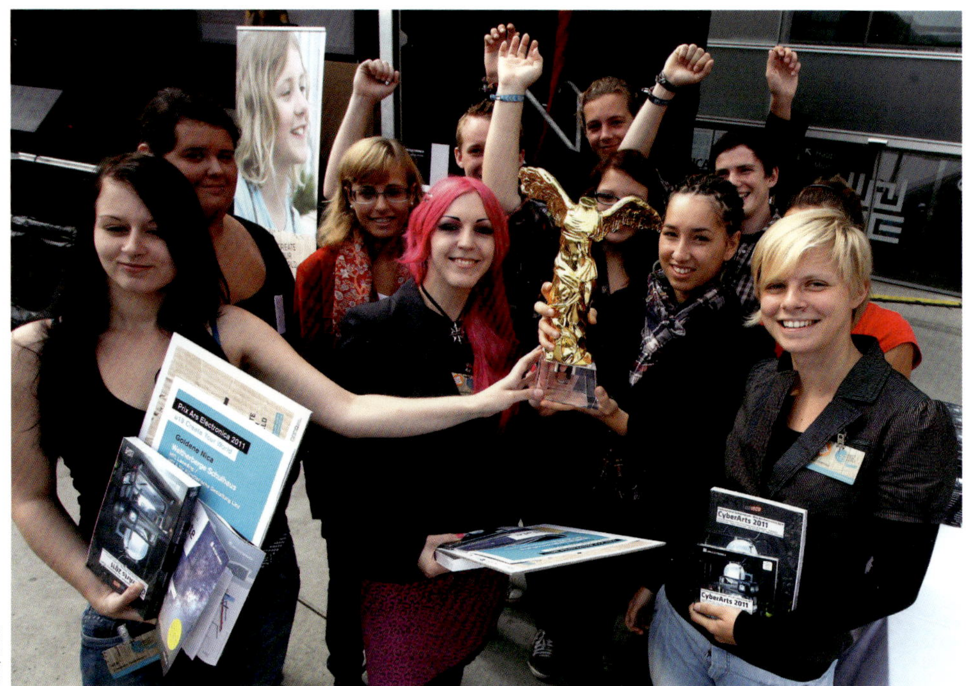

Rosi Grillmair

The Brain Comes up with Ideas
... without ever having searched for them before

"We don't know how creative we really are. We're unaware of just how much we can accomplish." These words were uttered by Ines in the course of an otherwise typical day at Linz's High School for Artistic Design. What they accomplished was to make it clear to herself and lots of her classmates that their thoughts and deeds didn't just vanish without a trace amidst the deluge of worldwide current events. And ultimately it garnered first place in the 2011 Prix Ars Electronica's u19 category. Which is precisely the point of u19 – CREATE YOUR WORLD, Ars Electronica's future festival of the next generation.

Everybody who has an idea and the desire to implement it gets the chance to do just that and to present their concept to others. u19 – CREATE YOUR WORLD encourages youngsters to take their own ideas seriously and to imagine how they might be able to change this world. It teaches you to think big. And there are lots of kids who've already done just that. The festival consists of projects that young people make available to it. The occasion lends itself to scrutinizing what's on display and maybe figuring out how to take it to the next level.

If you just stroll around the exhibition areas, labs and workshops surrounding the Ars Electronica Center and, for instance, watch somebody present a ball that isn't round but you can still use to play soccer, or check out 10-year-old Tobi as he puts his talent on display and answers all imaginable queries, then you realize where this festival is coming from. As children, we can imagine everything, call anything into question, and invent all sorts of new stuff. This is the most powerful advantage that young thinkers have! Everyone thinks freely about the world before they explain you the rules according to which it seems to function. A key skill you learn as you grow

400

up is differentiating between the possible and the impossible. But when you attend this festival, you quickly realize that the best way to bring about something new is simply to forget about this differentiation.

u19 – CREATE YOUR WORLD also shows those who have already been confronted by the fact that you can't divide by 0 and that pigs don't fly at night when nobody's looking (no matter how much they'd just love to do so) that a good reason to at least familiarize yourself with the so-called realm of possibilities is to be in a better position to expand it. In order to arrive at good solutions, it's often necessary to have several hands and heads—those who can bring their own individual strengths and new points of view to bear.

For *Weltherberge. Schulhaus,* our 2011 prizewinning project, students at Linz's High School for Artistic Design had the idea of taking a new approach to the internet, which most of us experience as a social platform in a virtual space. This time, we would design it as a real space in which the furniture and fixtures could be stuffed with information, and the people in this space could then use them to access the status reports previous visitors left behind. In the broad spectrum of fields our students were trained in—ranging from textiles to video art—no feasible solution was to be found as to how to enable a bed to store and play back information, to say nothing of recognizing that there was somebody in the room to begin with. So we contacted students at the Leonding Upper Secondary Technical & Vocational College and got them on board. They possessed the technical know-how and probably had nothing cooler to do than to equip a table and a cushion with recorders and sensors. Jointly, abstract ideas became a reality, and as the winner of the u19 – CREATE YOUR WORLD competition, the project could be made public, exhibited and sent on tour.

If you're interested in seeing ideas that inspire you to get busy on a spinoff in a slightly—or totally—different direction, then start rethinking your world right now! This is what brings about change. And once in a while, a revolution.

The winner in the u19 – CREATE YOUR WOLRD category also receives a Golden Nica, the grand prize awarded by the Prix Ars Electronica competition. What might be called the big brother of the festival within a festival for young people is a great opportunity to nurture fresh ideas. It not only shows what media artists have already re-conceptualized and created; it also actively brings forth more!

Technical college undergrads confronted with art and up-and-coming artistic designers with a newfound delight in sensors are definitely not the only ones to recognize that taking advantage of what Ars Electronica has to offer can sometimes bring about quite peculiar reactions inside your head. The brain comes up with ideas without ever having searched for them before. You suddenly find yourself implementing a project you didn't even know you'd begun. Workshops, exhibitions and project groups are the means of intentionally provoking this sort of behavior.

And since last year, those who aren't in a position to quickly pop over to the Ars Electronica Center are no longer excluded. Now, u19 – CREATE YOUR REGION comes almost to your front door. This division of u19 – CREATE YOUR WORLD has established a presence designed to make exciting things happen in other parts of Upper Austria: Vöckla-Ager, Traunviertler Alpenvorland, Nationalpark Kalkalpen, Mühlviertler Kernland and Linz-Land.

According to my calendar, u19 – CREATE YOUR WORLD starts on August 30, 2012. But anytime is a good time to have impossible ideas and to bring them to fruition. If it's inspiration, free-thinkers and visions with great future promise you seek, then you'll fit right in to this year's container city surrounding the Ars Electronica Center. A visit is a great start to making utopian ideas more realistic and more feasible.

Rosi Grillmair

Das Hirn findet Ideen
... ohne sie vorher gesucht zu haben

„Wir wissen nicht, wie kreativ wir sind. Wir sind uns nicht bewusst, wie viel wir bewirken können." Diese Aussage stammt von Ines aus der HBLA für künstlerische Gestaltung Linz und ist im Schulalltag gefallen. Was ihr und vielen anderen aus ihrem Jahrgang dann klarmachte, dass ihre Gedanken und ihr Tun nicht im Weltgeschehen untergehen, und brachte den ersten Platz in der u19-Kategorie des Prix Ars Electronica 2011. Und genau das ist das Ziel von u19 – CREATE YOUR WORLD, dem Zukunftsfestival der nächsten Generation.

Alle, die Ideen haben und sie verwirklichen wollen, bekommen die Gelegenheit, das zu tun und den anderen ihr Konzept zu zeigen. u19 – CREATE YOUR WORLD ermutigt Kinder und Jugendliche dazu, die eigenen Ideen ernst zu nehmen und sich vorzustellen, wie diese die Welt verändern könnten. Man lernt dadurch, im Großen zu denken. Es gibt viele, die das schon getan haben. Das Festival besteht aus den Projekten, die junge Menschen dafür zur Verfügung stellen. Es bietet sich an, dass man diese genauer betrachtet und in Gedanken weiterspinnt.

Wenn man so durch die Ausstellungsflächen, Labore und Werkstätten rund um das Ars Electronica Center spaziert und sieht, wie jemand einen Ball vorstellt, der nicht rund ist, mit dem man aber trotzdem Fußball spielen kann, oder ein zehnjähriger Tobi sein Talent beweist und alle nur erdenklichen Fragen beantworten kann, bemerkt man, welchen Ursprung dieses Festival hat: Als Kinder können wir uns alles vorstellen, alles, was da ist, in Frage stellen, und Neues entstehen lassen. Das ist der gewaltigste Vorteil, den junge Denkerinnen und Denker haben!

Jede und jeder denkt frei über die Welt nach, bevor einem die Regeln erklärt werden, nach denen sie zu funktionieren scheint. Eine wichtige Unterscheidung, die man beim Erwachsenwerden lernt, ist die zwischen möglich und unmöglich. Beim Festival bemerkt man bald, dass etwas Neues am besten entstehen kann, wenn dieser Unterschied nicht berücksichtigt wird.

u19 – CREATE YOUR WORLD zeigt auch denen, die schon damit konfrontiert wurden, dass man nicht durch Null dividieren kann oder dass Schweine nicht fliegen können (auch wenn sie es sich noch so sehr wünschen), dass man den sogenannten Rahmen des Möglichen zumindest deshalb kennen sollte, um ihn auszuweiten. Um zu guten Lösungen zu gelangen, sind auch oft mehrere Hände und Köpfe nötig, die ihre individuellen Stärken einbringen und Blickwinkel verändern können.

Für das Gewinnerprojekt des Jahres 2011 – *Weltherberge. Schulhaus* – hatten die SchülerInnen der HBLA für künstlerische Gestaltung Linz die Idee, das Internet, das ja vor allem als soziale Plattform im virtuellen Raum erlebt wird, einmal als realen Raum zu gestalten, dessen Möbel mit Informationen gefüttert werden konnten. Den im Raum Anwesenden sollte dann die Einrichtung die von anderen hinterlassenen Statusmeldungen entgegensprudeln. In den großen Weiten von Textil bis Videokunst, mit denen die Schülerinnen vertraut waren, fand sich leider keine real umsetzbare Lösung dafür, ein Bett dazu zu bringen, Aufnahmen zu speichern und wiederzugeben, geschweige denn, von alleine zu wissen, ob sich überhaupt jemand im Raum befand.

So holten sie sich Schüler der HTL Leonding mit ins Boot. Die hatten das technische Know-how und wahrscheinlich auch noch nie etwas Lässigeres zu tun, als einen Tisch und einen Polster mit Recordern und Sensoren auszustatten. Gemeinsam setzten sie also die abstrakten Ideen in die Realität um, und als Gewinner beim Wettbewerb u19 – CREATE YOUR WORLD konnte das Projekt veröffentlicht, ausgestellt und auf Reisen geschickt werden.

Wenn du Ideen sehen willst, an die du anknüpfen oder von denen du dich komplett unterscheiden willst, dann beginn, damit die Welt umzudenken! Dadurch entsteht Veränderung, immer wieder eine Revolution.

Der Prix Ars Electronica selbst und dessen erste Preise, die Goldene Nica, die auch an den Gewinner oder die Gewinnerin von u19 – CREATE YOUR WOLRD verliehen wird, bietet als großer Bruder des Zukunftsfestivals der nächsten Generation auch die beste Gelegenheit, junge Ideen wachsen zu lassen. Er zeigt nicht nur, was Medienkünstler und -künstlerinnen schon neu gedacht und erschaffen haben, sondern ruft auch nach mehr!

Mit Sicherheit haben nicht nur die kunstkonfrontierten HTLer und die sensorbegeisterten HBLA-Schülerinnen erkannt, dass es schon manchmal zu eigenartigen Reaktionen im Kopf kommt, wenn man das Angebot der Ars Electronica nutzt: Das Hirn findet Ideen, ohne sie vorher gesucht zu haben. Plötzlich befindet man sich in der Verwirklichung eines Projekts, von dem man noch nicht einmal wusste, dass es begonnen hat. Durch Workshops, Ausstellungen und Projektgruppen wird dieses Verhalten bewusst provoziert.

Seit letztem Jahr sind auch jene, die nicht schnell mal zum Ars Electronica Center spazieren können, von diesem Zustand nicht mehr ausgeschlossen. u19 – CREATE YOUR REGION verleitet schon fast vor der Haustür dazu, sich mit der Zukunft der näheren Umgebung auseinanderzusetzen. Gerade wächst dieser Bereich von u19 – CREATE YOUR WORLD nach Vöckla-Ager, ins Traunviertler Alpenvorland, in den Nationalpark Kalkalpen, ins Mühlviertler Kernland, nach Linz-Land und in die Traunsteinregion.

u19 – CREATE YOUR WORLD startet laut Kalender am 30. August 2012. Unmögliche Ideen haben und diese realisieren geht aber jederzeit. Wer Inspiration, frei denkende Menschen und Zukunftsvisionen sucht, kommt am besten zur heurigen Containerstadt rund um das Ars Electronica Center. Utopische Ideen erscheinen nach einem Besuch viel realistischer und vor allem auch umsetzbar.

Rosi Grillmair (AT) was born in 1991. She's studying Time-based & Interactive Media at Linz Art University. In 2011, the year she graduated from Linz's High School for Artistic Design, she and a number of fellow students produced *Weltherberge: Schulhaus,* the project that was honored with the Golden Nica grand prize in the Prix Ars Electronica's category for young people, u19 – CREATE YOUR WORLD, and was exhibited at the festival of the same name.

Rosi Grillmair (AT), geb. 1991, studiert „Zeitbasierte und Interaktive Medien" an der Kunstuniversität Linz. 2011, in ihrem Maturajahr an der HBLA für Künstlerische Gestaltung Linz, gewann sie mit MitschülerInnen und dem Projekt *Weltherberge: Schulhaus* die Goldene Nica bei u19 – CREATE YOUR WORLD, der Kategorie für unter 19-Jährige des Prix Ars Electronica. Im gleichnamigen Festival wurde das Projekt ausgestellt.

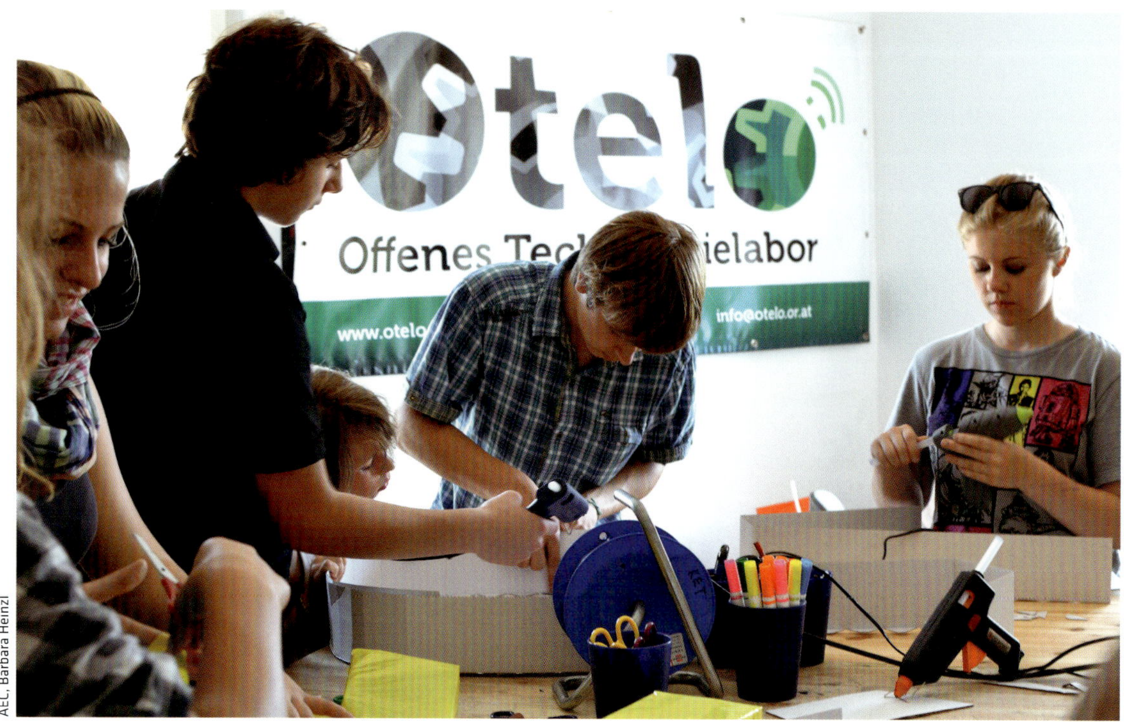

Martin Hollinez / OTELO

Create Your Region
Participation Becomes Active Commitment

Where is the future emerging? Kids and young people as the ones configuring our future form the basis for the development of our society. Grown-ups are well-advised to offer young-sters a chance not only to consider new ideas but also to get experience implementing what they come up with.

Especially in an increasingly regimented society, it's difficult to implement a nurturing matrix for ideas that foster the ongoing development of our habitat. Rural regions in particular, areas pervaded by traditional ways and rigid structures offering scant latitude, often make it impossible for young people to bring their ideas to fruition.

Decisions about the future are made in the present; nevertheless, it is far too seldom that kids and young people—the ones who will have to live with the results—are involved on an equal foot-ing with adults in the process of designing the future of their region.

But freedom to think and act upon those thoughts, independence from institutionalized sys-tems and systematically utilitarian considerations are absolutely indispensible for encountering ideas solely for the sake of enjoying the use of one's mental faculties. This, in turn, can consti-tute the key to constructive-innovative changes, and act as a catalyst of more significant changes to come. This is how a new Big Picture of the future can materialize!

Create Your Region is now making things happen in a very real way at precisely that point that has often been the end of the line for young people: where it comes to actually effectuating their ideas.

404

This project is making a significant impact by affording youngsters age 11-19 a real chance to get actively involved, to show what they're capable of, and to really make a difference in the development of their region and the circumstances of their day-to-day life.

Create Your Region is a cooperative undertaking under the aegis of the EU's LEADER Program, one of the aims of which is to improve the quality of life in rural areas and encourage diversification of the rural economy.

Six Upper Austrian regions—Traunsteinregion, Region Vöckla-Ager, Nationalpark Region oberösterreichische Kalkalpen, Traunviertler Alpenvorland, Region Linz-Land and Mühlviertler Kernland—as well as Ars Electronica and the OTELO open technology labs are participating in the *Create Your Region* initiative.

The project encompasses 113 communities in the Province of Upper Austria. The insights and experience gleaned from CREATE YOUR WORLD, the very successful festival Ars Electronica and OTELO launched in 2011, have flowed into the configuration of this project and thus provided yet more impressive proof of the suitability of artistically motivated modes and fields of action serving as models for much larger-scale social initiatives and developments.

Thus, *Create Your Region* isn't just an invitation to work out wondrous concepts; it offers user-friendly framework conditions to quickly make them happen. Within this project of remarkable scope—it's a joint initiative of Ars Electronica, the OTELO open technology labs, and six regions and 113 communities of the Province of Upper Austria—youngsters age 11-19 are getting a real chance to get actively involved, to show what they're capable of, and to really make a difference in the development of their region and the circumstances of their day-to-day life.

In each respective region, OTELOs or equivalent facilities are being made available as supporting home bases. Here's where you can consider the ideas of the festival, think them through and adapt them to regional facts & circumstances. Here's where young people serve as prime facilitators of how the world of the future ought to be!

This cooperative effort with the *u19 – Create Your World* festival is how *Create Your Region* is initiating a vibrant process of interaction between the region and the city as well as the region and the world. *u19 – Create Your World* is a hub, a launching pad, a network node and a meet & greet—for the creation of new images from the perspective of members of the young generation, who'll take them back with them to their respective regions to change life there.

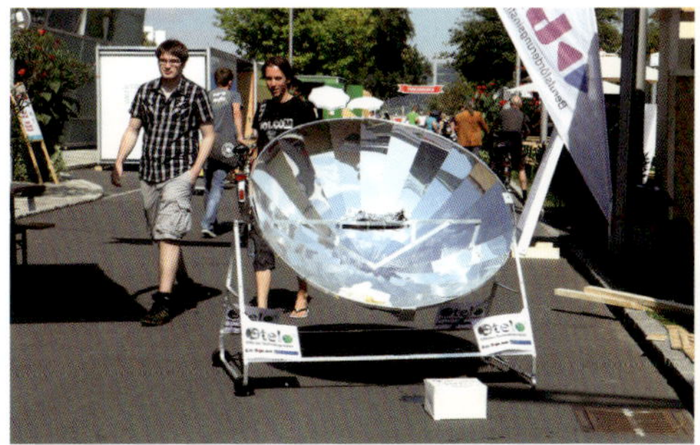

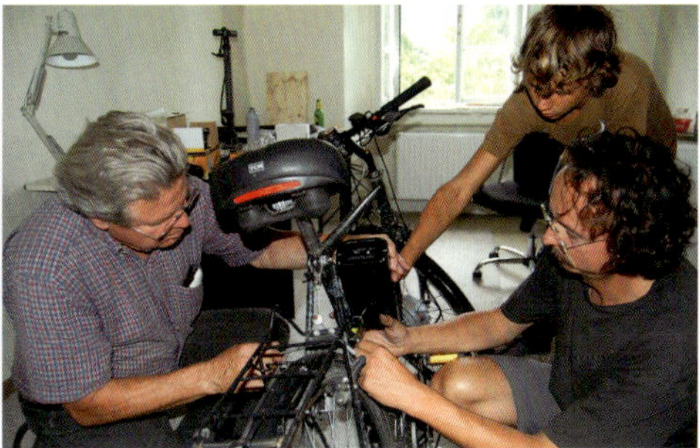

Martin Hollinez / OTELO

Create Your Region
Beteiligung wird zu Gestaltung

Wo entsteht Zukunft? Kinder und Jugendliche als Gestalter unserer Zukunft sind die Basis für die Entwicklung der Gesellschaft. Die Erwachsenenwelt tut gut daran, den Jugendlichen eine Chance zu bieten, nicht nur über neue Ideen nachzudenken, sondern sich auch in der Umsetzung zu erproben.

Gerade in einer zunehmend reglementierten Gesellschaft ist es schwierig, einen Nährboden für Ideen zu finden, die eine Weiterentwicklung des Lebensraums ermöglichen. Besonders regionale Lebensräume, die geprägt sind von Traditionen und festen Strukturen mit wenig Spielraum, machen es jungen Menschen oft unmöglich, ihre Ideen zu realisieren.

Über die Zukunft entschieden wird jedoch in der Gegenwart. Allerdings werden Kinder und Jugendliche – obwohl vor allem sie es sind, die mit dem Ergebnis leben müssen – viel zu selten auf Augenhöhe mit den Erwachsenen in die Zukunftsgestaltung ihrer Region eingebunden.

Dabei ermöglicht nur ein Freiraum im Denken und Handeln, der unabhängig von institutionalisierten Systemen oder Verwertungsgedanken ist, eine kreative und lustbetonte Auseinandersetzung. Diese wiederum kann den Schlüssel für konstruktiv-innovative Veränderungen darstellen und ein Andocken an große Veränderungen ermöglichen. Hier können neue Bilder von Zukunft entstehen!

Create Your Region setzt konkret dort an, wo für die Jugendlichen oft Endstation ist – bei der Umsetzung ihrer ureigenen Ideen: *Create Your Region* lädt daher nicht nur zum Ideenspinnen ein, sondern ermöglicht durch unkomplizierte Rahmenbedingungen deren rasche Realisierung. Die Tragweite ist bemerkenswert, bekommen doch Kinder und Jugendliche von 11 bis 19 Jahren eine reelle Chance, sich, entsprechend ihren Möglichkeiten aktiv an der Entwicklung ihrer unmittelbaren Lebenswelt, ihrer Region zu beteiligen.

Create Your Region ist ein Kooperationsprojekt im Rahmen des sogenannten LEADER-Programms, einem Förderprogramm der Europäischen Union, mit dem Ziel, die ländlichen Regionen Europas auf dem Weg zu einer eigenständigen Entwicklung zu unterstützen.

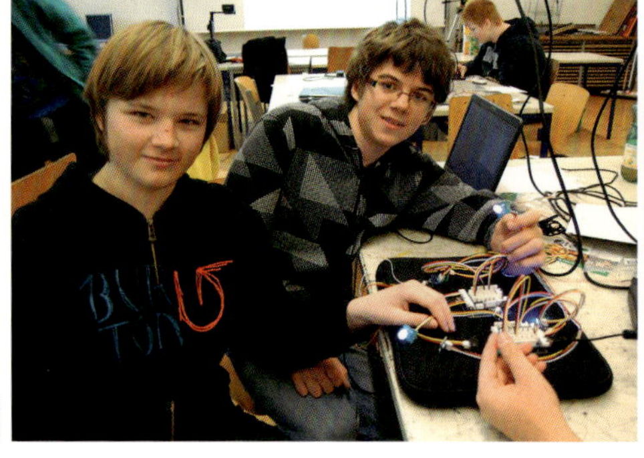
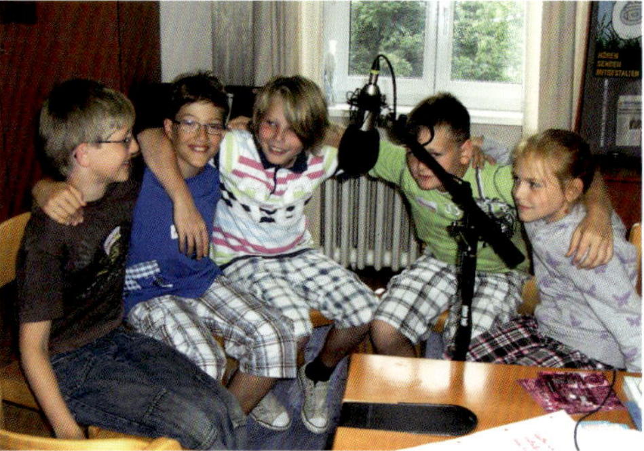

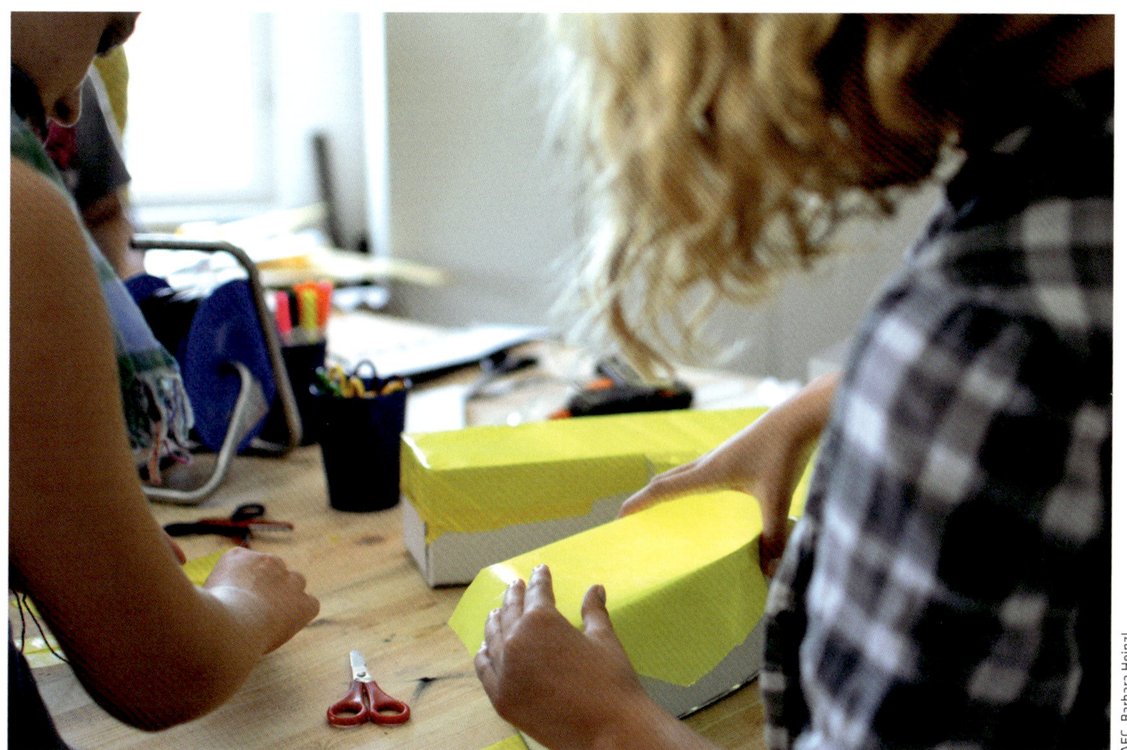

Am *Create Your Region*-Projekt sind die oberösterreichischen Regionen Traunsteinregion, Region Vöckla-Ager, Nationalpark Region oberösterreichische Kalkalpen, Traunviertler Alpenvorland, Region Linz-Land, Mühlviertler Kernland sowie Ars Electronica und die Offenen Technologielabore OTELO initiativ beteiligt. Das Projekt erstreckt sich auf 113 Gemeinden aus Oberösterreich und ist in seiner konkreten Ausformung stark aus den erfolgreichen Erfahrungen des 2011 von OTELO und Ars Electronica ins Leben gerufenen Festival CREATE YOUR WORLD hervorgegangen. Die Tauglichkeit künstlerisch motivierter Handlungsweisen und Aktionsfelder als Modell für darüber hinausreichende gesellschaftliche Initiativen und Entwicklungen ist damit einmal mehr eindrucksvoll unter Beweis gestellt.

Als unterstützende Homebase stehen in den jeweiligen Regionen OTELOs – Offene Technologielabore – oder ähnliche offene Räume zur Verfügung. Hier können die Ideen des Festivals landen, weitergedacht werden und sich mit den regionalen Gegebenheiten verbinden. Die Jugend als zentrale Vermittler der Weltbilder für die Zukunft!

Create Your Region startet durch diese Kooperation mit dem Festival u19 – CREATE YOUR WORLD einen pulsierenden Kreislauf zwischen Region und Stadt – zwischen Region und Welt. u19 – CREATE YOUR WORLD ist Drehscheibe, Sprungbrett, Netzwerkknoten und Treffpunkt – für die Erschaffung neuer Bilder aus dem Blickwinkel der jungen Generation, die wiederum in die Region mitgenommen werden und das Leben dort verändern.

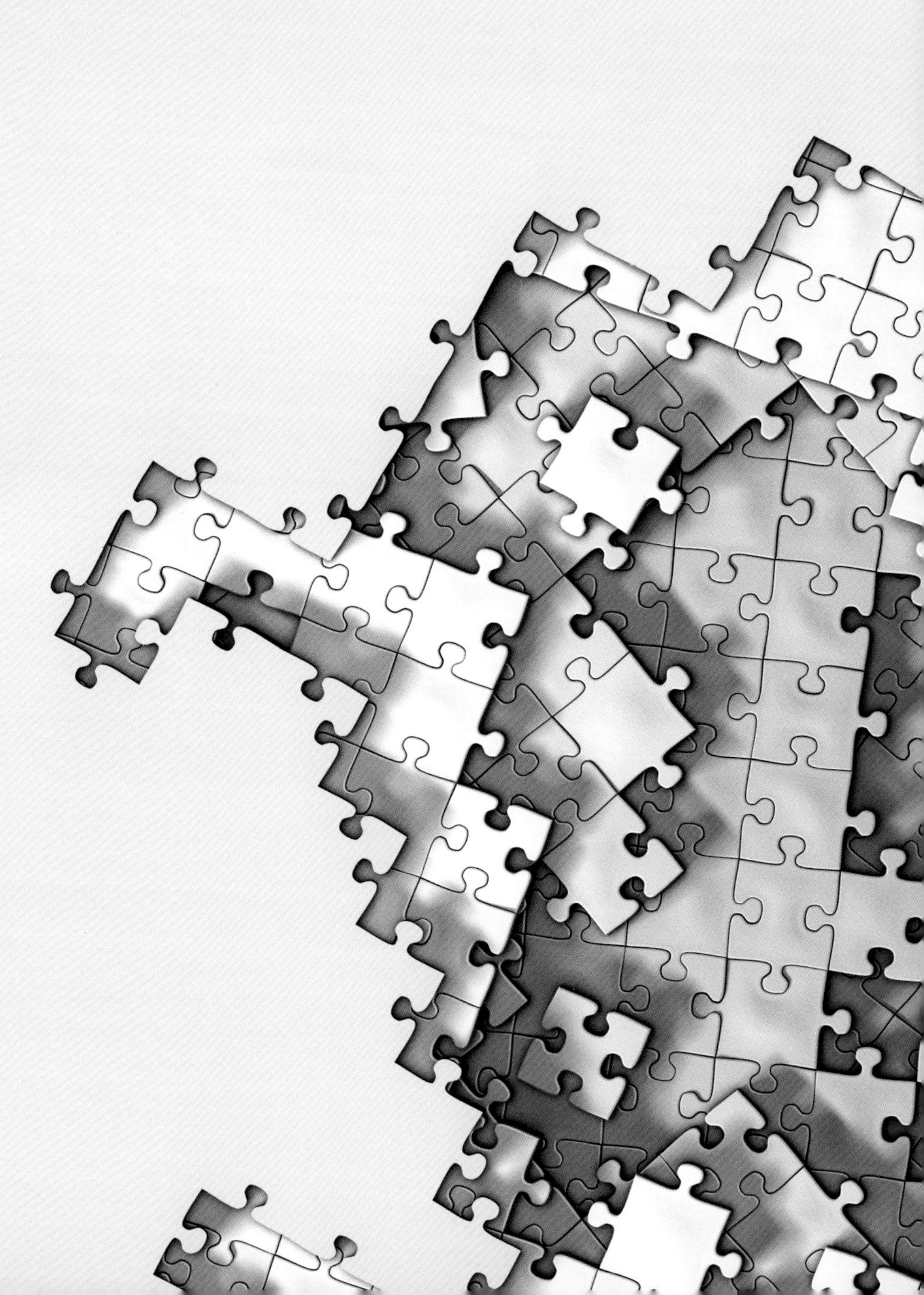

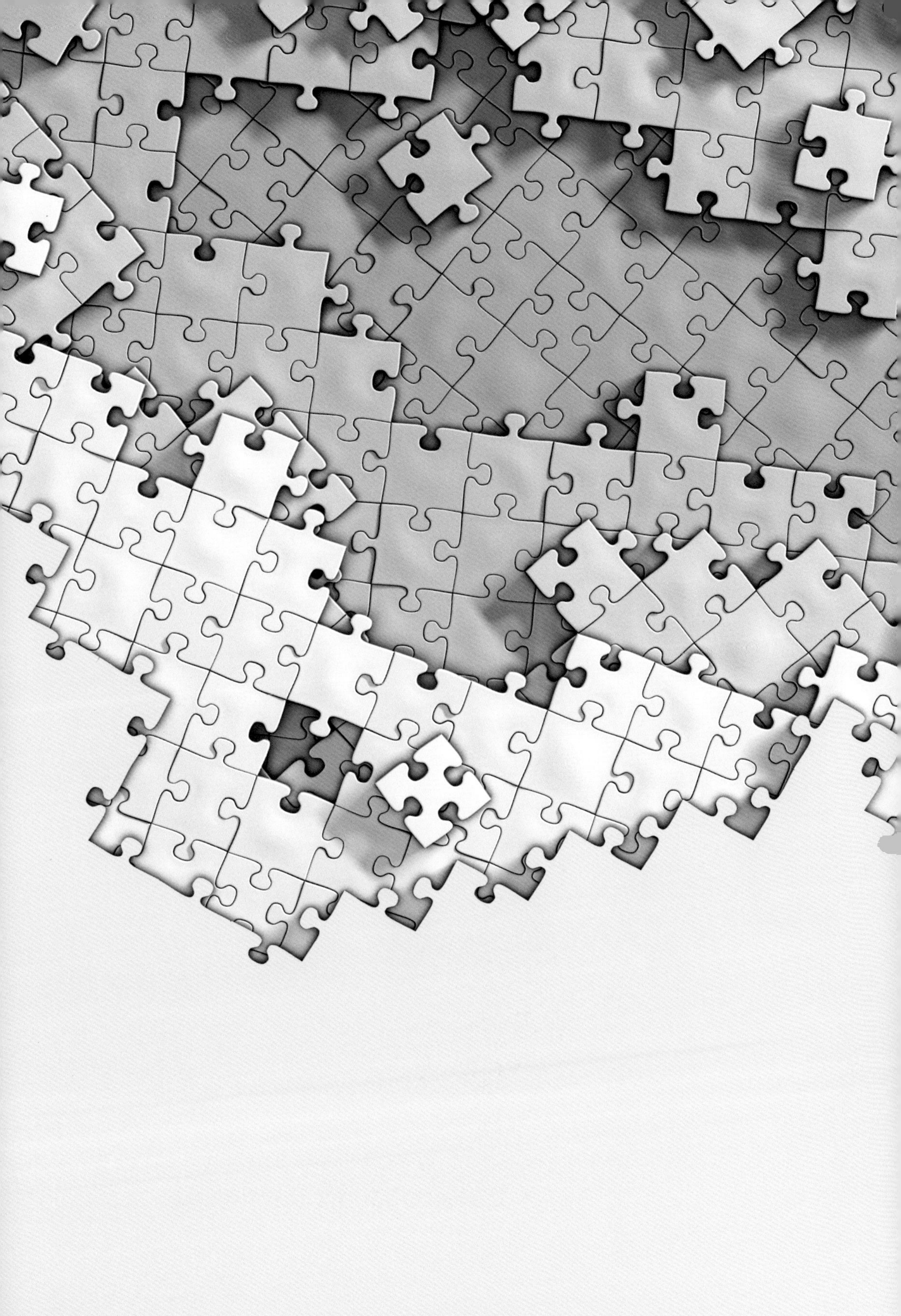

Prix Ars Electronica 2012
International Competition for CyberArts

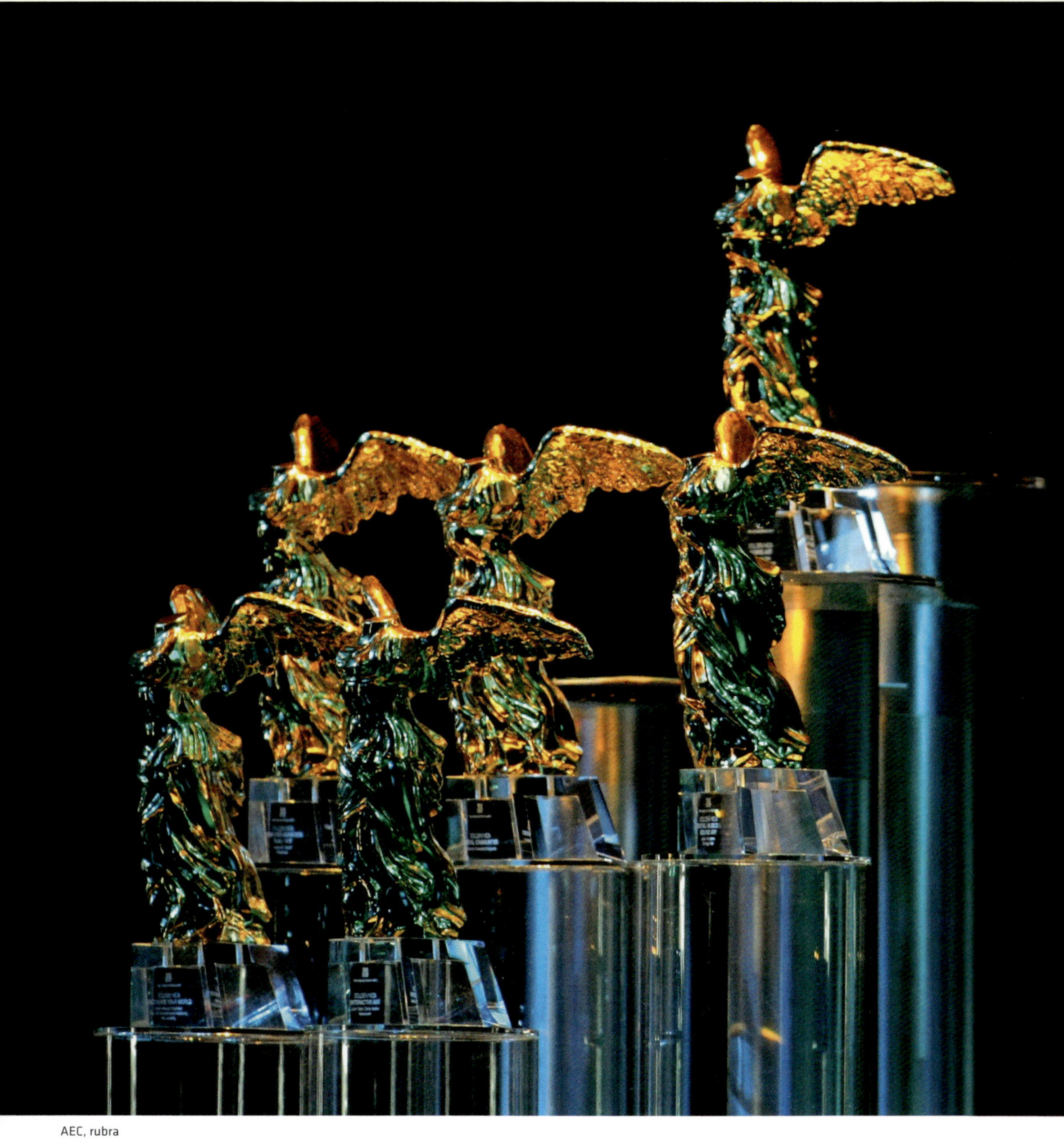

AEC, rubra

Since 1987, the Prix Ars Electronica is a seismograph for the latest innovations at the interface of art, technology and science, and thus an important barometer of trends in the digital arts. With 3,674 entries submitted from 72 countries, the Prix Ars Electronica has once again underscored its status as key bellwether in the dynamic field of cyberarts. The 2012 Prix Ars Electronica invited submissions in the following seven categories: Computer Animation/Film/VFX, Digital Communities, Digital Musics & Sound Art, Hybrid Art, Interactive Art, [the next idea] voestalpine Art and Technology Grant and u19 – CREATE YOUR WORLD that reflect the ongoing diversification of digital media art as well as the continuing development of the Prix Ars Electronica itself. Juries made up of prominent experts from all over the world selected the winners of 6 Golden Nicas, 12 Awards of Distinction, 1 [the next idea] Grant and 72 Honorary Mentions. Honorees also received a total of 117,500 euros in prize money.
This year, a jury also selected the first recipient of the Prix Ars Electronica Collide@CERN Recidency Award, the new artist-in-residence program established by CERN and Ars Electronica.

Der Prix Ars Electronica ist seit 1987 Seismograph für aktuelle Innovationen an der Schnittstelle von Kunst, Technologie und Wissenschaft und damit wichtiger Trendbarometer der digitalen Künste. Mit 3.674 eingereichten Projekten aus 72 Ländern unterstreicht der Prix Ars Electronica einmal mehr seinen Stellenwert als wichtiger Indikator im dynamischen Umfeld der Cyberarts. Folgende sieben Kategorien wurden im Rahmen des Prix Ars Electronica 2012 ausgeschrieben: Computer Animation/Film/VFX, Digital Communities, Digital Musics & Sound Art, Hybrid Art, Interactive Art, [the next idea] voestalpine Art and Technology Grant and u19 – CREATE YOUR WORLD. Allesamt spiegeln die fortschreitende Diversifizierung digitaler Medienkunst, aber auch die kontinuierliche Weiterentwicklung des Prix Ars Electronica wider. Internationale und hochkarätig besetzte Fachjuries entschieden über die Vergabe von 6 Goldene Nicas, 12 Auszeichnungen, 1 [the next idea] grant und 72 Anerkennungen. Es ergehen 117.500 Euro Preisgeld an die GewinnerInnen. Darüber hinaus wurde in diesem Jahr erstmals der Prix Ars Electronica Collide@CERN Residency Award vergeben, das neue von CERN und Ars Electronica ins Leben gerufene Artist-in-Residence-Programm.

You'll find the results of the 2012 Prix Ars Electronica and detailed descriptions of the prizewinning projects in: / Die Ergebnisse des Prix Ars Electronica und detaillierte Beschreibungen der Gewinnerprojekte finden Sie in:

CyberArts 2012
International Compendium – Prix Ars Electronica 2012
H. Leopoldseder / C. Schöpf / G. Stocker (Hrsg.)
Hatje Cantz, Ostfildern-Ruit
Ausgewählte Arbeiten des Prix Ars Electronica werden in der Ausstellung CyberArts 2012 im OK Offenes Kulturhaus im OÖ Kulturquartier Oberösterreich präsentiert.

Computer Animation / Film / VFX

Golden Nica Computer Animation / Film / VFX

Rear Window Loop
Jeff Desom (LU)
http://www.jeffdesom.com

Awards of Distinction Computer Animation / Film / VFX

Rise of the Planet of the Apes
Weta Digital (NZ) / Twentieth Century Fox
http://www.wetafx.co.nz/

Caldera
Evan Viera (US) / Orchid Animation
www.orchidanimation.com

Honorary Mentions Computer Animation / Film / VFX

Crossover
Fabian Grodde (DE)

The City, Five Years Older
Dirk Koy (DE) / Equipo
www.equipo.ch

Fat
Yohann Auroux Bernard, Gary Fouchy, Sébastien De
Oliveira Bispo (FR) / Supinfocom Arles
http://www.supinfocom-arles.fr/Supinfocom_Arles/
Accueil.html

L'ère bête
Thomas Caudron, Ingrid Menet, Laurent Meriaux,
Clement Tissier (FR) / Supinfocom Valenciennes
http://www.supinfocom.fr/

Christmas Card To Friends
Stephen Fitzgerald, Nathan Deceasar / Group Hug (US)
www.mono-motion.com

Countdown
Céline Desrumaux (FR) / Passion Pictures
http://groovythesushi.blogspot.fr/

unnamed soundsculpture
Cedric Kiefer, Daniel Franke (DE)
www.onformative.com / www.daniel-franke.com

Assassin's Creed Revelations
Digic Pictures
www.digicpictures.com

Zing
Kyra Buschor (CH), Cynthia Collins, Philipp Wolf (DE) /
Filmakademie Baden-Württemberg
www.zing-movie.com

Aalterate
Christobal de Oliveira (FR) / Sabotage Studio
aalterate.com / christobaldeoliveira.com

The Fantastic Flying Books of Mr. Morris Lessmore
William Joyce, Brandon Oldenburg (US) / Moonbot
Studios
http://www.morrislessmore.com/

The Visual Effects and Animation of Rango
Industrial Light & Magic (US)
http://www.ilm.com

Digital Communities

Golden Nica Digital Communities

Syrian People Know Their Way
http://sha3b3aref.blogspot.com/; https://www.
facebook.com/Syrian.Intifada

Awards of Distinction Digital Communities

Dark Glasses.Portrait
http://ichenguangcheng.blogspot.com

Apertus Open Source Cinema
http://www.apertus.org

Honorary Mentions Digital Communities

Texting for Democracy / Kubatana.net
http://www.kubatana.net

iStreet Lab
iStreet World http://istreetbhae.ning.com/

CRONICAS DE HEROES
http://www.cronicasdeheroes.mx/

iHub – Nairobi's Innovation Hub
http://ihub.co.ke;

Meine Abgeordneten
http://www.meineabgeordneten.at/

Europe versus Facebook
http://www.europe-v-facebook.org/

Safecast
http://safecast.org

YoungAfricaLive
http://www.praekeltfoundation.org/
young-africa-live.html

The Johnny Cash Project
http://www.thejohnnycashproject.com/

18 Days in Egypt
http://www.18daysinegypt.com

Lorea
http://www.lorea.org

XinCheJian: The First Hackerspace in China
http://www.xinchejian.com

Digital Musics & Sound Art

Golden Nica Digital Musics & Sound Art

Crystal Sounds of a Synchrotron
Jo Thomas (UK)
www.jothomas.me

Awards of Distinction Digital Musics & Sound Art

#tweetscapes – a HEAVYLISTENING experience
Anselm Venezian Nehls (DE), Tarik Barri (NL)
http://tweetscapes.de

scape-sequencer
Cheng Xu (CN)
http://jiahuiqingyu.com/xcss.mov

untitled #275
Francisco López (ES)
http://www.franciscolopez.net, http://www.
unsounds.com/26u.html

Terra Prosodia – Sound composition based on
European dialects
Antje Vowinckel (DE)
www.antjevowinckel.de

Years
Bartholomäus Traubeck (DE)
http://traubeck.com/years/

Forma II
Thomas Ankersmit (NL), Valerio Tricoli (IT)
http://www.thomasankersmit.net/; http://www.
pan-act.com/

Sonic Vista
by O+A (Bruce Odland, Sam Auinger)
http://www.sonicvista.de/

Organ of Corti
Liminal (UK)
http://www.liminal.org.uk/organ-of-corti

What does it matter how many lovers you have
if none of them gives you the universe
Bjørn Erik Haugen (NO)
http://bjornerikhaugen.com/Websted/What_does_it_
matter_how_many_lovers_you_have_if_none_of_
them_gives_you_the_universe.html

Project Integration / Intervention into Tenryu City
Dawang Huang, You-Sheng Zhang / Minkoku
Hyakunen (TW)
http://kandalarecords.blogspot.com/search/label/
Minkoku_Hyakunen

Benoît and the Mandelbrots
Juan A. Romero (CO), Holger Ballweg, Patrick Borgeat,
Matthias Schneiderbanger (DE)
http://www.the-mandelbrots.de

I am thinking in a room, different from the one you are
hearing in now
Samson Young (HK)
http://www.thismusicisfalse.com/?portfolio=2011-i-
am-thinking-in-a-room-different-from-the-one-you-
are-hearing-in-now-homage-to-alvin-lucier

BETWEEN | YOU | AND | ME
Anke Eckardt (DE)
www.ankeeckardt.org

Crackle-canvas #1
Tom Verbruggen (NL)
http://toktek.org/Site/Crackle-canvas_1.html

Hybrid Art

Golden Nica Hybrid Art

Bacterial Radio
Joe Davis (US) with support of Tara Gianoulis, Ido
Bachelet

Awards of Distinction Hybrid Art

Moon Goose Analogue: Lunar Migration Bird Facility
Agnes Meyer-Brandis (DE)
http://www.ffur.de/mga

The Free Universal Construction Kit
Golan Levin, Shawn Sims (US)
http://fffff.at/free-universal-construction-kit

Honorary Mentions Hybrid Art

Game Border
Jun Fujiki (JP)
http://www.youtube.com/watch?feature=player_
embedded&v=LvOxVPHQlec

Un Réseau Translucide
Prue Lang (AU)
http://www.pruelang.com

Dream Water Wonderland
Hörner/Antlfinger (DE)
http://www.h--a.org

The Great Work of the Metal Lover
Adam Brown (US)
http://adamwbrown.net/projects-2/the-great-work-
of-the-metal-lover/

MAQUILA REGION 4
Amor Muñoz (MX)
www.amormunoz.net

The Body is a Big Place
Peta Clancy (AU), Helen Pynor (AU)
www.thebodyisabigplace.com

Protei
Protei (UK)
http://www.protei.org

Irrational Computing
Ralf Baecker (DE)
http://www.rlfbckr.org/irrational_computing

50 Aktenkilometer - Ein begehbares STASI-Hörspiel
Rimini Protokoll (DE); Deutschlandradio Kultur
http://www.dradio-ortung.de<http://www.
dradio-ortung.de/

People Staring at Computers
Kyle McDonald (US)
http://fffff.at/people-staring-at-computers/

2.6g 329m/s
Jailia Essaidi (NL)
http://jalilaessaidi.com/2-6g-329ms/

Searching for the Ubiquitous Genetically Engineered
Machine
ArtScienceBangalore (IN)
http://artscienceblr.org

Interactive Art

Golden Nica Interactive Art

Memopol-2
Timo Toots (EE)
http://www.timo.ee

Awards of Distinction Interactive Art

Solar Sinter Project
Markus Kayser (DE)
www.markuskayser.com

It's a jungle in here
Isobel Knowles, Van Sowerwine with
Matthew Gingold (AU)
http://www.isobelandvan.com/jungle

Honorary Mentions Interactive Art

fly tweet
David Bowen (US)
http://dwbowen.com/fly_tweet_movie.html

Occupy George
Ivan Cash, Andy Dao (US)
http://occupygeorge.com

Cross Coordinates (MX-US)
Ivan Abreu (MX)
http://crosscoordinates.org/

LightType
François Chay, Léo Chéron (FR)
http://lighttype.qsdqsd.com

Versus
David Letellier (FR)
http://www.davidletellier.net/works.html#versus

Ideogenetic Machine
Nova Jiang (NZ)
http://www.novajiang.com/installations/
ideogenetic-machine

MNM v091
Christian Graupner (DE) feat.
Ming Wei Poon (SG) & Mieko Suzuki (JP)
http://mnm.humatic.net

Löschen/DELETE
Marcello Mercado (DE)
http://www.khm.de/~marcello,
http://vimeo.com/36645107

Menstruation Machine - Takashi's Take
Sputniko! (UK)
http://www.sputniko.com/?p=91600

Energy Parasites
Eric Paulos (US)
http://www.energyparasites.net

ADM8
RYBN (FR)
http://www.rybn.org/ANTI/ADM8/

Osadok / Aftertaste
Where dogs run (RU)
http://where-dogs-run.livejournal.com/

u19 – CREATE YOR WORLD

Golden Nica u19 – CREATE YOUR WORLD

state of revolution
Agnes Aistleitner / HBLA für Künstlerische
Gestaltung, Linz

Awards of Distinction u19 – CREATE YOUR WORLD

BioBookCover
BG/BRG Stainach
Derndler Lilian
Baumann Gerald
Berger Valerie
Ebner Aron
Edegger Christina
Greimeister Johannes
Lackner Nadine
Lemmerer Roland
Maringer Vera
Mayer Marco
Oßberger Raphaela
Rezar Thomas
Thalhammer Therese
Wegscheider Lisa
www.biobookcover.at

Bin Baum mit 2 Stämmen
Daniel Wieczorek
Asya Serimoglu
Stephan Friedl
Lorena Zorkic
Anita Simic
Radio Poly, PTS 3, Wien
radiopoly.wordpress.com

Non-cash prize u14

BALANCING ROBOT
Magdalena Kranjec
Sonja Stankovic
Christian Grill
Maximilian Tabelander
Sasa Vasiljkovic
NMS-Telfs-Dr.-Aloys-Weissenbach

Non-cash prize u10

Zukunftswürfel
Kindergarten Auwiesenstraße
Eriona Hoti
Rene Hausleitner
Leon Arslanovic
Ashab Mintulaev
Omar Sharef
Jelena Damjanovic
Emil Avdic
Edvin Memic
Alessandro Sasal
Kimberly Zagler
Anna Mae Steinerberger
Gwanza Durglishvili
Nicole Haslehner
Iman Chasiew
Lara Köck
Riccardo Moser
Laura Stockinger

Honorary Mentions

iTanky
Felix Krause
http://itanky.com

Weltrekord für eine bessere Welt
BG/BORG Kirchdorf

Das Superhirn
BG Wasagasse
Cornelia Auböck
Melanie Buchinger
Karin Cui
Ava Elahi
Miriam Freundlinger
Bruno Gstötterer
Laura Joichl
Felix Kriegerl
Andrea Klein
Oskar Lang
Oliver Lui
Tamara Manojlovic
Marko Popovic
Florentin Prammer
Laurenz Prammer
Florian Röder
Phillip Rössler
Anna-Sophie Schlemmer
Johannes Steindl
Thomas Vetter
Daphne Weber
Alden Weiss
Clara Wutti
Mag. Marlies Cermak

Fragment Planet
Simon Stix
www.indiedb.com/games/fragment-planet

Impressive Title (Paradise)
Laura Kaltenbrunner
Michaela Gehmayr

RiffGrabber
Peter Paikl
Alin Kalam
Wolfgang Schneiderbauer
Manmeet Singh
Christian Sorko
HTL Ottakring
www.riffgrabber.at

handsome
Anna Neubauer
William Mikulaschek
Gregor Eckmayr
Valentina Heinisch
Felix Brandstetter
Killian Sochor
C.LOUD

ConnectIn(g)
Robin von Mendel
Magnus Reinstadler
Franz Reinstadler
Dino Grgic
BORG Gastein

Quadrocopter
Tanja Roschanz
Lukas Pfeifhofer
HTL Mössingerstraße
quadrocopter.drseus.eu

Flat Water Bottle/ Evolution of Animation
Michael Schmidl

[the next idea]
voestalpine Art and Technology Grant

[the next idea] voestalpine Art and Technology Grant
qaul.net - tools for the next revolution
Christoph Wachter, Mathias Jud (CH)
http://www.qaul.net

Honorary Mentions [the next idea]
Designing Zero-Energy Building Components with
Smart Thermobimetal
Doris Sung (US) / DOSU Studio Architecture and
University of Southern California

Matopy
Sam Jewell (UK)
http://getaudioweb.com

Prix Ars Electronica
Collide@CERN Residency Award
Versuch unter Kreisen
Julius von Bismarck (DE)
http://www.juliusvonbismarck.com/

Honorary Mentions

How I learned to love the particle
Adrian Hornsby (UK), Arnoud Noordegraaf (NL)

Das Gestell
Eno Henze (DE)

0_0
Nataša Teofilović (RS)

Biographies

Bager Akbay (TR), born in 1976 in Istanbul, studied Visual Communication Design at Yildiz Technical University and Interface Cultures at Linz University of Arts. Bager was an actor and a puppeteer in Dark Theatre, Istanbul, worked as a lecturer for 6 years in his field, and enjoys living his life between art and science as an experimentalist. Bager's works focus mainly on artifical art and the human mind.

Alex Arteaga (ES/DE) studied Composition and Architecture in Barcelona and Berlin, and has a Ph.D. in Philosophy from Humboldt-Universität zu Berlin for his work on cognition and aesthetic practice. He currently heads the Auditory Architecture Research Unit and is a member of the faculty of the Sound Studies masters program (UdK Berlin) and a fellow of the "Bildakt und Verkörperung" research group (HU Berlin).

Sam Auinger (AT/DE) is a sonic thinker, composer and sound-artist. Together with Bruce Odland he founded O+A in 1989. Their central theme is "hearing perspective". Their work is known for large scale, public space sound installations that transform city noise into harmony in real-time, *www.o-a.info*. He collaborates with city planners and architects, gives lectures and is a frequent participant of international symposiums on urban planning, architecture, media, the senses and sound in particular. Besides his artistic work Sam Auinger is Professor for Experimental Sound Design at UdK Berlin. *www.samauinger.de*

Alexander Baratsits (AT) is an attorney at a Vienna commercial law firm. One of his fields of research is intellectual property, with special focus on free use and broadcast databanks.

Adam Bly (CA) is founder and CEO of Seed. He is the editor of *Science is Culture: Conversations at the New Intersection of Science + Society* and creator of the data visualization platform Visualizing.org. He served as Vice Chair of the World Economic Forum's Global Agenda Council on Design Innovation and currently serves as Vice Chair of the Global Agenda Council on Complex Systems. He has lectured at the World Economic Forum, MoMA, The Royal Society, Harvard University, and the US House of Representatives.

Joachim Böttger (DE) studied Computational Visualistics (University of Magdeburg) and has a PhD from the 'Explorative Analysis and Visualization of Large Information Spaces' graduate program as member of the Computer Graphics group (University of Konstanz). He worked in the Department of Neurosurgery at the Charité in Berlin and is currently a member of the "Neuroanatomy and Connectivity" research group at the Max Planck Institute for Human Cognitive and Brain Sciences in Leipzig.

Andreas Broeckmann (DE) is an art historian and curator based in Berlin and Lüneburg. As director of the Leuphana Arts Program at Leuphana University Lüneburg he is currently developing a new artist residency program. Broeckmann worked with the V2_Organisation (1995-2000) and was the artistic director of transmediale (2001-2007), TESLA media>art<lab Berlin, and of ISEA2010 RUHR.

George Church (US), Professor of Genetics, Harvard Medical School, Director of the Center for Computational Genetics. His 1984 Harvard PhD included the first direct genomic sequencing, molecular multiplexing and barcode tags, which led to automation and software used for the first commercial genome sequence (of the pathogen Helicobacter) in 1994. His multiplex solid-phase sequencing evolved into polonies (1999), ABI-SOLiD (2005), open-source Polonator.org (2007), and Complete Genomics (2008). Innovations in DNA reading, writing and cell/tissue engineering lead to consumer-directed genomics (23andme, Knome) , synthetic biology (SynBERC, Joule, LS9) and new ethics, safety and security strategies. He founded PersonalGenomes.org, which provides the world's only open-access information source for human genomic, environmental and trait data (GET). He is director of the NIH CCV Center for Excellence in Genomic Science. He is a member of NAS and NAE and was awarded the Hoogendijk Prize and the Franklin Laureate for Achievement in Science.

The CogniToo team (DE/IT/US) is an interdisciplinary group of neuroscience experts and award-winning artists (psychologists, physicians, physicists, computer scientists, philosophers, art historians, sculptors, painters, and tattoo artists). The company was founded in May 2012 by CEO Maurice Cabanis, who studied Art History, Philosophy and Medicine. He currently works at the Section of Brain Imaging at Philipps-University Marburg.

Dan Cosley (US) is an Assistant Professor in the Department of Information Science at Cornell University. His research focuses on studying existing online communities and designing new tools and systems that help support user engagement. Dan received his PhD in Computer Science from the University of Minnesota. He serves as the Technical Chair of Wikisym 2012.

CMoDA (China Millennium Monument Museum of Digital Arts, CN), is China's first museum dedicated to digital art and design. It aims to become the digital cultural incubator for creative future in China. CMoDA CoINNO Lab, the R&D body of CMoDA, focuses on collaborative innovation by bringing in international and local partners in joint project development on urban future and interactive media. *www.modachina.org*

R. Cameron Craddock (US), PhD, is Director of Imaging for the Center for the Developing Brain at the Child Mind Institute. He is a co-founder of the Neuro Bureau and has been involved with several open science initiatives such as the art @HBM art exhibition, 2012 Brainhack Unconference, and ADHD200 preprocessing.

Heidrun Friese (DE) is an anthropologist who completed her post-doc at Goethe-Universität Frankfurt a. M. and is on the staff of the Center for Mediterranean Research at Ruhr-Universität Bochum. She's working on *The Limits of Hospitality*, a project investigating undocumented mobility in the Mediterranean (Tunisia, Lampedusa) and *New Beginnings. Undocumented Mobility and the "Arab Spring"*, a study that focuses on cultural aspects. Her publications include 'Ya l'babour, ya mon amour – Raï-Rap und undokumentierte Mobilität', in M. Dietrich and M. Seeliger (Eds.), *Deutscher Gangsta-Rap. Sozial- und kulturwissenschaftliche Beiträge zu einem Pop-Phänomen.* Bielefeld (2012); *Geglücktes Leben.* Bochum/Berlin (2011) and "Willkommen, Nachbar. Die europäischen Grenzen der Gastfreundschaft", in Ch. Bartmann, C. Dürr and K.-D.. Lehmann (Eds.) *Illusion der Nähe? Ausblick auf die europäische Nachbarschaft von Morgen.* Göttingen (2011). *http://web.mac.com/hfriese*

Günther Friesinger (AT) lives in Vienna and Graz; he's a philosopher, university lecturer, artist, free-lance media producer, curator and journalist; organizer of the Paraflows Festival for Digital Art and Cultures in Vienna, the Arse Elektronika Festival and the Roboexotica Festival; tag cloud: contemporary art, activism, performance, media theory, cultural studies, science fiction, free software and copyright.

Sebastian Frisch (DE) studied Musical Art and Computer Science at Salzburg University of Applied Sciences and works in a wide range of media fields. He makes use of spatial audio, sound programming and augmented reality as a means of closing the gap between the digital domain and our own world. He has traveled to Kenya annually since 2007 to work together with aid organizations and artists there.

Rosi Grillmair (AT), born 1991, is studying Timebased and Interactive Media at the University of Art and Design Linz. In 2011, during her final year of school at the HBLA für Künstlerische Gestaltung Linz, she belonged to the group of pupils who won the Golden Nica in the u19 – CREATE YOUR WORLD, Prix Ars Electronica, for their project *Weltherberge: Schulhaus* (World Hostel–School House), which was exhibited at the Festival.

Amy Grumbling (Co-Producer): is currently producing and co-directing a documentary about the experiences of two photojournalists assigned to Ground Zero on 9/11/01. She recently travelled to Haiti shooting and editing a documentary about post-catastrophe reconstruction. She was Associate Producer for Celia Maysles' feature documentary *Wild Blue Yonder*, and worked as an Associate Programmer at UnionDocs, a non-profit documentary venue in Brooklyn.

Enrique Guitart (AR/AT) studied Business Administration in Buenos Aires; has been working in various sectors of the art world (production, exhibition organization, mediating people's encounters with art, consulting in artistic matters) for over 20 years. In 2009, founder (with Thomas Thurner and Günther Friesinger) of the Buckminster Fuller Institute Austria. Lecturer at Danube University Krems (Exhibition Management) and the Institut für Kulturkonzepte. Founder of Art Consulting & Production art production firm.

Bettina Habsburg-Lothringen (AT), PhD, is a museologist and head of the Museum Academy, Universalmuseum Joanneum, Graz

Yoshihiro Harano (JP) was born in 1955 and lives in Kobe. He is a Law graduate from Konan University. In 1984, he joined the Marketing & Communication Centre, specializing in company and government office communication strategies and event management.He was Director of the Communications Department before becoming self-employed and founding Landmark Japan Ltd. In 1999. Harano is committed to creating new urban landscapes by enhancing river surfaces, as in the *Inori Boshi*® project, in which he covers the river with lights. He is the director of *The Milky Way Project* (Japanese: *Amanogawa Project*−天の川プロジェクト®), and is actively involved in company and government office communication strategies, as well as revitalization projects of local communities involving culture and sports.

Roland Haring (AT) studied Media Technology and Design at Hagenberg Polytechnical University in Upper Austria, where he graduated with distinction on mobile interactions in public space. The year before he had joined the Ars Electronica Futurelab. One of the highlights of his successful work within the Ars Electronica Futurelab was *Gulliver's World*, a complex collaborative Mixed Reality project that has been singled out for recognition with numerous prizes in Austria and abroad. His later activities include research at the interface between academia, industry and the mission of the Ars Electronica. On the side, he's at work on a doctoral dissertation dealing with a novel open framework for urban information systems. Right now he is working as Co-Director of the Research and Innovation Group, and as Senior Research Lead he is establishing the research field of Interaction Ecology.

HEAVYLISTENING (DE) are Carl Schilde and Anselm Venezian Nehls, both born in Berlin, 1981. They studied Popular Music in England and Sound Studies at the University of the Arts Berlin with Sam Auinger and Robert Henke. Their first project, *TIEFDRUCKGEBIET*, garnered the 1st Art Prize at the 2011 48 Hours Neukölln Festival. Their second project, *#tweetscapes*, was honored with an Award of Distinction in the 2012 Prix Ars Electronica's Digital Music & Sound Art category.

Martina Hechenberger (AT) was born in Linz in 1978 as Martina Wagner. She studied Media Technology and Design at the University for Applied Science in Hagenberg and Timebased Media at the University of Art and Design in Linz. Since 2005 she has worked in the fields of film, photography and video and in different productions and projects. In 2008 she joined Ars Electronica and started to work with Jutta Schmiederer on the Ars Electronica Archive, developing and establishing a physical and digital archiving system. Since 2009 Hechenberger has been in charge of the Ars Electronica Archive.

Stephen Hetherington (UK) is Chairman of HQ Theatres and a founder of the OHMI Trust. He studied at the Royal Academy of Music, playing the trumpet with a number of the UK's leading orchestras, before moving on to produce theatre, opera, ballet and orchestras across the world with his partner Joseph Seelig. Stephen has acted as a consultant for the development of a variety of cultural buildings, operations and events, including the development of Britain's largest Lottery funded project (£106 million), *The Lowry*. He directed Birmingham's Bid for European Capital of Culture in 2002 and is currently completing a PhD in Political Science at Birmingham University, UK.

Martin Hochleitner (AT) was born in Salzburg. He is the director of Landesgalerie Linz and Professor of Art History and Theory at the University of Art and Design Linz.

Adi Hoesle (DE), born 1959. First trained as a special nurse for anaesthesia/intensive care, but changed to study Art at the Freien Kunsthochschule Nürtingen. Since the early Nineties Adi Hoesle has been concerned with reform measures in art, culture, research and the economy.

Martin Hollinetz (AT) is a social education worker and teacher, regional developer and passionate advocate of Digital Bohème. The desire to overcome the bourgeois values and norms that he perceives as restrictive, the wish to reconfigure his identity, and the longing for creative freedom have motivated and driven him, since 1993, to found and mentor a series of business start-ups, projects and associations concerning work, youth culture, IT and media. Martin Hollinetz is cofounder and chairman of OTELO.

Martin Honzik (AT) studied Experimental Design at the University of Art and Design Linz. From 2002–2006 he was a member of Ars Electronica's Futurelab staff. Since then, he's been in charge of organizing and producing the Ars Electronica Festival, the Prix Ars Electronica and international exhibitions.

John Van Horn (US) is an Assistant Professor of Neurology at the UCLA. He received his Ph.D. in Psychology from the University of London (UK), a Masters degree in Engineering from the University of Maryland College Park, and conducted post-doctoral training at the National Institute of Mental Health. His work on human brain imaging has been published in top-tier journals such as *NeuroImage, Biological Psychiatry, Nature Neuroscience, PNAS*, and *Science*.

Horst Hörtner (AT) is a media artist and researcher. He is an expert in the design of human-computer interaction and holds several patents in this field. Hörtner was a founding member of the Ars Electronica Futurelab in 1996 and since then he has been the director of this atelier/laboratory. He started work in the field of media art in the 1980s and co-founded the "media-art group x-space" in Graz, Austria, in 1990. Horst Hörtner works at the nexus of art and science and gives lectures and talks at numerous international conferences and universities.

Rupert Huber (AT), born 1967 and lives in Vienna. He is a freelance composer of "dimensional music", personal procedure of creation. Works commissioned for Wiener Festwochen, Centre Pompidou, Ars Electronica. Music for film and radio, electronic music duo tosca (huber/dorfmeister). His main interests are piano music, sound in public areas, sound networks. working on a theory for sounds controlled by machine data e.g. multichannel sound installation for an airport, the sounds being controlled by the airplanes. *www.ruperthuber.com*

Hiroshi Ishiguro (JP) received a D. Eng. in Systems Engineering from Osaka University, Japan in 1991. He has been a Professor in the Department of Systems Innovation at the Graduate School of Engineering Science, Osaka University since 2009 and Group Leader of the Hiroshi Ishiguro Laboratory at the Advanced Telecommunications Research Institute and ATR fellow since 2011. His research interests include sensor networks, interactive robotics, and android science.

Neda Jahanshad (US), PhD, is a post-doctoral scholar at the Imaging Genetics Center in the Laboratory of Neuro Imaging (LONI-IGC) at the University of California, Los Angeles (UCLA). Professor Victor Valcour, MD is Associate Professor of Geriatric Medicine at the University of California, San Francisco. Professor Paul Thompson, PhD is Professor of Neurology and Psychiatry and Director of the LONI-IGC at UCLA.

Michael Kaczorowski (AT) studied Music in Vienna. He's a musician and blogger, currently working for Ars Electronica in the field of Web communication and on the development of various projects. For the voestalpine Klangwolke, he's responsible for the Soundcloud miniatures. He deals with everything that's digital and that happens online.

Deniz Kader (BG), born 1983, graduated from the Animation Department, Eskişehir Anatolian University. He founded NOHlab studio in 2011. Deniz Kader recently realized Yekpare projection mapping within İstanbul 2010 European Capital of Culture activities. He works in the fields of visual and performance. Deniz 's works are mainly focused on time, space and experience.

Yoshiyuki Katayama (JP). After studying film at the Department of Cinema, College of Art, Nihon University, he has been active as a freelance film designer. He began to create works using digital media in 2008. He garnered attention with such works as *CONCH* and *Sou-Tyuu-Ji-Zu*, which was chosen for the Jury Selection of the 14th Japan Media Arts Festival.

Laura Kepplinger (AT), MA (UAM), is a historian and sociologist at the University of Linz and with Open Commons Region Linz. In addition to open commons and digital communities, she's interested in new biotechnologies and their eugenic implications.

Gerhard Kürner (AT) was active for several years in a number of Austrian media, film and television production companies in different capacities, including founder, business partner and managing director, before joining voestalpine AG in 2001 as Group Content Manager in Corporate Communications, responsible for designing and implementing the new Internet pages for the corporate group and its subsidiaries. Gerhard Kürner became responsible for establishing an efficient and international IT management structure in the voestalpine Automotive Division, the youngest business area of the voestalpine group, assuming responsibility for the communications department of this division in early 2004. In 2005 he became Head of the Department of Communications in the Steel Division and in August 2006 he was appointed Director of Corporate Communications at voestalpine AG.

Friedrich A. Kittler (DE), Ph.D., was a literary scientist and media theorist. He was born in 1943 in Rochlitz, Saxony (Germany) and he died on October 18, 2011 in Berlin. His research and work is focused on media, history, communications, technology, and the military. Friedrich Kittler has been called the "Derrida of the digital age". His innovative media theories have transformed the nature of technological scholarship and led the way in the field. Kittler is an innovative and hard to define theorist, who has pushed theoretical works of literary scholars into technological fields with unprecedented modes of critical thought. Through his unique brand of media determinism his work is influencing new generations of students across the world.

Margarita Köhl (AT) is a communications scholar who specializes in social acquisition of information & communication technologies, transcultural research and assessing the consequences of technology. She is currently a lecturer and researcher at the First Tech University (NKFUST) in Taiwan and in the Department of Journalism and Communications at the University of Vienna.

Cliff Lampe (US) is an Assistant Professor in the School of Information at the University of Michigan. He researches how technical systems enable large-scale distributed interaction, and how social interactions are changed by computer mediation. He has studied sites like Slashdot and Wikipedia, as well as creating new online communities for collective action. He serves as the General Chair of Wikisym 2012.

Hannes Leopoldseder (AT), PhD. He has worked as a television journalist for ORF Vienna, as Managing Director of ORF Upper Austria (1974–1998), and as Information Director of ORF Vienna (1998 - 2002). He was appointed Honorary Professor at the University of Art and Industrial Design in Linz in 2009. He co-founded the Ars Electronica and SoundCloud of Linz (1979) and initiated the Prix Ars Electronica (1987) and the Ars Electronica Center (1996). He is also the co-editor of Ars Electronica's catalogues.

Brandon Litman (US) is co-founder and executive producer for *One Day on Earth*. Brandon has shaped production partnerships with the United Nations and many of the world's leading NGOs to produce a flagship *One Day on Earth* film and the creation of the largest archive of cause-based media shot in a single day. Brandon is also founder and managing partner of a New York City based production and design studio, called Alien Kung Fu. He holds a business degree from the University of Southern California.

Manfred Litzlbauer (AT) was born in 1955 in Heiligenberg, Upper Austria. He is CEO of Energie AG Oberösterreich Data GmbH, which installs and operates a fiber optics cable network that serves essential infrastructure throughout the Province of Upper Austria. He studied electrical engineering at HTL Linz vocational school, studied Sociology with a dissertation on NLP Metaprograms, is a life consultant and a social counselor, has a Master's degree in Business, LIMAK, a Master's degree in Theology from the University of Salzburg and is a recipient of the Province of Upper Austria's prize for Achievement in Adult Education.

Thomas Macho (DE) studied Musicology and Philosophy at the University of Vienna (Doctorate 1976); he acquired the University Lecturing Qualification (Habilitation) in Philosophy at the University of Klagenfurt (1984). Since 1993 he has been teaching and carrying out research as a Chair of Cultural History at the Humboldt-University of Berlin. Recent publications: *Das Leben ist ungerecht* (Salzburg/St. Pölten 2010), *Vorbilder* (Munich 2011) and *Kulturtechniken der Synchronisation,* edited with Christian Kassung, (Munich 2012).

Daniel Margulies (US) is the head of the Neuroanatomy & Connectivity Research Group at the Max Planck Institute for Human Cognitive and Brain Sciences in Leipzig. He previously studied literature and philosophy in New York and Paris, before moving to Berlin in 2008 to pursue graduate studies in neuroscience. In addition to his scientific research, he has collaborated with artists and social scientists, and is a co-founder of the Neuro Bureau.

Jon McCormack (AU) is an Australian electronic media artist and academic. Since the late 1980s he has worked with computer code as a medium for creative expression, drawing on a process-oriented interpretation of the world. He is currently a research fellow and director of the Centre for Electronic Media Art at Monash University, Melbourne and was recently an artist-in-residence at the Ars Electronica Futurelab.

Seiko Mikami (JP) is an artist and Professor at Tama Art University. Large-scale installations on the information society and the human body since the 1980s. From 1990 till the present day the majority of her interactive media art installations incorporate human perception. Art works have been exhibited at Miro Museum, Musée des Beaux Arts de Nantes, Künstlerhaus Vienna, Kulturhuset Stockholm, National Art Museum of China, Canon ARTLAB, Yamaguchi Center for Art and Media/YCAM, InterCommunication Center/ICC, transmediale Berlin, DEAF Rotterdam, ISEA, Ars Electronica. Participation in numerous media art festivals.

Michael P. Milham (US), MD, PhD, is the Director of the Center for the Developing Brain at the Child Mind Institute, and Deputy Director of Human Imaging at the Center for Advanced Brain Imaging located at the Nathan S. Kline Institute for Psychiatric Research. He is a child and adolescent psychiatrist, and has also completed doctoral training in Cognitive Neuroscience and undergraduate training in Computer Science. In addition to his extensive record of scientific studies in neuroimaging and psychiatry, Dr. Milham is a lead figure in openscience efforts promoting data-sharing in the imaging community; in this capacity, he is co-founder of the *1000 Functional Connectomes Project* and founder of the International Neuroimaging Data-sharing Initiative.

Miraikan—The National Museum of Emerging Science and Innovation (JP) is a new type of science museum that links people directly with the new wisdom of the 21st century. At the heart of Miraikan's activities is the cutting-edge science and technology. This is the "state-of-the-art knowledge and innovation" which Miraikan aims to share with the whole society as part of enriched human culture. Founded in 2001.
http://www.miraikan.jst.go.jp/sp/tsunagari/index.html

Maki Namekawa (JP), pianist, is equally at home in the classical and contemporary repertoire. She performs regularly at international venues such as Suntory Hall Tokyo, Ruhr Piano Festival, Musik-Biennale Berlin, Festival Eclat in Stuttgart, ZKM Karlsruhe and Rheingau Music Festival and records frequently for the major German radio networks. Recent engagements include Seattle Symphony Orchestra, Concertgebouw Orkest Amsterdam, Münchner Philharmoniker, Munich Chamber Orchestra, Dresdener Philharmonie, Stuttgart Chamber Orchestra and Bruckner Orchester Linz. In 2012 she performed Arvo Pärt's "Lamentate" at Carnegie Hall New York and Igor Strawinsky's Concerto for Piano and Wind Instruments with the Bamberg Symphony Orchestra. Since 2005, Maki Namekawa and Dennis Russell Davies have been performing together as a piano duo in Europe and the US.

NOHlab is a multidisciplinary studio founded and directed by two vastly experienced creative partners: Deniz Kader & Candas Şişman, who both follow a unique and distinctive Art & Concept direction in their projects, focusing its work in the areas of art direction, audiovisual performance, motion design, projection mapping and new media for arts & culture and clients. *www. nohlab.com*

Dietmar Offenhuber (AT) has backgrounds in architecture, urban studies and digital media. He works on the spatial aspects of cognition, representation and behavior. Dietmar has degrees from the Technical University of Vienna and the MIT Media Lab. He was a key researcher in the Ars Electronica Futurelab and the Ludwig Boltzmann Institute for Media.Art.Research and taught in the Interface Cultures program as a professor at the Linz Art University. Currently he is researching his PhD dissertation in the Senseable City Lab at the Department for Urban Studies and Planning, MIT.

Emiko Ogawa (JP) is an artist, a curator and a researcher. She is in charge of creative direction, graphics and interaction design in the media artist group "h.o" *www.howeb.org*. Currently she also works at Ars Electronica, and is responsible for planning the exhibitions for the Ars Electronica Export, Ars Electronica Center and Ars Electronica Festival.

Hideaki Ogawa (JP) is an artist, curator and researcher in the field of art, technology and society. He is a representative and artistic director of the media artist group "h.o" *www.howeb.org*. Currently he also works in the Ars Electronica Futurelab Research & Innovation Group and has realized many projects for research, festivals and the AEC.

Stefan Pawel (AT) has been project director of Open Commons Region Linz since 2010. He manages Web projects, marketing and distribution, is co-author of *Freie Netze. Freies Wissen.* and *Freiheit vor Ort* and author on the subject of open government data. *http://www.blog.opencommons.at*

Ella Raidel (AT) was born in 1970. An artist and a filmmaker, she lived 2002–2009 in Taipei, Taiwan and presents her work at international exhibitions and film festivals. Her dissertation *Subversive Realitäten. Die Filme des Tsai Ming-Liang* was published in 2011 by Schüren Verlag. In 2011 she was artist-in-residence at Red Gate Gallery, Peking (BMUUK) and in Huantie Times Art Museum, Peking (exchange program with Salzamt Linz). Recipient of a 2011 Forum Grant from the University of Art and Design Linz for research about independent filmmaking in China.

Gunther Reisinger (AT), PhD, is an art historian and a member of the academic staff at the Museum Academy of the Universalmuseum Joanneum, Graz.

Arash T. Riahi (AT) was born 1972 in Iran and has lived in Vienna since 1982. Writer, director and producer. Studied Film and the Arts, founded the film production company Golden Girls Filmproduktion in 1997. Has written, directed and produced several award-winning documentaries, shorts, experimental films, music videos and commercials, including *The Souvenirs of Mr. X (www.HerrX.com)*, *Exile Family Movie (www.exilefamilymovie.at)* and *For a moment, freedom (www.foramomentfreedom.com)*.

Arman T. Riahi (AT) was born 1981 in Iran and has lived in Vienna since 1983. Writer and director. Studied Media Technologies and worked as a screen and graphic designer in London and Vienna. Since 2005, he has worked as a director and writer of TV shows, e.g. *Sendung ohne Namen* (ORF), *Sunshine Airlines* (ORF) and the TV documentary series *Momentum* (Red Bull Media House). In 2011, his first cinema documentary *Darkhead* opened the competition of the 17th Sarajevo Film Festival *(www.schwarzkopf-derfilm.com)*.

Kyle Ruddick (US) is the founder and director of *One Day on Earth,* a global media movement, community and film started in late 2008. *One Day on Earth* is the first film shot in every country of the world and has over 70 NGO partnerships. Prior to *One Day on Earth* Kyle founded an award-winning creative agency called Eyestorm Productions and worked at Lucasfilm in their documentary department. Kyle is a graduate of the University of Southern California School of Cinematic Arts.

Rúrí (IS) was born in 1951. She has presented her works in countless individual & group exhibitions worldwide. Most recently, she was honored with a major retrospective at the National Gallery of Iceland (2012) and a comprehensive book about her work (2011, Hatje Cantz). Rúrí has an international reputation and is regularly invited to show her work at ecological-political exhibitions, of late at Rethink in Copenhagen (2009) and Climate-Change-Minds (2012). Rúrí presented Overtures Environmental Office at the 2007 Ars Electronica Festival.

Sabine Sanio (DE) is currently guest professor teaching Theory and History of Auditory Culture in the University of the Arts Berlin's Sound Studies program. Publications: *Alternativen zur Werkästhetik,* Cage und Heißenbüttel (Saarbrücken 1999); *1968 und die Avantgarde* (Sinzig 2008) and as co-editor with Christian Scheib: *Das Rauschen* (Hofheim 1995).

Peter Sasowsky (AUS) is an award-winning producer and director and the founder and director of Serious Motion Pictures, a script to screen production company that produces documentary and narrative films, corporate communications, and media for foundations and philanthropies.

Alexander Schäfer (DE) is a PhD student in Neuroscience funded by the Max Planck Institute for Human Cognitive and Brain Science in Leipzig, Germany. His research is centered around networks derived from human brains. He is interested in the organization of these networks and the changes that occur due to aging or diseases. Alexander graduated in Computer Sciences from the Friedrich Schiller University Jena (2009).

Ingrid Schaumüller-Bichl (AT) is Professor at the Upper Austria University of Applied Sciences Department of Computer Science, Communications and Media and, at the school's Hagenberg Campus, the Department of Secure Information Systems.
She is also an instructor at the universities of Linz, Klagenfurt and Krems, vice-president of the OCG and Assistant Chairwoman of the Council of Research and Technology for Upper Austria.

Katja Schechtner (AT/US) has a background in architecture, urban studies and technology assessment. Her research interests focus on the understanding of urban mobility and the coupling of citizens' movements with urban automation systems and was stimulated by her international work experience in Asia, the US and Europe. She is Head of Dynamic Transportation Systems at the AIT Mobility Department, while at the same time being a Visiting Scholar at the MIT Media Lab.

Christine Schöpf (AT), PhD, studied German and Romance Languages. She has worked as a radio and television journalist and was the head of the art and science department at ORF Upper Austria (1981-2008). Recently she was appointed Honorary Professor at the University of Art and Industrial Design in Linz (2009). Since 1979, she has held a number of positions in which she has been able to contribute considerably to the development of Ars Electronica. She was responsible for conceiving and organizing the Prix Ars Electronica from 1987-2003. Together with Gerfried Stocker, she has been the artistic co-director of Ars Electronica since 1996.

Theresa Schubert (DE/AT) studied Media Art & Design at the Bauhaus University Weimar. She currently works as a researcher and project manager for the Ars Electronica Archive. She is also working on a PhD at the Bauhaus University Weimar, Faculty of Art & Design, where she is investigating the relationship between aesthetics, technology and experience.

Kotobuki Shiriagari (JP), born in Shizuoka. Joined Kirin Brewery Company after graduating from Tama Art University in 1981, in charge of package design and advertising. In 1985, he made his debut as a manga artist with the book *Ereki na Haru.* In 1994, he left Kirin Brewery and became an independent artist. While continuing his independent activities as a manga artist, he has expanded into a diverse range of fields, including essays, visual images, games and art.

Candas Şişman (TR) was born in 1985. He graduated from Eskişehir Anatolian University Animation Department. In 2011 he founded NOHlab. In 2011 he received an Honorary Mention from Ars Electronica in the Computer Animation/ Film /VFX category with his audiovisual work *Flux.* He works in the fields of visual, sound and installation. Candas's works are mainly focused on time, space and experience. The artist is representing PG Art Gallery in Istanbul, Turkey. *www.csismn.com*

Paul Stepan (AT) is an economist who has specialized in the fields of art, culture and copyright. Since 2003, he has taught at various European universities. He is a co-founder and member of the board of directors of FOKUS.

Gerfried Stocker (AT) is a media artist and electronic engineer. In 1991, he founded x-space, a team for the realization of interdisciplinary projects. In this framework numerous installations and performance projects have been carried out in the field of interaction, robotics and telecommunication. Since 1995 Gerfried Stocker has been a Managing and Artistic Director of Ars Electronica. 1995/1996 he developed the groundbreaking exhibition strategies of the Ars Electronica Center with a small team of artists and technicians and was responsible for the set-up (and establishment) of Ars Electronica's own R&D facility, the Ars Electronica Futurelab. Since 2004 he has been in charge of developing Ars Electronica's program of international exhibition tours. Since 2005 he has planned the expansion of the Ars Electronica Center and implemented the total substantive makeover of its exhibits.

Ronald Strasser (AT) studied Sociology with emphasis on organization, scientific research and STS in Vienna; particularly interested in practical research at the nexus of individuals, society, science and art. A freelance media producer active in the field of adult further education since 2000; planning and implementing educational concepts in communications, social skills, gender mainstreaming and diversity management; development of eLearning concepts and tutorials.

The Museum of Me—Team (JP), Koichiro Tanaka: Creative Director, Representative, Projector; Eiji Tanigawa: Director, Planner, Planning and Direction Division, Taiyo Kikaku Co., Ltd; Seiichi Saito: Technical Director, Representative, Rhizomatiks; Masanori Sakamoto: Art Director, Designer, Established Deltro Inc. in 2009; Ken Murayama: Interactive Director, Developer, Established Deltro Inc. in 2009.

Thomas Thurner (AT). Laboratory situations are his preferred environment. His career path has included work doing electronics R&D, radio-related publishing, fundraising management, webcasting, setting up an internet culture lab and consulting for innovation processes & spaces. He works at net culture lab and his interests include innovation, Web3.0, enabling spaces, radical innovation and creative industries. Blog: *http://polymatic.blogspot.com;* website: *http://lab.netculture.at;* selected projects: *http://docs.google.com/View?id=dggddrc4_71drdswxgb*

Wolfgang Winkler (AT) was born in 1945 in Graz. He studied at the University of Music and at the University of Graz (Medicine). He began his career at the ORF – Austrian Broadcasting Company's Styria Regional Studio as a freelancer keeping the music protocol. In 1978, he began his affiliation with the Bruckner Conservatory Linz. In 1979, he was named Director of the music department at ORF Upper Austria. Since 1998, he has served as Artistic Director of LIVA. He's also been involved in Ars Electronica, the Prix Ars Electronica and the Linz Klangwolke (SoundCloud) since 1979. He teaches at Anton Bruckner University and the University of Linz.

Dajuin Yao (US/TW) is a sound artist, producer, curator, radio host and art historian. Dajuin has created and promoted experimental music and sound art in China through concerts, radio shows, websites and teaching. He has curated international new media performances in China, including Sounding Beijing 2003 and the opening concerts for the 2008 Shanghai eArts Festival. In 1997 Dajuin founded *China Sound Unit,* a pioneering phonography project, devoted to the documenting and recontextualizing of Chinese urban sound phenomena. He is currently director of the Open Media Lab at the China Academy of Art, Hangzhou. *www.dajuin.com*

Jun Yoshihara (JP) was born in Kyoto in 1972. Graduated from the Faculty of Art at Kyoto Seika University. Involved in a wide range of work, from corporate branding to art directions, and design for SUBARU, YAMAHA, FUJIFILM, SoftBank, Mitsui Fudosan Residential, Tokyo Metropolitan Museum of Photography, LOFT etc.